HANDBOOK for BIBLE STUDY

A guide to
understanding,
teaching, and preaching
the Word of God

HANDBOOK for BIBLE STUDY

LEE J. GUGLIOTTO

REVIEW AND HERALD® PUBLISHING ASSOCIATION
HAGERSTOWN, MD 21740

Unless otherwise noted, the Bible citations are the author's own translation.
Texts credited to KJV are from the King James Version.
Scripture quotations marked NASB are from the *New American Standard Bible*, © The
Lockman Foundation 1960, 1962, 1963, 1968, 1971, 1972, 1973, 1975, 1977.
Texts credited to NIV are from the *Holy Bible, New International Version*. Copyright © 1973,
1978, 1984, International Bible Society. Used by permission of Zondervan Bible Publishers.
Texts credited to NKJV are from The New King James Version. Copyright © 1979, 1980, 1982,
Thomas Nelson, Inc., Publishers.
Bible texts credited to NRSV are from the New Revised Standard Version of the Bible, copy-
right © 1989 by the Division of Christian Education of the National Council of the Churches of
Christ in the U.S.A. Used by permission.
Bible texts credited to Phillips are from J. B. Phillips: *The New Testament in Modern English*,
Revised Edition. © J. B. Phillips 1958, 1960, 1972. Used by permission of Macmillan Publishing
Co., Inc.
Texts credited to REB are from *The Revised English Bible*. Copyright © Oxford University
Press and Cambridge University Press, 1989. Reprinted by permission.
Bible texts credited to RSV are from the Revised Standard Version of the Bible, copyright ©
1946, 1952, 1971, by the Division of Christian Education of the National Council of the Churches
of Christ in the U.S.A. Used by permission.
Bible texts credited to TEV are from the *Good News Bible*—Old Testament: Copyright ©
American Bible Society 1976; New Testament: Copyright © American Bible Society 1966, 1971,
1976.
Bible texts credited to Williams are from the *Williams New Testament, the New Testament in
the Language of the People*, by Charles B. Williams. © Copyright 1937, 1966, 1986 by Holman
Bible Publishers. Used by permission.

This book was
Edited by Richard W. Coffen
Designed by Patricia S. Wegh
Cover design by Bryan Gray
Typeset: 9.5/10.5 Times Roman

PRINTED IN U.S.A.

09 08 07 06 05   6 5 4 3 2

Library of Congress Cataloging in Publication Data
Gugliotto, Lee J.
    Handbook for Bible study: a guide to understanding, teaching, and
preaching the word of God / Lee. J. Gugliotto.
            p.   cm.
    Includes bibliographical references (p.   ).
    1. Bible—Study and teaching.   2. Bible—Hermeneutics.   3. Bible—
Criticism, interpretation, etc.   I. Title.
BS600.2.G84   95-19356
220' .07—dc20   CIP

ISBN 0-8280-1461-2

DEDICATION

To Jolynn,
Gina, Keith, Wendi, and Jessica—
God's circle of gifts to me

CONTENTS

CONTENTS

PART II—A CLOSER LOOK

CONTENTS

CONTENTS

APPENDICES

PREFACE

Lay leaders are often called upon to teach or speak in their churches. The members expect them to have a gift for sharing God's Word, even though they have had little or no formal training in biblical interpretation or public speaking. Sometimes gifted laypersons do a fair job of presenting truth in public, but more often than not the untrained worker simply converts a pet Bible study into an awkward message. The flip side of all this is that it does not take long to discover that successful speakers are also skilled interpreters. This handbook is for laity and professionals alike who want a practical guide to help them interpret the Bible and prepare sermons or lessons.

You may wonder Is it really necessary for me to interpret the Scriptures for myself? Our pioneers certainly thought so. When "a brother asked one of our leading denominational forebears, 'Sister White, do you think we must understand the truth for ourselves? Why can we not take the truths that others have gathered together, and believe them because they have investigated the subjects?'" she replied: "It is dangerous for us to make flesh our arm. We should lean upon the arm of infinite power. . . . We must have living faith in our hearts, and reach out for larger knowledge and more advanced light" *(Review and Herald,* Mar. 25, 1890).

Ellen White promoted regular, personal Bible study, urging that "the word of God must be studied as never before" *(ibid.,* Dec. 15, 1891) and "thoroughly studied" *(Testimonies,* vol. 2, p. 337). But the indifference of some Adventists and the lack of initiative in others led her to the conclusion that "little heed is given to the Bible" and to see in her own writings that "the Lord has given a lesser light to lead men and women to the greater light" *(Review and Herald,* Jan. 20, 1903).

Considered the dean of all Seventh-day Adventist expositors, she intended her books to bring people "back to the Word that they have neglected to follow" and to call attention to "general principles [from the Word] for the formation of correct habits of living" *(Testimonies,* vol. 5, pp. 663, 664). However, they were *not* to serve as a substitute for, or an alternative to, God's Word. She herself warned: "The *Testimonies* were not given to take the place of the Bible" *(ibid.,* p. 663). Because she and others hammered out what they believed from the Bible alone, she personally advised others to "prove their positions from the Scriptures and substantiate every point . . . claim[ed] as truth from the revealed Word of God" *(Evangelism,* p. 256). She echoed the sentiments of many founding fathers when she urged: "As the miner digs for the golden treasure in the earth, so earnestly, persistently, must we seek for the treasure of God's word" *(Counsels to Parents and Teachers,* p. 461).

From earliest times Adventists have considered truth to be progressive. A persistent searcher for truth herself, Ellen White once said that "whenever the people of God are growing in grace, they will be constantly obtaining a clearer understanding of His word. . . . But as real spiritual life declines, it has ever been the tendency to cease to advance in the knowledge of the truth" *(Testimonies,* vol. 5, p. 706). In other words, the Bible student who returns to a passage for further or renewed study can always receive fresh insights from the same text. A new situation, a different perspective, or an urgent need can provide an up-to-date setting in which the truth may correct earlier views, communicate something new, or advance understanding of what is already known.

In fact, every time we handle the Word it is important to remember that "we must not think, 'Well, we have all the truth, we understand the main pillars of the faith, and we may rest on this knowledge.' The truth is an advancing truth, and we must walk in the increasing light" *(Review and Herald,* Mar. 25, 1890). Otherwise we may fall into the light trap of traditionalism, that self-contained system made popular by certain Pharisees (Matt. 15:1-9). We should beware of perpetuating opinions that agree with what we believe. "A spirit of pharisaism has been coming in upon the people who claim to believe the truth for these last days. They are self-satisfied. They have said, 'We have the truth. There is no more light for the people of God.' But we are not safe when we take a position that we will not accept anything else than that upon which we have settled as truth. We should take the Bible and investigate it closely for ourselves. We should dig in the mine of God's word for truth" *(Review and Herald,* June 18, 1889).

"There is no excuse for any one in taking the position that there is no more truth to be revealed, and that all our expositions of Scripture are without error. The fact that certain doctrines have been held as truth for many years by our people, is not a proof that our ideas are infallible" *(ibid.,* Dec. 20, 1892).

Now, there is nothing wrong with clinging to the pillars—those "positions that cannot be shaken; but we must not look with suspicion upon any new light God may send, and say, Really, we cannot see that we need any more light than the old truth which we have hitherto received, and in which we are settled. While we hold to this position, the testimony of the True Witness applies to our cases its rebuke, 'And knowest not that thou art wretched, and miserable, and poor, and blind, and naked.' Those who feel rich and increased with goods and in need of nothing, are in a condition of blindness as to their true condition before God, and they know it not" *(ibid.,* Aug. 7, 1894).

Like so many other Christians, too many Seventh-day Adventists claim that they are "loyal to the message," the collection of doctrines as we have them, as though it were already perfected. The consensus of the rank and file, however, is that it would be better if Christians everywhere would be willing to reexamine and revise their message in newer light and claim loyalty to Christ, who is perfect and "the same yesterday and today and forever" (Heb. 13:8). It is His Spirit who will "teach you all things" and "guide you into all the truth" (John 14:26; 16:13) through "mental effort and prayer for wisdom" *(Counsels to Parents and Teachers,* p. 461).

Some Seventh-day Adventists labor under the misconception that Ellen White endorsed only God's Word and her own writings as the sole tools in the search for truth, but that simply is not true. Instead, she appealed to ministers: "Make the preaching of the truth a success. . . . A careful study of the Bible will not necessarily exclude all other reading of a religious nature; but if the word of God is studied prayerfully, all reading which will have a tendency to divert the mind from it will be excluded" *(Testimonies,* vol. 2, pp. 337, 338).

Although Scripture dominated her own sermons, Ellen White's writings show that she also used outside sources. "Most of the material in 1SM on inspiration is borrowed from Calvin Stowe *[Origin and History of the Books of the Bible,* pp. 13-20] with significant omissions" (R. Edward Turner, *Proclaiming the Word: The Concept of Preaching in the Thought of Ellen White*, p. 58).

Ellen White's grandson, Arthur White, wrote: "William C. White, my father, reports that when he was a mere boy he heard his mother read D'Aubigné's *History of the Reformation* to his father. . . . Her reading helped her to locate and identify many of the events presented to her in vision. . . . She was not always informed as to just where and when the events transpired" (*The Ellen G. White Writings*, p. 110). Even though the Spirit revealed truth to her, she still needed the help of outside sources to complete her study.

This in no way diminishes the quality of her inspiration or the reliability of her writings, as George Rice aptly explains in his book *Luke, a Plagiarist?* (See also Arthur White, "Toward a Factual Concept of Inspiration" and "Toward a Factual Concept of Inspiration, II: The Role of Visions and the Use of Historical Sources in the *Great Controversy*," *The Ellen G. White Writings*, pp. 13-48.) Although "she did not write essentially as a historian," "her reading of D'Aubigné, Wiley, and others proved to be helpful. She sometimes drew on them for clear historical statements to help make plain to the reader the things she was endeavoring to present. Also by thus corroborating with well-accepted historical evidence what had been revealed to her, she would win the confidence of the general reader in the truths she was presenting" (*The Ellen G. White Writings*, pp. 113, 114).

Yet "when *Spirit of Prophecy*, volume 4, came from the press and our ministers and members began to read it, they discovered that Mrs. White had employed a number of historical quotations, and this use led to some questions" (*ibid.*, p. 114). Some people wondered why she would do this if God were her sole source of inspiration, but she was simply making use of carefully researched nineteenth-century literature to explore and communicate biblical truth (see F. D. Nichol, *Ellen G. White and Her Critics*, pp. 403-407, and *The Ellen G. White Writings*, pp. 107-136). In fact, an inventory of her estate at the time of her death revealed a vast collection of study books among her possessions. (See "A Bibliography of Ellen G. White's Private and Office Libraries," compiled by Warren H. Johns, Tim Poirier, and Ron Graybill.)

Ellen White found outside sources helpful in preparing her books. She also found that "in daily Bible study the verse-by-verse method is often most helpful" (*Counsels to Parents and Teachers*, p. 461). In *Proclaiming the Word: The Concept of Preaching in the Thought of Ellen White*, author R. Edward Turner explains: "Ellen White recognized the importance of a sound methodology in using Scripture. Although she never wrote out her rules for interpretation in explicit form, she did, over a period of years, write concerning the ways to study and interpret Scripture. From these random statements an underlying methodology begins to appear" (p. 58).

First of all, she appreciated the place of *context* in interpretation: "The student should learn to view the word as a whole, and to see the relation of its parts. He should gain a knowledge of its grand central theme—of God's original purpose for the world, of the rise of the great controversy, and of the work of redemption. . . . He . . . should learn to trace their working through the records of history and prophecy, to the great consummation" (*Counsels to Parents and Teachers*, p. 462). She recommended that God's people take into full consideration the "time and place" of writing of the passage, or else they may "misinterpret and misrepresent" (*Selected Messages*, book 1, p. 57) what the author intended.

She, along with many of her colleagues, advocated *word study* as an essential step to getting at the author's original intent. Early denominational documents reveal the widespread conviction that "the writers of the Bible had to express their ideas in human language" and that "different meanings are expressed by the same word" (*Selected Messages*, book 1, pp. 19, 20). Furthermore, since "the language of the Bible should be explained according to its obvious meaning, unless a symbol or figure is employed" (*The Great Controversy*, p. 599), many of our pioneers were not satisfied with merely a surface view. They believed that biblical truths must be "searched" and "dug out by painstaking effort" (*Selected Messages*, book 1, p. 20).

Additionally, Seventh-day Adventists have always understood the need to grasp what the text meant to its original audience, before attempting to explain what the text means to a modern congregation. "Understanding what the words of Jesus meant to those who heard them," says Ellen White, "we may discern in them a new vividness and beauty, and may also gather for ourselves their deeper lessons" (*Thoughts From the Mount of Blessing*, p. 1). An integral part of the procedure of this handbook is the task of setting the text in its original *historical and cultural situation*.

A century and a half of Seventh-day Adventist interpreters have shared Ellen White's opinion that "the Bible is its own best expositor. Scripture is to be compared with scripture. . . . The Old Testament sheds light upon the New, and the New upon the Old. Each is a revelation of the glory of God in Christ. Christ as manifested to the patriarchs, as symbolized in the sacrificial service, as portrayed in the law, and as revealed by the prophets, is the riches of the Old Testament. Christ in His life, His death, and His resurrection; Christ as He is manifested by the Holy Spirit, is the treasure of the New. Both Old and New present truths that will continually reveal new depths of meaning to the earnest seeker" (*Counsels to Parents and Teachers*, pp. 462, 463).

She believed in exegesis before proclamation and advised gospel workers to "help them [those in every congregation upon whom the Spirit of the Lord is moving] to understand what is truth; break the bread of life to them" (*Gospel Workers*, p. 154).

Speakers are supposed to open up the Scriptures and pass on their nourishing truths to the hungry souls who hear them, but not with "flowery discourses" or "a flood of words without meaning" (*ibid.*). Those who break the bread of life must "call their [the people's] attention to vital questions [eternal issues]" (*ibid.*), "to fortify the hearers for the daily battles of life" (*ibid.*, p. 153)—something you cannot do without staying in touch with them to prepare practical, insightful messages that mean something to those who hear them. "The reception of the gospel does not depend on learned testimonies, eloquent speeches, or deep arguments, but upon its simplicity, and its adaptation to those who are hungering for the bread of life" (*ibid.*, p. 155).

A sermon is more than a glorified Bible study or an opportunity to persuade people to agree with your views. It is a life-or-death presentation of truth painstakingly discovered, carefully arranged, and simply told so as to "touch the common life experience, the daily necessities; bringing home to the heart the very truths which are of vital interest" (*Evangelism*, p. 182). You do this by preaching what is important to the congregation—not to you.

As a denomination, Seventh-day Adventists recognize that the Bible contains "textual variances due to emendations, copyist error, and differing source materials" (Turner, p. 61), which make difficult, at best, the exploration of biblical "mysteries too deep for the human mind to explain or even fully comprehend" (*Testimonies*, vol. 5, p. 699). Consistent with her views of revelation and inspiration, however, Ellen White also insisted that "variations found in the gospel narratives were not really an issue to be confused over, but one in which the expressions of [inspired] authors were the creative [and not the mechanical] product of individual personalities" (Turner, p. 61).

But even with the best resources at our disposal, we need to remember that the best exegete never forgets that "it is the efficiency of the Spirit that makes the ministry of the word effective" *(Gospel Workers*, p. 155).

So this handbook offers a full range of "tools" to mine the raw truth in its proper context and to polish the precious jewels you find into a finished presentation.

To God be the glory, now and always.

INTRODUCTION

The Bible claims that people can know God because He has chosen to reveal Himself and to unfold truths about Himself in *words* and *deeds* (2 Peter 1:16-21). According to the apostle Paul, God used human language, despite its limitations, to record this supernatural revelation (2 Tim. 3:16). Peter explains the "how" when he tells us that whether God supplied the information or supervised its writing, the Holy Spirit is ultimately responsible for *all* Holy Scripture (2 Peter 1:21). Any attempt to interpret the Bible must consider both its *human* and *divine* dimensions.

Let the Bible Speak for Itself

A wholesome lesson always begins with healthy interpretation. So you must come to terms with the text *before* you can have anything meaningful to share from it. That's why no-nonsense interpreters follow a *hermeneutic,* a sound system of principles that allows the text to speak for itself through *exegesis,* a procedure that consistently leads the truth out of Bible texts. *Hermeneutics* refers to the machinery, and *exegesis* to the method, of biblical interpretation. Hence Jesus could claim: "Whoever has seen me has seen the Father" (John 14:9), because according to John 1:18, He "led [the Greek verb is the root from which we get our word "exegete"] the Father out to us." The Father accurately expressed Himself through Jesus because Jesus allowed Him to represent Himself. Similarly, the only way truth can communicate with us through the text is for it to speak for itself.

Exegetical Method

This book will present a proven six-step procedure that, under the Holy Spirit's direction, should allow you to prepare faithfully the text for any practical application—whether it is for personal growth, public teaching, or pulpit preaching.

Contextual Analysis—Before working with a text, you must acquaint yourself with the *context,* the body of text surrounding a passage that sheds light on its meaning. You do this by locating the text in the larger stream of revelation that progressively flows from the Old Testament into the New Testament (sometimes called "cotext" by linguists) and then tracing the general flow of a specific author's thought, and fixing where and how your text fits into his book—the immediate context.

Structural Analysis—Every writer has a system for developing ideas. To capture the biblical author's overall pattern, you will analyze the literary style. Begin by identifying the type of literature, and look for characteristic features. Trace the way the biblical writer organized his or her [some recent authors have postulated female Bible writers] views, with main and supporting arguments, into a series of connected thoughts. Mark the starting and ending points of the topics and themes that you find along the literary-grammatical trail. Once you pinpoint all the building blocks of thought in their context, they are individually ready for study.

Verbal Analysis—Then you can focus on individual words and details to uncover what the author meant to say. Once you have the original setting, explore the author's language. Acquaint yourself with unfamiliar words. Word forms offer invaluable insights, so consider them carefully. Identify and decipher figures of speech. Examine and explain symbols. Try to define key terms in their context. It's time to get specific.

Cultural Analysis—Investigate the historical-cultural background to your text. Enrich your initial findings with insights from history, anthropology, geography, and the environment. If you allow the ancient world to speak for itself, you can recover the original setting and enter the writer's or speaker's world. Obscure terms will clarify themselves, difficult texts will yield their secrets, and you will move about the biblical terrain, so to speak, with enough familiarity to give your study a ring of authenticity.

Theological Analysis—Here is where you tie things together and bring out the whole story. You do this by expanding the range of study and by relating your text to the rest of the Bible. Place the biblical passage in the broader context of the plan of salvation. Trace it along the path from promise to fulfillment in order to see where it is coming from and going to. Consider its Old Testament roots and/or New Testament developments. Use earlier passages to understand later ones and later texts to capture the fuller sense of earlier ones.

Homiletical Analysis—The exegetical process is incomplete until it brings out the author's meaning to your audience. So you must explore the various ways that you may present what you have learned to your listeners. These approaches must make sense of the text and help your hearers reach a decision concerning its message. Before you can settle on a certain type or style of sermon, however, you should consider stylistic, physical, and psychological factors. Once you have done that, you can take what the author meant, organize your thoughts logically, and make it relevant for the congregation today.

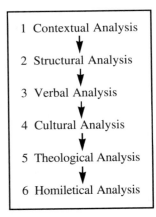

FIGURE 1

As you can see, this approach to Bible study is both cumulative and progressive. Each step builds on the preceding one and leads to the next. Sound exegesis is a process rather than a list of techniques. If you leave out or try to bypass a single step, the results will likely prove inaccurate.

The rest of this book attempts to explain this method in detail. Although any single chapter has the potential to improve your presentation, a grasp of the complete procedure will bring the best results.

However, a word of warning. Don't assume that you can sit down, read this book from the opening page to the closing page, and absorb in a single sitting or even two or three what is herein presented. Instead, take the book in "doses." Read a few pages or a short section at a time. Because of the size of this book, it can be quite daunting. But it need not be an overwhelming challenge if you take it in bite-size chunks. Read Section I—Survey first. Then if you wish to go into matters in more depth (and I urge you to do that), begin to read Part II—A Closer Look.

PART 1

SURVEY

CHAPTER 1

CONTEXTUAL ANALYSIS

Preachers and teachers should strive for the fullest message possible, because anything less may leave the congregation empty. For example, when Priscilla and Aquila first heard Apollos preach at the synagogue in Ephesus, they found that his messages were not quite right. Since Apollos based his studies on less than the whole story, his sermons were incomplete (Acts 18:24-28). As Aquila and Priscilla filled him in on what was missing, the Spirit gave Apollos deeper insights and richer doctrine. Eventually some of the Corinthian church members compared him favorably to Paul and Peter (1 Cor. 1:12).

The Only Authorized Context

In your study of God's Word, avoid incomplete conclusions. Don't isolate a passage from what comes before or after it in the text. Instead, get the whole picture. To do this you will need to acquaint yourself with the *context*, the entire body of text surrounding a passage, which sheds light on its meaning. The following diagram illustrates the relationship between the four principle Bible contexts:

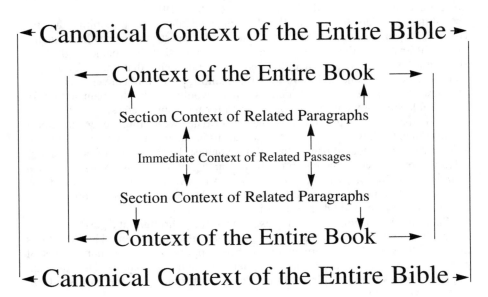

◄ Canonical Context of the Entire Bible ►

◄ Context of the Entire Book ►

Section Context of Related Paragraphs

Immediate Context of Related Passages

Section Context of Related Paragraphs

◄ Context of the Entire Book ►

◄ Canonical Context of the Entire Bible ►

FIGURE 2

25

The Canonical Context

Did you know that God revealed more to His people than just the collection of writings we call the Bible? For example, 1 Chronicles 29:29 mentions books by three ancient Hebrew prophets, yet God saw fit to preserve the words of only one—Samuel.

Although it took more than 300 years to finalize the New Testament group of writings, people who lived during biblical times apparently recognized and honored God's Word from the time it first appeared. In A.D. 350 Athanasius, bishop of Alexandria, was the first person to identify *ta biblia* (the Bible) with *kanon* (a Greek word that meant measuring stick). Later, in his 39th Festal Letter (Easter, A.D. 367), he was the first to propose the 27 constituent parts of the New Testament as it exists today.

The 66 books of the entire Bible constitute the Protestant *canon* of Scripture—the officially recognized body of inspired writings. (The Jewish canon differs from the Christian canon, of course, because it does not include the Christian writings. The Samaritan canon differs from that of the Jews because it includes only the first five books of the Hebrew Bible. And the Roman Catholic canon includes more books—the Apocrypha—than does the Protestant canon.) Even though different people wrote the books of the Bible during a span of some 1,500 years, the entire collection functions for us as a single unit—the Holy Bible.

The early church had two reasons for attaching its faith to this group of authoritative writings: (1) to maintain a direct connection with the apostles and prophets and (2) to establish a perpetual, divine standard of faith and practice.

Today the Christian community still believes that God continues to make Himself, His will, and His purpose known through the Scriptures. Even though the Bible is a record of what God has already said and done, the sacred writings are more than a memorial of the past. Indeed, they remain a fresh, living witness to the present and the future—until Christ returns (2 Peter 1:19).

Biblical scholars have argued with each other about the possibility that the Bible has a single overarching theme. Those who insist that it does have such a theme differ among themselves, however, regarding what that theme might be. I side with those who suggest that there is one overall theme that unifies every moment of history into one divine working plan, uniting every biblical verse into a single, powerful message. This all-inclusive motif would thus be the main setting for every Bible study—the ultimate context even for individual verses.

And just what do I think this theme is? The everlasting covenant. God's promise/plan to all who believe in Messiah Jesus is the grand story line that unfolds itself across every sacred page. "In both testaments, the same God offers the same salvation by the same Savior through the same actions" (John Marsh, *Biblical Authority for Today*, p. 189). Spread cover to cover, this canonical context can serve as the foremost framework for Bible study because it shows us both where a text is coming from and where it is going.

Salvation is a promise that unfolds progressively throughout a period of time, rather than a prediction that is limited to a particular fulfillment. The Scriptures attest to the way that the covenant has been appropriate for human beings of every age, accommodating itself to a variety of historical contexts. The covenant began prior to sin and continues in a redemptive format since the Fall (see Gen. 3:15; cf. verse 21).

When He installed Adam and Eve as royal caretakers of His creation (Gen.

1:28ff.), the Creator revealed the plans for His creation, and He intends to see these plans through.

The covenant with Noah confirmed the Creator's resolve to bless His creation—even if He had to re-create it.

The covenant with Abraham embraced all the nations of the world. The Creator installed the aging patriarch as both the object and agent of promise to extend the sphere of blessedness to people everywhere (Gen. 12:1-3).

The covenant with Moses called on Israel to demonstrate its appreciation of the Creator, who also redeems, with holy service according to His law (Ex. 19:6; 20:1ff.). Although fulfillment depended upon their loyalty, only the Creator has the attributes to keep the covenant in force (Ex. 34:6).

The covenant with David gave further structure to the agreement by placing it in a theocratic context (2 Sam. 7:8-16), thus symbolizing His royal presence and commitment with the Temple. During David's reign God continued to prepare Israel for the literal fulfillment of His promises to Abraham and Moses under Solomon (2 Sam. 8; 1 Kings 4:20-25).

The latter prophets used the covenant as a symbol of hope for the post-exilic future (Isa. 55:3).

The new covenant of which Christians speak is not a separate arrangement, but the ultimate expression of the Creator's faithfulness and determination to carry out His original plans for the Creation. It was progressively disclosed in the previous covenants. Israel's hope, revealed in the progression of divine covenants, reached climactic proportions in the person and ministry of Jesus. He was the promised King who was to perpetuate the covenant, make it possible for Israel to complete her original mission, and inaugurate the age that will usher in the final edition of the kingdom—the new earth.

Adam	Noah	Abraham	Moses	David	The New Covenant		
					FORETOLD	INTRODUCED	ESTABLISHED
Gen. 1-2	Gen. 9	Gen. 12, 15, 17	Ex. 19-20	2 Sam. 7	Jer. 31 Ex. 36	Matt. 26	Heb. 8

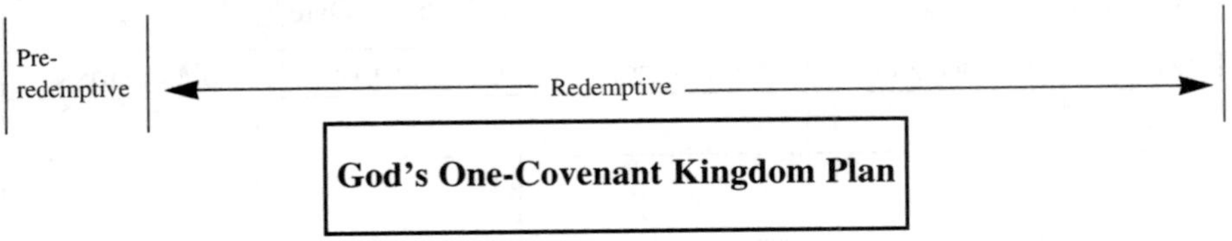

Pre-redemptive ◄——————————— Redemptive ———————————►

God's One-Covenant Kingdom Plan

FIGURE 3

It is so much easier to see where each part fits into the big picture when you have a view like this of the whole. Every verse is ripe for understanding if it is allowed to grow from its Old Testament roots into fruit on the New Testament branches of the Bible tree. (These are distinctly Christian terms, of course. Our Jewish friends do not think in terms of a "New" Testament added to an "Old" Testament. They refer to their Bible as the Tanakh, an acrostic made up of the initial letter of each of the three divisions of the Hebrew Scriptures—*Torah* [law], *Nebiim* [prophets], and *Kethubim* [writings].)

In terms of progressive fulfillment, we are still living during the stage when branches grow, bud, and bear fruit. God's people have always lived in the tension of present real-

27

ity on the way to future fulfillment. We still draw strength from God's record of faithfulness in the past in order to believe He will act according to His promises in the future. Like our Old Testament brethren, we live by faith, awaiting the "age to come."

So while it is important that you examine the historical context, it is equally critical that you relate the passage to God's unfolding plan as it appears throughout the Scriptures, because every word of God is for all God's people regardless of their nationality or era. Until you get a fix on your text in the flow of progressive revelation, you cannot relate its message to the past, present, and future of God's promises.

The Book Context

Once you have established solid contact with this overall theme, it is time to search for the overall plan and purpose of the book from which you have selected a passage. (See the *International Inductive Study Bible*. Its book-by-book work sheets make it a contextual analysis workbook.) Introduce yourself to the background and structure of the particular scriptural book by completing a biblical data chart. Consult at least three different sources for the information it takes to fill in its boxes.

Because you are in the preliminary stages of study, now is the time to get only a rough sketch of things. Fine details should come later. For example, if geography appears to play a major role in the passage, you may want to glance at a Bible atlas for a lay of the land, but that is all. For now, just get in touch with *who* wrote the book, *when*, *where*, and to *whom* he addressed it. Then try to figure out *why*. Read the entire book through, and jot down the reasons or motives the author may admit, whatever he challenges the readers to join him in doing, or anything he seems to be driving at so that you can determine the overall purpose.

As you begin to make out the general shape of the whole book, specific verses will stand out. Sort through and pick out the main ones, but it is too early to concentrate on any particular passage. Below (Figure 4) is a scaled-down version of the biblical data chart that appears in Appendix A.

FIGURE 4

Biblical Data for the Book of _____ Date _____				
DATA	DICTIONARY	INTRODUCTION	COMMENTARY	CONCLUSIONS
Author				
Date written				
From where?				
To whom?				
Why?				
Main theme				
Key verses				

The next step is to sketch a flow chart of the entire book. Draw a *horizontal* line to represent the author's flow of thought. Trace the progressive stops that unfold his purpose and lead to his goal. For example, in his *second* epistle, Peter seems to think along these lines:

BOOK OF THE BIBLE FLOW CHART "A"
FIGURE 5

Chapter 1	Chapter 2	Chapter 3
Foundation	Caution	Exhortation

But sometimes one line is not enough. Just as does Mark's gospel, your Bible book may require two sloping lines to get the author's point across:

BOOK OF THE BIBLE FLOW CHART "B"
FIGURE 6

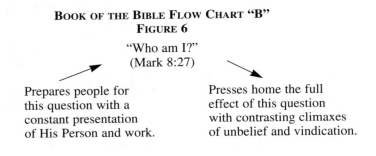

"Who am I?"
(Mark 8:27)

Prepares people for this question with a constant presentation of His Person and work.

Presses home the full effect of this question with contrasting climaxes of unbelief and vindication.

BOOK OF THE BIBLE FLOW CHART "C"
FIGURE 7

Matthew's gospel requires a stepladder:

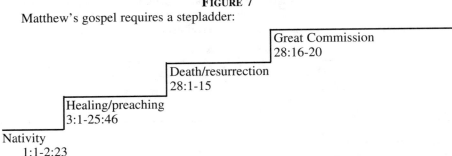

Great Commission
28:16-20

Death/resurrection
28:1-15

Healing/preaching
3:1-25:46

Nativity
1:1-2:23

Whatever shape your flow chart takes, a diagram of the biblical author's primary line of reasoning across the book is a must for mapping out the rest of the context.

The Section Context

During this aspect of your contextual studies, you focus your attention on the natural breaks in the text that divide it into sections. Read the entire book through *at one sitting* and try to concentrate on the larger relationships in the passage.

Be on the Lookout for *Repetition*—Sometimes repeated terms, phrases, clauses, and sentences act as headings to introduce sections. For example, you may read the words "And it came to pass" repeatedly. Or these elements may act as tailpieces to conclude each section. (See, for instance, Luke 1:80; 2:40; cf. 2:52.) Some authors repeat key words, propositions, or concepts to set the tone for entire sections—such as the word "love" in 1 John.

Search for *Grammatical Clues*—Some conjunctions and adverbs mark the place where the author made a transition. Hunt out such words as "then," "therefore," "wherefore," "but," "nevertheless," or "meanwhile." If you know Greek, pay attention to the words *oun, de, kai, tote,* or *dio.*

Watch Out for *Rhetorical Questions*—Verses such as Romans 6:1 could signal a switch to a new theme or new section. Sometimes you might find a series of questions designed to keep up the argument or plan of an entire section, as in Romans 3:1, 3, 5, 6, 7, 8, 9, etc.

Be Alert to *Psychological Indicators*—Occasionally an author will (1) leave out a conjunction (asyndeton) when in a hurry or excited or thinking fast; (2) insert an explanation (parenthesis) when wanting to throw in some guidelines for interpretation (see, for an example, Eph. 3:2-13); or (3) not bother to finish a sentence before going on to the next thought (anacoluthon) when really stirred up about something.

Be Sensitive to *Changes*—When the author switches the *time, location,* or *setting*—especially when either he or the speaker is narrating something—or modifies the *tense, voice,* or *mood* of a verb, it could signal the inception of something new. A shift in the *subject or object* or of *attention* from one group to another (usually with a vocative—"O man," [Rom. 2:1]) frequently establishes sectional limits in the epistles.

Don't Miss When the Author *Announces* the Theme—Paul clearly states the topic for the section (1 Thess. 4:13-18) when he says: "But we do not want you to remain uninformed, brethren, *about those who are asleep*" (verse 13).

After you have divided the book into its major sections, *prepare a map* to show the natural breaks in the text. Chart each turn in the author's flow of thought. For example, here is how you might map the main sections in Peter's second epistle:

THE SECTION MAP—FIGURE 8

Greetings	Foundation	Caution	Exhortation	Conclusion
	COVENANT			
Benediction	Cooperation	Desecration	Consummation	Benediction
1:1, 2	1:3-21	2:1-22	3:1-17	3:18

The Immediate Context

Once you locate your text in the stream of progressive revelation, it is time for you to pin down where and how it fits into its book and section. Unlike its forerunners, however, this step presents some unique challenges. As A. Berkeley Mickelson points out: "The first responsibility of every interpreter is to note carefully what precedes and what follows any verse or passage which he is interpreting. This often involves going back two or three paragraphs and ahead two or three paragraphs. Chapter divisions do not necessarily serve as boundary lines. One may need to go back to the preceding chapter or ahead to the next chapter to get the true context" (*Interpreting the Bible*, p. 102).

Each section of a biblical book can be broken down into paragraphs, that is, distinct blocks of related thought. (The Old Testament was not originally written in paragraphs—just as the entire Bible was not originally written in verses. The paragraph was originally considered a form of punctuation among the Greeks and was the only punctuation mark that Aristotle ever mentioned. Aristophanes, in developing his theory of rhetoric, subdivided long segments of writing into periods, colons, and commas, which, of course, we now consider punctuation marks and not sections of copy. The Hebrew books of Scripture were divided into *parashiyyot*, not paragraphs, and at least some of these parashiyyot were given names. For example, the *parashah* [singular of *parashiyyot]* of Moses' encounter with God in the wilderness was called "the bush" and appears that way in Mark 12:26; Luke 20:37; Acts 7:35.)

Even if your text is only a fragment of a paragraph, your search for its connection with what comes before and after it may span the entire section. At times your investigation may extend to other sections—especially if your text is part of a section that resumes or develops an earlier topic or theme that differs from those of bordering sections. The connection may be:

1. *historical* if the text is tied to actual facts, people, places, or events—possibly in chronological order.

2. *logical* when the text is involved in a chain of reasoning, either depending on what the writer or speaker said previously or as part of a developing argument.

3. *theological* if the text develops some historical fact or circumstance along Christological, ecclesiological, or eschatological lines (see chapter 5, the section on typology under the subdivision of the analogy of faith).

4. *psychological* when the author or speaker seems to go off on a tangent for some inexplicable reason. Actually, something in the preceding text most likely triggered a somewhat different but related idea that interrupted the flow of thought. The result is usually an *asyndeton* (the omission of conjunctions that normally link together words or phrases), a *parenthesis* (a digression or explanation), or an *anacoluthon* (inconsistent or incoherent syntax within a sentence that breaks off the original line of reasoning to launch into what at first appears to be out-of-place). The mood of a verb is also a key to the speaker or writer's psychology. (See chapter 3.)

For example, more is at stake than Samson's personal fall in Judges 16. The angel of the Lord announced in 13:5 that Samson would begin to deliver his people—not just himself. So taking the larger context into account, we discover that God meant for Samson's individual Nazirite vows to commence the process of separating both him and Israel from a pagan Philistine environment.

God used the Hebrew strongman as a symbol of cultural differences to instigate division between His people and their oppressors. For instance, the Philistines relied on military prowess to give them the advantage over their neighbors. Archaeologists have uncovered evidence that the Philistines shaved their heads for hand-to-hand combat. Imagine how Samson's uncut locks stood out against a sea of Philistine "skinheads." So Samson's final blow against the Dagon worshipers was more than an act of personal vindication; it was a blow toward Israel's freedom.

Interpreters need to remember that there is a danger of bypassing the historical situation and reading the text as if God spoke directly to them and contemporary society. The opposite risk is also possible—that interpreters may get bogged down in the immediate situation and draw the incorrect conclusion that God spoke only to

Israel. As you attempt to understand Scripture, stay in touch with the everlasting covenant and explore how God's people related to your text in pre-Exilic, Exilic, and post-Exilic times, and both before and after Christ's first advent.

Notice the summarizing guidelines for contextual analysis, adapted from Mickelsen's book, *Interpreting the Bible* (p. 113).

---

1. Keep everything in perspective. Never lose sight of the big picture. The smaller the quantity of material under investigation, the greater the danger of ignoring context. The entire Bible is the eventual context for your verse or passage. Build your study on a canonical framework.

2. Examine the book as you zero in on the more local setting for your text. Discover its overall plan and purpose. Prepare a biblical data chart of background information and a Bible flow chart of the author's thought.

3. Concentrate on the larger relationships in the text. Map the entire book, separating it at those points where it naturally divides into major segments of thought. Your verse or passage belongs to one of these sections of the book.

4. Explore the immediate context of your verse or passage. Observe any parallels between it and other material in the same section. You may have to go outside the local section to establish a historical, logical, theological, or psychological connection with what comes before and after it.

5. Expand the context to canonical proportions. Observe any parallels with other material, first in the same book and then in another book by the same author, and finally in other books by different authors. Try to find genuine parallels that come from the same time period.

CHAPTER 2

STRUCTURAL ANALYSIS

There is more to locking in the meaning of a word than just looking it up in a dictionary. When you single out and apply one of the definitions for a word under consideration, you might plug a meaning into the text that forces the verse to say something it does not. You could even distort the sense of the entire passage.

To Begin With

Language experts recognize that the literary *context* reflects an author's overall flow of connected thoughts. It provides the framework for each word and even directions as to how the sentence should function. Every sentence gets its instructions, so to speak, from the words, phrases, and clauses that precede it, and it influences those that follow. That is why experienced interpreters investigate larger textual segments instead of individual words in the process of trying to get a sense of what the author meant. They work with clauses, phrases, and sentences, while paying strict attention to the details of each component word.

Since the Bible writers expressed themselves both by the word forms they chose and by the way that they arranged those forms, grammatical analysis is not enough. Grammar may tell us how words are used in their various forms, but *syntax* explains how word forms are arranged into phrases, clauses, and sentences. *Structural analysis*[1] aims to expose the overall pattern by which an author develops his ideas, with main and supporting arguments, into a series of connected thoughts—without disturbing the original context or stripping the writer's original intent from a single word.

Instead of concentrating on individual words, structural studies focus on the way the author assembled them into a single whole—in order to separate the text into distinct blocks of thought called paragraphs—without tearing the text apart. The contribution of each word becomes clear, as you trace the way the author organized his views. (See Walter C. Kaiser, Jr., *Toward an Exegetical Theology*, p. 89.)

THE SYNTACTICAL PROCESS—FIGURE 9

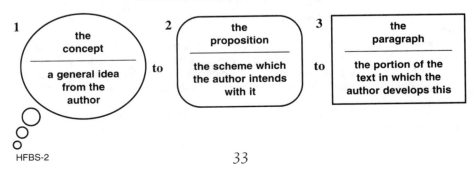

1. the concept
   _____
   a general idea from the author

to

2. the proposition
   _____
   the scheme which the author intends with it

to

3. the paragraph
   _____
   the portion of the text in which the author develops this

33

Generally, an author progressively develops his thoughts the usual literary way:

FIGURE 10

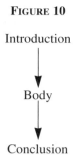

Introduction

Body

Conclusion

The Introduction—If the author has written a narrative, the unifying principle is most often chronology, and the author usually gives the basics about time, place, characters, and other important information in the introduction.

New Testament stories, for example, often compress this information into a single sentence, as in Matthew 8:5-13 (KJV). Matthew quickly establishes what follows as the next event in a sequence ("And when"); tells us where (Capernaum); gives the reason for the encounter ("my servant . . . sick of the palsy"); indicates the social positions of the characters (centurion, Lord, servant); and reveals the centurion's genuine concern for his servant's welfare ("beseeching him"). Thus he gives us a clue to the centurion's character and attitude.

Old Testament narratives tend to stress historical data, such as time and place in their introductions. Esther 1:1-3, for example, supplies the background to the feast (time, date, occasion, and guest list), which is the occasion that queen Vashti refused to appear before King Ahasuerus and to impress the VIPs at his court.

If the writer intends to *persuade* readers about something, the introduction takes whatever form appeals to the widest audience. In 1 Corinthians the first thing Paul does is to establish himself and his position to his readers. Instead of tooting his own apostolic horn, he displays the affection and concern of a genuine shepherd, which makes the reprimands that follow easier to take. As Christ's emissary he can accomplish a great deal more than as a leader in his own right.

When a writer intends to express clear, incisive thoughts or the importance of cause and effect, he frequently uses *lead-in* sentences to introduce each progressive step in the development of thought, linking each step clearly to what has gone before. Lead-in sentences focus the readers' or listeners' attention, preparing them for what follows. Each paragraph picks up an idea (or more often an exact word) from the closing sentence of the preceding paragraph and that idea, finally linking it clearly with the next paragraph.

Therefore, each chapter, and especially each paragraph, in 1 Corinthians has its own organization within the greater organization of the whole. Each unit has its own introduction, body, and conclusion as Paul elaborates on an idea introduced in a preceding chapter or verse. The conclusion leads into the next major unit, and the pattern repeats itself.

The Body—After the introduction accomplishes its purpose, the writer frequently amplifies a thread, a detail, or concept set forth in the introduction (1) by presenting examples, (2) by taking a more detailed look at various aspects of it, or (3) by developing it into a larger issue.

In a narrative the body begins after the introduction has presented the time, place, and characters and has developed the plot and action. In nonnarrative prose, it is usually easy to detect when the writer moves on to the body of the work.

In the book of Romans, for instance, Paul finishes his introduction with the theme he will follow (1:16, 17) and immediately shifts into an explanation of what he means (verse 18).

Jude rushes right into his purpose for writing (verse 3), and after he exposes the false teachers, he repeatedly reminds his readers of the danger they present to the faithful. These reminders clearly define the way that Jude organized his thoughts as he leads us from one major thought unit into the next.

The Conclusion—The conclusion is the place where the writer or speaker pulls together the main threads of the introduction and the high points of the body. He can (1) summarize things, (2) deductively or inductively reason his way to a principle, (3) call readers to action, or (4) ask a significant question, to mention only a few.

Conclusions to the New Testament epistles usually stand out sharply as they return the reader to the tone found in the introductions. Frequently they summarize things in the form of a doxology followed with final greetings and blessings. Biblical narratives usually have a brief conclusion, simply telling about the action that resulted from the climax or noting that the characters left the scene and went to another place.

In Summary—Biblical writers organized their thoughts in the usual literary way: with an introduction, a body, and a conclusion. This overall format even appears within the chapters or smaller units.

Those ideas grouped together in paragraphs, or in stanzas of poetry, work very closely together and form a cluster of associated minor thought units. Structural analysis explores the way that these clusters contribute to the overall progression of thought.

The ability to analyze the author's style will help the interpreter see how everything works together to achieve a total effect. Style reflects the complex attitudes and environmental influences directly responsible for the thought patterns and habitual vocabulary that the author uses to express himself or herself in writing. As structural analysis recaptures the writer's pattern for putting words together, it simultaneously reconstructs his thread of thought and so reproduces the original meaning from the text.

Here is the basic syntactical procedure:

1. Identify what type of literature you are working with.

2. Trace the way that the author develops the idea into a full-fledged proposition by (a) identifying the form of each word; (b) recognizing the way that the author organized the words into groups to form phrases, clauses, or sentences; (c) determining the relationship of one group to another; and (d) measuring the rhythm of groups as a result of stresses and pauses.

3. Define all paragraphs, the basic units for any further study. This is the aim of the first two steps.

Identifying the Type of Literature

There are five basic literary types.

Prose—Plain, free-flowing language that isn't organized according to the rules of poetry is prose. There are three classes of biblical prose: (1) speeches—sermons (for example, Deut. 6; Acts 7:2-53) and prayers (for instance, Nehemiah's prayer in Neh.

1:5-11); (2) records—contracts (Gen. 15), letters (Galatians), lists (Ex. 1:1-5; Matt. 1:1-16), laws (Ex. 20:1-17), and ritual observances (Lev. 16); and (3) historical narratives (for example, Acts 17:10-15).

Poetry—This type of literature makes up almost one third of the Old Testament and frequently appears in the New Testament, especially in the gospels. In fact, only Leviticus, Ruth, Ezra, Nehemiah, Esther, Haggai, and Malachi lack some form of poetry. Poetry presents issues in black and white with mostly figurative language. It generally avoids certain devices found in Hebrew prose (such as the definite article—*heh*, the definite direct object marker—*eth*, the relative pronoun—*asher*, and either the *waw* consecutive or conversive).

The dominant feature, however, of biblical poetry is the way it arranges two (a couplet), three (a triad), and even four (a quatrain) lines in parallel.

The three basic kinds of parallels used in Hebrew poetry are:

1. Grammatic—The lines are parallel in form but not in meaning. For example, both lines may have the same word order:

subject	verb	direct object
subject	verb	direct object

But none of the words used need to have the same meaning.

2. Semantic—The lines are parallel in meaning or thought and also can match up grammatically. There are two subdivisions of semantic parallelism:

(a) *synonymous parallelism*, in which the second or succeeding lines repeat the thought from the first line but use different words; for example,

"Israel	does not	know,
My people	do not	consider" (Isa. 1:3, NKJV)

"Love	your enemies,
Do good to	those who hate you, . . .
Bless	those who curse you,
Pray for	those who abuse you" (Luke 6:27, 28).

[Matt. 5:39, 40; 39:46, 47; 6:25; 7:6; 7:7, 8; 10:24, 25; 10:41; 12:30; 12:41, 42; 13:16; 23:39; Mark 2:21, 22; 3:4; 3:24, 25; 3:28; 4:22; 4:30; 8:17, 18; 9:43-47; 10:38; 10:43, 44; 13:24, 25; Luke 6:37, 38; 12:48b; 13:2-5; 15:32; 17:26-29; 19:43, 44; 23:39; John 3:11; 6:35; 6:55; 12:31; 13:16]

(b) *antithetic parallelism*, in which the second or succeeding lines are in contrast with the thought from the first line, but again using different words; for example,

"A soft answer	turns away	wrath,
But a harsh word	stirs up	anger" (Prov. 15:1).

| "A good tree cannot | bear | bad fruit, |
| Nor can a bad tree | bear | good fruit" (Matt. 7:18). |

[Matt. 5:19; 6:2, 3; 6:5, 6; 6:22, 23; 7:17, 18; 10:32, 33; 13:16, 17; 22:14; Mark 2:19, 20; 3:28, 29; 4:25; 7:8; 7:15; 8:35; Luke 6:21a and 25a; 6:21b and 25b; 7:44, 45; 7:46, 47; 16:10; John 3:6; 3:12; 3:17; 3:20, 21]

3. Rhetorical—This type of parallelism uses certain literary devices to balance, beautify, or simplify meaning, and it uses seven different ways to do this:

(a) *climactic*, in which the thoughts repeat and progressively build to a peak; for example:

"The Lord	is	in	his holy temple;
The Lord	is	on	his heavenly throne;
He	observes		the sons of men;
His eyes	examine		them" (Ps. 11:4, NIV).

or they might climb a staircase; for example:

"for	he cometh,				
for	he cometh	to	judge	the earth:	
	he	shall	judge	the world	with righteousness,
		and		the people	with his truth"
					(Ps. 96:13, KJV).

"Do not think that	I have come	to abolish the law and the prophets;
	I have not come	to abolish
	but	to fulfill" (Matt. 5:17).

[Matt. 6:6; 6:22, 23; 6:34; 10:34; 10:40; 12:28, 29; Mark 2:27, 28; 9:37; Luke 10:16; John 6:37; 8:32; 10:11; 11:25; 13:20; 14:2, 3; 14:21; 16:7; 16:22]

(b) *synthetic*—in which thoughts are added to one another and so fill out the idea; for instance:

"Blessed is the	man			
	who does	not walk	in the counsel	of the wicked
		or stand	in the way	of sinners
		or sit	in the seat	of mockers"
				(Ps. 1:1, NIV).

"The law of the wise is a fountain of life,
to turn one away from the snares of death" (Prov. 13:14, NKJV).

Sometimes both lines seem to express entirely different or unrelated ideas, yet they share a common theme:

"He that hideth hatred with lying lips,

and

he that uttereth a slander   is a fool" (Prov. 10:18, KJV).

Although the first person hides his true feelings and the second makes no effort to conceal his, both improperly use their tongues to produce the same results—injury.

[Matt. 23:5-10; Mark 12:38b, 39; Luke 12:49-51]

(c) *chiastic*—in which the thoughts alternate, usually going from thought A to B and then back from B' to A'. If you diagram the pattern, you discover that the thoughts crisscross to form an X, which is the shape of the Greek letter *chi*, hence the words "chiastic" and "chiasm."

FIGURE 11

"The alternation of ideas . . . indicate that this . . . structure is not accidental, but rather an ingenious design of the poet . . . the Hebrew poet deliberately decided not to parallel precisely the word order of his poem by using the chiastic pattern." Although B may complement or even complete A, "Chiastic parallelism clearly avoids expressing the same idea twice. It rather aims at a sequence of thought which brings out the essence of the point more fully and sharply" (LaRondelle, *Deliverance in the Psalms,* pp. 27, 28).

There are at least three chiastic patterns.

The simple chiasm:

A	"Ephraim		
B		shall not envy	
	C		Judah,
	C'		and Judah
B'		shall not harass	
A'	Ephraim" (Isa. 11:13, NKJV).		

The line chiasm:

A	"My son, if thine heart be	wise,
B	My heart shall rejoice, . . .	
B'	My reins shall rejoice,	
A'	When thy lips speak	right things" (Prov. 23:15, 16, KJV).

```
A        "Whoever exalts himself
   B            will be humbled, . . .
   B'           whoever humbles himself
A'       will be exalted" (Matt. 23:12, NIV).
```

The stanza chiasm:

```
A        "By his power      he stilled the Sea;
   B          by his understanding      he struck down      Rahab.
   B'         by his wind      the heavens were made fair;
A'       his hand pierced      the fleeing serpent" (Job 26:12, 13, NRSV).
```

[Matt. 6:24; 7:6; Mark 2:22, 27; 8:35; 9:43, 45, 47; 10:31]

(d) *comparative*—in which the second line, in comparison with the first, illustrates and explains it

figuratively:

```
"As the deer pants      for      the water brooks,
     so pants my soul    for      You, O God" (Ps. 42:1, NKJV).
```

directly:

```
"A continual dropping on a very rainy day
 and a contentious woman are alike" (Prov. 27:15, NKJV).
```

sensibly:

```
"Better is a little with the fear of the Lord,
 than great treasure and turmoil" (Prov. 15:16, NASB).
```

(e) *merismus*—in which a part is used to indicate the whole, and vice versa.

```
"For from the rising of the sun
 even unto the going down of the same
 my name shall be great among the Gentiles" (Mal. 1:11, KJV).
```

(f) *paronomasia*—in which similar sounds are placed side by side; poets used paronomasia to achieve a play on words:

```
[God] "looked for      justice            [mishpat],
       but saw          bloodshed          [mishpach];
       for              righteousness      [tsedaqah],
       but heard        cries of distress  [tseaqah]"  (Isa. 5:7, NIV).
```

(g) *ballast-variant*—when couplets or triads occur in which one grammatical unit has no counterpart to balance it, the Hebrew compensates by lengthening the shorter line with the missing part:

A	"He made known	his ways	to Moses,
B		his acts	to the people of Israel" (Ps. 103:7).

(Note that the verb translated "he made known" in the first line has nothing to match it in the second line, but David adds "of Israel" to the second line as sort of ballast to compensate for the lack of the verb.) For more information about these insightful parallelisms, see Nils Lund's *Chiasms in the New Testament*.

Narrative—The writer tends to stay in the background of a narrative. Instead of addressing us with direct statements, he usually allows the words and actions of the people in the story to get across the main thrust of the message. As you try to figure out what is going on in the narrative, ask these questions of the text: (1) What details did the author select from the maze of possible speeches, persons, or events? (2) How did he arrange this selection? (3) Does the author allow a person or a group of people to go on speaking at the climax of a sequence of events, or does he personally interrupt the narration to offer an inspired estimate of what took place?

Wisdom—There are two basic strains of biblical wisdom writing: (1) Philosophic or reflective wisdom thought tends to carry a sustained argument across a large body of text in either a persuasive tone (for instance, Job or Ecclesiastes) and/or in a pleading tone (for example, Prov. 1-9; Matt. 5-7). It asks how and why in search of answers to life's most basic questions about the ways of God and the purpose of life. (2) Prudential wisdom thought tends to come in smaller, disconnected units of thought that often stand alone (for example, Prov. 10-31; Psalms 1, 37, 49, 112; James). It consists of practical statements that answer the question "What?"

Here is a complete list of the wisdom writings of the Bible: Job, Psalms 1, 19, 32, 34, 37, 49, 73, 78, 112, 127, 128, 133; Proverbs; Ecclesiastes; Song of Solomon; Matthew 5-7 (the Sermon on the Mount); and James.

Apocalyptic—Ezekiel; Daniel; Zechariah; Matthew 24, Mark 13, and Luke 21 (the Olivet discourse); the book of Revelation; and brief prophetic sections in the Old Testament (for instance, Isa. 24-27) are all examples of biblical apocalyptic thought. Apocalyptic writing generally (1) stresses God's freedom to act and power to rule, (2) emphasizes dreams and visions, (3) uses sometimes bizarre symbolism, (4) puts everything in historical sequence, (5) focuses on the end time rather than the present, (6) features angels, and (7) proclaims a powerful ethical warning.

Whether in ancient literal Babylon or presently symbolic Babylon, God's people often find themselves caught between their difficult present circumstances and the glorious promised future. At first the Old Testament prophets spoke to their own day, but as time wore on and their dreams were not realized, new generations of prophets shifted their perspective from a contemporary to an end-time focus, projecting the fulfillment of their announcements into the remote future. As a result, they resorted to typology in order to reach beyond their current circumstances to the promised realities.

Unlike classical prophecy, apocalyptic writing attempts to answer contemporary questions and dispel current doubts by describing the time between the disturbing *now* and the wonderful *then* as a divinely controlled delay of inevitable victory. Apocalyptic literature reveals God as the permanent Lord of history, and no matter how bad things seem to get, the glories of the new age are sure to come—but in His good time. It relieves the pressure of our frustration by reminding us that the worse things seem to get, the nearer we are to Christ's blessed return.

Apocalyptic also inspires perseverance by insisting that, finally, just as the earth is about to give out and the heavens brace themselves for collapse, Jesus will come with heavenly armies to overthrow the enemy and to install the kingdom for those who remain faithful to the end.

The Importance of Grammatical Details

Most of us hated English class in elementary school and high school. Remember all those sentences the teacher made you diagram? Who cared? You surely didn't. It might have been useful learning the times tables, but you'd never have any use for learning the parts of speech, for knowing the difference between a noun and a verb. But most of us managed to slog through those tedium-filled classes. Boring!

But if you stop to think about it for a moment, anyone who sets out to interpret Scripture needs to have a working knowledge of basic grammar. After all, how can you exegete the Bible properly if you cannot distinguish between a subject and the direct object? And this cluster of words here—what role do they play in the sentence? Do they form an adverbial clause? Prepositional phrase? Participial phrase? And how can you explain what is going on in a sentence unless you know the difference between a declarative, interrogative, and imperative sentence? Similarly, it is important for you to know what kind of action is taking place in a sentence, but the only way you will know that is if you understand the difference between a transitive verb and an intransitive one.

And who cared about participles and gerunds and infinitives? Well, now that you want to understand Scripture better, *you* care. But all those puzzling terms you met so many years ago that you hardly know how to spell them now, let alone know what they mean. Yet you are serious about exegeting the Bible so that your congregation can understand God, His will, and His plan more clearly. So what can you do? How do you make up for all that lost time when you daydreamed through English classes?

Well, all is not lost. In Part 2 of this book—"A Closer Look"—you will find in chapter 7 a crash course in some of the niceties of basic grammar—especially adapted to English Bible study. Some of it may seem confusing, but read it through carefully. Study the examples given. And, if need be, consult an English grammar book at your local library.

The section that immediately follows this paragraph relies heavily on syntactical and grammatical analysis. So you may want to read chapter 7 right now before you proceed to "A Strategy for Structural Analysis."

A Strategy for Structural Analysis

The purpose of "structural analysis" is to trace an author's train of thought by means of the literary-grammatical footprints left behind in the text. We do this by applying what we have learned about grammar and syntax to the text so that we can mark the starting and ending points along the trail where the author developed his topics or themes. The process should yield an accurate, detailed picture of what the author intended to communicate.

The first thing we want to do is to identify and define sentences. We accomplish this by acquainting ourselves with the *parts of speech* so that we can prepare a structural draft of the clauses and phrases that they form. After we figure out which clauses and phrases belong to one another, we count the number of related clauses and phrases and label each sentence as simple, complex, compound, or compound-complex. This will divide the text into units of complete thought.

Next, we need to figure out which sentences work together. We start by mentally lumping together those sentences that we suspect share the same topic or theme. Then we prepare a map to show where we believe the text divides into separate themes or topics.

Then we need to determine which topic sentences or theme propositions work together. To do this, we must prepare a structural analysis of the entire passage. Proceeding verse by verse, we carefully position every word, phrase, clause, and sentence to show the way that they parallel or support one another. This will bring out the precise relationship between every element in the passage.

Finally, we need to identify the relationship between related topic sentences or theme propositions. This last step is to convert the structural analysis into a structural diagram that shows how everything works. Color-coding each structural signal allows the structure to stand out more vividly. Grammatical-syntactical notes alongside key words further define the shape of the text and make it easier to isolate each stated or implied theme proposition or topic sentence so that we can syntactically bracket into paragraphs the ones that seem to share something similar into paragraphs. Then we can outline the entire structure as a whole, in the main margin, with main divisions at each paragraph, subdividing its sentences, clauses, or phrases into main points and subpoints.

Here are step-by-step instructions for the entire procedure—complete with detailed examples. A sample analysis appears in Appendix A.

Proceed *one sentence* at a time.

Step 1—Scan the Text—Mentally identify each part of speech.

FIGURE 12

PART OF SPEECH	QUESTIONS TO ASK
Noun	Does it name a person, place, or thing? Does it answer the question *who?* or *what?* before the verb; *whom?* or *what?* after the verb?
Pronoun	Does it stand for a noun?
Verb	Does it tell what someone or something did?
	Does it link one word with another that identifies or describes it?
	Does it merely show that something exists?
Adjective	Does the word tell *what kind, which one, how many,* or *how much?*
Adverb	Does the word tell *where, when, in what manner,* or *to what extent* the verbal idea occurs?
Preposition	Is the word part of a phrase that includes a noun or a pronoun as its object?
Conjunction	Does the word connect other words in the sentence?
Interjection	Does the word express emotion and function independently from the rest of the sentence?

Step 2—Prepare a Structural Draft—The basic unit for structural analysis is the sentence. It (1) shows how each clause and phrase functions, (2) organizes them according to the actual way they relate to each other, and (3) makes it possible to accurately compare their significance with that of other clauses and phrases in the text.

The three steps to sentence identification are:

1. *Identify clauses and phrases.* Examine the word group. Decide whether it is a clause or a phrase. Record the word or words that introduce it ("Intro"). Label the ("Type") of clause or phrase that these words introduce, not what part or parts of speech they are. Is it an adjective, adverb, noun, or main *clause*? Is it a prepositional, adjective, appositive, adverb, or verbal *phrase*?

2. *Figure out the relationship between clauses.* If it expresses a complete idea and can stand alone, it is independent. If it is connected to another independent clause by means of a coordinating conjunction, it is coordinate. If it is connected to an independent or coordinate clause by means of a subordinating conjunction, it is dependent. (Indicate whether it is independent [ind.], coordinate [coor.], or dependent [dep.] in the "Relation" slot.

3. *Count the number of clauses and phrases directly related to each other.* A single independent clause is a *simple sentence*. One or more subordinate clauses joined to a single independent clause form a *complex sentence*. Two or more independent clauses joined by either a comma and a coordinating conjunction or a semicolon make up a *compound sentence*. Two or more independent clauses plus at least one subordinate clause constitute a *compound-complex sentence*. (Label each sentence on the same line as its first clause.)

FIGURE 13

	CLAUSES			PHRASES		SENTENCES
Vs	Intro	Type	Relation	Intro	Type	Type
1	Jude	Subj.		a bondslave	Appo.	Complete Subj.
				and brother	Appo.	
				to those	Prep.	Incompl. Pred.
	who	Adj.	Dep.			
	who	Adj.	Dep./Coor.	by	Adv.	
	who	Adj.	Dep./Coor.	in	Prep.	
2	Grace	Noun				Simple
	peace	Noun				
	and mercy	Main	Ind.			
3				While	Verb	Complex
				about	Prep.	
	I	Main	Ind.	calling	Verb	
				to battle	Verb	
	that was	Adj.	Sub.			
4	because	Adv.	Sub.			
	those who	Adj.	Sub.			
	ungodly	Appo.				
	who turn	Adj.	Sub.			
	and deny	Adj.	Sub./Coor.			
5	So I	Main	Ind.			Complex
	though	Adv.	Sub.			
	that	Noun	Sub.			
	after			from	Prep.	
	who	Adj.	Sub.			
6	and He	Noun	Coor.			
	those who	Adj.	Sub.			
	who did not	Adj.	Sub.			
	but	Adj.	Sub./Coor.	in	Prep.	

	CLAUSES			PHRASES		SENTENCES
Vs	Intro	Type	Relation	Intro	Type	Type
				under	Prep.	
				for	Prep.	
7	Just as	Adv.	Sub.			
	which indul.	Adj.	Sub.	the same	Adv.	
	and went	Adj.	Sub./Coor.	as	Prep.	
				by	Adv.	
8	Well these	Main	Ind.	in	Prep.	Complex
9	Even Mich.	Main	Ind.			Compound
	when he	Adv.	Sub.	with	Prep.	
	and argued	Adv.	Sub./Coor.	about	Prep.	
				against	Prep.	
	but said	Main	Coor.			

Step 3—Prepare a Paragraph Map—We need to gather together those sentences that deal with a single topic or a series of events that relate to one actor or participant in the same time-setting and location. Since there may be many of these paragraphs in a single section, carefully trace each concept from the point at which the author starts developing an idea to its conclusion. Fortunately, most of the criteria for recognizing these units resemble those for setting off sections.

Repeated terms or concepts may give away the theme that unifies the author's arguments into one paragraph (for example, "love" in 1 Cor. 13).

Rhetorical questions (see Rom. 6:1) and *vocative* forms of address (for instance, Col. 3:18-4:1) often mark the start of a paragraph.

Sudden changes in the text usually betray the beginning of a paragraph—(a) a switch in the key actor or participant, (b) a shift in the action site, (c) a swing in topic, or (d) a change in the tense, voice, or mood of a verb.

What appears *at or near the end* of one paragraph frequently becomes the topic of more intense development in the next (for instance, "wisdom" in 1 Cor. 2:5; then from 2:6ff).

The *strophe*, the paragraph of poetry, gives itself away by:

1. the *recurring refrain*—lines that repeat themselves in the midst of a poem (for example, Psalms 39, 42, 43, 44, 46, 49, 56, 57, 59, 62, 67, 78, 80, 99, 107, 114, 136, 144, 145; Amos 1, 2, 4; Isa. 5:9, 10). For instance, the following refrain divides Isaiah 9:8-10:4 into four strophes (9:12, 17, 21; 10:4): "For all this his anger is not turned away; his hand is stretched out still."

2. the word *selah*, which occurs 71 times in 39 psalms, plus three times in Habakkuk (3:3, 9, 13). (The meaning of *selah* is unknown, but speculation has identified it as a sort of musical notation, as a pause in singing for narration, as a command to lift up the hands, as a command to bow in prayer, as instructions to the choir, as instructions regarding instrumental accompaniment, or as an ejaculation such as Hallelujah.)

3. the *alphabetic acrostic*, in which the first word of the first stanza begins with the first letter of the Hebrew alphabet and the first word in the second stanza begins with the second letter of the alphabet, etc. In some cases every line in the same strophe begins with the same letter. Acrostics are found in Psalms 9-10, 25, 34, 37, 111, 112, 119, 135 and Lamentations 1-4.

4. *miscellaneous devices*, such as (a) changes in rhythm or length of the last line, (b)

repeated catchwords (for example, "O Lord") or formulas like "Thus saith the Lord," (c) chiasms (see the subsection "Parallelism" under "Poetry"), (d) anacrusis, which is when a single word (for instance, an interrogative—"How"—in Lamentations 1:1 or an exclamation—"truly"—in Genesis 4:24) stands outside the basic pattern of balance and parallelism in couplets or strophes. This is found in especially expressive strophes, such as "If Cain shall be avenged sevenfold, then Lamech [ballast variant] seventy-seven fold" (NKJV).

5. *distant parallelism*, as when parallel paired words are sometimes separated from each other as in "I crushed them" (Ps. 18:38, NIV) and "I beat them" (Ps. 18:42, NIV).

Once you have consulted several Bibles and compiled some notes of your own, map out the divisions with a chart like this one. Use Malachi 1:1-14 as your text.

PARAGRAPH MAP—FIGURE 14

	AV	RSV	LB	NASB	NAB	NEB	NIV	Mine
1								
2		2		2	2	2	2	
3								
4								4
5								5
6	6	6		6	6	6	6	6
7								
8								8
9								
10								10
11								
12	12							
13								13
14								

Step 4—Prepare a Structural Analysis—1. Preserve the writer's flow of thought by (a) listing each verse in numerical order and without skipping lines between them and (b) working (in pencil) from left to right then from top to bottom, from main to subordinate clauses and from subject to predicate. See chart on page 421.

2. Carefully position each term in order to show (a) *coordination* of parallel words, phrases, clauses, and sentences, as well as balanced pairs and contrasts, lining them up directly under each other no matter how far apart they are from each other in the text.

For example,

Jude 3		Beloved
Jude 17	But	you, beloved

(b) *subordination* of adverb, adjective, and noun clauses; of adverb, adjective, appositive, prepositional, and verbal phrases; and of adverbs, adjectives, appositives, and most pronouns. Do this by indenting them (when it helps bring out the structure of the text) *above* (if they come before) or *below* (if they come after) and slightly to the right of the terms they modify.

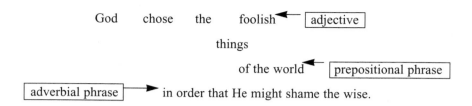

(c) *connection* between every term in the text with *arrows* pointing up to show dependency or support or pointing down to continue the flow of the text. For example,

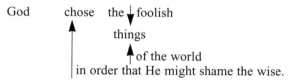

Or use *brackets* to lump together groups of terms, attaching distant terms to each other. For instance,

Jude (verse 3)		Beloved . . . ⌐
	But	you ───
Jude (verse 17)		beloved . . . ⌐

3. Set off the structural signals in the text by
(a) isolating
(b) using boldface or underlining to mark adverbs, adjectives, prepositions, pronouns, interjections, conjunctions.

FIGURE 15

Vs.	Conjunctions	
6	*Yet*	we do speak ⌐wisdom
		▲*among* those *who* are mature;
		┃ └wisdom,
		however, ▲*not* ▼ *of* this age, ─┐
		nor of the rulers
		▲*of* this age, ─┘
		┃ *who* are passing away.

(c) positioning (i) conjunctions that introduce independent clauses (like *yet* in the above diagram), before, and to the left of the main margin; coordinate clauses/ phrases or couple nouns, verbs, etc., (like *however* in the above diagram), before, and to the left of a connecting arrow; and subordinate clauses/phrases (like *nor* in the above diagram), after, to the right of a connecting arrow; (ii) brief quotes, idiomatic expressions, or introductory formulas where they best bring out the structure of the text; (iii) predicate nominatives, adjectives, or pronouns where a direct object would go to balance their subject; (iv) complementary infinitives immediately after the verbs they complete; (v) gerunds where their counterparts would go (that is, subject, direct object, indirect object, object of a preposition, appositive); and (vi) participles where adjectives would go.

(d) highlighting (i) appositives with parentheses ( ), (ii) controversial words from the original text in plain brackets [ ], and (iii) italicized words, missing from the original text, in braces { }.

2. Preserve the writer's syntax, by working from a formal translation (such as the King James Version, the New King James Version, the American Standard Version, the New American Standard Version, the Revised Standard Version, or the New Revised Standard Version), which aims at preserving the original grammar of the language and translates the original text form-for-form (for example, a verb with a verb and a noun with a noun). These translations are preferable to a dynamic translation (such as the New International Version, *The New English Bible*, Moffatt's translation, or Phillips' translation), which aims at preserving the original sense of the language and translates the original text thought-for-thought (for instance, a clause or a phrase for a word).

Because English strains to capture the original language, consult at least two formal translations for the grammar and several dynamic translations for the sense of the passage.

Step 5—Convert Your Structural Analysis Into a Structural Diagram—1. Code your analysis.

FIGURE 16

Part of Speech	Highlight in	or	Mark with
relative pronoun	orange		○
preposition	green		◇
adjective	yellow		□
conjunction	pink		▷
adverb	blue		△

2. Make appropriate grammatical/syntactical notes alongside key words, phrases, and clauses. (Consult chapter 7 in this book and a good English reference tool with a wide selection of definitions, such as the *Oxford Dictionary of Current English*.)

3. Isolate the stated or implied theme proposition or topic sentence for each paragraph and whether at the paragraph's beginning, middle, or end (a) by singling out the main clause syntactically rather than logically and (b) by tracing the flow of thought along the trail of phrases, clauses, and sentences that the author left behind in the text.

4. Outline the structure in the main margin, using Roman numerals lined up with theme propositions or topic sentences, and letters and working from capitals to lower case lined up with main and subordinate subpoints.

5. Reflect any insights gained so far by labeling the theme propositions or topic sentences and the subpoints.

SAMPLE STRUCTURAL DIAGRAM[2]—FIGURE 17

Book		Chapter	Verses	Bible Version	Date
Vs.	Conjunctions	MAIN Clause	SUBORDINATE Clause, SUBJECT		PREDICATE

	I. A. 1.	Topic Sentence ◄───────┐ ▲ │ Subordinate Clauses │ A Typical Paragraph ▼Coordinate Clauses ◄────┘	
	II.	── Theme Proposition ── Theme Proposition ── Theme Proposition ── Theme Proposition	**Alternate Paragraph 1** Sometimes the writer offers the same topic or theme several ways in the same paragraph. So, instead of displaying how subordinate clauses rank under the one main topic clause, this situation requires you to show how each clause shares the same status—by lining them up, one under the other, and bracketing them together as a single package.
	III.	── Theme Proposition ▲ Subordinate Clauses ── Theme Proposition ▲ Subordinate Clause ── Theme Proposition	**Alternate Paragraph 2** At times, the writer develops his theme over a series of clauses in the same paragraph—even though subordinate material may separate them from one another. But you can show their equal rank by disregarding the space between them, lining them up with one another, and bracketing them as a single package.

---

[1] The term *structural analysis* can have two meanings when we talk about exegesis.

A relatively recent discipline in biblical studies is based on the linguistic theories of A. J. Greimas, Ferdinand de Saussure, and others. In this kind of structural analysis, biblical scholars try to discern the "deep structures" that underlie the biblical passage.

Frequently these deep structures will reveal ideas that are polar opposites which are then mediated by a third idea. The assumption is that the larger act of verbal communication has a grammar to it just as do the sentences and paragraphs that constitute a literary work.

That is *not* the meaning of structural analysis as used in this chapter. In this chapter we are talking about the syntactical structure of written works—how words function in phrases, how phrases function in sentences, how sentences function in paragraphs, etc.

[2] Adapted from Kaiser, Walter C., Jr., *Toward an Exegetical Theology* (Grand Rapids: Baker Book House, 1981).

CHAPTER 3

VERBAL ANALYSIS

There is no sense in trying to get at the meaning of a passage without having a handle on unfamiliar words. That is like trying to understand what you hear on the radio when the signal fades in and out and all you get are bits and pieces of the broadcast. Although certain words play a key role in the passage, exegesis requires a basic understanding of every word involved—working from root meanings, the initial thrust carried to the sentence—to contextual meanings, the final sense picked up from the sentence and the rest of the Bible context.

Language

Pregnant, pivotal, or prominent words in the immediate or surrounding passages will eventually demand more intensive study (see "Word Studies"). For now, here is a simple way to acquaint yourself with the unfamiliar words in the text.

> 1. Refer to each word alphabetically in Strong's *Concordance* (or Young's *Concordance* if you don't have Strong's).
>
> 2. If you use Strong's, note the number to the right of each word. That's the code for its original root in either the Hebrew and Chaldee Dictionary or the Greek Dictionary, which are in the back of the book. Work through the suggested meanings and write down the one(s) that seem to best suit the text.
>
> 3. Then for help in understanding the root meaning check either of the following two word study tools, which are coded to Strong's dictionaries—R. Laird Harris, Gleason L. Archer, Jr., and Bruce K. Waltke, *The Theological Wordbook of the Old Testament* or W. E. Vine, *An Expository Dictionary of New Testament Words*.

FIGURE 18

Vs.	Unfamiliar Word	Part of Speech	Strong's Number	Root Meaning From Bible Dictionary, *Theological Wordbook of OT,* or Vine's *Expository Dictionary of NT*

As you zero in on the contextual meaning, look for some of these ways that the Bible writers gave meaning to the words that we find in their writings.

Defining Terms—Sometimes the author defines the meaning of the word, such as Paul did with the word "carnal" in Romans 7:14, KJV. He said that it meant "sold into slavery to sin" (NRSV).

Explaining Terms—Sometimes the author glosses a term, that is, attaches an explanation to it. See Ephesians 2:1; John 2:19; 7:37, 38 for examples.

Limiting Terms—Often the subject or predicate may either limit or define a term. When Matthew used the word *moraino* with salt, it meant tasteless (Matt. 5:13), but Paul used the same word with a human subject (Rom. 1:22), where it takes on the meaning "foolish" (Kaiser, p. 107).

Arguing by Contrast—At times an author develops the meaning of a term by arguing one thing in contrast with another. Compare, for instance, 2 Corinthians 3:6-14 with Romans 8:5-8.

Parallel Passages—Parallel passages may help you determine the meaning of a word when the same writer uses either (a) a verbal parallel, in which the same word is used in a similar context or in reference to the same subject (see for example, Gal. 5:6; 6:15; 1 Cor. 7:19) or (b) a topical parallel, in which similar facts, subjects, attitudes, or doctrines can throw light on the meaning, even though the exact words or phrases may be different (see Luke 14:26 and Matt. 10:37). Under these circumstances you then have something reliable to compare things with. The situation can be less certain, however, when you compare a parallel passage from a different Bible writer who used the same word or spoke on the same topic.

Word Forms—Word forms offer a treasure of understanding for those who are willing to do a little digging. Whatever part of speech a word appears in, you should explore its full grammatical-structural dimensions. All you need is patience, this handbook, and tools that enable you to study God's Word in its original languages.

The *Newberry Bible* is especially helpful for those without a working knowledge of Hebrew or Greek. In addition to labeling many words according to what they are and what they do, the *Newberry Bible* offers short but valuable grammars for both Hebrew and Greek.

The *Hebrew-Greek Key Study Bible* and the *Discovery Bible New Testament* offer rich insights into New Testament grammar. The former includes word studies for key Old Testament and New Testament words, and the latter explains subtle differences between some of the most frequent New Testament synonyms.

Both *The Complete Word Study Old Testament* and *The Complete Word Study New Testament* parse and break down every word in their texts according to its form. While they each include terse but powerful grammars for their respective languages, the former includes a thorough study of many key Old Testament words, and the latter has a comprehensive companion volume, *The Complete Word Study Dictionary: New Testament*. Neither work requires any knowledge of the original languages.

In addition to perennial favorites, *Strong's Exhaustive Concordance* and *Young's Analytical Concordance*, James Gall's *Layman's Greek-English Concordance* and *The Englishman's Greek Concordance of the New Testament* transliterate Greek root words into English letters and cite biblical references for illustrations. *The Englishman's Hebrew and Chaldee Concordance to the Old Testament* and Wilson's *Old Testament Word Studies* do the same but also provide a list of root words translated by the same English word, giving their definitions and including grammatical notes.

For those who have access to a personal computer, "there are several Bible Study packages on the market today that can make studying the Bible in its original languages easier and more meaningful" (*Christian Computing Magazine*, vol. 6, no. 11, p. 18).

Programs such as *The Online Bible* (The Online Bible Foundation), *The Logos Bible* (Logos Research Systems), and *SeedMaster for Windows* (White Harvest Software, Inc.), for example, contain the original language texts, lexicons, assorted resources, and selected grammatical information.

Others like *Bible Windows* (Silver Mountain Software), *The Word Advanced Study System* (Wordsoft), and *BibleWorks for Windows* (Hermeneutika Bible Software) enable you te explore all the words and their forms in both the Old and New Testaments, and the latter even includes the Septuagint.

You can also combine the capabilities of specialized but compatible word study products like two from The Gramcord Institute—*Bible Word Plus* and the highly regarded *Gramcord,* into a single, comprehensive, original language (DOS) study package. The Macintosh counterpart, *acCordance,* integrates the sophisticated grammatical capabilities of the Gramcord Greek New Testament and Gramcord Hebrew Masoretic Text with a full-featured search and display environment. The result is an enormously powerful research tool for advanced grammatical and syntactical study of scripture.

Original language Bible study books and software make it possible to take advantage of all the language insights in this handbook. Most of the software is available on CD-ROM as well as diskettes and includes a variety of additional study tools such as atlases, dictionaries, and commentaries. Which one is best for you? That depends on what you want to spend, your computer's processor and memory, the user-friendliness of the program, and how far you want to go in your language studies.

You would be amazed at how much you can learn from the form a word takes. The tense, voice, and mood of a verb can reveal a great deal. Compare the verbs in your text with the categories explained in chapter 8. Carefully work your way through the possibilities, and let the context decide which ones are appropriate. Don't just jump at the first one that makes sense. Unless you have some tool that offers grammatical notes, you won't be able to take advantage of these exciting insights.

Figures of Speech—Sometimes the Bible writers would use a figure of speech, thereby deliberately deviating from the literal or natural meaning of the word so as to "increase its power" and "image making ability" (Kaiser, p. 121). The Greeks identified more than 200 of these new forms of speech based on "resemblance or on certain definite relations" (L. Berkhof, *Principles of Biblical Interpretation*, p. 83), "called *tropes*, in which a word or expression is used in a different sense from that which properly belongs to it" (*ibid.*). The Romans picked up where their Hellenistic predecessors left off and called them *figura*; hence today we call them figures of speech.

---

1. Is there a mismatch between subject and predicate if you interpret the subject literally? For example, "God is our *Rock.*"

2. Is a colorful word followed by one that immediately defines it? For example, "We were *dead*—in our trespasses and sins."

3. Is it absurd, aside from a miracle, to take the statement literally? For example, "The mountains *clapped their hands.*"

4. Does the text require a heightened feeling, some dramatic emphasis, or some mnemonic device at this point? For example, "The stones would *cry out.*"

5. Does this same figure of speech appear elsewhere in the Bible?

At the bottom of page 51 are some guidelines (adapted from Kaiser, p. 122) to help you recognize when something is figurative:

Mickelsen lists three principal figure of speech types.

Short Figures—There are short figures (see Mickelsen, pp. 179-198), which Kaiser subdivides into four categories (pp. 123, 124): *comparisons, associations, additions,* and *contrasts.*

- **Comparisons** include:

Similes, which begin with the words "like" or "as"—"He shall be like a tree" (Ps. 1:3, KJV). (For additional examples see Matt. 6:29; 10:16; 12:40; 13:40, 43; 18:17; 23:27; 24:27, 37; 25:32, 33; Mark 10:15; 14:48; Luke 10:18; 11:36; 13:34; 17:6, 28-30; 21:34, 35; 22:31; John 15:6.)

Metaphors, which are implied or unexpressed comparisons, such as "Go and tell that fox" (Luke 13:32). According to Berkhof (p. 83) Bible writers employed two kinds of metaphors when they referred to God: *anthropopathisms,* which ascribe human emotions, passions, and desires to Him (see for example, Gen. 6:6; Deut. 13:17; Eph. 4:30) and *anthropomorphisms,* which attribute body parts and physical activities to Him (see for example, Ex. 15:16; Ps. 34:16; Lam. 3:56; Zech. 14:4; James 5:4).

- **Associations** include:

Metonymy, which is when the speaker exchanges a noun for a related one so that the cause stands for its effect, as in the expression "Moses and the prophets" stands for the books they wrote (cf. Gen. 23:8; Luke 16:29); or so that the subject stands for its subordinate (Gen. 41:13; Deut. 28:5), or vice versa (Gen. 25:23; Acts 1:18; Gen. 28:22; Job 32:37); or so that a sign stands for the thing it signifies, as in Acts 7:8, in which circumcision stands for the covenant.

Synecdoche, which is when the speaker exchanges an idea for a related one so that a part can be used to represent the whole and vice versa, as in "All the world [= the Roman Empire] should be taxed" (Luke 2:1, KJV). In Isaiah 2:4, beating swords into plowshares and knives into pruning hooks = total disarmament, the conditions for everlasting peace ("And never again will they learn war" [NASB]).

- **Additions** include:

Pleonasm, in which the redundant use of words multiplies the force of the first, as in "The chief cupbearer did not remember Joseph, but forgot him" (Gen. 40:23), which heightens the suspense as the reader awaits what will happen next to Joseph as at the same time it also sets the stage for a dramatic episode with the pharaoh's dream.

Pun, which is a play on words that sound alike or when the same word has two different meanings in the same context. Puns can be subdivided into (a) *paronomasia,* which is the repetition of words that sound the same but don't necessarily mean the same thing, as in "strain out a gnat [Aramaic *qalma*] but swallow a camel [Aramaic *gamla*]" (Matt. 23:24); and (b) *epanidiplosis,* which is a repetition of the same word, as in "The wind [Aramaic *ruha*] blows where it chooses, and you hear the sound of it. . . . So it is with everyone who is born of the Spirit [Aramaic *ruha*]" (John 3:8). (For additional examples see Matt. 16:16; Mark 1:17; 4:9; 8:35; 9:35-37; 10:31; 13:28; Luke 9:59, 60.)

Exaggeration, which is a conscious attempt to increase the effect by stating that something is greater than is actually the case. Exaggeration can be subdivided into (i) *overstatement,* which is a saying that could be taken literally even though the speaker has no such intention, as in "If anyone comes to Me, and does not hate his own father . . . , yes, and even his own life, he cannot be My disciple" (Luke 14:26, NASB), in which Jesus is emphasizing the cost of discipleship, not advocating hostility toward our loved ones; and (b) *hyperbole*, in which a statement is so grossly exaggerated that it is impossible to take it literally, as in "I am weary with my sighing; every night I make my bed swim [with tears]" (Ps. 6:6, NASB). (For additional examples of exaggeration see Matt. 5:9, 18, 23, 24, 29, 30, 32, 34, 38-42, 48; 6:6, 17, 24; 7:1, 6, 7, 8; 10:12, 13, 30, 34; 17:20; 18:19; 19:9; 23:3; 26:52; Mark 5:34; 9:43-47; 10:11; 11:24; 13:2; Luke 6:27; 10:19; 19:42. For additional examples of hyperbole see Matt. 6:2-4; 7:3-5; 23:23, 24; Mark 10:24, 25.)

Hendiadys, in which two words are used when only one thing is actually meant, as in "fire and brimstone" = burning brimstone, or "Thou shalt not multiply, thou shalt not speak" = thou shalt not talk much (1 Sam. 2:3). (For additional examples see Ex. 4:10; Ps. 143:2; Acts 23:6; 1 Thess. 1:3; 2 Thess. 1:4.)

- **Contrasts** include:

Subtle contrasts, as in (a) *irony*, in which the author intends the opposite of the literal meaning or proposes in a clever or amusing way an event or result that is opposite to what the audience would expect: "Behold, the man is become as one of us" (Gen. 3:22, KJV). Berkhof points out that sometimes irony passes over into sarcasm (p. 91), as in 1 Samuel 26:15; 1 Kings 18:27; 1 Corinthians 4:8, or (b) *paradox*, which is a statement that at first appears self-contradictory, absurd, or at odds with common sense, but upon further investigation or explanation proves to be logical, as in "Many that are first shall be last" (Matt. 19:30, KJV). (For additional examples of irony see Matt. 11:16-19; 16:2, 3; 22:1-14; 23:29-35; Mark 2:17; 7:9; Luke 7:35; 10:29-37; 12:16-20; 13:33; 15:7; 16:1-9, 19-31; 18:9-14; John 3:10; 5:43; 10:32. For additional examples of paradox see Matt. 5:5; 6:17; 7:15; 10:27, 34-36, 39; 11:11, 22-24; 18:3, 4; 21:31; 23:11, 24, 25, 27, 28; 25:29; Mark 4:22, 25; 6:4; 8:35; 9:35; 10:14, 31, 43, 44, 45; 12:41-44; Luke 4:23; 12:3, 32; 14:11, 24; 18:14; John 12:25.)

Litotes, which belittles one thing to magnify another, as in "hate his own father and mother" (Luke 14:26, NASB). Jesus here emphasizes how much more important our relationship with Him is than any other.

Euphemism, which exchanges a harsh or disagreeable word for a gentler, more pleasant one, as in "he fell asleep" for "he died" (Acts 7:60, KJV).

A fortiori, which is an argument that uses facts or conclusions to set up an inescapable punch line ("If such and such, . . . then how much more . . ."), as in "If the world hates you, [then] beware [how much more] that it hated me before it hated you" (John 15:18). (For additional examples see Matt. 6:23, 26, 28-30; 7:9-11; 10:25, 28, 29-31; 12:11, 12; Mark 2:23-28; Luke 13:15, 16; 14:1-6; 18:1-8; John 13:14; 15:20.)

Question, which is a device used to draw the audience into the learning process. There are three kinds of questions:

(a) *rhetorical*, which are designed to produce an effect more than to generate a verbal response, thereby guiding the audience to an inescapable conclusion, as in Matthew 7:16, Mark 3:23, and Luke 15:8; or emphasizing seriousness, as in Matthew 5:13 and Mark 8:36, 37; or driving home a point, as in Mark 3:33, 10:18, and 12:35-37; or revealing exasperation and frustration, as in Mark 9:19 and Luke 12:14;

(b) *didactic*, which are used to more convincingly and permanently impress truth upon the minds of the audience, as in "Who do people say that I am? . . . But who do you say that I am? . . . You are the Messiah. . . . And he sternly ordered them not to tell anyone about him" (Mark 8:27-32);

(c) *polemical*, which is the counterquestion, usually raised in response to a hostile question, either stated or implied, or an unfriendly situation to which the speaker or writer is expected or feels constrained to reply, as in "And they watched Him . . . so that they might accuse Him. . . . And He said to them, 'Is it lawful on the Sabbath to do good or to do harm, to save life or to kill?'" (Mark 3:1-4, NKJV). (For additional examples of rhetorical questions see Matt. 5:46, 47; 6:25-30; 7:3, 4, 9, 10; 10:29; 11:7-9, 23; 12:34; 14:31; 18:12; 23:17-19, 33; 24:45; 26:53, 54; Mark 4:13, 21, 30, 40; 7:18, 19; 8:12, 17, 18, 21; 9:50; 11:17; 12:9, 24-26; 13:2; 14:6, 37, 41, 48; Luke 2:49; 6:34, 39, 46; 11:5-7, 40; 12:51, 56; 13:2-4, 20; 14:28, 31; 16:11, 12; 17:7-9, 17, 18; 18:7, 8; 22:27. For additional examples of didactic questions see Matt. 17:25; 21:31; Mark 8:19, 20; 10:38; Luke 10:36; 22:35. For additional examples of polemical questions see Matt. 12:11, 12, 27-29; Mark 2:6-9, 19, 25, 26; 3:23, 24; 10:3, 37-39; 11:27-33; 12:14-16; Luke 7:39-42; 10:26; 13:15, 16; 14:1-5.)

Opaque Figures—There are also opaque figures (see Mickelsen, pp. 199-211). Sometimes obscure statements in the Bible defy understanding even after we have analyzed their context, structure, language, and historical-cultural background. These include riddles, fables, proverbs, and enigmatic sayings.

• **Riddles** are concise sayings during a match of wits, which challenge the audience to discover their shrouded meanings, as in "This calls for wisdom: let anyone with understanding calculate the number of the beast, for it is the number of a person. Its number is six hundred sixty-six" (Rev. 13:18). (For additional examples see Judges 14:14; Prov. 1:5, 6; Matt. 10:34; 11:11, 12; 13:52; 19:12; Mark 2:19; 9:12, 13; 14:58; Luke 13:32, 33; 22:36.)

• **Fables** are fictitious stories meant to teach a moral lesson. They frequently use animals or vegetables to portray the nature, emotions, and failures of human beings. (For examples see Judges 9:8-15; 2 Kings 14:9; Eze. 17.)

Here are some suggestions, adapted from Mickelsen (p. 206), for interpreting fables:

---

1. Find out about the current situation in which the speaker resorted to a fable.
2. Figure out if the fable is simple (trying to teach a lesson by stressing a single point) or complex (trying to teach several points).
3. Notice the influence the fable has on the audience and the way that the fable teller responds to them.
4. Update the lesson and make it meaningful for your audience.

• **Proverbs** are brief sayings full of meaning. Usually they are one sentence long and worth remembering. They generally fall into five classes.

(a) *Synonymous* proverbs are those in which both lines say essentially the same thing, only the second puts it slightly different from the first, as in "The liberal soul shall be made fat: and he that watereth shall be watered also himself" (Prov. 11:25, KJV). Generous people prosper because they live to be a blessing—not to receive one.

(b) *Synthetic* proverbs are those in which both lines seem to say something different but must be taken together in order to fully understand either one, as in "He that hideth hatred with lying lips, and he that uttereth slander is a fool" (Prov. 10:18, KJV). To not say anything and conceal true feelings is just as foolish as broadcasting them. Sometimes the second line completes the thought of the first, as in "Hear counsel, and receive instruction, that thou mayest be wise in thy latter end" (Prov. 19:20,

KJV). Never think you know it all—unless you want to stop growing.

(c) *Antithetic* proverbs are those in which the second line presents a thought opposite to or in contrast with that expressed in the first, usually to emphasize the first in some way, as in "A cheerful heart is like a good medicine, but a downcast spirit dries up the bones" (Prov. 17:22). A good attitude promotes health, but a bad attitude drains the life out of you.

(d) *Parabolic* proverbs are those in which the first line illustrates the second, which offers the main lesson, as in "As a jewel of gold in a swine's snout, so is a fair woman which is without discretion" (Prov. 11:22, KJV). A pig with a gold ring in its nose is about as ridiculous as a beautiful woman who lacks judgment and self-control.

(e) *Comparative* proverbs are those in which one line compares something with what is in the other in order "to illustrate a common trait or theme" (Bob Yandian, *Proverbs: Principles of Wisdom*, p. 26). "Like snow in summer and like rain in harvest, so honor is not fitting for a fool" (Prov. 26:1, NASB). Honor is as inappropriate for a fool as snow in the summer and rain during harvesttime. (For additional examples see Matt. 5:14; 6:21, 22, 24, 27, 34; 7:12, 17, 18; 8:22; 10:16, 24, 26, 27; 11:19; 12:30, 34, 35; 15:14; 24:28; 25:29; 26:52; Mark 2:17, 21, 22, 27; 3:24, 27; 4:21, 22, 25; 6:4; 7:15; 8:35, 36, 37; 9:40, 50; 10:25, 27, 31, 43, 44; Luke 4:23; 5:39; 9:62; 11:47; 12:15, 48; 14:11; 16:10; 20:18; John 3:3, 12, 20; 4:23; 12:25, 36; 15:14; Acts 20:35.)

• **Enigmatic sayings** are statements so saturated with meaning that they overwhelm an audience unprepared for them. (For examples see Num. 12:6-8; Ps. 49:4; 78:2; John 10:6; 16:25; Luke 11:33-36.)

Here are some suggestions for interpreting enigmatic sayings, adapted from Mickelsen (pp. 210, 211):

---

1. Strip away all the "nonessentials" that stand between you and understanding. Check the meanings of difficult words, and pay careful attention to syntax.

2. Trace the flow of thought again from your contextual analysis.

3. Watch for sudden shifts from literal to metaphorical language.

4. Wait until you have personally exegeted the passage before consulting any commentaries, otherwise you may miss the speaker's or writer's point while prematurely chasing solutions.

5. Write down what you think it means in your own words.

Extended Figures—There are also extended figures (see Mickelsen, pp. 212-235), which are the largest figures of speech. Unlike the short and opaque figures, extended figures sometimes stretch across entire chapters.

• **Similitudes and parables** are examples of extended figures of speech. The word parable comes from the Greek verb *ballein*, which means "to throw," and the preposition *para*, which can be translated "alongside." Teachers in Bible times frequently tossed something familiar and ordinary from everyday life alongside a deep, unfamiliar spiritual truth so that their audience could learn that truth by comparison or illustration. The parable is an extended simile that takes the form of stories (Eze. 17:2-10); acted-out lessons (Eze. 24:3-14); mysterious sayings intended to go over the heads of casual listeners (Matt. 13:1-9; cf. verses 10-17); paradoxical sayings (Mark 3:23); and sustained comparisons (Luke 15:11-32).

Mickelsen tells us how to distinguish between a simile, a similitude, and a parable (p. 213).

FIGURE 19

Simile	Similitude	Parable
One main verb	More than one main verb in present tense	More than one main verb in past tense
Formal comparison	Formal comparison	Formal comparison
Literal words	Literal words	Literal words
	One chief point of comparison	One chief point of comparison
	Customary habit almost a timeless truth	Particular example a specific occurrence
	Imagery kept distinct from what it signifies	Imagery kept distinct from what it signifies
	Story true to the facts and experiences of life	Story true to the facts and experiences of life
	Explained by telling what the imagery stands for in the light of the main point of the story	Explained by telling what the imagery stands for in the light of the main point of the story

• **Figurative actions** are not simply an illustration to support something said, but a nonverbal lesson contained in the action itself, like the time Jesus dined in Zacchaeus' house (Luke 19:1-10). (For additional examples see Matt. 11:4, 5; Mark 1:9; 2:15, 16, 18; 3:14-19; 4:10-12; 6:11, 32-44; 8:1-10; 9:36, 37; 10:33, 34; 11:1-10, 12-14, 15-17; 14:61; 15:5; John 2:1-11; 4:4-42; 11:38-44; 13:1-11; Acts 1:15-26.)

Here are some guidelines for interpreting parables that I have adapted from Mickelsen, pages 229, 230.

> 1. Try to get a handle on the "earthly details." Get in touch with the historic background to the parable—the manners, customs, culture, and symbolism of the day. For example, how can you understand the parable of the sower unless you have a good grasp of first-century farming?
>
> 2. Try not to make the parable "walk on all fours." A parable often may have a main point, with one principle message to get across. So instead of pressing home every detail, try to uncover the prime theme they all share. This will help you avoid the pitfalls of allegorization.
>
> 3. Spend most of your time trying to uncover the main emphasis in the places where most of the details are explained.
>
> 4. Note the attitude and spiritual condition of the audience.
>
> 5. Note the reason Jesus used the parable.
>
> 6. Try relating the main point (a) Jesus' message that the kingdom of God is at hand and (b) the way that God's kingship was the center of much that Jesus ever said and did.
>
> 7. Does Jesus make any general sayings in the parable? Encouragement may be central to, or on the fringe of, its main teaching.
>
> 8. Keeping in mind cultural, historical, etc. similarities and differences, relate the main emphasis to your audience.

• **Allegories** are also found in Scripture. Sometimes the Bible writers preferred to create an imaginative event from ordinary circumstances rather than tie themselves down to the literal sense. So they used extended metaphors to illustrate the way of the covenant. Isaiah used the vine and the vineyard (5:1-5; cf. 60:21; 61:3) to describe God's care for His transplanted people. Similarly, Jesus used an allegory of the vine and its branches to admonish His followers to depend on Him for the Father's continued care (John 15:1-11).

Mickelsen explains how to differentiate between a metaphor and an allegory (p. 230).

FIGURE 20

Metaphor	Allegory
One main verb	More than one main verb, plus a mixture of tenses
Direct comparison	Direct comparison
Figurative words	Figurative words
	Emphasis usually on timeless truths
	Imagery identified with the specific thing signified
	Story blends both factual and nonfactual experience to enable the narrative to teach specific truths
	Explained by showing why the imagery is identified with the reality and what specific truths are being taught

Here are some principles for interpreting allegories, which I have adapted from Mickelsen (pp. 234, 235):

1. Identify the original audience.
2. Note why the allegory comes into play.
3. Search out the basic points of comparison stressed by the original speaker or writer via emphatic elements in the story. Look for explicit identification (as in John 15:1) or implicit identification from context (as in 1 Cor. 3:1, 2).
4. State why both the original audience and your congregation need to hear it.

Symbols—Sometimes the Bible writers resorted to using symbols. "A symbol is a sign which suggests meaning rather than stating it" (Mickelsen, p. 265). Because a symbol is similar in certain respects to what it represents, it creates certain impressions in the observer that lead to an understanding of what it attempts to portray. As "a sign, pledge, or token, . . . its importance [is] derived from the fact that it was a representative object which guaranteed the reality of that which it symbolized" (*New Bible Dictionary*, ed. J. D. Douglas, p. 1225). The symbol ("that which is thrown together," from the Greek preposition *sum* [together] plus the verb *ballein* [to throw]) points beyond itself to a spiritual reality by bringing together invisible spiritual things and visible physical things in a single, literal object so that they can be readily compared. Bible writers frequently resorted to symbolism, painting pictures with literal objects to illustrate spiritual truth.

The Bible features four categories of symbols.

• **Material Symbols**—These are actual objects that the people could see and touch, but they conveyed "a meaning beyond their material use" (Mickelsen, p. 270).

For example, the tabernacle as a whole, with its services, sacrifices, and servants "all stand for basic elements in the [covenant] relationship between man and God" (*ibid.*, p. 272).

The altar symbolized the meeting place of God with humanity, just as it had in pretabernacle days, when the patriarchs used altars to mark the sites of encounters with God and claimed them for Him (*New Bible Dictionary*, p. 1225).

"The ark symbolized the presence of God because it contained the tablets of the Decalogue, and where the Word of the Lord was, there was the Lord Himself" (*ibid.*).

Men like Moses, Samuel, David, and Elisha, in and through whom the Lord operated, also symbolized the divine presence.

• **Visional Symbols**—Visional symbols are common, everyday objects presented in vision to the prophets but which stood for something else (Berkhof, p. 143). Because these symbols guaranteed the reality of what they represented, God expected His prophets to relay their significance to the people. For example, the basket of summer fruit let Amos know that the harvest of Israel's sin was ripe—that God's judgment on the rebellious northern kingdom was just around the corner. Sometimes the objects were surrealistic, especially in apocalyptic scenes, where bizarre things appeared and happened (for instance, a four-headed leopard that pops up from the sea). Contrary to nature, they are the twisted handiwork of the archenemy and symbolize opposition to God and His government. (See, for example, Zech. 1:10, 18, 19; 4; 5; 6:1-8; Rev. 11:3-12; Jer. 1:13; 24; Eze. 37:1-14; Dan. 2:31-35, 36-45; 7:1-8; 8.)

• **Miraculous Symbols**—These symbols also were significant. At crucial times in Israel's history, God saw fit to interrupt the daily flow of nature with miracles. The patriarchs called Him "El-Shaddai, because through the supernaturalism of His procedure He, as it were, overpowers nature in the service of His grace, and compels her to further His designs" (Geerhardus Vos, *Biblical Theology*, p. 82). Mickelsen says: "The God known to the people of the Bible was both a God of order and a God of freedom. The regularity of nature testified to God's order, the miracles to His freedom" (p. 267).

God sovereignly suspended the usual order, without losing control, to communicate something about Himself for humanity's benefit. The burning bush and the pillar of cloud and fire, for instance, were "ordinary objects of nature transformed to help both Moses and the people realize that God was not merely an idea, but a reality" (*ibid.*). Both symbolized God's presence. The bush made Moses aware of God's majesty and holiness, and the pillar assured the people of His never-failing guidance.

Sometimes the symbol itself was supernatural, like the "captain of the Lord's Host" or the "Angel of the Lord." At times the latter spoke in the first person as though He were God, and at other times in the third person as though God were someone else. Vos explains: "If the Angel sent were Himself partaker of the Godhead, then He could refer to God as His sender, and at the same time speak as God, and in both cases there would be reality behind it" (p. 73). Many scholars accept the Angel's visits as preincarnate appearances of the Lord Jesus Christ, and they believe that He symbolized the reality of God's burning desire to be near and with His people to assure them of His relentless concern for and care of them.

 • **Emblematic Symbols**—These include *numbers*. Normally numbers are units of measurement that tell us how far, how long, how big, etc. something was, is, or will be. But they may also indicate some spiritual significance in the Bible.

FIGURE 21

Number	Significance
One	*unity,* e.g., among the Trinitarian Godhead *(one* God)
	initiation, e.g., first item on a list is prominent, important
	uniqueness, e.g., "The Lord our God is *one* Lord."
Two	*difference,* e.g., *double* minded; so when *two* witnesses agree their testimony is conclusive
Three	*completeness,* e.g., the three dimensions, the Trinity
Four	*visible creation,* e.g., the four winds
Five	*divine grace;* 5 = 4 + 1 and symbolizes God adding His gifts and blessing to the work of His hands; e.g., it is the leading factor in the tabernacle measurements
Six	*humanity;* e.g., God created human beings on the sixth day; Athaliah usurped the throne of Judah for six years (cf. 666 and the efforts of the antichrist power to usurp God's throne): *"Six . . . is not seven and never reaches seven. It always fails to attain to perfection; that is, it never becomes seven. Six means missing the mark, or failure. Seven means perfection or victory . . . Rejoice O church of God. The number of the beast is 666, that is failure upon failure upon failure. It is the number of a man, for the beast glories in man; and must fail!"* (William Hendriksen. *More Than Conquerors.* Grand Rapids: Baker Book House, 1982, p. 151).
Seven	*the covenant relationship;* 7 = 4 + 3, symbolizing the perfect union of the Creator with His Creation; e.g., the high priest sprinkled the blood of the sin offering seven times before the Lord
Eight	*resurrection; regeneration;* e.g., Jews circumcised their children on the eighth day to signify a new beginning with God in the covenant relationship; the Father raised Jesus on the eighth day to signify the regeneration of the covenant and of the human race, the commencement of a new creation
Nine	*finality of judgment;* 9 = 3 x 3, the product of divine completeness; e.g., its factors or multiples always occur in a judgment context
Ten	*fullness, totality, or completeness;* e. g., the Ten Commandments are the transcript of God's character
Eleven	*disorder, disorganization,* because it is one short of the number twelve; e.g., the disciples sought a replacement for Judas to bring the 11 back up to 12 in Acts 1:21-26
Twelve	*God's chosen people; governmental perfection;* the 12 tribes; the 12 apostles

Similarly, there is the *year-day principle*. Scholars generally agree that the 70 weeks of Daniel 9 ("seventy 'sevens'" verse 24, NIV) are actually 490 literal years. God authorized this use of days to represent prophetic years from the time of Moses (Num. 14:34) to the exile (Eze. 4:4-6) and maybe into the New Testament era, if one sees Jesus, the antitypical "Son of God," perhaps reliving the 40-year wandering of national Israel, the typical "son of God" with 40 days (= 40 24-hour periods) in the wilderness (Matt. 4:1-11; see chapter 10). Old Testament scholar William H. Shea explains year-day symbolism in detail in *Selected Studies on Prophetic Interpretation*, pages 56-93.

Color can also be included among the emblematic symbols. Colors usually express something aesthetic to the senses, but they can take on significance from what they are connected with.

FIGURE 22

Color	Significance
Black or brown	*evil* (opposite of white); hence, *calamity/desolation* (Isa. 50:3); e.g., famine (Rev. 6:5, 6); *dirty, dark, or gloomy*; e.g., a visionless day (Micah 3:6); *treachery* (Job 6:16); *mourning* (Jer. 4:28)
Gray	*age*; e.g., gray hairs (Gen. 42:38; 1 Sam. 12:2)
Green	*prosperity*; hence, *luxuriant, flourishing, healthy*; e.g., green pastures = fields of thick, choice grass (Ps. 23:2); also *living, growing, fresh, new*
Yellow; pale	*diseased*; e.g., leprosy (Lev. 13:30, 32, 36); a pale horse (Rev. 6:8); a sick-looking, ashen animal symbolizing *death* and the *grave* (Hades)
Purple scarlet	*royalty; majesty*; e.g., the purple robe Belshazzar gave to Daniel
Red scarlet	*war; bloodshed*; e.g., bloody hands = caught red-handed (Isa. 1:15); the red horse in Rev. 6:4; the dragon in Rev. 12:3; the scarlet beast in Rev. 17:3, symbolizing an organization of political powers that have defected to the enemy who wages war against God; sin (Isa. 1:18).
White	*purity; unstained;* hence, *virgin; victorious* (over sin); *power; royalty;* e.g., white robes are given to the righteous who serve as "royal priests" (cf. Rev. 7:9-15 with 1:5, 6)

Emblematic symbolism also may extend to *metals*, which are usually found in lists, because of their qualities and uses. Take, for instance, the declining order of metals from gold, to silver, to brass, to iron, and iron mixed with ceramic in Daniel 2. The decreasing value reminds us of the decaying character of the empires as leadership changed hands from one pagan kingdom to the next. The increasing hardness can bring to mind the intensifying savagery of their operations as time grows short before the end.

We might also see emblematic symbolism in *jewels*, which again are found frequently in lists. We might find significance because of their value, beauty, rarity, durability, or splendor.

The most complete list occurs in Exodus 28:17-20, where God instructed the tabernacle workers to mount 12 stones on a breastpiece for the high priest. The valuable gems resting across his heart probably symbolized how precious the 12 tribes (Israel) should be to the chief priest. They could also remind us that spiritual Israel is dear to the heart of Christ, our Great High Priest in these last days (Heb. 4:14-16).

Another important list of gems appears in Revelation 21:19-21, where John describes the 12 foundations of the New Jerusalem (cf. Isa. 54:11, 12). Each foundation is decorated with a precious stone inscribed with the name of an apostle (Rev. 21:14) to symbolize the valuable role each played in laying the foundations of this spiritual city (cf. Eph. 2:20).

Proverbs 31:10 claims that a virtuous wife is priceless because she is worth more (that is, more rare) than precious jewels. John compares the ripples of splendor about God's throne with waves of shimmering light from a dazzling emerald (Rev. 4:3; cf. 9:17).

God compares bestowing His glory on Israel (Eze. 16:14) to adorning her with expensive gifts of beautiful jewels and jewelry (see also Eze. 16:11-13).

When Jeremiah wanted to emphasize how permanent the record was of Judah's sin, he said that it had been "engraved upon the tablet of their heart" "with a diamond pen" (Jer. 17:1).

Also among emblematic symbols are *names*, which often revealed what parents saw in and hoped for their children. Fathers and mothers in the ancient Near Eastern world waited to name their children until they had some hint of their character, abilities, or destiny. So, for example, in 1 Chronicles 4:9 Jabez' mother discloses her expectations from her son and her faith in God with a play on the Hebrew word for pain. Apparently reversing the last two consonants (*o-ts-b*), she called him Jabez (*y-b-ts*) because she hoped that God would turn things around for her son, who was born in pain under Adam's curse (Gen. 3:16) so that he might escape the gloomy future reserved for fallen humanity (1 Chron. 4:10).

In humbly acknowledging God's gift and giving Him all the glory for bringing their boy into the world, Zacharias and Elizabeth named their son John, which means "the Lord is gracious" (Luke 1:57-66), instead of after Zacharias.

The angel Gabriel told Mary to name her Son Jesus, which means "the Lord saves," because He would save His people from their sins (Matt. 1:21).

Isaiah named his son Maher-shalal-hash-baz, which can be interpreted as "Quick-loot/Easy-pickings." This name prophetically symbolized the ease with which Assyria would spoil Syria and the northern kingdom of Israel (Isa. 8:3, 4).

God told Hosea to name his children Lo-ammi ("not my people") and Lo-ruhamah ("not having obtained mercy") to show a reversal in national Israel's relationship with God (Hosea 1:6-9). Peter later applied the symbolic prophecy of these names to spiritual Israel and the fulfillment of literal Israel's original mission (1 Peter 2:10; cf. Rom. 9:23-26; 11:30-32) among the Gentiles.

Actions can also serve as emblematic symbols because they can be a dramatic way of representing something. So, for example, Hosea kept taking back his unfaithful wife to illustrate God's undying love for an unworthy Israel, who repeatedly disqualified herself from the covenant relationship (Hosea 3:1).

On one occasion Isaiah went around naked as a sign that Israel would be stripped of her divine blessings (Isa. 20:2), and Ezekiel even painted a picture of Jerusalem's future destruction with a toy siege of a miniature city (Eze. 4:1-3).

Circumcision dedicated the reproductive powers to God and His will. It symbolized the need to cut away the flesh before a person could be included in the covenant community or as regenerate future citizens for it.

The sinner praying with his hands over the head of his sacrifice and the priest eating the flesh of the sin offering or bringing shed blood into the holy place symbolized the transfer of sin. When the sin offering died, it did so in the place of the confessed sinner. Then the priest either ate its flesh to symbolize that he had personally taken the confessed sin upon himself (Lev. 10:17) or burned it outside the camp to symbolize the shame the sacrificial animal bore for the transferred sin (Lev. 4:21). If the priest did not eat the flesh, then he brought the shed blood into the holy place (Lev. 6:30).

But "it was not left to the judgment of the priest to choose which of these two . . . [symbolic acts] to do. He was specifically commanded to bring the blood into the sanctuary in the cases of the anointed priest and the whole congregation; in the other two cases [of the ruler, or an individual from the congregation] he was not to carry the blood into the holy place, but put it upon the horns of the altar of burnt offering, and then eat the flesh. He was not permitted to carry the blood into the sanctuary and *also* eat the flesh, nor could he omit eating the flesh when the blood was not carried in. He could do only one of two things, but that one thing could not be omitted. From this it seems to be indicated that the eating of the flesh was in some way considered the equivalent of carrying the blood into the sanctuary" (M. L. Andreasen, *The Sanctuary Service*, pp. 135, 136).

So if the sin was not transferred to the priest, it had to be transferred to the sanctuary. According to the Bible, adultery (Eze. 23:37, 38), Sabbathbreaking (verse 38), uncleanness (Lev. 15:31; 16:16), worship of false gods (Lev. 20:3), and ceremonial uncleanness (Num. 19:13, 20) defile the sanctuary. The blood of the sacrificial animal, properly applied, also defiled the sanctuary because of the specific sin it represented. We can infer from this that sin was similarly terribly defiling.

The priest sprinkled some of the sacrificial blood before (in front of) the veil in the holy place (Lev. 4:17) and thereby left blood stains on the curtain for a symbolic record of the actual sins dealt with there throughout the year, awaiting cleansing on the annual Day of Atonement. He also put some of the blood on the horns of the altar of incense, symbolic of the payment that had been made in the outer court (Lev. 4:18). That is why Jeremiah warned: "The sin of Judah is written down with an iron stylus; with a diamond pen it is engraved upon the tablet of their heart, and on the horns of their altars" (Jer. 17:1, NASB).

Ordinances are sacred rites celebrated with material elements designed to call forth a human response to what God has done, is doing, and will yet do in Christ.

For example, in washing the feet of His disciples during the Last Supper, Christ demonstrated true humility and unselfishness. He shocked Peter because foot washing was so degrading that only non-Jewish slaves performed it as a courtesy for their master's guests. Jewish men expected their wives and children to do it for them as a sign of submission and respect. In the absence of a slave, one of the disciples should have offered to do it, but they were too busy arguing among themselves about who was the greatest. Christ intended to end the strife with a towel, a basin of water, and a good example. Foot washing symbolizes a personal desire to serve, confess to, and forgive one another, and it is the ideal way to prepare for the Lord's Supper.

The *Lord's Supper* is an opportunity to express dependence upon the High Priest Jesus and hope in the second coming of the King of kings. It helps us benefit from

His sacrificial death. Each participant actually feasts by grace on Christ's body and blood through a faith meal with the emblems of real bread and wine (cf. John 6)—a meal that will not allow the people to forget what God has done, is doing, and will yet do for them (cf. Ps. 22:27-31 and 1 Cor. 11:23-26).

In the emblematic symbol of baptism Christians are "baptized into Christ" (Rom. 6:3), much as Israelites were "baptized into Moses" under water (that is, the cloud over them and the Red Sea heaped up on both sides of them) during the Exodus (1 Cor. 10:1, 2). We do the same with Jesus. Paul says that we are "baptized into his death" (Rom. 6:3). Whereas in the Old Testament the sinner prayed with his hands over the lamb's head, now we are baptized into Christ. Baptism is the occasion in which the candidate officially and publicly identifies with the Lamb of God as his or her sacrifice. Paul also says that "our old self [the person we used to be] was crucified with Him [Christ]." So in entering the baptismal pool, we march to our "death"—are buried with Jesus in a watery grave—only to reappear on the other side as a new creature who should "walk in newness of life" (Rom. 6:4-6).

Such ordinances are not mere "mechanical rituals" (Mickelsen, p. 278) but are actual faith experiences that look beyond the physical emblems.

Here are some guidelines for interpreting symbols (adapted from Mickelsen, pp. 278, 279 and Kenneth A. Strand, *Interpreting the Book of Revelation*, p. 29).

---

1. Look for an interpretation by Scripture. That's the safest route.

2. Remember that symbols are fluid. A symbol may have more than one meaning (for instance, a lion can represent either Christ or the devil). Different symbols may represent the same thing (for example, both a lion and a lamb can represent Christ). Various symbols may represent the same thing in the same context (Christ is both the good shepherd and the door in John 10). Details may vary in what is apparently the same symbol (for instance, each of the four living creatures in Ezekiel has four faces, whereas each of the four living creatures in Revelation has only one face, but each creature has a different face from each of the others).

3. List the qualities of the literal object operating as the symbol.

4. Try to discover the purpose for using the symbol from the context, tracing the source(s) of symbolism. Observe how often and where the symbol appears. Note its original and any derived meaning for the community now using it. Allow each context to control its meaning, and don't force the symbol to say the same thing in each context.

5. Let the context explain how the symbol is connected with the truth it teaches.

6. Note the relationship of the symbol to the main theme. Consider the symbol within its immediate literary context or setting.

7. Consider the way that other cultures at that time may have used this same symbol for clues to its meaning, but interpret the symbol according to the way the writing community used it at the time.

8. Don't press every particular but just get the big picture. Bible writers often filled in details to round out the picture.

9. Think about or meditate on your findings. Allow room to expand, reconsider, or confirm the results.

10. Why was the symbol effective for its original audience? List the barriers preventing your audience from grasping its significance. Build only on what you are sure of.

Word Studies—These can be helpful, once you have acquainted yourself with the unfamiliar words in the passage. It is then time to explore the sense that each key word or term lends to it. You can accomplish this with a word study—"a thorough analysis of the meaning(s) of a word, designed to arrive at its specific meaning in a given passage" (Douglas Stuart, *Old Testament Exegesis*, p. 124). But since a particular word may have more than one meaning, "it is especially important to remember that words function in a context. Therefore, although any given word may have a broad or narrow range of meaning, the aim of word study . . . is to . . . understand as precisely as possible what the author was trying to convey by his use of this word in this context. Thus, for example, you cannot legitimately do a word study of *sarx* [flesh]; you can only do a word study of *sarx* in (1 Cor. 5:5) or in (2 Cor. 5:16), and so on" (Gordon D. Fee, *New Testament Exegesis*, p. 83).

But the ultimate setting for word study is the canonical context, the entire remote body of text that affects meaning. Consider, for example, the word translated "soul." Since the biblical concept of the soul originated with the Hebrews, the New Testament writers imported the soul concept from the Old Testament—not from Greek philosophy. The Old Testament takes a wholistic view of human beings, claiming that the soul (*nephesh*) is a person with the breath of life. The soul is something a person is, not something that a person has. Upon death it sleeps, awaiting a bodily resurrection to eternal joy.

Greek philosophers, however, promoted a dichotomous view of human nature, insisting that the soul and human flesh are incompatible with each other so that an immaterial soul must eventually escape its evil body through physical death in order to enter the blissful, superior, bodiless realm. This pagan view of the soul is incompatible with the Old Testament, and any attempt to determine the meaning of soul that ignores or even minimizes its Old Testament roots and erroneously adopts this dichotomous view will inaccurately reinterpret the entire soul concept and improperly redefine it. So, for example, *The Living Bible*, apparently in sympathy with the pagan Greek view in an editorial note, insists that Solomon's holistic statements on the subject in Ecclesiastes 9:5, 10 are his own personal "discouraged opinion, and do not reflect a knowledge of God's truth on these points!"

Even though they substitute a Greek word *psychē* for the Hebrew *nephesh*, the New Testament writers do not redefine the Old Testament idea, because despite its socio-cultural connotations or even its explicit meaning, *psychē* must still convey the core concept of soul rooted in and consistent with its Hebrew heritage. The New Testament uses the nearest Greek equivalent to the Hebrew word in order to communicate with its Greek-speaking audience—even if the word meant something very different in Greek.

A valid word study recognizes that New Testament writers frequently "baptized" pagan words into Christian service and acknowledges both the Old Testament roots of New Testament words and the New Testament destination of words from the Old Testament. Word study must never ignore progressive revelation.

FIGURE 23

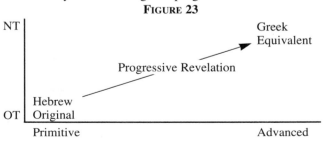

Cyril J. Barber outlines the classic threefold approach to word study in his *Introduction to Theological Research* (p. 104).

Etymology traces the historical origin and development of a word. It must be used with caution, because the original derivation of a word may no longer apply. For instance, atheists can say "Goodbye" without compromising their philosophy. Although the etymology of the word shows that it comes from "God bless ye," that meaning no longer inheres in the word.

Fee cautions us to "avoid the danger of becoming 'derivation happy'" (p. 83) because the etymology of a word helps very little with understanding its current meaning (see James Barr, *Semantics of Biblical Language*, pp. 107-160). Moises Silva goes so far as to say that "we learn much more about the doctrine of sin by John's statement, 'Sin is the transgression of the law,' than by a word study of *hamartia*, the word most commonly translated 'sin' [in the New Testament]" (*Biblical Words and Their Meaning*, p. 28).

For example, at the root of the word *hamartia* is the picture of missing the mark. But does the sinner miss the mark by overshooting it? by going off to one side or another? Not according to Romans 3:23: For we "all have sinned and *fall short* of the glory of God." Paul wants us to understand that no one is on God's level, and he uses *hamartia* to make it clear that sin is coming up short—a failure to reach, to live up to, the ultimate standard by which all righteousness is actually measured: God Himself (that is, His image). Of course, if we understand the concept to mean missing the mark set forth by the law, then it is possible to go beyond the requirements of the law, which may, therefore, also be sin.

So the root meaning is a good place to start, something to go on as we begin exploring the writer's overall thought in the sentence; but a word study is a thorough investigation into the contextual meaning of a term in the light of other inspired applications of that term or its cognates in biblical and other pertinent contexts.

Usage analyzes the way a word is employed both in its current and other contexts. This is extremely important.

Verification helps us check our findings against reference materials produced by specialists in the field. Sometimes our hunches may be correct, but they can also be very wrong, so authorities in the field of biblical languages are important.

The following is a procedure for word study that incorporates those important principles.

• Determine which words need special attention. Do you recognize or suspect any theologically pregnant words in the text, such as "body" in Ephesians 4? Are there any pivotal words crucial to a clear understanding of the text, such as "hinder" in 1 Peter 3:7? Do any prominent words stand out from the rest because of repetition, as "love" does in John 22:15-19; for their agreement with the paragraph theme, as "boast" does in 1 Corinthians 1:26-31; or by some other means of emphasis in the text?

• Describe the word or term in its context. What is it? A noun? A verb? What does it do in the sentence? Is it the subject? Object? A modifier? Is it literal or figurative? (Follow the appropriate guidelines.)

• Decide where you can learn the most about the word. Look up the word in Strong's *Concordance*. As mentioned earlier, the number to the right of each reference identifies its root in the Hebrew or Greek dictionaries at the back of the concordance. Each entry with the same identification number comes from the same root.

How many times does the root word appear in the Bible? If it is more than 25 times, be practical. Instead of checking every occurrence in detail, "think in terms of groups of occurrences" (Stuart, p. 125), like "What is its meaning in a particular book?" or "How does Paul use it?"

What historical period has the highest concentration of occurrences? Before the Exile? During the Exile? After the Exile? Before Christ? During Christ's earthly ministry (pre- or post-resurrection)? After Christ's ascension? Is the Bible book you are studying from this same period? If not, this could be an unusual application of it. Is your Bible writer the most frequent user of the word? If not, who is? How does he use it? Did he influence your writer (for example, did your writer quote from him?)?

Rely strictly on occurrences that really pin down the meaning of the word in a definite way and separate them into two groups (those earlier and those later than yours) in order to establish a range of meanings.

FIGURE 24

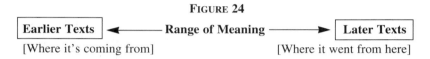

Look up the word in Nelson's *Expository Dictionary of the Old Testament*, Wilson's *Old Testament Word Studies*, Xavier Leon-Dufour's *Dictionary of the New Testament*, or Vine's *Expository Dictionary of the New Testament*. These tools offer a roundup of definite meanings for specific texts so that you will have something concrete to go on as you fix the range of meanings for your word.

Greek-speaking Old Testament scholars in Alexandria, Egypt, translated the Hebrew Scriptures into their native tongue for the benefit of fellow Jews who lived outside Palestine (*c.* 300-200 B.C.). Their work remains extremely important to modern interpretation because of its cross-cultural value. In choosing "Greek" equivalents for Hebrew and Aramaic words, they left us with a bridge between the testaments, a way to understand the transition from the Old Testament to the New. Frederick W. Danker devotes an entire chapter to "The Use of the Septuagint" in biblical studies (*Multipurpose Tools for Bible Study*, pp. 81-95).

Those who know the Hebrew and Greek alphabets can include input from the Septuagint translators in their analysis. To trace the Old Testament roots of a New Testament word; look up the word in Hatch and Redpath's *Concordance to the Septuagint* and make a note of the Hebrew or Aramaic equivalent(s) for the various scriptural references and record their meanings from Holladay's *A Concise Hebrew and Aramaic Lexicon of the Old Testament*.

How did your Bible writer's inspired contemporaries use the word in question? Can you make out any earlier, contemporary, or later trends? Was it used only or mostly in formulas? In certain kinds of expressions? On specific occasions? In some other way?

Does your Bible writer fit in with or deviate from any of these trends? Does he agree with any earlier, contemporary, or later authors? How does this affect your understanding of the word in question? If he does fit or agree, perhaps God used him to reinforce, revive, or reintroduce what others were trying to say. If he does not, maybe God gave him a unique, deeper, or progressive insight.

• Compare what you have learned so far with nonbiblical sources. This is especially helpful with *hapax legomena* (words that occur only once in the Bible), instances where you are still uncertain about the meaning or in cases where you need confirmation of your findings.

Determine the range of meanings in the Mesopotamian world for Old Testament words and in the Greco-Roman Jewish world for New Testament words.

For Old Testament words:

Look up the root meanings of Hebrew equivalents from related languages in the *Theological Wordbook of the Old Testament*. Those who read Hebrew should consult either Brown, Driver, and Briggs' *Hebrew and English Lexicon to the Old Testament*; Lisowsky's *Konkordanz zum Hebraischen Alten Testament*; Holladay's *Concise Hebrew and Aramaic Lexicon of the Old Testament*; or Ringgren's *Theological Dictionary of the Old Testament*.

Establish the range of meanings from both secular or religious inscriptions or relevant documents that predate and postdate your text. (Use references such as Edgar Jones' *Discoveries and Documents*; James B. Pritchard's *The Ancient Near East: An Anthology of Texts and Pictures*, vol. 1; D. Winton Thomas' *Documents From Old Testament Times*; John H. Walton's *Ancient Israelite Literature in Its Cultural Context*; and literature from the intertestamental period.)

How do your Bible writer's secular contemporaries use the word or its equivalents? Can you make out any earlier, contemporary, or later trends?

Does your Bible writer fit or deviate from any of these trends? Does he agree with any earlier, contemporary, or later authors? How does this affect your understanding of the word?

For New Testament words:

Look up the word in Vine's *Expository Dictionary of New Testament Words*. He transliterates the Greek word into English.

Establish the range of meanings by looking up the word in either Kittel's *Theological Dictionary of the New Testament,* Brown's *Dictionary of New Testament Theology,* or Balz and Schneider's *Exegetical Dictionary of the New Testament*. All three trace the secular and biblical path of these words from earlier classical Greek to later patristic Greek, frequently cross-referencing them with Hebrew, Aramaic, and other related language equivalents. You don't have to know Greek or Hebrew to use either of these tools, but it would help.

Those who read Greek can get a feel for the word in classical and Hellenistic Greek from Liddell-Scott's *Greek-English Lexicon*; Moulton and Milligan's *Vocabulary of the Greek New Testament*; Arndt-Bauer-Gingrich's *A Greek-English Lexicon of the New Testament and Other Early Christian Literature* (although it offers earlier and later Greek references); and for patristic Greek from Lampe's *A Patristic Greek Lexicon*.

Additional sources from the classical period include: Stanford's *The Odyssey of Homer*, two volumes; Xenophon's *Anabasis*; and Herodotus' *History*.

Additional sources from the Hellenistic period include insights from ancient papyri and inscriptions presented in Adolph Deissman's *Bible Studies*.

Additional sources from the intertestamental period include: *The Old Testament Pseudepigrapha*, edited by J. H. Charlesworth; C. G. Montefiore and H. Loewe's *A Rabbinic Anthology*; George Nickelsburg and Michael E. Stone's *Faith and Piety in Early Judaism: Texts and Documents;* Martin McNamara's *Targum and Testament: Aramaic Paraphrases of the Hebrew Bible: A Light on the New Testament;* F. H. Colson, G. H. Whitaker, and R. Marcus' *Philo* or N. N.

Glatzer's *Philo Judaeus, the Essential Philo*.

Additional sources from the post-biblical period include: Tixeront's *Handbook of Patrology*; J. B. Lightfoot's *The Apostolic Fathers*; *The Later Christian Fathers*, edited and translated by Henry Bettenson; Eusebius' *Ecclesiastical History*; Harry R. Boer's *A Short History of the Early Church;* and J.N.D. Kelly's *Early Christian Doctrines*.

How did your Bible writer's contemporaries use the word?

For parallels from the Dead Sea Scrolls see *John and Qumran*, edited by J. H. Charlesworth; Frank Moore Cross, Jr.'s *The Ancient Library of Qumran and Modern Biblical Studies*, rev. ed.; *Qumran and the History of the Biblical Text*, edited by Frank Moore Cross, Jr., and Shemaryahu Talmon; William Sanford LaSor's *The Dead Sea Scrolls and the New Testament*; and Geza Vermes' *The Dead Sea Scrolls in English*.

For parallels from rabbinic writings see W. D. Davies' *Paul and Rabbinic Judaism*; E. P. Sanders' *Paul and Palestinian Judaism*; Herbert Danby's translation of *The Mishnah*; Charles Gianotti's *The New Testament and the Mishnah*. You need to remember that most rabbinic parallels are much later than the New Testament, so any parallels should be used with great caution.

For actual examples from New Testament era papyri and all sorts of documents from everyday life in New Testament times see James Hope Moulton and George Milligan's *Vocabulary of the Greek New Testament*; F. F. Bruce's *Jesus and Christian Origins Outside the New Testament*; David R. Cartlidge and David L. Dungan's *Documents for the Study of the Gospels*; *New Testament Apocrypha*, edited by Wilhelm Schneemelcher and translated by R. McL. Wilson; *The Nag Hammadi Library in English*, edited by James M. Robinson. Consider also Flavius Josephus' *Complete Works*.

Can you make out any earlier, contemporary, or later trends?

Does your Bible writer fit or deviate from any of these trends? Does he agree with any earlier, contemporary, or later authors? How does this affect your understanding of the word?

• Consider the context of the word under consideration. Does the author define conventionally what he means? Or does he depart from the conventional use of the term and either stipulate what the word means by attaching a unique or at least unconventional meaning to it? Or does he persuade us to accept what he would have it to mean by passing off opinion as fact? Perhaps the inspired author is attempting to correct an earlier or current misconception, to advance a fresh insight, or to establish his understanding as the norm.

Does the author attach any explanations to the word? Does the structure of the author's (i) argument, (ii) logic, (iii) syntax, or (iv) semantics affect the term? (For example, for effect, to keep from repeating himself, to present another side of something, to rhyme, to play on words, etc.)

What about the writer's *argumentation*? An argument is "any group of propositions (true or false statements) one of which [that is, the conclusion] is said to follow from the others [that is, the premises]" (Vincent E. Barry, *Practical Logic*, pp. 5, 6). Perhaps the sequence is logical but not necessarily structural. Premises do not always have to come at the beginning, or conclusions do not have to come at the end, of the argument. So, for example, in Luke 20:21, 22 the Sadducees bring up a touchy subject for the Jews, hoping to trap Jesus into taking an unpopular position. Here the argument begins with the premises "[Since] You speak and teach correctly" + "You are not partial to any, but teach the way of God in truth," and it ends with the conclusion [it follows that You can be counted on to give us an honest answer to this question]: "Is it lawful for us to pay taxes to Caesar or not?"

Certain words frequently signal either a premise (*since, as, for, because, inasmuch as, for the reason that*, etc.) or a conclusion (*so, thus, therefore, it follows that, consequently, as a result, hence, finally, in conclusion*, etc.). But "signal words are no substitute for contextual analysis" (Barry, p. 9). They may lead us to suspect an argument, but only the context can confirm one.

Arguments generally fall into two categories: deductive and inductive. When the conclusion follows its premises with logical certainty, it is *deductive* (for example, Rom. 5:7, 8). When the conclusion comes with only logical probability, it is *inductive* (for instance, 2 Peter 3:4).

Paul's claim that the divine love is evident from Christ's willingness to die for the ungodly is a valid argument (that is, it is one in which the premises of Romans 5:7 necessarily lead to the conclusion in Romans 5:8).

The scoffers' assumption that since the creation does not appear to have changed any throughout the years, there is reason to doubt Christ's return is unwarranted. Only when the premises lend a high degree of probability to the conclusion is an inductive argument justified, although true premises don't always justify an inductive argument (for example, Matt. 19:3, 7). It is true that Moses did tolerate divorce in Israel (verse 7), but only as a reluctant concession to the stubborn Israelites of his day, who were too proud to make a go of tough marriages (verse 8), not because the law authorizes a man to divorce his wife for any reason (verse 3).

What about the author's *logic*?

Language can *reflect* our view of things because it "inevitably reveals values" (*ibid.*, p. 22). It shows how we see our world and what we think about it, by revealing our "assumptions, biases, and interests" and by disclosing "what's important and what's trivial in our lives. So developing a sensitivity to language and its usage can help foster invaluable insights into ourselves and others. Such insights can be extremely helpful in understanding and analyzing arguments, in uncovering their hidden assumptions" (*ibid.*, p. 23). For example, if the author uses euphemism, slang, or jargon, his presentation may rely more on emotion and psychology than it does on reason and communication. All three tend to reinforce what we already are and embrace, rather than introduce or lead us to something new.

Euphemism is a polite way of putting things. It tends to reflect what we prefer to think about unpleasant facts or "undignified circumstances, positions, events, or conditions, . . . and we are inclined to talk around the fact and what it actually represents. . . . [The trouble is], these viewpoints [which frequently evade reality] often serve as assumptions for arguments . . . and introduce emotion and obscurity into argument" (*ibid.*, p. 26). In Genesis 42:38, Jacob gets very emotional when Reuben asks to take Benjamin to Egypt. Instead of appealing to his son's reason, he argues that if anything should happen to Joseph's younger brother on the journey there, then "you would bring down my gray hairs with sorrow to Sheol" (that is, he will send an old man in tears to his grave).

Slang is the language used and accepted by a subgroup of society. It is up-to-date, to the point, and full of meaning. With a single word, slang betrays "more of the user's mental, psychological, and social background than most autobiographical statements could" (*ibid.*, p. 27). So, for example, the scribes and Pharisees used socially charged words like "publican" and "sinner" to reinforce their own identity more than to identify others. They referred to the people at large as "the common herd" because they neither belonged to nor saw themselves as a part of that larger group. Slang helped them both to unite themselves and to remain separate or distinct from everyone else. As such, slang was an expression of their loyalty to the subgroup in which they functioned, and it helped them identify who they were, not in terms of society, but in terms of the subgroup.

The slang user attempts neither to reason nor communicate with others; he simply wants to assert his membership in the subgroup. So, when some of the scribes and Pharisees said to Jesus' disciples, "Why does your teacher eat with the tax collectors and sinners?" they probably meant to reinforce or recapture their self-appointed role of pious leadership by putting Jesus, they thought, on the defensive *(ibid.,* pp. 27-30).

Jargon is shop talk, "the technical language of a trade, profession, or a membership" *(ibid.,* p. 31). Jargon differs from slang in that it is acceptable even outside the subgroup circle. The people of Israel admired the scribes and Pharisees and considered their teachings to be true (see John 12:34). The tradition of the elders—supposedly handed down to the "doctors of the law" from Moses—was rabbinic jargon for the collection of scholarly opinions preserved and circulated by the scribes and Pharisees since the post-Maccabean revolt era. It was widely regarded with the same respect as the written law. So it is no surprise that some of the scribes and Pharisees from Jerusalem dared to confront Jesus one day by saying, "Why do Your disciples transgress the tradition of the elders? For they do not wash their hands when they eat bread" (Matt. 15:1, 2, NKJV). Neither should it shock us that Nicodemus dropped in on Jesus one evening to talk shop (John 3:1-21). Jesus rebuked the Pharisees for teaching human precepts as though they were divine commandments (Matt. 15:9), and He also questioned Nicodemus' credentials to teach, because he couldn't grasp a fundamental spiritual concept (John 3:10).

The rabbis handed down the *halakah* (rules of conduct) and *haggadah* (homiletical illustrations) of the scholars before them, as though they did not have authority to teach directly from the Scriptures for themselves, but Jesus presented fresh truth directly from the Word without having to quote the recognized scholars, as someone with authorization to teach directly from God (Matt. 7:28, 29).

Language also can *affect* our view of things. Words "of high emotional content . . . invite a psychological, not a logical response" *(ibid.,* p. 41). "Often our feelings are so identified with such [emotionally loaded] words [and phrases such as "Calvary," "Gethsemane," and "the upper room"], that their mere mention sets off an emotional reaction" *(ibid.,* p. 39). The apostle Paul's emotionally charged speech before King Agrippa in Caesarea, alternating the terms "Jew" and "Gentile," brought an excited response from the king (Acts 26:24) and a concession that Paul's moving testimony had nearly persuaded him to convert (verse 28). But the emotion of the moment passed, and Agrippa never did come around to Paul's way of thinking.

What about the author's use of *syntax* versus *semantics*?

Semantics deals with the connotation or customary (but not necessarily exhaustive) meaning of words. *Syntax* focuses on the way the author arranged words to form phrases, clauses, and sentences. As Kaiser puts it: "Usually the particular meaning a word has in a particular situation is clearly specified by the grammatical constructions in which it occurs . . . the *syntactic* sign of meaning. Thus the same word . . . may appear in one sentence as a noun, but in another as a verb. In these instances, then, the meaning of the term is indicated by the grammar, that is by the syntactic construction. In other situations, the meaning of a word may be marked by the interaction of that word with the meaning of the terms which surround it. This is called the *semotactic* sign of meaning" (p. 105).

A definition is a concise statement that attempts to express the meaning of a term—either explicit (denotation) or implicit (connotation). On the one hand, "defining denotatively is defining through example" (Barry, p. 34). A term is the sign or symbol or name of the objects it can be extended or applied to. On the other hand, to define connotatively is to know how to use the term correctly. "You don't need to know everything it can be applied to. [Just] . . . the criterion for deciding whether or not an object is denoted by a term" *(ibid.,* p. 34). A term suggests certain "properties shared by all and only those objects" *(ibid.)* to which it extends or applies. So Christ's "cross" exemplifies any "tree" upon which sinners are "crucified."

Study the logical, syntactic, and semantic features of your text. As the author argues or develops his case—his line of thinking—choice or placement of terms, or the meaning he expresses throughout the entire context may have a profound influence on the meaning of your term.

Does the author use this same word in another context? How? Does he use any other words in this or another book to communicate the same idea? How does this affect your understanding of the word?

• Attempt a definition—in pencil.

• Verify your work. Compare your findings with reliable reference materials (such as commentaries, dictionaries, Bible translations, etc.). If they agree, write the word "agree" in the second column; if not, spell out what the differences are.

FIGURE 25

Source	Differences

• Adjust or affirm your definition. If verification turns up enough evidence so that you suspect your attempted definition may be in error, review the word-study process until you are satisfied with the results. Then reword the definition in pencil.

CHAPTER 4

CULTURAL ANALYSIS

Studying the Bible is a lot like traveling in a foreign country. Unless you acquaint yourself with the language, customs, and places of its people, you will never understand it, and your trip will be far less enjoyable and meaningful than it could be. (An especially helpful nontechnical book that deals with such matters is Bruce J. Malina's *Windows on the World of Jesus* by Westminster/John Knox.) That's why today's interpreters familiarize themselves with the "ways, methods, manners, tools, institutions, and literature" (Bernard Ramm, *Protestant Biblical Interpretation,* p. 96), of the Bible writers. They know that any attempt to understand them without factoring in the history and culture behind their words will fail. "The Bible was not written to introduce us to an ancient people with seemingly strange ways. It was written to introduce us to the ways of God Himself. But we live so far away from the people in the Bible, both in distance and in time, that we are puzzled and confused by certain elements that were neither puzzling nor confusing to the writers themselves or to their earliest readers" (Miller, *Harper's Encyclopedia of Bible Life,* p. 1).

The Author's Meaning

So in order to understand what the authors meant, make every effort to get a feel for "how they lived, what values they stressed, and why they did or did not prosper" (Mickelsen, *Interpreting the Bible,* p. 160). Norval F. Pease once said: "Horrible blunders have been made by preachers who neglected to acquaint themselves with the contextual and historical background" ("Preaching and Biblical Interpretation," in *A Symposium on Biblical Hermeneutics,* p. 259).

Authentic interpretation calls for an honest attempt to reconstruct the background to the passage (1) from information within the passage itself and (2) from reliable outside sources. As you go about this procedure, remember that reclaiming the historical situation (what) is more important than setting a precise historical date (when).

Sources of Information—The Bible

History is the record of what has happened. As Siegfried Schwantes points out, however: "History [is not] concerned with all the events in which man plays a role; it deals only with events which have *significance* in the overall drama" (*The Biblical Meaning of History,* p. 7; emphasis supplied). So, for example, when the apostle John closed his Gospel with the words: "Jesus did many other things as well. If every one of them were written down, I suppose that even the whole world would not have room for the books that could be written" (John 21:25, NIV), he candidly admitted that his version of Jesus' life and ministry was not an exhaustive account of everything that had happened during the Saviour's time on earth.

Should John have included everything he knew about Jesus? Does the fact he did not affect the accuracy of his Gospel? Is it any less reliable than say, Luke's rendition, which claims to be the full story of "all that Jesus began to do and to teach until the day that he was taken up" (Acts 1:1, 2, NIV)? When the Old Testament chronicler cut short the story of king after king with the words: "The rest of the acts of [so-and-so] . . . are written [elsewhere]" (see 2 Chron. 13:22), did he sabotage his credibility? If he did, he did so deliberately. He obviously had something else in mind besides telling everything he knew.

First of all, how much you tell does not determine the accuracy of what you report. History, said Schwantes: "deals *only* with [the *significant*] events . . . in the overall drama." So the Bible writers had the flexibility to pick and choose what was important and meaningful to them—and still be historical.

Second, no two people see or experience things *exactly* the same way. So it is only fair to expect different accounts of the same events from Bible writers who viewed things from their own individual perspectives—and still consider them truthful.

Third, no two situations are identical. Hence it is only reasonable to expect different slants on the same events from Bible authors who wrote in and to different, specific situations—and still consider them accurate.

The Bible writers were more than mere collectors or dispensers of facts. They did not write simply to preserve or report what had happened. They were "witnesses" who testified to others, either as history-makers themselves or as Spirit-led chroniclers of people, places, and things who made history. They wrote what they knew from their various experiences or the experiences of others—in specific contexts—painting a picture of God for the audience (or readers, though most common people at that time were illiterate) in each situation so that they could see Him as the writers saw Him and share their experience with Him. John made this very clear in the introduction to his first epistle when he said: "That which we have seen and heard we declare to you, that you also may have fellowship with us; and truly our fellowship is with the Father, and with His Son Jesus Christ" (1 John 1:3, NKJV). He and his fellow witnesses (he used the plural "we" and "us") wrote to make God real and near to others. They enjoyed sharing facts more as writers than as simple historians (verse 4).

The Bible writers themselves made it clear, then, that "although the Bible covers many centuries, it is more than just a book of ancient history. It is a whole library of different kinds of literature, written by various men over a long period of time" (*Harper's Encyclopedia of Bible Life*, p. 12). "Unless this basic fact is kept in mind," warn the Millers, "the reader tends to approach the reading and study of the Bible with the wrong presuppositions" (*ibid*, p. 12).

So the Bible is both historical and literary. Its writers select significant portions of the overall picture and apply them in and to specific historical contexts. If we want to understand why they drew on certain experiences and said the things they did to a particular audience, we have to study their words in context. As Gordon Fee points out: "Contextual questions are of two kinds: historical and literary. Historical context has to do with the general historical setting of a document (e.g., the city of Corinth, its geography, peoples, religion, economy, etc.) and with the specific occasion of that document (i.e., why it was written). Literary context has to do with why a given thing was said at a given point in the argument or narrative" (*New Testament Exegesis*, p. 25).

The first major literary difference is obvious: The Bible divides into old and new testaments (see the discussion beginning on page 266 of this book regarding the framework of biblical history under the subsection "The Progressive Fulfillment Model" in chapter 10, entitled "Typology"). At first the Old Testament stood alone. The Jews called it the "Tanakh," creating a word from the first letter of each of its three sections: "T" from the "Torah," the five books of Moses: Genesis to Deuteronomy; "N" from the "Nebiim," the prophets, historically dividing them into the "former prophets" from Joshua to 2 Kings, and the "latter prophets" from Isaiah through Malachi (with the exception of Daniel, which was included in the third and final group); and "kh" from the "Khethubim," the "Writings" (the rest of the Old Testament).

After Jesus burst on the redemptive scene, however, perspectives changed. He radically altered the understanding of the Old Testament. As the apostles reexamined it in the light of Christ and His ministry, they reshaped the overall revelation picture. First, they noticed that the Old Testament chronologically preceded the New. It came first and covers events that led up to the New Testament. So Matthew began his gospel: "Therefore all the generations from Abraham to David are fourteen generations; and from David to the deportation to Babylon fourteen generations; and from the deportation to Babylon to the time of Christ fourteen generations" (1:17, NASB).

The disciples understood that Christ's coming into the world marked the beginning of a new era in history, but they failed at first to see the connection between the two testaments. So when they struggled to understand the significance of what had happened at Calvary, Jesus told them: "O foolish men and slow of heart to believe in *all that the prophets* have spoken" (Luke 24:25, NASB), explaining that more than *preceding* the New Testament, the Old Testament actually *pointed* to it. Then, thanks to Bible studies with Christ like the one on the road to Emmaus in which, "beginning with Moses and with all the prophets, He explained to them the things concerning Himself in all the Scriptures" (Luke 24:27, NASB), they recast the Old Testament in the role of setting the stage for Christ's arrival and His fulfillment of its promises.

The church came to feel so strongly about this that it added new writings to the Scriptures (the New Testament) that it had inherited from Judaism. Commissioned to transmit the truth by Jesus Himself, the apostles considered their message from Him as valid and compelling as any Old Testament prophecy: "Remember the words spoken beforehand by the holy prophets and the commandment of the Lord and Savior spoken by your apostles" (2 Peter 3:2, NASB). Although Peter valued this New(er) Testament equal in authority to the Old—"Brother Paul . . . in all his letters . . . as . . . the rest of the Scriptures" (2 Peter 3:15, 16, NASB)—because of its advanced light, at least Paul promoted it ahead of the Old(er) Testament in its present significance to God's endtime people—"You . . . are God's household, . . . built upon the foundation of the *apostles* and prophets" (Eph. 2:20, NASB).

Subsequently the editors of the English Bible rearranged the Old Testament into three new groups of books that reflected this Christian view of salvation history. The first 17 books, from Genesis through Esther, explain the origins of God's covenant people. The next five, from Job through Song of Solomon, describe life from the covenant point-of-view. The last 17 books, from Isaiah through Malachi, give the reasons for Israel's less-than-glorious situation after centuries of being in covenant with God. With the stage dramatically set at the conclusion of the Old Testament for the arrival of an Elijah-like figure to usher in the new age (Mal. 4:5, 6; cf. Isa. 40:3), the New Testament then announced the good news, through Elijah-like John the Baptist (Matt. 3:3; 11:14) among others (the angel Gabriel; Jesus' mother, Mary; John's father, Zacharias; righteous Simeon; Anna the prophet; et al.), that the long-awaited Messiah had arrived to fulfill what God had promised in the Old (Matthew through John), and explained that Jesus works out this fulfillment through who He is and what He does in, through, and for His church, throughout the New Testament era (Acts through Revelation).

Books written in Palestine from the time of Moses to the days of Ezra that agreed with the Torah gained gradual acceptance among God's people (*Harper's Encyclopedia of Bible Life,* pp. 17, 18). At least "no Jewish book earlier than *c.* 250 B.C. has been preserved except for those in the OT canon" (Donald E. Gowan, *Bridge Between the Testaments,* p. 325). Whether the Old Testament was "presented 'as is' to God's people" or "it grew to its present limits and attained its present authority by a long and complex process" *(ibid.,* p. 314), the Jewish community considered this canon, this "closed body of writings . . . inspired and authoritative for their faith and life" *(ibid.,* p. 505).

Lamentably, the Jews lived in a changing world, and they soon underwent some changes of their own. "Among the changes in the lives of the Jews in Palestine must have been a shift in the daily, spoken language from Hebrew to Aramaic" *(ibid.,* p. 63). Outside of Palestine, which resisted Hellenization, most of the world spoke Greek, including the surviving, thriving Jews, scattered from the Promised Land. As time wore on, services entirely in Hebrew failed to meet the needs of Jews, regardless of where they lived. Rabbis reacted to the problem by translating Hebrew Scripture readings at the synagogue into the "daily language of the congregation, Aramaic in Palestine and Greek in much of the Diaspora. It had to be done orally and without notes, in the early days, and interpretation, rather than word-for-word translation was expected, so considerable freedom was permitted. In the second century A.D. an attempt was made to standardize the Aramaic translations and put them into writing. Later Targums became more and more literal, but the earliest examples tend to be midrashic in nature [see the discussion of midrash beginning on p. 129 of this book in the subsection "Quotations, Allusions, and Commentary"] freely adding explanations and illustrations to the text" *(ibid.,* p. 286).

Hellenized Hebrew scholars in third century B.C. Alexandria, Egypt, translated first the Torah, then the rest of the Old Testament into Greek, for the "large Greek speaking community there" *(ibid.,* p. 307). Gowan points out that this Septuagint version of the Old Testament, the Bible of the early church used extensively even by Jews outside of Palestine, "contained longer forms of some of the old books plus some new works which had been written during the first and second centuries B.C." *(ibid.,* pp. 327, 328).

With the Temple in ruins after the fall of Jerusalem in A.D. 70, Israel turned from sacrifices to pure synagogue worship, and a council of 72 rabbis met at Jamnia, near Joppa, in A.D. 90 to settle on a Hebrew canon. In order to come up with a distinctively Hebrew collection "a number of the books which had in fact been thought of as holy Scripture by the Greek speaking Jews had to be rejected" (*Harper's Encyclopedia of the Bible,* p. 18). Some early church leaders questioned these books because they did not appear in the Jewish canon, but did not object strongly enough to have them removed. When Christians, however, continued to use the Septuagint with great evangelistic success among Jews, another council in A.D. 130, "under the leadership of Rabbi Akiba condemned the Greek translation for ordinary religious use" *(ibid.,* p. 18).

The church, on the other hand, continued to include the disputed books in its manuscripts, and as Gowan says, "they continued in use until the Reformation" *(Bridge Between the Testaments,* p. 309). That is the time when the Reformers, who turned from the church to the Scriptures as their only source of authority, investigated the differences between the church's then official Bible, the Vulgate (Jerome's Latin translation of the Bible, *c.* 400 B.C.), and the Hebrew Bible. Whatever they found in the Vulgate that did not appear in the Hebrew canon, they "called Apocrypha (from the Greek word meaning "hidden") and refused to accord them the same authority as the other books. Eventually they dropped out of Protestant translations of the Bible" *(ibid.,* p. 309).

For details of how the New Testament gelled into written form and the way the church determined which books it should add to the Old Testament, see the discussion regarding transmission of the New Testament text beginning on page 313 of this book in the chapter "Is the King James the Most Accurate Version of the New Testament?" and the story of New Testament canonization beginning on page 347 in this book in the chapter "How Did We Get the New Testament?"

Sources of Information—Extrabiblical Literature (See chapter 9 for an exhaustive list)

Ancient Near Eastern Documents*—*The Bible is a product of the ancient Near East. Although it is true that the Israelites received special revelation from God that made them distinctively different from their neighbors in many ways, they were nevertheless ancient Near Easterners who reflected the culture of the world in which they lived. Even a casual reading of the Old Testament and New Testament plunges us into the world of desert nomads, marketplace potters, and itinerant scribes.

Abraham, for instance, came from Ur, where he and his ancestors had worshiped foreign gods (Joshua 24:2, 3). It comes as no surprise, then, that "God tested Abraham" (Gen. 22:1), essentially checking the former pagan for any residual Mesopotamian ties and tendencies (verse 12). To complicate matters, "the descendants of Abraham spent centuries in Egypt and then came to dwell in the midst of Canaanite civilization" (John H. Walton, *Ancient Israelite Literature in Its Cultural Context,* p. 13) under the influence of other ancient Near Eastern cultures. For example, when Moses warned the Israelites about to enter Canaan, "The land, into which you are entering to possess it, is not like the land of Egypt, from which you came, where you used to sow your seed and water it with your foot like a vegetable garden. But the land into which you are about to possess it, a land of hills and valleys, drinks water from the rain from heaven" (Deut. 11:10, 11, NASB), he tells them that the farming techniques they had learned from the Egyptians would not work in the Promised Land.

It is obvious, then, that the children of Israel added to their native Mesopotamian ways the cultural features they assimilated from peoples they encountered in their travels. As a result of these accumulated influences, "the language spoken by the Israelites is historically related to the languages of the Semitic world around them. Copies of ancient Near Eastern literature have been discovered in the excavations of Israelite cities, . . . and the Israelites' awareness of the cultures and literature of the ancient Near East is demonstrable from the biblical record as well as from the archaeological data" *(ibid.,* p. 13).

And if the Israelites did, in fact, embrace things in common with their neighbors, it is only reasonable to conclude that "Israelite thinking cannot be understood in isolation from its ancient Near Eastern cultural context" *(ibid.).* Furthermore, since it is a primary source of information and written by actual people of that region and era, "ancient Near Eastern literature should and can instruct us about the common worldview of biblical times. . . . The similarities that exist can be very instructive and should not be ignored" *(ibid.)*. So are the differences.

It is important to note here that the Bible writers did not derive their material from secular sources. In *The Babylonian Genesis,* author Alexander Heidel offers three possible explanations for the similarities between the biblical and Babylonian creation stories: "First, the Babylonians borrowed from the Hebrew account; second, the Hebrews borrowed from the Babylonian; third, the two stories revert to a common fountainhead" (p. 130).

If the Israelites did, in fact, receive a special revelation from God, and that is the position of this handbook, then Heidel's third suggestion makes the most sense: both the Hebrews and the Babylonians referred to the same phenomena or event—except the Bible writers had more than natural revelation to go on. They simply shared what God had revealed to them, and then they borrowed, reshaped, and reapplied the popular cultural materials of their day to correct the misconceptions of those who did not have the benefit of special relevation. So, for example, the inspired psalmist correctly ascribes to the Lord characteristics popularly attributed to Baal by the Canaanite world. It is He, not the mythical Canaanite deity, "who makes the clouds His chariot, who walks on the wings of the winds," "who laid the foundations of the earth, so that it should not be removed forever" (Ps. 104:3, 5, NKJV).

In this way the Scriptures can simultaneously fortify God's people with truths intended to restore the world's view of God and reinstate Him to His rightful place as Lord and Creator of all. As Paul said: "All scripture is given by inspiration of God, and is profitable for doctrine, for reproof, for correction, for instruction in righteousness" (2 Tim. 3:16, KJV).

As we move from the Old Testament to the New, the sweep of history also leaves its impression on the biblical environment. Changes in the political arena brought corresponding modifications in the socioreligious situation of the region. The transition from one dominant power to the next caused Israel to live in an Egyptian, then Mesopotamian, next Medo-Persian turned Greco, and finally Roman world. While kingdoms fell, however, they did not disappear from the scene. Fallen realms may have "had their dominion taken away," yet they survived these takeovers because "their lives were prolonged for a season and time" (Dan. 7:12, KJV). Conquerors absorbed rather than exterminated their victims, who continued to influence the resulting situation. For example, the *iron*-toothed fourth beast (verse 7) representing Rome in Daniel 7 (cf. 2:40) had nails of *bronze* (see verse 19), which represented residual Greek presence and influence (cf. 2:39). Consequently, it is proper to say that the early church during the Roman era still lived in a *Greco-Roman* world.

Chapter 9 lists specific literary documents that have the potential of helping us better understand not only the Old Testament world but also the world of the New Testament and the developing Christian church.

Ancient documents that help us understand the ancient Near Eastern background to the Old Testament include Creation and Flood stories, law codes, covenants and treaties, historical literature, religious literature, wisdom literature, and prophetic literature.

Intertestamental Documents—There are also documents that give us insight into the intertestamental period. Scholars intently study such literature as the Septuagint, the Apocrypha, the pseudepigrapha, and expansions of the Old Testament.

Additionally, Jewish targumim, Mishnah, midrashim, and Talmuds offer interesting glimpses into the ancient Jewish milieu. And the Dead Sea Scrolls help the student of Scripture understand some of the sectarian thought that was so rampant during intertestamental times. Chapter 9 offers summaries of these literary documents.

Apocryphal Documents—After the rise of Christianity additional literature had an influence on the growing church. There are apocryphal gospels, acts, epistles, and apocalypses that the student of the Bible cannot afford to ignore.

Church Fathers and Doctors—Although the writings of the Church Fathers and Doctors come to us considerably later than the New Testament world itself, they too offer a glimpse into how the developing church understood Scripture and itself.

"Patrology," says Patrick J. Hamell, "is the science which deals with the life, writings, and doctrine of the orthodox writers of Christian antiquity" *(Handbook of Patrology,* p. 9), consisting of the *Fathers* and *Doctors* of the church.

The title *father* originally referred to bishops (Polycarp, the Bishop of Smyrna, was called *"the Father of Christians" (The Martyrdom of Polycarp* 12. 2 [c. A.D. 155]). By the fifth century, however, it came "to designate the old ecclesiastical [church] writers—ordinarily bishops—who died in the faith and in communion with the church" (Tixeront, *Handbook of Patrology,* p. 2). Only those with "orthodox" doctrine, a holy life, and ecclesiastical approval, who ministered during the first eight centuries qualified as fathers. While they do not have to meet the fourth requirement of antiquity, "an eminent degree of learning is also necessary, together with a special declaration by ecclesiastical authority" to be considered a *doctor (ibid.).* Such illuminaries as Tertullian, Origen, Eusebius, etc., held erroneous views at one time or another, and are known as ecclesiastical writers. Only Ambrose, Jerome, Augustine, and Gregory in the west; Basil, Gregory of Nazianzus, and John Chrysostom in the east—hold the elusive title of *doctor.* Scholars divide patrology into *three* eras:

The First Period (A.D. 100-300)—Closest to the beginning of Christianity, these authors are the most respected witnesses to the apostolic tradition. Three main issues were addressed during this period:

Gnosticism. The world of the New Testament was very concerned about having an experience with the divine. The intellectuals may have been satisfied with philosophy, but the masses found it and the routine religions of state and of nature unable to deliver what they wanted. So a large number of people turned to mystery religions because these cults claimed to have the secret knowledge that opens the door to real fellowship with the gods. Toward the end of the first century, Gnosticism (knowledge), a religious movement that claimed to have such esoteric information, came on the scene and grew very popular among early Christians. *Syncretists* (mixers), who adopted the best of rival beliefs, made Jesus and the gospel a part of their religion.

According to Gnosticism, God, the Unknown Father, originally existed alone. He found this situation undesirable and created Mind and Truth, the first two *aeons* (celestial beings) of the *Pleroma* (the fullness of the divine being). These aeons set in motion a process of reproduction until the number of aeons totaled 30. The last aeon, Wisdom, the weakest of them all, wanted to know the unknowable Unknown Father, and in her frustration brought forth a female aeon, Achamoth, without the help of her male partner. An unnatural child, Achamoth could not remain in the Pleroma and fell out of it. Mind and Truth produced two other aeons, Christ and the Holy Spirit, to comfort her. With harmony restored to the Pleroma, the other aeons combined their efforts and produced one more aeon named Jesus. Meanwhile, Achamoth had a son,

Demiurge (workman, Creator), and through him became the mother of all matter. Because she is inferior and thus unworthy of the Pleroma, matter is evil, making it unworthy of contact with the all-good Unknown Father. Demiurge formed and shaped all matter, and even created human souls.

Wisdom is the link between the wholly spiritual realm (the Pleroma) that comes out of the Unknown Father, and the lower material world that comes out of Wisdom's unnatural daughter, Achamoth, and Achamoth's son, Demiurge. As such, Wisdom still has influence over her grandson and causes him to make people with positive spiritual qualities . . . even though they are still trapped in evil flesh. Since the creation of the world, then, was not the result of a divine plan, but of an accident, the world and everything in it, including us, is evil—but not without hope. Our spiritual souls can be redeemed from these evil bodies if we receive this knowledge from Christ, an aeon born of the virgin Mary, and return to the Pleroma from which we received our spiritual existence.

Valentinus, an Alexandrian who taught at Rome in the early second century, was probably Gnosticism's most powerful spokesperson. A group of Gnostics, the Docetists (named for the Greek word *dokein,* which means "to seem"), claimed that Jesus only *seemed* to be human, because the aeon Jesus evacuated the earthly body that died on the cross and was not actually crucified.

The early writers battled this heresy, arguing against the idea that only Gnostics had worthwhile knowledge of God. They refuted the notion of a Creator who was supposedly different from and inferior to the Redeemer. They discredited the concepts of evil matter (which made resurrection unnecessary), a ghost-saviour (who only seemed to die), and that only those created with positive spiritual qualities by Demiurge could be saved.

Marcionism. As Gnosticism gained momentum toward the middle of the second century, a Christian named Marcion moved to Rome and began to study with a Gnostic there called Cerdo, who said that the God of the Old Testament was not the Father of Jesus. This principle led Marcion to believe that the Old Testament, the Law, and Israel of the Creator were separate from the New Testament, the gospel, and church of the good Father of Jesus. Following this line of reasoning to its logical conclusion, Marcion figured that if the God of the Old Testament, then, is inferior to God the Father, then the Law and the prophets inspired by the Old Testament God are also inferior to Jesus, the pure revelation of the unknown New Testament Father. The New Testament, however, teems with Old Testament-Jewish ideas that, for Marcion, prevent it from presenting a clear picture of Christ, so he cleansed it by reducing it to the Gospel of Luke and Paul's Epistles (except the pastorals), and by removing all references to the New Testament Redeemer as the Old Testament Creator.

For Marcion, Jesus only appeared to be material, because He came directly, incorporeally, and suddenly from heaven to reveal the previously Unknown Father. The cruel Old Testament God crucified the perfectly just Christ, but in doing so broke His own Old Testament Law. When Christ accepted the souls of the redeemed in exchange for what the Old Testament God had done to Him, He paid the price of their salvation. He purchased them so that they could join Him in the Pleroma. Having escaped the flesh, He is not coming back. Since we will not require physical bodies in that place, there is no need to resurrect the dead. Christians should live ascetic lives now, escape the flesh at death, and go on to the spiritual realm. Like our physical bodies, this evil, material world has no future either.

The early Christian writers battled this heresy by showing that God the Creator is also God the Redeemer—a God of love and justice. Furthermore, they also argued that this truth is revealed in Christ Jesus, the incarnate Creator/Redeemer.

Montanism. Montanus, a former Phrygian priest, held orthodox views of God the Father and God the Son, but misunderstood the person and work of the Holy Spirit. Not only did he superimpose the ecstatic spiritual experiences from his wild, prophetic, pagan past onto his life in Christ, but he emphasized them. At first he stood out alone from the church. Then two women, Maximilla and Priscilla, left their husbands to assist him with his ministry. Too radical to stay, they eventually separated from the Catholic Church and organized their own.

Montanus taught that the Father appeared in the Old Testament and the Son in the New and that the age of the Paraclete had come. In this new age God spoke exclusively through the prophet Montanus and his two female assistants. He called on his followers to fast, leave their earthly tasks, and proceed to the nearby town of Pepuza to await the descent of the New Jerusalem. As time wore on, Montanus taught his followers many other things that put him at odds with the organized church: that they must marry only once (although they could walk out on a spouse for spiritual reasons); that true Christians have only recognizable spiritual gifts and desire martyrdom (it was a sin to avoid it); that women could hold office (like his two female coprophets); that Christians should completely separate from the world (when church leaders wanted to keep channels open); that people of high spirituality (himself included) could forgive sins (the clergy refused to share that authority).

At first Montanism appealed to many people. For those under persecution, prophecies of the end brought welcome relief. Others, like Tertullian, a popular and powerful defender of the faith, appreciated the call for a stricter lifestyle, because the church had gradually grown worldly. Eventually, however, Montanus, Maximilla, and Priscilla died, and the delay in Christ's return neutralized the belief in an imminent Second Coming. And the failure of the New Jerusalem to come down at Pepuza took the urgency out of Montanus' prophecies. The Montanist church then settled down to the business of the long haul, organized itself into a number of small churches, and with nothing to attract significant numbers of people from the mainstream of Christian society, it eventually disappeared sometime between A.D. 500 and 550.

The Second Period (A.D. 300-430)—This was the *golden age* of patrology. The greatest ecclesiastical minds ever wrestled with the trinitarian problem *doctrinally* (300-360) and *practically* (360-430). Also at this time these Christian thinkers investigated the doctrine of grace.

The Third Period (A.D. 430-750)—This was the era of the great Christological controversies, from the Council of Ephesus (431) to the Second Council of Constantinople (553). The period witnessed a great decline in Christian literature, probably because of the inferiority of its writers compared to those of the first two patrological economies. Many of its writers overlapped with those of the golden age.

As already mentioned, two issues predominated these important writings.

The Trinitarian and Christological Controversy—The apostolic fathers simply repeated the New Testament and did not elaborate on the subject. This left the door wide open to speculation and opinion in the years that followed. Eventually the problem boiled down to three prevailing views of the relationship between the divinity and humanity of Christ: (1) the Western understanding insisted that the fully human nature and fully divine nature coexist united though unmixed in the person of Christ, but is this person the eternal Son or the human being miraculously born of the virgin Mary? (2) The Antiochan view emphasized Christ's humanity, but anything less than a fully divine Saviour could not save anyone. (3) The Alexandrian position emphasized Christ's divinity, but anything less than a fully human Saviour could not save anyone either.

And there were variations, of course, among these viewpoints.

Subordinationism—Justin Martyr and the other apologists taught that Christ was a creature—begotten by and subordinate to the Father. The Bible, they maintained, calls Christ God's Son because He was born and was not coeternal with His Father.

Adoptionism—A Greek named Theodotus, who relocated to Rome, taught that Jesus was conceived by the Holy Ghost and grew up a good and righteous man. Because Jesus was filled with the Holy Spirit and was obedient to the death of the cross, God raised Him from the dead and adopted Him as His Son.

Adoptionists were also called Dynamic Monarchianists, because the *self-ruling one* (Monarch) revealed Himself powerfully (dynamically) in Jesus.

Sabellianism—Concerned about the unity of God, first Praxeas, then Noetus, and finally Sabellius taught that the one God revealed Himself in three successive ways or modes: first as the Father-Creator; then as the Son-Saviour; and finally as the Holy Spirit-Comforter. Since the Father took on the form of the Son, who suffered and died, some people called the Sabellians "Patripassians" or Father-sufferers (patri: father; passion: suffer). Others called them Modalistic Monarchians because the *self-ruling one* revealed Himself in all three modes.

Arianism—Arius, an elder in the Alexandrian church, taught that the Father alone is true God because He existed alone in the beginning. He created the Son, separate and distinct from Himself, so that the Son could make the world. He is a Son only by adoption, and He is able to work directly with matter because, although He is the greatest of all created beings, the Son is inferior enough to the Father that He can. The Son is, therefore, neither God nor man. The second creature is the Holy Ghost.

Apollinarianism—In A.D. 360 Apollinaris, the bishop of Laodicea, taught that Christ was not completely human. He believed that the divine *Logos*, or *Reason*, took the place of the human spirit in Jesus. So Apollinaris' Christ is fully divine, but incompletely human.

Nestorianism—Nestorius of Antioch became the patriarch of Constantinople in A.D. 428. The idea there that the virgin Mary was the "mother of God" offended his high regard for the humanity of Christ. So he preached that the Lord's humanity and divinity existed as two separate entities in Jesus. By denying the personal unity of Christ, he also rejected the God-man.

Pneumatomachianism—With Arian roots, this group denied the divinity of the Holy Ghost and, therefore, the entire Trinity. They were also called Semi-Arians.

Monophysitism—The followers of Cyril of Alexandria believed that the two natures of Christ became one combined divine-human nature at the Incarnation. Although it came out of two natures, they could not accept the idea that Christ always has two natures. So they were called Monophysites from the Greek *mono* (one) and *physis* (nature).

The Controversy Over Grace—Once again there was a difference of opinion among Christians during these formative years.

Manichaenism—These Christians taught an absolute dualism between eternal evil and good. Light and darkness have been battling each other throughout eternity

81

and now contend in the world and in each human heart. So God, the absolute light, is not responsible for evil. It is also all right to indulge the flesh and to concede the flesh to evil, because the body is only a minor part of a person when compared to the spirit. Christ Himself never wore human flesh.

Donatism—In A.D. 311 Carthage received a newly ordained bishop named Caecilian. One of the bishops who ordained him was Felix of Aptunga, who stood accused of handing over the Scriptures during the Diocletian persecution. Felix' accusers believed that his participation in the rite invalidated Caecilian's ordination. In other words, they believed that the effectuality of rites and sacraments depended on the holiness of the ministers involved. The dissenters elected their own bishop, Marjorinus. Several councils later, Marjorinus' successor, Donatus, gave this schismatic movement its name.

Pelagianism—An Irish monk living at Rome, Pelagius taught that God gives everyone the possibility of living a sinless life. Human beings have the *will* to live and the *power* to lead such a life. We are by nature good, but the will to do good is weak from repeatedly giving in to evil example. So God assists our innate will to do good by giving us the law and sending Christ to be an example. Baptism puts the weaknesses and failures of the past behind us so that we can begin to live the sinless life.

Sources of Information—Archaeology

While history is the study of what happened, archaeology is the study of what history has physically left behind—its "material remains," which "include all tangible things made by man" (G. W. Van Beek, "Archaeology," in *The Interpreter's Dictionary of the Bible,* vol. 1, p. 195). Archaeologists explore for and examine what they can see and touch from the past—*"written* documents, including texts of ancient languages on stone, metal, clay, parchment, and papyrus; and *unwritten* documents, comprising all other objects—*e.g.,* fortifications, buildings of various kinds, sculpture, household vessels, tools, weapons, and personal ornaments" *(ibid.).* According to Abraham Terrian, coins excavated at Heshbon by a team from Andrews University revealed volumes of fresh insights into that city's history ("Coins From the 1976 Excavation at Heshbon," in *Andrews University Seminary Studies,* vol. 18 [Autumn 1980]: 173-180).

Biblical archaeology deals with relics from the past "that touch directly or indirectly upon the Bible and its message" (Merrill F. Unger, *Archaeology and the Old Testament,* p. 9). Artifacts recovered by biblical archaeologists shed light on the past, which helps us reconstruct the biblical background to passages of Scripture. Their discoveries illuminate and illustrate texts by bringing the remote and unfamiliar biblical past into the present.

History of Biblical Archaeology—The science of archaeology began on the banks of the Nile River in 1798, the year artists and scholars among Napoleon's expeditionary force to Egypt came face-to-face with mummies and monuments from the ancient world. They wiped the first layers of dust off a neglected past just waiting to be rediscovered.

Thousands of years had built up a language barrier between the modern world and ancient Egypt. Unfamiliar with its out-of-date symbols, Napoleon's men of letters could not even begin to decipher the record of Egypt's past. On the brink of discovery, at the foot of a canyon of differences, they needed a bridge—some link with the past to move ahead with their investigations. A French military engineer named Bouchard found it in 1799. While working at Rosetta, near the western mouth of the

Nile, he uncovered a slab of black basalt with three bands of writing on it. It turned out to be the record of a single decree, written in three different languages: hieratic, a simplified form of hieroglyphics, at the top (the same Egyptian picture writing that previously stumped the scholars); demotic, a cursive form of hieratic, in the middle; and familiar Greek at the bottom. Working from their knowledge of Greek to decipher the cryptic symbols of long ago, first Sir Thomas Young and then Jean-François Champollion used the Rosetta stone as a bridge to cross over the language chasm into the ancient world of the pharaohs.

In a similar way scholars finally solved the puzzle of cuneiform, the wedge-shaped writing of Mesopotamia. For centuries they had tried unsuccessfully to crack the ancient Near Eastern code. Then a German schoolteacher from Göttingen, Georg Friedrich Grotefend, boldly tackled another trilingual inscription, this time from Persepolis. Through a process of elimination, he figured out 13 of its symbolic signs, a significant step toward solving the cuneiform riddle.

Then in 1835 Henry Creswicke Rawlinson came to the end of the cuneiform trail. Generations of curious passersby on the road from Ecbatana to Babylon had wondered about an enormous inscription nearly 200 feet up on the cliff face of Mount Behistun, but no one had ever deciphered its message—until the young Englishman came along. Employed by the East India Company, Rawlinson spent his free time transcribing, deciphering, and translating ancient cuneiform texts. Intrigued by Behistun, he took four years to copy its 14 columns of curious cuneiform.

Eighteen years of intensive study later, Rawlinson concluded that Mount Behistun had been a natural billboard and the inscription an announcement of Darius the Great's heroism, prominently advertised in three languages: Old Persian, Elamitic, and Babylonian.

Rawlinson's translation turned the orientalist world on its ear, provoking an army of fortune hunters in the decades that followed, treasure-hunting rather than excavating the sites of past civilizations until Flinders Petrie turned archaeology into a science. After excavating Egypt's Tanis, Naukratis, and Hawara in the 1880s, Petrie spent six weeks digging Tell el-Hesi, a mound near Gaza in Palestine and sucessfully dated the successive strata of settlements there from its *pottery*—a method still in use today. In 1908 George A. Reisner and Clarence S. Fisher conducted the first American excavations in Palestine—at Samaria. Reisner went on to develop the first systematic methods of analyzing, surveying, and recording archaeological discoveries. Another American, William F. Albright, late president of the American School of Oriental Research, enhanced the reliability of pottery chronology while excavating Tell Beit Mirsim from 1926-1932. One of his students, Nelson Glueck, president of Hebrew Union College-Jewish Institute of Religion and an ordained rabbi, explored Transjordan and the Negev with his Bible in hand, trusting what he called "the remarkable phenomenon of historical memory in the Bible" (Keith N. Schoville, *Biblical Archaeology in Focus*, p. 163).

Dame Kathleen Kenyon, one of the foremost of modern Palestinian archaeologists, refined techniques of analyzing soils and debris while excavating Samaria from 1931-1935 and Jericho from 1952-1958. Her contributions to the science of archaeology had such an impact that the government of Israel permitted her to excavate at Jerusalem from 1961-1967, an honor generally reserved for Hebrew nationals (e.g., Benjamin Mazar, Nahman Avigad, and Yigal Shiloh). While excavating Masada from 1963-1965, Yagael Yadin began the modern practice of using volunteers on digs in place of paid staff. Both Harvard's G. Ernest Wright, a student of W. F. Albright, and William G. Dever, Wright's protégée and a president of the American School of Oriental Research, trained young volunteers on their digs at Shechem (1956-1964) and Gezer (1964-1971).

Modern archaeological teams continue to use volunteers, but they also include a host of specialists in the fields of geology, architecture, photography, pottery, and ancient civilization. Laboratories use the latest techniques to date objects and determine their places of origin. Despite this high-tech approach, serendipity still has a place in archaeology. In addition to the accidental recovery of the Dead Sea Scrolls at Khirbet Qumran, unsuspecting nonprofessionals also stumbled upon the ancient city of Ugarit at Ras Shamra, Syria, and the Amarna Letters and the Nag Hammadi Library in Egypt.

Archaeological Methods—Ancient Mesopotamians did most of their building with bricks. Unfortunately, "unseasonably wet winters, accidental fires, or demolition by invading armies could quickly turn houses, palaces or whole towns into desolate ruins" (K. A. Kitchen, *The Bible in Its World,* p. 10). In the event the inhabitants wanted to stay and rebuild, "they often just levelled-off the debris and built on top. Thus, through the centuries, towns grew ever upward upon their own former ruins" (*ibid.*, p. 10). To recover the material remains of earlier civilizations, then, the archaeologist "excavates the town-mounds of the ancient Near East, beginning at the top levels left by the last occupants . . . working his way downward through ever earlier periods of settlement to reach bedrock on which the first inhabitants had built" (*ibid.*). Archaeologists then sift through the layers for material clues to the identity and situation of the civilizations buried in the mound to record and evaluate what they find.

Sometimes, however, finds await discovery in caves or tombs. The Dead Sea Scrolls, for example, sat undisturbed for nearly 1,900 years until Muhammed Adh-Dhib, searching for a wayward goat, entered one of the caves in the cliffs overlooking the west coast of the Dead Sea and found them stored in jars. Tombs, as a rule, did not fare as well. Robbers usually plundered them for valuables, leaving very little besides skeletons and pottery for posterity. But whatever the circumstances or the magnitude of the find, archaeologists have developed a procedure to make the most of what they discover.

Most of the materials recovered are worth very little themselves. "In every excavation tens of thousands, and often hundreds of thousands of objects are found. . . . For the most part potsherds; broken bits of stone, metal, and glass vessels; flint and metal tools; implements and weapons; clay figurines; bits of sculpture in stone or metal; architectural fragments; bones; rings; stone and metal beads; scarabs; seals; etc." (G. W. Van Beek, "Archaeology," in *The Interpreter's Dictionary of the Bible,* p. 200). Seemingly worthless at face value, these objects "are extremely important because they enable the archaeologist (a) to date the occupation levels and strata in the site, and (b) to describe and compare material cultures" (*ibid.*).

Things do not remain the same indefinitely. As time passes, no matter how popular something is, it undergoes change and eventually goes out of style—only to be replaced by some newer version of itself or by something different that improves upon it. Archaeologists trace this history of each class of object by tracking its progress or decline as they work through a tell (mound). When excavation is complete, they simply take all the samples of a single class, starting with the most remote nearest the bottom of the tell, and trace its history, in sequence, from one strata to the next. After doing this with each class of object, the archaeologist correlates the results and develops a profile for each period of settlement.

If there are no other means of dating the objects, archaeologists work on the assumption that strata from different sites with similar object profiles are probably contemporary with each other. So to date the occupational periods in the tell where they are working, archaeologists compare the objects they find with similar objects of known dates. They don't have to be identical to belong to the same culture. As it is today, where styles of the same thing betray their place of origin, archaeologists can tell an object of one region from another. When different versions of contemporary objects turn up at a site, they have reason to suspect trade or commerce occurred between it and other sites or that it "was subject to a foreign power" *(ibid.,* p. 201).

By keeping track of how many and what kind of foreign objects are imported to a site or a region, archaeologists can calculate balances and patterns of trade, which could fluctuate from one strata to the next. Sometimes local craftsmen put their own spin on objects from elsewhere, or made them from different materials than the original. Archaeologists believe that "the existence of the local imitation proves that there was contact with the land where the prototype was made at that time, in spite of the fact that the genuine imported object which served as a model may never be found" *(ibid.).*

If classes of objects common to a site suddenly disappear and completely different objects replace them, it probably indicates a change in occupation. By comparing the new objects with similar objects elsewhere, archaeologists can usually tell where the new settlers emigrated from. The sudden appearance of new pottery, for example, along the coastal plain of Palestine *c.* 1150 B.C. indicated the fresh arrival of people from the sea, the Philistines, who colonized the region. Furthermore, comparison of this pottery with possible sources revealed similiarities to Mycenaean ceramics and suggested the Aegean as a general point of origin.

In addition to pottery, archaeologists use other objects to date their finds: (1) *literature* at one site may mention names, locations, and dates that help to trace the origin and date of objects at other sites; (2) *inscriptions* may name contemporaries, mention dates, or provide helpful locations (unfortunately they frequently turn up far from their points of origin, either reused as building material at a later date or kept for generations as family keepsakes); (3) *coins* are useful for dating strata or companion objects—when they come in large quantities (Even though comparison with similar coins elsewhere may point to a definite date, the results can be misleading. People tended to stash coins in their homes and hand them down to later generations, and sometimes they end up out of place in the debris because of their small size.); (4) *other objects* are valuable for dating only when they contribute *as a class* to a chronology or history of development; (5) *architectural* types and style of buildings, layout and elevation, methods and materials of construction, are essentially indigenous to regions and not only help to date finds, but also reveal the origins and contacts of the people who occupied them.

Specialists help reconstruct probable models of occupation from the evidence at hand. "Botanists classify samples of wood and grain; zoologists and physical anthropologists classify animal and human bones" *(ibid.,* p. 203) to reconstruct original ecosystems and cultural prototypes. Geologists fix places of origin by classifying building materials. Laboratory techniques include carbon dating, petrographic analysis of minerals, neutron activation of elements, and spectrographic analysis of incandescent samples to determine composition, plus qualitative and quantitative analysis of what and how much is present. It's all part of the high-tech assault on the past to help today's archaeologist fix dates and identify origins more accurately than ever.

The Role of Archaeology in Biblical Studies—Archaeology can serve many roles for serious students of Scripture.

Archaeology can supplement or enrich the ancient record. As a source, archaeology may provide information or details that the biblical text does not. For example, "when it comes to the synagogues of ancient Palestine, much of the data comes from famous sites, such as Baram, which are not even remembered in the literary record" (Eric M. Meyers and James F. Strange, *Archaeology, the Rabbis, and Early Christianity,* p. 28).

Artifacts and documents can help explain customs, acquaint us with cities, sketch biographies, or introduce us to physical, natural, or political background elements that the writer or speaker takes for granted. When Paul discloses the facts about the resurrection and the reunion that awaits us all at Christ's return (1 Thess. 4:13), he refutes the local misconception that "after death no reviving, after the grave no meeting again" as expressed in an ancient inscription recovered at Thessalonica.

Max Miller cautions, however, that "artifactual evidence is not very useful for dealing with *these* [political-historical] kind of questions; for the specifics of history, we must depend primarily on written records" ("Old Testament History and Archaeology," *Biblical Archaeologist* 50 [March 1987]: 59). Generally more specific and subject to less interpretation, written evidence speaks for itself to us and carries more weight than silent relics.

Archaeology can help clarify obscure texts or improve our understanding of difficult ones. Cultural insights from archaeological evidence can help scholars translate the unfamiliar idiom of the past into language that we can grasp.

For example, an investigation of Jewish burial customs helps us understand how the "sign" of a "babe wrapped in swaddling cloths, lying in a manger" (Luke 2:12) is a sign that a Saviour had been born to Israel.

Travelers in those days took their burial cloths with them on long journeys so they could avoid burial without them in the event of an untimely death on the road. So the swaddling cloths were probably strips of Mary's burial garment. In addition to funerary wrappings, the sign included a manger—an animal feeding trough probably carved out of stone like the ones found at Megiddo and other places in the Holy Land. Now, a manger bears a strong resemblance to the sarcophogi, or stone coffins, found in the Herodian and other royal family tombs—minus the lid, of course.

So when the shepherds entered the stable, they saw a baby wrapped like a corpse, lying in what appeared to be a miniature, royal coffin—a sign to them that here is your King, born to die! More than just a means of telling the Saviour apart from other infants in Bethlehem, the sign showed the shepherds a glimpse of who Jesus was and what He would do on their behalf.

Archaeology can confirm the reliability of historical information in the text. For example, "the Bible mentions 'the Hittites' over forty times in Scripture, and ranks their power with that of Egypt. But up to 1860, the Bible record stood as the solitary witness to Hittite greatness. They are never mentioned in classical historical sources. They disappeared so completely from history that 150 years ago some critics of the Bible declared boldly that the Hittites never existed. Then, by means of Egyptian and Babylonian inscriptions, and more recently by painstaking research among the ruined cities of Asia Minor, this long forgotten empire has been dramatically rescued from oblivion. Fully a score of Hittite cities have been excavated since 1892. . . . So great has been the volume of Hittite inscriptions unearthed, that there are now 20,000 Hittite tablets in the Berlin Museum alone" (Frank Breaden, "The Spade Confirms the Bible," in *The Instruction Manual for the New Pictorial Aid*, p. 34).

Unwritten material remains are a good source for clarifying the material culture of the past but a very poor source of information about specific people and events. As Miller puts it: "When such evidence is cited in support of the historicity of a biblical text or of the certainty of a particular historical position, this means nothing more than the data in question can be interpreted to fit the particular text or position" ("Old Testament History and Archaeology," *Biblical Archaeologist* 50 [March 1987]: 59, 60).

Miller illustrates this principle from the various positions taken on the basis of the same artifactual evidence for the Israelite conquest and settlement of Canaan. William F. Albright dated the event to the *thirteenth* century B.C., whereas John Bimson, using a very similar methodological approach, arrived at a *mid-fifteenth* century date.

Joseph Callaway sees from the same evidence a gradual "non-military settlement of the central Palestinian hill country" *(ibid.,* p. 60), whereas Albrecht Alt, using a similar approach to Callaway's, concludes that "the settlers [of Canaan] came primarily from the coastal regions to the west rather than from the desert fringe to the east and that they were agricultural folk forced inland by the Sea Peoples rather than seminomads coming in search of pastorage" *(ibid.).*

And Norman Gottwald sees the disturbances at the end of the Late Bronze Age, which led Albright to set a *thirteenth* century date for the conquest and settlement of Canaan, as evidence that Israel came into existence as a nation not by conquest but "from a widespread peasant revolt" *(ibid.)* in Palestine.

Making the Most of Archaeological Discoveries—Here is additional information about biblical archaeology that can help you in your study of the Bible as you attempt to understand God's message and make it accessible to your congregation.

Table of archaeological eras. Archaeologists divide history into epochs according to the natural sequence of cultural development and significant technological changes. Because it is difficult to set dates archaeologically with pinpoint accuracy, archaeologists frequently make general references to these broad "ages" rather than to specific dates. Based on Ussher's chronology (see the discussion of "history" later in this chapter), the chronology looks something like this:

Chalcolithic Age	4000-3200 B.C.
Esdraelon Age	3200-3000 B.C.
Early Bronze Age (EB)	
EB I	3000-2800 B.C.
EB II	2800-2600 B.C.
EB III	2600-2300 B.C.
EB IV (or IIIB)	2300-2100 B.C.
Middle Bronze Age (MB)	
MB I	2100-1900 B.C.
MB IIa	1900-1700 B.C.
MB IIb	1700-1600 B.C.
MB IIc	1600-1550 B.C.
Late Bronze Age (LB)	
LB I	1550-1400 B.C.
LB IIa	1400-1300 B.C.

LB IIb	1300-1200 B.C.
Iron I or Early Iron (EI)	
Ia	1200-1150 B.C.
Ib	1150-1025 B.C.
Ic	1025-950 B.C.
Id	950-900 B.C.
Iron II or Middle Iron (MI)	
IIa	900-800 B.C.
IIb	800-700 B.C.
IIc	700-600 B.C.
Iron III, Late Iron or Persian	600-300 B.C.
Hellenistic	300-63 B.C.
Roman	63 B.C.-A.D. 323
Byzantine	A.D. 323-636
Islamic	A.D. 636-present

Arrangement of Finds. Archaeology books lend themselves to different types of study, depending on the way they organize their information. Most of them report finds in one or more of three ways:

1. In some sort of *biblical* order:

By book. Drawing on many sources that refer to or have significance for the same Bible book, some archaeology books (e.g., Thompson's *Archaeology of the Bible*) unfold their material from Genesis to Revelation, book by Bible book. This makes them the handiest sources for working up the historical-cultural profile of a particular book or passage of Scripture because they concentrate all the information relating to the book or passage in one place.

By historical divisions. Some books (e.g., *The Oxford Companion to the Bible*) provide general insights from archaeology for an entire period of biblical history rather than book-by-book specifics. Proceeding from the Old Testment to the New, they make sweeping statements about primeval history, the patriarchal age, the Exodus, the conquest, the judges, the united and divided monarchies, and the Hellenistic and Roman periods. This makes them the handiest sources for sketching the overall historical framework of your Bible book because they provide a wide-angle view of the entire era in a few comprehensive snapshots.

2. According to themes or categories. Drawing on many sources, some books (e.g., *Harper's Encyclopedia of Bible Life*) group archaeological evidence under particular or general headings (e.g., the Flood, the covenant, the Temple, medicine, family events, religious events, nomadic life, professional life, civil life, agricultural life, military life, and industrial life). This makes them the handiest sources for compiling material on a subject because they gather and focus the bulk of what antiquity has to say about it in one place for you.

3. According to excavated sites. Some books (e.g., Schoville's *Biblical Archaeology in Focus*) profile historic sites from what archaeologists recovered on location, evaluated on its own merit and in comparison with other relevant material cultures. This makes them the handiest sources for studying a particular place, people, or region because the description relates most or all of the evidence gathered to date from and native to the local site. Here is a list of the most significant excavation sites to date:

FIGURE 26

Outside Palestine

Mesopotamia	Asia Minor	Syria/Lebanon	Egypt	Mediterranean Area
Ashur	Assos	Antioch of Syria	Alexandria	Athens
Babylon	Boghazkoy	Byblos	Elephantine	Corinth
Hamadan	Colossae	Damascus	Pe-Ramses	Philippi
Khorsabad	Didyma	Ebla (Tell Mardikh)	Pithom	Rome
Nineveh	Ephesus	Mari	Sinai	Thessalonica
Nimrud	Hieropolis	Sidon	Tell el-Amarna	Crete
Nippur	Laodicea	Tyre	Thebes	
Nuzi	Miletus	Ugarit (Ras Shamra)		
Pasargadae	Pergamos			
Persepolis	Philadelphia			
Persia	Sardis			
Susa	Smyrna			
Ur	Thyatira			
Uruk				

FIGURE 27

Palestine

Within the Holy Land		Transjordan
Ai	Hazor	Amman
Arad	Herodium	Bab edh-'Drah
Ashdod	Jaffa	Dibon
Beer-Sheba	Jericho	Heshbon
Bethel	Jerusalem	Jerash
Tell Beit Mirsim	Lachish	Petra
Beth-Shan	Masada	Succoth
Bethlehem	Megiddo	Teleilat el-Ghassul
Capernaum	Nazareth	Zarethan
Caesarea	Qumran	
Dan	Samaria	
Gezer	Shechem	
Gibeon		

Sources of Information—Environment

History—

Factors to Consider	Biblical data chart items (in greater depth); events that lead up to, occur during, and after the text

Biblical history begins with Creation and extends into the first century A.D. The Creation, however, is more than the first event mentioned in the Bible. It is also the starting point of the biblical record. The dates of subsequent biblical events, then, depend on the time you fix for this momentous event. Scholars call the discipline of dating biblical events "chronology."

Since "a correct reconstruction of history is impossible . . . [without chronology] . . . Bible commentators have from the earliest periods of church history been engaged in the reconstruction of the chronological framework of Biblical history" (Siegfried H. Horn, "From Bishop Ussher to Edwin R. Thiele," *Andrews University Seminary Studies* 18, No. 1: 37). Bishop James Ussher, "who dated the creation of the world in 4004 B.C.," worked out a chronology for the Bible with the help of biblical and nonbiblical sources (*ibid.*, p. 42). He "was therefore able to date the events of the later part of biblical history quite accurately" (*ibid.*, p. 43).

While scholars may quibble over dates—between a higher, more conservative and a lower, more liberal chronology—they generally divide biblical history into the following periods of significant events:

FIGURE 28

SACRED HISTORY	SECULAR HISTORY
CREATION	
From Adam to Moses [4004-2250 B.C.]	
Creation Week	Akkadian dynasties in Mesopotamia
Fall of humanity	Old Kingdom in Egypt
The Flood	Ebla flourishes in Palestine
Tower of Babel	Early Minoan civilization on Crete, Helladic in Greece
PATRIARCHS	
From Ur to Egypt [2250-1900 B.C.]	
Abram's call	Neo-Sumerian period in Mesopotamia
Lot's fall	First Intermediate period in Egypt
Isaac's miracle birth	Amorite period in Palestine
Esau and Jacob	Middle Minoan period on Crete
Rachel and Leah	Middle Helladic period in Greece
Jacob's 12 sons	Elamite dynasties in Persia
SOJOURN IN EGYPT	
From Joseph to Moses [1900-1446 B.C.]	
Joseph sold to Egypt-bound caravan	Isin-Larsa and Old Babylonian periods in Mesopotamia,
Dream/Joseph's interpretation/promotion	Middle Kingdom, 2 Intermediate (Hyksos) Period, New
Canaanite famine	Kingdom in Egypt, Hittite Old Kingdom in Anatolia
Jacob relocates Israel to Goshen	Hyksos and Late Canaanite periods in Palestine
Moses' birth in Egypt	Middle Minoan period on Crete, Helladic in Greece
Moses' flight to Canaan	Elamite dynasties in Persia
EXODUS AND CONQUEST	
From Moses to Joshua [1446-1375 B.C.]	
Moses returns to Egypt	Kassite and Mitannian periods in Mesopotamia
The ten plagues	New Kingdom in Egypt
The First Passover/Feast of Unleavened Bread	Late Canaanite period in Palestine

SACRED HISTORY	SECULAR HISTORY
Crossing the Red Sea	Hittite Empire in Anatolia
40 years wandering in the wilderness	Late Minoan period on Crete
Joshua succeeds Moses	Elamite dynasties in Egypt
Jericho falls	Late Helladic (Mycenean) period in Greece
The 12 tribes settle the land	Achaemenian and Median dynasties in Persia

JUDGES
From Othniel to Samson [1375-1050 B.C.]

Othniel [1367-1327 B.C.]	Kassite, Mitannian, Middle Assyrian periods in Mesopotamia
Ehud [1309-1229 B.C.]	New Kingdom in Egypt
Deborah [1209-1169 B.C.]	Late Canaanite and Sea Peoples periods in Palestine
Gideon [1162-1122 B.C.]	Hittite Empire and Phrygian periods in Anatolia
Samuel [1105- B.C.]	Late Minoan period on Crete
Jephthah [1078-1072 B.C.]	Late Helladic (Mycenean) period in Greece
Samson [1075-1055 B.C.]	Achaemenian and Median dynasties in Persia

UNITED KINGDOM
From Saul to Rehoboam [1050-930 B.C.]

Saul [1050-1010 B.C.]	Kassite, Middle Assyrian, Assyrian Empire in Mesopotamia
David [1010-970 B.C.]	Late Dynastic period in Egypt
Solomon [970-930 B.C.]	Phoenician/Aramean/Neo-Hittite states in Palestine
Rehoboam [930-913 B.C.]	Dorian States on Crete and in Greece, Achaemenian and Median dynasties in Persia

DIVIDED KINGDOM: North
From Israel to Samaria's fall [930-722 B.C.]

Jeroboam I [931-909 B.C.]	Assyrian Empire in Mesopotamia and Palestine
Nadab [910-908 B.C.]	Late Dynastic period in Egypt
Baasha [909-885 B.C.]	Phoenician/Aramean/Neo-Hittite states, Assyrian
Elah [886-884 B.C.]	Empire in Palestine
Zimri [885-884 B.C.]	Dorian states on Crete and in Greece
Tibni [885-880 B.C.]	Achaemenian and Median dynasties in Persia
Omri [885-873 B.C.]	Etruscan states in Italy
Ahab [874-853 B.C.]	
Ahaziah [853-852 B.C.]	
Joram [852-841 B.C.]	
Jehu [841-813 B.C.]	
Jehoahaz [814-798 B.C.]	
Jehoash [798-781 B.C.]	
Jeroboam II [793-753 B.C.]	
Zechariah [753-752 B.C.]	
Shallum [752 B.C.]	
Menahem [752-741 B.C.]	

SACRED HISTORY	SECULAR HISTORY
Pekahiah [742-739 B.C.] Pekah [740-731 B.C.] Hoshea [732-722 B.C.]	
DIVIDED KINGDOM: South From Judah to Jerusalem's fall [930-586 B.C.] Rehoboam [930-913 B.C.]	Assyrian and Neo-Babylonian empires in Mesopotamia and Palestine
Abijah [913-910 B.C.] Asa [911-869 B.C.]	Late Dynastic period and Saite Dynasty in Egypt
Jehoshaphat [872-848 B.C.]	Kingdom of Lydia in Anatolia
Jehoram [853-841 B.C.]	Dorian states and city states on Crete
Ahaziah [841 B.C.]	Dorian states and Classical period in Greece
Athaliah [841-835 B.C.]	Achaemenian and Median dynasties in Persia
Joash [835-796 B.C.]	Etruscan states and Early Roman state in Italy
Amaziah [796-767 B.C.] Azariah (Uzziah) [792-739 B.C.] Jotham [750-731 B.C.] Ahaz [735-715 B.C.] Hezekiah [716-686 B.C.] Manasseh [697-642 B.C.] Amon [643-640 B.C.] Josiah [641-609 B.C.] Jehoahaz [609 B.C.] Jehoiakim [609-598 B.C.] Jehoiachin [598-597 B.C.] Zedekiah [597-586 B.C.]	
EXILE From Jerusalem to Babylon [586-538 B.C.] City and Temple sacked and destroyed Captives taken to Babylon Those who stay behind murder Governor Gedaliah	Neo-Babylonian and Persian empires in Mesopotamia and Palestine Saite Dynasty and Persian Empire in Egypt Kingdom of Lydia and Persian Empire in Anatolia
flee to Elephantine, Egypt Medo-Persia Conquers Babylon	City states and Persian Empire on Crete Achaemenian and Median dynasties, Empire in Persia
Cyrus decrees Jews may return and rebuild Temple	Classical period in Greece Early Roman state in Italy
NATIONAL RESTORATION From Babylon to Jerusalem [538-432 B.C.] Zerubbabel leads return, begins reconstruction of Temple	Persian Empire in Mesopotamia, Egypt, Palestine, Anatolia, Crete, Persia

SACRED HISTORY	SECULAR HISTORY
Temple work stops	
Temple work resumes	Classical Period, Peloponnesian Wars in Greece
Temple finished	Roman Republic in Italy
Ezra returns	
Nehemiah returns and rebuilds city	
INTERTESTAMENTAL PERIOD	
From Ezra to Herod [432-4 B.C.]	
Macedonia conquers Medo-Persia	Persian Empire gives way to Alexander and
	Greece
Lysimachus, Cassander, Seleucis,	
and Ptolemy succeed Alexander and	Ptolemies in Egypt and Palestine
divide his empire four ways	Seleucids in Syria and Palestine
Ptolemies dominate Israel	Rome supplants Greece
Seleucids dominate Israel	Julius Caesar [63-44 B.C.]
Maccabees revolt and Hasmoneans rule Israel	Octavian Caesar [44-27 B.C.]
Pompey captures Jerusalem	Augustus Caesar [27 B.C.-A.D. 14]
Herod begins rebuilding the Temple	Roman governors rule Palestine [63-37 B.C.]
John the Baptist miraculously conceived	Herod the Great rules Palestine [37-4 B.C.]
Christ supernaturally conceived by the	
Holy Ghost	
Caesar Augustus orders census by	
hometown	
MESSIANIC RESTORATION	
From stable to church [4 B.C.-A.D. 100]	
John the Baptist's birth	Archelaus rules Judea, Samaria, Idumea
	[4 B.C.-A.D. 6]
Jesus' birth	Philip rules Batanea, Trachonitis, Auranitis
	[4 B.C.-A.D.33]
Herod's death	Antipas rules Galilee and Perea [4 B.C.-A.D. 6]
Jesus' baptism	Tiberius Caesar [A.D. 14-37]
Jesus calls the 12	
the Crucifixion	Pontius Pilate governs Judea [A.D. 26-36]
the Resurrection	
the Ascension	
the outpouring of the Spirit at Pentecost	
the church at Jerusalem grows	Caligula [A.D. 37-41]
Jerusalem church persecuted, scattered	Herod Agrippa I rules Palestine [A.D. 39-44]
Christianity spreads across empire	Claudius [A.D. 41-54]
Death of Paul and Peter	Nero [A.D. 54-68]
	Glaba, Otho, Vitellius [A.D. 68, 69]
Titus destroys Jerusalem	Herod Agrippa II rules Palestine [A.D. 44-100]
Masada falls	Vespasian [A.D. 69-79]
	Titus [A.D. 79-81]
	Domitian [A.D. 81-96]
	Nerva [A.D. 96-98]
Trajan persecutes church	Trajan [A.D. 98-117]

In applying the historical background to the biblical passage you are studying, ask yourself:

1. What is going on in this passage? What events lead up to its situation? Review your biblical data sheet. Investigate more closely and thoroughly such items as Who wrote or speaks in the passage? Who is the original audience in the passage/historical situation? Where did they live? What were their present circumstances? What is the author's reason for writing/speaker's reason for talking in the passage? How do the passage and its circumstances fit into the author's flow of thought?

2. Is the situation in the passage strictly the result of internal developments in Israel, or did other parts of the ancient world have something to do with its realization? Do other passages dealing with the same or similar situations shed any light on its circumstances?

3. What comes next? Does the passage *conclude* an episode, or is it the *start* of any new developments? How does the passage fit into the flow of Old Testament/New Testament history? into the sweep of redemptive history?

Anthropology—

Factors to Consider	*social and civil institutions; psychology of writer, speaker, key characters; occupation, titles; relationships, property*

People living in the Mediterranean area—then as well as today—display what anthropologists call a dyadic personality. They prefer to maintain relationships rather than exercise their individuality. Bruce J. Malina explains that "a dyadic personality is one who simply needs another continually in order to know who he or she really is. . . . Such a person internalizes and makes his own what others say, do, and think about him because he believes it is necessary for being human, to live out the expectations of others" *(The New Testament World,* p. 55).

In such a society, the individual doesn't count for much, as in our western culture. Instead, everyone is in some way interrelated to others. Indeed, how a person perceives himself or herself depends almost entirely on this web of relationships. This explains why Scripture places so much emphasis on kinship and why the connection with Jesus—"in Christ"—is so important.

A byproduct of the dyadic outlook is the concept (sometimes repeated today but repudiated by thoughtful people) that if you know one member of a group, you know them all. That is clearly not true of groups in our culture, and probably not totally true in the ancient Near East either, but it likely had more truth then than now. This phenomenon probably accounts for blanket statements in the Bible such as "Cretans are always liars" (Titus 1:12); "Jews have no dealings with Samaritans" (John 4:9, NKJV); and "Can any good thing come out of Nazareth?" (John 1:46, NASB).

In addition, concern for shame and honor governed just about all relationships. People either acquired honor by what they did, or others ascribed it to them for who they were. "Honor," says Malina, "is the value of a person in his or her own eyes . . . *plus* that person's value in the eyes of his or her social group. Honor is a claim to worth along with the social acknowledgment of [that] worth" *(The New Testament World,* p. 27). Honorable people, then, not only considered themselves worthy of honor, but the community also agreed with them and treated them accordingly.

"Consequently, one who is in [ancient Near Eastern] society depends on his honor rating, which situates the person on the status ladder of the community" (*ibid.*, p. 28). The community, however, had only so much honor to go around. So individuals engaged in a frequent tug-of-war (as Malina calls it) when it came to honor and shame.

The ancient Near East considered honoring the honorable a social duty. More than a breach of etiquette in the eyes of the community, failure to do so virtually robbed honorable people of what they owned or had earned. Obviously, then, the command to honor one's parents is much more than a demand for obedience on the part of children. Disobedience in our culture may connote a refusal to accept the authority of another, but in the ancient Near Eastern world, honor (which may have involved the issue of authority) went a whole lot deeper than that.

Ancient Near Eastern people constantly defended themselves against dishonor in their highly stratified society. Under no circumstances would they permit themselves to suffer shame in the presence of social inferiors—something like not losing face among modern Asians. They also divided honor along male and female lines corresponding to family roles (husband, wife, children) and created a double standard.

"Honor has a male and a female component," says Malina. "When considered from this perspective, the male aspect is called honor, while the female aspect is called shame" (*ibid.*, p. 48). Shame in this context refers to a person's sensitivity to what others think, say, and do with regard to his or her honor. This distinction derived from physiological and spatial considerations. Females maintained their sexual purity and the honorable reputation of their husbands by "thwarting off even the remotest advances of their symbolic space" (*ibid.*, p. 43).

"The male clearly lacks . . . the physiological basis for sexual exclusiveness or sexual 'purity' (he cannot symbolize invasion into his space as the female can). [He can] protect, defend, and look after the purity of his women (wife, sister, daughter), since their dishonor directly implied his own" (*ibid.*).

To maintain such relationships required a great deal of time and energy, because each party involved must not lose honor or gain shame. Greetings, for instance, evolved into elaborate, extensive rituals. So Jesus ordered His disciples not to greet anyone while they were on a mission (Luke 10:4). The ceremonies could distract them and waste important time.

Negotiators also consumed time with a lot of bickering back and forth—"What is it to me?" "I give it to you." "It is worth nothing." "But, no . . ." "Far be it from me to . . ." So when Lot did not hesitate to choose the best acreage for himself from the land that Abraham offered, he betrayed a lack of respect for his uncle. He should have deferred to his elder and superior. Instead, he left Abraham with a great deal of shame—not honor—by choosing selfishly as he did.

Ancient Near Easterners considered resolving differences in court "highly dishonorable and against the rules of honor" (*ibid.*, p. 39). The publicity from a trial increased the likelihood that the parties involved might lose honor and gain shame. In addition, the suing party publicly admitted, by resorting to the courts, that he or she could not deal with his or her peers. These insights into the legal side of honor help us understand why Paul warned the Corinthian Christians not to take each other to court (1 Cor. 6:1-8).

Only two classes existed in the social world of the ancient Mediterranean— "those who had to work with their hands and those who did not" (John Dominic Crossan, *Jesus: A Revolutionary Biography*, p. 24), or as we might put it today—the

95

lower and upper classes. The lower class included the peasants, who turned over about 66 percent of their harvest to the upper class; the artisans, who made up about 5 percent of the population; the degraded, who had "origins, occupations, or conditions rendering them outcasts" (*ibid.*, p. 25); and the expendable 10 percent of society made up of beggars, outlaws, day laborers, and slaves. Among the upper class, the rulers (who formed only 1 percent of society) owned about 50 percent of the land, while the priests owned 15 percent of it. The retainers held positions as generals or bureaucrats, and the moderately wealthy merchants enjoyed modest political clout.

A knowledge of these New Testament social strata helps explain the radical nature of Jesus' ideas concerning classes. He could pronounce blessings on the previously despised poor and beggars, saying, "theirs is the kingdom of heaven" (Matt. 5:3), because the kingdom of God He came to establish would revolutionize society and remove its social distinctions (Gal. 3:28).

Meals held tremendous significance in those days. Eating together, especially in that society, had specific cultural overtones. A strict social code did not allow just anyone to eat with someone else. For example, women usually ate in a different room from men. Jesus, however, allowed a significant contingent of women to eat with Him and the disciples—even though His contemporaries considered women who ate with men to be forward and indiscreet.

And when the master of the house in Jesus' parable ordered his servant to "Go out into the highways and hedges, and compel them to come in, that my house may be filled" (Luke 14:23, NKJV), he violated every tradition of hospitality—because an open invitation would bring all sorts of people to his table and fail to preserve conventional class distinctions.

"Think for a moment, if beggars came to your door, of the difference between giving them some food to go, of inviting them into your kitchen for a meal, of bringing them into the dining room to eat in the evening with your family, or of having them come back on Saturday night for supper with a group of your friends. . . . Those events are not just ones of eating together, of simple table fellowship. [They are] *miniature models for the rules of association and socialization*" (*ibid.*, p. 68).

"What Jesus' parable advocates, therefore, is . . . eating together without using the table as a miniature map of society's vertical discriminations and lateral separations. [It is] an absolute equality of people that denies the validity of any discrimination between them and negates the necessity of any hierarchy among them" (*ibid.*, pp. 69, 71).

As different as our culture is from that of the ancient Near East, the church today still continues to struggle with Jesus' radical concept that "there is neither Jew nor Greek, there is neither bond nor free, there is neither male nor female: for ye are all one in Christ Jesus" (Gal. 3:28).

In applying the anthropological background to the biblical passage you are studying, ask yourself:

1. Is the milieu of my passage Israelite or Gentile? This will help you find the right track for further investigation. Avoid generalizations. Carefully track down the particulars for this passage.

2. What social, civil, or religious institutions does the passage involve? At what stage in Israel's history do they occur? What is their meaning or significance in this particular context? Do the people, places, or things in the passage relate only to ancient Israel, or are they Old Testament projections/New Testament editions of realities to come during the Messianic Age?

3. Do any other passages or outside sources help explain the cultural situation of the author and audience? Does the author refer to something common and universal, or local and provincial? Gordon Fee warns: "When Dio Chrysostom laments the decay of the custom of veiling *(Orationes* 33. 46f.), is he reflecting his own tastes, the peculiar circumstances of Tarsus, or a more universal custom?" *(New Testament Exegesis,* p. 100). Don't be too eager to transfer what you find elsewhere to your passage. Things, though similar, are not necessarily identical. "For example," says Fee, "1 Tim. 2:14 says that Eve, because she was deceived, became a sinner. It is common to argue, in the light of some of the language in verses 9, 10, and 15, that this refers to a rabbinic and apocalyptic tradition that Satan seduced Eve sexually. But there is an equally strong contemporary tradition that implies she was deceived because she was the weaker sex. Furthermore, several other sources speak of her deception without attributing to it either cause. Caution is urged in the light of such diversity" *(ibid.).*

Geography—

Factors to Consider	*the climate; relation to the sea, rivers, desert, mountains, roads, and kind of terrain; population density/distribution*

It is vitally important to learn what you can about the place where Bible history happened. Various geographical factors influenced Bible life and the language of Bible writers. For example, the land of Israel occupied a strategic place in the ancient world. Palestine served as a natural "land bridge between the vast centers of civilization in Egypt to the south and Mesopotamia and Anatolia (modern Turkey) to the north" (Madeline S. and J. Lane Miller, *Harper's Encyclopedia of Bible Life,* p. 3). Difficulties crossing the Mediterranean Sea to its west or the Arabian Desert to its east left ancient armies and merchants no alternative route. Consequently, the Bible, with distinctively geographic language, records frequent occasions when the superpowers crossed this "bridge" on their way to confrontations with each other. So, for example, Pharaoh Necho "went up" (from Egypt in the south) to the river Euphrates (to his northeast) for a showdown with the king of Assyria—and slew king Josiah of Judah for obstructing his northward march (2 Kings 23:29).

Except for a brief period under Solomon (1 Kings 4:21, 24), when its borders approximated the boundaries promised to Abraham (from Egypt's Nile to Mesopotamia's Euphrates and Tigris rivers, Gen. 15:18), Israel rarely embraced more square miles than today make up the state of Vermont *(ibid.,* p. 2). Consequently, a term like "from Dan even to Beersheba" (1 Kings 4:25) may "indicate the full length of the country, as if it were big, but this north-south extent measures only about 150 miles" *(ibid.).* The emphasis, then, with the terms such as this is not so much on size (the distance between the two reference points) as it is on extent (how much of the country lies between them). So when 1 Kings 4:25 (KJV) says that "Judah and Israel dwelt safely, every man under his vine and under his fig tree, *from Dan even to Beersheba,*" it means *"from one end of the country to the other,"* emphasizing the extent of blessedness under Solomon's kingship. Palestine also possesses an amazing variety of landscapes for a country its size, "from high mountains to flat plains and sub-sea level rifts and valleys" *(ibid.,* p. 4). Along with these differences in topography also come correspondingly different climates, "from desert conditions to conditions permitting intensive agriculture" *(ibid.).* As you can imagine, "if the Israelites ever were a homogeneous people, the varied landscape of the Promised Land soon produced regional differences among them, depending on the geography of their settlement" *(ibid.).*

The characteristic weather, in particular the amount of rainfall, had something to do with the kind of people indigenous to each zone and the kind of lives they led. The peoples in the west and north settled down and worked the land, while those in the south and east wandered from place to place in search of water and grazing land for their flocks.

Rain, of course, depends on moisture. While the prevailing winds in Palestine blow from west to east—from the humid Mediterranean coast—breezes originating from the arid south have no moisture and do not bring any rain as they head north. Accordingly, Jesus could say: "And when you see the south wind blowing, you say, 'There will be scorching heat'; and it happens" (Luke 12:55). On the other hand, as the damp Mediterranean winds sweep eastward, the steep countryside forces them upward over the fertile plains to the peak of Jerusalem, and they discharge their moisture as rain. This is why Jesus could say: "When you see a cloud rising in the west, you immediately say 'It is going to rain'; and so it happens" (verse 54). By the time the winds descend into the Jordan Valley, however, the moisture is gone, and in the absence of rain, the land turns to desert within a few miles of Jerusalem.

Farming played a major role in the economic, social, and religious life of ancient Palestine. Agriculture in Palestine, however, differed greatly from that in Egypt. There are no overflowing rivers and few bodies of water to dam or wells to pump. Palestinian farmers are entirely at the mercy of the rain. Consequently, Moses could tell the Israelites about to enter the Promised Land: "The land which you go to possess is not like the land of Egypt . . . , where you sowed your seed and watered it by foot. . . ; but the land which you cross over to possess is a land of hills and valleys, which drinks water from the rain of heaven" (Deut. 11:10, 11).

The parable of the sower in Matthew 13 spells out some of the other difficulties facing farmers both preparing and harvesting the rugged Palestinian landscape. Incidentally, Palestinian farmers did not plow the land before they seeded it. They scattered the seed first and then plowed it under, which explains some of the terminology and circumstances in this passage. Despite these hardships, the Israelites were about to settle "a land that the Lord your God cares for . . . from the beginning of the year to its end. So if you faithfully obey the commands I am giving you today . . . then I will send on your land in its season both autumn and spring rains, so that you may gather in your grain, new wine and oil. I will provide grass in the fields for your cattle, and you will eat and be satisfied " (Deut. 11:12-15, NIV). Whether settled or nomadic, the people of Palestine had nothing to fear. Throughout the year God would supply His obedient people with enough rain to harvest their crops and feed their flocks.

Life in the land of Israel revolved around agriculture. Religious festivals coincided with the various harvests throughout the agricultural year. As the promised rain fell and brought a time of reaping, the people celebrated God's goodness, especially at Passover (the Feast of Unleavened Bread/Firstfruits), Pentecost (the Feast of Weeks), and Tabernacles (the Feast of Ingathering)—the three times a year God expected every adult male to show up at His Temple (Deut. 16:16). The people came, not only to express thanks for what they had harvested so far but to pledge their obedience and to demonstrate their faith that God was able to bless them until the last crop came in and filled their barns to capacity.

Jesus used this cycle of feasts to explain His work of redemption, and the rain to represent the role of the Holy Spirit (cf. Joel 2:23-32 with Acts 2:17-21, 33) in God's plan of salvation. The *early* rain comes at the beginning of the agricultural cycle, around late October or early November. At first these fall/winter rains are very light—just enough to soften the ground for plowing. Then around December they pick up intensity to nourish the planted seeds and start them growing—with the heaviest rainfall in early January.

The first great farming festival of unleavened bread, or firstfruits, celebrated the beginning of the harvest year. Two days after the Passover, the priests waved a sheaf of barley over their heads toward the Lord to thank God for it and to look forward by faith to the rest of the harvest season. Jesus dramatically fulfilled this symbolic ritual when He emerged from the tomb two days after Passover, "lifted up from the earth" (John 12:32). His resurrected body marked the beginning of the harvest season for souls.

Fifty days after the first day of Unleavened Bread, or seven weeks from the waving of the barley sheaf, the second great farming festival of Pentecost, or Weeks, marked the beginning of the wheat harvest. Jesus referred to human souls awaiting harvest as wheat that grows up side by side with look-alike weeds (Matt. 13:24, 25). When God poured out His Spirit on Pentecost, seven weeks after He had raised His Son from the grave, the disciples harvested 3,000 souls from the field that Jesus had sowed (Acts 2:41).

The *latter* rain (still part of the single rainy season that Palestine experiences) falls in the spring, during the months of March and April. God sent it to ripen and mature the crops already initiated by the early rain. Even a spectacular early rainfall could not make up for light or no latter rains. The Jews had to wait until October—after the long, hot, dry summer—before they could harvest olives, figs, dates, grapes, and nuts. Only substantial latter rainfall could saturate the land with enough water to give these crops time to ripen in spite of the summer heat and drought.

Then the Jews wound up the harvest year with the third and final harvest festival of Ingathering, when they gathered in all there was to harvest that year. The feast symbolizes the time when every soul is gathered in for God and the Messiah finishes His work. As James puts it, "Be patient, therefore, brethren, until the coming of the Lord. Behold the farmer waits for the precious produce of the soil, being patient about it, until it gets the early and the latter rains" (James 5:7, NASB).

The earth will be ripe for harvest when Jesus comes again as a result of the spiritual early and latter rains. The souls He will reap in the end with His sickle are a tribute to Messiah's patience and power (Rev. 14:14-16).

In applying the geographical background to the biblical passage you are studying, ask yourself:

> 1. Does the passage have a geographical setting? "In which nation, region, tribal territory, and village do the events or concepts of the passage apply? Is it a northern or southern passage? Does it have a national or regional perspective?" (Douglas Stuart, *Old Testament Exegesis*, p. 28).
>
> 2. Do climate, topography, or local features figure prominently in the passage? If so, what is their significance? What can they tell us about the significance of people, places, and things in the text? Can other passages or outside sources (maps, etc.) help explain these issues and open up our understanding of the passage?

Material Goods—

Factors to Consider	*everyday living items; homes, furnishings, clothing, tools, weapons, transportation*

Archaeology has confirmed that the people of Palestine lived in caves northwest of the Sea of Galilee at Mugharet ez-Zuttiyeh; at Wadi Khareitun, between Bethlehem and the Dead Sea; and at Wadi el-Mughara in the Mount Carmel range long before they moved into tents and houses. Cave homes had passed over into cave shelters by the time the patriarchs roamed the promised land, serving "as places of seasonal residence, temporary refuge, and burial" *(Harper's Encyclopedia of Bible Life*, p. 25) (cf. Gen. 19:30; 1 Kings 19:9; 1 Sam. 13:6; 22:1; Judges 6:2). Only the Edomites, especially those at the cave-city, Petra, continued to occupy caves and prosper in biblical times.

The patriarchs and early Israelites lived in tents. While some of them continued to live in tents as shepherds, the vast majority of Israelites took up the settled life in permanent dwelling places. The Feast of Tabernacles, however, gave them an annual opportunity to camp out in tents and recapture their heritage. At first, nomads used animal skins, but eventually they wove their tents of heat- and water-resistant goat's hair. The apostle Paul financed his ministry as a tentmaker. Tents came to symbolize the temporary, portable life of a pilgrim wandering through this world, headed by faith, toward a better land (Heb. 11:9, 10).

The average Israelite lived in "a small boxlike structure with walls made of mud bricks, sealed by one or more layers of mortar and whitewash" *(Harpers Encyclopedia of Bible Life*, p. 33). People in the central highlands used stones for their homes. "Though a well-to-do man might hire the services of a stonecutter, most had to settle for walls of uncut, ill-fitting stones held together with mortar" *(ibid.*, p. 34). Structures of stone lasted longer and served their occupants better, so it is no surprise that Christ is building a dwelling-place for God from "living stones" (1 Peter 2:5), taken from the quarry of mankind (verse 9) and stonemasoned into place by His own hand (Eph. 2:20). Regardless of location, cloth doors eventually gave way to wooden ones, either barred from the inside or equipped with primitive locks.

Most Israelites lived in modest homes and still slept on straw mats as their ancestors did during the wilderness wanderings. Domestic life was so humble that the average Israelite ate on the floor with a mat or animal skin for a table and pillows for chairs (*"reclined* at the table," Luke 7:36; 22:14, NASB). Furniture (e.g., a sofa) was a sign of wealth. So when the book of Esther wants to give us an opulent picture of king Ahasuerus, it mentions among other things his "couches of gold and silver" (Esther 1:6).

To cook over open fires indoors, Israelites ventilated their homes with one or two high, narrow windows. Generally the windows were covered with shutters "to discourage intruders" *(ibid.,* p. 37), so even the poorest families kept a ceramic *lamp* burning 24 hours a day. One of the ways a wife demonstrates her excellence, says Solomon, is that "her lamp does not go out at night" (Prov. 31:18) so that "it gives light to everyone in the house" (Matt. 5:15, NIV).

Israelites often looked to the roof of the house as a "refuge from its dim, cramped living quarters" *(ibid.,* p. 39). In order to have a paralytic healed, some friends once removed a section of thatched mud, brush, grass, reed, and clay to outflank a crowd and lower him from the roof into a house where Jesus was speaking (Mark 2:4). The roof was an ideal place for women to sew, bake, or dry the wash, for families to socialize, and people to relax or pray. Some Israelites set up temporary quarters on the roof to accommodate guests (2 Kings 4:10), or they converted the roof to a second floor, like the person who allowed Jesus and the disciples to celebrate the Lord's Supper in "a large furnished upper room" (Luke 22:12, NKJV).

Israelites believed in opening their doors to strangers. The patriarchs set the example of sharing food and drink with visitors (Gen. 18:1-8) and of offering strangers a place to spend the night under their protection, if necessary (Gen. 19:1-8), to which Paul (Heb. 13:2), John (3 John 5-8), and Jesus (Matt. 25:35, 36) appealed in their day. The main staple of Israel's diet was barley bread, "generally baked at home each day" *(ibid.,* p. 43). Jesus probably had these routine loaves in mind when He advised His disciples not to take anything for granted but to appreciate every blessing, no matter how mundane, as an unmerited gift from God, praying, "Give us this day our daily bread" (Matt. 6:11).

Most Israelites depended on springs or wells for drinking water and cooking purposes (see the discussion of rainfall under the previous subsection "Geography" in this chapter).

While wine enjoyed universal popularity as a pleasure beverage, water from heaven filled the wadis (dried-up riverbeds) and quenched the everyday thirst of the people. Between rainfall, most Israelites made up for a shortage of water with goat's milk and even bought rainwater from street vendors, but in general, mothers and their daughters went daily to the community source to fetch water for the household. Knowing this, Abraham's servant waited by a spring to find a wife for Isaac (Gen. 24:13, 14), and Jesus stopped at Jacob's well to meet a certain Samaritan woman (John 4:6, 7).

"For most Israelites, meat was a special treat, reserved for holidays, weddings, and other important occasions. Their animals were too valuable as sources of wool and milk—and of such labor as plowing and carrying—to be slaughtered for their meat" *(ibid.,* pp. 44, 45). Dietary laws also regulated the consumption of meat by differentiating between what flesh was "clean" and "unclean" (Lev. 11; Deut. 14).

So Solomon warned the wide-eyed commoner not to be overwhelmed by the fancy foods set on royal tables. Rulers often wined and dined their guests with hidden motives, using delicacies intended to impress company and please the palette—usually with little or no redeeeming nutritional value (Prov. 23:1-8).

Although many people ate fish, either freshly caught or pickled and dried, most Israelites ate vegetables (e.g., beans, lentils, peas, onions, leeks, garlic, lettuce, beets, cucumbers) with their bread, and usually capped off the evening meal with delicious fruit (e.g., figs, melons, pomegranates, dates). The Bible frequently uses fruit to paint a picture of *present* contentment as a man with a wife who produces children and goodness "like a fruitful vine in the very heart of your house," and children blossoming "like olive plants" around the family table (Ps. 128:3, NKJV), and of *future* bliss, as everybody's sitting under his own vine and fig tree (Micah 4:4).

Ancient Near Eastern people had a practical view of life. As such, everything had to be functional—including clothes. Those who worked outdoors in the sun wore simple loincloths "made of wool, sackcloth, or animal skin . . . worn loose like a skirt, or pulled between the legs and tucked in at the waist" *(ibid.*, p. 49). Both men and women wore tunics, snug knee-length shirts made from wool or linen and held at the waist by a girdle or belt. This girdle doubled as a money belt for men and a place to carry swords for soldiers. When people needed maximum freedom to move so that they could put every ounce of strength into something, they could tuck the tunic, like a loincloth, into its girdle. That's why the Bible frequently advises soldiers going into battle or anyone else about to undertake an arduous task to show their grit and determination to see it through by girding up their loins (e.g., 2 Kings 4:29; 9:1; 1 Peter 1:13).

Ever practical, Israelites wore heavy woolen cloaks or mantles over their tunics, which doubled "as rugs to sit on and blankets at night" *(ibid.*, p. 50). Mantles made from animal hair distinguished kings and prophets from the rank and file of Israel. John the Baptist wore such daily (Matt. 3:4), and Herod put such on for special public appearances (Acts 12:21). Herod put a similar robe on Jesus to mock His royalty (Luke 23:11). Priests wore sleeveless white linen robes called ephods as a badge of their sacred office. Since Christ fulfills the covenantal promise to make His people "a kingdom of priests" (Ex. 19:6, NASB; cf. 1 Peter 2:5, 9; Rev. 1:6), He endows them with the garments of their office, His own robe of righteousness (Rev. 6:11; 7:9, 13, 14; cf. Isa. 61:10).

The main garment of New Testament times (Jesus and His disciples wore them) was the colobium, "a long, close-fitting tunic with openings for the head and arms" *(ibid.*, p. 54). The one Jesus wore was "seamless, woven of one piece," so the soldiers who divided His outer garments agreed, "Let us not tear it, but cast lots for it, to see who will get it" (John 19:23, 24).

The Israelites wore simple leather sandals, and although footwear wasn't a high priority, "to be barefoot (except in times of mourning or on holy ground, when it was customary) was a sign either of extreme poverty or humiliation, as in the case of war prisoners" *(ibid.*, p. 50; cf. Isa. 20:1-6). Israelites went bareheaded for the most part, except for turbaned priests and helmeted soldiers. Long hair for men, long admired in Oriental circles (e.g., Absalom cut his hair only once a year, 2 Sam. 14:26), came under criticism in circles under Greek influence (1 Cor. 11:14, 15).

People of the ancient Near East relied principally on two species of animals for riding and for carrying their burdens: the camel and the ass.

According to the *Seventh-day Adventist Bible Dictionary,* the biblical camel was more likely the one-humped dromedary than the two-humped Bactrian camel that appears in Mesopotamian and Persian art (p. 175). Domesticated camels date to patriarchal times. Joseph's brothers sold him to Midianite traders passing by with "an Ishmaelite caravan coming from Gilead on the way down to Egypt, with camels bearing aromatic tragacanth and balm and myrrh" (Gen. 37:25-29, REB). Camels were so plentiful in the days of the judges that "the Midianites . . . the Amalekites and the sons of the east" "would come in like locusts for number, both they and their camels were innumerable" (Judges 6:3, 5, NASB).

The ass was "an all-purpose working animal" and the beast of burden of the Bible seminomads" (*Harper's Encyclopedia of the Bible,* p. 128). Though much smaller than camels, asses "could carry an impressive load of household goods or be ridden by a man, or by a woman and a child" (*ibid.,* p. 128). Horses became the mount of choice only after the Exile. Before then, people of rank (Judges 10:4) and wealth (1 Sam. 25:20) rode asses. So Zechariah prophesied that the Messianic King would come, riding on an ass (Zech. 9:9).

In applying the information about material goods to the biblical passage you are studying, ask yourself:

> 1. Does the text mention any everyday items? What are they? What do they tell me about the origins, the practices, the social-commercial contacts of the people in this passage?
> 2. What can I tell about the people in the passage from what they wear? where they live? what they eat? what animals they own?.

Socioreligious Situation—

Factors to Consider	*customs at birth, marriage, death; place of worship—tabernacle, Temple, synagogue, Christian congregation; priests, ministers; roles of the city gate to the legal side of life and of the city itself to law and order and labor*

In the ancient Near East, midwives delivered most babies (Gen. 35:17; Ex. 1:15-21) with the help of "older, experienced, married women of the family" (*Harpers Encyclopedia of Bible Life,* p. 90). A child was considered a gift from God (1 Sam. 1:19, 20), and the task of cleaning the infant was a joy, not work that violated the Sabbath. After they cut the umbilical cord, Israelites would rub newborns with salt, partly because of its alleged medicinal properties and partly because of a notion they picked up from their pagan neighbors that it was "a safeguard against demons and the evil eye" (*ibid.,* p. 91).

Israelite parents took naming their children very seriously. Instead of simply passing on the name of a favorite relative or calling them something that sounded pleasant, parents put their hopes and dreams into their children's names. Sometimes they included the name for God, *El* (as in *El*kanah or Dani*el*), or the personal name of the Lord, *Jah,* short for *Yahweh* (as in Jerem*iah*). These religious names "proclaimed the name-giver's faith and trust in the Lord, or expressed the parental hopes for the child at God's hands" (*ibid.,* p. 93). So, for example, in 1 Chronicles 4:9 a woman named her son, Jabez, "because," she said, "I bore him in pain." The name Jabez, however, is apparently a play on the word for the pain associated with childbirth since the Fall (Gen. 3:16), reversing two of its letters—and it does seem to include God's personal name Jah. It is a name that seems to betray a mother's desire to see the Lord reverse her son's fallen situation; her hope that Jabez would one day escape the curse and its restrictions to become all God wanted him to be. In verse 10 his mother's dream became Jabez' own wish, which God granted and made come true.

Parents tended to name their girls after plants and animals (e.g., Deborah, bee; Tamar, palm tree), although they sometimes did the same for their boys (Jonah, dove). After the Exile, however, names began to reflect the influence of their captors or oppressors (e.g., Zerubbabel, offspring of Babylon).

Circumcision, the cutting away of the male foreskin, was another birth ritual borrowed from the ancient world and given an Israelite twist. After Israel became a nation, fathers carried out the law and circumcised their sons on the eighth day of their young lives (Lev. 12:3). The rite required them to use stone knives like Joshua did at Gibeath-ha-araloth (Joshua 5:2, 3)—even during the bronze and iron ages. Heads of families circumcised all the males in their households—their sons and the sons of their servants as God instructed them to do in Genesis 17:12, 13. Circumcision is, however, more than a health measure. The apostle Paul, no doubt with the prophetic promise God made to Israel in mind to "circumcise your heart and the heart of your descendants, so that you will love the Lord your God with all your heart" (Deut. 30:6), explained the fuller significance of circumcision to the Romans: "For he is not a Jew, which is one outwardly; neither is that circumcision, which is outward in the flesh: but he is a Jew, which is one inwardly; and circumcison is that of the heart" (Rom. 2:28, 29, KJV). "In baptism," he later told the Colossians, "you were also circumcised with the circumcision made without hands, by putting off the body of the sins of the flesh, by the circumcision of Christ" (Col. 2:12, 11).

When a firstborn child reached the age of 30 days, the father, or both parents after the mother completed the period of purification from the blood of childbirth, took their little one to the sanctuary for a special transaction: the redemption of the firstborn. The firstborn human or animal belonged to the Lord (Ex. 13:12; 22:29-31), and parents were to redeem their firstborn by paying five shekels of silver to the priest (Num. 3:47, 48). The Israelites owed the lives of their firstborn to God for sparing them during the tenth plague when He killed the firstborn of Egypt (Ex. 13:14-16; Num. 3:13; 8:17). At first the firstborn entered the Lord's service, but as time wore on "the Levites . . . took over entirely the religious functions apparently first assigned to the firstborn . . . [Num. 3:41; 8:16-18] . . . [and] . . . in the ceremony of redemption, the father in effect paid five shekels of silver at the sanctuary to pay for a Levite to provide the service due by the firstborn son (Num. 3:46-51; 8:18; 18:16; Ex. 34:20)" (ibid., p. 97).

Fathers were the main players in the rite of marriage; first the father of a son of marrying age and then the father of an eligible daughter. "Marriage was an agreement between two heads of families, not between two individuals who were in love" (ibid., p. 98). Once the fathers reached an agreement, the two children had no choice but to go along with it. The daughter knew that "her father had authority to sell her into concubinage if he wished" (ibid., p. 99). The father of the groom stood to gain more from the arranged marriage than did the father of the bride. So the groom's father paid a mohar to the bride's father, a sum intended to compensate him "for the loss of her services as a helper to his wife in the running of his household" (ibid.). Without the help of his father to negotiate a fair mohar, Jacob paid off his father-in-law Laban with years of service (Gen. 29:18-21, 27, 28). Fathers often kept the mohar as a kind of indemnity for the bride against the loss of her husband.

Scholars figure that the average mohar probably ran around 50 shekels of silver, because that was the amount due a father if a man raped his virgin daughter (Deut. 22:28, 29). So the young groom-to-be worked with his father to help him save up enough money for the mohar and to deck out his bride with jewelry for her wedding and to wear throughout her married life. This custom helps us understand why God, recalling His covenant wedding to Israel, reminds His bride: "I decked thee also with ornaments. . . . And thy renown went forth among the heathen for thy beauty: for it was perfect through my comeliness, which I had put upon thee" (Eze. 16:11a-14, KJV). God gave Israel the perfect *mohar,* making her the most beautiful bride in the world. He had done everything required of a bridegroom and a husband. She had no reason to leave Him for other lovers after the wedding and trash her marriage (verse 43). Similarly, Christ has paid the ultimate *mohar* for His bride, the church, in order to make her the most beautiful woman possible (Eph. 5:25-27).

The fathers sealed the agreement when the groom and his father paid the *mohar* to the bride's father. During this season of betrothal the bride-to-be wore a veil in the presence of men outside the home (Gen. 24:65), while Israel excused the groom from any military service until after his marriage (Deut. 20:7).

The transfer of the bride from the house of her father to her husband's home began the bridal procession on the day of her wedding. A large group of friends escorted her to a rendezvous with her husband-to-be (1 Maccabees 9:37-39) with singing, dancing, and love poems (Ps. 78:63; Eze. 33:32; Jer. 7:34; S. of Sol. 3:6-8). The bride wore a thick veil (S. of Sol. 4:1, 3; 6:7) and did not remove it until she and her husband con- summated the marriage that evening (Gen. 24:65), which explains how Laban sucess- fully substituted Leah for Rachel at Jacob's wedding (Gen. 29:23-25).

Both the bride (Eze. 23:42) and the bridegroom (Isa. 61:10) wore a type of crown, just as Christ and His bride, the church, will wear crowns when He comes for her on their wedding day (Rev. 2:10; 3:11; 14:14). They were treated like a king and queen, obeyed by bridesmaids (Ps. 45:14), groomsmen, and best man (Judges 14:20; John 3:29). Some of the groom's procession carried swords "as if they were royal body- guards" *(ibid.,* p. 102), just as angels will accompany Jesus when He comes (Jude 14, 15). The procession then went to the groom's home, and the celebration began. At the marriage feast, the guests celebrated with wine (John 2:1-10), music, dancing, and singing (Judges 14:10-12). Eventually the couple retired to the bedchamber to physically consummate the marriage. Although the celebration lasted for a week (Gen. 29:27; Judges 14:17), most guests had to work during the daylight hours for a living and returned in the evenings to continue the festivities.

"The most popular times of the year for weddings were spring, after the rainy sea- son had ended (S. of Sol. 2:10-14) and before the harvesting of grain crops began, and autumn, after the harvesting of fruit crops and the work of the year was over for farming families" *(ibid.,* p. 103).

For a discussion of the biblical view of death, see the introductory paragraphs to "Word Studies," beginning on page 63 of this book. The loss of a loved one in the ancient Near East immediately impacted any survivors. Everyone in the family, in- cluding slaves, entered into the mourning ritual, which usually lasted a week (Gen. 50:10), and freely showed their grief with frequently public, dramatic gestures such as tearing off their clothes, putting on sackcloth, beating their chests, plucking out hairs, sitting in ashes and tossing them on their heads, and loud screaming (Gen. 37:34; 50:10; Lev. 10:6; 2 Sam. 1:11, 12; 3:32-34; 14:2; Esther 4:3; Job 1:20; Judith 8:4-6; Mark 5:38). When Jonah prophesied that God would destroy Nineveh, the king of that great city "arose from his throne, laid aside his robe from him, covered him- self with sackcloth, and sat on the ashes" (Jonah 3:6), mourning in advance the loss of his kingdom, symbolically stripped of his royal robes and seated on its ruins. Friends often joined the bereaved family in expressing grief (2 Sam. 1:11, 12; John 11:33), while relatives customarily hired professional mourners, usually women, who wailed or sang laments to musical accompaniment (Jer. 48:36; Matt. 9:23) to amplify their display of sorrow (2 Chron. 35:25; Eccl. 12:5; Jer. 9:17-20; Matt. 9:24). Funerary poems/laments found in Scripture contain "a eulogy that was careful to name the deceased; a recounting of what had caused the person's death; and a word of consolation that focused not on the hope that the deceased lived beyond the grave but on the good name left behind by the deceased and the posterity to perpetuate that name (2 Sam. 1:18-27; 3:33, 34; cf. Eze. 19:1-14; 32:2-16; Rev. 18:9-24)" *(The Oxford Companion to the Bible,* p. 531). The promise of resurrection from the dead with Christ toned down such expressions of grief during the New Testament era with the hope of future restoration and reunion (1 Thess. 4:13-18). Sometimes the mourners fasted (1 Sam. 31:11-13) and relatives voluntarily refrained from washing and using perfume throughout the official mourning period (2 Sam. 12:20; 14:2).

The family prepared the body for burial and secured a resting place for it. Unlike their neighbors, the Israelites did not cremate or enbalm the corpses of their loved ones, or lay them to rest in coffins. Archaeological evidence indicates that the poor used ditches, the middle class either purchased or dug out a cave on the family property, and the rich carved out ledges or niches in the soft limestone walls of tombs, to bury their dead. They wrapped the body in strips of cloth with a sticky mixture of spices (John 19:39, 40) and put a napkin over the face (John 11:44). Since families that could afford it burned incense in the tombs of their dead, the "very great fire" at King Asa's funeral (2 Chron. 16:14) seems to suggest that his survivors burned a large amount of incense in his honor. When the burial caves or tombs became over-crowded, the Jews reburied the dried-up bones of their ancestors in stone boxes or coffins called ossuaries to make room for fresh corpses *(The Mishnah, Moed Katan, 1.5)*. Burials occurred without delay, and caves or tombs were sealed with "a hinged door or a heavy, wheel-shaped stone" *(The Oxford Companion to the Bible,* p. 96) to prevent hungry, roaming dogs or jackals from entering *(Harper's Encyclopedia of Bible Life,* p. 106).

For a discussion of the Temple and the synagogues, see chapter 12, "Jewish Institutions and the Spiritual Condition of Israel in the Time of Jesus," beginning on page 306 in this book. Unlike the massive edifice on Mount Zion, the *tabernacle* was a portable replica of the heavenly sanctuary, which served as God's sacred dwelling place during Israel's wilderness wanderings and early occupation of Canaan. God used it to "tabernacle" among humans, so the people called it the "Tent of Meeting" and the "Tent of Testimony" because it was the center of Israelite worship for more than four centuries. Together with its furnishings, the tabernacle served as an object lesson of redemptive truths. In fact, "the whole worship of ancient Israel was a promise, in figures and symbols, of Christ; and it was not merely a promise, but an actual provision, designed by God to aid millions of people by lifting their thoughts to Him who was to manifest Himself to the world" (Ellen G. White, *Testimonies to Ministers and Gospel Workers,* p. 123).

Structurally, the tabernacle consisted of two principal parts: the courtyard and the sacred precincts of the holy and Most Holy Places. Made from wood and animal skins secured on the way to Canaan and precious metals, together with linen spoiled from the Egyptians (Ex. 12:35; 35:21-29), it took nearly six months to construct. In terms of its layout, proceeding from the gate, the first item in the courtyard was the altar of sacrifice, also called the brazen altar or the altar of burnt offering, made of acacia wood overlaid with bronze. Next came the laver, the bronze water basin that the priests used to wash up for ministry. At the far end of the courtyard stood first the holy and then the Most Holy Place of the rectangular tent, called the tabernacle proper.

Facing the Most Holy, the holy place housed the golden, seven-branched candlestick on the left, and two items made of acacia wood overlaid with gold: the table of showbread on the right and altar of incense straight ahead in front of the veil separating the two sacred places. In the Most Holy stood the ark of the covenant, an acacia wood chest overlaid with pure gold inside and out. The Israelites stored the two tables of stone from Mount Sinai, a pot of manna gathered in the wilderness, and Aaron's rod that budded in it. Atop the ark sat the mercy seat, above which rested the shekinah cloud of God's presence, flanked by golden figures of cherubim, one on each side.

The layout of the tabernacle was a progression of holiness so that the journey from its gate to the Most Holy Place traced a path that both prepared and led priests into God's holy presence. In this way, the tabernacle taught Israel both how to approach and fellowship with God, and it continues to instruct New Testament believers, whom Christ has installed as "priests to His God and Father" (Rev. 1:6) "to offer up spiritual sacrifices acceptable to God through [that is, under the high priesthood of] Jesus Christ" (1 Peter 2:5).

The personal gratitude that motivated the Israelites to approach the gate was supposed to escalate into public praise as they entered the court (Ps. 100:4) and elevate into the highest form of praise, which is submission to God, at the altar of substitutionary sacrifice. This would make the advancing worshipers willing to change when they saw less-than-flattering reflections of themselves in the laver and to depend upon both the oil of God's Spirit and the wick of the righteous priest's robe at the candlestick (Edersheim, *The Temple*, p. 283). All this was reiterated when the priest ate from the table of showbread in the light of the candlestick and was reinforced when the incense (typifying the Spirit) sizzled on hot coals transferred from the altar of sacrifice to the altar of incense, standing for divine intercession. The vaporized incense as it wafted over the veil prepared the Most Holy Place for the entrance of the high priest. By both shielding and accessing the way to God, the veil underscored the continuing need for a bridge between God and humanity all the way into the divine throne room. The high priest's ministration of sacrificial blood between the law in the ark and the divine presence above it showed how welcome the right sacrifice, the right priest, and God's Spirit can make repentant sinners in God's presence.

The early Christians continued to worship at the Temple (Acts 2:46), but as the Jews disassociated themselves from the so-called "sect of the Nazarenes" (referring to Jesus), the Christian community began to develop a separate identity and to meet on its own. It was not feasible, for example, for the church at Jerusalem to meet as a single body after God added 3,000 converts to the 120 first Christians on Pentecost (Acts 1:15; 2:41). So while they were enjoying steady growth as a church, still on good terms with the Jewish community (Acts 2:47), the Jerusalem church members already began meeting in small house churches, breaking the bread of the Lord's Supper from house to house (Acts 2:46; cf. Luke 22:19 and 24:30, 31). But as the Sanhedrin sought to silence Christ's followers, attacking them for their beliefs (Acts 4:1-21), the Christian community began to lump the "people of Israel" with the Gentiles, Herod, and Pontius Pilate as enemies of the cause of Christ (verses 23-30). One Jerusalem church met at the home of Mary, Mark's mother (Acts 12:12). Priscilla and Aquila opened their home to a group of believers (1 Cor. 16:19), and Paul asked Philemon to greet "the church in your house" (Philemon 2).

For a while some Christian groups clung to their Jewish roots. A Franciscan scholar, Father Bagatti, has presented archaeological evidence (e.g., graffiti, amulets, lamps, flasks, mosaics, and inscriptions) that "some Christians remained with their fellow Jews to resettle the Galilee and surrounding areas after the [A.D. 66-70] revolt. . . . He cites such villages and towns as Nazareth, Capernaum, Sepphoris, Cana, Cochaba, Tiberias, Gush Hal-av, and Caparasima as centers of Jewish Christianity in this period" (Eric M. Meyers, "Early Judaism and Christianity in the Light of Archaeology," *Biblical Archaeologist*, vol. 51:2, June 1988, p. 71). Although Jewish-Christians observed the Torah in the letter, the Jews, in an identity crisis of their own, gradually labeled all Christians *minim* [heretics], making it impossible for any of Christ's followers to worship at the synagogue, where they had to recite the mandatory Birkat haMinim, a ritual benediction of condemnation for any group with divergent views from orthodox Judaism.

Christians made it unmistakably clear that they assembled for worship in the name of Jesus (see Matt. 18:20). "At their liturgical assemblies . . . [they] . . . hailed the presence of the risen Jesus and called for his return: 'Maranatha' (1 Cor. 16:22; cf. Rev. 22:20; 1 Cor. 11:26)" *(The Oxford Companion to the Bible*, p. 820). Although forced out of the synagogues to gather elsewhere, the Christian community did not instantly or uniformly adopt a different day of worship.

Christians have observed both the seventh day and the first day of the week throughout the church age. Xavier Leon-Dufour, the premier New Testament scholar in France and one of the foremost Catholic New Testament scholars in Europe, says: "Jesus observed the Sabbath" and that His "disciples first of all kept on observing the Sabbath and made use of it to proclaim the Gospel. But very rapidly, the day after Sabbath, the first day of the week, Sunday, became 'the Lord's Day.' With regard to the Sabbath—our Saturday—it conserves only a figurative value, that of the heavenly rest" *(Dictionary of the New Testament*, p. 355).

And, in fact, the apostle Paul, as he went about his mission to the Gentiles, customarily "went into the synagogue on the Sabbath day" to proclaim the gospel to Jews and Gentiles alike (Acts 13:14, NKJV; cf. verse 44; 16:13; 17:2; 18:4). Furthermore, since he kept "reasoning in the synagogue every sabbath, trying to persuade Jews and Greeks" (Acts 18:4, NASB), as though there were no separate Christian meetings on Sabbath or otherwise, this suggests a belated move toward Sunday worship during the post-apostolic age—a change instigated by Christian separatists (see, for instance, the obvious anti-Jewish rhetoric by apologists such as Justin Martyr in his *Dialogue With Trypho)* rather than by Christ or His apostles or any scriptural mandate.

The designation "Lord's day" for Sunday is also somewhat misleading, since the Lord Himself already claims that the seventh-day Sabbath is "my holy day" (Isa. 58:13). The notion that Sunday, the first day of the week, commemorates Jesus' resurrection and His appearances to the disciples at a meal (e.g., Justin Martyr *First Apology* 66. 1-3) is redundant, since the New Testament presents overwhelming evidence that Christ Himself had already instituted an official sacrament to experience, by faith, the benefits of His death, burial, and resurrection: baptism (Col. 2:12; Rom. 6:3-5).

A liturgy of worship was slow to develop. Latourette says that "no single pattern was followed" by early Christians, and because "the Holy Spirit was believed to be impelling and guiding," most worship was spontaneous rather than formatted *(A History of Christianity*, p. 196). As evidence of this, the apostle Paul presents the atmosphere of worship at Corinth as borderline confusion in need of order—what with people selfishly exercising their gifts (e.g., tongues, prophecy at the same time, and wives disturbing the service with questions that distracted attention from the speaker (1 Cor. 14).

The church commonly practiced the Lord's Supper in conjunction with the "love feast," a sort of potluck or fellowship dinner. Paul had to correct their view of the ordinance, because the meal separated, rather than united, the members, who brought food only for themselves and thus defeated the supper's sacramental purpose, since some of them participated in it as though it were an ordinary meal.

When Justin Martyr wrote a defense of Christianity to emperor Antoninus Pius (A.D. 138-161), he wanted to correct any misconceptions of the faith held by outsiders, and devoted chapters lxi-lxvii to a description of what took place at worship. At Rome the people gathered—on Sunday—to hear "the writings of the prophets" and the "memoirs of the apostles." The president preached, and the congregation prayed for the church and the world. Then the president gave thanks over a loaf of bread and a cup of wine, which the congregation ate and drank. After he saw to their distribution, the deacons took them to those who could not attend. By the end of the fifth century the worship service reflected clerical and liturgical influences from the Jewish synagogue: "the clergy . . . had become priests patterned consciously after the Jewish priesthood of pre-Christian times and offering a bloodless sacrifice at an altar" (Latourette, *History*, p. 201), and the service followed a similar format of "readings and prayers" *(The Oxford Companion to the Bible,* p. 820).

Cities were centers of society, technology, industry, and commerce, and represented the epitome of ancient civilization. They enjoyed a wider sphere of influence than villages did and attracted the services of scribes, who left written records behind for posterity. Each city housed at least one temple, providing rulers with one or more patron gods to support their authority. In addition to maintaining a standing army, most cities in the ancient world were deliberately built on hilltops like Jerusalem, or along mountain slopes to make them easier to defend against attack. Jerusalem, for example, was vulnerable only to the north. So the Israelites relied on the Temple and their God to defend against attack from that direction. Scripture refers to Nebuchadnezzar (of Babylon to the southeast) and his allies as the peoples of the north, because they swooped down from that direction—not because they lived there.

Inhabitants also erected stone walls around the cities—with towers at regular or strategic intervals to guard against other dangers and to keep out wild animals, as well as enemy troops. Major cities like Nineveh and Babylon prided themselves on the length, thickness, and height of their walls. A city was only as strong as its gate— the weakest spot in its wall. So when God wanted to show utter contempt for the so-called Philistine iron advantage, He enabled Samson to walk right through a force waiting to ambush him at the iron gate at Gaza, rip it out hinges and all, hoist it over head, and plant it on a mountaintop 38 miles away in Hebron. Strategic to the city's defense, sentries were posted at the gate to keep watch (2 Sam. 18:24; 2 Kings 9:17). As the place of highest traffic, the gate was also the ideal place for business (2 Kings 7:1), public hearings (1 Kings 22:10), legal transactions (Ruth 4:1-11), and trying legal cases (Deut. 21:18-21).

In applying the information about the socioreligious situation to the biblical passage you are studying, ask yourself:

1. Are there any customs in this passage that I can recognize from what is said? or implied? from items mentioned? from the times? from frequency? or seasons? from the location? from places of origin? from names? What do these customs tell me about the people involved?

2. Does the text offer any clues about the society in which these people lived? Were they agrarian? nomadic? urban? suburban? What can I deduce or infer from these clues concerning their views of law and order? of justice? of government? of opportunities to succeed? of keeping safe?

3. Where did they worship? How did they worship? When do they worship? daily? weekly? seasonally? Are there any traces of religious syncretism? extremism?

Economics—

Factors to Consider	*trade and commerce; agriculture; craftsmen and products; travel by sea and land; lingering effects of catastrophes, weather, and war*

Merchants sold or exchanged goods on a professional level. Shop owners, craftsmen, and farmers brought their goods to town and offered them to the public at the marketplace, usually at the city gate (2 Kings 7:1) or at bazaars (1 Kings 20:34), streets lined with awning-covered stalls or shops. The Greeks introduced the open square to the Orient during the fourth century B.C., as excavations in Marisa and Samaria have confirmed. Each city had a superintendent in charge of the market (2 Maccabees 3:4), a powerful position, as witnessed by the fact that Herod Agrippa I served as the superintendent in Tiberias before he became a king. Abraham and the patriarchs probably transported goods across Syria and Palestine with donkey caravans. By the time the monarchy came to Israel, camel caravans became a regular thing between Arabia and Palestine (1 Kings 10:2). In the book *Ben Hur,* Lew Wallace drew on extrabiblical sources to define the role of the steward of the house of Hur, who kept records of all expenses and received an allowance to oversee the operation of such a caravan.

The Israelites as a people were more agricultural than commercial. First the Canaanites, then the Phoenicians, controlled most of the commerce in the ancient Near East. In the ancient world, the term "Canaanite" was a synonym for merchant (see note to Zech. 14:21, NIV). Solomon opened the door to trade with King Hiram of Tyre, exchanging grain, oil, and wine for the timber he needed to conduct an agressive building campaign (1 Kings 5:6-11; 2 Chron. 2:15). He also contracted with Tyre to build a fleet of ships at the port of Ezion-geber on the Gulf of Aqabah (1 Kings 9:26, 27), and sold horses he had acquired from the north and chariots secured from Egypt to the kings of Syria for a royal sum (1 Kings 9:28). It wasn't until the exile in Babylon, however, that the Jews turned more as a people toward commercial pursuits. Solomon compares the woman who finds bargains to stay within her family budget to merchant ships that sail in and out of ports to get the best buy for their money.

Potters plied one of the most important trades in the ancient world. With copper and bronze being terribly expensive and leather so temporary, clay pots were in great demand for carrying water and storing oil, honey, and meal. As easily as clay shattered, the market never stagnated. The first thing the potter did was to tread the clay into the right consistency (Isa. 41:25). Then he placed a lump of it on the upper disk of his potter's wheel (Jer. 18:3), and working the lower disk with his foot, spun the clay into shape with his hands, water, and a wooden tool. When the pot turned out different from the potter's expectations, he collapsed the vessel and with the help of water prepared it for a second try. Both Jeremiah 18:4 and Paul, in Romans 9:20, 21, refer to this process when they describe God's prerogative to shape and mold people as He pleases. The brittleness of pottery became a symbol of how fragile and helpless people and even nations are when it comes to divine judgment. God promises the Messiah that He will "dash" kings who rebel against His authority "in pieces like a potter's vessel" (Ps. 2:9; cf. Jer. 19:11). Useless fragments of pottery were called potsherds, which (according to Isa. 30:14) were used to carry coals or water (e.g., drinking cups, or ladles to fill jars). Job used a potsherd to scrape his sores (Job 2:8).

Carpenters did most of their work in the shop—on benches. Isaiah lists four of the tools used in their woodworking craft: the ruler, probably a reed measuring some 10-11 feet in length according to Eze. 40:5; the pencil, most likely a stylus used to leave a mark; the plane, to smoothe the wood; and the compass, to mark circles (44:13). To this array of tools archaeologists have added metal saws, axes, chisels, awls, nails, and files (Ex. 21:6; Deut. 19:5; 1 Chron. 22:3; 2 Chron. 3:9; Isa. 10:15; Jer. 10:4).

Carpenters used imported cedar and cypress from Phoenicia (1 Kings 5:8) and almug wood from Ophir (1 Kings 10:11), and domestic sycamore (1 Kings 10:27) and olivewood (1 Kings 6:31). They made beams for ceilings and support columns (1 Kings 6:9), window frames and doors (1 Kings 6:31-35); furniture (1 Kings 10:18-20), musical instruments (1 Kings 10:12), roof and window panels, doors, and ceilings (1 Kings 6:18, 29, 32, 35), plus yokes for oxen, plows, tables, chairs, benches, chests, wooden locks, keys, and sandals. People also called upon them to repair and restore items as well.

Shipbuilders could put together seacraft of any size, from the simple fishing boat designed for local use (Luke 8:22) to large merchant ships capable of sailing across the Mediterranean Sea, so-called "ships of Tarshish" (1 Kings 10:22). Since the Israelites lived inland (the Philistines occupied the Palestinian coast and the Phoenicians the Syrian shore), few Israelites had the expertise to build or sail merchant-sized ships, which explains why Solomon contracted with Phoenicians from the coastal city of Tyre to build a fleet of ships for him at the port of Ezion-geber on the Gulf of Aqabah (1 Kings 9:26) and hired foreigners, "sailors who knew the sea" (verse 27, NASB) to sail them. According to Ezekiel, the Phoenicians at Tyre outfitted both merchant and military ships with fir planks, cedar masts, oak oars, pine decks, sails of fine Egyptian linen, and dyed deck covers (Eze. 27:5-7), while experts from neighboring Byblos caulked them (verse 8). The Phoenicians marketed two kinds of ships: a coast-hugging short one with a rounded hull for cargo, and a streamlined long ship designed for combat, with two rows of oars on each side and an upper deck to hold warriors' shields.

From the coast of the Mediterranean to the shores of the Sea of Galilee, Palestinian fishermen engaged in a major enterprise. Even in the wilderness, recalling their days along the Nile, the Israelites remembered the "fish which we ate . . . in Egypt" (Num. 11:5, NKJV). Some ancient fishermen used hooks to catch fish (e.g., Peter in Matt. 17:27). Isaiah in a negative way (Isa. 19:8) and Amos in a positive way (Amos 4:2) compared the sureness of hooking fish to the certainty of judgment. Others used harpoons or spears (Job 41:7) and two types of nets: the casting net, ringed with lead weights on its outer edge, and the dragnet. Fishermen tossed the former from the shore or in shallow water so that it would fall over, sink around, and trap fish (see Matt. 4:21, 22). The latter depended on motion, supplied either by people or a pair of boats working together (Matt. 13:47, 48), to trap the fish. Jesus compared the kingdom of God to such a net, which hauls in both good and bad fish and requires separation in the end (verses 49, 50).

Masons had the important task of shaping stones and forming arches. Their work required enough precision that they used a plumb line, a piece of metal or stone fastened to a string, suspended from the top of a structure to make sure that a wall was square. Amos used the image of a plumb line to emphasize how precisely God was checking His people at the time to see if they were on the square or worthy of demolition by judgment (Amos 7:7, 8). The mason also used the measuring reed, a cane used to lay straight foundations and to guage the distances between doors and windows.

The mason began his work by digging a trench and filling it with a stone and lime foundation. Jesus compared people who hear what He has to say and build their lives on it, to a mason who "dug deep and laid a foundation upon the rock" (Luke 6:48). Once the first layer of stone was in place on the foundation, the mason set a large square stone in each corner to hold the walls together at the base (Job 38:6). When the walls were finished, the mason set a thin square stone at the top of each corner to hold them together at the ceiling. A stone rejected as too thin for the walls often turned out right to be "the head of the corner." Matthew used this imagery to show how Israel's leaders had misjudged Jesus, "the stone which the builders rejected," but who nevertheless became the chief cornerstone (Matt. 21:42).

Metalworking is an ancient art. Zillah, the wife of Lamech, Enoch's great-great-great grandson, gave birth to a son she named "Tubal-cain, the forger of all implements of bronze and iron" (Gen. 4:22, NASB). Metalwork was a complete industry with a high impact on the ancient economy. First of all, slaves or prisoners mined for ore (Job 28:1-11). Then smelters separated metal from the ore by fire and cast it into handy ingots for delivery to the smith, who refined the metal over a fire fanned by a foot-driven goatskin bellows, and pounded it into a desired shape on an anvil of iron and wood with his hammers (Isa. 41:7; 44:12; Jer. 6:29).

Metals also influenced the political as well as economic scene. During Saul's reign, for example, the Philistines banned blacksmithing for anyone except themselves so that they could monopolize metals in that region and maintain a military advantage over their Palestinian neighbors (1 Sam. 13:19). Once the ban was lifted, however, the Israelites became very active, making all kinds of things from simple nails to sharp swords.

Blacksmiths made a variety of useful devices, including plowshares, hoes, axes, forks, and goads—pointed rods about eight feet long used to motivate oxen (Judges 3:31). When Jesus told Saul on the Damascus road, "It is hard for thee to kick against the pricks" (Acts 26:14, KJV), He was comparing His poking Saul's conscience with people and events with the farmer goading an ox. A smith named Hiram also manufactured the polished brass basins, shovels, pails, bowls, and stands for Solomon's Temple (1 Kings 7:40-45). A silversmith at Ephesus named Demetrius made a living producing images of the goddess Artemis (Acts 19:23-27), and Peter compared the quality of faith purified through trials with the purity of metal prepared by goldsmiths, saying: "The proof of your faith, being more precious than gold which is perishable, even though tested by fire" (1 Peter 1:7, NASB).

When Peter went to Joppa, "he stayed many days . . . with a certain tanner, Simon" (Acts 9:43, NASB). People of the ancient Near East used to carry, hold, and store liquids of all kinds in animal skins after the hide or skin was converted into leather. Tanners were experts at this conversion process that left the hide permanently soft and flexible. Step one called for soaking the skin in lime to loosen the hair. Then the tanner removed the hair and fat from the treated skin by dunking it in a solution made from oak bark and other plant juices. After the skins hung out to dry for two or three days, the tanner skillfully treated the skin with various additional solutions until it was in the desired condition. Simon probably lived by the Mediterranean Sea because tanners needed so much water in their work (Acts 10:6).

Financial concerns generated numerous employment opportunities for people in Bible times. In addition to caravan managers and house stewards, bankers, tax-collectors, and money changers all made a living handling money. Although the Bible does not explicitly refer to bankers per se, it does mention banking. In the parable of the talents the nobleman chastises a slave for not depositing his mina in a bank so that it could have earned interest (Luke 19:23).

Scripture does, however, discuss money changers (Matt. 21:12). Every village and city had at least one, sitting at a table in public, changing people's money from one currency to another—sometimes charging an exorbitant fee for each transaction. They monopolized the market and did a thriving business, especially at the Temple, where every male Israelite 20 and older had to pay the Temple tax, or atonement money (Ex. 30:12-16). Jews from outside of Palestine had to exchange their foreign cash for the proper currency, because only the half-shekel, a native Hebrew coin, satisfied the scriptural requirement. Not only did the money changers perform this service, at a rate of about 12 percent, according to the Talmud, but they also provided pilgrims with the right coinage to purchase animals for sacrifice.

By law Israelites could not charge interest on loans to their countrymen (Lev. 25:36, 37), but they could take interest from strangers and Canaanites (Deut. 23:20). While reasonable interest was acceptable in New Testament times (Matt. 25:27), Jesus said it was better to lend without expecting anything in return (Luke 6:35), and He chased the money changers from the Temple for desecrating its sacredness with their unscrupulous practices (Matt. 21:12). No wonder the people considered money changers and their less-than-ethical procedures contemptible.

The people despised tax collectors even more than money changers. While the latter may have extorted or exploited their clients, they did not collect taxes for the enemy Roman government, as did the former. The Romans hired Jewish tax collectors to raise taxes for them from their fellow Jews and paid them a portion of what they brought in. Unfortunately, as long as they got their money, the Romans did not care just how much the publicans (tax collectors) actually did take in—or pocketed for themselves. The people referred to publicans as "sinners" (Matt. 9:11) and put them in the same class as "harlots" (Matt. 21:31). Because Jesus spent time with and showed concern for tax collectors like Zacchaeus (Luke 19:2) and called a former publican named Matthew to join His close circle of disciples (Mark 2:14), some people labeled Him "a friend of publicans and sinners" (Matt. 11:19, KJV).

The textile industry thrived in the ancient world. While women initially did their own spinning and weaving, "in time, home shops were formed and weaving became specialized and industrialized. Guilds were formed and districts of a town or city— even entire villages—became the centers of a textile industry" (Harper's Encyclopedia of Bible Life, p. 376), which depended on domestic wool and imported flax (linen) from Egypt.

First the woolen or flaxen fibers were washed, bleached, and thickened to prepare them for spinning. This task fell to professional "fullers," usually men, who could handle the strenuous work involved. After they soaked the raw flax in cold water, fullers boiled it in a vat of alkali and water, beat and scraped it with wooden clubs, rinsed it in water, and laid it out to dry (Mal. 3:2; Job 9:30). The process gave off such an odor that fullers did their work outside the city wall, like the "fuller's field" near Jerusalem (2 Kings 18:17; Isa. 7:3).

Before the fibers could be spun into continuous threads, however, professionals dyed them red, blue, yellow, purple, and a variety of other less popular colors. Purple, the most prized of all colors, came in various shades, from crimson to deep purple, depending on the duration of soaking and type of dyes used. Processed from a secretion of the hypobranchial gland of the murex shellfish, it was very valuable because each mollusk yielded only a single drop of dye. It took 12,000 murex to make 1.4 grams of crude purple dye. Accordingly, it became the color of royalty, and since the Phoenician (the root for Phoenician probably comes from a word meaning purple; the same is undoubtedly true for "Canaan") coastal community monopolized its manufacture, the ancient world labeled it "Tyrian Purple" (Judges 8:26; Eze. 27:7). Clothing colored with murex dye was colorfast and could be washed again and again. At Philippi, in Macedonia, a woman from Thyatira named Lydia, "a seller of purple fabrics," became Paul's first Christian convert in Europe (Acts 16:14, NASB).

Dyers processed red from a grub, blue from pomegranate rind, and other colors from a variety of sources. In addition to the varying colors of purple obtained from differing species of murex, the dried bodies of the female kermes scale insect, the root of the madder plant, henna, alkanet, archil, rattan palm, woad, and indigo plants were used.

Dyeing processing factories discovered by archaeologists at Gezer, Beth-zur, Beth-shemesh, Tell en-Nasbeh, and Tell beit Mirsim have helped to recreate the procedure for dyeing. First the dyes were put into stone vats and the cloth or yarn was soaked in them. When the expert eye of the dyer was satisfied that the process had achieved the targeted color, he would wring out the excess dye and set the color by soaking the dyed material in a lime solution.

Although women originally did the spinning at home (Prov. 31:13, 19), later on professional spinners stretched and twisted the dyed fiber into thread "by rotating a spindle in the hand while feeding the threads . . . from a staff or an open bowl with interior 'handles' . . . [that] . . . prevented the threads from becoming entangled" *(Harper's Encyclopedia of Bible Life,* p. 379). Weavers interlaced the thread into fabric on a loom. Either men (Ex. 35:35) or women (2 Kings 23:7) stretched the warp or lengthwise threads on the loom, and passed the woof threads perpendicular to and over and under the warp threads. Although looms generally must have been quite massive, Samuel having compared Goliath's spear to "a weaver's beam" (1 Sam. 17:7), Job could compare the fleeting nature of his life to the speedy way adept professionals handled the loom. He lamented: "My days are swifter than a weaver's shuttle" (Job 7:6), referring to the handy device that helped the woof deftly weave its way through the warp.

The textile industry relied on flocks of sheep for wool, and the sheep depended on shepherds to watch over and care for them (Ps. 23). The Holy Land never wanted for lack of sheep. Just about every family had some, and nearly everyone in the home took a turn caring for the flock. Although most shepherds were men, at times women saw to the watering of the sheep (Gen. 29:6-10; Ex. 2:16-19). Finding food and water was a top priority. Green pastures in the spring and gleanings left in the fields from the harvests of late summer easily supplied the nutritional needs of most flocks, but come the dry fall weather, the shepherd had to guide his sheep to the hill country, where he could cut down leafy branches to supplement their diet. As for water, the shepherd always tried to keep his flock near a running stream. When the pools and streams went dry, he watered the sheep from a well. Without water every day the sheep would die.

The sheep needed constant protection because wild beasts, thieves, or inclement weather could strike at any time (Gen. 31:38-40). There wasn't much he could do for the sheep to protect them from excessive heat or freezing temperatures, but he did carry a long rod—a tree branch with a knot at one end—to defend them from dangerous beasts and ruthless thieves. Shepherds also carried a sling, a string with a piece of leather at the middle to hold a stone. When he spied an animal or robber, the shepherd placed a stone in the leather, grabbed both ends of the string, whirled it around his head, and then released one end to let the stone fly toward the target. That shepherds developed uncanny accuracy with the sling is obvious from the story of David and Goliath. Even under pressure and on the dead run, David was able to hit the Philistine giant squarely in the forehead—the only vulnerable spot available to him (1 Sam. 17:48-50). At any event, shepherds defended their sheep with their own lives. David told Saul about hand-to-hand encounters with lions and bears that had threatened his father's flock to alleviate any fears the king may have had about his credentials for combat with Goliath (1 Sam. 17:33-37).

The shepherd also carried a staff—a cane or walking stick with a crook at one end—about five or six feet long. He used it to help him climb rocky cliffs and retrieve sheep from brambles and other such places. It was not as a weapon (see also the story in Luke 15:4-7 about the shepherd who left the 99 to find a lost sheep. Aware of how encouraging shepherds were to his flock, David told the Lord, his Shepherd, "Thy rod and Thy staff, they comfort me" (Ps. 23:4, NASB). Shepherds usually wore simple sandals and a camel's hair cloak or mantle and carried their food in a girdle or in a primitive knapsack called a scrip. In addition to a water bag, since many shepherds also tended herds of goats, they usually had a plentiful supply of curdled goat's milk on hand, the main staple of their diet. Some shepherds were skillful musicians, like David (1 Sam. 16:18), usually playing the pipes—flutes made from reeds—or as in David's case a small harp or lyre (1 Sam. 16:23).

At night the sheep were placed in a sheepfold, a makeshift corral, formed from bushes, branches, rocks, or logs. Shepherds often took advantage of natural topography and set up the sheepfold against the slope of a hill. A lean-to roof at one corner of the fold protected the sheep from snow or rain. At night shepherds usually separated the sheep from the goats, tallied the number of each, and inspected them for injuries or signs of disease (see Matt. 25:32). They often mingled their flocks into one fold for defensive purposes, knowing that they could separate their sheep from the rest of the fold in the morning. The shepherd simply stood at the gate or door to the fold and called for his sheep. The close relationship between the shepherd and his flock did the rest—only his own sheep responded to his voice, as Christ's own respond to His voice when He calls for them, and so they separate from the rest of the world's sheep (John 10:2-16). With the sheep safely in the fold, shepherds might sit around a campfire, playing music, singing songs, and telling stories—like the shepherds were probably doing that night the angel visited them to announce the Messiah's birth (Luke 2:8-14).

When the Israelites settled the Promised Land, "forests and woodlands spread over the central highlands, making large-scale farming impossible. The land was also hilly and rocky, limiting the size and intensity of true farming. As the lowlands and plains were absorbed or taken over under Israelite control, and as areas of alluvial soil and forests were cleared, larger areas could be farmed" (*Harper's Encyclopedia of Bible Life*, p. 157). Then the Israelites grew wheat "on the better drained areas of the Sharon and Esdraelon Plains, and in the downfaulted basins of Manasseh. Olive trees were at home on the well-watered slopes of Ephraim, and in the somewhat drier climate of Judah the vine predominated, although wheat and olives were grown as well. Grain crops, such as wheat and barley, could also be cultivated in the southern coastal zone" (*ibid.*, p. 157).

Sporadic rainfall in this area made crops such an iffy proposition that archaeologists have located several underground storage pits there and in the southern foothills of the Judean highlands dug to preserve grain for future seasons of drought or crop failure.

Farmers sowed grain by hand, then plowed it under (Mark 4:3-8; for a thorough exposition of the parable of the sower, with a detailed description of the way farmers prepared the land, see W. Phillip Keller's *A Gardener Looks at the Fruits of the Spirit*). They used either crude wooden plows pulled by oxen or a mattock to break up the soil. When the grain ripened, early harvesters cut it with sickles made of flint; later, reapers of iron. Then the women tied the grain into bundles (i.e., sheaves), for transport to the threshing floor. The Israelites used several methods of threshing, depending on the amount of grain. For example, Ruth (2:17) and Gideon (Judges 6:11) beat small amounts with a wooden stick or flail to separate the actual grain from the husk and straw.

If the thresher had a team of animals, he could either drive them around and around on the grain to tread it (Deut. 25:4; cf. 1 Cor. 9:9; 1 Tim. 5:18) or have them pull a threshing sledge, either the *morag*, with sharp pieces of metal or stone along the bottom to pull out the grain (2 Sam. 24:22; 1 Chron. 21:23; Isa. 41:15) or the *charus*, with two or three axles of toothed wheels to cut into the grain and separate the kernels from the straw (Job 41:30; Isa. 28:27; Amos 1:3).

Then the farmer separated the wheat from the straw with a winnowing fork, tossing the threshed grain into the air so that the wind could blow the lighter chaff away and the heavier heads of ripened grain would fall to the ground on the spot (Ps. 1:4). God promised downtrodden Israel: "Behold, I have made you a new sharp threshing sledge with double edges; you will thresh the mountains and pulverize them, and will make the hills like chaff. You will winnow them, and the wind will carry them away, and the storm will scatter them" (Isa. 41:15, 16, NASB). Comparing Israel to the familiar farm implement, the faithful covenant God told His trampled (treaded) and overwhelmed people that He would use them as His instrument to decide the fate of their powerful enemies—to keep the promise He made to Abraham long ago that He would "bless those who bless you, and . . . him who curses you" (Gen. 12:3, NKJV). Similarly, John the Baptist compared Jesus and His ministry to a farmer threshing with a winnowing fork, saying: "His winnowing fork is in his hand, and he will clear his threshing floor and gather His wheat into the granary; but the chaff He will burn with unquenchable fire" (Matt. 3:12). In accordance with the prophecy Simeon made on the day of Jesus' dedication: "Behold this child is destined for the fall and rising of many in Israel" (Luke 2:34, NKJV), John said that Jesus would separate the faithful from the counterfeit in Israel, like a farmer separating kernels from straw at the threshing floor—and so decide the eternal destiny of both groups.

Of particular interest in the area of agriculture is the vineyard. Vinedressers usually planted their vines on a hillside, apart from the rest of the crops (Isa. 5:1; Deut. 22:9) in rows about 10 feet apart. To improve the vines' chances of taking root the vinedresser "dug" the vineyard "all around" and "removed its stones" (Isa. 5:2, NASB), just as God cleared the land of Canaan by driving out its inhabitants, replanted His people there, and they took deep root and filled the land (Ps. 80:8, 9). Once the vines were planted, the vinedresser took precautions to ensure the best possible harvest: he built a wall of stones or a hedge of bushes around the vineyard, terraced the hill by filling in earth from the valley, and erected a watchtower of fieldstones in its middle (Isa. 5:2, 5). Otherwise, predators or thieves could come along at any time to eat or steal the grapes and trample the vines (Matt. 21:33; Ps. 80:12, 13), especially during harvest season.

Vinedressers initially "propped up their vines to keep the grapes above the soil" (Merrill T. Gilbertson, *The Way It Was in Bible Times,* p. 107), because "artificial trellises apparently were not used until the Roman period" *(ibid.,* p. 183). Yet "by growing close to the ground, the vines were able to soak up the moisture of the dew which covered the slopes of the hill" *(ibid.).*

The vineyard required attention after the grain harvest, during the summer, when its vines blossomed, and when they ripened (S. of Sol. 2:11-13). That's when the vinedresser pruned the vines, cutting them back to the main stem to improve their productivity and removed the unproductive branches for firewood (Isa. 18:5; John 15:1, 2, 6). Jesus used this symbolism to describe the fate of those who claim a personal relationship with Christ, the True Vine: the faithful produce Christlike fruit because they depend on the Vine at all times—and more so during trials—to produce even more fruit, but the unfruitful produce nothing Christlike because they have only a surface relationship with the Vine, the shallowness of which really shows during trials—any Christlikeness they once may have had eventually withers, the relationship dries up, and they sever their connection with Him—only to return once again to the ranks of those who are destined for destruction (John 15:2-6).

When the grapes were ready, the vinedresser cut them from the vine in clusters with a sickle-shaped tool and carried them from the vineyard in baskets covered with vine leaves. Some of the grapes were eaten fresh, others were soaked in oil and water and dried into raisins (1 Sam. 30:12), but the majority found their way to the winepress to be trampled in a large shallow basin, hollowed out of bedrock, for their juice (Job 24:11; Amos 9:13)—just as one day, when "her grapes are ripe" (Rev. 14:18, NASB), one of God's angels will swing "his sickle to the earth," and gather "the clusters from the vine of the earth," to throw "them into the great wine press of God's wrath" (Rev. 14:19, NASB). The juice ran into another, deeper vat, below the pressing basin. After the pulp and seeds settled to the bottom, the remaining liquid was funneled from the settling basin into storage jars and sealed with a layer of olive oil.

In applying the information about the economic situation to the biblical passage you are studying, ask yourself:

---

1. How do the people in the passage earn a living? What effect would this have on their view of society? of life? of God? of religion?

2. What can I tell about the people in the passage from their occupation? What does it say about what others thought of them? about what they thought of themselves? about their roots? contacts? any influence they may have? any influences on them?

3. Are the people in the passage living in a war-torn, weather-driven, or disaster-prone economy? What does this tell me about their views of society? of life? of God? Would they interpret natural, social, or historical events differently from people living elsewhere and/or under different conditions? Would they be less, more, or equally superstitious? extremists? indifferent?

Politics—

Factors to Consider	*ruler/newsmaker vital statistics; past history; international situation*

The pages of the Bible "are full of kings and empires, armies and wars, cries for justice" *(The Oxford Companion to the Bible,* p. 599), all in historical context. Ancient kings were powerful political figures. When Samuel explained the ramifications of having a man rule them in place of God, he warned the tribes that human kings conscripted young men for service, assigning them tasks as the rulers saw fit, and indentured young women to perform chores at their palaces. They also fed their servants with food seized from their subjects and took the servants, beasts of burden, and even flocks of their subjects for their own—in short, everyone within the king's jurisdiction wound up serving him (1 Sam. 8:11-17). Because kings *rose* to power, their past shed light on them and their activities in the present and for the future; so it pays to study, for example, David's pre-ascension background for the insights into his monarchial behavior.

The Bible identifies kings so closely with their kingdoms that they are synonymous with each other (cf. Dan. 7:17, 23), because as heads of state they made decisions for their nations and often shaped the attitudes of their subjects. So, for instance, when King Herod heard the wise men speak about a rival who was "born king of the Jews" (Matt. 2:2), "he was troubled, and all Jerusalem with him" (verse 3, NASB). In fact, what occurred on the monarchial level affected not only local subjects but also the peoples around them.

Consider the time Pharaoh Necho, the king of Egypt, decided to help Ashurubaleit II, the last king of Assyria, against the Babylonians at the River Euphrates. Necho passed through Israel on his way north along the Fertile Crescent, and when he entered Judean territory, King Josiah deliberately intercepted him at Megiddo and lost his life during the furious battle that followed. A senseless death? Well, a background check reveals that Josiah had worked hard to restore Israel to her former greatness—the level of spirituality and prosperity, even the extent of Israel's national boundaries under Solomon's rule—during his reign. Maybe Josiah believed that the glorious future prophesied for Israel had actually materialized with him on the throne and that no earthly power, including Egypt, had the right or might to trespass on covenant property. Perhaps he believed the time had come to test Judah's sovereignty against Egypt, or to prove to the world that the prophecies had come true with a victory over Egypt. It's also conceivable that he simply wanted to prevent Egypt from rescuing Assyria, or to keep it from rearming the brutal Assyrian military machine.

Your understanding of the rulers, "newsmakers" like the patriarchs, the judges, Jesus, and the apostles, or statesmen like Ahithophel—in the passage—can either hinder or enhance the recovery of the historical-cultural setting of the text and may significantly affect the way you interpret, teach, or preach it.

In applying the information about the political situation to the biblical passage you are studying, ask yourself:

> 1. Are there any rules or key political figures in or influencing the text? Who are they? Where do they come from? What do they do?
>
> 2. Does anything about them deserve further investigation? Look into the past. How did they get to occupy their current positions? Does their childhood, a crisis, or some other significant person or event explain anything you need to know?
>
> 3. Turn your attention to the international situation. Are forces in motion that have a bearing on them or their situation? on the people with whom they are intimately connected? How do these factors fit into the current political picture?

General Historical-Cultural Guidelines

Do your best to measure both dimensions of existence for all the people in your passage: the *horizontal* (humans and their environment) and the *vertical* (humans and their relationship to God). The Bible is not just a book about ancient people. It is also the record of God's revelation of Himself to human beings and His challenge to them to choose whom they will serve.

It is also important to keep in mind that the Bible writers borrowed, reshaped, and reapplied the popular cultural materials of their day (for example, the Canaanite sea monster, Leviathan [Ps. 74:13, 14]; the mythological dragon, Rahab [Job 26:12, 13]; and the Hittite Vassal Treaty as the prototype for the covenant in Deuteronomy). So the Bible student often must decide when to adopt both the *content* and the *form* of a cultural item (see Walter C. Kaiser, Jr., *Toward an Exegetical Theology*, p. 115; also the discussion on p. 64 of this book regarding Greek equivalents for Old Testament terms under "Word Studies").

Following is a procedure for effective historical-cultural study that I have adapted from Mickelsen (p. 176).

> 1. Know the people(s) involved in your text.
>
> 2. Do your best to fix the time period, but remember that the situation is more important than the precise date.
>
> 3. Check the place(s) of geographical setting.
>
> 4. Note the customs, material objects, and socioreligious relationships in and behind the passage.
>
> 5. Recognize how the history leading up to their time influenced the responses and attitudes of the original hearers or readers.
>
> 6. Examine the factors that either stabilized or unsettled the economy of the people in the passage.
>
> 7. Show the similarities and point out the differences between what is happening in the passage and the surrounding history and culture.
>
> 8. Stay aware of historical-cultural similarities and differences between you and the writer and his audience.

CHAPTER 5

THEOLOGICAL ANALYSIS

So far in this handbook the focus has been entirely on the text at hand. But no text is an island. The "local" context is too narrow to bring out its fullest sense. If we want to preach the gospel in its fullness, we must preach both the Saviour proclaimed in the New Testament *and* the Redeemer foretold by the Old Testament prophets and symbolized by the sanctuary services of ancient Israel.

Introduction

So the first thing we want to do after verbal analysis is to extend our sphere of study to the "canonical" context, which I identified earlier as the everlasting covenant—God's promise-plan to all who believe in Messiah Jesus.

Although the Christian Bible is divided into the Old and New testaments, one testament is incomplete without the other. We sometimes might assume that the truths we find in the New Testament are more important than those found in the Old Testament, but that oversimplifies the concept of progressive revelation. Jesus Christ was the Redeemer for Old Testament believers as well as for those living during and after New Testament times.

Theological analysis is the best way of expanding the context because it relates your text to the rest of Scripture by placing it in the broader context of the plan of salvation. God's salvific work will increase in its importance as we work carefully to understand its height and depth and breadth.

Theology is by definition the science, or study, of God. But it is unlike any other object of study; God took the initiative to communicate with us: "We love him, because he first loved us" (1 John 4:19, KJV). At first there was only God. No one forced Him to communicate. He freely chose to open up, reveal the secrets of His mind, and extend His thoughts into space. By the sheer force of His will He created the heavens and the earth and everything that is in them. Continuing to reach out, He voluntarily began to reveal the mystery of His nature, something we humans could never have discovered on our own. He disclosed Himself to us.

In the beginning God spoke regularly, on a personal basis and through nature, to Adam and Eve. But after sin separated humanity from God and also corrupted nature, revelation shifted into a redemptive mode. The Creator began to supplement the incomplete testimony of nature with a special revelation of Himself as the world's Redeemer.

And since the time of the Fall, Jesus Christ's character, life, and mediatorial work have intrigued the human mind. Since that time He has unfolded this truth in progressive installments, side by side with His efforts to redeem us (see Num. 15:41). In fact, "God disclosed . . . Himself . . . in response to the practical religious needs of His people as these emerged in the course of history" (Geerhardus Vos, *Biblical Theology*, p. 9).

Furthermore, because the Bible is the living Word of God, the Holy Spirit uses it to keep the plan of salvation always fresh. The concept of our infinite God's work to save us is so broad and deep that it is always a rich field for us to mine. Though the truths presented in Scripture are old, the Holy Spirit makes them look ever more glorious and powerful. As a result, every new generation can find rich resources in Scripture.

But the process of revelation is more than simultaneous with history. It is embodied in history. Some of the very people (for example, Moses), places (for instance, Mount Zion), and institutions (such as the Temple) of history themselves actually have a revelatory significance. So, for example, the Creator says: "And also I gave them My sabbaths to be a sign between Me and them, that they might know that I am the Lord who sanctifies them" (Eze. 20:12, NASB).

At times "redemption and revelation coincide" *(ibid.,* p. 7) when God personally discloses Himself in an unmistakable, powerful way (as at the Exodus or the Crucifixion). Such divine acts are both *redemptive landmarks* and *revelatory milestones.* For instance, not only did Jesus' earthly ministry take the work of redemption to new heights, but it also initiated a powerful surge in the flow of revelation. It marked both a significant step toward the fulfillment of God's ancient promises and the transition from the Old Testament to the New.

But such acts "are never entirely left to speak for themselves" *(ibid.).* Like Amos said, "Surely the Lord God does nothing unless He reveals His secret counsel to His servants the prophets" (Amos 3:7, NASB). Key divine acts "are preceded and followed by word-revelation" *(ibid.)* to announce in advance what will happen and then to explain the significance of what has occurred. So, for example, the Old Testament anticipated Christ's arrival and prepared Israel for His coming. The Gospels record His visit and announce that the Old Testament promises are fulfilled in who He is and what He does, and the Epistles interpret and explain the fuller significance of Jesus' life and work and how it should motivate the lives of Christians.

So when Jesus of Nazareth told His parables and instructed His disciples, what He said sounded like new truth, but in reality He was reiterating and expanding what had been revealed to the Old Testament writers. Additionally He predicted that the coming Holy Spirit would serve the same function and present to the disciples further amplification of scriptural truth.

The Spirit gave Jesus and the New Testament writers a supernatural understanding of the Old Testament and led them to draw advanced, insightful conclusions from it. As they applied truth to the New Testament situation, it unfolded in much the same way as a seed develops into a flower. This is the basic format for New Testament interaction with the Old Testament canon.

It is clear, then, that we cannot understand the law revealed in the Old Testament without understanding the gospel of grace presented in the New. And the opposite is also true. We can best understand the gospel of grace only as we relate it to the law revealed in the Old Testament.

Just as flora gradually bloom through a definite process in successive stages, so Bible truth gradually crystallized through a definite process in progressive installments. The Bible writers presented truth in a particular order, building on and clarifying what God said previously. Theological analysis expands the context by proceeding along the inspired lines of development. Unless you know where your text is in the stream of revelation as it progresses from the Old Testament to the New, you could take it out of sequence and draw incorrect conclusions concerning what it has to contribute overall to revelation and how it is supposed to make that contribution, thereby neutralizing its effectiveness in any presentation.

Revelation goes through stages of development as it progresses from the Old Testament to the New. Since every passage has a real connection with the rest of Scripture, every text has a specific relation to what comes before and after, which reflects this growth and development. Just as a growing thing becomes more defined as it develops, later texts can clarify what God said previously. Just as the level of growth represents how far a living thing has developed to that point, later texts climax the progress of revelation to their time. Just as the development so far indicates how something will grow thereafter, later texts build on the foundation of earlier texts that influence their development.

In order to grasp what the author meant to communicate to his original audience, you should explore the connection between your text and those that came before it in time. Earlier texts help us understand later ones by putting us in touch with their redemptive roots.

But looking back is not enough to get the whole picture. Since texts also set the stage for what follows, look ahead and investigate the influence of your passage on later, more advanced texts so that you can draw "analogies of faith" (that is, connect it with remote passages of Scripture that seem to further develop the same line of truth). This is especially important, because sometimes in the process of declaring the end from the beginning, the Holy Spirit went beyond the limits of human authorship and actually meant more than the human author may have understood or intended.

There are even occasions when the only way to understand the full sense of a passage is to see the way that things worked out. In other words, try to view it from the 20/20 hindsight of later Scripture. In bringing the message of your text into final focus, you must identify the role it plays in the flow of revelation. Once you understand how God used the text, then you can put it to work as God intended it and through it prepare, announce, or explain things to your audience. Ask yourself: Does the text anticipate, announce the arrival of, or explain the significance of, the Messiah and His work? Does it preview, confirm, or explain the significance of the everlasting covenant?

Sometimes the Old Testament writers had a compressed view of things. Despite seeing the main features of Jesus' Messianic career, the prophets did not always have sufficient depth perception from their remote vantage point to separate, for instance, His arrival into two distinct events. Events before, between, and after the two advents seemed to overlap in the distance and occur around the same time. So the Old Testament writings paint an indefinite picture of the last days.

In addition, the ancient Hebrew writers also made an enormous leap of faith to reach for the glories of the future. It is likely that in some instances, at least at first, they thought that the symbols God used to teach them supernatural truth were themselves the glories they represented. But God eventually led them to see that the symbolic people, places, and things of their time were only a foretaste of what He intended for them.

These symbols became *types*, which applied to ancient Israel and continue to apply to Messianic Israel in the last days when Messiah will complete His work of redemption and God will eventually fulfill all His promises. What may have been typical and symbolic to people in Old Testament times has become—and will become—a reality to us.

Typology is the word used to describe our human endeavor to see what may be a hidden or deeper meaning than a mere literal reading of Scripture might afford. It draws analogies by Israel's, Christ's, and the apostles' faith to trace this gradual realization of God's promises from shadowy beginnings to glorious conclusion. This trail allows you to track the truth developed in your text along the whole course of redemption and the parallel stream of revelation so that you can bring out its fullest sense.

For example, many Christians believe that the ancient Hebrew sanctuary and its services is pregnant with meaning that we may yet not fully understand. But as we come to a clearer understanding of the symbolic value behind and through these rituals, we can gain a more penetrating understanding of the plan of salvation. Based on this assumption, one author described the ancient tabernacle and its ministration as a passion play in the ancient Near Eastern desert.

Since the New Testament unfolds what we discover in the Old Testament, prophecy follows this typological trail from the Old to the New Testament as it works from promise to fulfillment. Such an approach, therefore, requires an understanding of typology for its proper interpretation. For instance, it may be possible that Zephaniah's prophecies about an impending judgment to come upon Judah just might offer us insight into the judgments that will accompany Jesus' second advent.

A warning: Typology can provide a very fruitful field for interpreters with vivid imaginations. As a result, farfetched interpretations can be read into the Old Testament—spiritual lessons that are not even logical or consistent with the literary context of the passage under consideration. There is a danger in seeing so much "hidden meaning" that we sound preposterous and strain the credulity of a thinking congregation. In these cases typology is not an exegetical tool to help unlock the theology of the biblical writers but instead a process of eisegesis, in which the interpreter reads all sorts of fanciful ideas into God's Word. This is poor theological analysis and even poorer homiletical practice. Biblical interpreters need controls to help corral the tendencies toward flights of fancy when it comes to typological interpretation.

Wick Broomall writes: "Some have so embellished the OT history with types that the simple history is all but ignored. At the other extreme are found those who refuse to see in OT history any typical meaning. The true view is found between these extremes" (*Baker's Dictionary of Theology*, p. 534).

Perhaps partly because of these extremes John E. Alsup states that "*typos*, in the main, is not part of a hermeneutical method as we normally think of it" (*Anchor Bible Dictionary*, vol. 6, p. 683).

Although scholars are not agreed on just when typological analysis began historically, it "had been employed earlier in Judaism and became in early Christianity, a basic key by which the Scriptures were understood" (E. Earle Ellis, *The Old Testament in Early Christianity*, p. 105). Some see it originating in Qumran, others look to the apostle Paul, but "The Exodus provided the model or 'type' by which the Old Testament prophets understood God's subsequent acts of redemption of Israel (Isa. 40-66) and of Gentiles" (*ibid.*, p. 105). Clearly, typological analysis has biblical roots, and "a number of writers" (including D. L. Baker, Walter Eichrodt, E. Earle Ellis, R. T. France, L. Goppelt, W. Kummel, and G. R. Osborne) "have argued a typological understanding of the Bible was fundamental for the New Testament apostles and prophets" (*ibid.*, p. 141).

During the early church the use of typology soon became a controversial matter. Irenaus of Lyons continued to view the Scriptures from a similar perspective, as did the patristic school of Antioch—but, typology had its rivals.

(1) The *Judaizers* subscribed to literal rather than typological interpretation of the Old Testament and not only failed to see the fulfillment of their shadowy Jewish rituals, but also insisted that the New Testament church continue to observe them.

(2) The heretic *Marcion* (c. 100-160 A.D.) and his followers (c. 140-650 A.D.), on the other hand, had no use for the Old Testament—at all. They believed that "the God proclaimed by the law and the prophets [the Old Testament] was not the Father of our Lord Jesus Christ" (Irenaus, *Against Heresies,* I, 27:1). So far as they were concerned, different Gods inspired the two testaments—and the God of the Old was inferior to the God of the New. Consequently, they saw no connection between the testaments and rejected the Old. Marcion even issued his own edition of the New Testament—purged of any Jewish ideas and influences.

(3) The church father, Origen (c. 185-254) and the Alexandrian school of thought saw great value in an allegorical approach to Scripture and so also embraced its cousin, typology. The Antiochene school, on the other hand, was more conservative in its approach. Although it did not forbid the practice of typological analysis, it "used typology as a hermeneutical aid in the service of the literal sense" (*ibid.*, p. 684).

The Alexandrian school of thought gained the day. "The development of typological thinking into the patristic period and beyond is marked by considerable excess" *(ibid.).* Frequently it seemed as though the sky was the limit when it came to digging out the hidden meanings of the biblical types. It all became quite ridiculous.

During the Reformation Martin Luther and John Calvin resurrected the emphasis of the Antiochene school of thought. They urged Christian leaders to "break with allegory and . . . return to the literal sense in combination with typology" *(ibid.).*

The debate over the usefulness and appropriateness of typology continues among biblical scholars, and the battle will likely continue for many more decades. The matter has definitely not been settled to everyone's satisfaction, but typological interpretation continues to be significant for current biblical studies. As the fundamental perspective of Jesus and the New Testament writers, typological interpretation is, has been, and always will be *indispensable* to our understanding of the relation between the testaments—to grasp the way the New Testament brings the Old Testament up-to-date for Messianic Israel and the world. Ellis points out, however, that "Competing alternatives to typological exegesis that were present in early Christianity and in the surrounding Judaism are again, under other names, bidding for acceptance in the church today . . . [including] . . . Allegorical interpretation . . . not currently advocated under that label . . . [and] . . . the revival of a Marcionite attitude toward the Old Testament, an attitude that has apparently arisen from a distortion of the law/gospel dialectic of traditional Lutheranism" *(The Old Testament in Early Christianity,* pp. 144, 145).

This handbook tries to take the middle-of-the-road approach to typological matters, which has historically been the fundamental position of the Seventh-day Adventist Church. We cannot repudiate typology because of our historical interest in and understanding of the ancient Hebrew sacrificial system, which we label "typical." On the other hand, Seventh-day Adventist biblical scholars by and large have taken a cautious stance toward the use of typological analysis lest excesses shift our focus away from the historical and literal meaning of God's Word.

Anyone undertaking typological analysis must adhere carefully to specific guidelines. By following such strictures the interpreter will be more likely able to avoid the silly results that can accompany an enthusiastic embracing of typology.

Wick Broomall feels that "a few simple distinctions will safeguard the student of typology. 1. One must distinguish between the type backed by NT authority and the type based on the speculation of the modern interpreter. . . . Sober exegesis must prevail over wild fancies. 2. One must distinguish between the type that definitely corroborates a doctrine and the type that has no relevance to a supposed doctrine. . . . 3. One must distinguish between what is essential in a type and what is peripheral in the same type. Some typologists have become so bogged down in details that absurdities and puerilities have swallowed up the essential truth. 4. One must distinguish between the type that is completely fulfilled in the antitype and the type, though partly fulfilled, that still retains its typical significance for the future world" *(Baker's Dictionary of Theology, p. 534).*

Some New Testament Methods of Using the Old Testament

The New Testament is both an explanation and extension of the Old. Jesus and the New Testament writers made the original meaning of the law and the prophets contemporary and compelling for their audience. They helped to keep the sacred writings a fresh, living witness to the present and the future. The Christian community still believes that God continues to make Himself, His will, and His purpose known through the Old and New testaments. Doesn't it make sense to follow the proven perspectives, principles, and procedures of Jesus and the inspired writers in our own expositions of Scripture? Here are some ways they led the truth out of God's Word.

Hillel's Rules of Interpretation—

According to later rabbinic tradition, the great first-century teacher Hillel taught and practiced seven rules of interpretation. "They represent," says E. Earle Ellis, "general hermeneutical principles of inference, analogy, and context that were probably in use before that time" *(The Old Testament in Early Christianity, p. 87).* David Daube argues, for example, that these maxims could be derived from rules of Hellenistic rhetoric already operative in first century B.C. Alexandria *("Rabbinic Methods of Interpretation and Hellenistic Rhetoric," HUCA 22 [1949], pp. 239-264).* Hillel died around 10 A.D., so the following rules were already in place as the New Testament era began:

1. *[Kal wa-homer = "*light and heavy"]

Hillel drew inferences from a minor premise to a major (and vice versa) and arrived at conclusions with greater logical necessity. As Siegfried Horn explains it, "any rule applicable to an item of inferior quality must be applied much more strictly to a superior item" ("Jewish Interpretation in the Apostolic Age," in *A Symposium on Biblical Hermeneutics,* Gordon M. Hyde, ed. [Washington, D.C.: Review and Herald Publishing Association, 1974], p. 20).

So, for example, the warning not to boil a kid in its mother's milk (Exodus 23:9) eventually led to a ban on the combined use of any meat and dairy products at the same meal *(Chullin* 115b).

This kind of argument is fairly common in the New Testament. Paul used it when he warned the Hebrew Christians of the greater penalties for profaning the New Testament realities than for violating their Old Testament shadows: "Anyone who has violated the [ceremonial] law of Moses dies without mercy 'on the testimony of two or three witnesses.' How much worse punishment do you think will be deserved by those who have spurned the Son of God, profaned the blood of the covenant by which they were sanctified, and outraged the Spirit of grace?" (Hebrews 10:28-29, NRSV).

2. [*Gezira Shawa* = "an equivalent expression"]

Hillel explained terms and texts by analogy—by comparing them with easily understood, equivalent expressions in other parts of the Scriptures. While this is a sound principle of interpretation, it can be taken to extremes. For example, the rabbis concluded that to "afflict your souls" on the Day of Atonement (Leviticus 16:29) required the people to fast, because Deuteronomy 8:3 uses the same word translated "afflict" in connection with hunger.

Jesus used this principle to defend Himself and His disciples against the charge of Sabbathbreaking, for plucking and eating grain on the Sabbath. Jesus says: "Have you not read what David did when he and his companions were hungry? He entered the house of God and took and ate the bread of the Presence, which it is not lawful for any but the priests to eat, and gave some to his companions?" Then he said to them, "The Son of Man is lord of the sabbath" (Luke 6:3-5, NRSV). In other words, Jesus appealed to David's similar royal status and circumstances to explain why He could also violate the law and yet remain blameless.

3. [*Binyan 'ab mi-katub 'ehad* = "developing a family from one passage"]

Hillel applied texts by analogy "to cases that were not expressly mentioned in the texts, although they dealt with situations of a similar nature" (Horn, *Jewish Interpretation,* p. 21). Transforming the teaching of a single verse into a general principle, he and his followers literally developed a family of applications from one passage. Working from this premise, however, the rabbis took the immunity from vengeance extended in Deuteronomy 19 to those who unintentionally kill, and erroneously applied it to any situation where accidental death occurs on a killer's private property (Maccoth II.3).

Jesus once told the scribes, "And the fact that the dead are raised Moses himself showed, in the story about the bush, where he speaks of the Lord as the God of Abraham, the God of Isaac, and the God of Jacob. Now he is God not of the dead, but of the living; for to him all of them are alive" (Luke 20:37, 38). He reasoned that if God continued to acknowledge His covenant relationship with Abraham after the patriarch's death, He must have intended to raise him from the dead. "From this one passage," says Ellis, "one may infer the resurrection of all the dead who have a similar covenantal relationship with God" (*The Old Testament in Early Christianity,* p. 132).

4. [*Binyan 'ab mi-shenei ketubim* = "developing a family from two passages"]

Hillel and his followers also made applications similar to those of the previous rule on the strength of analogy from two passages rather than one. Exodus 21, for example, says that a slaveowner must set a servant free if he destroys the servant's eye (verse 26), or a tooth (verse 27). The rabbis reasoned that since eyes and teeth are both parts of the body that cannot be replaced, the mandate to set a servant free extends to the destruction of any body part (Kiddushim 24a).

New Testament writers frequently deduced the general implications of related Old Testament texts. The apostle Paul, for instance, concluded from injunctions to let the ox eat as it works (Deuteronomy 25:4) and to give the temple priests a share of the sacrifices (Deuteronomy 18:1-18), that ministers in general have a right to a living from their labor for the gospel (1 Corinthians 9:9, 13).

5. [*Kalal weperet* = "general and particular"]

Hillel taught that Jewish expositors could either develop a specific application of a general term, or make a general application of a specific term. So, when the rabbis read Exodus 22:9: "In any case of disputed ownership involving ox, donkey, sheep, clothing, or any other loss of which one party claims, 'This is mine,' the case of both parties shall come before God; the one whom God condemns shall pay double to the other," they reasoned that the general term "any other loss" reduced the previous list of specific items to examples—and instructed the people to make double restitution of *any* borrowed thing they lost (Mekhilta on Exodus 22:9).

This type of thinking served as the rationale for Paul's conclusion that the particular commandments against adultery, killing, stealing, bearing false witness, "and any other commandment," are summed up in the one, general injunction to "love your neighbor as yourself" (Romans 13:9). Apparently, the general term "and any other commandment" reduces the previous list of specific orders to examples of the general rule.

6. *[Kayotse' bo mi-makom 'aher* = "something similar from another passage"]

Hillel also encouraged his students to compare similar passages as well as equivalent terms (rule two), so they could use one passage to interpret another. For example, "The law provided that the Jews had to keep the Passover 'at its appointed time' (Num. 9:2, RSV). Hillel was asked whether this meant that the Passover lamb had to be killed even on a Sabbath if the 14th of Nisan, the Passover eve, fell on a Sabbath day. He replied that the law expressly decreed that the 'daily' sacrifices had to be offered also on the Sabbath (Num. 28:10). Consequently, the expression 'at its appointed time' means, by analogy, that the Passover lamb had to be slain on the 14th of Nisan, whether that day fell on a Sabbath day or on any other day of the week" (Horn, *Jewish Interpretation,* p. 22).

New Testament authors, especially Paul, applied this principle in their writings. In the light of Jeremiah 31:31-34, he interpreted the Sinai covenant (Exodus 19:5f.) as provisional, temporary, and superseded by the new covenant (Hebrews 8:7-13).

7. *[Dabar halamed me-'inyano* = "explanation from the context"]

Hillel recommended that "a passage should not be interpreted as an isolated statement, but only in the light of its context" (Horn, *Jewish Interpretation,* p. 22). He evidently worried that Jewish expositors might take a passage out of context and misinterpret its true meaning. For example, "the statement of Ex. 16:29, 'Let no man go out of his place on the seventh day,' taken out of context could be interpreted to mean that no man was allowed to leave his home for any reason whatsoever on the Sabbath. However, a reading of the preceeding and following passages clearly shows that this prohibition applied to those gathering manna in the wilderness, saying that the Israelites should not go out on the Sabbath day to look for manna, which they would not find anyway on that day (Erubin 51a)" *(ibid.,* pp. 22, 23).

Jesus provides a practical demonstration of this principle during a verbal exchange with some Pharisees in Matthew 19. When they approached Him to test His views on marriage and appealed to the Mosaic practice of divorce, He referred them to the pre-Mosaic context for marriage in Genesis 1:27 and 2:24. Not only does this creation context predate the Mosaic custom, but, in Jesus' view, it also "takes priority over the later provisions for divorce and provides the regulative standard by which other biblical teachings on this subject are to be understood and applied" (E. Earle Ellis, *The Old Testament in Early Christianity,* p. 132).

Jewish methods of exposition, especially as outlined by Hillel, definitely influenced the way the Lord and His disciples interpreted the Old Testament. Although "the Jewish writings . . . reveal that the rabbis frequently employed farfetched interpretations and made the Scriptures say things they hardly implied" (Horn, *Jewish*

Interpretation, p. 25), it is also true that "Jesus employed, for the most part implicitly, Hillel's rules in his exposition of Scripture. Not all of Hillel's rules are clearly attested in the Gospels, and the rules of Jesus' usage appear less stylized than in the later rabbinic writings. But they are present, and they form a part of the hermeneutical framework for our Lord's biblical interpretation" (E. Earle Ellis, *The Old Testament in Early Christianity*, p. 132). The same holds true for the rest of the New Testament.

Quotations, Allusions, and Commentary

Anyone who spends time with the Bible eventually notices the influence that the Old Testament has on the New. Its themes, concepts, and expressions appear frequently throughout the New Testament, but not always word-for-word. As E. Earle Ellis points out: "Most often Old Testament wording appears in the New . . . in the form of citations or intentional allusions or reminiscences" *(Prophecy and Hermeneutic in Early Christianity*, vol. 18, p. 147).

This should not surprise us, because devout Jews during the first century were steeped in their Scriptures. Education, what little of it there was, relied heavily on memorization. A young man tutored under first-century rabbis would have committed to memory vast portions of the Torah. Synagogue services were also Bible-centric. Reading portions of the Hebrew Bible and expounding on their significance was what Sabbath worship at the synagogue was all about. (This was in contradistinction to the Temple services, which revolved around animal sacrifices and the ministration of their bodies, parts, and blood.)

Scholars suggest that New Testament references to the Old Testament are not always exact, because the writer (1) may have used a different translation from the popular Septuagint version, (2) couldn't recall every word from memory, or (3) even made a habit of wording things "Old Testament style," thus expressing himself with familiar but not always precise, scriptural language.

At first, Jesus' followers circulated the gospel by word of mouth, via the same high fidelity method their Lord adopted from the rabbis to transmit and preserve His Father's Word. One scholar proposes that "despite the many similarities among the Synoptic Gospels, each evangelist has produced a distinctive presentation of the common gospel message. The most obvious reason which accounts for their variety is that each writer had access to a somewhat different body of oral traditions regarding Jesus' words and works" (Bruce M. Metzger, *The New Testament: Its Background, Growth, and Content*, p. 89).

But the New Testament writers included words and events in their gospels not only because they figured in the life of Jesus, but also because they spoke to the vital needs in the life of the early church. Metzger goes on to say: "Moreover, since each evangelist had in mind a special reading public, he would naturally choose to emphasize those details which in his view were most suited to communicate the message of the Gospel to that reading public. The natural consequence is that each evangelist as a literary artist has drawn his own distinctive portrait of Jesus Christ" *(ibid.)*.

So the New Testament writers functioned both as authors and theologians, reinterpreting and developing the material in their books while not distorting the truth. (The concepts of truth and fact are not identical but may overlap.) They brought out the full vitality of the original meaning by aiming the truth at actual needs and by shaping it to meet contemporary challenges. All this was done, of course, under the Spirit's supervision.

The New Testament writers quoted the Hebrew Scripture for various reasons: to lean on its authority for arguing a case or for expressing its truths still in effect during their day, to illustrate a point of truth, or to obtain a desired effect by using familiar and sacred words regardless of their original usage and/or intent.

Explicit Quotations—These are the easiest to identify, because the New Testament writers frequently introduced these selections with a word formula that included verbs of "saying" or "writing," just like the ones we find in the Old Testament itself, the Dead Sea Scrolls, and the writings of Philo and later the rabbis. These formulas helped the New Testament writers identify the source of a citation for their audience, as in "This is he who was spoken of by the prophet Isaiah" (Matt. 3:3, NKJV).

These citations served to emphasize the divine authority of the New Testament to interpret the Old or to apply what the Old Testament teaches, as in "This was to fulfill what the Lord had declared through the prophet" (Matt. 2:15, REB).

Some formulas, such as "it is written," could even stamp approval on a writer's interpretation of Scripture, as Romans 9:33 does for Paul's preceding argument.

Allusions—Vague references to the Old Testament are more difficult to verify, since they consist of fragments from the original text. Just because the New Testament is strewn with clauses, phrases, and words from the Hebrew Bible does not necessarily mean that the New Testament writers intended for their readers to make an Old Testament connection in every case. We must determine where New Testament language "deliberately recalls key words, promises, and incidents found in the OT" (Walter C. Kaiser, Jr., *The Uses of the Old Testament in the New*, p. 2).

We do know, however, that the New Testament writers frequently combined quotations.

1. Sometimes two or more texts were combined into (a) a chain of passages (Rom. 15:9-12), (b) a commentary pattern (Rom. 9-11), or (c) a composite or merged reference (Rom. 3:10-18).

Just like Jewish scholars who employed techniques a and b (the so-called *haraz* method), the New Testament writers (for example, Paul in Rom. 10:18-21) approached the text from the standpoint of a, b, and c to develop themes from the Law, the Prophets, and the Writings by blending quotes and tying them together with certain catchwords like "stone" or "chosen" as in 1 Peter 2:6-9.

2. Other times they combined passages from the Old Testament that testified to Messiah Jesus.

At first some scholars argued for the existence of a single, exact source for these compound citations—a collection of Old Testament proof texts already combined according to methods a, b, and c, from which the New Testament writers drew direct citations.

In 1916 J. Rendall Harris, the primary spokesperson for this school, suggested that the early church used "testimonies"—groups of passages related to a single theme—to educate converts and opponents concerning the faith (for instance, Heb. 1). Similar combinations from Qumran (such as 4QTest) imply that these testimonies may have circulated among churches during the apostolic period.

In 1957 the New Testament scholar C. H. Dodd rejected Harris' hypothesis. Instead of randomly chosen proof texts, he considered these to be compounds—select quotations—picked by means of a popular method for Jewish exposition known as *midrash* to represent their larger Old Testament contexts. The particular text quoted and the modifications in it reflected the essence of that larger context according to the exegetical insights of that writer. So when Matthew cited only Isaiah 7:14 in Matthew 1:23, he probably had the entire section of Isaiah 6-9 in mind. Occasionally Scripture is the starting point for the pattern, working from quoted Scripture to the current event, which was the rabbinic norm of operation. But most New Testament *testimonia* from current event back to the quoted Scripture, as in "This took place to fulfill what by the Lord had been spoken" (Matt. 1:22).

Then in 1959 A. C. Sundberg, Jr., pointed out the different ways that various New Testament writers used the same biblical passage. For instance, "The prophecy in Zechariah 12:10 is quoted in John 19:37 as a prediction of the piercing of Jesus' side after His death. . . . Revelation 1:7 uses the same passage as a prediction of the second coming (cf. Matt. 24:30)" ("On Testimonies," *Novum Testamentus 3*, pp. 272, 273). Sundberg's findings successfully moved the thrust of biblical scholarship away from a quest for the original source to an analysis of the methods by which the New Testament writers selected and applied Old Testament texts. Research has revealed five broad systems: the literal-historical, the allegorical (for instance, Hagar and Ishmael in Gal. 4:21-31; see section on allegory in chapter 3), the typological (see chapter 10), the theological, and the *midrash*, or *pesher.*

3. In still other instances the New Testament writers used the midrashic method. *Midrash* comes from a Hebrew word meaning to search with care or to seek details and so came to refer to a commentary. It is both a noun and a verb. It designates "a way of expounding Scripture as well as the resulting exposition" (E. Earle Ellis, *Prophecy and Hermeneutic in Early Christianity*, vol. 18, p. 151).

By means of midrash, Judaistic interpreters updated God's Word from the past and applied it to their current situation. In a similar way New Testament writers modernized certain Old Testament passages in the light of recent developments in the history of salvation, namely, the person and work of Jesus Christ. Midrash made passages from the remote past come alive and be current and meaningful again for God's last-day people.

During the first century the chief forms of midrash included three specific types.

1. *Implicit midrash* was within the actual text itself. A shift from Hebrew to Greek as the language spoken by Jews outside Palestine and to Aramaic for Jews living in Palestine made it necessary to translate the Old Testament into these replacement languages. Influenced by current social and cultural factors, the various logic systems implicit in different languages, the varying semantic range of "equivalent" terms, etc., translators can produce in the receptor language a translation that is only an *interpretation* of the source text. Consequently, both the Greek Septuagint (commonly abbreviated as LXX) and the freely paraphrased Aramaic *targumim* (or targums) frequently deviated from the original Old Testament Hebrew source. (There is also the possibility that the LXX translators, for example, had yet another Hebrew source in front of them, one that varied from what we now know as the Masoretic Hebrew text.)

Two *basic varieties* of implicit midrash occur in the New Testament.

There are *double meanings*, which contain a play on the words involved. For instance, Matthew says that because Jesus lived in the town of Nazareth, thus fulfilling the prophecies that suggested the Messiah would be a Nazarene, someone who was either a pious Nazirite (see Judges 13:5-7 in the LXX), or a *netzer*, someone who was the branch of Isaiah 11:1 (see also Isa. 49:6; 60:21; 61:3).

There were also *interpretive alterations* made in the original text itself. These were made by inserting words or phrases that do not appear in the original passage, such as the way Paul slipped in the term *everyone* in Romans 10:11 (NIV) so as to make Isaiah 28:16 fit better into his argument. Or sometimes the New Testament writers substituted words or phrases, such as when Paul in Galatians 4:30 (NASB) wrote "son of the free woman" for the expression "my son Isaac" so as to better adapt Genesis 21:10 to his line of reasoning.

Two *complex varieties* of implicit midrash occur in the New Testament. Sometimes the authors altered composite passages or merged citations as in 1 Corinthians 2:9 and 2 Corinthians 6:16-18. Or they might describe a current or future event by using biblical phrases, which had the effect of linking this new event with an Old Testament passage. Such an approach put the spotlight on the event by using allusions either to illustrate it or explain it. (See, for instance, Luke 1:26-38, which alludes to Isa. 6:1-9:7.)

FIGURE 29

verse 27	Isa. 7:13
verse 31	Isa. 7:14; Gen. 16:11
verses 32, 35	Isa. 4:3; 9:6, 7; 62:12; 2 Sam. 7:12-16
verse 33	Dan. 7:14

2. *Explicit midrash* consisted of the text plus exposition, such as we commonly find in rabbinic commentaries. The form most often used in the New Testament is known as the *proem* midrash. The synagogue version of the proem midrash went something like this: (a) a text from the Pentateuch was assigned for use that Sabbath; (b) a second text—the *proem* or opening—served to begin the oral discourse; (c) the exposition or discourse contained additional Old Testament verses, parables, or other commentary, all of which were linked to the initial texts by repeated catchwords; and (d) a final text, which usually repeated or alluded to the text for the day.

Pesikta Rabbati 33:7, a festival midrash, reveals this basic pattern.

FIGURE 30

Original text	Isa. 51:12
Second text	Hosea 6:1
Exposition	Parable and application linked to the second text
Additional text	Lam. 1:13
Concluding text	Isa. 51:12

"The general outline of this pattern, with some variation, occurs rather frequently in the NT" (*ibid.*, p. 155). Here are some examples.

HEBREWS 10:5-39 (WITHOUT THE PENTATEUCHAL TEXT FOR THE DAY)

FIGURE 31

Verses 5-7	Initial text: Ps. 40:7-9
Verses 8-36	Exposition with additional quotes (verses 16ff., 30) *linked* to the initial text by the *catchwords* "sacrifice" (verses 8, 26); "offering" (verses 8, 10, 14, 18); "for sins" (verses 8, 17, 18, 26)
Verses 37-39	Final text and application alluding to the initial text with the verbs "to come" and "to please" (Isa. 26:20; Hab. 2:3ff.)

ROMANS 9:6-29 (WITH THE PENTATEUCHAL TEXT FOR THE DAY)
FIGURE 32

Verses 6-8	Theme and initial text: Gen. 21:12
Verse 9	A second, supplemental text: Gen. 18:10
Verses 10-28	Exposition containing additional quotes (verses 13, 15, 17, 25-28), and linked to the initial texts by the catchwords "call" and "son" (verses 12, 24ff., 27)
Verse 29	A final text alluding to the initial texts with the catchword "seed"

1 CORINTHIANS 1:18-31 (MERGES THE PROEM TEXT WITH THE INITIAL TEXT; FINAL TEXT DOES NOT ALLUDE TO THE INITIAL TEXT)
FIGURE 33

Verses 18-20	Theme and initial texts: Isa. 29:14; 19:11ff. cf. 33:18
Verses 20-30	Exposition linked to the initial and final texts by the catchwords "wise" (verses 26ff.), "wisdom" (verses 21ff., 30), "foolish" (verses 25, 27), "foolishness" (verses 21, 23), and "glory" (verse 29)
Verse 31	Final text (cf. Jer. 9:22ff.)

1 CORINTHIANS 2:6-16 (INITIAL TEXTS ARE A COMPOSITE AND HIGHLY INTERPRETED QUOTATION.)
FIGURE 34

Verses 6-9	Theme and initial texts: cf. Isa. 64:4; 65:16
Verses 10-15	Exposition linked to the initial and final texts by the catchwords "man" (verses 11, 14; cf. verse 13), "know" *[idein]* (verses 11ff.), and "know" *[ginosko]* (verses 11, 14)
Verse 16	Final text and application; Isa. 40:13

GALATIANS 4:21-5:1 (INSTEAD OF A COMPOSITE QUOTATION, THE INITIAL TEXT OF THE COMMENTARY IS ITSELF A SUMMARY OF A GENESIS PASSAGE; THIS IS A IMPLICIT MIDRASH INTRODUCING THE KEY WORD "FREEWOMAN.")
FIGURE 35

Verses 21ff.	Introduction and final text: cf. Gen. 21
Verses 23-29	Exposition with an additional quote, linked to the initial and final texts by the catchwords "freewoman" (verses 22, 23, 26, 30), "bondwoman" (verses 22, 23, 30, 31), and "son" (children) (verses 22, 25, 27, 28, 30, 31)
Verses 30ff.	Final text and application, referring to the initial text (cf. Gen. 21:10)

2 PETER 3:5-13 (THE PATTERN HERE IS SIMILAR TO, THOUGH LESS CLEAR THAN, THAT IN GAL. 4; THE INITIAL TEXT IS A SELECTIVE SUMMARY OF A SECTION OF SCRIPTURE.)

FIGURE 36

Verses 5ff.	Initial text [with eschatological application; see section "Pesher Midrash"]; cf. Gen. 1:6
Verses 7-12	Exposition (with an additional quote, verse 8), linked to the initial and final texts by the catchwords "heaven" (verses 5, 7, 10, 12), "earth" (verses 5, 7, 10), "destroy" (verses 6, 9; cf. verse 7), and "day" (verses 7, 8, 10, 12)
Verse 13	Final text and applications; cf. Isa. 65:17

These examples show how the New Testament writers used composite, interpreted quotes, and an interpretive selective summary of a larger section of Scripture for a midrash.

A more elaborate commentary pattern made use of short explicit midrashim as "texts."

1 CORINTHIANS 1:18-3:20 (CATCHWORDS LINK EACH SECTION [FOR EXAMPLE, "WISDOM"].)

FIGURE 37

1:18-31	Initial text
2:1-5	Exposition/application
2:6-16	Additional text
3:1-17	Exposition/application
3:18-20	Concluding texts

MATTHEW 21:33-44 (AN ANCIENT FORM OF SYNAGOGUE ADDRESS)

FIGURE 38

Verse 33	Initial text: Isa. 5:1ff.
Verses 34-41	Exposition by means of a parable, linked to the initial and final texts by a catchword, "stone" (verses 42, 44; cf. verse 35; Isa. 5:2) cf. "build" (verses 33, 42)
Verses 42-44	Concluding texts: Ps. 118:22ff.; Dan. 2:34ff., 44ff.

LUKE 10:25-37—FIGURE 39
(THIS FOLLOWS THE PATTERN CALLED *YELAMMEDANU RABBENU*—
"LET OUR RABBI TEACH US," EVEN THOUGH IT USUALLY INVOLVES
A SINGLE RABBI AND NOT A DIALOGUE. IT BEGINS BY POSING A QUESTION
OR A PROBLEM AND THEN PROCEEDS TO ANSWER IT. ROM.
9-11 MORE CLOSELY FOLLOWS THE RABBINIC MODEL THAN DOES
LUKE OR MOST OTHER GOSPEL MIDRASHIM.)

Verses 25-27	Dialogue including question and initial texts (Deut. 6:5; Lev. 19:18)
Verse 28	Second text (Lev. 18:5)
Verses 29-36	Exposition. A parable linked to the initial texts by the catchwords "neighbor" (verses 27, 29, 36) and "do" (verses 28, 37a, 37b)
Verse 37	Concluding allusion to the second text ("do")

MATTHEW 15:1-9 (A SIMILAR PATTERN IS FOLLOWED HERE.)
FIGURE 40

Verses 1-4	Dialogue including a question and initial texts: Ex. 20:12; 21:17
Verses 5, 6	Exposition/application linked to the text and dialogue by the catchwords "honor" (verses 4, 6, 8) and "tradition" (verses 3, 6); cf. "commandment," "commandments" (verses 3, 9)
Verses 7-9	Concluding text: Isa. 29:13

MATTHEW 19:3-8—FIGURE 41

Verses 3-5	Question answered by the initial texts: Gen. 1:27; 2:24
Verse 6	Exposition linked to the initial text by the catchwords "two" and "one flesh"
Verses 7, 8a	Additional quote (Deut. 24:1), posing a problem, with exposition
Verse 8b	Concluding allusion to the initial inserted text ("from the beginning")

Although they closely resemble each other, there are differences between New Testament and rabbinic exegesis. New Testament midrashim may not (a) have an initial text from the Pentateuch, (b) have a proem or second text, or (c) end with a final text that corresponds or alludes to the initial text. Generally, New Testament midrashim have an eschatological bent.

But as Ellis points out: "Nevertheless, in their general structure they have an affinity with the rabbinic usage that is unmistakable and too close to be coincidental" (*Prophecy and Hermeneutic in Early Christianity*, vol. 18, p. 159).

3. *Pesher midrash* is found in some of the writings from Qumran. The name comes

from the way some of the Dead Sea Scrolls start off the explanation of the passage by using the formula "the interpretation [*pesher*] is . . ." Qumran scholars followed the Old Testament example and introduced quotations or commentary following a quote with the above formula or its equivalent, "this is the interpretation."

Pesher adapts a text or texts to the current interpretation or commentary, links the texts and commentary with catchwords, and arranges the material into certain commentary patterns. Among these patterns are the single quote, a collection, or a consecutive commentary on an Old Testament book.

Usually there were two dimensions to the exegesis found in a *pesher*:

There was a clear *eschatological* dimension, because pesher exegesis presupposes that the Old Testament prophecies and promises had their fulfillment during the interpeter's own time and community. He and his people were the society that was to inaugurate the new covenant of the last days (see Jer. 31:31; 1QpHab 2:3-6). They were the final generation of God's people prior to Messiah's coming and the inbreaking of the kingdom of God (see CD 1:12; 1QpHab 2:7; 7:2).

The New Testament offers many examples of the pesher formula in an eschatological setting. "It is written that Abraham had two sons. . . . These women are two covenants" (Gal. 4:22-24). "Jesus Christ of Nazareth" "is the stone that was rejected" (Acts 4:10, 11). Other examples include Acts 2:4, 16-21; Romans 9:7-9; 10:6-8; Ephesians 4:31, 32; and 1 Corinthians 10:1-5.

There was also a *charismatic* dimension to pesher. Those who lived at Qumran got the idea for their pesher midrashim from the book of Daniel. Nebuchadnezzar's dream remained a secret until God gave Daniel the pesher, or solution, or interpretation (Dan. 2:25-28). So the people at Qumran considered pesher exegesis to be the work of inspired persons such as their founder, the so-called Teacher of Righteousness, and other wise teachers (supposedly the *maskilim* of Dan. 12:3). They understood the Old Testament prophecies to be secrets (cf. the New Testament "mystery"), which needed an interpretation (*pesher*), which only the *maskilim* could supply (see Dan. 2:19, 24; 9:2, 22; 1QpHab 7:1-8; 1 Cor. 15:51-58; Rev. 1:20).

Pesher exegesis also appears in Paul's writings, as he frequently used readings that disagreed with the most reliable Hebrew text or any of the popular biblical versions. Keep in mind that *pesher* quotation builds the interpretation or exposition right into the text itself. This means that differences from the established and most respected versions of the texts are most likely deliberate rather than accidental.

"Paul uses a selective interpretation. . . . Variations [from customary texts] should not be viewed as capricious, or arbitrary, or merely incidental. . . . This procedure has a more significant purpose: Paul utilzes *ad hoc* [that is, on the spot, for a specific purpose, case, or situation] renderings and the deliberate selection and rejection of known readings to draw out and express the true meaning of the OT passage as he understands it" *(ibid.*, pp. 174, 175).

In other words, Paul sorted through the available readings to find or develop renderings that did the best job of expressing his inspired view of the text. For example, the most reliable Hebrew wording of Deuteronomy 32:35 (the Masoretic text) says "To me belongs vengeance and retribution," whereas a targum says "Vengeance is before me, and I will repay." When Paul quotes this verse in Romans 12:19, he prefers the targumic reading and says "Vengeance is mine, I will repay" because it fit best into his argument.

Paul usually followed the LXX when it deviated from the Masoretic text, not just because he preferred it on a daily basis but because of the way its interpretive readings usually agreed with the sense that he had found in the passage (cf. "faith" in Rom. 1:17). Paul usually selected a particular version over another or even created a fresh rendition of an Old Testament verse to more accurately express its true meaning. This *pesher* technique really stands out the 20-some times that his version varies from both the LXX and the Masoretic text.

"In almost all of these, the variation seems to be a deliberate adaptation to the NT context; in some cases the alteration has a definite bearing on the interpretation of the passage. Changes in person and number are especially prevalent. The deviations from the catena [a closely linked series] in 2 Corinthians 6:14-18 are evidently designed for a messianic-age interpretation of the prophecies. God's command to Israel regarding Babylon ('her') is now applied to the relation of Christians to unbelievers ('them'); the promise given to Israel, 'personified' in Solomon ('to him . . . he') is fulfilled in the true Israel, the members of Christ's body ('to you . . . ye'). Similarly, 'the wise' in 1 Corinthians 3:20 and 'the first man Adam' in 1 Corinthians 15:45 show an elaboration or interpretation of the OT text to fit it to the NT context" *(ibid.,* p. 177).

Jesus amazed His contemporaries when He bypassed the traditions handed down from the elders of Israel and returned to the Old Testament to teach the people (Matt. 7:28, 29). He expected His apostles to continue this trend by passing on what He had taught them (Matt. 28:19, 20; 1 Cor. 11:2, 23; Gal. 1:12; 2 Peter 3:1, 2) under the Holy Spirit's direction (John 14:26; 15:26, 27). Apparently the apostles understood this (cf. Paul quoting Jesus in 1 Cor. 7:10 and then soloing from verse 12 and claiming in verse 40, "I think that I too have the Spirit of God)" and considered themselves authorized to make inspired alterations to the text for the sake of truth (2 Peter 1:12-21; cf. 3:1, 2, 15, 16).

"For Paul as for the rabbis, the 'letter' was sacred, but unlike some of the rabbis, Paul valued the letter not for itself alone, but for the meaning which it conveyed. His idea of quotation was not a worshiping of the letter or a parroting of the text; neither was it an eisegesis [a reading into] which imposed a foreign meaning upon the text. It was rather, in his eyes, a quotation-exposition, a midrash pesher, which drew from the text the meaning originally implanted there by the Holy Spirit and expressed that meaning in the most appropriate words and phrases known to him" *(ibid.,* pp. 179, 180).

And so in 1 Corinthians 15:54 Paul goes against both the LXX and the targum on Isaiah 25:8 and follows the Masoretic text, which says: "He will swallow up death in victory [the Hebrew word is *lanetsach*]." The word *lanetsach* is usually translated "forever" or "utterly" (see 2 Sam. 2:26; Job 36:7; Amos 1:11). Its root meaning is "leader" or "success," from which we derive the secondary meanings of excel, eminence, or overcome. So Paul was not off in left field when he translated *lanetsach* with the Greek *eis nikos* (in victory). Although it was customary to translate this passage "He will swallow up death forever," Paul quotes it *pesher* style: "Death is swallowed up in victory" (KJV) to set the stage for an outburst of praise for Christ and the eschatological triumph that God gives us in Him (verse 57).

"Midrash pesher . . . [should be] understood as an interpretive moulding of the text within an apocalyptic framework . . . [either] ad hoc or with reference to appropriate textual or targumic traditions" *(ibid.,* p. 181). Here are some guidelines for identifying and interpreting New Testament examples of *midrash.*

1. Is there a quotation associated with the verbs "saying" or "writing"?
2. Is there a sequence from current events back to Scripture or vice versa?
3. Is this a sample of implicit midrash? Look for double meanings and plays on words and words or phrases that the writer inserted into or substituted for those in the text. Check the context for his reasons for so doing.
4. Is this a sample of explicit midrash? Look for a pattern of text plus commentary with catchwords. Study the relationship of all its parts.
5. Is this a sample of pesher midrash? Do the words "the interpretation is" or "this is" introduce a citation or a commentary following a quotation? Is there an eschatological or apocalyptic setting? Compare the New Testament text with its Old Testament roots. Has the author adapted the text to suit his own purpose? Ad hoc? Selectively? Check the context for his reason(s) for so doing. How does this affect the meaning of the Old Testament passage?

The Analogy of Antecedent Scripture

The Bible did not come all at once. God spoke in a progressive way, continuously building on and clarifying what He had already said. That is how He unfolded the everlasting covenant—the promise-plan for all who believe in Messiah Jesus. Any place you pick in Scripture, the text depends on what came before it and represents the limits of revelation up to that point in history. If you want to know what the author meant at that time, limit your study to the passage and those texts that preceded it in time. The same is true when you investigate any theological connections between your passage and the rest of the Bible. The first touchstone for any text is its redemptive roots. Get in touch with the Scripture that came prior to it in time.

For example, Isaiah spoke initially to the people of the northern kingdom (c. 740 B.C.), yet his message continued to address the needs of God's people in the southern kingdom during the Assyrian campaigns, the Babylonian siege of Jerusalem, and the ensuing Exile. The ungodly Judeans saw the appropriateness of the earlier counsel to their own later situation. They recognized that the same fate awaited them as befell Israel unless they responded to Isaiah's message. The same, unchangeable God confronted them through Isaiah's words.

Here are some guidelines to understanding antecedent theology.

1. Suspect an antecedent connection if the study text has (1) key terms that frequently appear in previous biblical passages, such as seed, servant, inheritance; (2) a direct reference or an indirect allusion of an earlier redemptive event, such as the Exodus, the epiphany at Sinai; (3) a direct quotation from or mention of some previous text; and (4) a reference to the covenant, its promises, or its formulas.
2. Remember that antecedents help us see the connection between the passage and the collection of sacred writings at that time.
3. Your passage can help clarify what God has already said, building on scriptural antecedents and upgrading what they have to say.
4. Antecedent theology is merely the beginning, because it considers only past salvation history. To capture the fuller sense of your passage, you should also include in your study its future, when the promises that sparked and supported Israel's faith are finally fulfilled. Both the Old and New testaments testify how Israel tried to define God's promises with her limited vision. Unless you see the progress of fulfillment, it is impossible to get the whole picture of what God really promised in the first place. Remember, the Bible is God's revelation of Himself and His purposes. Stay in touch with the canonical context to unite your passage with the rest of the Bible into one divine working plan and single powerful message.

The Analogy of Faith

The Protestant Reformers opposed the Church of Rome's traditions. They saw no need to go beyond the Bible when it comes to what Christians should believe and how they should live. Scripture alone was sufficient for them, but Scripture still needed interpretation. So, in time, they developed a very simple rule: Scripture interprets Scripture. They championed the idea that the Bible is its own best expositor.

And so interpreters speak of the *sensus plenior* of the Bible. As the Reformers used earlier passages to understand later ones, they also found that later passages can help bring out the "fuller sense" *(sensus plenior)* of earlier ones. They discovered that when you study the words of Scripture in the light of what God revealed later on, a deeper meaning intended by God but not clearly intended by the human author comes to the surface.

"The prophetic word has a bearing on the historical context of the prophet, but its relevance goes far beyond what the prophet said and how it was fulfilled. . . . The prophetic oracles are God's Word to each new generation in its own historical context" (Willem VanGemeren, *Interpreting the Prophetic Word*, p. 75).

That is why we sometimes refer to the Bible as the living Word of God, which is another way of affirming that its ancient message can inform us even in our contemporary situations.

For instance, the prophet Hosea clearly referred to ancient Israel and the exodus when he said, "When Israel was a child, I loved him, and out of Egypt I called my son" (Hosea 11:1). In this passage a disappointed God looks back to better days before His "son" Israel turned out to be a rebellious adult and so broke God's great heart of love. Here God through Hosea referred to the Israelites' Exodus from Egypt while Moses led them. Matthew, however, reapplied this statement to the young child Jesus, who returned from Egypt to Nazareth upon the death of Herod (Matt. 2:15).

Was Matthew using some sort of midrash or pesher at this point? It appears that in the light of Israel's continuing failure to carry out God's plans, Matthew sees Jesus reliving key events from Israel's past. Jesus in Matthew thus became the model child that God wanted Israel to be. Just like Israel, the next significant event following Jesus' exodus from Egypt is a baptism experience (cf. Matt. 3:16, 17 and 1 Cor. 10:1, 2). But whereas the nation received the law at Mount Sinai, failed in the wilderness, and suffered death for its own sins, Jesus Himself (as the ideal son) emerged victorious from the wilderness, gave the "law" from the mountain, and died for the world's sins as He carried out the mission that God had assigned to Israel (cf. Dan. 9:24-27 with Hosea 6:1, 2).

This *sensus plenior* is not limited just to New Testament light for the Old Testament. Because God's revelation constantly developed throughout the Old Testament period, later passages in the Hebrew Scriptures may reveal the fuller sense of earlier passages. For instance, it appears that Daniel 9:24-27 brings out the fuller meaning hidden in Genesis 12:1-3.

"The message of Hosea, originally addressed to Israel in 750 B.C. also functioned as God's word to the godly in Judah during the Assyrian crises, the Babylonian siege, and the subsequent exile. They interpreted Hosea's oracles of judgment in the light of Samaria's fall and reread the prophecy as also given to Judah. The godly in Judah who heard the prophecy received it as God's word to them. They believed that what happened to Israel could also happen to them because God's nature and expectations are the same.

. . . In other words, God's revelation in space and time extended beyond the fall of the northern kingdom (722 B.C.) to the fall of Judah (586 B.C.)" *(ibid.,* pp. 80, 81).

Another classic example of the *sensus plenior* occurs in Paul's epistle to the Galatians. God made promises to Abraham and his "seed" (descendants) in Genesis 15. But Paul insisted that "the promises were spoken to Abraham and to his seed. He does not say, 'And to seeds,' as referring to many, but rather to one, 'And to your seed,' that is, Christ" (Gal. 3:16, NASB).

You would not normally come to such an interpretation by the usual methods of grammatical analysis of Genesis 15. Nevertheless, Paul reviewed the promises made to Abraham and his heirs in the light of redemptive history and apparently concluded that although Moses may have had Abraham's descendants in view, God had Jesus in mind all along.

The apostle, continuing to review things in progressive light, refined "seed" in terms of Christ and His accomplishments. And so Paul was able to say: "And if you belong to Christ, then you are Abraham's offspring, and heirs according to promise" (Gal. 3:29).

Here are a couple of guidelines to help you deal with the *sensus plenior* of Scripture.

---

1. Look for a later passage that interprets an earlier one in a more than literal way.
2. Look for a later passage that develops what the human author may have wanted to say, that is, he expands the literal sense of the earlier text.

CHAPTER 6

HOMILETICAL ANALYSIS

Exegesis is more than an expedition to *bring back* what the biblical author meant. Exegetes do not stop until they *bring out* the biblical author's meaning to *their* audience. They do this by presenting what they have learned in such a way that the present listeners are able to make sense of the text and reach a decision concerning its message.

Introduction

Sermons, lessons, and devotionals are actually *extended* arguments, longer compositions that combine argument with persuasion "to compel the listener or reader to adopt another position, another manner of thinking, or another solution to a problem" (Vincent E. Barry, *Practical Logic*, 2nd ed., p. 391). They generally include an analysis of a problem, a proposal of how to solve it, a refutation of opposing points of view, and a climactic or summary restatement of the proposed solution.

Every extended argument has a *thesis*—a main idea—and a *thesis proposition*—a statement of what the argument is all about. This is where speakers or writers introduce, identify, or admit to their subject and their attitude toward their subject.

FIGURE 42

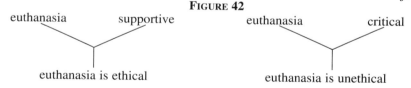

The most common extended argument states its thesis right away and adds supporting material as it draws to a conclusion. In other words, it moves from the general to the specific. As the argument proceeds to develop, it promotes its thesis from one feature to the next, which is the common thread that binds every element together from start to finish. A second and less frequent format begins with supporting materials and concludes with a thesis. In other words, it works from the specific to the general.

The most crucial feature of the extended argument is the series of main points it uses to support that thesis as it works toward a conclusion. These main points generally follow a pattern as the argument unfolds. When it comes to a sermon that unfolds the meaning of a scriptural passage, you have already separated the entire biblical text into paragraphs to trace how the biblical author carried out his overall purpose in this particular book of the Bible. So the theme sentences, which summarize what the scriptural author had to say in each paragraph, serve as the main points of any lesson or message from the text. You may restate individual paragraph themes to make them easier to remember (for example, rhyme or alliteration), but be careful not to water them down or to add out-of-context notions to them (see Walter C. Kaiser, Jr., *Toward an Exegetical Theology*, p. 152). If the theme is only implied in your biblical passage, you will have to propose one. If it consists of a series of independent sentences rather than a single explicit statement, you will have to weave them all into a single compound theme. Work first from the actual theme sentences in your structural diagram. Later on, you can refine your theme sentences into their final main point form.

This extended argument layout will allow you to structure what you have reaped from the previous five exegetical steps into a workable teaching, preaching, or devotional format like this:

I. *Introduction*
    A. Strong opening remark
    B. An illustration
    C. An explanation that leads into your . . .

II. *Theme* [of the Topic Sentence(s) or Theme Proposition(s)]
    A. Stated from brief background into pointed proposition
    B. A transitional sentence that leads into your . . .

III. *Exposition and application*

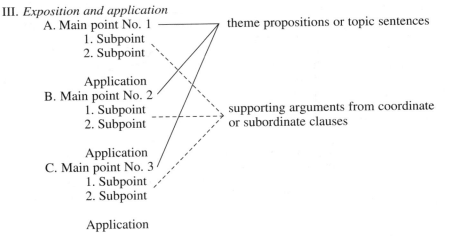

    A. Main point No. 1   theme propositions or topic sentences
        1. Subpoint
        2. Subpoint

        Application
    B. Main point No. 2
        1. Subpoint   supporting arguments from coordinate
        2. Subpoint   or subordinate clauses

        Application
    C. Main point No. 3
        1. Subpoint
        2. Subpoint

        Application

IV. *Conclusion and challenge*
    A. A summaraizing or climactic illustration
    B. Stirring appeal/call for a decision

What Is the Author's Topic of the Text?

The main topic of your message should reflect the Bible writer's principal, overall concern in the text—not your own. Avoid forcing the text (1) to answer one of your favorite questions or (2) to offer society a solution for some up-to-the-minute issue (see *ibid.*, p. 153). You can do this by reviewing what you have learned so far. Retrace the author's flow of thought as it weaves its way through *his* contemporary situation.

Consider, for instance, Paul's exhortation: "Let the women keep silent in the churches" (1 Cor. 14:34, NASB). Is he saying that females should never make a sound at church? Or be barred from teaching or preaching when the saints assemble? The rest of verse 34 would seem to agree with this: "for they are not permitted to speak, but let them subject themselves, just as the Law also says."

But on closer inspection of the context, we discover that Paul is already in the process of discouraging anything that would disturb the peace at church gatherings (verse 33). He especially singles out the selfish exercise of individual gifts at group expense. That is why Paul advises (1) the *wife* who wants her husband to explain something she does not understand (verse 35) along with (2) the tongues speaker without an interpreter (verse 28) and also (3) the prophet who sees that another person is ready to prophesy (verses 30-32) to "keep silent" during the services.

So Paul is not discriminating against women. He is simply relating the norm: "Let all things be done decently and in order" (verse 40, KJV) to the church at large. His solution of keeping silent is not a timeless norm but an inspired example of how to apply a divinely ordained norm to real-life situations—even in our day.

What Is the Author's Thrust in the Text?

The passage you have selected contains important words and key terms that stand out from the rest of the text by how often the author used them and where he placed them. These words often make or break the passage. If he linked a series of sentences or clauses together with "the same introductory word [such as] 'because,' 'therefore,' 'since . . . ,' etc. (*ibid.*, p. 155), then you should build your outline from the same point of view. For example, the word "therefore" suggests main points that discuss consequences of the author's topic. The word "because" indicates the reasons for it. In 1 Corinthians 14, Paul repeats the words "keep silent" three times (verses 28, 30, 34)—once for each of the three groups he singles out as examples from those contributing to the confusion at Corinth.

Sometimes the repetition is grammatical, such as the three hortatory subjunctives (that is, "let us . . .") such as we find in Hebrews 10:22-24, which are used to develop the topic "Appropriating the Combined Benefits of Christ's Earthly and Heavenly Ministries." Or perhaps the same word closes out each thought, as "forever" does in Psalm 111:3, 5, 8, 9, 10. At any event, always rely on the author's own stylistic, grammatical, or rhetorical emphasis, which shows up as a pattern in the text (see *ibid.*, p. 156).

Other Factors to Consider

Sermon presentation—You will want to give much prayer and thought to your *delivery* of the message. The purpose of exegesis is to communicate effectively, not just to investigate accurately biblical truth.

Communication experts tell us that when we attempt to express ourselves only 7 percent gets across with our words (vocabulary, outline, and illustrations), about 38 percent comes through our tone of voice (diction, resonance, and inflection), and nearly 55 percent drives home via body language (stance, gestures, and expression).

Ideally, the best preachers give brief sermons, use vivid illustrations, and are very enthusiastic. Ardor breathes life into a presentation by animating what is on the mind. Like currents of electricity, waves of enthusiasm carry our innermost feelings, convictions, and ideas to the surface and deliver them in an interesting way. Then the

Holy Spirit can bring them home to the hearts of those who hear and see us.

Preachers are not born fervent but become that way because they believe intensely in the subject; are confident to present it; have thoroughly researched their material, rehearsed their message, and know the opening well; are eager to address the congregation; and deeply want to help those who listen (Perry, *Biblical Preaching for Today's World*, p. 160).

You will also want to give thoughtful consideration to your audience. By learning all you can about the people you address, you will increase the effectiveness of your delivery, because then you can speak to them from the heart, not just the head. The heart of the preacher must reach the heart of the listener. Take the feelings you have become aware of into consideration. Your message should "infuse grace into the pain of the human situation" (Turner, *Proclaiming the Word*, p. 119). Always talk *to* the people, never at them. The better acquainted you are with the people in the pew, the more likely you will be to interact with them on an interpersonal level. Ask yourself the following questions:

- How well do I know the congregation?
- Am I acquainted with its needs?
- Am I on good terms with the group?
- What is its cultural, economic, and social background?
- Where is it emotionally? Spiritually?
- How well does the audience know the subject I want to present?
- Does the congregation include individuals or subgroups with an unorthodox slant?
- How can I reach its individuals or subgroups?
- Is there a real mixture, or do most of my listeners have pretty much the same knowledge and background?

Based on the profile generated by your analysis, identify your audience from among the main group types listed below. Target them and their specific needs, and develop your presentation according to the guidelines suggested for them. The following is adapted from Lloyd M. Perry, *Biblical Preaching for Today's World:*

1. Apathetic. Because their attitude toward you is one of indifference, your task is to get and maintain their attention. Here are some recommendations.

Physically—Eliminate distractions by making frequent eye contact; avoiding notes as much as possible; varying your rate of delivery and force of speech; pausing frequently; getting close to the people; arranging for effective lighting, platform decor, and seating; dealing with potential problems in advance; and aiming for a building temperature of 65 degrees, allowing body heat to bring the temperature up to an optimum 68 to 70 degrees.

Psychologically—Get off to a good start by avoiding both overelaborate preliminaries (get to the podium as soon as possible and steer clear of time pressures) and boring introductions. Instead, capture the listeners' attention early, and do not begin with sweeping abstract statements, rambling backgrounds, or apologies. Do not give away your main points. Arouse curiosity throughout your message by using questions, startling or paradoxical statements, graphic descriptions, and drama. Utilize familiar facts, quotations, and people with whom the audience can identify. Do not shy away from a novel approach, humor, and especially inside stories.

2. Believing. Because their attitude toward you is one of acceptance, your task is basically to motivate them to action. Here are some recommendations.

Instead of announcing what is in your head, describe things in terms of their own experiences. Avoid principles and generalizations, for they are too indefinite, unclear, and abstract. Take time to develop your conclusions. The congregation cannot make the leap to a life application merely from your opinions and principles. Give the listeners sufficient reasons to change.

Be specific. Describe each major item down to the finest details—those details that the average person tends to overlook. Use illustrations, visual aids, comparisons (between things that have a lot in common), similes (between things that are basically alike), and metaphors (which challenge the audience to imagine the connection).

Encourage audience participation without embarrassing anyone.

3. Hostile. Because their attitude toward you is unfriendly, your task is to establish your authority to deliver the message to them. Consider these recommendations:

Ride the coattails of some reputable authority whom they will accept. Quote others who belong to an organization for professionals, have educational or professional credentials, or have written a book on the subject. Stand on your own authority as a spokesperson for God. And prepare thoroughly so that you can show poise, confidence, sincerity, compassion, kindness, and enthusiasm.

4. Doubtful. Because their attitude toward you remains undecided, your task is to persuade them to form a definite opinion. Following are some suggestions:

Know how to develop theories, thus formulating a basis for action that the congregation can tell agrees with the facts. Draw logical conclusions from your theory. Talk factually. Avoid stating inferences as though they were facts; avoid giving the impression that you are a know-it-all; avoid references to variables as though they never change; and avoid oversimplification. Aim at making contact with the audience rather than merely giving them information.

Give the congregation time to evaluate what you have said. Then evaluate their responses, respect their new position, and continue from there.

Sermonic Methods

Every sermon should aim for clarity and coherence to present truth in a straightforward way that listeners can easily follow. That's why you should organize your message into distinct units (that is, more or less the paragraphs from your structural diagram) and unify them with a single theme so that your congregation will not lose track as you advance from one unit to the next.

Here are several proven methods for developing sermons.

Motivational Approaches—

Monroe's Motivational Sequence (adapted from Alan H. Monroe, *Principles and Types of Speech*, rev. ed.).

Text: Romans 6:1-14

Body:

I. Get their attention: Is sin invincible? (verse 1)

II. Show the need: Overcoming the sin problem (verses 2, 3)

III. Satisfy the need: how we overcome (verse 4)

IV. Help them visualize it: show how (verses 5-10)

V. Call them to action: Challenge them to overcome (verses 11-14)

R.C.H. Lenski Method (adapted from R.C.H. Lenski, *The Sermon: Its Homiletical Construction*).

144

As determined by responsible exegesis, the theme from the text is also the theme of the sermon, and the parts of the text are also the parts of the sermon.

Text: Psalm 24:3-6
Theme: Who may ascend God's holy hill? (verse 3)
Body:
I. Describe the person (verse 4)
II. Describe the reward (verse 5)
Conclusion: Seek Him! (verse 6)

The Perry Method (adapted from Lloyd M. Perry, *Biblical Preaching for Today's World*).

I. Determine the author's subject in the text: God
II. State your theme: God's love
III. Propose a timeless truth in terms of:
    A. *evaluation* or *judgment*—God's love is knowable.
    B. *obligation* or *duty*—You ought to know God's love.
    C. *emphasis* on *ability*—You can know God's love.
IV. Introduce the rest of the sermon by means of a transitional sentence to explain how, what, where, or why concerning the proposition. For example: How can you know God's love?

Repeat the proposition as you answer the question—"You can know God's love *by* reading the instructions in our text." "Instructions" here is the plural key word that lays out the major divisions for the rest of the sermon:

    a. The first instruction
    b. The second instruction
    c. The third instruction

V. Recap all previous points as you progress from one point to the next.
VI. Close with a stirring appeal, and call for a decision.

Inductive Storytelling—

Two principal factors lie behind the current storytelling trend: the media, both audio and visual, have conditioned the public to expect a story format—even from the pulpit; and an increasing number of people regard the Bible as literature, because of the insistence of liberal scholars that the Scriptures are actually a collection of stories handed down throughout the course of centuries to capture and memorialize God's heroic deeds.

The typical story line starts with a simple situation, the plot thickens and complicates things, and then everything is resolved in the end.

The Crum Method (adapted from Milton Crum, Jr., *Manual on Preaching*).
Text: Matthew 13:1-23
Body:
I. Present a symptomatic behavior, so that the listener can identify with it:
    Disappointing results of evangelism (verses 1-9)

II. Show the root cause, so that the listener will see where this behavior origi- nates: Deeper than eyes and ears (verses 10-15)

III. List the resulting consequences, so that the listener will notice the general out- come of those who behave this way: Dismal failure (verses 19-22)

IV. Introduce some gospel content so that the listener understands that a helpless situation does not have to be a hopeless one: But you are definite proof that evangelism works (verses 16-18)

V. Display the new results so that the listener will choose the gospel and the re- sultant beautiful ending it will give to his or her life in contrast with his or her current behavior and its ugly results: A delightful outcome—many times over (verse 23)

The Lowry Method (adapted from Eugene M. Lowry, *The Homiletical Plot*).
Text: Romans 3:10-26
Body:

I. Disturb the listener's status quo (verses 10, 11, 23)

II. Analyze the discrepancy (verses 12, 18)

III. Disclose the clue to resolution (verses 19, 20)

IV. Challenge him or her to a gospel experience (verses 21-24)

V. Anticipate the consequences (verses 25, 26)

Logical Approaches—

The inductive method (arguing from the parts to the whole—building a case)
Text: Romans 4:1-3, 18-22

I. Introduction—How does the Scripture say we get right with God? (verses 1-3)

II. Body

    A. Against all hope, believe (verse 18)

    B. Without weakening, face the facts (verse 19)

    C. Don't waver (verse 20)

III. Conclusion—That's why . . . (verses 21, 22)

The deductive method (arguing from the whole to its parts—working from the general to the specific)
Text: Hebrews 10:19-25

I. Introduction—On the basis of Christ's combined earthly and heavenly min- istries . . . (verses 19, 21)

II. Body

    A. "Let us draw near" . . . (verse 22)

    B. "Let us hold fast" . . . (verse 23)

    C. "Let us consider" . . . (verses 24, 25)

III. Conclusion—Challenge them to take up these activities now, because Christ will return soon—"And so much the more, as ye see the day approaching" (verse 25).

Sermon Types

Following is a summary of the three basic sermon types that preachers use:

Doctrinal—The aim of a doctrinal sermon is instruction, so it tends to emphasize truth rather than duty. Nevertheless, it always combines exposition with application to reflect what the church believes and understands the Scriptures to teach and what God expects. As a result, it builds up the listener, lays the groundwork for sound Christian living, and allows each church to maintain its unique identity for generations to come.

There are three basic types of doctrinal sermons: *apologetic*, which shows that the faith does not disagree with the body of authentic truth (for instance, scientific truth) that is acknowledged by the secular community; *polemic*, which sorts through the various opinions, theories, and differences within the local church, the denomination, and the larger Christian community; *declarative*, which reviews the historical development of a truth up to the present day to show that the pillars of truth have withstood the test of time and how other truths have developed and progressed in increasing light.

Life-Situation—The aim of a life-situation sermon is to confront the congregation with the gospel so that the members will be drawn to God, their only source of strength and safety, and to preach the message in such a way that they are able to put its truth into practice.

The most effective sermons come from a balanced ministry of preaching and pastoral care *(Proclaiming the Word*, p. 87). "We need more sermons which try to face the real problems of the people, help meet their difficulties, answer their questions, confirm their noblest faith, and interpret their experiences with sympathetic, wise understanding and cooperation" (Perry, *Biblical Preaching*, p. 104).

While the primary purpose of preaching is the conversion of souls, the sermon as a vehicle for this purpose arouses, convicts, persuades, and teaches. It cuts its way to the heart, fortifying listeners in the struggle to live, teaching them the science of salvation *(Proclaiming the Word*, p. 46).

Life-situation sermons are a species of prophetic preaching aimed at bringing Spirit-filled comfort. It is not to console the hearers in their problems but to encourage them out of them (see George A. F. Knight, *Servant Theology*). To accomplish this you must tie biblical content to specific life problems so that people can come to grips with them and subdue them. They can face their problems, recognize the true cause(s) for them, and adopt God's method of dealing with them.

The life-situation sermon should deal with problems discovered firsthand through pastoral visitation, hospital visitation, conversations with members, feedback, news and magazine articles, denominational literature, and questions raised by young people. Additional issues can be discovered from contacts at prayer meeting; after worship services; over the phone; and by observing church members during fellowships, formal meetings, special functions, and times of crisis.

Perry says that there are two principle strategies for life-situation preaching—investigation and modification.

The strategy of *investigation* is especially suited to a professional or university congregation.

    Text: 1 Kings 19:1-18
    Subject: Discouragement
    Theme: Overcoming discouragement
    Title: "God's Cure for Human Discouragement"
    I. Introduction
        A. Strong opening statement: "Our courage seems to rise and fall with the

way the news media present what is happening in the world around us."
B. An illustration to make the problem real to listeners
C. An explanation
    1. What is the problem? How would you define it?
    2. How widespread is the problem? Is it something new? Chronic? Local? Universal? Do we find examples of it in the Bible?
    3. What are some of the human solutions to this problem? Where did you read or hear about them? Who recommends them? What are their results? Do you recommend them?
II. Theme: How should a Christian deal with life's disappointments?
    Explanation: Show the connection between discouragement and disappointment (1 Kings 19:1-18). Transitional sentence: "By following the method that Elijah used in this passage, we also can overcome discouragement."
III. Exposition and Application
    A. By becoming physically prepared (verse 8)
    B. By becoming spiritually prepared (verse 13)
    C. By becoming involved in service (verse 15)
    D. By becoming supportive of others (verse 19)
IV. Conclusion and Challenge
    A. Summary and illustration
    B. Stimulating appeal: To help the congregation implement Elijah's four-point plan in their own lives. A summarizing illustration would lead to a "so therefore" appeal. Main point D could also be presented as the conclusion of the sermon via a climactic illustration.

The strategy of *modification* is especially suited to a traditional, biblically oriented congregation.
    Text: 1 Kings 19:1-18
    Subject: Discouragement
    Theme: Overcoming discouragement
    Title: "God's Cure for Human Discouragement"
I. Introduction
    A. Strong opening statement: "Our courage seems to rise and fall with the way the news media present what is happening around us."
    B. Illustration (a gripping story of a news-related suicide)
    C. Explanation: Discouragement is a fact of life, but many people have overcome it. (Show the relationship between discouragement and several Bible characters, especially Elijah in 1 Kings 19:1-18.)
II. Theme: Christ makes it possible to overcome even the worst disappointments. Transitional sentence: "If you have the Spirit Christ alone can give, then you can appreciate the ways Elijah overcame discouragement in 1 Kings 19."
III. Exposition and Application
    A. Get in physical shape (verse 8)
    B. Get in spiritual shape (verse 13)
    C. Get involved for God (verse 15)
    D. Get behind others in the work (verse 19)
IV. Conclusion and Challenge
    A. Summarizing illustration

B. Stirring appeal to implement Elijah's four-point plan in their own lives.

Evangelistic—The evangelistic sermon aims to "bring the people to a decision" by presenting truth in such a manner that people can "weigh the evidence and decide" (*Proclaiming the Word*, pp. 44, 45). This kind of sermon, then, should "arouse, convict and persuade" *(ibid.*, p. 45). Perry reminds us that the evangelistic message should appeal to ordinary people and therefore be down to earth, not abstract; have human interest; and be simple, personal, direct, and urgent (see *Biblical Preaching*, p. 158).

Evangelistic preaching requires a "healthy balance between the heart and head" (*Proclaiming the Word*, p. 45) so as to avoid the extremes of dry intellectualism and excessive emotionalism. "The preaching of the Word should appeal to the intellect and impart knowledge, but it comprises more than this. The heart of the minister must reach the heart of the hearers" *(ibid.)*.

So the evangelistic sermon should be biblical, informative, and heartfelt. It should be delivered in a simple, clear, and specific way that communicates a real burden on the part of God and the speaker for souls. Instead of rushing through a lengthy presentation, it is best to repeat "a few essential points . . . often so they can be readily remembered . . . and avoid overwhelming people with a 'mass of matter' which in reality buries the truth" *(ibid.)*.

Furthermore, the evangelistic sermon should be a balanced presentation of truth, blending an offer of Christ's love with a call for obedience to God. So climax the message with a stirring appeal to a sense of duty (Christ, the Lord), or a sense of morality (Christ, the Example), or a sense of romance (Christ, the Hero), or even a sense of shame over moral failure (Christ, the Answer). But never end with an appeal to fear.

In an unpublished M.A. thesis from 1950 (*An Examination of the Philosophy of Persuasion in Pulpit Oratory Advocated by Ellen G. White*) Leslie Hardinge concludes: "Ellen White was opposed to persuasive techniques that appealed to the impelling motives of fear, excitement, sensationalism, exhibitionism, sentimentality and witticisms" (cited in *Proclaiming the Word*, p. 93). Her sermonic method was simple and overt: "First . . . melt and subdue the soul by presenting our Lord Jesus Christ as the sin-pardoning Saviour. . . . [Next] keep before the people the cross of Calvary. Show what caused the death of Christ—the transgression of the law. Let not sin be cloaked or treated as a matter of little consequence. It is to be presented as guilt against the Son of God. Then point the people to Christ, telling them that immortality comes only through receiving Him as their personal Saviour" (*Testimonies*, vol. 6, pp. 53, 54).

Sermon Styles

Sermons usually differ from each other more as a matter of style rather than subject. While there are numerous subclassifications, they generally fall into three main groups: topical, textual, and expository.

Topical—These sermons are probably the most common. Sometimes speakers develop their outlines from a biblical topic rather than a text. Instead of working from a particular passage, they weave independent texts into a single, systematic presentation, supporting each division in the outline with a Scripture reference.

Reference works such as Bible handbooks, Bible dictionaries, exhaustive concordances, *Nave's Topical Bible*, the *Topical Chain Study Bible*, the *Topical Reference Bible*, or the Thompson Chain Reference Bible are all excellent sources of headings and supporting verses of Scripture for this style of sermon. Simply locate the subject you wish to discuss and select from the references under it the verses that best express the topic. Since these entries are usually very broad, you should select your references according to some organizing principle that narrows down the selection to a manageable few, while it unites the ones you choose into a single, coherent message.

For example, the *Topical Chain Study Bible* lists 23 references under the topic "Patience." You could study patience as a divine attribute, as a reason for human tribute to God, or even as a human need. For example:

I. Humans need patience in affliction (Heb. 12:11).
II. Humans need patience in listening (Prov. 18:13).
III. Humans need patience in prayer (Psalm 40:1).

The doctrinal sermon is ideally suited to this style of preaching, because the doctrine itself (for example, righteousness by faith) serves as the topic of the message. The topical approach is especially helpful when you preach a series of messages on a broad subject such as the early and latter rains of the Holy Spirit:

"The *Parable* of the Early and Latter Rains"
"The *Promise* of the Early and Latter Rains"
"The *Purpose* of the Early Rain"
"The *Pouring Out* of the Early Rain"
"The *Potential* of the Early Rain"
"The *Preparation* for the Latter Rain"
"The *Pouring Out* of the Latter Rain"
"The *Power* of the Latter Rain"

Topical sermons come in a variety of categories.

Category: *Analysis* (a thorough, well-rounded investigation of a topic)
Text: Various
Subject: Evangelists
Title: "Fishers of Men"
I. Introduction
    A. Strong opening statement: "Fishing is a lot of fun—when the fish are biting."
    B. An illustration: Story of unsuccessful fishing trip
    C. An explanation: Fishermen catch fish. But all I ever catch when I go fishing is a cold.
II. Theme
    A. Stated: "Some people bring in souls by the bushel. They throw out the nets and close in whole mobs of people for Christ. But the rest of us angle for souls one at a time."
    B. Transitional sentence: "The Scriptures have a lot to say about these fishers of men. If we analyze some of these passages, the light will help us recognize an evangelist when we see one and understand what God has called him or her to do."
III. Exposition and Application
    A. Their ordination (1 Tim. 4:14)
    B. Their authority (Acts 18:24-27; 1 Tim. 1:3; 5:20, 21; Titus 1:5)

    C. Their work (1 Thess. 3:1, 2)

IV. Conclusion and Challenge

    A. Climactic illustration about a successful evangelistic campaign

    B. Stirring appeal to prepare a pond stocked with souls gathered through one-on-one evangelism by the members for the evangelist

Category: *Biography* (compiled from different texts)

Text: Various

Subject: Barnabas

Title: "What an Encouragement!"

I. Introduction

    A. Strong opening statement: "Some people are a pleasure to be around. They always leave you feeling better than they find you."

    B. An illustration: Revolutionary War story of Mrs. Richard Shubrick, who made a habit of shielding people from danger, even at the risk of her own life.

    C. An explanation: Mrs. Shubrick had plenty of courage, and she shared it.

II. Theme

    A. Stated: "She represents that rare breed of people who are not afraid to get between other people and their problems—even if it might cost her her life."

    B. Transitional sentence: "She reminds me of another person who was always full of compassion for those who were down, needy, unpopular, or forgotten. His name said it all: Barnabas, 'Son of Encouragement.' His life story is an object lesson of courage that always makes a difference."

III. Exposition and Application

    A. Sold his land for the church family (Acts 4:36)

    B. Stuck out his neck for a former enemy (Acts 9:26, 27)

    C. Supported the underdog (Acts 11:25, 26; 15:36-40)

IV. Conclusion and Challenge

    A. Climactic illustration that shows the positive influence of courage.

    B. Stirring appeal to imitate Barnabas and become an encourager.

Category: *Catchwords* (the same word appears in each of the biblical texts used)

Text: Various

Subject: Life in Christ

Title: "The Only Thing That Matters"

I. Introduction

    A. Strong opening statement: "Every Christian ought to know what really matters in the Christian life."

    B. An illustration: Story of woman frantic to land her husband's plane after he had a heart attack. But she kept switching channels, so no one got through with instructions, and she crashed.

    C. An explanation: Most of us are like that woman. We are so used to polling our friends, depending on others, or looking here, there, and everywhere for answers that God cannot get through to us. So we live by opinions instead of facts.

II. Theme

    A. Stated: "The Bible is the best place to find out what really matters in the Christian life."

    B. Transitional sentence: "Paul has three inspired opinions to share with us. All we have to do is look for the catchwords 'neither circumcision nor uncircumcision counts for anything' to find what really matters in Christ."

III. Exposition and Application

    A. What really matters in Christ is keeping God's commandments (1 Cor. 7:19)

    B. What really matters in Christ is faith that works by love (Gal. 5:6)

    C. What really matters in Christ is a new creation (Gal. 6:15, 16)

IV. Conclusion and Challenge

    A. Summarizing illustration that shows that these different opinions are actually three ways of saying the same thing.

    B. Stirring appeal to set aside our pet opinions and to focus on what the Bible says really matters in the Christian life.

Category: *Comparisons* (similarity or contrast)
Text: Various
Subject: The believer's witness
Title: "An Effective Testimony" (adapted from James Braga, *How to Prepare Bible Messages*, rev. ed.)

I. Introduction

    A. Strong opening statement: [Where is it?]

    B. An illustration: Story of child who is surprised what salt can do once it comes out of the salt shaker and gets sprinkled on her food.

    C. An explanation: God scatters His people like salt sprinkled from a shaker, . . . and you would be surprised what they can do once they come out of the church building and get sprinkled on their neighbors.

II. Theme

    A. Stated: "The believer's testimony should be like salt."

    B. Transitional sentence: "If we compare the believer's testimony to the things that salt can do, we can learn what constitutes an effective witness for Jesus Christ in this desperate world."

III. Exposition and Application

    A. Like salt, the believer's testimony should season (Col. 4:6).

    B. Like salt, the believer's testimony should purify (1 Thess. 4:4).

    C. Like salt, the believer's testimony should not lose its savor (Matt. 5:13).

IV. Conclusion and Challenge

    A. Climactic illustration that shows the results of an effective testimony.

    B. Stirring appeal: Like salt, the believer's testimony should create thirst (1 Peter 2:12).

Category: *Definitions* (a word study using several independent texts)
Text: Various
Subject: Forgiveness
Title: "Letting Your Brother Off the Hook!"

I. Introduction

    A. Strong opening statement: "Many people say they are willing to for-

give, but few are actually prepared to forget."
    B. An illustration
    C. An explanation

II. Theme
    A. Stated: "The Bible is the best place to find out what God means by for-giveness."
    B. Transitional sentence: "Let's develop a biblical meaning of forgiveness by defining an assortment of words that the Bible uses for forgiveness from a variety of Bible contexts."

III. Exposition and Application
    A. In Psalm 78:38 the word is *kaphar* (to cover) and brings out the idea that the injured party starts the process of forgiveness.
    B. In Psalm 25:18 the word is *nasa* (to lift up or away) and brings out the idea that the injured party offers to bear the weight of guilt or punishment himself or herself.
    C. In Luke 7:43 the word is *charizomai* (to cancel a debt), and it brings out the idea that the injured party deals with sin at his or her own expense.
    D. In Psalm 103:3 the word is *shalach* (to send away) and brings out the idea that the injured party sets the other party free by dropping the charges.

IV. Conclusion and Challenge
    A. Summarizing illustration that draws on the parable of the unforgiving servant in Matthew 18:21-35, climaxing with a challenge to forgive others from the heart—as God does—or else (verse 35).
    B. Stirring appeal to follow Christ's example.

Category: *Examples* (compiled from independent texts to prove a point)
Text: Various
Subject: Discovering sin
Title: "Cover-up or Catch-up?"

I. Introduction
    A. Strong opening statement: "There are some really incredible stories of how dogs sniff out drugs and other illegal things that criminals try to hide from the authorities."
    B. An illustration: One of them is the story of Dox, a dog assigned to a homicide squad in Italy. Dox eventually uncovered evidence that a suspect who had previously maintained his innocence had actually murdered a man while robbing a jewelry store. The suspect finally confessed.
    C. An explanation: People do not like getting caught with their hand in the cookie jar. We will do anything to keep from admitting our guilt—denying everything—until overwhelming evidence leaves us no other choice except finally to confess.

II. Theme
    A. Stated: "If you can count on one thing in this life, it is this: Your sins will always catch up with you."
    B. Transitional sentence: "The Bible offers many examples of how our sin always catches up when we try to cover up."

III. Exposition and Application
    A. David tried to hide adultery and murder (2 Samuel 11)

B. Achan tried to bury the forbidden spoil (Joshua 7)
C. Ananias and Sapphira tried to deceive the Holy Spirit (Acts 5)
IV. Conclusion and Challenge
    A. Summarizing illustration that climaxes on the note that only Christ can cover up sin—and then only after we have brought it out into the open.
    B. Stirring appeal to let nothing come between us and a forgiving God. It is better to confess sin and gain Christ than to hide our sin and lose everything.

Textual—These sermons are perhaps nearly as common as topical sermons. Sometimes speakers derive their sermons from a brief passage of Scripture—usually three verses or less. The theme and points of the textual sermon are the topic sentences/theme propositions and their supporting arguments discovered through analysis of the text.

Consider, for example, Micah 6:6-8:

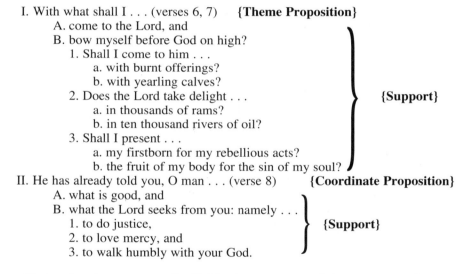

I. With what shall I . . . (verses 6, 7)   **{Theme Proposition}**
    A. come to the Lord, and
    B. bow myself before God on high?
        1. Shall I come to him . . .
           a. with burnt offerings?
           b. with yearling calves?
        2. Does the Lord take delight . . .
           a. in thousands of rams?   **{Support}**
           b. in ten thousand rivers of oil?
        3. Shall I present . . .
           a. my firstborn for my rebellious acts?
           b. the fruit of my body for the sin of my soul?
II. He has already told you, O man . . . (verse 8)   **{Coordinate Proposition}**
    A. what is good, and
    B. what the Lord seeks from you: namely . . .
        1. to do justice,   **{Support}**
        2. to love mercy, and
        3. to walk humbly with your God.

Notice that the text naturally divides into two parts. It is easy to see the connection between them. The first part (verses 6, 7) is a question that attempts to answer itself three times. The second part (verse 8) offers a single answer in three parts. But the textual approach, focusing on a short passage, runs the risk of taking things out of context. So in preparing a textual sermon be exceptionally careful to *let the writer or speaker speak for himself.*

• He determines the subject and the thrust of the text.
• He determines the order of your points by the sequence of his ideas in the text.
• He determines how the text relates to what comes before and after it.

In this particular case, verses 6-8 must be proclaimed in the light of verses 1-5, or else the sermon will miss the point that God is trying to make through His prophet Micah.

At first glance, verses 6 through 8 appear to be a simple question-and-answer session between God and His people. Actually, verses 6 and 7 are the people's extended response to the covenant lawsuit that God brought against them in verses 1 through 5. Verse 8 is Micah's crisp counterresponse to the people's defense.

Summoned to appear in court and to answer charges of covenant breaking, the people used ignorance for a defense: "What is Micah talking about? Maybe we have sinned in the past, but we always repaired any damage to our relationship with God by offering sacrifices at the Temple." Even then they were willing to do whatever it took to make things right with Him. So they asked if they should offer *different* sacrifices? *more* sacrifices? *more valuable* sacrifices? "How dare Micah accuse us of covenant breaking?" They confidently entered a plea of innocent and rested their case.

But they could not fool the jury. The ancient mountains and hills had been around long enough to see for themselves what God put up with through the years with Israel. In the first place, nobody accused Israel of failing to repair the damage with sacrifices at the Temple—only of breaking the covenant in the first place so that it needed repair. In the second place, their record of prompt sacrifices again and again only underscored them as repeat offenders.

The fact is, said Micah, God had explained long ago precisely what He expected from His covenant people: "To obey is better than sacrifice" (1 Sam. 15:22). So while the people looked outside of themselves for answers, Micah redirected their attention to the real source of the problem—inside. "When we come before God . . . it is not so much what is in our hands but what is in our hearts that finds expression in our conduct that is important" (Ralph L. Smith, *The Word Biblical Commentary*, vol. 32, p. 51). Outward ceremony is not enough. A healthy covenant relationship also requires godly character and upright conduct.

There are several ways to preach this text, but they all relate verses 6 through 8 to the *covenant lawsuit context*, which begins at verse 1. To compare the various formats more easily, we will use condensed outlines. Let us begin with some that use all three verses.

Category: *Comparisons* (similarity or contrast)
Text: Micah 6:6-8
Subject: Covenant living
Title: "To Obey Is Better Than Sacrifice"
Transition: God is displeased with people who keep on sinning the same sins, even though they promptly take steps to make things right with Him. What, therefore, will it take to make God happy?
    I. Human questions: sacrifice? (verses 6, 7)
    II. Divine answer: obedience! (verse 8)
This message aims at the answer given in verse 8, and it uses an exposition of verses 6 and 7 to get there. After explaining the circumstances in verses 1 through 5, it discusses Israel's questions for the sole purpose of featuring God's answer. By contrasting her off-base inquiry with God's on-target reply, it accentuates the superiority of obedience to sacrifice in the covenant life.

The following presentation, on the other hand, is more concerned with *why* the people have missed God's point throughout the years, rather than *what* they missed. It explores Israel's questions to expose the perspective that fails to see things from God's point of view, as explained from verse 8.

155

Category: *Comparisons* (similarity or contrast)
Text: Micah 6:6-8
Subject: Covenant living
Title: "Double Vision"
Transition: Some people are very good at keeping up the formal side of religion, but they have missed the point about covenant living. Although they have no trouble pointing to the law's requirements for sacrifice, they are also mysteriously blind to its demand for right living. Why can't they see what God really expects from them?
   I. Religious people are concerned about (verses 6, 7)
      A. which sacrifice?
      B. how much sacrifice?
      C. what to sacrifice?
 II. But God is concerned that (verse 8)
      A. we act fairly,
      B. we think compassionately, and
      C. we walk properly.
We can also craft a textual sermon from verse 8 alone.

Category: *Verbatim* (points quoted verbatim from the text)
Text: Micah 6:8
Subject: Covenant living
Title: "What Does God Want From Me?"
Transition: Some people really do not know what God expects from them, so they keep asking questions. A frustrated Israel once asked God what He wanted from her. He reminded her of what He had already said.
   I. To do justice (verse 8b)
  II. To love mercy (verse 8c)
 III. To walk humbly with God (verse 8d)
This format allows more time for developing the concepts in verse 8 than the previous outlines, because it focuses entirely on God's answer. But as an even shorter portion of text, it requires a very thorough discussion of the context, beginning with verse 1 either as an introduction to or a touchstone during the sermon.

The following message is very similar but with one major difference—it views the points in verse 8 more as desirable characteristics of true covenant people, the product of, rather than the indispensable divine requirements for, covenant living.

Category: *Deductive* (conclusions drawn from the text)
Text: Micah 6:8
Subject: Covenant living
Title: "What Is God Looking For?"
Transition: Our covenant God has covenant goals. That means the covenant is more than a perpetual relationship. It has long- and short-term objectives. If we are God's covenant people, then whatever He aims to see happen is supposed to involve us. Just what is God looking for, anyway?
   I. Considerate actions (verse 8b)
  II. Compassionate motives (verse 8c)
 III. Cooperative relationship (verse 8d)
Textual sermons also lend themselves to preaching a series of messages. Unlike

a topical series, however, in which the unifying topic is determined independently of the text, a textual series derives the topics for its messages from the various texts but unites them with a common theme. So, for example, here is a series of textual messages from a youth revival entitled "God Loves Me No Matter What!"

"God Loves Me No Matter What It Costs" (1 John 4:9)

"God Loves Me No Matter What It Takes" (John 15:13-15)

"God Loves Me No Matter What He Does" (Heb. 12:6)

"God Loves Me No Matter What Happens" (Rom. 8:38, 39)

"God Loves Me No Matter What I Do" (Heb. 4:15, 16)

Notice that while each message has a common theme ("God Loves Me No Matter What!"), the topics are different, because each text determines its own topic.

That is the beauty of textual preaching. Nothing appears either contrived or coerced, because it allows the author of each text to present his points in the same order and manner that he originally developed them. The biblical flavor of such messages is unmistakable. So are the results.

Expository—These sermons are frequently the more difficult to prepare. Speakers occasionally derive their sermons from a broad passage of Scripture, at times even chapters in length. Too long for a running commentary (a biblical homily) or a detailed study (an exegetical lecture) of every verse, the passage lends itself best to a message that summarizes rather than spells out the text. The speaker and the audience stay in touch with the biblical text throughout the expository sermon, though not as frequently as with a textual address, because unlike the latter, the expository text is the primary not the precise, framework for the presentation.

An expository sermon has a different format. A textual message usually develops a single topic sentence or theme proposition, and the dependent clauses and phrases supporting it serve as the main points of the message. But an expository sermon proceeds from either one paragraph or section to the next, using either topic sentences/theme propositions or section headings for main points, supported by selected subpoints consisting of dependent clauses, phrases, or paragraphs.

So, for example, although Luke 15 consists of three distinct parables, each of which could serve as a sermon text in its own right, the chapter actually divides into two main parts:

I. A complaint by the scribes and Pharisees that "this man [Jesus] welcomes sinners and eats with them" (verses 1, 2, NIV)

II. A three-part response by Jesus to this charge (verses 3-32)

    A. The parable of the lost sheep (verses 3-7)

    B. The parable of the lost coin (verses 8-10)

    C. The parable of the lost son (verses 11-32)

It is unclear from the text whether Jesus responded with all three parables on the same occasion to a single accusation or during a period of time to relentless criticism from His pious rivals, but one thing is certain: None of the parables is a complete response in itself. Taken together, however, as Luke presents them, they offer a well-rounded illustration of God's relentless love for people, including those whom society often despises, rejects, and writes off as a loss.

The sheep, coin, and prodigal all appear at first to be lost causes, but as Jesus points out, in each case the patient owner is rewarded with rediscovery, reunion, and restoration of what had been lost. Taken in the light of Ezekiel 34, where the prophet warned that selfish shepherds would scatter God's sheep and make it necessary for

God Himself to find them and put them in the care of a shepherd from the line of David, these parables both justified Jesus' mission to seek and to save the lost (that is, the outcasts) and indicted those who criticized Jesus for seeking sheep that they did not consider worth rounding up.

An expository outline of the passage would take into account this larger context as it relates the three parables to the outcasts of this world. Whether they have wandered from their Creator or strayed from their Redeemer, Christ longs to reclaim all from the world and restore them to His flock. Proceeding from one paragraph to the next, you could develop a message that is

1. directed to the church, in view of the Great Commission:

   I. Search for strays (the ninety-nine)
  II. Sweep the house (the nine pieces of silver)
III. Support returnees (the brethren)

2. directed to the lost, in view of the gospel:

   I. You are missed. (the lost sheep)
  II. You are precious. (the lost coin)
III. You are welcome. (the lost brother)

3. directed to either the church or the lost, in view of God's promises:

   I. I rescue (the seeking shepherd)
  II. I illuminate (the shining lamp)
III. I wait (the sleepless father)

Expository sermons are the ideal way to preach through a Bible book, because instead of focusing on every verse, you can hit the highlights of the text. For example, the "Everything You Wanted to Know About Righteousness—But Were Afraid to Ask" series from the book of Romans.

"God's Righteousness" (1:16, 17)
"Human Unrighteousness" (1:18-3:20)
"Imputed Righteousness: Justification" (3:21-5:21)
"Imparted Righteousness: Sanctification" (6:1-8:15)
"Implemented Righteousness: Glorification" (8:16-39)
"God's Program of Righteousness" (9:1-11:32)
"Man's Practice of Righteousness" (12:1-15:13)

Or consider "The Lonesome Dove" series from the book of Jonah (the Hebrew word "Jonah" means dove).

"The Lonesome Dove Turns Into an Albatross" (chapter 1)
"The Lonesome Dove Flies Like a Homing Pigeon" (chapter 2)
"The Lonesome Dove Soars Like an Eagle" (chapter 3)
"The Lonesome Dove Cooks His Goose" (chapter 4)

Expository sermons come in all shapes and sizes. Since they depend on the same structural signals as other sermon styles, categories often resemble those of topical and textual sermons. Here are some ways you might generate expository outlines.

Category: *Applications* (the inspired author's inspired application of a divinely supported norm in a historical situation)

Text: Jonah 1

Subject: God's sovereignty

Title: "Who's in Charge?"

I. Introduction
   A. An illustration
   B. An explanation

II. Theme
   A. Stated: By the way God operated in the lives of Bible people, Scripture offers a lot of evidence that God is in charge.
   B. Transitional sentence: "When we see the amazing ways that a rebellious Jonah applied this teaching to his own life, maybe that will clear things up for us about who is in charge of our own lives."

III. Exposition and Application
   A. God designates those who work for Him (verse 1): Jonah learned that God chooses His workers (cf. John 15:16).
   B. God directs those who work for Him (verse 2): Jonah learned that God decides where His workers will go.
   C. God disciplines those who work for Him (verse 4): Jonah learned that God is able to reach His workers wherever they are.

IV. Conclusion and Challenge
   A. Summarizing illustration
   B. Stirring appeal to follow Christ

Category: *Collections* (lists or groups of related people, places, or things in the text)

Text: Colossians 3:18-4:1

Subject: The healthy Christian family

Title: "The Apple of God's Eye"

I. Introduction
   A. Strong opening statement: "It does not take a genius to see that the American family is in big trouble."
   B. An illustration
   C. An explanation

II. Theme
   A. Stated: "America needs healthy families, and the only way to have a healthy family is for all its members to live their lives for God."
   B. Transitional sentence: "The apostle Paul saw the need for healthy families, and he wrote to several churches about it, because as Vince Lombardi used to bring out the best in his teams by keeping each player in touch with the basics for his position, so Paul hoped to bring out the best in Christian homes by spelling out the fundamentals for each of the family members. That is how Lombardi built his championship teams; that is how we can build healthy families."

III. Exposition and Application
   A. Wives should give their husbands a special place of authority in their lives (3:18).
   B. Husbands should give their wives a special place of affection in their

lives (3:19).

C. Children should give their parents a special place of honor in their lives (3:20).

D. Fathers should give their children a special place of understanding in their lives (3:21).

E. People should give the families they serve a special place of respect in their lives (3:22).

IV. Conclusion and Challenge

    A. Summarizing illustration

    B. Stirring appeal to follow Christ, based on three charges:

        1. Do everything as if it is to the Lord (3:23).

        2. The Lord will reward your faithfulness (3:24).

        3. If you do not live for the Lord, serious consequences follow (3:25; 4:1).

Category: *Comparisons* (either similarity or contrast)
Text: Hebrews 12:1-17
Subject: The Christian life
Title: "Running the Race!"

I. Introduction

    A. Strong opening statement

    B. An illustration

    C. An explanation

II. Theme

    A. Stated: "The Christian life is like running a race."

    B. Transitional sentence: "Let's spend some time picking up pointers on how to run the course with Christ from the apostle Paul. According to 2 Timothy 4:7, he crossed the finish line just before the Romans executed him, and in Hebrews 12 he shares his dynamite training tips and winning strategy."

III. Exposition and Application

    A. Just as former champions in the stands bring out the best in runners, heroes of faith who line the track should bring out the best in the Christian race (verse 1).

    B. Just as runners streamline themselves to run a race, so the Christian should shed anything that slows down the Christian race (verse 1).

    C. Just as runners keep the finish line in view, so the Christian should always keep Christ's goal in mind (verse 2).

IV. Conclusion and Challenge

    A. Summarizing illustration that climaxes on the note that just as successful runners follow their coach's instructions, so Christians should always follow their Lord's directions (12:5-11).

    B. Stirring appeal to follow Christ all the way into the kingdom.

Category: *Steps/parts/stages/phases* (inductively develops the whole from its parts)
Text: John 9
Subject: The way God works
Title: "There's a Method to His Madness!"

I. Introduction
    A. Strong opening statement
    B. An illustration
    C. An explanation
II. Theme
    A. Stated: "Most Christians can describe the things that God does, but few can explain why or how. When people ask us to make the plan of salvation plain for them, we should have more than just a story to tell. They expect more than simply a list of facts. So instead of merely memorizing what God does, we must also learn the method behind His actions."
    B. Transitional sentence: "If we take the time to analyze one step at a time a story of Jesus in action—such as the time He healed a man born blind (John 9)—maybe we can put things together and understand the way God works."
III. Exposition and Application
    A. When Jesus explains why He healed the man, we see that *God works by grace* (verses 1-6).
    B. When John describes how Jesus healed the man, we see that *God works, providing we obey* (verses 7-15).
    C. When the text tells us what happened after the healing, we see that *God works to build relationships with people* (verses 16-41).
IV. Conclusion and Challenge
    A. Summarizing illustration
    B. Stirring appeal to follow Christ

Choosing a Title

Speakers should always aim for positive first impressions. They can create a favorable atmosphere for presentations from the pulpit. One of the ways a speaker can obtain a good first impression is through the careful crafting of the sermon title. Whether it appears in advance or on the day the sermon is presented, the title should appeal to the congregation and attract interest for the message.

Sermon titles should be terse—brief enough for the audience to memorize—and interesting—catchy enough for them to want to memorize it. Speakers should, however, tailor the title to the situation, the congregation, and the material they intend to present. That is why the title appears so near the beginning of the process of sermon preparation. It often sets the mood and indicates the direction speakers will take as they go about the process of putting their sermons together.

Composing an Introduction

The introduction is the part of the sermon that makes clear why your congregation should listen to what you have to discuss. When you present it in a friendly, tactful, and direct way, the introduction should help you gain your audience's interest and confidence in less than 15 percent of your speaking time. So you will need to be brief, clear, and to the point. The introduction is not an end in itself but merely points to what is on the way (Lloyd M. Perry, *Biblical Preaching for Today's World*, pp. 57, 58).

Begin with a strong opening statement. From the theme select a word or an idea that you need to define, make clear, or develop for your audience. This will become the heart of your opening statement and the subject for the rest of your introduction. Expand on this word or idea in terms of the listeners' daily lives. Start by meeting your congregation members where they are.

Illustrate the point you made in the opening statement. Work toward your theme. Use only one illustration for each idea. Present material that is relevant, in good taste, and builds credibility right away. Gather your illustrations from a variety of sources and rotate them frequently.

Explain what you've said. Move away from your real-life illustration toward the biblical setting of your message. By including features unique to the particular type of sermon you have chosen to deliver, the explanation can actually prepare the listeners to follow along in their Bibles as the message unfolds.

The Theme of Your Message

The body of the sermon develops the subject of the introduction. Before you can proceed to list the points of the message, however, you must have a clear theme to weave your points into a coherent presentation. The author of your passage will supply this for you. Your text, depending on its length and structure, has at least one theme proposition or topic sentence. This should be the main thought of your presentation. If there is more than one, determine what they all have in common, put it into a single summary statement, and make this the guiding principle throughout your sermon. Every sermon should have one theme.

Do not repeat word-for-word the theme proposition or topic sentence. Update the language and abbreviate what it has to say. The theme is the main thought of the sermon—distilled to its essence. It is clear, concise, and precise. The ideal theme is both pointed and comprehensive so as to penetrate the listeners' defenses at the beginning of the sermon and remain relevant throughout its presentation—otherwise the message may fail to generate and hold the listeners' attention.

The Transitional Sentence

Once you have stated the theme, it is time to make the transition from your proposition to the body of the sermon. You accomplish this with a transitional sentence that summarizes what you have already said in such a way that you can logically proceed with your presentation. The transitional sentence does this either (1) by asking a question concerning the theme on behalf of the congregation or (2) by proposing something from the theme for the audience so that you can spend the rest of the sermon answering or developing it for them.

The Theology of the Text

In addition to the analogies of antecedent Scripture and faith, Hebrews 10:19-25 offers an additional insight into developing Christ-centered messages. A message is incomplete and unbalanced unless it focuses on the complete person of Jesus Christ and the full scope of His work. In this passage the audience is challenged three times (in verses 22-24) to live the fullest possible Christian life, *looking back* to Calvary's cross and Lamb (verses 19, 20), *looking up* to the heavenly sanctuary and our High Priest (verse 21), and *looking ahead* to the second coming of the King of kings (verse 25). This is the only way to take all that Christ is and does into account for balanced and full applications of the text.

The Main Points of Your Message

It is time to refine your theme sentences into your main point. Keeping in mind the author's topic and his thrust in the text, carefully reword what he says (whether implied or expressed) so that it appeals to your audience. The author is addressing a problem that goes deeper than the in-text behaviors, so update the text from the situation in the Bible writer's days to what is happening where you are. Strip away any socio-historical-cultural differences so that your listeners can identify with the people in the text. By using contemporary language, make your points as here-and-now as possible.

As Kaiser points out: "It is of utmost importance that the restated theme not be a purely descriptive narration of past events. This will immediately prejudice moderns against giving it their attention. Thus it is imperative that each main point . . . avoid the *past tense* of the verb and use of *proper names* (with the understandable exception of God's names)" (Walter C. Kaiser, Jr., *Toward an Exegetical Theology*, p. 152). The people must see each point as fresh advice and not as something over and done with or out-of-date. Do everything you can to draw their attention away from *then* so that they will not miss what is happening *now*!

Consider this outline from 1 Corinthians 14:20-40:

I. Tongues-speakers without an interpreter should keep silent (verses 27, 28).

II. Prophets should keep silent when others are ready to prophesy (verses 30-32).

III. Women should keep silent in church (verses 34, 35).

This kind of preaching clings to the letter of the text but misses its spirit. Although the past tense is gone, it still brings the past into the present. Paul had a reason for insisting that these groups be silent in the church. They were disturbing the peace at church gatherings. Detaching these three injunctions from that purpose disconnects them from the norm that Paul applied to the Corinthian situation, namely, "Let all things be done decently and in order" (verse 40, KJV). As a result, these injunctions might be taken out of context. The apostle had a higher purpose in mind than simply attacking these groups. Perseverance must replace confusion at the public meetings in Corinth.

So instead of focusing on the Corinthian details, the exegete should ask, What is Paul *really* saying here? Is he merely out to silence egotistical tongues-speakers, long-winded prophets, and talkative women?

What is actually happening in the passage is that Paul tests the Corinthians by the principle: "Let all things be done decently and in order." And he uncovers what all three groups have in common: selfishness. The indiscriminate use of individual gifts, frustration of others who want to exercise their gifts, and satisfaction of personal curiosity while someone else exercises his or her gift are the unmistakable symptoms of a deeper spiritual problem at Corinth—pride. First Corinthians 14 deals with the desperate need to set self aside for the good of the church.

A more appropriate outline would propose that a church test itself by this principle so that its members will

I. Unselfishly exercise their spiritual gifts (verses 20-28)

II. Yield unselfishly to others who want to exercise their gifts (verses 29-32)

III. Behave unselfishly while others exercise their spiritual gifts (verses 34, 35).

Keep the main points in the same order as the paragraphs in your structural diagram. This is the easiest format for your congregation to follow. Make sure that the main points are parallel and uniform. Stay with the same form all the way through, using all single words, or all phrases, or all sentences. Match nouns with nouns, verbs with verbs, and prepositions with prepositions. Do not mix commands with questions. Once you have come up with a set of main points, keep refining them through meditation and prayer.

The Subpoints of Your Message

While the main points only summarize what you want to share with the congregation, the subpoints allow you to pause and develop each one of these former theme sentences by going into detail with their dependent clauses, phrases, words, and related sentences from the structural diagram.

Open up each of these points with a solid exposition of the text, describing the way things actually were at the time of writing. Be sure to make the transition to your own local situation before going on to the next point. Segue smoothly from the socio-historical-cultural particulars in the text to the specifics in your own situation. Make each point as here-and-now as possible.

It is best to limit the number of subdivisions; otherwise your outline might become too complicated for the congregation to follow. Let the structural diagram—your copy of the original writer's blueprint for the book—decide which sentences, clauses, or phrases get the nod over others for subpoints. To make it easier for the listeners to trace the author's flow of thought in the text, keep your subpoints in parallel and do not get out of order from the biblical text. After all, that is the sequence that the congregational members have at their disposal in their Bibles.

Since the subpoints get pretty detailed, help the audience stay with you by frequently announcing where you are in the text. Let the Scriptures shape and develop your message. Drive the text home as you challenge, encourage, or advise the people from God's Word. They may not memorize your outline or catch everything you say, but if they associate the message with its particular text, they can return home, reread it for themselves, and relive the encounter they have had with God. So develop your main points as the original writer did—with a list of reasons where he used a series of because clauses, or a chain of conditions where he had a string of if clauses. All this, of course, should be supported by reliable background information.

Framing a Conclusion

The introduction and theme get across the idea that the subject applies to people in general, but starting with the exposition/application segment of your message, begin driving home the personal nature of the subject until the members of the congregation suspect that it applies to them. Then bring the people to the goal that God intended for the text. You do this with a strong conclusion so that each listener can identify with the subject on an individual basis.

Wrap up your message with a stirring challenge. End with a powerful, Christ-centered appeal, calling for a decision. Aim your message from the start at the heart and mind, not just at the emotions and the brain. Bring the fullest intention of the text to the listeners so that they cannot escape its supernatural impact. God expects a certain response from both the speaker and the listeners. God's people should apply what the speaker has explained.

Since this is the part of the sermon that summarizes what you have said and challenges the congregation to live by it, use the opportunity to make on-the-spot adjustments to the specific audience. Anticipate objections. Do not allow the enemy time to build a wall of resistance in people's hearts.

• Start the conclusion with a summarizing illustration that dramatically recaptures the essence of your message in a practical way.

• Follow it with a stirring appeal that calls for a response on the listener's part. You can recap your main points, restate the most important applications, or list specific ways that the members of the congregation can personally apply these truths to their lives. You may even want to challenge the audience to accept your main points through an appeal to kindness, vision, interest, duty, love, or reason—but never through fear.

In Summary

We can summarize the material presented in this chapter on a sermonic worksheet. These work sheets will help you organize your ideas into a coherent, workable format.

Homiletical Analysis of *[Scripture passage]*

A. What is the biblical author's topic of the text?
B. What is the biblical author's thrust in the text?
C. What type of congregation will I face?
D. What type, style, and category of sermon should I use?
E. What is the title of my message?
F. What is my strong opening statement?
G. How can I illustrate this?
H. What can I explain to move into the biblical setting?
I. What is the theme of my message?
J. What is my transitional sentence?
K. What are the main points, subpoints, and applications of my message?
L. What is my summarizing or climactic illustration?
M. How will I make an appeal and call for a decision?

The closing section of this chapter will provide some examples of how to use these work sheets.

Homiletical Analysis of . . .

Psalm 22
A. What is the author's topic of this text? A desperate time in David's life.
B. What is the author's thrust in the text? David vowed to celebrate his deliverance even before God rescued him.
C. What type of audience will I face? Believing.
D. What type, style, and category of sermon should I use? Doctrinal (declarative). Topical. Typological (tracing the fullest sense of the text from the Old Testament shadows to the New Testament realities).
E. What is the title of my message? "I Just Can't Wait!"
F. What is my strong opening statement? "Suffering puts such a drain on the human spirit that even the toughest people can break under the strain unless they see some purpose to it."
G. How can I illustrate this? No one wants to bid for an old violin at an auction until its owner produces beautiful music from it. Then everyone wants it.
H. What can I explain to move into the biblical setting? We are all very much

like that old violin. What becomes of us depends on who plays us. For some people, suffering is only a tragedy without purpose or meaning, but when God plays our life, even suffering has a different sound to it.

Psalm 22 records the most painful episode of David's life. Words of agony and confusion drive home his anguish and despair nonstop for 21 verses. Then suddenly David's moans and groans give way to shouts of gratitude and praise. David still needs rescue from his desperate situation, but the tune of the last 10 verses has a different sound to it.

I. What is the theme of my message? David sings a new song in an old trial because he remembers that he is in God's hands.

J. What is my transitional sentence? "Psalm 22 is music to the Christian's ears. Familiarize yourself with its lyrics and get to know the tune, because Jesus used it for His theme song at the Last Supper, and we are going to sing it ourselves at our wedding feast in the kingdom."

K. What are the main points, subpoints, and applications of my message?

1. David invited national Israel to share a meal with him at the Lord's table in literal Jerusalem, because God would deliver its king from death (verses 22-31).

2. Jesus invited Messianic Israel to share supper with Him at His table in spiritual Jerusalem, because God would deliver its king from death (Luke 14:16-24).

3. The Father invites His Israel to share a banquet with Him at His table in the heavenly Jerusalem, because He has delivered its King and will also deliver His bride from death (Luke 14:15; Rev. 19:9).

L. What is my summarizing or climactic illustration? Story of Tiny Tim, the pitiful Dickens' character from *A Christmas Carol*, who looked beyond his suffering to Christmas dinner with his family.

M. How will I make an appeal and call for a decision? David could not wait to celebrate. Jesus could not either. If you cannot wait to celebrate with Jesus and David, let Jesus bring you up-to-date on the song David sang, with a taste of the future now at the Lord's Supper in order to get you ready for the day you will sing it at the marriage supper in the kingdom of God.

1 John 1:5-2:2

A. What is the author's topic of this text? Walking in the light.

B. What is the author's thrust in the text? What it takes to walk in the light.

C. What type of audience will I face? Believing.

D. What type, style, and category of sermon should I use? Life situation (modification). Expository. Explanations.

E. What is the title of my message? "You Have to Be Real!"

F. What is my strong opening statement? "Every organization has three main groups: two at the extremes (right and left) and the largest group of all—the so-called people in the middle."

G. How can I illustrate this? An incident with two parties at the extremes (a victim and an attacker) and those who stood by and let it happen.

H. What can I explain to move into the biblical setting? While conservatives and liberals take turns attacking each other, dominating and upsetting the church, the silent majority retreats to the legendary neutral zone—the so-called gray area between. Why do they camp there? To escape the cross fire, lick their wounds, and avoid feelings of guilt brought on by the finger-pointing extremists. Uneasy and unsettled by what they have heard, they are not taking any chances. But their strategy will not work. Gray is just a whiter shade of black, and hiding there is just a futile attempt to mix darkness with light (1:5, 6). The light shows everything—good and bad (1:7). David knew that when he said: "The darkness and the light are both alike to" God (Ps. 139:12, KJV). The psalmist understood that the darkness will not hide us and our failures from God any more than it did Adam and Eve.

I. What is the theme of my message? God wants us to come out of the darkness and into the light. The good news is that Christians do not have to be perfect to walk in the light—only honest about their sins (1:7).

J. What is my transitional sentence? "The apostle John explains the three ways that we must deal with our sins (verses 8-10) in order to stay out of the darkness and walk in the light."

K. What are the main points, subpoints, and applications of my message?

> 1. Be honest with yourself (verse 8).
> 2. Be honest with God (verse 9).
> 3. Be honest with each other (verse 10).

L. What is my summarizing or climactic illustration? I once sneaked into the kitchen in the dark to steal some cookies. I felt safe until Mom flipped on the lights and caught me with my hand in the cookie jar.

M. How will I make an appeal and call for a decision? Point them to the exciting promise in 2:2.

Genesis 14

A. What is the author's topic of this text? Stewardship.

B. What is the author's thrust in the text? Abraham's willingness to be a blessing with what God gave him.

C. What type of audience will I face? Believing.

D. What type, style, and category of sermon should I use? Life situation. Expository. Heroes.

E. What is the title of my message? "God's Little Dividend"

F. What is my strong opening statement? "Too many people conduct their lives cafeteria style—self-service only."

G. How can I illustrate this? A little boy and his younger sister were riding a rocking horse together. After a while the boy said, "If one of us would get off this thing, there would be more room for me."

H. What can I explain to move into the biblical setting? When Abraham returned from Egypt, he was a very wealthy man, and he cut his nephew Lot in for a share of his financial success. Not only did he give Lot a piece of the action, but when the time came to separate, Abraham allowed his nephew to take the best part of his real estate and as much of it as he wanted.

I. What is the theme of my message? Abraham never forgot that God blessed him to be a blessing (Gen. 12:1-3). Every time God invested in him, Abraham remembered that he was supposed to be God's little dividend to the world.

J. What is my transitional sentence? "One day word came to Abraham that his nephew had been captured, along with many others and a great deal of property from the cities of Sodom and Gomorrah. Would Abraham care? Hadn't he given Lot too much already? Should the people and goods from Sodom and Gomorrah matter to him? Matter enough to risk his life and the rest of his property? Enough to put his own reputation and future on the line? What does God expect us to do with our time, money, and talent? Well, we can learn a lot by studying a real hero of the faith in action and under fire. He sets a terrific triple example for us to follow."

K. What are the main points, subpoints, and applications of my message?
1. A true steward shares God's gifts (verses 13-16).
2. A true steward supports God's ministers (verses 17-20).
3. A true steward sings God's praises (verses 21-24).

L. What is my summarizing or climactic illustration? The story of Arland D. Williams, Jr., a bank examiner with the Federal Reserve system in Atlanta, who unselfishly refused to grab the rescue line lowered to him from a helicopter the night he died after an airplane crash in the frigid Potomac River. President Reagan told Williams' children, "You can live with tremendous pride in your father."

M. How will I make an appeal and call for a decision? "You do not have to be a hero to become one! All you have to do is give what you have—like Arland Williams and Abraham. God could always count on him to give 100 percent. Whatever He invested in Abram became a dividend to the people around him. Since the same God who equipped him long ago is supplying us today, can we give or be anything less?"

Hebrews 10:19-25
A. What is the author's topic of the text? The benefits of Christ's ministry.

B. What is the author's thrust in the text? Understanding the different aspects of Christ's ministry that lead to a balanced Christian life.

C. What type of audience will I face? Believing.

D. What type, style, and category of sermon should I use? Life-situation. Expository. Transitions.

E. What is the title of my message? "Keep Your Eyes on Him!"

F. What is my strong opening statement? "You know, it doesn't take a major overhaul to sabotage something completely; just a little modification of the guidance system is all it takes."

G. How can I illustrate this? Story of a ship that ends up hundreds of miles off course because a tiny magnet deflected its heading by a couple of degrees.

H. What can I explain to move into the biblical setting? It does not take much to lose your way in this life. It never has. Just before the fall of Jerusalem (*c.* 70), for example, shortsighted Hebrew Christians threatened to desert Christ and return to Judaism. Circumstances had gradually led them to underestimate Christ and underrate His ministry to the point that He no longer appeared able to lead them into God's promises. Paul attempted to reclaim these straying sheep with a sweeping presentation of Jesus and His work. He hoped that the sight of a cosmic, all-powerful Saviour would restore their confidence in Him and get them back on track.

I. What is the theme of my message? The enemy does not have to destroy our faith in Christ all at once to keep us out of the kingdom. All he has to do is keep us from seeing and appreciating a small part of all Christ is and does to put us ever so slightly off course, so eventually we will miss the port.

J. What is my transitional sentence? "The apostle spends the better part of 10 chapters developing the significance of Christ and His ministry for us. Then suddenly in Hebrews 10:19 he makes the transition from theological arguments to practical instructions. And in six short but powerful verses, he sums up everything that Christ is and does, and how it should affect our lives."

K. What are the main points, subpoints, and applications of my message?
1. Look back to the Lamb and His cross and remember (verses 19, 20)
2. Look up to the High Priest and His sanctuary and react (verses 21-25)
    a. Privately "draw near" (verse 23)
    b. Publicly "hold fast" (verse 24)
    c. Personally "consider" (verses 24, 25)
3. Look forward to the King of kings and His return and rush (verse 25).

L. What is my summarizing or climactic illustration? A man's wife calls in an expensive repair person for her electric stove when her husband could have fixed it at no charge. She says, "I didn't know you could fix the stove." He says, "There's a lot about me you don't know yet."

M. How will I make an appeal and call for a decision? Study Jesus. Familiarize yourself with all that He is and does. Otherwise the day may come when you leave Him out of the equation and wind up costing yourself an emotional, and maybe even an eternal, fortune.

PART 2

A CLOSER LOOK

CHAPTER 7

A GRAMMAR FOR ENGLISH BIBLE STUDY

The Parts of Speech and a Grammar Review

Nouns—Remember when you were in elementary school and Miss Wortfinger taught English? One of the first lessons she taught was that a noun is a word that refers to a person, place, or thing.

FIGURE 43

Person	Place	Things	
Jesus	Calvary	Visible things	cross
		Ideas	covenant
		Actions	faith
		Conditions	fear
		Qualities	truth

There are many different ways to classify nouns.

Is it concrete or abstract? If a noun names something you can physically see, touch, taste, hear, smell, or measure—such as flower, bird, or rock—it is *concrete*. If not—such as idea, thought, or opinion—it is *abstract.*

Is it singular, plural, or collective? If a noun names one person, place, or thing (for instance, trooper), it is *singular*. If it refers to more than one (troops), it is *plural*. If it points to a group (troop), it is *collective*.

Is it compound? If two or more words act as a single unit, they form a compound noun. The words can either be separated (crab apple), hyphenated (son-in-law), or combined (dragonfly).

Is it common or proper? A *proper noun* (Jericho) names a specific person, place, or thing, whereas a *common noun* (city) names people, places, or things in general. (Proper nouns are always capitalized.) The name of a person directly spoken to is always proper (Yes, Mom), as is a family title before a personal name (Uncle Barnabas).

Pronouns and Antecedents—Pronouns are words that stand for nouns or for words that take the place of nouns. They help the speaker or writer to avoid awkward repetition of nouns. Antecedents are nouns (or words that take the place of nouns) for which pronouns stand.

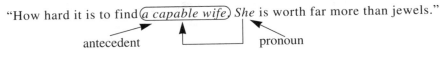

"How hard it is to find *a capable wife.* She is worth far more than jewels."

antecedent   pronoun

173

Although antecedents usually precede their pronouns, they can also follow their pronouns. For example:

"When *they* saw it, (the wise men) rejoiced."

Pronouns can be subdivided into various categories. For example, there are *personal pronouns*.

FIGURE 44

REFER TO	PERSON	SINGULAR	PLURAL
person speaking	first	I, me, my, mine	we, us, our, ours
person spoken to	second	you, your, yours	you, your, yours
person, place, or thing spoken of	third	he, she, it, him, her, his, hers, its	they, they, their, theirs

There are also *reflexive* and *intensive pronouns.*

Reflexive pronouns add essential information to a sentence by pointing back to a noun or pronoun near the beginning of the sentence. For instance,

"(Wives) submit *yourselves* to your own husbands."

Intensive pronouns add emphasis to a noun or pronoun, but can usually be removed from the sentence without changing its basic meaning. For example,

"(You) *yourselves* give them something to eat."

Compare with "You give them something to eat."

FIGURE 45

PERSON	SINGULAR	PLURAL
first	myself	ourselves
second	yourself	yourselves
third	(him, her, it)self	themselves

There are *demonstrative pronouns*, which point out a specific person, place, or thing and also indicate whether it is near or distant. Demonstrative pronouns may come either before or after the antecedent.

"*That* (over there) is (the city)"

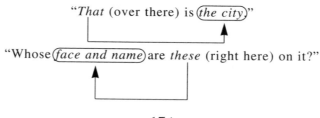

"Whose (face and name) are *these* (right here) on it?"

174

FIGURE 46

INDICATES	SINGULAR	PLURAL
Near	this	these
Distant	that	those

There are *relative pronouns*, which begin a subordinate clause and relate it to another idea in the sentence by linking the information in a subordinate clause to a word in an independent clause. The antecedent for the relative pronoun is located in another clause of the sentence. (See the section on "Clauses and Phrases" for more information.) The most common relative pronouns are *that, which, who, whom, what,* and *whose.* For example,

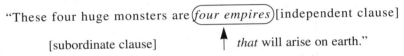

"These four huge monsters are *four empires* [independent clause]

[subordinate clause]   *that* will arise on earth."

There are *interrogative pronouns*. An interrogative pronoun begins a direct or indirect question. There are five interrogative pronouns: *what, which, who, whom,* and *whose.* Sometimes the antecedent for an interrogative pronoun is not clear. For instance, "*What* did you go out to see?"

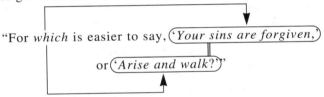

"For *which* is easier to say, *'Your sins are forgiven,'*

or *'Arise and walk?'*'"

And there are *indefinite pronouns*, which do not require specific antecedents, because they refer to persons, places, or things, often without specifying which ones. For example, "If *anyone* thirsts, let him come to me and drink."
Sometimes, however, they can have specific antecedents.

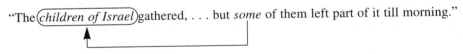

"The *children of Israel* gathered, . . . but *some* of them left part of it till morning."

FIGURE 47

SINGULAR			PLURAL	BOTH
another	everyone	nothing	both	all
anybody	everything	one	few	any
anyone	little	other	many	more
anything	much	somebody	others	most
each	neither	someone	several	none
either	nobody	something		some
everybody	no one			such

175

Sometimes the speaker or writer uses the indefinite pronoun when he or she wants to make a person, place, or thing more definite without giving away its identity ("A *certain* man had two sons") or to remove all doubts about its identity

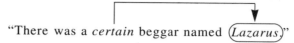

"There was a *certain* beggar named (*Lazarus*)"

Adjectives—Adjectives are modifiers; that is, they add to the meaning of other nouns or pronouns by describing them or by making them more precise. An adjective can answer four questions about a noun or pronoun:

FIGURE 48

QUESTION	ANSWER
What kind?	in *green* pastures
Which one?	at My *right* hand
How many:	to the *seven* churches
How much?	*abundant* life

An adjective usually precedes the noun or pronoun it modifies, but occasionally it may follow. "The Lord is *gracious*." "They are *sensual*."

The *definite article* ("the") in Scripture can function as a kind of adjective to particularize a noun or pronoun in order to emphasize it in some way. Nathan told David, "You are *the* man," that is, "You are *the* man I was just talking about in my story." The indefinite article ("a," "an") does not particularize a noun or pronoun.

Sometimes nouns can be used as adjectives and help answer the questions What kind? or Which one? about another noun ("*sheep* [noun used as adjective] herder" or "*fruit* [noun used as adjective] pincher").

Proper adjectives are proper nouns used as adjectives or adjectives formed from proper nouns. They usually begin with a capital letter. "The *Lord's* day." "The *Mediterranean* Sea."

If two or more words that are separated (*North American* continent), hyphenated (*ready-made*), or combined (*nearsighted*) act as a single modifier, they form a *compound adjective*.

Sometimes pronouns may be used as adjectives. The seven personal pronouns (also known as possessive adjectives or pronouns) are both pronouns (because they have antecedents) and adjectives (because they answer the question Which one?) at the same time. The rest of the pronouns act as adjectives rather than pronouns when they stand before nouns and answer the question Which one?

FIGURE 49

TYPE	PRONOUNS	EXAMPLES
Possessive	my, your, his, her, its, our, their	The dragon shook *its* tail.
Demonstrative	this, that, these, those	*These* four huge monsters are four kings.
Interrogative	which, what, whose	*Which* orchard do you own?
Indefinite Singular	another, each, either, little much, neither, one	A *little* horn came up.
Plural	both, few, many, several	The sound of *many* waters.
Either/or	all, any, more, most, other, some	*Most* brethren are bolder to speak.

176

Verbs can even be used as adjectives. Verbs called *participles* used as adjectives usually end in *ing* or *ed*. For example, "*running* water" or "*enlightened* wisdom." (See the section on "Verbals and Verbal Phrases" for more detailed information.)

Adverbs—An adverb is a word that modifies a verb, an adjective, or another adverb. It helps answer certain questions, depending on what it modifies.

FIGURE 50

WORD MODIFIED	QUESTION ANSWERED	EXAMPLES
Verb	Where?	as the sparks fly *upward*
	When?	*afterward* we sailed
	In what manner?	God has dealt *graciously* with me.
	To what extent?	it came up *immediately*
Adjective	To what extent?	*exceptionally* strong
Adverb	To what extent?	*much* more bold

Adverbs can also serve as parts of verbs. Some verbs require an adverb to complete their meaning. Adverbs used this way are considered part of the verb they complete. For instance, "Moses *turned aside* to examine the burning bush."

Nouns, too, can be used as adverbs. Several nouns that answer the questions When? or Where? can function as adverbs.

FIGURE 51

SAMPLE NOUNS		QUESTION	EXAMPLE
yesterday	home	When?	I preach *weekends*.
tomorrow	nights		
mornings	week	Where?	They turned *home*.
afternoons	year		
evenings	month		
weekends	today		

Is the word an adverb or an adjective? The majority of adverbs end in *ly*, but so do some adjectives (for example, *nightly*, which can function either as an adjective or adverb). So the best way to tell adjectives from adverbs is to check the way the word functions in the sentence. Adjectives modify nouns or pronouns, whereas adverbs modify verbs, adjectives, or other adverbs.

Prepositions—Prepositions are connectors. They express the relationship between words or ideas. A preposition relates the noun or pronoun that appears with it to another word in the sentence. Prepositions do not necessarily function in the same way in all languages. (See Figure 52 on page 178.) For example, the Greek *en tois sabbasin* (Luke 4:31) literally reads "*in* the Sabbath" but should be translated into English as "*on* the Sabbath."

Since words like *around, before, behind, down, in, off, on, out, over,* and *up* can function as either prepositions or adverbs, check to see if an *object* accompanies the word. Prepositions have objects; adverbs do not. A good dictionary will help you sort through the possibilities to determine the precise nuance of a preposition in its literary context.

Here is some important information about cases and prepositions. *Case* is the function of a word, determined by its form, which (a) decides its place in a sentence and (b) shows how it relates to the rest of the sentence. A preposition is a word that helps a noun express its case relationship by sharply defining its relationship to the rest of the sentence.

FIGURE 52

TABLE OF PREPOSITIONS

aboard	before	in front of	over
about	behind	in place of	owing to
above	below	in regard to	past
according to	beneath	inside	prior to
across	beside	inspite of	regarding
across from	besides	instead of	round
after	between	into	since
against	beyond	in view of	through
ahead of	but	like	throughout
along	by	near	till
alongside	by means of	nearby	to
along with	concerning	next to	together with
amid	considering	of	toward
among	despite	off	under
apart from	down	on	underneath
around	during	on account of	until
aside from	except	onto	unto
as of	for	on top of	up
at	from	opposite	upon
atop	in	out	with
barring	in addition to	out of	within
because of	in back of	outside	without

Although English has lost most of its cases, New Testament Greek has five cases.

1. The *nominative* case (a) names or designates the subject of a sentence or its equivalents; for example, "And the word was God" (both "the Word" and "God" are in the Greek nominative case; "the Word" is the subject, and "God" is its equivalent or a predicate noun); (b) further describes a previous noun; for example, "Paul, an apostle" (consider both nouns to be equal); and (c) expresses sudden, sharp, surprised, or emotional speech; for instance, "Wretched man that I am!"

2. The *vocative* case identifies the person or thing being addressed. "*Lord*, to whom shall we go?"

3. The *genitive* case describes and defines nouns by

(a) crediting them with certain qualities, as in "the body of [characterized or dominated by] sin";

(b) clarifying whether action nouns like "faith" in passages such as "the faith of the Son of God" emphasize *performance*, as in "the faith demonstrated by the Son of God" (by voluntarily going to His death for us, according to God's plan); *experience*, as in "the faith directed toward the Son of God" (by devoted followers); *ownership*, as in "the faith that belongs to the Son of God" (the Son of God's faith," emphasizing the owner, not his property); *source*, as in "the faith that comes from the Son of God" (emphasizing the place or person from whom this kind of faith springs); or *origin*, as in "the faith that comes as a result of the Son of God" (emphasizing the kind of faith Christ generates);

(c) *indicating relationships*; for example, "James *of Zebedee*" actually means "James descended from" or "a son of Zebedee"; *material or contents*, as in "the net *of fish*," which means "the net containing fish"; *kind of time*, for instance, "he came to

178

Him *by night*" means "he came to Him during the night"; *price or value*, as in "sold *for a farthing*," which actually means "sold at the price of [worth] one farthing"; or the *whole* of which something is a part, for example, "*certain* of the scribes" means "some of the scribes" [a group within and representative of the scribal school];

(d) *explaining* other nouns, as in "the *earnest of* the Spirit," which actually means "the down payment that is the Spirit."

4. The *accusative* case

(a) supplies the *direct object* upon which the verb acts or shows the extent of that action in time and space, as in "They saw my works *for 40 years*," which actually means "They saw my works during a period of 40 years" (Both "my works" and "for 40 years" are in the accusative case; even though "my works" tells us what they saw, the direct object and "for 40 years" tell us how long they saw them, the extent of that action.);

(b) supplies *double direct objects* when necessary; for example, "He shall . . . bring all things to your remembrance" actually means "He shall remind you of everything";

(c) generally refers to the *person other than the subject*, who is involved in the action, usually the subject of an infinitive, as in "I want you to know";

(d) supplies the direct object with *a complement* to complete the intention of the verb; for example, "I will make *you* fishers of men" or "They had *John* as their [for a] minister";

(e) appears as an *object* with the same meaning as its verb, as in "I have fought the good *fight*" or as an *adverb* to specify the manner in which something is done, as in "You have received freely; give as *freely*" or in *oaths*, as in "I beg you *in God's name*."

5. The *dative* is the case of the indirect object, which tells us whether the verbal idea is performed:

(a) in the *interest of* or *on behalf of* someone or something, as in "I decided this *for* myself";

(b) *with reference to* someone or something, as in "Consider yourself dead [with reference] *to* sin";

(c) in a certain *sphere or territory*, as in "He fell *among* [in the company of] *thieves*";

(d) at a precise *location*, as in "They put it *upon* His *head*";

(e) at a certain *time*, as in "*on* the first *day* of the week";

(f) with a particular *instrument*, as in "He killed James . . . *with* the *sword*";

(g) by a specific *means* or *agency*, as in "bound *by means of fetters and chains*";

(h) in a specific *manner*, as in "*In every way*, whether *in pretense* or *in truth*";

(i) *in association with* others, as in "This man accepts sinners and eats *with them*"; and

(j) as the *cause* of an action, as in "They were broken off *because of unbelief*."

Here are some general guidelines concerning the cases:

Don't jump to conclusions. For example, "to" could be a preposition frequently associated with the accusative ("to town"), a help translating the dative ("to him"), or part of an infinitive ("to believe").

Identify, note the function, and label the relationship between the various clauses and phrases in your structural diagram before you attempt to troubleshoot the cases. Then mark all possible indicators or any group of words in which you suspect a case.

Next, ask questions to flesh out any subjects, object complements, direct or indirect objects, infinitives, etc., and compare what you find with the examples in this section to confirm or repudiate your suspicions. For instance, you might suspect that the phrase "in Jesus Christ" is possibly a dative of location, sphere, or territory.

179

Then investigate further to clarify the sense of the text. The phrase "In Jesus Christ" is part of a clause that describes "those who are called." It answers the question Where are the called ones kept? This seems to imply that Jesus is the Christian's refuge.

Finally, compare this sense of the text with related passages. When you lay one passage (Jude 1) alongside verses that involve the same phrase (for instance, Gal. 5:6; cf. 1 Cor. 7:19; Gal. 6:15), the meaning of the phrase becomes clear: those who take a stand in Jesus are safe and secure as long as they conduct themselves within His boundaries (that is, live as He would).

Conjunctions—A conjunction is a word used to connect other words or groups of words.

1. *Coordinating* conjunctions connect similar parts of speech or groups of words of equal grammatical weight.

FIGURE 53

COORDINATING CONJUNCTIONS	
and but for nor or so yet	
Link up . . .	**Examples**
Nouns and pronouns	Paul *and* I sailed on the ship.
Verbs	He answered *and* said . . .
Adjectives	It was terrible, dreadful, *and* exceptionally strong.
Adverbs	He spoke quickly *but* timely.
Prepositional phrases	I will go to Rome *or* to Spain.
Subordinate ideas	I have the desire to do good, *but* not the power to carry it out.
Complete ideas	He delivers and rescues, *and* He works signs and wonders.

2. Working in pairs, *correlative* conjunctions join elements of equal grammatical weight in much the same manner as coordinating conjunctions do.

FIGURE 54

CORRELATIVE CONJUNCTIONS	
both/and either/or neither/nor not only/but also whether/or	
Link up . . .	**Examples**
Nouns	*both* man *and* beast
Nouns and pronouns	Call *either* Paul *or* me.
Adjectives	*not only* cruel *but also* vicious
Prepositional phrases	*either* on the table *or* in the drawer
Complete ideas	*Neither* did they bow *nor* did they serve the image.

3. *Subordinating* conjunctions join two complete ideas by making one of the ideas dependent upon the other. The dependent idea always begins with a subordinating conjunction to form what is called a subordinate clause. The subordinate clause may either follow or precede the main idea in the sentence. (See the section on "Clauses and Phrases.") For example, "Let the priests sanctify themselves [main idea] *lest* the Lord break out against them [subordinate idea]" or "Even if anyone

should sin [subordinate idea] we have an Advocate with the Father [main idea]."

FIGURE 55

TABLE OF SUBORDINATING CONJUNCTIONS			
after	but (that)	lest	till
although	even if	notwithstanding	unless
as	even though	now that	until
as if	for the purpose of	provided (that)	what(ever)
as often as	how	since	when(ever)
as long as	if	so (that)	where(ever)
as much as	in case	so as (that)	which(ever)
as soon as	inasmuch as	such (as) (that)	while
as though	in order that	than	whither
because	in spite of	that	who(ever)
before	in that	though	why

FIGURE 56

MAIN IDEA	SUBORDINATE IDEA
Let the priests sanctify themselves	*lest* the Lord break out against them.
We have an Advocate with the Father	*even if* anyone should sin.

Some subordinating conjunctions also act as prepositions (*after, till, before, since,* and *until*) or as adverbs (*after, before, when,* and *where*). Here's how to tell them apart:

FIGURE 57

PART OF SPEECH	EXAMPLE
Subordinating conjunction	*After* 12 months he was walking around the palace grounds.
Preposition	War broke out *after* talks broke down.
Adverb	The fighting began at noon and ended an hour *after*.

4. *Conjunctive* adverbs act as transitions between complete ideas by indicating comparisons, contrasts, results, and other relationships.

FIGURE 58

TABLE OF MOST COMMON CONJUNCTIVE ADVERBS			
accordingly	furthermore	likewise	otherwise
again	hence	meanwhile	so
also	however	moreover	still
besides	indeed	nevertheless	then
consequently	in fact	notwithstanding	therefore
finally	in the first place	on the contrary	thus
for that reason	in the meantime	on the other hand	

FIGURE 59

COMPLETE IDEA ONE	COMPLETE IDEA TWO
O My Father, if it is possible, let this cup pass from Me;	*nevertheless,* not as I will, but as You will.

5. An *interjection* is a word that expresses feeling or emotion. It functions independently of a sentence. Interjections can express happiness, fear, anger, pain, surprise, sorrow, exhaustion, hesitation, etc.

FIGURE 60

TABLE OF COMMON INTERJECTIONS				
ah	dear	hey	ouch	well
aha	goodness	hurray	psst	whew
alas	gracious	oh	tsk	wow

An exclamation mark or comma often follows an interjection to set it off from the rest of the sentence. Sometimes the exclamation mark is at the end of the sentence: "*Oh!* You surprised me," "*Oh,* wretched man that I am!*" or "*Oh, my Lord!* Please do not charge this sin against us."

The Sentence, Verbs, and Complements—A sentence is a group of words with two main parts: (a) a complete subject and (b) a complete predicate. Together these parts express a complete thought.

The *complete subject* consists of a noun, pronoun, or group of words acting as a noun—plus any modifiers that tell who or what the speaker or writer has uppermost in mind.

The *complete predicate* contains the verb or verb phrase, plus any modifiers and complements that tell what the complete subject does or is.

FIGURE 61

SENTENCE TYPE	COMPLETE SUBJECT	COMPLETE PREDICATE
Direct statement	I	must needs go through Samaria.
	Our Father	which art in heaven, hallowed by Thy name.
The question	He	is . . . God of the Jews only?
The command	You all (unstated but understood)	stand fast in the liberty wherewith Christ has made us free.

In some sentences a portion of the predicate may actually precede the subject:

FIGURE 62

COMPLETE —————————————— PREDICATE

In the second year of his reign,	Nebuchadnezzar	had dreams
partial predicate	*subject*	*partial predicate*

A *sentence fragment* is a group of words that does not express a complete thought.

FIGURE 63

FRAGMENT	ADD	COMPLETE SENTENCE
People with problems	complete predicate	People with problems need a personal relationship with Christ.
Always leads us in triumph in Christ	complete subject	God always leads us in triumph in Christ.
In His time	complete subject and predicate	God makes all things beautiful in His time.

A *subject* either (a) confines the action to itself, (b) acts upon something or someone else, or (c) acts on someone else's behalf or in someone else's best interest.

A verb supplies subjects with action. It is a word (or group of words) that expresses time while showing an action, a condition, or the fact that something exists. (See the section on "Time and Kind of Action" for a more detailed explanation of biblical verbs.)

A *complement* is a word or group of words that completes the meaning of the predicate. Active verbs may require *direct objects, indirect objects,* or *object complements.* Linking verbs require *subject complements*; that is, *predicate nominatives* or *predicate adjectives.*

Action verbs tell what mental or physical action someone or something is performing. There are two kinds of action verbs.

1. *Intransitive* verbs provide the subject with action that it confines to itself, so it doesn't need any complements.

"Jesus wept."
[verb]

(If you want to know the subject, just ask Who? or What? before the verb. In this case, Who wept? Jesus did. So Jesus is the subject.)

2. *Transitive* verbs provide the subject with action to perform either

(a) upon a noun, pronoun, or group of words acting as a noun—the direct object, as in

"I   thank ——▶ my God."
[subject] [verb]   [direct object]

(If you want to identify the direct object, just ask Whom? or What? after the verb—in this case, Whom did I thank? My God, so "my God" is the direct object); or

(b) on behalf of/with the person or thing in mind, named by the noun or pronoun that appears with the direct object—the indirect object, as in

"I   will give ——▶ the morning star ——▶ to him."
[subject] [verb]   [direct object]   [indirect object]

The indirect object usually appears with verbs like *ask, bring, buy, give, lend, make, promise, show, teach, tell,* and *write.* If you want to find the indirect object, that is, in whose interest the subject acts, just ask To whom? or To what? after the verb; on whose behalf the subject acts, just ask For whom? or For what? after the verb. In this case, To whom did I give the morning star? To him. So "him" is the indirect object in whose interest I promise to act.

An *object complement* is an adjective or noun that appears with a direct object and describes or renames it. Whereas an indirect object usually comes before a direct one, an objective complement generally follows a direct object. Often mistaken at first for a second direct object, an objective complement actually occurs only with specific verbs like *appoint, call, consider, declare, elect, judge, label, make, name, think,* or *select.* This simplifies its identification.

For example,

| "The priest | pronounced ⟶ | the lepers | clean." |
| [subject] | [verb] | [direct object] | [object complement] |

The word "clean" is an adjective that describes the new condition of the lepers and is pronounced by the priest.

Linking verbs express a subject's state, condition, or character instead of action and do so by linking the subject to another word or group of words called the *subject complement,* which acts like a noun and is generally found near the end of the sentence.

A *subject complement* is a noun, pronoun, or adjective that appears with a linking verb and tells us something about the subject.

A *predicate nominative* is a noun or pronoun that appears with a linking verb and renames, identifies, or explains the subject of a sentence.

A *predicate adjective* is an adjective that appears with a linking verb and describes the subject of a sentence much the same way any adjective modifies a noun or pronoun.

FIGURE 64

SUBJECT	VERB	SUBJECT COMPLEMENT	TYPE OF SUBJECT COMPLEMENT
I	am	the good Shepherd	predicate noun
I	am	He	predicate pronoun
The Lord	is	gracious	predicate adjective

Although a linking verb serves as a sort of equal sign, it doesn't always equate the subject and its complement. For example, 1 John 4:8 says that "God is love." This doesn't mean that the adjective "love" captures everything there is to know about God, but it does tell us that God has a loving nature, that love is a regular feature of His unchanging character.

Although English translations usually place a subject before its complement, the more definite term is the subject—even if it doesn't come first in the sentence. Generally, a proper name, the term with a definite article, or the term with the narrower reference is the subject. When one of the two terms, however, has already been referred to in the immediately preceding context, it is the subject. So, for example, in "The rock was Christ," the rock, not Christ, is the subject. And in "This one is the antichrist," this one, not the antichrist, is the subject.

FIGURE 65

TABLE OF LINKING VERBS			
Forms of the Verb "To Be"			
am	am being	can be	have been
are	are being	could be	has been
is	is being	may be	had been
was	was being	might be	could have been
were	were being	must be	may have been
		shall be	might have been
		should be	shall have been
		will be	should have been
		would be	will have been
			would have been
Other Linking Verbs			
	appear	look	sound
	become	remain	stay
	feel	seem	taste
	grow	smell	turn

Every verb has tense, voice, mood, person, and number. (See chapter 8 for a detailed explanation.)

Tense tells us about the kind of action, whether it is (a) momentary, frozen at a point in time; (b) persistent and ongoing; or (c) perfective and completed.

Voice tells us whether the stress is (a) on the subject, (b) the agent acting on the subject, or (c) the action.

Mood tells us how the writer or speaker relates to reality.

Person indicates (a) who is speaking or writing—in the *first person*, (b) who is spoken to—in the *second person*, or who is spoken about—in the *third person*.

Number indicates whether the subject is (a) one person or thing—in the singular or (b) more than one—in the plural.

FIGURE 66

TABLE OF PERSON AND NUMBER		
Person	Singular	Plural
1st	I	We (us)
2nd	You	You (all)
3rd	He, she, it	They (them)

Sometimes a collective noun, representing a group of people or things, is linked with a singular verb. When this happens, the individual members recede into the background so that the group can take center stage. At other times, a collective noun may be linked with a plural verb. In this instance the group fades out of sight to feature the individual members.

The *simple subject* is the essential noun, pronoun, or group of words acting as a noun that cannot be left out of the complete subject.

The *simple predicate* is the essential verb or verb phrase that cannot be left out of the complete predicate.

Keep in mind that the object of a preposition can never be the simple subject of a sentence.

FIGURE 67

SIMPLE SUBJECTS AND SIMPLE PREDICATES	
Complete Subjects	Complete Predicates
Small pocket *calculators* *Ronald Reagan* *Pictures* of Saturn	*fit* nicely into coat pockets. *starred* in many films during his early career. *have* certainly *revealed* much about the ringed planet.

A *compound subject* is two or more subjects that share the same verb and are joined by a conjunction, such as "and" or "or." For example, "Then Peter *and* the other disciple [compound subject] went to the tomb" or "Jews *or* Gentiles [compound subject] may find rest in Messiah Jesus."

A *compound verb* is two or more verbs that share the same subject and are joined by a conjunction, such as "and" or "or." For instance, "Jesus replied *and* said [compound verb] . . ."

Types of Sentences

The sentence is the basic unit of thought within the larger units of paragraphs and sections.

Declarative—These flow briskly from ["who" or "what"] ──► [the action.] Brief and conclusive, they supply a satisfying sense of completion because they do not hold us in suspense, waiting for qualifying phrases and clauses. Sprinkled between longer, more complex sentences, they give us a chance to gather our thoughts about previous statements or to focus on a new idea.

Interrogative—These are either direct or rhetorical. Answers follow direct questions, which usually appear in dialogue or drama. Writers or speakers use rhetorical questions to introduce a topic or to underscore a point but do not expect an answer. Sometimes the question is unanswerable or the answer is so familiar to the audience that there is no need to spell it out. Paul used rhetorical sentences to press his audience toward the response he wanted. Many of them were lead-in or topic sentences. The writer of Job alternated progressively more rhetorical questions with descriptive declarative sentences in order to gradually silence Job's objections and emphasize God's power and majesty.

Imperative—These sentences cut right into the minds of the audience because they call for some action or decision on its part. Sometimes, as in the Genesis Creation account, God challenges an outside agent whose response will directly affect those who listen. Direct statements introduce each day's activities, expressing God's will with imperative challenges. The sentences get more complex with phrases and clauses as the days progress, but each day's activities conclude with similar, brief direct statements and identical declarative sentences so as to help us gather our thoughts before going on.

Exclamatory—These add something to the sense of the preceding word or words. Because they are usually incomplete sentences, they stand out as interjections within the complete thought. Although they usually mark an emotional rise, they actually add to or comment on what has already been said or done or, even more frequently, what is about to follow.

The structure of a sentence can be simple, compound, or complex.

186

A *simple sentence* consists of a single independent clause, as in

"No one has ever seen God."
[independent]

A *compound sentence* consists of two or more independent clauses joined by a comma and a coordinating conjunction or by a semicolon, as in

"God gave the law through Moses,   *but* grace and truth came by Jesus Christ."
[independent]   [independent]

A *complex sentence* consists of one independent clause and one or more subordinate clauses, as in

"We will do   whatever you say."
[main]   [subordinate]

A *compound-complex sentence* consists of two or more independent clauses and one or more subordinate clauses, as in

"I assure you,   whoever declares publicly that he belongs to me,
[independent]   [subordinate]
the Son of man will do the same for him before God's angels."
[independent]

Clauses and Phrases

There are many different types of clauses and phrases.

A *prepositional phrase* contains a preposition and a noun or a pronoun, which is called the object of the preposition. The object may have its own modifiers and can be compound. For example,

"beside   the still   waters."
[preposition]   [modifiers]   [object of preposition]

An *adjective phrase* is a prepositional phrase that modifies a noun or pronoun by telling what kind or which one. It can modify any sentence part occupied by a noun or pronoun. More than one adjective phrase may modify the same word. For instance,

"that   the body   *of sin*   might be destroyed."
[adjective phrase—either what kind or which one]

(For a detailed explanation of phrases beginning with the word "of" see "Cases and Prepositions.")

An *adverbial phrase* is a prepositional phrase that modifies a verb, adjective, or adverb by pointing out where, when, in what manner, or to what extent. For example,

"And they overcame him   *by the blood of the Lamb*
          and   *by the word of their testimony.*"

[adverb phrases—in what manner]

An *appositive* is a noun or pronoun placed near or next to another noun or pronoun to identify, rename, or explain it, as in

"Paul, ◄——— *an apostle.*"
[appositive—identifies Paul as one sent]

Commas are used only when the appositive contains nonessential (nonrestrictive) material that you could leave out without altering the meaning of the sentence. Essential (restrictive) appositives do not require commas.

An *appositive phrase* is a noun or pronoun with modifiers placed near or next to a noun or pronoun to add information and details. One-word adjectives, adjective phrases, or other groups of words acting as adjectives can modify an appositive. Appositive phrases can modify nouns or pronouns occupying any part of the sentence, including the subject, a direct object, an indirect object, an object complement, a predicate nominative, and the object of a preposition. For instance,

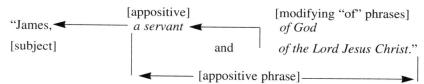

An *adjective clause* is a subordinate clause that modifies a noun or pronoun by telling what kind or which one. These clauses follow the nouns or pronouns they modify and usually begin with a relative pronoun (such as *that, which, who, whom,* or *whose*) that acts as a subject, direct object, object of a preposition, or an adjective in the clauses or sometimes with a relative adverb (such as *before, since, when, where,* or *why*) that can act only as an adverb in the clause.

Nonrestrictive clauses, which are not essential to the basic meaning of the sentence, are set off by commas; restrictive or essential ones are not. For instance,

"Are you that Daniel ◄——— *who is one of the captives from Judah?*"
[adjective clause]

(The restrictive, essential clause answers the question Which Daniel? Answer: The captive from Judah.)

FIGURE 68

THE USES OF RELATIVE PRONOUNS WITHIN ADJECTIVE CLAUSES	
A subject	The fish *that was just reeled in* set a record. What was just reeled in? That was.
A direct object	Someone broke that window *that I recently fixed.* I recently fixed what? That.
An object of a preposition	This is my aunt *of whom I have spoken.* I have spoken of ——➤ whom.
An adjective	I have a friend *whose witty remarks amuse me.* "Whose" modifies remarks.

FIGURE 69

THE USE OF RELATIVE ADVERBS WITHIN ADJECTIVE CLAUSES	
An adverb	The place *where we stayed* was called an inn. We stayed where?

An *adverbial clause* is a subordinate clause that modifies a verb, adjective, adverb, or verbal. It does this by pointing out where, when, in what manner, to what extent, under what condition, or why. This clause begins with a subordinating conjunction and contains a subject and a verb, though not the main subject and verb in the sentence.

FIGURE 70

ADVERB CLAUSES	
Modified words	Examples
Verb	We called ◄——— *because we were worried about you.*
Adjective	Jo looked confident ◄——— *as she took her exams.*
Adverb	He finished sooner ◄——— *than we expected.*
Participle	My sisters, arguing ◄——— *as I sat down to study,* made concentration impossible.
Gerund	I relax by reading the newspaper ▲ *after I study.*
Infinitive	I wanted to ski ◄——— *while the snow lasted.*

Sometimes adverbial clauses beginning with the words "as" or "than" are elliptical—that is, the verb or both the subject and the verb are understood but not stated.

FIGURE 71

UNDERSTOOD	BUT NOT STATED
Verb	I ate as much dessert *as he [did].*
Verb and subject	The pastor had more candidates *than [he had] baptismal robes.*

A *noun clause* is a subordinate clause that acts as a noun in a sentence. It can perform any function that any other kind of noun can.

FIGURE 72

USES OF NOUN CLAUSES IN SENTENCES	
Functions	Examples
Subject	*That David had escaped* was told to Saul.
Direct object	The Lord saw *that man's wickedness on earth was great.*
Indirect object	The youth sent *whoever requested it* a brochure of their activities.
Predicate nominative	The happiness of others is *what I live for.*
Object of preposition	Jesus offered love to *whomever He met.*
Appositive	If it is proven true *that this detestable thing has been done among you,* . . .

189

Noun clauses frequently begin with the relative pronouns *that, which, who, whom,* or *whose,* just as adjective clauses. Other words found at the beginning of noun clauses include *how, if, what, whatever, when, where, whether, whichever, whoever,* and *whomever.* Besides introducing a noun clause, these words sometimes serve a function within the clause as well.

FIGURE 73

SOME USES OF INTRODUCTORY WORDS IN NOUN CLAUSES	
Functions	Examples
Adjective	She finally decided *which* ——▶ *cut of bread she wanted.*
Adverb	I don't know *when the paint will dry.*
Subject	*Whoever reads this* shall be blessed.
Direct object	*Whatever He asks* you, do.
Quotation marker	Jesus said *that we should pray unceasingly.*

Since some of the words that introduce noun clauses also launch adverb and adjective clauses, try substituting the words "fact," "it," "thing," or "you" for the clause and check to see if the sentence still makes sense.

Grammarians also speak of connected clauses, which are illustrated in the following table:

CONNECTED CLAUSES—FIGURE 74

RELATIONSHIP	CONNECTORS
When clauses **AGREE,** the second may:	
1. carry forward the thought of the first 2. set forth another step in a series 3. provide another detail 4. make a comparison	too, also, as, just as, so also, likewise, and, besides, like, furthermore, in like manner, moreover
5. illustrate the first with a specific example	for example, for instance, thus
6. explain or practically repeat the first in more specific terms	that is, namely, in other words, (or some kind of punctuation)
7. emphasize what was said in the first	yea, certainly, in fact, indeed, truly, surely
When clauses **DISAGREE,** the second either:	
1. opposes the first, or 2. stands in contrast to it	but, even though, much more, nevertheless, yet, although, then, however, on the other hand, on the contrary, except, not only . . . but also
3. offers an alternative or choice	or, either . . . or, neither . . . nor, otherwise, else
When clauses express **CAUSE** and **EFFECT,** the second may:	
1. be a consequence of the first or 2. draw a conclusion from it	therefore, hence, consequently, thus, so, accordingly, so that, as a result, for this reason
When clauses act as a **SINGLE** part of speech, they may function:	
1. like an **Adjective** modifying nouns or pronouns by telling	*relative* pronouns (that, which, who, whom, whose) which act as a subject,

RELATIONSHIP	CONNECTORS
What kind? or Which one?	direct object, object of a preposition, or an adjective within the adj. clause; *relative* adverbs (e.g., before, since, when, where, why), which function as adverbs within the adj. clause *"restrictive"* clauses (which point out or restrict the statement to a particular person or thing and cannot be left out of the sentence) usually begin with **"that"** and no comma; **"nonrestrictive"** clauses (which describe or explain a person or thing that stands out without its help, and can be left out of the sentence) usually begin with **"who,"** or **"which"** preceded with a comma.
2. Like a *Noun* as a subject, direct object, indirect object, object of a preposition, predicate nominative, or an appositive in the sentence	*relative* pronouns (that, which, who, whom, whose), or *other* words (how, if, what, whatever, when, where, whether, whichever, whoever, whomever), which act as an adjective, adverb, subject, direct object or, (as in the case of **"that"** sometimes without any function at all). *Try substituting the words *"fact, it, thing,* or *you* for the entire clause: Does it retain its smoothness? Does it still make sense?
3. Like an *Adverb* modifying verbs, adjectives, adverbs, or verbals by pointing out where? when? in what manner? to what extent? under what condition? or why?	*temporal* (now, until, when, before, whenever, after, while, since) *conditional* (if) *purpose* (that, so that, in order that, lest, perchance, perhaps) *concessive/contrastive* (though, even though, although, whatever, however much, no matter what) *causal/reason* (because, for this reason, for this purpose, since, for, inasmuch as, on account of, for which cause) *locative* (where, whither, whence, wherever, from where, in what) *comparative* (than + verbs ending in -er, or -est; more + a word ending in -ly; more than, [sometimes] that

Sometimes biblical authors used correlative connectors, working in pairs, to join nouns, nouns and pronouns, adjectives, prepositional phrases, or complete ideas when they share equal grammatical weight, as in *as . . . so also, for . . . as, so . . . as, as . . . therefore, although . . . nevertheless, both . . . and, on the one hand . . . on the other, when . . . then, where . . . there, whether . . . or.*

A *verbal* is a word derived from a verb that combines the action of a verb with either the descriptive power of an adjective or the naming power of a noun, but it is used as a noun, adjective, or adverb and not as a verb.

A *participle* is a verbal (a form of the verb) that acts like:

1. an adjective, so it modifies or describes nouns or pronouns [for instance, "*running* water"], preceding or following the word it modifies, by answering the questions Which one? ["*roaring* lion"] or What kind? ["*aching* muscles"].

2. a verb, and so it takes a subject ["from the words of my *roaring*"], or it may have an object ["*having taken* the bread"], and it can be modified ["*turning* quickly, he faced his accusers"].

3. an adverb, so it describes circumstances determined by the context. It can denote cause ["*When* they *saw* the star, they rejoiced"], concession ["*Though* they *found* no offense, they asked . . ."], condition ["How shall we escape, *if* we *neglect* . . ."], manner ["He emptied himself, *by taking* the form . . ."], means ["Who *by means of worry* is able to add . . ."], purpose ["He had come to Jerusalem *to worship* . . ."], and accompaniment ["they went forth and preached the Lord, *working* with them and *confirming* . . ."].

In Greek a participle acting as an adverb can also indicate time as a *present* participle, indicating that time simultaneous with the main verb; as a *future* participle, indicating time after the main verb; as an *aorist* (Greek) or *past* participle, indicating time before the main verb; or a *perfect* participle, indicating the result of a previous action.

An adverbial participle can also complete the idea of the main verb, describing an actual experience with verbs of mental action, as in "for I felt that power *went out* from me . . ." Additionally, it can paraphrase the main verb. In Greek, when the participle accompanies the imperfect, present, or future of the verb "to be," it highlights the *time* of the action. When it is the present, aorist (past), or perfect participle, it features the *kind* of action.

A *participial phrase* is a participle plus a modifier (an adverb, as in "burning brightly," or an adverb phrase, as in "broken in two pieces." Sometimes it is a participle plus a complement, as in "the man, reading the book, . . ." The entire phrase functions like a participle.

A comma sets off a participial phrase at the beginning of a sentence. Commas, however, set off only nonessential (nonrestrictive) phrases within the sentence.

A *nominative absolute* is a noun or pronoun followed by a participle or participial phrase that functions independently of the rest of the sentence. It can express time ("*Three hours having passed,* I decided to wait no longer"), reason ("*My stomach growling with hunger,* I made a sandwich"), or circumstance ("Many students missed final exams, *a flu epidemic having struck at the end of the semester*").

The participle "being" is sometimes understood rather than expressed in some nominative absolutes, as in "*The team [being] out of time,* we had to rush on."

It is sometimes easy to mistake a nominative absolute for the main subject and verb in a sentence. However, the nominative absolute is a phrase and cannot stand independently as a complete sentence.

A *gerund* is a form of a verb that acts as a noun. It ends in "ing."

FIGURE 75

SOME USES OF GERUNDS IN SENTENCES	
Subject	*Striking* is considered subversive in some countries.
Direct object	A successful chef must enjoy *cooking*.
Indirect object	He gives *gardening* all his attention.
Predicate nominative	Her ear is *swelling*.
Object of preposition	Lock the door before *leaving*.
Appositive	One field, *engineering*, has an open market.

A *gerund phrase* is a gerund with modifiers or a complement.

FIGURE 76

GERUND PHRASES		
Modifiers or Complements	Examples	Function
Adjectives	*His loud yawning* woke me up.	Subject
Adjective phrase	*Worrying about the deadline* kept me up.	Subject
Adverb	I estimated the cost by *calculating quickly*.	Adverb
Adverb phrase	*Fishing from the pier* is permitted.	Subject
Direct object	*Reproducing copies* gets pretty expensive.	Subject
Indirect and direct objects	He suggested *writing them a letter*.	Direct object

Is it a verb, participle, or gerund? Here are some examples. "Mission teams *are traveling* [verb phrase] to Mexico." "A *traveling* [participle] preacher came to our church." "*Traveling* [gerund] tires me out."

Only the possessive form of a personal pronoun is appropriate before a gerund. Not "We were intrigued by *them* witnessing" but "We were intrigued by *their* witnessing."

An *infinitive* is a form of a verb that generally appears with the word "to" and acts as a noun, adjective, or adverb. After the verbs *dare, hear, help, let, make, please, see,* and *watch,* the "to" is usually understood rather than stated, as in "John Mark helped [to] preach." Although some prepositional phrases also begin with the word "to," you can tell them from infinitives because an infinitive links the word "to" to a verb, as in "to brag" or "to have finished," whereas a prepositional phrase links the word "to" to a noun or pronoun, as in "to them" or "to dad."

FIGURE 77

INFINITIVES USED AS VERBS	
May have its own subject	I know *them* to be burners of books.
May take an object	to know *Him* and *the power* of His resurrection
May be modified by adverb	to speak the word *fearlessly*
May stand as command	*[to]* weep, with those who mourn
May express time	*before, during,* or *after* the main verb

Can express
        purpose
        result
        cause
	I have come [in order] *to fulfill*.
	[so as] *to be* without excuse
	[on account of] not *[to be]* having deep soil

FIGURE 78

INFINITIVES USED AS NOUNS		
subject"		*To eat* is necessary." "*To have* her is not lawful for you." "*To live* is Christ."
direct *object*	of the main verb *complementary* use begin, wish, able, will, about to, ought	They kept looking for ways *to arrest* Him.
object	of a preposition	She has no choice except *to obey*.
predicate noun		His ambition is *to study* law.
apposition		Pure religion and undefiled is . . . *to visit widows and orphans*.
articular	translates as a noun	For to me (to live =) *living* is Christ.

FIGURE 79

INFINITIVES USED AS MODIFIERS	
As an adjective	The doctor gave me some vitamins *to take*.
As an adverb	Ice cream is easy *to freeze*.

An *infinitive phrase* is an infinitive accompanied by a modifier, complement, or a subject, all acting together as a single part of speech.

FIGURE 80

INFINITIVE PHRASES	
With an adverb	The baby wanted *to wiggle continuously*.
With an adverb phrase	I plan *to visit during the afternoon*.
With a direct object	The foghorn helped *[to] warn incoming ships*.
With indirect and direct objects	The bank decided *to lend the family the money*.
With a subject and complement	A student asked *the college to send a catalog*.

In Hebrew the infinitive has two aspects.

The *infinitive construct* appears in connection (in construct) with its subject, and it functions like a traditional infinitive.

The *infinitive absolute* acts more like an adverb itself, emphasizing the verbal idea, as in "Thou shalt *surely* die," (Gen. 2:17), which literally reads "*dying* [infinitive] you will die [verb]" or complementing the idea of the main verb, as in "and he walked along eating," which literally would read "and he walked [verb], walking and eating [two infinitives]."

Sometimes the infinitive absolute does not have to depend on the main verb. Instead of emphasizing or complementing the main verb, it often describes action that is on a par with the main verb, as in "All this I have seen [verb] and *applied* [infinitive] my heart to every deed." At times it may seem even to stand alone in place of a finite verb, as in "*Go* [infinitive] and cry [verb] into the ears of Jerusalem."

Sample Sentence Diagrams

The trick to diagramming sentences is to do it properly and uniformly. The best way to develop a structural diagram is to diagram correctly one sentence at a time, and you must line up the various clauses and phrases in a consistent way for the overall structure of your text to stand out. The following diagrams are guides as well as examples. Not only do they show *how* to relate the various clauses and phrases to each other, but they also point out *where* to place them for maximum structural effect.

1. *Subject, verb*
   John   visited.

2, *Subject, helping verb, verb*
   John   should have visited.

3. *Subject with modifier, helping verb, verb, adverb*
   A *remorseful* John   should have visited
                                                       ▲ *sooner.*

4. *Subject with modifier, helping verb, verb, direct object, adverb*
   A *remorseful* John   should have visited   Mary
                                                       ▲ *sooner.*

5. *Implied subject, imperative verb, adverb*
   (You)   Call
                                    ▲ *home.*

6. *Inverted Sentence: Subject, helping verb, verb, adverb*
   (you)   Have telephoned
                                       ▲ *yet?*

7. *Definite article, compound adjective, subject, helping verb, verb, compound adverb*
   The | *long*
   and ▼ *difficult*
       report   was read
                                       ▲ *quickly*
                                    but | *not easily.*

8. *Compound subject, helping verb, compound verb, adverbs*
   Both | you
   and ▼ I   must | pack
                                          ▲ today
                                    and ▼ move
                                          ▲ tomorrow.

195

9. *Adverb, compound subject, compound verb*

                                        Yesterday

    the ↓ campers

   and ▼ counselors

                       and ▼ swam

                                   fished.

10. *Subject, verb, direct object, indirect object*

    Richard   bought   a ***floral*** arrangement.

                          ▲ (for) us

11. *Definite article, subject, verb, direct object, object complement with modifier*

    The supervisor   named   Lee/manager

                                     ▲***division.***

12. *Subject, linking verb, subject complement (predicate adjective) with modifier*

    Jolynn   is   ***very*** pretty.

13. *Subject, verb, pronoun, compound indirect objects, compound direct objects*

    We   gave

                ▲ (to) ***our*** ↓ grandmother

                   and ▼ grandfather   ↓ ***airplane*** tickets

                                   and ▼ money.

14. *Definite article, subject, adjective phrase, linking verb, verb, adverbial phrase*

    The man

      ▲ ***with*** a beard   is waiting

                        ▲***at*** the ***train*** station.

15. *Definite article, subject, linking verb, adverbial phrase, modified by an adjective phrase*

    The keys   are

                       ▲***on*** the table

                           ▲***by*** the door.

16. *Subject, verb, adverbial noun, adverb, modified by an adverbial phrase*

    I   arrived

                    ▲ ***home***

                     ↑ ***late***

                    ▲***at*** night.

17. *Subject, helping verb, verb, direct object, modified by two adverbial phrases with conjunction, direct object*

    I   will meet   you

                   ▲***at*** the entrance

             or | ***in*** the mall.

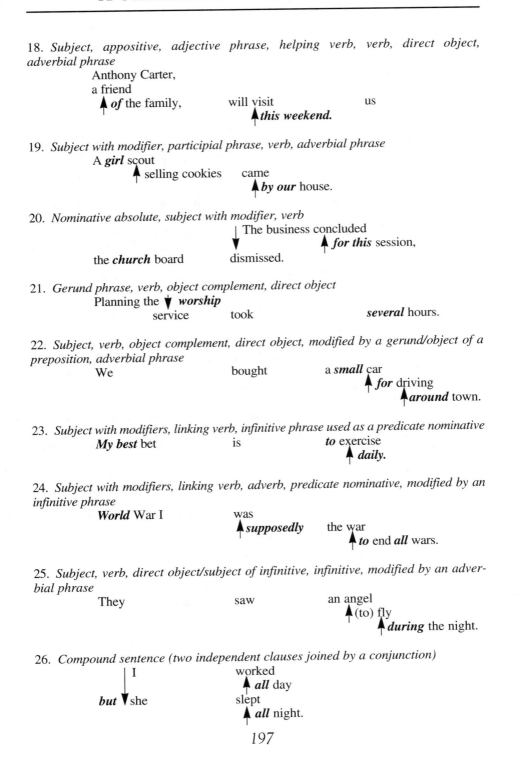

18. *Subject, appositive, adjective phrase, helping verb, verb, direct object, adverbial phrase*

        Anthony Carter,
        a friend
        ▲ *of* the family,   will visit   us
                           ▲ *this weekend.*

19. *Subject with modifier, participial phrase, verb, adverbial phrase*

        A *girl* scout
            ▲ selling cookies   came
                        ▲ *by our* house.

20. *Nominative absolute, subject with modifier, verb*

                    | The business concluded
                  ▼   ▲ *for this* session,
        the *church* board   dismissed.

21. *Gerund phrase, verb, object complement, direct object*

        Planning the ▼ *worship*
            service   took   *several* hours.

22. *Subject, verb, object complement, direct object, modified by a gerund/object of a preposition, adverbial phrase*

        We   bought   a *small* car
                                  ▲ *for* driving
                                  ▲ *around* town.

23. *Subject with modifiers, linking verb, infinitive phrase used as a predicate nominative*

        My best bet   is   *to* exercise
                                   ▲ *daily.*

24. *Subject with modifiers, linking verb, adverb, predicate nominative, modified by an infinitive phrase*

        World War I   was
                  ▲ *supposedly*   the war
                          ▲ *to* end *all* wars.

25. *Subject, verb, direct object/subject of infinitive, infinitive, modified by an adverbial phrase*

        They   saw   an angel
                             ▲ (to) fly
                                  ▲ *during* the night.

26. *Compound sentence (two independent clauses joined by a conjunction)*

           | I   worked
                    ▲ *all* day
      but ▼ she   slept
                    ▲ *all* night.

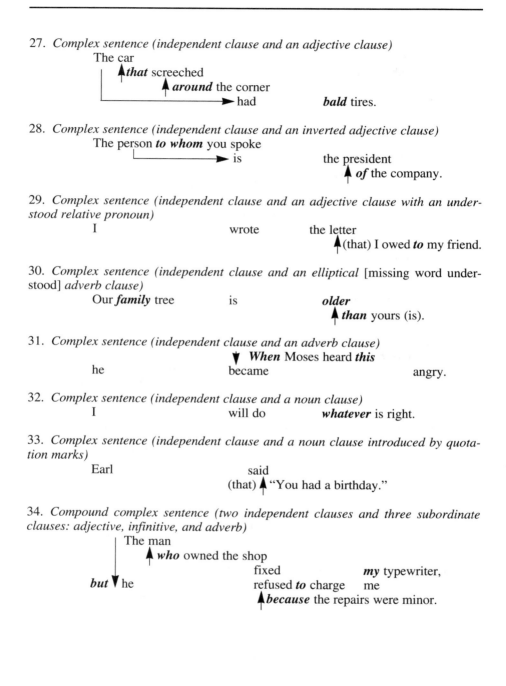

27. *Complex sentence (independent clause and an adjective clause)*

The car
   ▲*that* screeched
      ▲ *around* the corner
         → had   **bald** tires.

28. *Complex sentence (independent clause and an inverted adjective clause)*

The person *to whom* you spoke
      → is   the president
                  ▲ *of* the company.

29. *Complex sentence (independent clause and an adjective clause with an understood relative pronoun)*

I   wrote   the letter
                     ▲(that) I owed *to* my friend.

30. *Complex sentence (independent clause and an elliptical* [missing word understood] *adverb clause)*

Our **family** tree   is   ***older***
                        ▲ *than* yours (is).

31. *Complex sentence (independent clause and an adverb clause)*

           ▼ **When** Moses heard ***this***
he   became   angry.

32. *Complex sentence (independent clause and a noun clause)*

I   will do   **whatever** is right.

33. *Complex sentence (independent clause and a noun clause introduced by quotation marks)*

Earl   said
     (that) ▲ "You had a birthday."

34. *Compound complex sentence (two independent clauses and three subordinate clauses: adjective, infinitive, and adverb)*

    The man
      ▲ *who* owned the shop
         fixed   *my* typewriter,
but ▼ he   refused *to* charge   me
          ▲*because* the repairs were minor.

CHAPTER 8

<h1>CATEGORIES OF VERBS</h1>

Norma Youngberg's instructions to neophyte writers can be just as appropriate to those learning how to intepret a biblical passage. "Every craftsman is concerned first of all with his material: the builder with wood, cement, brick; the tailor with cloth; the cook with food. Words are the writer's basic material. He must know words, their use and their quality, as a builder knows wood, as a tailor knows fabric, as a cook knows foods and seasonings.

Time and Kind of Action

"Words can kill and words can make alive. Every shade and degree of power between these two extremes is within the capacity of words. A writer must first of all have a working vocabulary. He must know the quality of words and their functions, methods of handling them, and their power or futility. . . .

"A writer needs to know the strength of simple words, the effectiveness of few words, the power of the unsaid word" *(Creative Techniques for Christian Writers*, p. 5).

So in trying to understand the meaning in any passage of Scripture, it is important to know how the verbs function. Because verbs express the action intended, they are extremely significant, and to give them slight attention serves only to hamper the communication process.

It is common knowledge that the Scriptures were written in two languages—Hebrew and Greek. (Aramaic, a cousin to Hebrew, is used in a few isolated instances.) What is not commonly known is that the rules governing verbs in Hebrew and, to a lesser extent, Greek are not the same rules describing English verbs. It is important, then, to understand how verbs functioned in these ancient languages.

New Testament Greek

Although Koine Greek actually has six tenses, the kinds of action found in the New Testament boil down to three groups:

1. momentary action that is frozen at a point in time includes (a) an action that is isolated at its beginning ("He began, or started, to teach") or at its end ("He effectively, or successfully, or completely taught"); (b) an entire action viewed at a glance, regardless of how long it actually lasted ("If he ever teaches" or "His teaching as a whole, or on the whole, is poor"); (c) an action captured as a single or one-time occurrence, regardless of when it happens ("If he teaches even once"); and (d) an anticipating action that is a fact or reality ("If he indeed, or in fact, or actually, or really does teach . . .").

2. persistent and ongoing action includes (a) continuous and uninterrupted action ("He continuously, or uninterruptedly, shines"); (b) action in progress ("He is already, or is constantly, or keeps on shining"); (c) recurring action ("He repeatedly

shines" or "He shines again and again" or "He keeps trying, or kept trying, to shine"); (d) customary or habitual action ("He customarily, or habitually, or regularly shines" or "He used to or began to shine").

FIGURE 81

COMMANDS OR CHALLENGES		
POSITIVE		
Category	Momentary Action	Persistent Action
Purpose	urges to choose	commits to a process
Situation	particular, specific	general, recurring
Calls for	a decisive choice	a long-term plan
Focus	on the spot decision	a lifestyle commitment
Example	"Put on the whole armor."	"Follow me."
NEGATIVE		
Purpose	to prevent an action from ever occurring	to stop an action already in progress or to turn down an action each time it comes up again
Example	"Never begin to quarrel."	"Stop being quarrelsome."
	"Do not quarrel at all."	"Do not allow quarreling to continue any longer."
	"Don't even start to quarrel."	"Go on refusing to quarrel."

3. perfective or completed action includes (a) action that combines both of the above to express the continuation of a completed action or (b) action that focuses on either the complete and finished act, for which no further effort is required, or on the effect of that completed act, which lingers on.

Compare the verbs in your text with the examples in the catalog of tenses. Work through the various possibilities until you find the type of action for each one that is demanded by the context.

The Significance of Greek Voices—The *voice* of a verb tells us how the *subject* relates to the action.

Active—Here the subject produces the action, but the stress is on the action itself and not on the subject.

1. *The Simple Active*—When John wrote: "For God so *loved* the world that He *gave* His only begotten Son" (John 3:16, NKJV), he was not emphasizing the Creator as much as what the Creator did. In fact, John did not bother to explain why God loves the world or how God's Son could allow Himself to be offered as a sacrifice. He simply announced the fact of God's love and then traced Christ's sacrifice back to it.

2. *The Causative Active*—Sometimes the subject *causes* the action to occur rather than personally performs it, as in 1 Corinthians 3:6. Taken literally, the text seems to say, "I planted, Apollos watered, and God *was growing*." The verse makes better sense, however, if we translate the last verb causatively—"and God *caused the growth*," so that God does not grow—He makes growth happen.

200

3. *The Reflexive Active*—When an active verb occurs with a reflexive pronoun, the subject acts upon itself, much as it does in the Reflexive Middle voice (see below). In Luke 23:39, for example, one of the thieves crucified beside Christ sarcastically tempted Him to use His power and so, avoid death: *"Save yourself and us."* By choosing the *reflexive active* instead of the middle voice, Luke emphasizes the sinister nature of the temptation. Motivated by his own self-interests, the thief attempted to trick Jesus into saving him, by appealing to the basic human need for self-preservation. If Jesus had rescued Himself, however, He would have abandoned His sacrificial calling—and failed to save anyone else.

4. *Deponent-Active*—Deponent verbs are *middle* or *passive* in form—but *active* in meaning. Their subjects either *cause* the action or perform it in a *simple* or *reflexive way.*

Passive—Here the subject participates in the action, so the stress is usually on the agent that produces it.

1. *Emphatic Agency*—In Ephesians 2:13 Paul wrote: "But now in Christ Jesus you who once were far off *have been brought near* by the blood of Christ." The emphasis here is not on those who were once cut off or on their new status with God, but on Christ's blood, which miraculously makes this happen. There are two possible agencies when the verb is passive:

Direct Agency—(1) when the agent that *personally* acts upon the subject
    (a) appears without a preposition
        "Come, you who have been blessed *by My Father"* (Matthew 25:34)
    (b) is accompanied by one of the following prepositions:
    [apo] "Let no one who is being tempted say, I am being tempted *by God"* (James 1:13) [emphatically denies that anyone can trace temptation back to God as its source]
    [ek] "God sent forth His Son, made *by a woman"* (Galatians 4:4) [focuses on the incarnation by emphasizing Christ the man's very human beginnings]
    [hupo] "They were being baptized in the river Jordan *by him"* (Matthew 3:6) [emphasizes John the Baptizer as the primary agent who personally performed this rite]
    [para] "This was done *by the Lord"* (Matthew 21:42) [emphasizes the Lord as the source of what was done]
    (2) the agent that *impersonally* acts upon the subject is accompanied by the preposition:
    [en] "For *by grace* you are saved" (Ephesians 2:8).
Intermediary Agency—when the agent that acts as the medium through which the direct agent acts upon the subject is accompanied by the preposition:
    [dia] ". . . so that the world might be saved *through Him"* (John 3:17).

2. *Omitted Agency*—A passive sentence does not need to mention the agent. For example, "they will be shown mercy," is the passive of, "God will be merciful to them." The Bible writers omitted agents for *three* principle reasons: (1) to avoid repeating God's name (the so-called, *Theological Passive),* (2) when the agent was irrelevant, or (3) when the agent was obvious from the context.

Thematic Passive—When authors wanted to keep the topic, theme, or previous subject as the subject of the sentence, they resorted to the passive voice. In Romans 1:17, for instance, the passive verb *"is revealed"* allows Paul to feature and stay on the theme of *the righteousness of God* which he began to develop in verse 16.

Middle-Passive—Although it eventually replaced the middle, the passive had middle roots and Greeks commonly interchanged the two voices. It comes as no surprise then that there are occasions where a middle verb has passive overtones and vice versa. For instance, the verb *baptized* in Acts 22:16, normally translated *passive,* *"be baptized,"* is actually a *permissive middle—"get yourself baptized,"* and the verb *humble* in 1 Peter 5:6, normally translated *middle, "humble yourselves under the mighty hand of God,"* is actually a *passive of emphatic agency—"Become humble by the mighty hand of God."* The sense is not so much passive, however, emphasizing God's powerful agency, but middle, stressing the willingness of God's people to accept what happens to them because it is all part of their powerful God's plan. If they will do this, the God who resists the proud and *"gives grace to the humble"* (verse 5), will *"lift* [them] *up at an appropriate time."*

Middle—Here the subject produces and then participates in or expresses deep concern for the results of the action. The stress is on the subject in one of four ways:

1. *intensive*, which is the most important of the four. It accents the subject's role in producing the action, as in "Be imitators [yourselves] of God, therefore, as dearly loved children" (Eph. 5:1, NIV). Paul wanted the Ephesians to reflect personally the heavenly Father in their own lives; no one else could do it for them.

2. *reflexive*, which is second in importance to the intensive. It accents the subject's participation in the results of the action (to act in one's own interest). "Lay aside the old man *for yourselves*, from the old way of life . . . and put on the new man" (Eph. 4:22). Here Paul emphasized that the only way to make room for the new man is to personally discard the old one.

3. *reciprocal*, which accents plural subjects as they interchange action. "Submit *[yourselves] to one another* out of reverence for Christ" (Eph. 5:21, NIV). Respect for Christ is the spirit in which the Ephesians could show humility to each other. Only as they bowed to Him would wives and husbands, children and parents, even servants and masters swallow their pride and serve other's interests.

4. *permissive*, which accents the subject as he or she allows himself or herself to yield to the results of an action. "That we *permit ourselves* to be children no longer, tossed and carried about by every wind of doctrine" (Eph. 4:14). If the Ephesians were tired of being pushed around like children, then all they had to do was allow the ministry of the apostles, the prophets, the evangelists, and the pastor-teachers to equip them for service. As a result the church would grow and mature into a full grown person with the dimensions of Jesus Christ.

The Significance of Greek Moods—The *mood* tells us something about the psychology of the speaker or writer.

FIGURE 82

INDICATIVE	SUBJUNCTIVE	OPTATIVE	IMPERATIVE
Certainty	Probability	Conceivability	Intentionality
Factual	Objective	Subjective	Desirable
Actuality	Hinges on little	Hinges on much	Pure appeal
Reality	Objectively possible	Subjectively possible	Voluntary possible
Is happening	Should happen	Could happen	Let it happen
INDEPENDENT	D E P E N D E N T		

Indicative—In the form of simple statements or questions, the indicative mood expresses certainty or what is actually going on. All other moods depend on the indicative because it is the only one entirely rooted in the facts. Verbs in this mood set the time frame for the context.

Verbs in the indicative mood function in the following ways:

The *declarative* indicative states a simple fact: "We *have seen* His star and *have come* to worship Him" (Matt. 2:2).

The *interrogative* indicative asks a simple question in search of a factual answer: "Who *do* men *say* that the Son of Man is?" (Matt. 16:13).

The *cohortative* (future) indicative compels rather than predicts what will happen in the future: "You *shall call* his name John" (Luke 1:13).

The *potential* indicative expresses something that should, would, or could occur. Something in the nature of the verbal idea, the context or some other word in the sentence (usually the particle "an") tempers its certainty with contingency:

Obligation—"It *should have appeared necessary* to you to have invested my money with the bankers" (Matt. 25:27).

Wish or impulse—"I myself *have been wanting* to hear the man" (Acts 25:22).

Condition—"If God so loved us, [and as a matter of fact, He did], we also ought to love one another" (1 John 4:11). "Lord, *had* You *been* here, [but we know that You were not], my brother *would not have died*" (John 11:21).

Subjunctive—The subjunctive mood expresses probability in the form of a thought presented as an objective possibility as the writer or speaker begins to speculate. The writer or speaker assumes that although the verbal idea is not yet a fact, it may become one—but the whole thing hinges on certain objective factors.

In *independent* [main] clauses

• the **hortatory** subjunctive encourages others to join the speaker or writer in a course of action: "*Let us* also *go*, that we may die with Him" (John 11:16).

• the **prohibitive** subjunctive (the aorist subjunctive with the negative particle *me*) attempts to head off an action before it has a chance to occur (see "Commands or Challenges," *Negative, Momentary Action*, pp. 331, 332).

• the **deliberative** subjunctive allows the speaker or writer to ask a rhetorical question or challenge the audience to think something over carefully before they make a decision: "*Should* I *crucify* your king?" (John 19:15).

• the **emphatic negative** subjunctive (the aorist subjunctive with the double negative *ou me*) expresses the impossibility of something: "Unless your righteousness exceeds that of the scribes and Pharisees, you *will never enter* the kingdom of heaven" (Matt. 5:20).

In *dependent* [subordinate] clauses

• in a **purpose** clause the subjunctive expresses the purpose of the action of the main verb: "They love to pray standing . . . for the purpose of being seen by people" (Matt. 6:5).

• in a **result** clause the subjunctive indicates the results of the action of the main verb: "These things are contrary to one another, and *as a result* you *cannot do* what you want" (Rom. 11:11).

• in a **conditional** clause, the subjunctive expresses a probable future condition: "If her husband *should die* [and he probably will], she is released from the marriage bond" (Rom. 7:2).

• in an **imperative** clause the subjunctive expresses a command: "The wife *is to* *respect* her husband" (Eph. 5:33).

• in a **relative** clause the subjunctive expresses either a probable future condition (as subjunctives in conditional clauses do) or results: "He is worthy and *as a result* you *should do* this for Him" (Luke 7:4).

• in a **comparative** clause the subjunctive compares the subject of the main verb with its own: "The kingdom of heaven is similar to a net that *was cast* into the sea" (Matt. 24:28).

• in a **temporal** clause the subjunctive expresses something probably in the indefinite future: "Whenever you *see* all these things, recognize that [the end] is near" (Matt. 24:33).

• in a **concessive** clause the subjunctive concedes something hypothetical: "Brethren, even if someone *gets caught* in [the act of doing] something wrong, you who are spiritual restore him" (Gal. 6:1).

• in a **substantival** clause the subjunctive supplies potential action to the subject of a noun clause:

1. when the noun clause acts as a *subject*: "That one of these little ones *should perish* is not the will of your Father who is in heaven" (Matt. 18:14).

2. when the noun clause acts as a *predicate nominative*: "My meat is [that I am] *to do*" (John 4:34).

3. when the noun clause acts as an *object*: "If you are the Son of God, order that these stones *should become* bread" (Matt. 4:3).

4. when the noun clause acts as an *appositive*: "This is my commandment, [namely] that you *should love* one another" (John 15:12).

Optative—The optative mood is less optimistic and expresses something conceivable, but it hinges on many factors. It is possible as the writer or speaker sees it, and so he or she presents the whole thing in the form of a wish.

In *independent* [main] clauses

• the **voluntative** optative expresses a wish or a prayer: "There are times I *could almost wish to be accursed*" (Rom. 9:3).

• the **potential** optative expresses what would happen if an expressed or implied condition were fulfilled: "How *can* I unless someone will guide me?" (Acts 8:31).

• the **deliberative** optative expresses a very doubtful state of mind in the form of an indirect rhetorical question: "A discussion arose among them about which of them *was* the greatest" (Luke 9:46).

In *dependent* [subordinate] clauses

• in **conditional** clauses the optative expresses a possible future condition: "Even if you *should suffer* because of righteousness [and it is possible that you will], (you will be) blessed" (1 Peter 3:14).

Imperative—The imperative mood is the weakest of all moods because it expresses something that is entirely out of the speaker's or writer's control. What he desires or intends depends entirely on people or things outside of himself. He presents in the form of a command or urgent request that which he would like to see happen, but he knows that the whole thing is up to the other party or parties. The speaker or writer appeals to the indicative as the ground for the demand. That's where he got the idea in the first place. He finds the possibility in the indicative fact, appeals to it, and intends for the audience to carry it out.

In *independent* [main] clauses

• the imperative of **command** expresses a direct appeal to the will of another person either to commence and/or continue an action (see "Commands or Challenges, Positive" on p. 331).

• the imperative of **prohibition** (the present imperative with the negative particle *me*) expresses an appeal to another person to stop an action already in progress or to turn down an action each time it comes up again (see "Commands or Challenges, Negative, Persistent Action" on pp. 331, 332).

• the imperative of **entreaty** softens the force of the imperative to a request, sometimes with a note of urgency. It frequently occurs when a subordinate addresses a superior: "*Please give* us this day our daily bread" (Matt. 6:11).

• the imperative of **condition** causes an independent clause to function as though it were dependent and conditional. So the literal translation "*Destroy* this temple, and I will rebuild it in three days" is more accurately translated "*If you destroy* this temple [hypothetical case], I will rebuild it in three days" (John 2:19).

• the imperative of **permission** expresses compliance with the desire or consent to the request of another: "But if the unbeliever leaves, *let him go*" (1 Cor. 7:15).

• the imperative of **concession** concedes something hypothetical: "Be angry and sin not" would be better rendered "*Although you may become angry*, you must not sin" (Eph. 4:26).

In *dependent* [subordinate] clauses

• in a **relative** clause the imperative expresses duty or obligation toward or concerning the subject of the main clause: "Your nemesis the devil . . . whom you *must resist*" (1 Peter 5:8, 9).

The Significance of Greek Tenses—The **present tense** normally describes action going on in the present from the writer's or speaker's point of view. The present tense functions several ways in New Testament Greek:

1. The *descriptive* present—"Our lamps are going out" (Matt. 25:8). Although these lamps continue to burn at present, they *are growing* dim on the way to being extinguished.

2. The *progressive* present—"For three years, I *have been coming* . . ." (Luke 13:7, NASB). Here is an action from the past that continues into the present, and it is captured in a single expression. The gardener is not griping about a three-year journey, but he is expressing the frustration and disappointment from three unsuccessful annual attempts to find fruit on his fig tree.

3. The *iterative* present—"I *fast* twice a week" (Luke 18:12). The Pharisee here brags about his custom of fasting two times each week.

4. The *conative* present—"You . . . [*keep trying* to] stone me" (John 10:32). Jesus reminds the crowd that this is not the first time that they have tried—unsuccessfully—to stone Him.

5. The *historical* present—"And she . . . [*sees*] two angels in white" (John 20:12). Although John describes something that has already happened, he tells us about it as though we are there while it is going on. That makes the act from the past really come to life.

6. The *gnomic* (proverbial) present—"Every good tree *bears* good fruit" (Matt. 7:17). This is a timeless truth that even continues to be true in the present.

7. The *futuristic* present—"I . . . [*am going* to] rise" (Matt. 27:63). Instead of just announcing something in advance, Jesus adds a note of confident assurance here. Although the resurrection lies in the future—on the other side of the cross—Jesus gives it an unbroken connection with the present. It is one of the steps in the walk He

had already begun.

8. The *perfect* present—"Your brother *has come*" (Luke 15:27). Certain Greek verbs stress either the past verbal act or its results by using the present tense. This is one of those verbs that plugs into the present. The brother successfully ends his journey by arriving at the destination he intended to reach. But enough about the trip! The big news is that he is here!

The **future tense** generally refers to a point in time that is yet to come as far as the speaker's or writer's point of view is concerned.

1. The *volitive* (intentional) future—"You *shall call* His name Jesus" (Matt. 1:21, NKJV). The Father is determined that when His Son is born, Mary should call Him Jesus, and the angel communicates this divine intent in the form of a command.

2. Simple *futurity*—"For he *will save* His people from their sins" (Matt. 1:21, NKJV). Jesus will definitely rescue His people, but the day of their deliverance is still in the future.

3. The *deliberative* future—"How *shall* we . . . *live* any longer in it?" (Rom. 6:2, NKJV). Paul pondered how anyone who has died to sin with Christ and come alive to God can live any longer under the tyranny of sin.

The **imperfect tense** shows action going on in past time from the writer's or speaker's point of view.

1. The *inchoative* (inceptive) imperfect—"He . . . *began to teach*" (Mark 1:21, REB). When Jesus arrived at Capernaum, the first thing He did on the Sabbath was to head straight for the synagogue, where He spread the good news. Mark catches Jesus the teacher just as He begins His first class there in the synagogue.

2. The *progressive* imperfect—"Why *were* you *searching* for me?" (Luke 2:49). Jesus wanted to know why Mary and Joseph went about searching for Him. His question includes all the activity they had spent trying to locate Him—from the past right up to that moment—in a single expression.

3. The *iterative* (repetitive) imperfect—"A certain man . . . *[used to be] carried* . . ." (Acts 3:2). Luke wrote about a man lame from birth whom others carried to the Temple so that he could beg alms every day. This was a customary, habitual, repeated, ritual act carried out in the past, from the writer's point of view.

4. The *desiderative* imperfect—"[There are times] I *could* [almost] *wish* that myself were accursed" (Rom. 9:3, KJV). Paul wrote about a feeling that he had felt for some time, though he did not cherish it at the time he was writing. Even though he still felt the same way, Paul realized that he could never carry it out. So he deliberately toned down a remark that would normally shock or offend God's true people. This frees Paul to express how much he wanted to win his natural brothers to Christ while at the same time not compromising his loyalty to God.

5. The *conative* imperfect—"John . . . *[kept trying]* to prevent . . ." (Matt. 3:14, NKJV). John kept interrupting Jesus, trying to hinder Him from going under the water, but eventually John gave in and baptized Him.

The **aorist tense** views action as a moment in time that was usually in the past from the writer's or speaker's point of view. In the imperative the aorist calls for an immediate start or an abrupt end to something.

1. The *ingressive* aorist—"Jesus *burst out weeping*" (see John 11:35). John looked at the action as it broke into the story to emphasize its suddenness. He caught Jesus about to have a good cry—just as He exploded into tears.

2. The *effective* aorist—He "*has triumphed*" (Rev. 5:5, NIV). John looked at the

conclusion of an action to emphasize the success of an effort. He caught Jesus, "the Lion of the tribe of Judah," at the glorious moment of victory, having won a smashing triumph over all the forces of darkness.

3. The *constantive* aorist—"Nevertheless death *reigned* from Adam to Moses" (Rom. 5:14, NKJV). Paul summarized what is happening for us by reducing the time of action to a point so that we can look at the entire period as a whole—at a glance. Here he spotlighted the stranglehold death had on humanity from the fall of Adam to the days of Moses by emphasizing the way it thoroughly dominated every person who lived throughout that period.

4. The *narrative* aorist—"We . . . *stayed* . . ." (Acts 28:12). Luke presented the real order of events by showing that one past event had preceded another that was either mentioned or implied in the context. Here he points out that he and Paul spent three days at Syracuse after a three-month stay at Malta and just before arriving by ship at Rhegium.

5. The *gnomic* aorist—"He is like a branch that *is thrown away* and withers" (John 15:6, NIV). Scholars are split over how to interpret this one. Some believe that the author chose the aorist instead of the present tense to express timeless truths in a more abrupt and startling way: Fruitless branches are good for only one thing—the woodpile. Others say that this is a dramatic New Testament version of the Hebrew perfect. John may have chosen the aorist to dramatize the seriousness of the situation by emphasizing the sudden end that awaits fruitless branches—how complete and final it is.

6. The *dramatic* aorist—"I *know* what I will do!" (Luke 16:4, TEV). Sometimes writers or speakers use the aorist in place of the present tense in order to more graphically present a state of mind just reached or an act that expresses it. Here the manager is about to lose his job. Unable to perform manual labor—and ashamed to beg—he hits on a shrewd idea. Luke dramatically interrupts the text to capture vividly the way that the idea suddenly popped into the manager's head.

7. The *epistolary* aorist—"See what large letters I use as I *write* to you" (Gal. 6:11, NIV). Paul here put himself in the place of his readers by describing his present writing activity as though it were in the past—the way it was by the time the Galatians actually received it. In this case Paul took the pen from his scribe's hand to write the closing paragraph himself with noticeably larger letters.

The **perfect tense** describes an action completed in the past that may have results that continue into the writer's or speaker's present. Whereas the aorist testifies that something actually did happen, the perfect tense confirms that it reached the normal result.

1. The *extensive* perfect—"I *have fought* . . . I *have finished* . . . I *have kept* . . ." (2 Tim. 4:7). Paul described a completed effort. Nothing remained undone to reach the intended result. God had given him a task and had the means to accomplish it. When Paul summed up his life as one big thrust toward winning the contest, finishing the course, and keeping the faith, he meant that he had carried things out God's way. As a result, no additional effort was required. The task stood completed.

2. The *intensive* perfect—"That he was buried, and . . . *[remains raised* since] the third day" (1 Cor. 15:4). Sometimes the past act disappears from view, leaving only its results. Here Paul testified that Christ really died, because He was buried (aorist), and he assured the readers that the Saviour truly accomplished His earthly mission through the Resurrection. The only successful way for Jesus to finish His ministry on

earth was to conquer death. Since God had rescued Jesus from the grave (the act) on the third day, Jesus had remained triumphantly raised to life (the abiding result) since.

3. The *iterative* perfect—"Did I exploit you through any of the men I *sent* you?" (1 Cor. 12:17, 18, NIV). This is a special use of the extensive perfect, which indicates repeated action in the past at intervals. Unlike the present or imperfect, this iterative perfect does not necessarily refer to the same act performed again and again. But it does spotlight action that was repeated at intervals, and these repeated actions worked toward the same goal and had the same normal result. Paul first, then Titus and Timothy, whom he sent, all worked in the same spirit and pursued the same course. They all strengthened and built up the Corinthian church and never took advantage of the Corinthian Christians.

4. The *dramatic-historical* perfect—"John bore witness of Him and *cried out* . . ." (John 1:15, NKJV). This use of the intensive perfect dramatizes a narrative by vividly bringing a past event into the speaker's or writer's present. John wrote his Gospel nearly 70 years after John the Baptist's death. Yet the use of the perfect tense here allowed him to vividly bring the forerunner's testimony out of the past and dramatically into the present. The apostle had heard those immortal words back then, and now his readers could also hear John "cry out" on behalf of Messiah Jesus.

5. The *gnomic* perfect—"A woman *is bound* to her husband as long as he lives" (1 Cor. 7:39, NKJV). This use of the perfect describes a custom of society that is the abiding result or state left behind by some past action. In this case the marriage vow had established a state of affairs that remained in effect until the husband died.

6. The *allegorical* perfect—"But God *dealt* graciously with Abraham through a promise" (see Gal. 3:18). Some Bible writers used the perfect tense for a New Testament exposition of an Old Testament verse. Since the perfect expresses continuation from the past to the present time, this particular usage represents Old Testament events as more than history—they stand recorded in the abiding Christian tradition, contemporary with and relevant to New Testament people. References to Christ or the church, however, are more than relevant; they are still in operation (abiding results). In this passage, Paul told the Galatian Christians that because even Abraham had nothing more than God's word for it, the covenant promise always was, still is, and ever shall be the only means by which human beings can receive the title to the inheritance. The law determines only their fitness to keep it.

7. The *prophetic* perfect—"And I *am* glorified in them" (John 17:10, KJV). Jesus confidently expressed His expectation that the disciples would do Him honor in the future—expressed it as though it had already happened.

The **pluperfect tense** normally represents a state or result in the past that was generated by a completed action that was still further in the past. (Note that the perfect tense represents a present state resulting from a past action, but the pluperfect tense represents a past state resulting from a yet previous action.)

1. The *extensive* pluperfect—"It *had* its foundation" (Matt. 7:25, NIV). The builder completed the foundation of the house prior to the flood. Designed to withstand the flood, it did not fall because the builder's efforts had reached their normal result—a foundation built to last.

2. The *intensive* pluperfect—"For the Jews *had already* agreed" (John 9:22). Verbs that express the present intensive aspect of the perfect also stress the past intensive aspect of the pluperfect. When the Pharisees investigated the healing of a man born blind, his parents denied knowing by whom he had been healed or how this mir-

acle had happened. And verse 22 explains why. They were afraid (still) of the Jewish leaders, based on a previous agreement with them that anyone who acknowledged Messiah Jesus should be barred from the synagogue.

Old Testament Hebrew

The Hebrew language has only two tenses—the *perfect* and the *imperfect*, either of which can occur in the past, present, or future. In other words, the tense does not determine when the action occurs. It reveals only the *kind* of action: (a) the short or decisive tense expresses an action complete and finished, rounded off to a point in time, or (b) the long or continuous tense expresses an incomplete and ongoing action.

The context and certain grammatical devices decide whether the verbal idea occurs in the past, present, or future. Generally speaking, time depends on whether a *chain of verbs* begins with either a perfect (short) or an imperfect (long) verb. Unless the context indicates otherwise, the short tense is in the past and the long is in the future, and the verbs that follow connect their kind of action to the time set by this first verb with the conjunction *waw* (and). For example: [long] + [waw + short] = [long] + [long].

Many grammarians say that the conjunction *waw* converts one tense into the other. Actually, the *waw* doesn't convert. It *connects*:

1. the *completeness* of the perfect (usually past; for instance, Gen. 1:5; Ex. 1:1) with:

   a. the *present* to express decisiveness (Ex. 3:7, 9) or

   b. the *future* to express certainty (Ex. 4:9; Lev. 4:20) or decisiveness (Ex. 3:20) or

2. the *incompleteness* of the imperfect (usually future; for instance, Gen. 9:26; Ex. 3:19) with

   a. the *present* to express habit, custom (Gen. 10:9; Ex. 13:15), or persistence (Ex. 5:4; 14:15) or

   b. the *past* to express long-lasting activity or results (Ex. 3:17) or permanency (Gen. 1:3).

At times both tenses can work together, as in the case where something in the future depends on whether certain conditions are met first. For example, when Moses said, "If a priest who is anointed *should sin* [imperfect, long tense] then *let* him *bring* [perfect, short tense] a sin offering" (Lev. 4:3), he meant that if an anointed priest should sin tomorrow, the next day, or later, the Lord expects him to bring an appropriate sin offering to the sanctuary/Temple and do so without delay.

Sometimes the Old Testament writers omitted verbs from the text to focus attention on the condition or state of the characters rather than on their activity. In such cases the translator supplies the missing verb. (In most King James Bibles, this verb is in italics.)

Characteristically, however, the *perfect* (short and decisive) tense translates as the simple past ("I wrote") or the present perfect ("I have written").

With verbs that signify *perception* or the *attitude* of the subject toward an object (rather than an action performed on the object), the *perfect* can be translated as "I love," "I loved," or "I have loved"; or "I know," "I knew," or "I have known."

With verbs that signify the *mental or physical state* of the subject and consistently do not have a direct object, the *perfect* can be translated as the present of the verb "to be" plus an adjective ("I am old," "I have become old," or "I grew old") or as "I aged."

With verbs that frequently occur in *poetic and proverbial expressions* but only rarely in prose, the *perfect* expresses habitual activity with no specific tense value and so is translated in the general present ("I write").

The *imperfect* (long and continuous) tense expresses specific and simple futurity ("I will write").

If the *imperfect* refers to a general and nonspecific action that occurs by *force of habit* or is a *regular, customary* action, it is translated as "I write" or "I used to write."

If the *imperfect* refers to a *potential or probable action*, It can be translated "I can (or could or may or might or would or should or will or shall [probably] write."

Sometimes the *imperfect* is used in a special manner, as when it is used to *challenge* others to take up a certain course of action: in the *first person* it is *cohortative* ("Let us stand firm!") and in the *second person* it is *imperative* ("[You] stand firm!") and in the *third person* it is *jussive* ("Let him stand firm!").

When the *imperative* is part of a verb chain, there are four possibilities: **time**—(a) the imperative plus imperative with the *waw* indicates a list that *may be* in chronological order, or (b) the imperative plus the perfect with the *waw* indicates a list that is *definitely* in chronological order; or **intention**—(a) the imperative alone or (b) the imperative plus the imperative or the jussive alone or the jussive plus the cohortative indicates purpose or result.

FIGURE 83
OVERVIEW OF THE HEBREW TENSES
(Adapted from the Newberry Bible)

TENSE	TIME OF OCCURRENCE		
	PAST	PRESENT	FUTURE
Short w/o *waw*	Complete, finished action or event	Decision	Certainty or probability
Long w/o *waw*	Incomplete action still in progress	Incomplete action, habit, custom, or practice	Promise or prediction
Short with *waw*	Complete, finished action or event	Contemporary with chain	Decision, certainty, or probability
Long with *waw*	Permanence; estab-templishes a fact; long-lasting act or results	Contemporary with chain	Futurity or con-temporary with chain

The Significance of Hebrew Voices—Hebrew also employs the active, passive, and middle voices but in a more restricted manner than in New Testament Greek. The **active** expresses itself in the *Qal, Piel*, and *Hiphil* themes; the **passive** in the *Qal, Niphal, Pual*, and *Hophal* themes; and the **middle** in the *Niphal* theme.

The Significance of Hebrew Verb Themes—The simplest form of a Hebrew verb normally consists of three letters. This root provides the fundamental idea of the verb and acts as a stem to which are added prefixes or suffixes that modify its form and develop its idea along seven basic lines or *themes*.

The *Qal*

• The **stative Qal** expresses a state or condition: "So he and his garments *shall* *be holy*" (Ex. 29:21).

• the **fientive Qal** expresses an action: "In the beginning, God *created* the heavens and the earth" (Gen. 1:1).

The *Niphal*

• the **resultitive** Niphal. Passives normally reverse the active sense. For instance, in the active sentence "The boy *walked* the dog," the boy is the subject who walks the dog. In its passive counterpart "The dog *was walked* by the boy," the boy still walks the dog, but the dog, formerly the direct object, is recast as the subject in order to emphasize it. For example, in the question "Why *is* the house of God *neglected*?" (Neh. 13:11), Nehemiah features the deplorable condition of the Temple as the result of withholding tithe from God's workers and he does so to rekindle the spirit of giving among the people.

• the **passive** Niphal stresses the agent (in the following case the agent is "my glory") that acts upon the subject: "And [the tabernacle] *shall be treated as holy* by my glory" (Ex. 29:43).

• in the **middle** Niphal the subject acts in its own interest: "I *will prove Myself holy* in you, before their eyes" (Eze. 36:23).

• in the **reflexive** Niphal the subject acts upon itself: "*Hide yourselves* there three days" (Josh. 2:16).

• in the **reciprocal** Niphal plural subjects interact: "Provide me a man that we *may fight one another*" (1 Sam. 17:10).

• in the **tolerative** Niphal the subject allows itself to yield to the results of an action: "But if the watchman sees the sword coming . . . and the people *do not let themselves be warned* . . ." (Eze. 33:6).

The *Piel* and *Pual*

For every Piel verb there is also a passive counterpart (the Pual).

• The **factitive** Piel/Pual forms active transitive verbs from roots that appear as intransitive or stative verbs in the Qal. For instance, the root *qadosh* (to be holy) in the Qal becomes "to sanctify" in the Piel/Pual: "I *will sanctify* My great name" (Eze. 36:23).

• The **causative** Piel/Pual (rare) takes roots that appear as fientive verbs in Qal and forms verbs that express the person or thing that produces an effect. In this way the root *yalad* (to bear a child; to beget) becomes "to assist or attend as a midwife" in the Piel/Pual: "When you *help* the Hebrew women *at childbirth* . . ." (Ex. 1:16).

• The **intensive** Piel/Pual pluralizes or magnifies the action that roots express in the Qal. The root *shaal* (to ask) in the Qal, for instance, becomes "to beg" in the Piel/Pual: "Let his children wander about and *beg*" (Ps. 109:10).

• The **delocutive** Piel/Pual transforms idiomatic expressions into verbs. So, for example, the root *tsaddiyq* (right, which also came to mean innocent or in the right) becomes "pronounce innocent" or "pronounce in the right" in the Piel/Pual: "Speak, because I want to *pronounce* you *in the right*" (Job 33:32).

• The **privative** Piel/Pual recasts the root idea in a privative (deprived) sense. Thus the root *caqal* (stone) expresses the loss or absence of stones in the Piel/Pual: "And he *rid* it *of stones*" (Isa. 5:2).

The *Hiphil* and *Hophal*

For each Hiphil verb there is also a passive counterpart (the Hophal).

• The **causative** Hiphil/Hophal forms verbs (from their Qal counterparts) that express the person or thing that produces an effect. Consequently, the root *'alah* (to go up, to ascend, to climb) becomes in the Hiphil/Hophal "to bring up" or "to cause to ascend or climb": "For this man Moses who *brought* us *up* out of the land of Egypt . . ." (Ex. 32:1).

- The **permissive** Hiphil/Hophal is closely related to the causative. Is Jeremiah saying "The Lord *showed* [caused me to see] me" (causative) or "The Lord *allowed* me *to see*" (permissive) "two baskets of figs set before the temple of the Lord" (Jer. 24:1)? The context is the decisive factor in cases like this.

- The **delocutive** Hiphil/Hophal transforms verbs derived from idiomatic expressions into causative verbs. As a result, the root idea of *qalal* (to be small or to be of little account) becomes "to belittle" or "to treat with contempt" in the Hiphil/Hophal: "Why then did you *treat* us *as insignificant* [and therefore make us small or of little account]?" (2 Sam. 19:43).

- The **factitive** Hiphil/Hophal produces stative verbs from roots that are also stative in the Qal. The root idea of *qarab* (to draw near or to approach), for example, becomes "to bring near" in the Hiphil/Hophal: "And when Samuel *brought* all the tribes of Israel *near* . . ." (1 Sam. 10:20).

- The **intransitive** Hiphil/Hophal—The Hiphil/Hophal can develop verbs that are doubly transitive (that is, that take *two* objects). One is the object of what is caused; the other is an object of the root verbal idea. In the case of "I will *make* them *hear* my words" (Deut. 4:10), God reminds Moses of the day at Horeb when He made the people (*them*, the object caused) hear what He had to say (His *words*, the object of the root verbal idea). If the second object is missing, however, the verbal idea is intransitive. Intransitive Hiphil/Hophal verbs chronicle a person's or thing's entry into a lasting state or condition: "Train up a child in the way he should go, and when he *is old*, he will not depart from it" (Prov. 22:6). In this case, the Hiphil verb points to that time in life when a child grows up, enters adulthood, and remains an adult.

- The **denominative** Hiphil/Hophal transforms a noun root into a verb, as in the case of the root *qaran* (horn). When the psalmist says that "this also shall please the Lord better than an ox or a bull that *displays horns*" (Ps. 69:31), he explains that God appreciates praise and recognition through song and gratitude more than the sacrifice of costly, fully grown animals (whose maturity is indicated by the horns that have been caused to grow until they show).

The *Hithpael*

Hithpael verbs are intransitive. Their subjects always participate in the action.

- The **reflexive** Hithpael may have a direct or indirect sense. In "Let the priests also . . . *sanctify themselves*" (Ex. 19:22), the subjects act directly upon themselves. In "So Abraham *prayed* to God" (Gen. 20:17), however, the patriarch engates in an activity either on his own behalf ("Abraham *himself prayed*") or for his own benefit ("Abraham *prayed for himself*"). The context helps decide which is the proper sense in the passage.

- The **reciprocal** Hithpael expresses interaction, as in Ezekiel 2:2, where the prophet says that after the Spirit entered him and set him on his feet "I heard him *conversing* with me." That is, he heard the Spirit and himself speaking back and forth to each other.

- The **iterative** Hithpael expresses repetitive action: "And they heard God's voice as they *walked about* [walked here and there in] the garden" (Gen. 3:8).

- The **denominative** Hithpael expresses action from noun roots. Hence, the root *nabiy'* (prophet) becomes in the Hithpael "to prophesy," "to behave or speak as a prophet," or "to behave or speak under the influence of the divine Spirit" as in: "So

I *prophesied* as He ordered me" (Eze. 37:10).

Auxiliary Verbs

Bible verbs generally demand more than one word to express themselves in English, so translators frequently resort to auxiliary verbs to help bring out the fullest sense of the text. Although an auxiliary verb can stand alone as an independent verb (for instance, "He *is* Lord"), as a helper it exists for the sole purpose of clarifying the meaning of the main verb in the sentence (as in "The king *is* coming"). For example, the verb "will" in the clause "He *will* return" grammatically tells us that Christ's return is *still future*, but also in the context it helps communicate that His coming is *sure*.

In using or understanding auxiliary verbs, select from the following possibilities the meaning that best fits the context.

1. *Be, being, been, am, are, is, was,* and *were* (in all tenses) (a) describe position, quality, condition, or state; (b) express continuous or repeated action with the present and imperfect tenses, regardless of voice; (c) form intensive perfect verbs in all voices (for instance, "He *is* risen"); and (d) form the passive voice in all tenses (for example, "has been," "is being," and "will be."

2. *Can* and *could* occur with the present, imperfect, and aorist (past) tenses in the indicative and optative moods. *Can* is used with the present tense, implying ability, know-how, right, or permission. *Could* is the past tense of *can* and represents a less certain condition than does the word *can.*

3. *Continue* and *keep* occur with the present tense and express (a) repeated, regular action in the present ("He continues to . . .") or (b) ongoing action from the present and into the future ("Keep on going").

4. *Do* and *does* (with the present tenses) or *did* and *done* (with past tenses) (a) add force to commands, pleadings, promptings, and challenges; (b) emphasize action ("I *do* believe"—Mark 9:24, NIV); (c) substitute for another verb to avoid repetition ("does not live" means in Acts 7:48, NIV, "is not living"; and (d) put Greek sentences into question form ("Did you offer?"—Acts 7:42).

5. *Has, have,* and *had* form extensive perfect and pluperfect verbs in all voices (for instance, "Your faith *has* saved you") and imply possession, prominence, relation, experience, or obligation.

6. *Let* is used with the present and aorist tenses of the imperative and hortatory subjunctive moods and serves to lay down a challenge or extend an invitation with respect to the verbal idea ("*Let us consider* one another"—Heb. 10:24, NKJV).

7. *May* is used in the present tense and *might* in the past tense. *Might* expresses more doubt and a greater dependence on circumstances than does *may* in the imperative, subjunctive, and optative moods. The two words express likelihood, possibility, or probability; concession or contingency; purpose or expectation; a wish or desire in prayer, an imprecation, or a benediction; and an implied doubt, permission, or possibility.

8. *Remain(s)* and *stand(s)* occur in the present and perfect tenses. They strengthen commands or challenges to stick things out (for instance, "Remain firm"), or they emphasize the intensive aspect of the perfect tense ("It *stands* written" instead of "It *has been* written").

9. *Shall* appears in the future tense and expresses a command, prompt, or challenge; what is mandatory (for instance, laws, regulations, or directives); what seems inevitable or likely to happen in the future; simple futurity (in the first person); or de-

termination (in the second and third persons).

10. *Should* is the past of *shall* and rarely expresses time past. It occurs in the aorist and present tenses in the subjunctive and optative moods, and it appears in all three persons—singular or plural. *Should* implies duty or fitness, doubt or hesitancy, and supposition or condition. It expresses condition ("If such-and-such *should* occur, then . . ."); obligation, propriety, or expediency; futurity (from a point of view in the past); what is probable or expected; a polite request; or a direct statement made in a softer way.

11. *Used (to)* occurs in the past tense and expresses customary or habitual action as in "He *used to* go down."

12. *Will* appears in the future tense. It expresses desire, choice, willingness, consent, or refusal in a "will not" construction; frequent, customary, habitual action, or a natural tendency or disposition; simple futurity in the second and third person; capability or sufficiency; probability or inevitability; determination, insistence, persistence, or willfulness when used in the first person; or a command, challenge, or charge.

13. *Would* is the past tense of *will*. It expresses futurity from a point of view in the past; preference with the words "rather" or "sooner;" wish, desire, or intent; willingness; plan or intention; custom or habitual action in the past ("I *would* go to the store . . ."); consent or choice ("I *would* do anything for you"); contingency or possibility in a conditional sentence ("If such-and-such should happen, then I *would* . . ." or "If he *would* do such-and-such, then I could . . ."); a statement of desire, request, or advice to completion in a noun clause ("We wish that he *would* go"); probability or presumption in the past or present; a request that expects voluntary compliance ("*Would* you . . . ?"); or doubt or uncertainty.

14. *Wish* occurs in the optative. It expresses a desire for something that appears unattainable, confers something unwanted on a person ("It is my *wish* that you . . ."), or invokes something good or evil on a person.

Here is a simple and effective procedure for interpreting verbs:

1. Work one sentence at a time.

2. Make a note of all the verbs in each sentence.

3. Are the verbs transitive or intransitive, expressing action, or copulative, expressing state, condition, or character?

4. Record each verb's tense, voice, and mood or theme.

5. Does the *voice* emphasize (a) the action, (b) the subject, or (c) an agent? In what way?

6. What kind of action, state, condition, or character does the *tense* indicate? (a) momentary/complete—isolated at its beginning, viewed in its entirety at a glance, captured as a one-time occurrence, or anticipated? (b) persistent/incomplete—uninterrupted, in-progress, recurring, customary, or habitual? or (c) perfective/complete—finished or lingering?

7. Does the *mood* relate the action or state/condition/character to reality or to some degree of possibility?

8. Along what lines does the *theme* develop the action?

9. What do auxiliary verbs, if any, help bring out?

10. Can you derive any insights from the order in which these verbs appear? Do they contrast, complement, or compound each other? Do they indicate chronological order, purpose, or result?

11. What influence does the context have on the verbal idea?

CHAPTER 9

INFORMED SOURCES

In our discussion of cultural analysis (see chapter 4), ancient Near Eastern literature was mentioned as one of the cultural sources that can help us understand better the messages of the biblical writers. At that point, however, we did not go into detail, specifically mentioning by name these individual resources. Here we do so.

The following selective list is adapted from Edgar Jones, *Discoveries and Documents;* J. Finegan, *Light From the Ancient Past,* Volumes I-II; J. B. Pritchard, *Ancient Near Eastern Texts;* D. Winton Thomas, *Documents from Old Testament Times;* and John H. Walton, *Ancient Israelite Literature in Its Cultural Context.* It is intended to direct you to appropriate literary sources for background information.

Old Testament Period

Creation/Flood Stories

Document	Origin	Date	Brief Description
Eridu Genesis	Sumerian	*c.* 1600 B.C.	Civilization gets out of hand; flood sent; king Ziusudra forewarned, builds a boat.
Atrahasis	Babylonian	*c.* 1700 B.C.	Civilization gets out of hand; flood eventually sent; Atrahasis forewarned, builds a boat and saves animals and birds.
Enuma Elish	Babylonian	*c.* 1800 B.C.	Conflict getween the gods and fresh/salt waters; Marduk champions gods, subdues the waters, creates heaven and earth from salt water, man from the blood of slain accomplice; grateful gods build Babylon for Marduk, crown him king, and bow to him each New Year's Day.
The Baal Epic	Canaanite/Ugaritic	*c.* 1400 B.C.	Baal subdues Yam, the sea, and Nahar, the river god, and brings order to creation; succumbs to Mot, god of death, then defeats him and returns from the dead, restoring fertility to the land; reigns supreme over pantheon of gods atop Mt. Saphon, under the emperorship of El.
Gilgamesh Epic	Sumerian	c. 2000 B.C.	Gods decide to destroy mankind with a flood; Utnapishtim forewarned, builds an ark, saves animals, relatives, possessions; rains for six days and nights; sends dove, swallow, and raven out; ark rests on a mountaintop; serpent steals plant from Gilgamesh and robs him of immortality.
Shabaka Stone	Egyptian		Creator is intermediary god; supreme deity is god of thought and spoken word.

Document	Origin	Date	Brief Description
Pyramid Texts	Egyptian		Creator god product of primeval waters, spawns gods (air and moisture) from his mouth, who generate gods (earth and sky).
Coffin Texts	Egyptian		Primeval waters are deep, dark, endless, and invisible.

Patriarchal Narratives

Document	Origin	Date	Brief Description
Nuzi Archives	Nuzi	c. 1400 B.C.	

Document	Genesis Parallels	Brief Description
HSS V 67:35-36	29:24, 29	New bride receives a handmaid.
HSS V 67:17-18 G 51	31:50	Contractual agreement not to take other wives.
PS 56 (AASOR XVI)	27:2	Deathbed declarations.
JEN 204	25:33	Birthright transfers.
HSS V 67:19-21	16:2	Provision for a 2nd wife in case of barrenness.
HSS V 11	31:14-16	Dowry privileges of daughters.
G 51	31:19, 30-34	Privileges of ownership of household gods.
HSS IX 22; HSS V 60	15:4	Childless people and adoption of heirs.
G 51	29:14	Heir adoption.
HSS V 80:5-6; 69:1; 25:1	12:13; 20:2; 26:7	Women given in marriage by brothers, become their husband's sisters.

(HSS = Harvard Semitic Series; JEN = Joint Expedition with the Iraq Museum at Nuzi; G = Nuzi texts published by C. J. Gadd in *Revue d'Assyrologie et d'archaeologie orientale* 23 [1926] 49-61; PS = Nuzi texts published by Pfeiffer and Speiser in *Annual of the American Schools of Oriental Research* 16 [1936].)

Document	Origin	Date	Brief Description
Adapa	Mesopotamian	Unknown	Lost opportunity for immortality.
Story of Sinuhe	Egyptian	c. 1800 B.C.	Triumphant return from exile to a foreign land.
Journey of Wen-Amon	Egyptian	c. 1100 B.C.	Negotiations in a foreign land.
Legend of Keret	Canaanite/Ugaritic	c. 1400 B.C.	Kingship and social orthodoxy in pre-Israelite Canaan.
Legend of Aqhat	Canaanite/Ugaritic	c. 1400 B.C.	Miraculous son; kingship and social orthodoxy in pre-Israelite Canaan.
The Tale of Two Brothers	Egyptian	c. 1210 B.C.	A wife's attempt to seduce her brother-in-law.

Ancient Law

Document	Origin	Date	Brief Description
Reform of Uru'inimgina	Sumerian	c. 2350 B.C.	Bureaucracy and taxes.
Laws of Ur-Nammu	Sumerian	c. 2060 B.C.	Family matters, bodily injury, slavery, false witness, property case law.
Laws of Lipit-Ishtar	Sumerian	c. 1875 B.C.	Family matters, inheritance, property, and slave law.
Laws of Eshunna	Old Babylonian	c. 1900 B.C.	Family matters, property, business, criminal, and slave law.
Code of Hammurabi	Old Babylonian	c. 1790 B.C.	Civil and criminal law.
Edict of Ammisaduqa	Old Babylonian	c. 1640 B.C.	Release from indebtedness.

216

Document	Origin	Date	Brief Description
Middle Assyrian Law	Middle Assyrian	*c.* 1200 B.C.	Civil and criminal law.
Hittite Law	Old Hittite	*c.* 1700 B.C.	Revision of civil and criminal law.

Covenants and Treaties

Treaty between

Document	Origin	Date	Brief Description
Hattusil III/Hatti and Ramses II/ Egypt	Hittite	*c.* 1275 B.C.	Parity type: oath binding on both parties.
Treaty between Suppiluliuma I/ Hatti and Matti-zawa of Mittani	Hittite	*c.* 1350 B.C.	Suzerainty type: oath binding only on vassal.
Grant of Ashurbanipal to his servant Balta	Assyrian	*c.* 650 B.C.	Royal grant type: oath binding only on sovereign.

Historical Literature

Document	Origin	Date	Brief Description
King of Battle	Assyrian	*c.* 714 B.C.	Describes Sargon's campaign into Asia Minor.
Epic of Tukulti-Ninurta I	Assyrian	*c.* 1250 B.C.	Celebrates victory over Babylon and its Kassite king, Kashtiliash IV.
The Merneptah Stele	Egyptian	*c.* 1208 B.C.	Celebrates victory over Libyans and Sea Peoples, inscribed on 150-yr.-old black granite stele previously used by Pharaoh Amenhotep III.
The Moabite Stone	Moabite	*c.* 845 B.C.	Celebrates successful revolt by Mesha, king of Moab against Israel under King Jehoram, despite help from kings of Judah (Jehoshaphat) and Edom, and the presence of the prophet Elijah.
The Black Obelisk of Shalmaneser III	Assyrian	*c.* 827 B.C.	Commemorates his achievements, including the payment of tribute by King Jehu of Judah.
The Siloam Inscription	Israelite	*c.* 700 B.C.	Commemorates construction of the pool and its conduit under Hezekiah, diverting the waters of Gihon from the Virgin's Fountain to prevent the enemy from tampering with its water supply and thereby successfully enabling the city to withstand an Assyrian siege.
The Lachish Letters	Israelite	*c.* 589 B.C.	A firsthand account of the military and political conditions just before the fall of Jerusalem, written by Hosha'yahu, an officer in charge of a nearby town, to Ya'osh, the military governor of Lachish, during that last, lethal Babylonian campaign against Judah.

Document	Origin	Date	Brief Description
The Taylor Prism	Assyrian	*c.* 691 B.C.	Describes Sennacharib's campaign against the Chaldean king of Babylon, Merodach-balaadan, and the subsequent reprisal against Hezekiah of Judah, including the siege of Lachish, and the demand he sent from there for Jerusalem's surrender.
The Babylonian Chronicles	Babylonian	*c.* 626-539 B.C.	Series of tablets reporting Babylonian history by contemporaries of the period 626-539 B.C., incuding the chronicle of its founder, Nabopolassar, 625-605 B.C., the fall of Nineveh (612 B.C.), Nebuchadnezzar's victory over Egypt at Carchemish (605 B.C.) and Judah's subsequent vassalhood, Jerusalem's capture on March 16/17, 597 B.C., and Babylon's fall to Cyrus on October 29, 539 B.C.
Verse Account of Nabonidus	Babylonian	*c.* 545 B.C.	Condemnation from priests of Marduk at Babylon or abandoning their god and city for the moon-goddess Sin and the city of Haran.
The Cyrus Cylinder	Medo-Persian	*c.* 539 B.C.	Cyrus' own account of the victories that led to his rise to power, and his policies and attitudes toward conquered nations.
The Behistun Inscription	Medo-Persian	*c.* 500 B.C.	Darius' version of his victories over rivals who led a revolt after his accession to the throne.
The Elephantine Papyri	Jewish	*c.* 495-400 B.C.	Aramaic legal documents and religious letters of a military colony of Jewish mercenaries who settled on the island of Elephantine, Egypt, after serving the Egyptian and Persian governments. Topics include marriage settlements, lawsuits, property deals, Passover observance, gifts for other gods besides Yahweh, and an appeal to Bagoas, governor of Judea, for help to rebuild the Elephantine temple—destroyed at the instigation of rival priests of the Egyptian god Khnub—restored with compromise, since five Jewish property owners actually petition for permission to forgo animal offerings and offer only incense, meal offering, and drink offering.

Religious Literature

Document	Origin	Date	Brief Description
Hymn to Enlil	Sumerian	*c.* 1800 B.C.	Hymn that surveys the current religious situation in Nippur, acknowledges Enlil's legendary role in building the temple, and offers descriptive praise to him for sustaining life and civilization.
Hymn of Enheduanna to Inanna	Sumerian	*c.* 2200 B.C.	Hymn of praise-lament-petition by Enheduanna, the daughter of King Sargon and high priestess of the moon god Nannar. After flattering Inanna, she registers her complaint, and ends on a confident note that powerful Inanna has heard her request.
Prayer to Any God	Sumerian	*c.* 2000 B.C.	Petition for pardon with confession of sin, a description of sinner's misfortunes, and a promise to worship the deity, but without any hint of a relationship with the god, or that the sinner needs a change of character or attitude in the future.

Document	Origin	Date	Brief Description
Hymn to Ishtar	Akkadian	*c.* 1600 B.C.	Hymn of praise that opens with flattery to get Ishtar to grant a list of blessings for King Ammiditana. He expresses his hope that they will come true by presenting them as already bestowed.
Hymn to Shamash	Akkadian	*c.* 1100 B.C.	Hymn of pure descriptive praise to the sun god.
Hymn to Marduk	Akkadian	*c.* 600 B.C.?	Fragments found in Assyrian city of Nineveh.
Hymn to Aton	Egyptian	*c.* 1360 B.C.	Written from a monotheistic perspective by the innovative Pharaoh Akhenaton to praise the sun disc for the generous distribution of its creating-recreating power all over the world.
"Ersemma" Wail of the Shem Drum	Sumerian	*c.* 2000 B.C. *c.* 1500 B.C.	Incantation; mythological narratives. Incantation; psalm to appease an angry deity.
"Ersahunga" Lament to Calm the Heart	Sumerian		Incantation; individual lament to calm the heart over sorrow or calamity caused by a deity.
"Suilla" Raising of the Hand	Sumerian	*c.* 1600-1200 B.C.	Action plus formula, without complaint, combine to activate divine power; call on gods for help.
	Akkadian		Out-and-out prayer of incantation, with lament.
"Ki-UTU-kam" Incantation of Utu/Shamash	Sumerian		Directed to the rising sun—to purify from sin, uncleanness, or illness.
"Surpu" (Burning)	Akkadian		A series of prayers addressed primarily to Marduk— with magical rites (burning is a rite of purification). People used these incantations when they did not know what offense they had committed.

Wisdom Literature

Document	Origin	Date	Brief Description
Man and His God	Sumerian	*c.* 2000 B.C.	The "Sumerian Job" (Samuel Kramer, "Man and His God," VT Supp. 3, 170). A poetic essay in which the author registers a first-person complaint with his god for neglecting him during a time of suffering he doesn't deserve. He requests a hearing for relief, and in the end discovers the reason for his distress, so that he can deal with it.
Akkadian Fable	Akkadian		A debate between a tamarisk and a date palm in which each attempts to prove itself better than the other.
Counsels of Wisdom	Akkadian		A series of Solomonlike proverbs from a father. Wisdom to his son (see line 81, "My son, if it be . . .").
Ludlul Bel Nemeqi "I Will Praise the Lord of Wisdom"	Akkadian	*c.* 1400-1200 B.C.	The "Babylonian Job." A monologue in which the author relates suffering a series of disasters and credits Marduk with fully restoring him.

Document	Origin	Date	Brief Description
The Babylonian Theodicy	Akkadian	*c.* 1000 B.C.	An acrostic dialogue between a sufferer and a friend who defends the prevailing views of society against his complaints. Each line begins with a letter that forms the sentence, "I Saggil-kinam-ubbib, the exorcist, am an adorant of the god and the king."
Instruction of the Vizier Ptah-hotep	Egyptian	*c.* 2450 B.C.	A series of 37 wise sayings intended for the son of Ptah-hotep's sovereign, King Izezi.
Instruction of Amen-em-Opet	Egyptian	*c.* 1200 B.C.	Unpretentious advice that closely parallels Proverbs 22:17-24:22.
A Dispute Over Suicide	Egyptian	*c.* 2200 B.C.	A man who is tired of life tries to convince his soul that suicide and death are the best thing for him. He reminds us of Job, except he is sick of what goes on around him, whereas Job suffers from what happens to him.
Instruction for King Merikare	Egyptian	*c.* 2100 B.C.	A king, possibly Khety II, who ruled during the turbulent aftermath of the Old Kingdom's fall, offers his son and heir, Merikare, practical pointers on government plus advice on how to live right and treat people fairly.
Instruction of Any	Egyptian	*c.* 1500 B.C.	A father, who serves in the temple of Neferteri, offers his recalcitrant son advice from the school of life.
ANET 425 "Proverbs From Mesopotamia"	Sumerian	*c.* 2000 B.C.	A series of sayings resembling those in the book of Ecclesiastes (1:9, 10; 9:11).
The Words of Ahiqar	Aramaic	*c.* 600-500 B.C.	Eleven sheets of palimpsest (reused) papyrus, the first four of which contain Ahiqar's story of betrayal and restoration, and the last seven, his wise sayings.
A Pessimistic Dialogue Between Master and Servant	Akkadian	*c.* 1000 B.C.	A dialogue in which the master proposes to first undertake, then reject, a series of strategies, to the servant's (a "yes" man) yea, in either case. In the end, the master threatens to kill the servant, who sarcastically replies, "Then would my lord wish to live even three days [without a "yes" man] after me?—

Prophetic Literature

Document	Origin	Date	Brief Description
Mari Letters ANET 623-626; 629-632	Mari	*c.* 1800 B.C.	Also published in Archives Royales de Mari (ARM). These texts include interesting parallels to OT passages, such as the fish-god Dagon commissioning a prophet with the words, "Now go, I send you. Thus shall you speak to Zimri-Lim saying . . ." (ANET 623; cf. Jer. 1:7; Eze. 2:4), among others.
Oracles Concerning Esarhaddon	Akkadian	*c.* 681-670 B.C.	The goddess Ishtar of Arbela expresses joy over king Esarhaddon and announces that he will have a victorious and prosperous reign.
A Letter to Ashurbanipal	Akkadian	*c.* 668-633 B.C.	Ashurbanipal has the god Ashur's promise that he will add victories of his own to his father's, Esarhaddon's, conquest of Egypt, and bring other countries under the jurisdiction of the gods Ashur and Sin.

Document	Origin	Date	Brief Description
Oracular Dream Concerning Ashurbanipal	Akkadian	c. 668-633 B.C.	The goddess Ishtar quiets Ashurbanipal's fears with a promise of victory and prosperity.
ANET 606-607	Akkadian	c. 700-600 B.C.	A series of pessimistic revelations about the rise and fall of kings in the land of Akkad.
Admonitions of Ipuwer	Egyptian	c. 1800 B.C.	A wise man called Ipuwer confronts Pharaoh about the deplorable state of the economy and the sad social situation in Egypt.
Prophecy of Nefer-rohu	Egyptian	c. 1991-1962 B.C.	Supposedly, Pharaoh Snefru of the Fourth Dynasty sought entertainment one day, and Nefer-rohu the priest foretold the demise of the Old Kingdom and the restoration of order in the Middle Kingdom under Amen-em-het I, the first pharaoh of the twelfth dynasty.
The Zakir Stele	Canaanite	c. 755 B.C.	Prophets allegedly predict victory for Zakir, the king of Hamath and Luash, over Ben-Hadad, the son of Hazael, king of Syria whom Jehoash smote three times, and recovered the cities of Israel formerly in his father's grasp (see 2 Kings 13:25).

Intertestamental and New Testament Period

The Septuagint

Document	Origin	Date	Brief Description
	Jewish	c. 250 B.C.	(See the previous subsection on "The Bible.")

The Apocrypha

Document	Origin	Date	Brief Description
	Jewish	c. 165 B.C.	15 Jewish books, that Jews themselves banned from the Hebrew Bible, but Christians included in their OT until the Reformers set them apart from Scripture in a section of their own. The Roman Catholic Church continues to include 12 of them in its Bibles, while Protestants generally do not. Catholics call these books "deuterocanonical," a "second canon," and apply the term "apocrypha" to another body of extracanonical literature that Protestants call "pseudepigrapha" or "falsely titled," because they claim to be written by OT people who obviously did not write them. So far as Protestants are concerned, the term "apocrypha" means hidden, either in the sense of "secret" and "hidden from the general public," or "removed" from the main body of canonical writings and "withdrawn from circulation."
1 Esdras		c. 165 B.C.	Also known as 3 Esdras/3 Ezra; an expanded version of Ezra-Nehemiah. Neither Catholics or Protestants accept it as canonical. It is essentially a translation of 2 Chronicles 35:1-36:21, the whole book of Ezra, and Nehemiah 7:73-8:12 "with one long and two shorter insertions" (Gowan, *Bridge Between the Testaments,* p. 343). The most famous addition (3:5-4:63) is a battle of wits between three

Document	Origin	Date	Brief Description
			of the king Darius' bodyguards over the question, "What is the strongest thing in the world? The first says "wine;" the second, "the king;" and the third, "women;" "but truth is victor of all things."
2 Esdras		*c.* A.D. 90-100	Esdras in Latin Bible, because Ezra and Nehemiah are called 1 and 2 Esdras, and 1 Esdras is labeled 3 Esdras). An apocalyptic work, it offers reasons for God's delay in fulfilling His promises to Israel. Chapters 3-14 are seven visions that unveil the future as they answer questions about Israel's past.
Tobit		*c.* 200 B.C.	Fictitious historical romance about a Jewish captive in Assyria called Tobit and his son Tobias. Though devout and generous, Tobit is stricken with blindness. A quarrel with his wife leads to a death wish. At the same time in Media, a virgin named Sarah, widowed seven times by a killer-demon named Asmodeus, prayed that she might die too. God sent the angel Raphael to give them both relief, to guide Tobias to Media to pick up 10 talents of silver that his father left there, and to cure Tobit's blindness. He marries Sarah, whom the angel said was destined for him from all eternity.
Judith		*c.* 150 B.C.	Fictitious religious romance built around the beautiful, devout heroine for which it is named. When Nebuchadnezzar sent his general to punish the nations to his west that refused to help him conquer the Medes, the Jews defied him. Judith rescued her people by enticing, tricking, and then beheading the intoxicated general Holofernes with his own sword while he slept.
The Greek Esther		*c.* 100-63 B.C.	Addition to the Book of Esther that "introduced discrepancies and contradictions into the account" (Siegfried Horn, *Seventh-day Adventist Bible Dictionary*, p. 54). Though originally scattered throughout the book, Jerome placed it at the end of his Vulgate version, and Luther "made a separate book of the non-Hebrew parts, printing it with the apocrypha" (Gowan, *Bridge Between the Testaments*, p. 345). Additions of "prayers, quotation of edicts and a dream with its interpretation . . . contain typical expressions of post-exilic Jewish piety" (*ibid.*, p. 346) that distinguish it from the original Hebrew parts that never get "religious" or even mention God's name.
The Wisdom of Solomon		*c.* 100-63 B.C.	"A religio-political treatise combining OT theological concepts with Alexandrian philosophical ideas derived from Platonism and Stoicism" (Horn, *SDA Bible Dictionary,* p. 54). The author claims to be Solomon, and credits the preservation of God's people to wisdom. In fact, "The histories of Israel and Egypt are a special demonstration of the results of wisdom on the one hand and of folly on the other" (*ibid.*, p. 54).

222

Document	Origin	Date	Brief Description
Ecclesiasticus		*c.* 180 B.C. *c.* 132 B.C. (translated into Greek by author's grandson)	(Also known as the Wisdom of Jesus, the son [Hebrew] of Sirach, a teacher, whose classroom lessons are considered by many to be the substance of the book, (Pfeiffer, *History of NT Times,* pp. 353, 354). The title "Ecclesiasticus," meaning "churchy," may possibly mean that its author considered it worthy of reading in church, and for catechizing converts. Patterned after Proverbs, it presents practical advice for daily life and even teaches morality and practical godliness.
Baruch		*c.* 165-63 B.C.(Hebrew) *c.* A.D. 70-100 (translated into Greek, to explain Jerusalem's fall in A.D. 70	The book is in three parts: a ritual of repentance among the Babylonian exiles, including Baruch (presumably Jeremiah's scribe) that led them to send funds to Jerusalem for the high priest who was still offering sacrifices there (1:1-3:8; cf. Dan. 9); a wisdom poem that explains the Exile as the consequence of deserting God, the fountain of wisdom (3:9-4:4; cp. Job 28); and a poem of consolation promising restoration to Israel and retribution to her oppressors (4:5-5:9; cf. Jer. 30-31 and Isa. 40-66).
The Letter of Jeremiah		*c.* 400-200 B.C.	A separate piece of writing frequently attached to Baruch as its sixth chapter. It "is not a letter at all, nor was it written by Jeremiah. It is a fervent dissertation based on Jeremiah 10:11, urging the Jews to cling to the God of their fathers and not to become fascinated with the idols of the lands of their captivity (Horn, *SDA Bible Dictionary,* p. 55).
The Prayer of Azariah and the Song of the Three Young Men		*c.* 100 B.C.	Unauthentic addition to the book of Daniel, inserted between (verses 23, 24) of chapter three. In the form of a traditional lament, Azariah (Abednego) petitions God while he, Shadrach, and Meshach are in the fiery furnace (verses 1-22). The Lord's angel then transforms the flames of the superheated furnace into "a moist wind . . . whistling through it" (verses 23-28), and all three worthies sing a psalm of thanksgiving for their deliverance (verses 29-68; cf. Ps. 148).
Susanna		*c.* 100 B.C.	Unauthentic addition, inserted either before chapter 1, or at the end, as chapter 13 of the book of Daniel, just before Bel and the Dragon. The story is a thriller about Susanna, the gorgeous wife of a Babylonian Jew named Joakim, who is accused by two unscrupulous elders of adultery because she turned down their amorous advances. Originally convicted and sentenced to death, she is set free after Daniel cross-examines her accusers and proves that their testimony is false.
Bel and the Dragon		*c.* 100 B.C.	Unauthentic addition to the Book of Daniel, inserted at the end of Daniel, sometimes after Susanna. These are two more stories/folk tales like

223

Document	Origin	Date	Brief Description
			Susanna that celebrate Daniel's legendary cleverness. The first is another thriller in which Daniel exposes the 70 priests of Bel and their families as the ones who ate offerings left overnight at Bel's temple. All too human footprints from the offering table to secret doors in the ashes that Daniel had sprinkled on the temple floor led to the culprits. In the second story, Daniel kills the monster/dragon that the Babylonians worshiped as a god by feeding it a goulash of fat pitch, and hair. Rewarded with six days in the lions' den, Daniel escapes harm thanks to help from the prophet Habakkuk. An angel miraculously transports him to Babylon from Judea to cater a meal for the legendary Jew.
The Prayer of Manasseh		*c.* 100-50 B.C.	2 Chron. 33:12, 13 says that Manasseh, one of Israel's most wicked kings (2 Kings 21:1-18), came to his senses when the Assyrians carried him off to Babylon, where he offered a prayer that led to his return home and restoration to the throne. The writer of this brief apocryphal work wants us to identify it with that prayer. Only 15 verses long, it is, on the one hand, sincerely repentant in tone and strangely self-righteous, on the other, when it insists that Abraham, Isaac, and Jacob never sinned. Neither Protestants nor Roman Catholics consider it canonical, though the Greek and Russian Orthodox churches recognize it as Deuterocanonical.
1 Maccabees		*c.* 110 B.C. (written in Hebrew by a Palestinian Jew)	Named for its heroes, the sons of Mattathias, a priest who resisted the Hellenization of Israel, and in particular its corrupting influence on the Temple. This led to 40 years of conflict known as the Maccabean Wars, from the days of Antiochus Epiphanes (175 B.C.) to those of John Hyrcanus (135 B.C.). A fairly reliable account of what happened, it focuses on the military at the expense of the social, economic, and religious factors for the period. The author obviously supported the Hasmoneans, the descendants of Hashmon, including the Maccabees, who ruled Judea from 142 to 63 B.C., when Pompey brought Palestine under Roman control.
2 Maccabees		*c.* 100 B.C. (written in Greek by a Diaspora Jew)	This is an entirely separate piece of work rather than a continuation of 1 Maccabees, and unlike his counterpart, the author of 2 Maccabees is more theologian than historian. In fact, after opening with two letters from Jews in Jerualem to exiles in Egypt about Chanukah observance (1-2), "the greater part of the book, which covers the first 15 years of the Maccabean wars, is admitted to be a condensation of the five-volume historical work of Jason of Cyrene (chap. 2:19-32)" (Horn, *SDA Bible Dictionary,* p. 56). Throughout the book he introduces legendary

Document	Origin	Date	Brief Description
			material, expanding on the events of the original Maccabean revolt (3-5), featuring persecution and martyrdom for religious faith (6-7), and playing up the successes of Judas Maccabeus up to the defeat of Nicanor (8-15), "to edify, strengthen and encourage the religious reader" (Gowan, *Bridge Between the Testaments,* p. 370).

The Pseudepigrapha

Document	Origin	Date	Brief Description
	Jewish Christian	*c.* 300 B.C.- to A.D. 200	A collection of some 65 documents written by Christian Jews and/or Christians, but attributed to one or another well known OT figure. Borrowing on, alluding to, or extrapolating from the OT, they can be grouped into five broad classes of literature:

Apocalyptic

Document	Origin	Date	Brief Description
			"Revelations" or "disclosures" of what is happening in the heavens or will happen in the future that impact the present. (See the discussion in this book about "Apocalyptic" beginning on p. 40 in the subsection "Type of Literature.")
1 (Ethiopic Apocalypse of) Enoch		*c.* 300 B.C. to A.D. 200	Being the longest pseudepigraphic work and the most important noncanonical apocalypse, it is the product of several authors, probably Jewish and Christian. Horn says that "it consists of a series of alleged revelations to Enoch concerning the origin of evil, the nature and destiny of angels, and includes such eschatalogical themes as the judgment, the resurrection, and the nature of gehenna and paradise" (*SDA Bible Dicitonary,* p. 914).
2 (Slavonic Apocalypse of) Enoch		*c.* 63 B.C. to A.D. 70	Though written originally in Greek, only two Slavonic versions survive of Enoch's guided tour of the seven heavens, record of oracles by an angel who spoke for 30 days and nights, and the appeals Enoch made to his children before his translation.
3 (Hebrew Apocalypse of) Enoch		*c.* A.D. 500-600	The alleged account of Rabbi Ishmael "of how he journeyed into heaven, saw God's throne and chariot, received revelations from the angel Metatron, and viewed the wonders of the upper world" (P. Alexander, "3 (Hebrew Apocalypse of) Enoch," in *The OT Pseudepigrapha,* vol. 1, p. 223).
Sybilline Oracles		*c.* 200 B.C. to A.D. 600	A collection of 15 alleged pagan, Jewish, and Christian apocalyptic communications from God, predicting future woes and calamities in the poetic style of the pagan "sybilline books." Only 12 survive (9, 10, and 15 are missing).
Treatise of Shem		*c.* 31-20 B.C.	Astrological document attributed to Shem, Noah's son. Divided into 12 chapters, one for each sign of the zodiac, the author proceeds to describe the characteristics of the year according to the house of the zodiac in which it begins.

Document Origin	Date	Brief Description
Apocryphon of Ezekiel	*c.* 50 B.C. to A.D. 50	Only four quotations and one small fragment of the work itself found in the writings of the fourth-century Church Father Epiphanius and the Babylonian Talmud, the story of the lame man and the blind man, have survived. Essentially the writer, allegedly the prophet Ezekiel, claims that the resurrection is a reunion of body and spirit. Anything less than body with the spirit in it is not a whole person and cannot be judged.
Apocalypse of Zephaniah	*c.* 100 B.C. to A.D.175	A description of Zephaniah's glorious tour of heaven and shocking views of sinners as they suffer what they deserve for their sins. Only fragments remain.
4 Ezra	*c.* A.D.100-120	Originally composed by a pessimistic Jew in the wake of Jerusalem's fall in A.D. 70, this book of seven alleged visions given to Salathiel (Ezra) while he was in Babylon underwent an attitude adjustment by a third-century Christian who prefixed two chapters and appendixed two others to it.
Greek Apocalypse of Ezra	*c.* A.D. 150-850	A mixture of Jewish and Christian sources reporting Ezra's alleged visions of heaven, hell, and the antichrist. It ends with a narrative of Ezra's own death and burial.
Vision of Ezra	*c.* A.D.400-700	The alleged vision begins at the fiery gates of hell, moves into Tartarus, passes on to Paradise, and ends in God's presence. "It is a recurrent feature of the vision that the just pass through the infernal regions unscathed, whereas the damned are unable to escape" (J. R. Mueller and G. A. Robbins, "Vision of Ezra," in *The OT Pseudepigrapha,* vol. 1, p. 581).
Questions of Ezra		This Christian work claims to be a dialogue between Ezra and the Lord's angel about the fate of human souls after death. It includes an interesting discussion about freeing of souls from Satan's grasp through expiatory prayer, and ends with a prediction of the resurrection and final judgment.
Revelation of Ezra	before A.D. 900	This "is a *kalandologion*, or almanac, describing the nature of the year depending on the day of the week on which the year begins" (D. A. Fiensy, "Revelation of Ezra," in *The OT Pseudipigrapha*, vol. 1, p. 601). Not only does this permit predictions of the usual natural phenomena, but also enables one to foresee the fate of national rulers.
Apocalypse of Sedrach	*c.* A.D. 150-500	A Christian work with many Jewish elements, recording the supernatural experiences of Sedrach, who resists the attempts of Christ to take him to paradise because he is concerned about the fate of sinners. Only after Jesus reduces the requirements of repentance for others does he at last allow himself to enter. A curious feature is the substitution of "Christ" for the name of the archangel Michael.

Document Origin	Date	Brief Description
2 (Syriac Apocalypse of) Baruch	c. A.D. 100	A more optimistic Jewish work written in reaction to the fall of Jerusalem in A.D. 70. It is a collection of various dirges, questions, prayers and unveilings of truth including a letter to the Jews scattered as a result of Jerusalem's temporary demise.
3 (Greek Apocalypse of) Baruch	c. A.D. 100-300	The work reports an alleged tour an angel gave Baruch, Jeremiah's scribe, through five heavens in order to comfort him when he cries over the destruction of Jerusalem and the way its pagan destroyers are laughing over it. Either a Christian wrote it with the help of Jewish sources, or it began as a Jewish work that was revised and reissued by a Christian.
Apocalypse of Abraham	c. A.D. 70-100	Written in reflection of the fall of Jerusalem in A.D. 70 (chap. 27), the writer, in the identity of Abraham, relives his youth, and especially the rejection of his father Terah's idols as gods (1-8). He obeys a command to sacrifice, and God sends the angel Iaoel to lead Abraham to heaven, where he sees seven visions and God announces that 10 plagues will punish the Gentiles, and the just will end up victorious (chaps. 9-32).
Apocalypse of Adam	c. A.D. 1-400	This is supposed to be a gnostic (secret) revelation from Adam to his son Seth, "for Seth's posterity, the race of the gnostics" (G. Macrae, "Apocalypse of Adam," in *The OT Pseudepigrapha*, vol. 1, p. 707). Just before his death, Adam retells the story of the fall in a gnostic way and the truth about the future revealed to him in his fallen state by three strangers. According to them, the Flood, the repopulation of the world, and a destructive fire were attempts by a jealous God to wipe out Seth's line, but heavenly beings saved them every time, and they will eventually emerge victorious in the end.
Apocalypse of Elijah	c. A.D. 150-275	The combination of Jewish and Christian materials, the work begins with a homily that encourages fasting and prayer (chap. 1), proceeds to a prophecy concerning the coming of the antichrist (chap. 2), the antichrist himself (chap. 3), three martyrdoms (chap. 4), and the institution of of the millennium, after Elijah and Enoch slay the antichrist (chap. 5).
Apocalypse of Daniel	c. A.D. 400-800	This work divides into two main sections; the first puts the events of the 8th century Byzantino-Arab wars into the form of a prophecy from Daniel (chaps. 1-7); the second (chap. 8-14), "draws upon earlier traditions and sources . . . [as the author, in the assumed person of Daniel] . . . "presents his own version of the end of the world as a direct continuation of the series of historical events described in chapters 1-7" (G. T. Zervos, "Apocalypse of Daniel," in *The OT Pseudepigrapha*, vol. 1, p. 755). In an ironic twist on the biblical account, the antichrist attempts to change a stone into bread, but it

227

Document	Origin	Date	Brief Description
			becomes a dragon that instead of being his ally, "shames him before the Jews" (13:13).

Testaments

Document	Origin	Date	Brief Description
			Legendary OT patriarchs on their deathbeds gather their sons and followers to share their (last wills and) testaments, filled with moral instructions, often "dramatized by visions into the future" (*Harper's Bible Dictionary,* p. 838).
Testaments of the Twelve Patriarchs		*c.* A.D. 150	In this Christian work, each of Jacob's 12 sons gathers his children around for a deathbed farewell, "reflecting on aspects of his life, confessing his misdeeds, exhorting his family to avoid his sins and exemplify virtue, concluding with predictions about the future of Israel. . . . In the process, each patriarch calls for special honor to be given to Levi and Judah, progenitors, respectively, of the priestly and kingly lines of the nation" (H. C. Kee, "Testament of the Twelve Patriarchs," in *The OT Pseudepigrapha,* vol. 1, p. 775).
Testament of Job		*c.* 100 B.C. to A.D. 100	This Jewish work urges its readers to imitate the patience of its assumed namesake, who calls his children to his bedside, to offer his own version of what happened to him and to distribute his estate (1:4-45:4). This time Satan surrenders to Job, his three friends are cast as three kings, and he uses magic to persuade his three daughters to turn away from the earthly inheritance he divided among their seven brothers to spiritual things. They wind up speaking with the tongues of angels, singing hymns, and blessing God as a heavenly chariot carries their father's soul to heaven (chaps. 46-52). Nereus presides over the burial of his brother Job's body (chap. 53).
Testament of the Three		*c.* A.D. 100	Three organically connected documents: two similar Christian writings, "The Testament of Isaac" and "The Testament of Jacob," evolving from and dependent upon the first century Jewish "Testament of Abraham."
Abraham		*c.* A.D. 100	A Jewish work dealing with Abraham's death, an alleged tour he made of the inhabited world, and his view of the judgment.
Isaac		*c.* A.D. 100-200	A Christian work derived from and deliberately attached to "The Testament of Abraham" that deals with an alleged visit from the archangel Michael to Abraham, and the story of the old patriarch's death.
Jacob		*c.* A.D. 100-200	A Christian work derived from and deliberately attached to "The Testament of Abraham," which commemorates the deaths of Abraham and Isaac.
Testament of Moses		*c.* A.D. 1-30	This is supposed to be Moses' farewell to his successor Joshua just before he died and Israel entered the Promised Land. It turns into a prophecy of what

Document	Origin	Date	Brief Description
			will happen from the time they go in until the end of history. He foretells the conquest, the periods of the judges, of the united and divided kingdoms, of the fall and exile, and the return to rebuild Jerusalem and the Temple. Then going on to explain the disappointing first-century situation, he predicts another apostasy brought on by hellenizing influences, along with its evil consequences. After forecasting victory for the faithful, Moses encourages a reluctant Joshua to assume the reins of leadership.
Testament of Solomon		c. A.D. 200	This is a folktale about Solomon's building the Temple with a magic ring from Michael, the archangel, which makes him able to call up demons and force them to help with its construction. He warns his readers against repeating his sin of idolatry, recalling how he fell so deeply in lust with a Shummanite woman that he sacrificed five locusts to the pagan gods Raphan and Moloch to possess her, built temples to her idols, and disqualified himself from God's attending glory.
Testament of Adam		c. A.D. 100-250	A composite work of Jewish and Christian elements, in three parts: the *Horarium* (chaps. 1-2), in which Adam allegedly lists the hours of the day and night for his son Seth, and tells him what part of the created world worships God at each hour; the *Prophecy* (chap. 3), in which Adam first divulges new information about Creation and the Fall, then predicts the Flood, the Messiah's life and death, and the end of the world; and the *Hierarchy* (chap. 4), a list of the nine different orders of heavenly beings with an explanation of what each is ordained to do.

Expansions of the Old Testament

Elaborate versions of Old Testament narratives and stories.

Document	Origin	Date	Brief Description
Letter of Aristeas		c. 200-150 B.C.	Written by a zealous Alexandrian Jew named Aristeas to his brother Philocrates to defend the Temple and the Septuagint translation of the OT from Hebrew into Greek by 72 Jewish scholars sent to Alexandria for this purpose.
Jubilees		c. 161-140 B.C.	Midrashic expansion (see the discussion concerning "Midrash" in this book beginning on p. 129 in the subsection, "Quotations, Allusions, and Commentary") of Gen. 1:1-Ex. 12:50, enlarging on what God revealed to Moses during his 40 days on Mount Sinai. After God forecasts apostasy and restoration in Israel's future (chap. 1), the angel of the presence retells many biblical narratives (chaps. 2-50) in a conservative way "that celebrates the supremacy of the Law and the Sabbath, directs polemics against a lunar calendar, and extols Jewish exclusiveness" (*Harper's Bible Dictionary*, p. 839).

Document Origin	Date	Brief Description
Martyrdom and Ascension of Isaiah	*c.* 100 B.C. to A.D. 300	An amalgamation of three works: the Jewish *Martyrdom and Ascension of Isaiah* (chap. 1-5), *c.* 100 B.C. (the legend of Isaiah's death at the hands of King Manasseh); the Christian *Vision of Isaiah* (chaps. 6-11), *c.* 200 A.D. (the story of Isaiah's journey to heaven for a vision of seven heavens); and the Christian, *Testament of Hezekiah* (3:13-4:22), c. A.D. 100. The process of combination ended sometime around 300 A.D.
Joseph and Asenath	*c.* 100 A.D.	A romantic takeoff on Genesis 41:45 to explain how Jacob's son, Joseph could marry Aseneth, the daughter of Pentephre, priest of Hieropolis and Pharaoh's chief counselor (cf. Potiphera, Priest of On, Gen. 41:45): she falls in love with Joseph, destroys her idols, and repents. Then they survive a plot by Pharaoh's son to kill them, Pharaoh and his son die, and Joseph reigns over Egypt for 48 years.
Life of Adam and Eve	*c.* 100 B.C. to A.D. 200	An extended version of Gen. 1-4 that retells the story of the Fall and claims that Eve survived Adam's death and witnessed "the awesome return of God to the earthly Paradise" (M.D. Johnson, "Life of Adam and Eve," in *The OT Pseudipigrapha,* vol. 2, p. 249), and died six days later.
Pseudo-Philo	*c.* 70 A.D.	An "imaginative retelling" of Genesis through 2 Samuel, the history of Israel from Adam to David that "interweaves biblical incidents and legendary expansions" (D. J. Harrington, "Pseudo-Philo" in *The OT Pseudipigrapha,* vol. 2, p. 297). The author attributes this work to Philo, the Alexandrian Jew, whose imaginative attempts to wed the Scriptures to Greek philosophy through allegorization resemble (though slightly) his innovative mingling of Scripture and legend.
Lives of the Prophets	*c.* A.D. 1-25 A.D.	This brief document claims to report the names birthplaces, circumstances of death, and resting places of three major (plus Daniel), 12 minor, and seven nonliterary prophets from the Bible. It also includes noncanonical information from popular folklore (*e.g.,* Jonah was the son of the widow of Zarephath whom Elijah visited in 1 Kings 17) to embellish some of its biographies.
Ladder of Jacob	*c.* A.D. 100?	The only surviving fragment of this fictitious expansion of Jacob's dream at Bethel (Gen. 28:11-22) occurs within the Slavonic *Explanatory Palaia,* a work from a genre notorious for freewheeling use of its source materials. Chapters 1-6 appear to come from a first-century Jewish source, whereas "chap. 7 is a Christian work, once independent, but now an appendix" (*Harper's Bible Dictionary,* p. 839), to (chaps. 1-6).
4 Baruch	*c.* A.D. 100	This expansion of what happened between the destruction of Jerusalem and the stoning of Jeremiah

Document	Origin	Date	Brief Description
			claims that prophet's scribe as its author. The actual writer was a mental gymnast who introduces miracles at will and interprets them as he pleases. For example, when Jeremiah tricks a friend into leaving the city and the friend allegedly sleeps safely under a tree for 66 years, the author considers his awakening as "proof of the resurrection of the dead, individually, and also as an indication that God is about to restore his people, collectively" (S. E. Robinson, "4 Baruch," in *The OT Pseudipigrapha,* vol. 2, p. 413). A Christian probably edited this originally Jewish writing.
Jannes and Jambres		*c.* A.D. 300	A Christian edited this originaly Jewish tale of the Pharaoh's magicians who "opposed Moses" (cf. Ex. 7:11 with 2 Tim. 3:8). It "is essentially a confession (*poenitentia*), a genre of literature that was manifestly Christian but not Jewish" (A. Pietersma and R. T. Lutz, "Jannes and Jambres," in *The OT Pseudipigrapha,* vol. 2, p. 433). In this legendary account of the ancient wizards, Jannes dies as result of judgment and leaves his brother a legacy of lessons learned from his experience, with a strong appeal for repentance and reform to avoid a similar fate.
History of the Rechabites		*c.* A.D. 100-300	A Christian expansion of Jer. 35 based on an early Jewish work. It is the alleged story of a pious man named Zosimus, who goes to the island of the blessed ones (chaps. 1-3), a distant rather than future utopia, an intermediary state between the corruptible world and the heavenly realm, where he learns their history (chaps. 4-7), that they fled Jerusalem in Jeremiah's day (chaps. 8-10), and an assortment of *doctrine* including the virgin birth of the Word, Lent, and the ascent of the soul with angelic assistance when the body dies, to await the resurrection of the rest of the blessed ones (chaps. 11-16). Content, he then returns home via the same miraculous means by which he came (chaps. 17, 18).
Eldad and Medad		*c.* A.D. 100	An expansion of Num. 11:26-29 concerning Eldad and Medad, the two prophets from the elders in the wilderness who continued to prophesy in the camp of Israel. The only surviving fragment appears as a quote in the Shepherd of Hermas, but "according to rabbinic sources . . . apparently contained references to Gog and Magog, the end of time, and the coming of a royal Messiah" (E. G. Martin, "Eldad and Medad" in *The OT Pseudipigrapha,* vol. 2, p. 463).
History of Joseph		*c.* A.D. 300	A Jewish midrashic elaboration of Gen. 41:39-42:38 recounting the major events during the Egyptian episode of Joseph's life. It exalts Joseph to regal status ("king of the people") and repeatedly mentions "Joseph remembering Jacob," which G. T. Zervos suggests may date this document to "a

Document	Origin	Date	Brief Description
			time of oppression of the Jews, when adherence to their ancestral traditions would be difficult" ("History of Joseph" in *The OT Pseudipigrapha,* vol. 2, p. 469).

Wisdom and Philosophy

Document	Origin	Date	Brief Description
			Writings that "preserve some of the insights of ancient wisdom, not only within early Judaism but also in surrounding cultures. Here we confront the universalistic truths so essential for sophisticated and enlightened conduct and behavior in all facets of life, secular and religious. Jews tended to borrow philosophical truths from other cultures, frequently but not always recasting them in light of the Torah" (*Harper's Bible Dictionary,* p. 839).
Ahiqar		*c.* 600 B.C.	A two-part work that first recounts the story of Ahiqar, the wise counselor of Assyrian kings, who fled his homeland when an ungrateful nephew convinced King Esarhaddon to execute him as a traitor. It then presents a collection of more than 100 of his Biblelike sayings. Although it is non-Jewish and predates the actual pseudipigraphic era "by the end of the Old Testament period, the story was not only known in some parts of the diaspora, but had even been reworked to portray the pagan sage as a Jew" (J. M. Lindenberger, "Ahiqar," in *The OT Pseudipigrapha,* vol. 2, p. 479). Even the author of Tobit cites it (1:21, 22).
3 Maccabees		*c.* 100 B.C.	This is "a humorous account of divine intervention that saved the Jews from persecution by Ptolemy IV Philopator" (*Harper's Bible Dictionary,* p. 840), king of Egypt from 221-204 B.C., who had recently defeated the Syrian king, Antiochus III (the Great), at the battle of Raphia. When Philopator supposedly ordered the Jews trampled by a herd of 500 elephants, angels terrorize the king by turning the herd on him and his supporters. As a result, Philopator reverses his position concerning the Jews, authorizing them to celebrate a week-long festival at his expense and instructing his governors to protect rather than persecute them. The whole episode is academic, however, since Antiochus soon ruled Palestine in Philpator's place after he defeated the Egyptian general Scopus at the Battle of Paneas in 198 B.C.
4 Maccabees		*c.* 63 B.C. to A.D. 70	A philosophical discourse, extolling the alleged triumph of reason over passion and emotion—demonstrated by the willing martyrdom of Eleazar, the seven sons, and their mother in the best OT heroic tradition. The main text pits Eleazar, portrayed as a devout philosopher-Jew driven by unswerving loyalty to the law and tradition, against the stoical King

Document	Origin	Date	Brief Description
			Antiochus, who recommends expediency to strict lawkeeping, because the latter is unreasonable, preposterous, and nonsensical if it leads to death (5:11).
Pseudo-Phocylides		c. 50 B.C. to A.D. 100	A collection of Jewish precepts disguised as the work of a renowned Ionic poet who lived in Miletus in the 500s B.C. To produce a monotheistic model for life consistent with truth, but also acceptable to the world, the author puts OT teaching into Phocylides' Stoic's mouth, without giving away its Jewish origins.
Sentences of the Syriac Menander		c. A.D. 250	A *florilegium* (collection) of practical, rather than philosophical, wisdom sayings, attributed to a Greek from the New Comedy in Athens (c. 300 B.C.), written in Syriac and designed to show people the best way to live in a mixed-up world. The author probably "drew on a source of monostichs . . . [one-liners] . . . ascribed to Menander and took this opportunity to connect this famous name with his collection of sayings" (T. Baarda, "The Sentences of the Syriac Menander," in *The OT Pseudipigrapha,* vol. 2, p. 584).

Prayers, Psalms, and Odes

Document	Origin	Date	Brief Description
			Poetic compositions either resembling biblical psalms or reflecting the style of early Jewish hymns.
More Psalms of David		c. 300 B.C. to A.D. 100	A collection of five additional psalms and part of a sixth, supposedly composed by David. As a continuation of the Hebrew canon, they are numbered 151A, 151B, 152, 153, 154, and 155. Four of them (151A, 151B, 154, 155) predate the Christian era, because they are included in the Dead Sea psalms scroll (11QPsa) [see the discussion, "Dead Sea Scrolls" in this book, p. 368]. J. H. Charlesworth and J. A. Sanders suggest that "there may be an organic relationship between" these seemingly unconnected works and that "earlier ones may have inspired later ones," because four of them (151A, 151B 152, 153), "are all influenced by the tradition recorded in 1 Samuel 16 and 17" ("More Psalms of David," in *The OT Pseudipigrahpa,* vol. 2, p. 609).
Psalms of Solomon		c. 50-1 B.C.	This is the collective response of a group of pious Jews to Pompey's capture of Jerusalem in 63 B.C. They are by nature messianic, *condemning* illegitimate, incompetent rulers for setting Israel up for an oppressive foreign takeover, *promising* that a rightful king will come, remove the invaders, and establish an independent Jewish state, and *explaining* how the people should live in the interim.
Hellenistic Synagogal Prayers		c. A.D. 150-300	Probably the remnants of *Jewish* synagogal prayers, these 16 Christian pieces are scattered among volumes seven and eight of the liturgical *Apostolic Confessions.* They "share numerous parallels of

Document	Origin	Date	Brief Description
			thought with Philo, . . . the Wisdom of Solomon and Aristobulus. All these works reflect the profound influence of Greek thought . . . so typical of Jewish authors living in the Diaspora" (D. A. Fiensy, "Hellenistic Synagogal Prayers" in *The OT Pseudipigrapha,* vol. 2, p. 674). The "prayers" touch on a variety of topics, including God, man, angels, law, wisdom, and the afterlife. The author of Prayer Five, for example, argues that Sunday, the day on which he apparently celebrated "the resurrection day festival" (verse 7), "surpasses" the seventh-day Sabbath (verse 20), because it revealed Jesus and His NT accomplishments (verses 20-22).
Prayer of Joseph		c. A.D. 70-135	An expansion of Gen. 32:24-31, this work alleges that the patriarch Jacob was actually the incarnation of the angel Israel. It recasts the legendary wrestling match between Jacob and the Lord's angel as a conflict between Jacob (Israel) and the angel Uriel, who envied Jacob and fought with him over "the rank he held among the sons of God" (verse 7). The author even ascribes to *Israel* titles usually reserved for Jesus ("the firstborn of every living thing to whom God gives life" (verse 3; cf. Col. 1:15) and the angel Michael ("archangel," and "chief captain" (verse 7; cf. Rev. 12:7, and Dan. 12:1).
Prayer of Jacob		c. A.D. 100-300	Only 26 lines of the original document have survived. It is probably Jewish, written by a Diaspora patriot in Egypt. It reminds us of the *Prayer of Joseph,* with its insistence that Jacob is "an earthly angel . . . having become immortal" (verse 19), and may allege that those who repeated its four invocations, three petitions, and one injunction "seven times to the north and east" (verse 20) may receive the same immortality as a gift from God (verse 19).
Odes of Solomon		c. A.D. 100	A "Christian collection of forty-two odes significantly influenced by the literature of early Judaism, especially the Qumran Scrolls . . . and is strikingly similar to the Gospel of John" (*Harper's Bible Dictionary,* p. 840). Although they have a very Jewish tone, they are actually "a collection of very early Christian hymns" (J. H. Charlesworth, "The Odes of Solomon" in *The OT Pseudipigrapha,* vol. 2, p. 725). The author never quotes the Old or New Testaments, or any apocryphal books, but he nevertheless shows direct OT influence, and does share both "significant traditions . . . with the New Testament" and "numerous ideas and symbols with many apocryphal compositions" (*ibid.,* p. 732).

Targumim

Document	Origin	Date	Brief Description
	Jewish		To accommodate the shift to a new daily language, Palestinian synagogues followed Hebrew readings of Scripture with oral translations into Aramaic that eventually came to be written out. The object of the translator was to explain the text, rather than generate a word-for-word rendition of it. As Gowan says: "Targumim contain modifications and expansions which help to reveal what the text meant to those who worshiped in the synagogue (*Bridge Between the Testaments,* p. 385). The most important Targums include:
The Palestinian Targum			A translation of the Torah.
Targum Onqelos		*c.* A.D. 200	An almost literal translation of the Torah.
Targum Jonathan		*c.* A.D. 300	A translation of the Prophets.
The Jerusalem Targum (also known as, Targum Pseudo-Jonathan)			A translation of the Torah.

Mishnah

Document	Origin	Date	Brief Description
	Jewish	*c.* 200 B.C. to A.D. 200	The written codification of the oral law. The Saduccees clung to the *written* law alone. The Torah, however, did not take into account the changing customs and circusmsatances of the Jewish people. It needed adaptation to everyday life, so the scribes and Pharisees, believing that God also gave an oral law to Moses, which he in turn passed on to the elders, who added their contribution to God's commandments through discussion and application of the written code. Although they considered both sacred, Jewish scholars kept oral law separate from the written Torah by passing it on exclusively by word of mouth. This large body of traditional law came in two forms: *halakah,* rules of conduct, and *haggadah,* interpretations of Scripture, such as stories, parables, allegories, proverbs, and plays on words intended to edify rather than to regulate behavior. The *halakoth* (plural of *halakah*—a *collection* of *halakah*) were originally a fence around the sacred law to protect it from corruption, and an extension of the law to adapt the Torah to the changes of everyday life. "Haggadah is concerned with the problems of life, Creation, the function of man in Creation, his relation to God and the universe, the problem of good and evil . . . the place of Israel among the nations . . . reflections on a future life . . . [and] . . . the political and social circumstances of the various periods in which particular scholars lived" (R. C. Musaph-Anriesse, *From Torah to Kabbalah,* p. 61). The earliest agents to hand down this tradition were the *Soferim,* "scribes" or "scholars" of the oral law.

Document	Origin	Date	Brief Description
			The five *zugoth* (pairs), were the leaders of soferim groups from 160 B.C. to the beginning of the Christian era: Jose b. Joezer and Jose b. Johanon; Joshua b. Perahiah and Mattai of Arbela; Judah b. Tabbai and Simeon b. Shetah; Shemaiah and Abtalion; and Hillel and Shammai. After the soferim came six generations of *Tannaim* (scholars), beginning with Rabbi Johanan B. Zakkai, who founded a school at Yavneh (Jamnia) that took over for the defunct Sanhedrin after Jerusalem's fall in A.D. 70. Every rabbi and his school had their own collection of *halakah* and *haggadah,* including Rabbi Aqiba (*c.* A.D. 50-135), and one of his disciples, Rabbi Meir (A.D. 110-175). The final redactor of the Mishnah was Rabbi Judah haNasi (A.D. 135-217), the great grandson of Gamaliel. His collection came to be what we call the Mishnah today.

The Mishnah divides into six parts called *seder:*

Document			Brief Description
Zeraim ("Anything That Is Sown")			Regulations about agriculture, and contributions that must be set aside for the priests, the Levites, and the poor.
Moed ("Appointed Time")			Regulations for festivals and special days in the calendar year.
Nashim ("Women")			Laws about marriage, conjugal rights, and divorce.
N°ziqin ("Damages")			Procedures and practices in civil and penal law.
Qodashim ("Holy Things")			Sacrificial laws and services in and for the Temple.
Teharoth ("Cleannesses")			Guidelines concerning ritual impurity.

Each division subdivides into approximately 63 tractates called *masseket,* which further subdivide into 525 chapters called *pereq,* and embrace some 4,187 chapters called *mishnah,* from which the book gets its name.

Midrash

Document	Origin	Date	Brief Description
	Jewish	*c.* 200 B.C. to A.D. 1350	A system of *investigating* Scripture to *explain* or *expound on* it. The noun became a "technical term for the exposition and explanation of passages from the Tanach, the Mishnah, and the Talmud" (Andriesse, *From Torah to Kabballah,* p. 50). A midrash follows the text and comments on it along the way. The interpreter could either subjectively derive a rule from it as he adapted it to the changes of everyday life (*halakah*), or use haggadah (stories, etc.) to explain objectively and expand it. These techniques proved especially useful in the ongoing task of converting the ancient Torah into a modern code for daily living. Most of the earliest midrash, the Midrash Halakah, found its way into

Document	Origin	Date	Brief Description
			the Mishnah. Midrash Haggadah (also known as *narrative* Midrash) came later in the form of sayings, legends, and popular stories. Even though Hagadah also made its way into both versions, the most important collections of midrash stand independent of the Talmud.
Midrash Rabbah		From the beginning of the Christian era to A.D.1000	Haggadic literature of the Torah and the Five Megilloth ("scrolls"). Bereshith (Genesis) Rabbah; Shemoth (Exodus) Rabbah; Wayyiqra (Leviticus) Rabbah; Bemidbar (Numbers) Rabbah; Debarim (Deuteronomy) Rabbah; Ruth Rabbah; Esther Rabbah; Shir haShirim (Song of Songs) Rabbah; Qoheleth (Ecclesiastes) Rabbah; Ekah (Lamentations) Rabbah.
Tannaitic Midrashim		From the beginning of the Christian era to A.D. 220	Halakic and haggadic collections that were eventually edited and produced in their final form by the Amoraim (A.D. 220-500): the Mekilta ("measure, form") [Exodus]; the Sifra ("book") [Leviticus]; the Sifre ("books") [Numbers/Deuteronomy].
the Midrash haGadol (the Great Midrash)		c. A.D. 1350	Includes and edits many lost works of Midrash.
Tanhuma		c. A.D. 775-900	All the stories in this collection begin with the phrase, *yelammedenu rabbenu* ("Let our rabbi teach us").
Festival Midrash (usually called "Pesiqtoth").		c. 500-640 B.C.	Pesiqta de Rab Kahana; Pesiqta Rabbati; Aboth de Rabbi Nathan

Tosefta

Document	Origin	Date	Brief Description
	Jewish	c. beginning of Christian era to A.D. 200	The Tosefta ("addition") is an independent collection of explanations and points of discussion by Tannaim (probably Rabbi Nehemiah, a student of Rabbi Aqiba), closely related to the Mishnah. It deals with the same subject and also has six divisions subdivided into tractates and chapters.

Baraita

Document	Origin	Date	Brief Description
	Jewish	c. beginning of Christian era to A.D. 220	The Baraita ("standing outside") are pronouncements by Tannaim that never made it into the Mishnah, but many of which found a place in the Babylonian Talmud. Introduced by the words *teno rabbanan* ("the rabbis have taught") they are *halakoth* (plural of *halakah*) "standing outside" the Mishnah. The Tosefta, then, are actually a collection of baraitoth.

Gemara

Document	Origin	Date	Brief Description
	Jewish	c. A.D. 220-500	The collective material gathered from the discussions of the Amoriam ("interpreters"), who wrote volumes of commentary on the Mishnah. R. C. Musaph-Andriesse says: "We might compare it

Document	Origin	Date	Brief Description
			with the detailed minutes of a scholarly society"(*From Torah to Kabbalah,* p. 35). Together with the Mishnah, the Gemara ("Teachings") form the Talmud ("teaching/study") so that it "has the function of a commentary and also a supplement" (*ibid.*, p. 35). Six generations of detailed discussion and commentary of the Mishnah made the Gemara ("completion") a more extensive work than its parent document.

Talmud

Document	Origin	Date	Brief Description
	Jewish	*c.* 200 B.C.	Two rabbinic centers, one in Palestine, the other in Babylon, produced Gemara independently of each other. Each combined the parent Mishnah with its own Gemara to produce its version of the Talmud. Neither group added Gemara to every tractate in the Mishnah, although they did incorporate both halakah and haggadah to generate a document with something to say about every facet of Jewish life. Besides historical notes and prayers, even incidental remarks made their way into the two works. The result is not a law book, but a treasury of thoughts on a variety of subjects. Instead of one set rule per topic, the Talmud presents a text of Mishnah with the spectrum of views, at times in conflict with each other, contributed by rabbis who participated in the Gemara process.

The Saboraim ("those who reflected"), who succeeded the Amoraim as agents for handing down oral tradition to Israel, put the finishing touches on the Talmud during the fifth century A.D. Sometime between A.D. 500-650 they revised and arranged the material in its present format.

At first, both the shorter Jerusalem (*Yerushalmi*) and later Babylonian (*Babli*) Talmud enjoyed equal status, but the spiritual decline among Jews in Palestine allowed the *Babli* to surpass and eventually supersede the *Yerushalmi* as the one and only international standard of all Judaism.

The Geonim took over the process from the Saboraim until A.D. 1050. With the Talmud in place, they functioned as teacher-lawyers who interpreted the Law when communities needed it, in the light of changing circumstances.

Dead Sea Scrolls—

Document	Origin	Date	Brief Description
	Jewish	*c.* 150 B.C. to A.D. 70	An Arab shepherd named Muhammed el Dib accidentally discovered the first scrolls at a cave while searching for a stray goat along the northwestern shore of the Dead Sea during the spring of 1947. Scholars labelled the site *Cave One* and call this

Document	Origin	Date	Brief Description
			region of the Judean Wilderness "Qumran." "About three hundred caves in the region of Qumran have been excavated, and eleven of these yielded thousands of fragments believed to contain different manuscripts. The many different types of discovered manuscripts consisted chiefly of biblical writings, apocryphal manuscripts, Old Testament pseudepigrapha, sectarian literature, and commentaries on biblical books. Only about 10 scrolls have been preserved complete, and some texts are represented by only one fragment" (Mansoor, *The Dead Sea Scrolls,* p. 5).

The Main Scrolls Discovered

Document	Origin	Date	Brief Description
	Texts from the OT		Every OT book with the exception of Esther.
	Fragments from the Apocrypha and Pseudepigrapha		Tobit, Enoch, Jubilees, Testaments of Levi and Naphtali, Psalms of Joshua, and assorted apocryphal Daniel literature.
	Commentaries		Genesis, 2 Samuel, Psalms 37 and 68, Isaiah, Micah, Nahum, Habakkuk, Hosea, and a Midrash on the Book of Moses.
	Nonbiblical Sectarian Documents		The Thanksgiving Hymns, The War Scroll, The Manual of Discipline, The Genesis Apocryphon, The Temple Scroll, The Damascus Document, Testimonium of the Messianic Era, Benedictions, Copper Scrolls, Description of the New Jerusalem.

Major Manuscript Finds

Cave	Type	Reference	Description
1 Q		Is a	The complete (just a few words are missing) Isaiah scroll from the second century B.C.
1 Q		Is b	The badly damaged, fragmentary manuscript, containing portions of chapters 10-66.
1 Q	p	Hab	The Habakkuk Commentary (see the discussion of "Pesher" in the subsection, "Quotations, Allusions, and Commentary," beginning on page 134 of this book) that quotes the text of chapters 1-2, and interprets its meaning for the people of the commentator's day.
1 Q		S	The Manual of Discipline (also known as The Rule of the Community), which details what the Dead Sea people believed, the way they admitted people into the sect, and how they lived as a community.
1 Q	ap	Gen	The Genesis Apocryhon, a midrash on Genesis from which scholars have recovered sections about Noah and Abraham.
1 Q		M	The War Scroll (also known as The War of the Sons of Light Against the Sons of Darkness), a full description of the militant end-time scenario, in which the people of Qumran expected to play a significant part.

239

Cave	Type	Reference	Description
1 Q		H	The Hodayoth (also called The Thanksgiving Scroll), a collection of distinctly Qumranian hymns that resemble the biblical psalms.
3 Q		15	The Copper Scroll, a list in two parts, of alleged buried treasure sites.
4 Q		D	The Damascus Document (also called The Zadokite Fragment)—seven fragments of the same document discovered first at the Cairo Geniza in 1896-1897. Similar to the Manual of Discipline, this work presents a serious problem to today's scholars because it features the "sons of Zadok," a term some have maintained alludes to the Saduccees and a possible connection with that sect. The problem is the people of Qumran held the prophets in very high regard, whereas the Saducees did not even consider them inspired. It is probably best to consider Zadok a reference to the high priest who served under David and Solomon, and "sons of Zadok" as the label devout priests claimed for themselves "to signifiy their authentic priestly lineage and their attachment to the traditional faith and cult" (Menahem Mansoor, *The Dead Sea Scrolls,* p. 145), rather than the aristocratic Saducees, who claimed descendency but collaborated with the Greeks and Romans to compromise the Jewish way of life.
4 Q		Hen	Fragments of several manuscripts of 1 Enoch in the original Aramaic.
11 Q		Ps a	The Psalms Scroll, a collection of biblical, apocryphal, and previously unknown psalms.
11 Q	tg	Job	The Targum of Job, an early Aramaic translation of the biblical book.
11 Q		Temple	The Temple Scroll, an extensive list of religious rules (halakah) concerning ritual cleanliness, sacrifices and offerings by festivals, another (rival) temple, and regulations for the king and his army.

New Testament Apocrypha

Document	Origin	Date	Brief Description
	Christian		The group of noncanonical and often unorthodox documents written either by various heretics, mostly gnostic, to authenticate and promote their often strange opinions or by well-meaning zealots who wanted to preserve popular but erroneous traditions about the lives of Christ, the apostles, and other prominent NT figures.
			They come in the form of gospels, acts of the apostles, epistles, and apocalypses—just like the NT—

Document	Origin	Date	Brief Description
			but that is where the similarities end, because unlike the NT environment, the characters in these works "move about in an unreal world where the marvelous is the rule" (J. Tixeront, *Handbook of Patrology,* p. 63). Furthermore, the church never sanctioned these often popular works, so people felt free to tamper with them and frequently revised or amended them as they saw fit. "This accounts for the many recensions [versions, e.g., Slavonic, Coptic, Ethiopic, etc] of the same work . . . and also renders it very difficult . . . to determine the origin and date of these writings . . . to distinguish between the primitive work and later alterations" (*ibid.*, p. 63). Although the majority probably originated during the first and second centuries, recensions continued into medieval times, often correcting many earlier heresies.

Gospels

Document	Origin	Date	Brief Description
Protoevangelium of James		*c.* A.D. 150-200	An infancy gospel written by a non-Jewish Christian to glorify Mary, the mother of Jesus.
Infancy Gospel of Thomas		*c.* A.D. 100-200	A collection of exaggerated legends concerning the childhood of Jesus written in Greek.
Gospel of Peter			A brief pro-Gnostic account written by someone other than Peter between the latter half of the first and second centuries. It comes across more as a "proof of truth" than a "testimony of belief" (Edgar Hennecke, *New Testament Apocrypha,* vol. 2, p. 181).
Gospel of Nicodemus		*c.* A.D. 300	An apologetic work written by a zealous Christian to counter a pagan forgery entitled, "The Acts of Pilate." Chapters 1-12 were formerly called by this name, while chapters 13-22 came to be known as "Christ's Descent Into Hell."
Gospel of the Nazaraeans		2nd cent.	A synoptic-like account written in Syriac or Aramaic.
Gospel of the Ebionites		2nd cent.	A synoptic-like account written in Greek.
Gospel of the Hebrews		2nd cent.	A very different account from the canonical Gospels, written as the Gospel of Greek-speaking Jewish-Christians.
Gospel of the Egyptians		2nd cent.	A very Gnostic account written as the Gospel of Gentile-Christian Egyptians.
Gospel of Thomas		*c.* A.D. 50-200	A pro-Gnostic, synoptic-like "collection of traditional sayings, prophecies, proverbs, and parables of Jesus" (Helmut Koester, "The Gospel of Thomas," in *The Nag Hammadi Library,* p. 117), written in Greek.
Gospel of Phillip		*c.* A.D. 250	A Gnostic collection of statements regarding sacrements and ethics, written in Syria.
Gospel of Mary		*c.* A.D. 200	A Gnostic account written in Greek in which Mary Magdalene occupies a pivotal place among Jesus' followers.

241

Acts

Document	Origin	Date	Brief Description
John		c. A.D 150-200	A narrative account of the apostle John's ministry, reconstructed from citations and later recensions of the missing original.
Peter			A pro-Gnostic account of Peter's healing ministry that urges "rigorous self-control of the sexual life" (James Brashler and Douglas M. Parrott, "The Acts of Peter" in *The Nag Hammadi Library*, p. 475).
Paul	Asia	c. A.D. 170	A massive work including *The Martyrdom of the Holy Apostle Paul, The Correspondence of St. Paul, Third Corinthians,* and *The Acts of Paul and Thecla.*
Andrew		c. A.D. 150-200	A work partially recovered from citations in Eusebius and other ancient writers who labeled it heretical. Three other compositions used it as the source of their subject matter: *The Acts of Andrew and Mathias in the Town of the Anthropophagi, The Acts of the Holy Apostles Peter and Andrew,* and *The Martyrdom of the Holy Apostle Andrew.*
Thomas		c. A.D. 200-250	A Gnostic work recounting the activities of Didymas Judas Thomas, the alleged twin of Jesus (both Didymas and Thomas mean "twin").
Phillip		c. A.D. 300	A work that seems to confuse Phillip the apostle with Phillip the deacon.
Thaddeus		c. A.D. 300	Also known as the *The Edessan Acts,* this work re-counts the exploits of Thaddeus, one of the 72 disciples. It refers to the famous letter that Jesus supposedly sent to King Abgarus of Edessa.
Peter and Paul		c. A.D. 200-250	An account of the journey of Paul to Rome, where Peter was already a resident, their adventures together, and their martyrdom.
Martyrdom of Matthew			An account of the apostle Matthew's ministry and martyrdom at Myrne that scholars conjecture served as the conclusion to a larger work perhaps called *The Acts of Matthew,* though none of the ancient writers mention such a document.
Peter and the Twelve Apostles		c. A.D. 100-200	A pro-Gnostic work extolling the work of Christ as "Lithargoel," "the god of the pearl" as the basis for any apostolic activity.

Letters

Document	Origin	Date	Brief Description
Laodiceans			A brief communication allegedly written by the apostle Paul from prison to the well-known church in Asia Minor. It bears a striking resemblance to his canonical epistle to the Philippians (cf. verses 7, 8 with Phil. 1:19, 21; verses 10-12 with Phil. 2:12-14; et al).
Paul and Seneca		2nd cent.	A work purportedly written by the apostle Paul as part of an ongoing dialogue through correspondence with the well-known Roman scholar, who is cast as a Christian member of Caesar's household.

Document	Origin	Date	Brief Description
Jesus and Abgar		before 4th cent.	A work that was supposedly sent by Jesus via "Ananias the footman," to Abgarus, the king of Edessa.
Barnabas		2nd cent.	A piece of correspondence accepted as authentic in antiquity but rejected as apocryphal by modern scholars, supposedly written by Paul's first missionary partner to converts under pressure from some Jewish Christians to accept the old law. Antagonistic to Jews, it was probably written by someone else after the apostolic age.
Clement			Two epistles allegedly written to the Corinthians by the disciple of Peter who later became the Bishop of Rome. According to the great historian Eusebius, the first and longer of the two (which used the legend of the phoenix, a bird that supposedly rose up from its own ashes, to argue for a future resurrection) enjoyed immense popularity and nearly ended up part of the official canon.
The Doctrine of the Twelve Apostles (*The Didache*)			A very popular treatise in the early church, regarded by many as inspired. It claims to present the collective teaching of the 12 apostles in four parts: the Way of Life and the Way of Death (morality); baptism, fasting, prayer, and the Lord's Supper (liturgy); dealing with local and itinerant figures of authority, and the format for worship (discipline); and an exhortation to get prepared for Christ's imminent return, with a description of the signs that will precede and accompany His second advent (eschatology). An anonymous author blended the four parts into a single work sometime between A.D. 50 and 150.
Didascalia Apostolorum	Syria	*c.* A.D. 250-300	A pseudo-apostolic work written by a former Jew turned bishop. It borrows from the Didache and various other Christian writings, but unlike Western documents, it offers lenient guidelines for readmission to the church. The author, however, has very little tolerance for Judaizers.

Apocalypses

Document	Origin	Date	Brief Description
Peter		c. A.D. 150-250	This Gnostic work comes to us in two parts: one of heaven, the other of hell. It attempted to comfort the persecuted Gnostic community vis-á-vis three visions Peter had of Jesus' suffering, which the Saviour Himself sympathetically explains to them.
Paul			This Gnostic document was probably written around the time it claims that it was discovered under the house where Paul lived at Tarsus—during the reign of Theodosius (A.D. 379-395), who allegedly sent it to Jerusalem. Expanding on Paul's journey to the third heaven (2 Cor. 12:2-4) in a very Jewish apocalyptic way, it gives a detailed account of his visit to the homes of the elect and the damned

Document	Origin	Date	Brief Description
			and the Garden of Eden. The Coptic version extends the trip to a tenth heaven.
First Apocalypse of James			A Gnostic composition that focuses on suffering, "particularly the passion and death of the Lord and the ascent of the soul after death" (Douglas M. Parrott, "The First Apocalypse of James," in *The Nag Hammadi Library,* p. 242). It was probably written to encourage the Gnostic community under persecution. None of them need fear death because Christ's redemption is sure, and the Gnostic rite of extreme unction can seal the dying for safe passage to heaven. The emergence of a second apocalypse made it necessary to number this earlier document the first.
Second Apocalypse of James			In this sequel to the first apocalypse, James again relates what the risen Jesus has revealed to him, but "while the *First Apocalypse of James* stresses the period prior to the martyrdom of James and offers certain predictions, the *Second Apocalypse of James* describes the suffering and death of James in line with these predictions" (Douglas M. Parrott, "The Second Apocalypse of James" in *The Nag Hammadi Library,* p. 249). To further neutralize the fear of death, faithful James eventually attains near divine stature (like pseudepigraphic Enoch).
Apocryphon of John			A Gnostic mythological document of the Creation and Fall—built around an alleged revelation to John by the risen Jesus. It answers two of the Christian life's basic questions: "What is the origin of evil?" and "How can we escape from this evil world to our heavenly home?" (Frederick Wisse, "The Apocryphon of John," in *The Nag Hammadi Library,* p. 98).
Letter of Peter to Phillip			A Gnostic work in which Christ answers the questions of His disciples, of which Peter is the leader. The author explains that Christ suffered because of others, but we must suffer because we ourselves have a hand in the downfall of Wisdom (Sophia). [See, the discussion of *Gnosticism* under the heading "Issues" in the first subsection of "Church Fathers and Doctors" immediately below.]

Church Fathers and Doctors
Apostolic Fathers

Name	Dates	Works	Issues
Clement of Rome	? - 102	Epistles to Corinthians and Virgins	Appeals to submit to ecclesiastical authority and to live a life worthy of Christ's calling.
Ignatius of Antioch	? - 107	Epistles to Ephesus, Rome, Magnesia,	Warnings against heresies, appeals to submit to ecclesiastical authority.

Name	Dates	Works	Issues
		Tralles, Smyrna, Philadelphia, and Polycarp	
Polycarp of Smyrna	70-156	Epistle to Philippians	Guarantees the authenticity of Ignatius' letters.
Papias of Hieropolis	c. 130	Explanation of the Oracles of Our Lord	Origin of Matthew and Mark's Gospels.
Hermas	c. 140-145	The Shepherd	Repentance that leads to baptism, at which all past sins are forgiven, after which it is possible to repent and be forgiven one more time.

Apologetes

Name	Dates	Works	Issues
Quadratus of Asia Minor	c. 124	Apology to Hadrian	
Arsitedes of Athens	c. 125	Apology to Hadrian	Unlike Greeks and Jews, Christians have the full truth and live it.
Aristo of Pella	c. 140	A Discussion Between Jason and Papiscus Concerning Christ	Messianic prophecies are all fulfilled in Jesus.
Justin Martyr	c. 165	Dialogue with Trypho	The church is the true (anti-Marcionist) Israel.
		Two Apologies	Christians are good, pious citizens; Christ is the fulfillment of the Jewish prophecies.
(Justin)?	c. 200	Letter to Diognetus	Answers questions of interested party about worship, conversion, and historical timing.
Tatian the Assyrian	c. 172	The Apology	Points out Greek errors about God, the world, sin, and redemption.
		The Diatessaron	A harmony of the four canonical Gospels.
Miltiades (anti-Montanist/ Gnostic)	c. 192	Apologies against, Jews, heretics and heathen	None preserved.
Apollinaris of Hieropolis (anti-Gnostic)	c. 172	Apologies, etc.	None preserved.
Melito of Sardis (anti-Gnostic)	c. 190	Apology to Marcus Aurelius	No separation of church and state.
		Homily on the Passion	A Good Friday sermon.
Athenagoras of Athens	c. 177	Supplication for the Christians	Refutes charges of atheism and immorality.
		On the Resurrection of the Dead	Proves reality of the Resurrection from man's eternal destiny, separation of body and soul at death, and a higher end in the life to come.

Name	Dates	Works	Issues
Theophilus of Antioch (anti-Gnostic)	c. 181	Discourse to Autolycus	Faith, idolatry, and inspiration.
Hermias	c. 200	The Mockery of Heathen Philosophers	Ridicules conflicting opinions among Greek thinkers concerning the soul and also the universe.
Minucius Felix	c. 200	Octavius	Dialogue that refutes the typical charges, defends monotheism, and argues against polytheism.
Hegesippus	c. 110-180	Memoirs	Anti-Gnostic.
Apollonius of Ephesus			Anti-Gnostic.
Gaius of Rome	c. 199-217		Anti-Montanist.
Irenaeus of Lyons	c. 135-203	Proof of the Apostolic Teaching	Summary of Christian teaching.
		Adversus Omnes Haereses	Detection/exposition/refutation of errors, and exposition of the truth.

Eastern Writers
Alexandrian

Name	Dates	Works	Issues
Clement	c. 150	Protrepticus	Exhorts pagans to abandon errors so that he can convert them.
		Paedagogus	Promises to teach the pagans how to live a genuine Christian life.
		Stromateis	Pledge to instruct them in the doctrines.
		Hypotyposes	Allegorical notes on the OT and the epistles of Paul, 1 and 2 John, Peter, and the Acts of the Apostles.
		Quis di ves Salvetur?	Homily on Mark 10—love of money is the root of all evil.
Origen	c. 185-255	The Hexapla	OT in Hebrew/Greek, and four Greek versions.
		Scholia	Notes on tough passages of Scripture.
		Homilies	Appealing expositions of Scripture.
		Commentaries	Extensive treatment of Scripture.
		Contra Celsum	A point-by-point refutation of Celsus' defense of state religion and attack on Christianity (*Alethes Logos*).
		De Principiis	Disciplined exposition of the Christian fundamentals.
		On Prayer, On the Lord's Prayer, Exhortation to Martyrdom	Ascetic/Homiletic works.

Name	Dates	Works	Issues
		Epistles to Julius Africanus and Gregory Thaumaturgus	
Dionysius	c. 264	On Nature	Against Epicureanism.
		On Temptations	Trials outside persecution.
		On the Promises	Against Nepos, bishop who defended the historical interpretation of Scripture.
		Epistles to Novatian	Urges him to abandon separation from the church and to resubmit to Pope Cornelius.
		Epistle to Council of Antioch	Urges them to reject Paul of Samosata's view that God adopted Christ after the crucifixion and Resurrection and then gave Him a kind of deity.
		Epistle to Bishop Basilides	Duration of fast during Lent; purity needed to receive Communion.
Theognostus	264-280	Hypotyposes	Seven books of essays steeped in Origenistic views of all Christian doctrines.
Pierius	282-300	On the Mother of God	Veneration of Mary.
Peter	300-311	On the Divinity	The divine nature of Christ dominated the human.
		Against the Pre-existence of Souls, On the Resurrection	Anti-Origen.

Syro-Palestinian

Name	Dates	Works	Issues
Julius Africanus	c. 240	Chronographia	Attempt to harmonize Judeo-Christian history with the history of the Gentile world.
		Embroidered Girdles	An encyclopedia of science, medicine, magic, farming, and warfare.
		Epistle to Origen	About Susanna in the Greek version of Daniel.
Paul of Samosata	c. 260		Overemphasized the humanity of Christ.
Malchion of Antioch	c. 268	Epistle from Council of Antioch to the Churches	Announced Paul of Samosata's excommunication.
Lucian of Samosata	c. 312	Revised Septuagint and Gospels	Pro-Paul, excommunicated, then recanted.
Pamphilus of Caesarea	c. 240-309	Apology for Origen	Defended Origen against charges of heterodoxy.

247

Asia Minor

Name	Dates	Works	Issues
Gregory Thaumaturgus	c. 213-270	Panegyric on Origen	
		Creed of Gregory	The Trinity
		Canonical Epistle	Mild treatment of Christians who had violated discipline and morality during the Gothic raids.
Methodius of Olympus	c. 311	The Banquet on Virginity	Praise for virginity.
		On the Freedom of the Will	Anti-Gnostic attack on dualism/determinism.
		On the Resurrection	Dialogue.

Western Writers

African

Name	Dates	Works	Issues
Tertullian	c. 160-220	Apologeticum	Refutes charges of secret and public crimes (refusal to honor state religion; high treason).
		Ad Nationes	Accusations against Christianity are likewise true of paganism.
		Ad Scapulam	Letter to the proconsul in Africa warning him of what happened to other persecutors of Christians.
		Adversus Judaeos	The Israelites rejected God's grace.
		De Praescriptione Hereticorum	The origin and nature of heresy.
		Adversus Marcionem	Refutation of Marcion's dualism and canon of Scripture; proof that the historical Jesus is the Messiah foretold in the OT.
		Adversus Hermogenem	Attack on dualism.
		Adversus Valentinianos	Anti-Montanist.
		De Baptismo	Declares heretical baptism invalid.
		De Carne Christi	Anti-Gnostic attack on Marcion's Docetism, maintaining Christ as a real man with a human body.
		Scorpiace	Presents a defense against Gnosticism as an antidote against the bite of a scorpion.
		De Resurrectione Carnis	Anti-Gnostic proof of the reality of a bodily resurrection.
		Adversus Praxeamon	Defends the orthodox view of the church the Trinity against the Patripassian concept of God ceasing to reveal Himself as the

248

Name	Dates	Works	Issues
			Father and taking on the form or mode of the Son (Modalistic Monarchianism).
		De Oratione	On prayer.
		De Poenitentia	Public canonical penances for various sins.
		De Pudicitia	A Montanist attack on forgiveness of adultery and fornication.
		Ad Martyres	Encouraging letter.
		Ad Uxorem	A Montanist view of marriage; rejection of second marriages.
		De Exhortatione Castitatis, De Monogamia	Second marriages are a sin (adultery).
		De Idolatria	The dangers and occasions of idolatry.
		De Corona	Soldiers have the right to refuse to wear a crown.
		De Cultu Feminarum	Denounces female vanity in dress and ornamentation.
		De Virginibus Velandis	Contra De Oratione, he insists that virgins everywhere should wear veils.
		De Fuga in Persecutione	A Montanist demand to stand one's ground at all times.
		De Anima	A Montanist, anti-Gnostic psychology of the soul.
Cyprian	c. 200-258	Letters	Eighty-one, dealing with persecution, schism, praise for the faithful, consolation, encouragement.
		Quod Idola Dii non Sint	Idols are not gods.
		Ad Donatum	The new life through baptism.
		De Habitu Virginum	Call for modest female dress.
		De Lapsis	Guidelines for the readmission of those who caved in to Decian persecution and renounced the faith.
		De Catholicae Ecclesiae Unitate	Attack on schism and argument for the need to unite with mother church.
		De Dominica Oratione	On prayer.
		Ad Demetrianum	Argues that natural disasters are the result of persecuting Christians rather than Christian neglect of pagan gods.
		De Mortalitate	Consolation for victims of the epidemic of A.D. 252.
		De Opere et Eleemosynis	Exhortation to show charity.

Name	Dates	Works	Issues
		De Bono Patientiae	The benefit of patience during the baptism controversy.
		De Zelo et Livore	Denounces envy.
		Ad Fortunatum	Urges saints to suffer martyrdom during the Valerian persecution.
		Ad Quirinum	A collection of texts to show that the Jewish Law is temporary, the fulfillment of OT prophecies in the person and work of Christ and in the Christian life of faith.
Arnobius	c. 280-310	Adversus Nationes	Polemic against heathenism, defense of his own conversion.
Lactantius	c. 250-317	De Opificio Dei	An anthropology to argue against the Epicureans that the human body is a creation of God.
		Divinae Institutiones	Refutes erroneous charges, defends true Christian teaching.
		De Ira Dei	Anti-Stoic and Epicurean.
		De Mortibus Persecutorum	Argues for the truth of Christianity by reporting the terrible deaths of its persecutors.
		De Ave Phoenice	A short poem about the mythical phoenix.

Roman

Name	Dates	Works	Issues
Hippolytus	c. 160-235	Philosophumena	Polemic against all heresies, tracing them to Greek philosophy rather than Scripture.
		Syntagma	Anti-heretic.
		Treatise on Antichrist	Describes the antichrist's brief triumph and swift downfall.
		Exhortation to Severina on the Economy	The Incarnation.
		Liturgy, Canon Law	Fasting on Saturdays, daily Communion.
		Apostolic Tradition	History and practice of Roman liturgy.
		Commentary on Daniel, Commentary on Canticle of Canticles	Not verse by verse, but explanations of ideas and select passages.
		Against the Greeks and Plato, Against the Jews, Against Marcion (Gnostics), Concerning Charismata (Montanists),	Attack on every form of error.

Name	Dates	Works	Issues
		Against the rabid anti-Montanists, Against the Modalists and Adoptionists, Against Artemon	
Novatian	*c.* 251	De Trinitate	Thorough treatise on the Trinity.
		De Cibis Judaicis	Unlike the Jews, Christians only have to avoid meat sacrificed to idols and to practice temperance.

At-large

Name	Dates	Works	Issues
Commodian	*c.* 250	Instruction	Poems against Jews and pagans, urging Christians to live up to their calling.
		Carmen Apologeticum	Defense of a wide variety of doctrine.
Victorinus of Pettau	*c.* 304	Commentary on the Apocalypse	Exegetical, millennial treatment.
		Adversus Omnes Haereses	Against heresies.
Rectitius of Autun	*c.* 313	Commentary on the Canticle of Canticles	Stylish but mediocre treatment.
		Against Novatian	Anti-heretic.

Greek Writers

Name	Dates	Works	Issues
Eusebius of Caesarea	*c.* 263-340	Chronicle	Chronology of different nation's events, synchronized and coordinated to show a connection between remote history and his own.
		Ecclesiastical History	Ten volumes covering the life of the early church from its beginning to 323.
		Evangelical Preparation	Christianity and even Judaism are superior to paganism.
		Evangelical Demonstration	Christianity is the divine development of Judaism.
		Against Marcellus	Proves Arians right for deposing him for his Sabellianism.
		On Ecclesiastical Theology	Exposition/defense of the Logos doctrine.
Athanasius	*c.* 295-373	Oratio Contra Gentes	Attack on pantheism.
		Oratio de Incarnatione Verbi	Against pagans and Jews.

Name	Dates	Works	Issues
		Orationes Contra Arianos IV	Relationship of God the Father to God the Son.
		Letters IV to Serapion	Refutes those who say the Son is eternal, but the Holy Ghost is not.
		Epistula ad Epictetum	Christology.
		Apology Against the Arians	Historical.
		Historia Arianorum	Proceedings of the councils of Rimini and Seleucia.
		Commentary on the Psalms	Allegorical interpretation.
		Biography of St. Anthony	Model of the dedicated life.
		Festal Letters	Historical value.
Cyril of Jerusalem	c. 315-386	The Catacheses	Complete body of doctrine.
Basil the Great	c. 329-379	Against Eunomius	The Trinity.
		De Spiritu Sancto	The Trinity.
		The Hexameron	Homilies on Gen. 1:1-26.
		On the Psalms	Literal interpretation.
		Ascetica	Monastic life.
		Regulae Fusius Tractatae, Regulae Brevius Tractatae	Rules of monaastic life and their application to daily life.
		De Baptismo	Rules for baptism.
		Liturgy of St. Basil	Reduces prayers and ceremonies at Caesarea to a fixed format.
Gregory of Nazianzus	c. 329 - 390	Five Theological Orations	Defense of the Godhead.
		Epistle 101	Christology.
		De Vita Sua	Defense of his actions in response to the challenges of life.
		Apology	Treatise on the priesthood.
Gregory of Nyssa	c. 335-394	De Hominus Opificio, Explicatio Apologetica in Hexaemeron	Completed older brother Basil's homilies; follows Origen's allegorical style.
		On the Witch of Endor	It was not a prophet but a demon that appeared to Saul.
		De Vita Moysis	On spiritual progress.
		In Canticum Canticorum	God is the Bridegroom, the soul is His bride.

252

Name	Dates	Works	Issues
		Homiliae XV	
		Adversus Eunomium	Counterattack to Eunomius reply after Basil's death.
		The Great Catechism	How to seize opponent's argument and point of view and to proceed from there; deals with all the fundamental doctrines.
		Ad Eustathium de S. Trinitate	The Trinity.
		Ad Alabium	"There are not three gods."
		De Anima et Resurrectione	Eschatological dialogue about the soul, death, and resurrection.
		Contra fatum	A defense of free will.
		Ad Hierium	Explanation of why God permits children to die untimely deaths.
		De Virginitate, To Harmonius, To Olympius	Praises virginity as a state of perfection and the foundation of the virtues.
		Letter to Eustathia and Abrosia	Complaint about ecclesiastical conditions in Palestine.
		Letter to Pilgrims	Complaint about abuses in pilgrimages.
Didymus the Blind	c. 398	De Trinitate	The Trinity.
		De Spiritu Sancto	The Holy Spirit, written against the *pneumatomachi*.
		Contra Manichaeos	Attack on the Manicheans.
		On the Death of Little Children	Explanation.
		Two books against the Arians	Anti-Arianism.
Epiphanius	c. 315-403	Ancoratus	The Trinity, especially the Holy Ghost, to anchor those tossed by waves of Arianism and semi-Arianism. Two creeds at the end to be used at baptism.
		Panarion	The *Medicine Chest*, from which readers could get the antidote for heresy-bites.
		On Measures and Weights of the Jews	Canon and versions of the OT, biblical meaures and weights, Palestinian geography.
		Twelve Precious Stones	Allegorical explanation of the symbolism of the stones in the high priest's breastplate.

Name	Dates	Works	Issues
Diodore of Tarsus	c. 393	Commentaries (on the whole Bible)	Uses the historico-grammatical method and rejects the mystico-allegorical system of the Alexandrian school.
		On the Difference Between Theory and Allegory	Milestone in the study of hermeneutical principles.
		Against Astronomers and Astrologers, Against the Manicheans, Against the Melchisedechians, Against the Jews, Against Plato on God and Gods, Against Photinus, Paul of Samasata, Sabellius, and Marcellus of Ancyra	Refutations of various heresies and ungodly practices.
		Against Porphyry	On animals and sacrifices.
Theodore of Mopsuestia	c. 428	Commentaries (on various books of the Bible)	Inferior view of inspiration; literal exegesis often turns into rationalization.
		On the Incarnation, On the Holy Ghost, On the Mysteries, On Faith, Priesthood, On Miracles	Against Arians, Apollonarists, Monophysites (who would not say that Christ always has two natures).
		Ad Patrophilum	Against Pneumatomachians.
		Against Those Who Say That Men Are Sinners by Nature and Not by Will	Against Jerome, but with Pelagius.
		Catecheses	Instructions for candidates.
John Chrysostom	c. 354-407	Homilies (the best of which are on the Psalms and Romans)	Popular and practical.
		De Statuis	Delivered to the people of Antioch, who had overturned the emperor's statues to protest taxes.

Name	Dates	Works	Issues
		De Incompre-hensibili	Twelve homilies against the Anomoeans concerning the Law.
		Against the Jews and Pagans on the Divinity of Christ	Shows from prophecy that our Lord is divine.
		De Inani Gloria et de Liberis Educandis	On education.
		De Sacerdotio	The dignity and function of a priest.
		On Pride and the Education of Children	The first handbook on Christian education.
		On the Virginal State, To a Young Widow, De non Iterando Conjugio	Virginity and self-control.
		Letters	News of his exile, the encouragement of his friends, evangelism, the state of the church, praise for virtuous suffering.
Cyril of Alexandria	c. 444	Apology Against Julian	Step-by-step answer to charges with text.
		De Adoratione et Cultu in Spiritu et Veritate	Allegorical-mystical interpretation of Jewish laws and institutions.
		Glaphyra	Strong insights into select Pentateuch passages.
		Commentaries	More literal than allegorical in the NT.
		Thesaurus de Sancta et Consubstantiali Trinitate	Refutes errors and affirms doctrine of "The Holy and Consubstantial [one common substance/essence/nature] Trinity."
		De Sancta et Consubstantiali Trinitate	Against Arians.
		Adversus Nestorii Blasphemias	A critical examination of Nestorus' sermons.
		De Recta Fide	Three anti-Nestorian memorials "On Right Belief."
		Homiliae Paschales	Moral and practical Easter sermons.
		Treatises on the Incarnation	The hypostatic union of Jesus' two natures.
		Contra Synusiastas	Against extreme Apollinarists.

255

Name	Dates	Works	Issues
		The 12 Anatahematisms	Alexandrian Christology.
Theodoret of Cyrus	c. 393-458	Graecarum Affectionum Curatio	Defense of apostolic authority and qualifications; comparison of Christian and pagan answers to life's basic questions.
		Pentalogium	Antiochene attack on Cyril, accusing him of Appolinarism and Monophysitism.
		The Beggar, or the Polymorph	Against Monophysitism.
		Commentaries	Antiochene rather than Alexandrian principles of exegesis; considered the finest exegete of the ancient Graeco-Christian world; mainly OT.
		Church History	Sequel to Eusebius, he traces the church's troubles from Arian to Nestorian controversies (323-428).
		History of the Monks	Story of the Eastern ascetics.
		A Handbook of Heretical Fables	A history of heresy in the Christian community.
		De Providentia Orationes	Intellectual sermons on God's providence.
John of Damascus	c. 675-749	Fountain of Wisdom	Condensation of his knowledge in three parts: Greek Philosophy, History of Heresy, and Orthodox Theology.
		Against Those Who Reject Images	Defense of image worship.
		Against the Manicheans, Against the Heresy of the Nestorians, Against the Monophysites	Anti-heretical.
		Sacra Parallela	Compilation of fathers and Scripture on the Christian life.
		Homilies	Three of his 13 sermons are on the death and assumption of Mary.
		Idiomela	Hymn composed for the office of the dead.

Syriac Writers

Name	Dates	Works	Issues
Ephraem Syrus	c. 306-373	Commentaries (on the whole Bible)	Translated into other languages; Antiochene rather than allegorical.
		Against the Scrutinizers	Against those who attacked the Trinity or the Incarnation.

Name	Dates	Works	Issues
		De Domino Nostro	On the Incarnation.
		Homilies and Sermons	Moral and practical, on paradise, Joseph, birth of Christ, Mary, the apostles, martyrs, and faithful, the Christian, priestly, and monastic lives.
		Carmina Nisibena	Christian morality.
		Funeral Hymns	Treasury of customs and liturgy of the time.
Aphraates	c. 367	Homilies	Dogmatic advice on a variety of subjects, in defense against Jews and their way of life.

Latin Writers

Name	Dates	Works	Issues
Firmicius Maternus	c. 360	Mathesis	Preconversion work on astrology.
		De Errore Profanarum Religionum	Attack on pagan mysteries directed to Emperor Constantine.
Hilary of Poitiers	c. 310-367	De Trinitate	Anti-Arian treatise on the Trinity.
		De Synodis	Proof to the Arians, who believed that Jesus and the Father had *similar* natures (*homoiousios*), that their position logically implies that the Father and Son are (*homoousios*) with the *same* nature.
		Apologetica	Replies to attacks on De Synodis.
		Liber ad Constantium Augustum	Request for audience with Constantius to discuss the deceit of Saturninus, the Arian bishop of Arles.
		Contra Constantium Imperatorum	When Constantius refused, Hilary compared him to Nero, Decius, and Maximian and denounced him as antichrist.
		Commentaries	Allegorical-mystical style.
Ambrose	c. 339-397	Hexameron	Lenten homilies.
		De Officiis Ministrorum	Christians are obligated to do what is lawful and good.
		De Virginibus, De Virginitate, De Institutione Virginis et Sanctae Mariae Virginitate Perpetua, Exhortatio Virginitatis	Praise of virginity.
		De Fide	Defends Christ's divinity to the Arians.
		De Spiritu Sancto	On the Holy Ghost.

Name	Dates	Works	Issues
		De Mysteriis	A catechism of Catholic sacraments: baptism, confirmation, and eucharist.
		De Paenitentia	On penance, refutes Novatianism.
		Sermons	Models of rhetorical composition, which impressed the unconverted rhetorician, Augustine.
		Letters	Historical value.
		Hymns	Well crafted, he introduced antiphonal singing. All hymns in his style after the seventh century were called Ambrosian.
		Liturgy	Innovative.
Prudentius	*c.* 348-405	Cathemerinon	12 daily hymns for various times and actions of the day.
		Peristephanon Liber	Fourteen songs praise Roman and Spanish martyrs.
Paulinus	*c.* 431	Carmina Natalitia	Thirteen hexametric poems in honor of Saint Felix for each of 13 years.
		Epithalamium Juliani et Jae	Christian wedding poem.
Sulpicius Severus	*c.* 420	Chronicorum Libri Duo	Summarized history of the OT.
		Life of St. Martin	Focus on his miracles.
		Dialogi	Complete life of Saint Martin.
Jerome	*c.* 349-420	The Vulgate	Translation of the Old and New testaments into Latin.
		Questiones Hebraicae in Genesim	On philology.
		Liber De Situ et Nominibus Locorum Hebraicorum	A geographical lexicon.
		Commentaries	Alexandrian style, but based the spiritual sense on a responsibly determined literal one.
		De Viris Illustribus	At times less than satisfactory first history of Christian literature, involving some 135 authors.
		Translations (of various other's works)	Origen, Theophilus of Alexandria, Epiphanius, and Didymus.
		Adversus Palagianos	A dialogue against the Pelagians.
		Letters	Treatises, exhortations, instructions.
Tyrannius Rufinus	*c.* 354-430	Translations (of various other's works)	Origen, Pamphilius of Caesarea, Sextus, Eusebius, Basil, Gregory of Nazianzus, Josephus.

Name	Dates	Works	Issues
		Historia Ecclesiastica	First Western history of the church.
Patrick	c. 432-461	Liber Epistolarum Sancti Patricii Episcopi	Seventh-century collection of letters, of which only two survive intact.
		Confession	An open letter defending his call and mission.
		Epistola ad Milites Corotici	A forceful indictment of the Christian prince for ordering his soldiers to carry off or kill some of Patrick's beloved converts.
Augustine	c. 354-430	Retractions	A recapitulation of all his works except the letters and discourses.
		Confessions	A book of praise and acknowledgement of God based on the life principle, "You have made us for Yourself and our heart is restless until it reposes in You."
		The City of God	Augustine interprets the whole of history from a prophetic perspective—to defend Christianity against the old charge of angering the pagan deities that had protected the empire.
		De Beata Vita	Happiness is knowing God.
		Soliloquia	On immortality.
		De Quantitate Animae	On the immaterial nature of the soul.
		De Magistro	Christ is the only Master.
		Adversus Judaeos	Against the Jews.
		De Haeresibus	On Heresies.
		Anti-Manichean works	Against Manicheans and their dualism.
		Anti-Donatist works	Against the Donatist contention that the effectiveness of rites and sacraments depends on the holiness of the minister; Augustine defended the concept of *ex opere operato,* that in their operation, the sacraments bestow grace regardless of the minister's or recipient's merits.
		Anti-Pelagian works	Make the case for fallen man's redemption from sin by grace.
		Anti-Arian works	Defend the consubstantiality (*homoousios*) of the Trinity.
		Enchiridion	Systematic dogmatic theology.
		De Doctrina Christiana	A virtual handbook of hermeneutics (how to investigate what the Scriptures mean), and homiletics (how to make it known to

Name	Dates	Works	Issues
			the faithful). (See the discussion of these terms in the "Introduction" to this book.)
		Treatises (on the NT)	Augustine was the first to say that there is more than one literal sense of Scripture and that whatever truth can be found in Scripture was intended by the Holy Spirit. (See the discussion of "Sensus Plenior" in the subsection "Analogy of Faith" beginning on p. 138 of this book.)
		De Agone Christiano	Instruction on how to overcome evil.
		Speculum	Collection of moral precepts from the Bible.
		Letters	Deal with pastoral, philosophical, and theological questions.
Leo the Great	*c.* 440-461	Homilies	More than half preached on feasts of Christ or the saints; the rest are dogmatic discourses.
		Letters	Defend doctrines of the church on Christ against the Monophysites, Council of Chalcedon, chronology of Easter.
		Epistola Dogmatica et Flavianum	Explains the doctrine of one person and two natures in Christ (also known as Leo's *Tome*) the definitive work on Christology.
Gregory the Great	*c.* 540-504	Registrum Epistolarum	848 generally pastoral and spiritual letters.
		Liber Regulae Pastoralis	The Pastoral Rule, spells out the responsibiities of a pastor.
		Dialogi	Biographies of the Italian fathers.
		Expositio in Librum Iob Sive Moralium Libri	Historical, allegorical, and moral exposition of Job with so much space devoted to the moral dimension, the entire work was called *Moralia.* It is a virtual handbook of Christian ethics.
		Homilies on the Gospels	A year of sermons with a fatherly tone.
		Gregorian Chant	Liturgical melodies.

CHAPTER 10

TYPOLOGY

The trend among Protestant interpreters today is to rely mainly on grammatical and historical studies to interpret Scripture, but an increasing number of scholars question the benefits from an intense study limited solely to the original historical situation. Hans K. LaRondelle says that "the meaning of single events can often be fully understood only in the light of their consequences in later history. . . . Among all the nations of the Oriental world, only Israel developed an eschatology, a hope in which God gradually unfolded His promise, corrected false, nationalistic hopes, and constantly transcended Israel's concepts of His kingdom by pointing to a future fulfillment that would exceed all Israel's earthly expectations" *(The Israel of God in Prophecy: Principles of Prophetic Interpretation,* p. 35).

Introduction

God originally called Israel to bless the world through her (Gen. 12:1-3). Yet by the time Jesus came on the scene, Israel had wandered so far from truth that it was impossible for her to bless anyone—even herself (Matt. 15:3; 23:13)! God could not carry out the purpose for His law or bring prophecy to completion with people who considered the kingdom a matter of simply overthrowing Rome (Matt. 5:17). Jesus found it necessary to correct these false impressions in order to restore God's crucial point of view to His people.

According to Matthew 5:17, Jesus disagreed with Israel's religious experts concerning both the law and prophecy. So He explained to them that righteousness goes deeper than human actions (cf. Matt. 5:20 and Deut. 5:1; 6:25). Jesus insisted that both the coming kingdom of God and true worship are matters of the heart—not something that you see with your eyes (see Luke 17:20, 21) or a ritual that people practice in a particular place (see John 4:20-23).

The Revelation Model

Although God had supernatural things to show Israel, He used natural ones to reveal these mysteries. And He did not present them all at once or in their most advanced form right away. Instead, He chose to progressively reveal supernatural realities with symbols: people, events, and institutions that the Israelites could see. He worked from elementary to more advanced levels as history unfolded so that His people would gradually grasp more and more of what these spiritual matters represented.

Because revelation is both progressive and cumulative, not only does it build to a climax, but it also adds up. Revelatory light gains intensity with the passing of time. Later texts offer brighter beams of insight because they focus rays of light accumulated to that time. Historically closer to the time when the supernatural realities will stand for themselves, later texts offer more advanced presentations, which bear closer resemblance to their higher realities than earlier ones. They thus help clarify as well as identify who or what is represented.

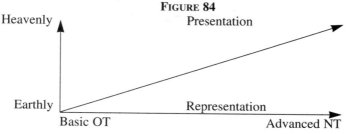

FIGURE 84

From early times it appears that Israel had trouble looking past these visible things to the much higher realities that they represented, which limited their understanding of God, righteousness, and the kingdom to what they could see. Even the early prophets—from the great prophetic revival under Samuel to the first writing prophets of the middle eighth century B.C.—did not fathom much more. Each had a word for his own day and generation, preaching so that the nation would repent and return to God. During the reign of Solomon, unable to imagine anything better than the literal fulfillment of the promises made to Abraham, they saw themselves as reorganizers sent by God to restore Israel to its former glory.

But later prophets saw past these restrictions. As God continued to unfold His everlasting covenant, His spokespersons continued to call for repentance, but the emphasis shifted from repair to regeneration as the remedy for Israel's problems.

Unfortunately, when Jesus came on the scene, Israel's spiritual condition had not improved much since the days of the prophets (cf. Isa. 6:9, 10 and Matt. 13:13-15). After centuries of limited thinking, Israel needed a loftier vision and a deeper insight into the true nature of things. So Jesus began speaking in parables to teach unfamiliar heavenly truths by placing them alongside corresponding, everyday earthly ones. Because the Creator had made both heaven and earth, natural things and processes reflect their heavenly counterparts and can be useful to illustrate the supernatural.

Jesus quoted Psalm 78:2 in Matthew 13:35 to explain why He spoke in parables: "I will utter things hidden since the creation of the world" (NIV). Not that God had deliberately kept truths out of sight or from being seen, but what He had to teach was more than met the eye. So Jesus sought to bring out the overlooked, deeper divine truth that was there all the time. Unlike the writers of pagan parables, Jesus presented things acting naturally—functioning as the Creator had made them—to place higher truths before the people in a dynamic way.

Few in Israel's history had seen what Jesus showed to His disciples (Matt. 13:17), including, tragically, the greatest "teachers" of His day. When Nicodemus dropped by to talk things over with Jesus, the Saviour told the scholar that no one in Israel could enter God's kingdom unless he or she was first "born again." Jesus used rebirth as a symbol of starting life over again with God for a Father.

Do you recall what Nicodemus said? "How can a man be born when he is old?" He can't enter his mother's womb a second time and be born, can he? (John 3:4, NKJV). Sad that Nicodemus, "a teacher of Israel" (verse 10), suffered the same chronic vision problem that had plagued God's people for centuries. He could not see past the symbol to the higher spiritual reality that it represented.

Israel had latched onto the symbols as though they were the higher realities themselves. She cherished the good times associated with the symbolic past (Luke 5:39 [NKJV]—"The old is better") and kept looking back, hoping that God would reinstate the old glory days sometime in the future. But instead of showing the prophets a revival of the best from the past, God gave them a glimpse of a future new creation that far surpassed Israel's limited expectations—"Eye hath not seen, nor ear heard" (Isa. 64:4).

Although these symbols—the best from the past—were merely shadows of things to come, the glorious future they represented was not something entirely new, because the symbols had been pointing to this glorious future all the time. The future is simply a continuation of God's original covenant plan—the final edition of what He intended and established from the beginning.

While most Israelites pined for the symbolic past, wondering how to link the ancient promises with the their seemingly hopeless present, the prophets reached into the future for the higher realities represented by the symbols in the first place.

The Typology Model

When a symbol that used to represent a spiritual truth to ancient, national Israel also prefigures this same truth for end-time Messianic Israel (sometimes called spiritual Israel), it is called a type. Yet "typology is not just a matter of collecting all the resemblances between the Old and New Testaments, but rather of understanding the underlying redemptive and revelational process which begins in the Old Testament and finds its fulfillment in the New" (C. T. Fritsch, "Principles of Biblical Typology," *Biblia Sacra* 104 [1947], p. 214).

Although a symbol pictured redemption in its own day and a type looks forward to the future, the things symbolized and typified are not different sets of things. They are the same with this one difference—the symbolical came first (at an earlier, preliminary stage of development in the work of redemption), and the typical came at a later, more advanced one.

FIGURE 85

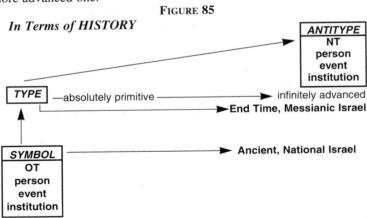

In Terms of History—In terms of history, a type has certain distinguishing features:

1. A type is always someone who really existed or something that actually occurred as presented in Scripture. Speaking of the letter to the Hebrews, Richard M.

Davidson writes: "The author takes for granted the historical reality of the OT persons, events, and institutions mentioned in the epistle. . . . 'His . . . concern throughout the sermon is to ground Christian confidence in objective *facts*. . . . *Real* deity, *real* humanity, *real* priesthood—and we may add, a *real* ministry in a real sanctuary'" *(Typology in Scripture*, p. 346).

2. A type always corresponds to its New Testament reality or realities in terms of people (see Rom. 5), events (see 1 Cor. 10; 1 Peter 3), or institutions (see Heb. 8 and 9). And this correspondence is also in terms of the crucial details determined by the type and by the fact that were already redemptively significant in the Old Testament as either a contrast (see Rom. 5) or a comparison (see 1 Cor. 10; 1 Peter 3).

For example, the main line of correspondence in Hebrews 8 is between the old and new covenants and in Hebrews 9 between the temporary Levitical offerings and the once-for-all sacrifice of Christ. Both chapters continue to match the Levitical priesthood with Christ's Melchizedek-like high priesthood down to crucial details: just as earthly priests had something to offer, so must Jesus have an offering (see Heb. 8:3), and just as the carcasses of sacrificial animals whose blood was brought into the sanctuary were burned "outside the camp," so Jesus "suffered outside the . . . gate" (13:11-13).

3. A type (the primitive Old Testament reality) is always a shadow of the absolutely superior and more advanced New Testament reality—its climactic, end-time edition.

Consider, for example, the Captain of the Lord's host who visited with Joshua. It is all right to recognize the supernatural military leader as the preincarnate Jesus, but it is inappropriate to plug the flesh-and-blood Son of God into His place and force the passage to say things that God chose to reveal about Himself and His Son at a later date and further along the redemptive-revelatory road.

The Captain and the Saviour are one and the same, but the Saviour's task is on a more advanced level than that of the Captain. As Captain of the Lord's host, the preincarnate Christ came to assure Joshua of victory and success in the city-by-city campaign to win the Promised Land from its natural occupants. Joshua needed to know that he would not be alone at the head of his Hebrew army. As Saviour of the world, Christ comes to assure us of victory and success in our stronghold-by-stronghold campaign to win the entire planet from its evil supernatural occupants, because He stands at the head of God's army.

The type is the first edition of the final truth and is itself a prophecy of the antitype, its much greater, fulfilled final edition. Thus the types allowed the prophets to reach for the fulfilled, ultimate realities, while still living in the symbolical shadows themselves. Their writings upgraded the ancient hopes and challenged the community of faith to reassess its views of God and His Word in the light of recent redemptive developments. They did this by reapplying the Word from the past to their current situation so as to bring Israel's view of the past, present, and future of God's promises up-to-date with the progress of redemption.

VanGemeren says: "The Law of Moses forms the hub of the canon, to which the Prophets, the Writings, the Gospels, the Acts, the Epistles, and the Apocalypse were gradually added. Each book expanded the horizons of the godly and challenged the previous interpretation and understanding of God, humankind, salvation, the kingdom, and the world" *(Interpreting the Prophetic Word*, p. 83).

Typology operates on the solid connection rather than any impressive correspondence between the Old and New Testaments. The Old Testament prepares us for the New. Its promises are fulfilled in the New. Revelation and redemption both move progressively from primitive beginnings in the Old to a much higher plane in the New.

FIGURE 86

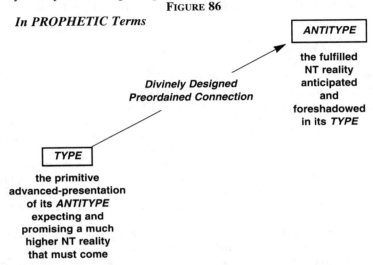

In PROPHETIC Terms

ANTITYPE

the fulfilled
NT reality
anticipated
and
foreshadowed
in its *TYPE*

Divinely Designed
Preordained Connection

TYPE

the primitive
advanced-presentation
of its *ANTITYPE*
expecting and
promising a much
higher NT reality
that must come

*In Terms of **Prophecy**—*In terms of prophecy, a type has certain distinguishing features:

1. A type is an advance presentation or preview of its actual corresponding New Testament reality or realities.

2. It is no coincidence that a type does this. God designed it that way. As the Lord of history He supervised people, events, and institutions so that they could actually present their corresponding New Testament realities in advance to teach Israel these last-day truths in an elementary way during the early stages of redemption without neutralizing human freedom or belittling their redemptive significance at the time.

3. More than any impressive correspondence, there is an inescapable connection between the type and its New Testament reality, which allows it to foreshadow, promise in advance, and look forward to something or someone greater to come. As the Holy Spirit opened the eyes of the New Testament writers, heavenly light illuminated the dimly understood truths of the sanctuary rituals, and the early Christians detected an amazing connection between God's Old Testament redemptive acts and the salvation that they witnessed in the person and work of Jesus Christ.

So LaRondelle rightly observes: "In other words, an Old Testament institution, event, or person only becomes a clear and understandable type in the light of Christ and His covenant people as the antitype. . . . It is the authority of the New Testament which establishes the divinely *pre-ordained* connection between a type and antitype and discloses the *predictive* nature of the type" *(The Israel of God in Prophecy*, p. 37).

For example, the sanctuary service, priesthood, and sacrifices gave themselves away as inadequate and temporary. These symbols actually revealed the need for the superior realities of Christ and His ministry, while at the same time they provided a shadowy presentation of them in advance. That is how the author of Hebrews argued from the Old Testament offerings to the necessity of Christ's sacrifice (Heb. 8:3, 4).

In fact, God arranged for the sacrificial law of the old covenant to function as "a shadow of good things to come" (Heb. 10:1). "The old covenant was *ordained by*

God (9:1), served its temporary function (9:10), but pointed forward as a shadow (10:1) to the realities of the New Covenant to be effected by Jesus" (Davidson, *Typology in Scripture*, p. 352).

The Progressive Fulfillment Model

The earliest Jewish Christians believed that Jesus was the promised Messiah and that they were His end-time people (see Acts 4:27; Rev. 12:17). They were equally convinced that Christ's resurrection and reign at God's right hand was the continuation of God's saving work for Israel in the past. But the types were neither instantly fulfilled at Christ's first advent nor postponed until His second coming. They were, instead, in the process of being fulfilled during the New Testament era, the climactic phase in the unfolding progress of God's redemptive work.

"Christ's first advent brought a basic fulfillment of the OT eschatological expectations of the New Age. The cross is the midpoint of salvation history. In Christ the powers of the Coming Age have irrupted into the Old Age. For the church living between the two advents of Christ, it is already true that upon them 'the end of the ages has come' (1 Cor. 10:11). They are living in the 'last days' (Heb. 1:2; Acts 2:16, 17). . . . The time between the two comings of Christ is thus a period with an overlapping of the two ages. The full consummation of the OT expectations is still future, to be experienced with the glorious, ultimate dawn of the Age to Come" (*ibid.*, p. 391).

FIGURE 87

OLD TESTAMENT	NEW TESTAMENT	
		Final Edition *ANTITYPE* Completely Fulfilled
	TYPE *ANTITYPE* Partially Fulfilled	
TYPE Shadowy First Edition *SYMBOL*		
PROPHET'S OWN DAY	FIRST ADVENT	SECOND ADVENT

God's people have always lived between the present and future realization of His promises: "During the present age the world is under God's judgment, but the children of God already receive their Father's goodness as tokens of the glory awaiting them. In the tension between creation and the new creation they live in faith, awaiting the fullness of salvation . . . the whole progress of redemption is *before the coming* [of Christ], that is, the era of climactic fulfillment at His second coming" (VanGemeren, pp. 90, 91).

God is "Israel's" King, but in the Old Testament He exercised only "a limited, patriarchal/nationalistic rule . . . incomplete and open-ended toward the future in its eschatological expectations. The coming of Christ fulfilled those Messianic/eschatological expectations" (Davidson, p. 391).

But Christ only inaugurated God's eschatological kingdom at His first coming. "This kingdom of grace [not glory], already experienced (proleptically) [that is, in advance] in OT times by the promise of God, was established in actuality by the death of Christ" *(ibid.)*.

While Christ continues to reign at God's right hand, He presently rules a kingdom of grace, not glory. His subjects are mystically connected to their ascended King through the Holy Spirit (see Eph. 3:16-19), but the ultimate, promised reality awaits consummation at His second coming. Meanwhile, just as "the Old Testament people of God lived . . . between the past acts of God and the promise of future acts of God" (VanGemeren, p. 91), the New Testament people of God live in the tension between what Christ has already inaugurated and what He has yet to consummate of God's promises.

"The kingdom of God still awaits the final consummation. At the consummation, the kingdom of grace will become the kingdom of glory; the powers of the present, evil age will be annihilated. God's tabernacle will be with men—the tension between the heavenly and earthly rule of Christ will be resolved by the transference of the very throne of God and of the Lamb to this earth. This kingdom of glory will therefore consist of a final, literal, universal reign, completely consummating the OT eschatological expectations" (Davidson, p. 392).

The Old Testament types focus on one or more of three time-related aspects of the postincarnation phase of God's gradually-being-fulfilled kingdom: (1) The *inaugurated* aspect is called *christological* because it focuses on Christ and His accomplishments during His earthly ministry at the First Advent; (2) the *appropriated* aspect is called *ecclesiological* because it focuses on the church (Greek—*ekklesia*) living by faith under Christ's heavenly ministry between His first and second advents; and (3) the *consummated* aspect is called *eschatological* because it focuses on the final (Greek—*eschatos*) and complete realization of God's promises before, during, and after the millennium.

The overall redemptive-historical picture looks like this:

FIGURE 88

SALVATION HISTORY			
OLD TESTAMENT	THE NEW TESTAMENT		
God actually rules in a limited way during the patriarchal national era	Preliminary fulfillment of the OT endtime hopes at Christ's first advent	Derived spiritual fulfillment by the church in the time of tension already/not yet	Utter fulfillment and complete ushering in of the age to come
THEOCENTRIC	CHRISTOLOGICAL	ECCLESIOLOGICAL	ESCHATOLOGICAL
EXPECTATIONS	PROGRESSIVE FULFILLMENT		
	INAUGURATION	APPROPRIATION	CONSUMMATION
TYPES	ANTITYPES		
SYMBOLS			

Because antitypes that occur during the New Testament era are not the final realities, they are also types—types of the ultimate realities/antitypes to come at the end of the age.

Inaugurated Typology

The *Christological* Interpretation of Scripture

The prophets expressed a hope rooted in the revelation to Israel through a progression of divine covenants. Reaching back to the promises made at Creation and to Abraham, Moses, and David, the prophets comforted God's people with a vision of the glorious future in which God would fulfill all His promises and covenants. They looked forward to the age to come, when God would be with His people and rule over them with His Messiah for eternity. The prophets recognized the unconditional nature of the promises God made to David, so they encouraged the people by tying their destiny to the house of David.

So Isaiah was authorized to promise the faithful in exile that God offered them "the sure mercies of David" (Isa. 55:3, KJV). In describing Israel's future after the exile to Babylon, Isaiah called what remained of the tree that was once Israel "the stump of Jesse" (11:1). The life of Israel was in the stump, and one day a leafy shoot would spring from it, with exclusive use of its roots. Since this descendant of David, Jesse's son, will develop into the righteous Branch of Israel (see Jer. 23:5), Jesus pictured Himself as God's chosen Vine with true believers as His branches (John 15:1).

The New Testament tells us that God is carrying out His original plan through Messiah Jesus (see Rom. 1:1-6; 2 Cor. 1:20). The promises fulfilled in and through Him go back to the days of Creation—before sin and redemption (see Gen. 1:28-30).

When Moses was facing the end of his role as leader of God's people, he assured them that "the Lord your God will raise up for you a prophet like me from your midst, from among you, from your countrymen. . . . Listen to Him" (Deut. 18:15, NASB). Those who heard these words would most certainly have been justified to expect that Moses' immediate successor—Joshua—was the fulfillment of this promise. And perhaps he was. But exactly what did it mean to be "like me"—like Moses? Being the same age? Having the same background? Having the same looks? Having the same personality? Doing the same job? At the end of the book of Deuteronomy and after Moses' death, someone added an interesting observation: "And there has not arisen a prophet since in Israel like Moses" (34:10, RSV).

Obviously the author of those words could hardly have been the deceased Moses. And why would Moses have apparently contradicted himself? The fact is that we do not know when these words were penned or by whom. Perhaps these words reflect a self-deprecating evaluation by Joshua himself who immediately succeeded Moses. Perhaps the words were added many years or centuries later—long after Joshua had passed from the scene.

As to the extent of likeness between Moses and his successor(s), Deuteronomy 34:10 explains what is meant by this lack of likeness: "whom the Lord knew face to face, none like him for all the signs and the wonders which the Lord sent him to do" (34:10, 11, RSV). Face-to-face communication with God and unprecedented supernatural power seem to be the points of dissimilarity that are being emphasized. So it is possible that Joshua may have been like Moses in some ways but not in these two particular aspects.

Whatever the case, it can be argued that because Joshua and his successors (the judges, for example) did not come close to equaling Moses in their relationship with God and their miraculous feats, Moses' promise remained open and basically unfulfilled until another amazing Person walked this earth—Jesus of Nazareth. Jesus had an unprecedented relationship to God and an unparalleled life accompanied by signs and wonders.

So it can be reasoned that God foresaw the need to redirect the course of wayward Israel in the last days and moved Moses to announce in Deuteronomy 18:15-18 Christ's first coming as the ultimate fulfillment of this promise (see Matt. 17:5; 23:37-39). Accordingly, Moses becomes a type of Christ.

So Jesus was not an outsider who offered the kingdom to Gentiles after the Jews had stubbornly rejected Him, but the prophet raised up from the stock of Israel to call His own people to repentance. John 5:46 seems to allude to Deuteronomy 18:15, 18, especially when compared with John 6:14.

When the nation rejected this final call to restore God's word and way (Dan. 9:24) so that she could resume her mission (Gen. 12:1-3) and go on to receive the kingdom, Israel was reduced to a single person, Messiah Jesus, who went on alone (cf. Isa. 11:1; 53:2). Jesus thus became the one announced in Genesis 3:15, where God promised that one of Eve's descendants would destroy the enemy, while sustaining personal injuries. The hope that this deliverer would eventually come continued through the line of election from Adam to Seth, to Noah, to Abraham, to Isaac, to Jacob, to Judah, to David, and to Jesus through Joseph (a descendant of Solomon) and Mary (a descendant of Nathan).

So when He turned to the Gentiles, Christ was not a spurned Saviour working an alternative plan but was Israel personified finally carrying out her original mission. All those who unite with Him by faith and bear fruit (that is, in character and by converts) are the branches attached to Jesus, God's true Vine.

Paul's explanation that the natural branches of Israel, the olive tree, had been broken off because of unbelief, leaving only a stump, was another way of saying that Israel had been reduced to a lonesome One—the Lord Jesus Christ, who singlehandedly stayed the course. Then as both the natural (unfaithful Israelites) and wild (enlightened Gentiles) branches exercised faith into Him (*pisteuontōn eis eme*, see Matt. 18:6) and were "grafted" into the stump to form a single Messianic Israel, all the families of the earth became blessed at last in Abraham (cf. Gen. 12:2; John 15:1-10; Romans 11).

And just as God told Abraham that He would bless those who blessed him, and curse those who cursed him, so God has promised to save those who respond positively to Christ's grace. He also refuses to save those who spurn it (see John 3:18, 36; cf. Heb. 10:29).

In addition, all the promises that God had made to His people throughout the unfolding of His everlasting covenant now belong to Christ. Thus Moses reported that the promises were made to Abraham and his "seed" (plural in Gen. 22:17, 18). But in the light from the cross, Paul informs us that God had Jesus uppermost in mind at the time, referring to a single "seed" rather than many (see Gal. 3:16, 19). The only way to be one of the "seed," in line to inherit the promises, is to belong to Christ. "Then you are Abraham's seed" (Gal. 3:29, NKJV).

No wonder VanGemeren wrote: "The focus of the hope in the fulfillment of God's promises is Jesus Christ, the midpoint of redemptive history" (p. 94). God has gathered everything together in one package in Him, to fulfill His original promises to all the families of the earth (Eph. 1:9-11). Typology recognizes that Jesus is the promised Messiah of Old Testament prophecy and that the New Testament is the continuation and completion of the Hebrew Scriptures. Whereas redemption progressed even before Christ's incarnation, "in Jesus the fulfillment of the prophetic hope is more real, as the nature of the hope gains greater clarity . . . correlative with the greater revelation of the Father in the Son, in Whom the fullness of the Godhead dwells incarnate (see Heb. 1:1, 2). In Jesus the eschaton (new age) is more present as evident in His miracles, the proclamation of the kingdom, and the Resurrection. The Resurrection is *the* sign of the new age (the eschaton). Another sign of the eschaton is the outpouring of the Holy Spirit. The Spirit indwells and ministers to believers in anticipation of the resurrection yet to come and the fullness of the eschatological age" (*ibid.*, p. 90).

Jesus radically altered the understanding of the Old Testament. The apostles re-examined it in the light of Christ and His ministry. While the prophets reached into the remote future for the promised heavenly realities, "the marvel is not that any prophet foretold. The marvel is that Jesus fulfills" (Gurdon C. Oxtoby, *Prediction and Fulfillment in the Bible*, p. 119).

When He spoke typologically of Himself, Jesus Himself introduced the idea that the age of antitypes had begun. He said that (a) His Messianic mission was greater than Jonah's prophetic one (Matt. 12:41), (b) His wisdom was greater than Solomon's (verse 42), (c) His kingship was greater than David's (see Mark 2:25-28), and (d) His once-for-all sacrifice was greater than the Temple with its centuries of of-ferings (Matt. 12:6). He even promised that greater works than He had performed would occur after His ascension (see John 14:12).

Jesus saw Himself as the ultimate reality to whom the entire Old Testament had pointed. The types had to be fulfilled for prophecy to go on to completion. So His mission to fulfill the Scriptures and Israel's historical types has both a redemptive and eschatological focus, because His typology, like Israel's prophecies, climaxes in the last days.

Typology is more than a matter of comparing related Old Testament and New Testament people, events, or institutions and recording points of similarity. "There is also messianic progress or intensification and eschatological completion beyond the similarity" (LaRondelle, p. 40).

For example, it can be argued that Jesus did not quote David's anguished cry "My God, my God, why hast thou forsaken me?" (Ps. 22:1, KJV) because He was merely going through a similar experience to that of David. It is possible to see a deeper dy-namic at work as the great Dutch scholar N. H. Ridderbos recognized: "Many of the statements of the psalm have become a deeper reality in the life of Christ" (Korte Verklarung, *De Psalmen*, Kampen: KOK, vol. 1, 1962; vol. 2, 1973). Jesus actually saw His own suffering on the cross as the extension and climax of the struggle be-ginning with David to establish God's anointed king over a hostile world.

Typology maintains that the New Testament realities are presently being fulfilled in Christ's redemptive work and will eventually be consummated when He asserts His kingship at the final judgment. Since every type began as a symbol rooted in his-tory and foreshadows some aspect of Christ's ministry, there is both a historical and theological correspondence between type and antitype.

Theologically, the Old Testament types are defined by their relation to YHWH, the God of Israel, whereas the New Testament antitypes are all qualified by their relation to Jesus Christ, God's Son. So the New Testament writers con-stantly reviewed Israel's history in the light of Messiah Jesus in order to determine the way that in Christ God has continued, is now performing, and will yet complete His Old Testament redemptive work.

FIGURE 89

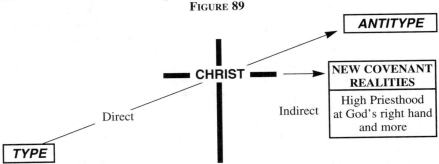

Christologically speaking . . .

(a) all the Old Testament types find their fulfillment in and through Jesus Christ.

(b) correspondence is either directly between an Old Testament reality and the person of Christ (Adam and Christ—Rom. 5; priesthood/sacrifices and High-Priest/sacrifice—Heb. 8, 9) or indirectly between an Old Testament reality and the various realities of the new covenant related to and brought about by Christ (ancient Israel, Noah and his family, and Christ's church individually, corporately, and sacramentally (see 1 Cor. 10; 1 Peter 3:18-22); earthly sanctuary and ritual of the old covenant and the heavenly sanctuary and Christ's high priesthood/once-for-all-sacrifice of the new—Heb. 8, 9).

(c) since the Old Testament types are redemptive realities that find their fulfillment either in Christ Himself or in His new covenant accomplishments, there is no salvation apart from Him. It is a matter of either responding to His grace and being saved or spurning it and going to destruction (see John 3:36).

(d) since Christ is the ultimate orientation point of the Old Testament types and their New Testament fulfillments, all correspondences are christocentrically determined. Old Testament types carry a plus or minus moral charge, depending on whether or not they are for or against Christ. So, for example, those who disobeyed God to their death in ancient Israel are negative types of those in the Christian church who disobey Christ (1 Cor. 10) and so deserve death all the more for it (Heb. 10:28, 29).

Appropriated Typology

The *Ecclesiological* Interpretation of Scripture

Since nothing enters the New Testament era without first passing through Christ's cross, everything imported into the New Testament has died a little and reemerged in a more advanced form. "The work of Christ is *continuous* with the work of God in the Old Testament but *discontinuous* with the religious structures of humankind. The coming of Christ marks the watershed in redemptive history. In Christ's coming the eschaton rushed in more evidently as the glorious Son of God became flesh. The distinction between Old and New may be explained by the difference in emphases: national and universal, material and spiritual, type and antitype, prefigurement and reality, promise and fulfillment. Yet as long as we await the universal, spiritual, and real fulfillment, we too live in hope of the promise that Jesus is the fulfiller of the promises of God" (VanGemeren, p. 95).

So the antitype is more than a simple repeat or a mere advanced form of the type.

It is actually a new, elevated, and unique work of God through Messiah Jesus. VanGemeren observes: "'The great lines of thought' of the Prophets come together in Christ 'in a wholly new combination, the spring of fresh forces and larger hopes for the world.'. . . But the advance in the progress of redemption only enhances the place of the Prophets as the 'old' becomes 'new'; that is, 'It is not fulfilled and exhausted, but fulfilled and illuminated'" (quoting A. F. Kirkpatrick, *The Doctrine of the Prophets*, pp. 528, 529, in VanGemeren, p. 96).

In some respects the antitype may actually oppose its type. National Israel, for instance, reduced to a single Israelite, Christ, passes through His cross and continues as Messianic Israel back on track with God and humanity (see Rom. 6:4). As VanGemeren says: "True discipleship demands that the disciples of Christ long for the consolation of Israel and for the restoration of all things" *(ibid.)*.

Stripped of all ethnic and geographic restrictions, Israel is no longer limited to natural descendants of Abraham or confined to the land of Palestine. Christ redefines the terms *Jew* (see Rom. 2:28, 29) and *Gentile* (see Acts 4:23-30). In the process of re-creation (Gal. 6:15, 16), Abraham's "seed" now includes all those who belong to Christ, regardless of their natural heritage and extends to the uttermost parts of the earth (see Gal. 3:29; Acts 1:8).

Christ broke down every barrier that Israel erected between itself and the rest of earth's families (see Eph. 2:12-22) so that Israel might complete its original mission. He unites converted Jews with those previously shut out to form a single, new people of God (see 1 Peter 2:9, 10).

So the gospel is the good news that the universal salvation originally promised through Abraham is now available and on its way to completion through Christ and His church (see Eph. 3:16-21). As the invitation goes out, souls from every tribe, tongue, people, and nation are grafted into the one tree/community of God's people (cf. Gen. 12:1-3 and Rom. 11:17 with Eph. 2:11-22 and Romans 6).

Israel may have failed as a nation naturally descended from Abraham, but supernaturally descended from Abraham through Christ, she will resume her mission and succeed in the last days as His church (see Matt. 28:19, 20).

This explains why the New Testament writers thought typologically as they applied the Old Testament to their own apostolic calling and gospel mission. Going far beyond the meaning of the original text as the human author intended it, the New Testament interprets Old Testament history by showing the way Christ continues and completes YHWH's work in and through His church.

LaRondelle sums it up this way: "The Church, as the eschatological Israel, with its new covenant in the blood of Christ, is the fulfillment of God's plan with ancient Israel" *(The Israel of God in Prophecy*, p. 40).

According to 1 Corinthians 10:6, Paul sees Israel's Exodus deliverance as a type that pointed forward to Christ's cross. The lambs offered in Egypt prefigured Christ, the actual Passover Lamb (see 1 Cor. 5:7), sacrificed in "the fullness of time" (Gal. 4:4).

All those who apply His shed blood to their hearts and lives are the Israel of the newer, grander Exodus (see Isa. 11:15, 16) on a pilgrimage through the wilderness of this world. They are bound for the ultimate rest, which will be the New Jerusalem (see Hebrews 4). Joined to their leader through the Holy Spirit, these citizens of the kingdom draw on the rich reserves of grace currently available through Christ.

Like Moses' leadership from the Red Sea onward, the rock in the wilderness, and the manna from heaven, Jesus' Lordship and death (through baptism), plus the Lord's

Supper sustain the faithful on their way and prepare them during this age of sanctification to enter the city's exclusive gates (Eph. 3:16-19; 2 Peter 1:2-11).

FITURE 90

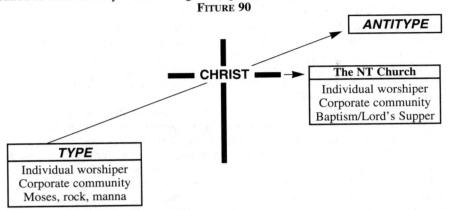

Ecclesiologically speaking . . .

(a) what the church lays claim to in the present depends on what Christ has already inaugurated and currently makes available through the Holy Spirit.

Messianic Israel is not merely the supernatural continuation of ancient Israel through Jesus Christ. "The working out of God's plan is progressive as the promises become more and more specific and as they are more fully enjoyed by the godly. This means that the benefits of God conferred on the post-exilic community were greater than those granted the pre-exilic people and also that the present benefits in Christ are greater than those of the post-exilic era of restoration" (VanGemeren, p. 94).

(b) in a sanctification setting appropriated typology has three aspects: (i) the individual worshiper (member), (ii) the corporate community (body), and (iii) the sacraments/ordinances (divine headship/strengthening presence).

For example, in 1 Corinthians 10 the experiences of ancient Israel in the wilderness happened typically as more than mere warnings or examples to Messianic Israel (see verses 6-11). So the experiences of the New Testament church are both the extension and climax of the pilgrimage to the heavenly city, which began with God's Old Testament people (see Heb. 11:39, 40).

There is also a striking connection between the ancient Israelite sacraments and the ordinances of Christian baptism and the Lord's Supper (see 1 Cor. 10:1-4). Paul can still appeal to them to call us to a personal decision whether to be faithful or disobedient (see verses 5-10).

In the book of Hebrews we find another example. Christianity is a pilgrimage through the wilderness. Its saints are separated from this world (see 11:16; 13:14) and on a way that is beset with hardship (see 3:12-18; 5:11-6:12; 10:23-26; 12:4), but they are journeying with a fixed purpose to the heavenly city of God (see 11:10, 16; 13:14).

The pilgrims are defiled by sin and need to deal with their sin problem now while en route. Christ's sacrifice perfects and purifies the conscience of individual worshipers (see 9:9, 14; 10:2, 14, 22), who are united by His accomplishments at the First Advent into an eschatological community (10:8-13; cf. 10:21; 12:22-24). Under the new covenant (Eze. 36:26-28) they are beneficiaries of His high priestly work in heaven and heirs to His exploits at the Second Coming (Heb. 7:25; 8:1; 9:14, 26-28).

Consummated Typology
The *Eschatological* Interpretation of Scripture

In his foreword to Geerhardus Vos's milestone work *The Pauline Eschatology*, theologian Richard B. Gaffin, Jr., says: "The title of this volume may be misleading. The reader who still understands 'eschatology' in its conventional, popular sense will expect a specialized study limited to those 'last things' associated with the second coming of Christ. The author, however, intends something more. His 'basic thesis is that to unfold Paul's eschatology is to set forth his theology as a whole, not just his teaching on Christ's return.'"

VanGemeren goes so far as to say: "In a sense the whole Bible is eschatological" (p. 88). That is because eschatology is more than a doctrine. "For in it the world-process is viewed as a unit. The end is placed in the light of the beginning, and all intermediate developments are construed with reference to the purpose . . . and the terminus" (Vos, p. 61).

Eschatology is the point of view that all history is moving toward a "definite final goal, beyond which a new order of affairs will be established, frequently with the further implication, that this new order of affairs will not be subject to any further change, but will partake of the static character of the eternal" *(ibid.*, p. 1). As such, eschatology detects the single thrust for everything that happens, unites past, present, and future, and "gives humans a perspective on their age and a framework for living in hope of a new age" (VanGemeren, p. 88).

As God gave them insight, the latter prophets abandoned reconstruction of the best of the past in favor of regeneration, and they began to see symbols in a progressive light, pointing simultaneously to wonderful things in the last days. Elevating them to the status of types, the prophets used the symbols to reach beyond their own shadowy times for the glorious future.

Reviewing the promise in this light, they "announce the *closure* of one era and the *opening* of a new era. The *new era in the progress of redemption* has elements of continuity with the past era as the new acts of grace flow out of the promises of God. Yet the new era has elements of discontinuity as God confirms an even grander fulfillment of the promises. The prophets also point beyond their time to an eternity of time when God will fulfill the promises and covenants. He will be with His people and rule over them with His Messiah from age to age" *(ibid.*, p. 89).

To which LaRondelle adds: "Among all the nations of the Oriental world, only Israel developed an eschatology, a hope in which God gradually unfolded His promise, corrected false, nationalistic hopes, and constantly transcended Israel's concepts of His kingdom by pointing to a future fulfillment that would exceed all Israel's earthly expectations" (p. 35).

So "the OT *tupoi* are eschatologically determined in that they find specific fulfillment [not just correspondence] in the community 'upon whom the end of the ages has come' [1 Cor. 10:11, RSV]" (Davidson, pp. 281, 282). In other words, New Testament hindsight helps clear up any misunderstanding of the way that the Old Testament type intensifies toward fulfillment and connects with its New Testament reality by providing it with a clear track to run on and a precise terminal to reach.

Consider, for example, the issue of the two ages: the world that is and the world that is to come. The Jews saw them as mutually exclusive and thus decisively consecutive, "the new being the outcome and termination of the forces of supernatural history propelling it towards the old. [But] This ancient point of view, while quite in accord with the Old Testament (and the Jewish) perspective to which the arrival of the Messiah still lay in the future, ceased to be in perfect harmony with a state of fact and belief looking back upon the arrival of the Messiah, and which in consequence had to recognize the eschatological process as in principle already begun" (Vos, p. 36).

The apostles recognized "that through the appearance and resurrection of Christ the eschatological process has been set in motion" (*ibid.*, p. 37) since His coming unfolds in two successive appearances and redemption progresses in stages of fulfillment between the two. So instead of a straight line

The age that is ⎯⎯⎯⎯▶ The age that is to come

the New Testament presents an overlapping, horizontal-vertical schematic.

FIGURE 91

The World to Come
Realized in Principle

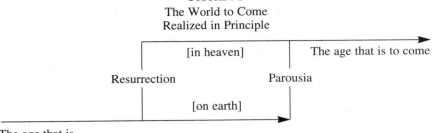

The age that is

Davidson suggests two eschatological models for the period of overlap through which Paul makes clear both the way and where the church is headed.

The first is an ascending time-line from Hebrews (*ibid.*, p. 348).

FIGURE 92

From YESTERDAY	Through TODAY	To the FUTURE
Christ's once-for-all act in the past	Christ reigns (1:3; 2:9) but victory is not complete (2:8; 10:13)	Future hope centered in the Second Coming (9:28; 10:25, 37) forever (13:8)

The second traces three stages of pilgrimage (p. 349).

FIGURE 93

THEN	[past]	separation	(baptism, persecution)
NOW	[present]	transition	(journey, participation in part and in advance)
NOT YET	[future]	incorporation	(reach the city and see God)

Here is how this eschatological perspective influences our understanding of biblical texts.

• Christ has inaugurated complete salvation with His once-for-all sacrifice and heavenly priesthood "at the end of the age" (Heb. 9:25, 26)—that is christological.

• His people cannot put off indefinitely dealing with the sin problem, because Christ will appear a second time "not to deal with sin, but to save those who are eagerly waiting for him" (Heb. 9:28)—that is eschatological.

• Therefore, they must appropriate the benefits of Christ's sacrifice during their journey, while Christ ministers above, before they arrive at their heavenly destination or else disqualify themselves from ever entering God's kingdom (cf. Matt. 5:20; Heb. 10:35-39)—that is ecclesiological.

The prophets spoke of an era called the "last days," during which God would re-instate His reputation through His renewed people (see Eze. 36:23). As early as Moses, they mentioned a time in the remote future when God's people would return to Him from their rebellious ways "with changed hearts" and "live in submission to God's revelation: 'The Lord your God will circumcise your hearts and the hearts of your descendants, so that you may love him with all your heart and with all your soul, and live' (Deut. 30:6, NIV; Rom. 3:30; Col. 2:11)" (VanGemeren, p. 357).

Because God had already announced His intention to replace "the heart of stone" with a "heart of flesh" (Eze. 36:26), Paul insisted that only those who have had the tough foreskin that resists God's attempts to get through and establish a love rela-tionship removed from over their hearts are true Jews (see Rom. 2:28, 29). Christ is the surgeon who circumcises "without hands" (Col. 2:11, RSV). He told His disci-ples, "It is to your advantage [cf. Eze. 36:27], that I go away; for if I do not go away, the Helper shall not come to you; but if I go, I will send Him to you. And He, when He comes, will convict the world concerning sin, and righteousness, and judgment" (John 16:7, 8, NASB).

In promising that the Spirit would convict (that is, get through to) the world, our eschatological High Priest (see Rev. 1:12, 13, 20) was also pledging to supply His church/candlestick/lampstand with the fuel/oil of the Holy Spirit, to be His light in the world and glorify (that is, reinstate the reputation of) His heavenly Father (see Matt. 5:14-16).

As VanGemeren observes: "The coming of the Holy Spirit at Pentecost . . . marked the coronation of our Lord Jesus Christ, at which time He shared gifts with His church through the Spirit . . . [who] applies the benefits of the new age by assur-ing the remnant of forgiveness, by drawing them closer to God, and by empowering them with the grace of the new age" *(ibid., p. 359)*.

Although Christ is physically absent from this world, the Spirit encourages a love relationship with the High Priest in heaven by making it possible for Him "to dwell in [y]our hearts by faith" (Eph. 3:16, 17). And "in this privileged relationship" true Jews "also know to do the will of God on earth. . . . By the Spirit they live in har-mony with God's will with enthusiasm and joy" *(ibid., pp. 359, 360)*.

This new situation in no way nullifies the law, since the promise to ancient Israel to deepen its bond to the law is fulfilled to Messianic Israel (cf. Jer. 31:33, 34; Heb. 10:16, 17). In fact, Paul insists that Christ's followers are bound to the law through Him (1 Cor. 9:21) and "under the law to Christ" (KJV; see Herman Ridderbos, pp. 284, 285 for a thorough discussion of the term *ennomos Christou]*. It is this closer re-lationship to the law through Christ that allows God to reach motives (see Matt. 5:21, 22), revise Israel's righteousness (verse 20), and carry out His original purpose for the law (verse 17).

Although the Spirit-powered witness of the renewed community will reveal that a supernatural work of God is already under way, "clearly the reality of this new and transformed relationship is still future. The fulfillment lies beyond this present age, but the tokens of the eschaton are [already] given to the children of God by the Spirit. He has begun a good work in us: transformation (renewal, regeneration), the fruit of the Spirit, the knowledge of God, and individual motivation . . . in the power of the Spirit our lights are bright as we enjoy victory upon victory and go from joy to joy (Rom. 8:26-39)" *(ibid.,* p. 360).

So sanctification is a process designed both to overturn the world's opinion of God and to prepare God's people for the age to come (cf. Phil. 2:12-16; Eph. 3:20, 21).

Besides confirming His covenant(s) and realizing His promises through internalization (that is, sanctification), the Spirit is also popularizing the covenant by using this witness to reverse the poor opinion that people outside the covenant community have of God and His true people (through conversion), and thus add souls to the church (cf. Acts 2:41). He holds "before us the vision of [His] empowering presence . . . in a greater number of people, permitting them to rise to new heights" *(ibid.),* thereby reinstating God's reputation among and through the greatest possible number of people.

The *Prophecy* Model
The *Threefold* Fulfillment of Old Testament Prophecy

When the prophets thought typologically to reach for the ultimate realities, they eschatologically projected the final fulfillment of their announcements into the remote future. So Old Testament prophecy essentially hangs on the same salvation/historical framework as typology.

FIGURE 94

OLD TESTAMENT PERIOD	NEW TESTAMENT PERIOD		
	1st Coming		2nd Coming
Typified	*Inaugurated*	*Appropriated*	*Consummated*
			Completely fulfilled
		"Already" "Not yet"	
Prophesied Initially fulfilled	Partially fulfilled		
LITERALLY/LOCALLY	SPIRITUALLY		LITERALLY/UNIVERSALLY
HISTORICAL	CHRISTOLOGICAL	ECCLESIOLOGICAL	ESCHATOLOGICAL

The Old Testament prophecies have a typological character. Just as the Old Testament types expect and promise infinitely advanced, absolutely superior final editions that must come, so the Old Testament prophecies also look forward to much greater fulfillments than initially imagined.

The New Testament teaches that Old Testament messianic prophecies and Israel's whole history of salvation are christologically fulfilled in progressive stages, distributed over two messianic appearances: provisionally at the First Advent and completely at the Second Advent.

FIGURE 95

OT PROPHECY	1st Coming	2nd Coming
Hosea 10:8	Luke 23:28-31	Revelation 6:16
Exodus 19:5, 6	1 Peter 2:9	Revelation 20:6
Jeremiah 51:63-64	Matthew 18:6	Revelation 18:21
Psalm 2:8	Matthew 28:18-20	Revelation 5:9
Genesis 3:15	Revelation 12:1f.	Revelation 12:17

The New Testament also presents the ecclesiological fulfillment of God's promises concerning the new covenant with Israel plus Israel's restoration or gathering (for instance Ex. 19:4-6 as applied in 1 Peter 2:9 and Rev. 5:10).

New Testament writers consistently remove all the geographic restrictions from Jerusalem and Mt. Zion and universalize Israel's territorial promises—even when they retain Middle East terminology and imagery (see Isa. 2:1-4 and Micah 4:1-4 as applied in Heb. 12:22-24 and 13:14).

So all Israel's apocalyptic visions and unfulfilled prophecies are realized in and/or through Christ on a cosmic rather than a local scale (Isa. 24:1-3, 21, 22 as applied in Rev. 20:1-3, 10-13).

The degree of their fulfillment depends on whether Christ is present spiritually (before) or physically (at and after the Second Coming).

LaRondelle points out that according to the New Testament the immediate and wider contexts of Revelation 20-22 (the millennium, New Jerusalem, the cosmic judgment, and even Satan's destruction) will find a literal, historical, and universal fulfillment. The events of Revelation 20 occur logically and chronologically after Christ's second coming:

First, in chapter 19—Christ returns at the head of heaven's armies (verses 11-18); the kings of the earth and their forces make war with Him (verse 19); and the beast and false prophet are captured and judged (verse 20).

Then, in chapter 20—Satan himself is captured and bound over for indictment before the saints of all ages during their 1,000-year session (verses 1-4); the saints are raised at the first resurrection (verses 4, 5); Satan is released at the end of the 1,000 years, and the wicked of all ages are raised at the second resurrection (verses 5, 7); and Satan deceives the wicked into attacking the holy city, is redefeated, recaptured, and destroyed along with the wicked (verses 8-15).

So Satan's personal capture and binding are determined by Christ's cosmic second coming rather than by His local first coming.

When Jeremiah announced Babylon's future destruction, his audience expected a literal, local fulfillment of the prophecy, but the outline series in the book of Daniel make it clear that God had a much greater overthrow in view of a more widespread and far more menacing "Babylon" than that ancient Near Eastern nation.

In revealing the sweep of future history, God deliberately chose a humanoid symbol to represent the kingdoms of the world to both Nebuchadnezzar and Daniel. Aside from their human origins and limitations, He wanted to disclose the close connection and relationship between them. So working from head to toe, Daniel 2 uses the continuous anatomy of the giant figure to project a nonstop history beginning with Babylon and ending with Rome, uninterrupted from Daniel's day to the end of time. Since the kingdoms are all part of the same body, they are successive stages of one continuous world empire, rather than a series of consecutive, unrelated world powers (verses 31-33).

Even though they arrived on the scene at different times and contended with one another for world supremacy, the four kingdoms were still united in their efforts to oppose God and oppress His loyal people. That is why they topple together at the close of earth's history—long after the heyday of literal Babylon, Medo-Persia, Greece, and Rome—when the "stone cut out, not by human hands" smashes the statue's feet and the empire falls (verses 34, 35). In fact, Daniel portrayed the entire sculpture as an image of Babylon right down to its toes by referring to Babylon as the head and to the rest of the kingdoms as its body (cf. verses 32, 33, 37-43). No wonder the apostle John called the end-time enemy "Babylon" (Rev. 14:8; 17, 18).

Daniel 7 parallels these truths but presents them in a more dynamic way. Instead of body parts from a lifeless icon, God used beasts that rose up from the sea of contentious humanity (verses 2, 3) to illustrate the kingdoms and their careers. One by one they ascended to world supremacy, then sank from sight, replaced but not removed by the next mighty monster from the deep (verses 4-7). God allowed the first three to live for a while after their fall (verse 12). What is the significance of their temporary survival?

Well, the fourth beast with iron teeth happens to have brass nails (see verse 19). Compare this with the sequence in chapter two, where the fourth kingdom of "iron" immediately followed, but did not eliminate the brass belly and thighs of kingdom number three. Apparently, then, the fourth beast swallowed up its immediate, predecessor predator, which continued to live as part of it. Actually, monster four assimilated, rather than annihilated, monster three, just as monster three dominated and absorbed monster two, and monster two overwhelmed and engulfed monster one. Eventually all three ended up in the fourth (see Rev. 13:1, 2), destined to perish together (see Dan. 2:34, 35), when the fourth was slain and its body burned with fire (Dan. 7:11).

FIGURE 96

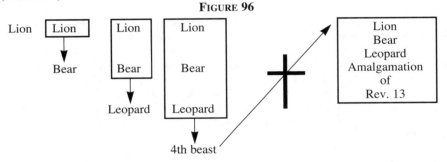

Can you see the typology? As the image fills out and the water show progresses, the presentation moves from the shadows into increasingly brighter light, with additional details appearing. We see that while the empire expands its territory and advances toward greater surface glory, each overthrown system brings both intrinsic and assimilated characteristics to its successor.

The decreasing value of the symbolic metals in Daniel 2, which decline from glittering gold to lackluster iron, illustrates the decaying character of the empire, whereas the increasing hardness of those same metals—from malleable gold to inflexible iron—vividly expresses its intensifying savagery as the empire steps up the use of force to impose its will on humanity.

So each kingdom is a type of its successor, which absorbs it and continues to display some of its characteristics. More than that, since they are part of the monster in Revelation 13, the original beasts are also types of the last-day edition of the enemy—even in its end-time phase.

But do not forget that each of these symbols is rooted in a specific, historical situation. Types are historical facts. So these are real kingdoms, and speaking literally, there was only one literal and physical Babylon, Medo-Persia, Greece, or Rome that rose and fell at a precise moment in history. The picture of a ram banging heads with a he-goat in Daniel 8 represents a historic milestone that can never be duplicated: the Greek transcendence over Medo-Persia. Remember also that each succeeding stage in the Danielic sequences represents an empire inferior to the one before it. Therefore, the symbol for a previous stage, only embracing the qualities of the ultimate reality already developed and accumulated to its own day, cannot be used to stand for a later edition of the empire without abusing its historical typological significance or distorting the facts.

Revelation 12 and 13 show us how the New Testament decides which symbols and in which way those symbols are imported from the Old Testament—through the cross.

1. It discloses enduring characteristics. Sometimes the New Testament repeats, thus renewing, an old symbol in a later time period of God's redemptive work in order to bring out the unchanging nature or repetitive activity of the thing or person represented. Such is the case with the archenemy of souls. The cross did not change him. Even in the last days, he is still the serpent of old, deceiving audiences and in rebellion against God. Time marches on, however. What began as hostility in the Garden (Gen. 3:15) blossomed as persecution (first of Christ, Rev 12:3-5; then of the church, verses 6-16; and finally escalated into all-out warfare against the woman's seed in an attempt to exterminate the last days' church from the face of the earth, Rev. 12:17).

2. It exposes greater detail than ever before. Sometimes the Bible presents progressively more advanced concepts by retelling an earlier version with fresh symbols so as to bring out something new in addition to what was previously known, as the ram and he-goat in Daniel 8 do for the bear and leopard of Daniel 7. But in the case of Daniel's struggle to describe the fourth beast, which he never does identify with any known creature, the New Testament has to blend several earlier symbols into a single, understandable later edition. So after reading Revelation 13:1, 2, we know why Daniel left us up in the air with the fourth beast—it is a nightmarish amalgamation of the earlier three.

3. It presents things at a future date and state. In Revelation 12:3 the beast with crowns on its heads is the empire at a time when Rome remained united under secular imperial rule. But in 13:1 the crowns have shifted from the seven heads to the 10 horns, because sometimes the New Testament has to update or upgrade an earlier symbol to present the same truth in a more advanced state, as Revelation 13 modernizes the beast from Revelation 12 to provide a glimpse of the empire after Rome divided into 10 smaller kingdoms, just prior to the rise and reign of Daniel 7's politico/religious emperor, the "little horn."

4. It sets the standard for their future use. Daniel already symbolized the first three kingdoms amalgamated under Roman rule as a single creature (Dan. 7). Since everything entering the New Testament must pass through Christ's cross, the New Testament imports (not the Old Testament exports) this 10-horned fourth beast from the Old Testament. The component creatures are the same, but their configuration is not. In this way the New Testament explains the end-time struggle with the enemy as an extension and climax of the conflict that began with and has continued ever since the days of ancient Babylon.

5. It renders parallel symbols obsolete. Have you noticed that the statue from Daniel 2 and the ram and he-goat from Daniel 8 do not reappear in the New Testament? That is because the New Testament screens out symbols that do not apply to later periods. For example, the combination of the first three beasts into a single sea monster recaptures, updates, and then surpasses the message of Daniel 2, so there is no need to revive its obsolete imagery. Neither is there any reason for the New Testament to reactivate the symbolism of Daniel 8, because Revelation 13 presents a much later edition of the empire—Rome after the cross—centuries after the Greek he-goat overwhelmed the clumsier but formerly invincible Medo-Persian ram. So it is unwise to uproot the Old Testament symbols for these one-time kingdoms, especially those that represent historical transactions between them, and replant them in the New Testament.

Here is an example of prophecy's typological character and interpretation:

FIGURE 97

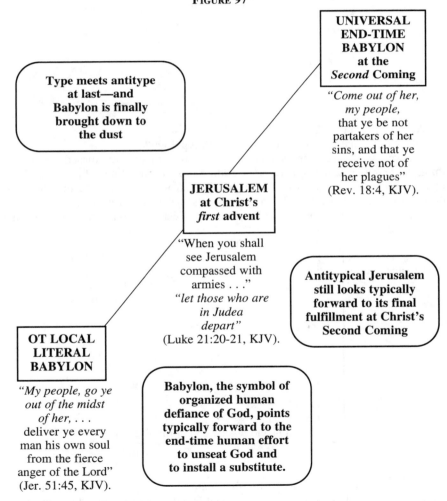

Stripped of geographic and ethnic limitations on this side of the cross, Babylon emerges as the worldwide, end-time enemy of God's universal Israel, the Christian

281

Church. This spiritualized or universalized Babylon will meet its literal end just as the Scriptures describe it. But before type meets apocalyptic antitype, Jesus surprises us by applying the doom prophecies for Babylon to the Jerusalem of His day. The fall of Jerusalem in A.D. 70 foreshadows the complete destruction of end-time Babylon, which has completely defected to the enemy.

Vertical Typology

The Closer Look at Typology's *Supernatural* Dimension

Question: What happens when two forces pull on an object in directions perpendicular to each other? Which way will the object move?

FIGURE 98

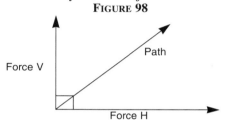

Answer: On a path between the two forces.

Question: What does this have to do with typology?

Answer: When we trace the path of development of symbols-turned-types, something very similar happens, because in addition to moving along a horizontal, historical time-sequence, typology also has "a strong vertical (earthly-heavenly) dimension" (Davidson, p. 352). In other words, types do not move exclusively on a straight historical, horizontal line from the Old Testament into the New Testament, because heaven exerts an upward influence on them like this:

FIGURE 99

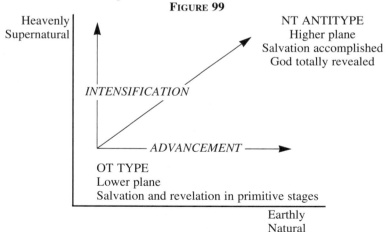

Types started out as symbols: familiar, natural, earthly people, events, and institutions, which God used in the early stages of Israel's supernatural education and salvation. Pointing ever forward to their specific supernatural realities, they are eventually fulfilled when God completes His saving work and totally reveals Himself to His people (cf. Isa. 12:6 and Rev. 22:3-5). Meanwhile, "in addition to a horizontal typology, the New Testament develops an explicitly vertical typology, in which Mount Zion, Jerusalem, Israel's tabernacle, and the Levitical priesthood serve as a shadow or reflection of *heavenly* originals (see Heb. 8:5; Acts 7:44 [cf. Ex. 25:40]; [Heb.] 12:22 [cf. Gal. 4:26])" (LaRondelle, p. 41).

According to Hebrews 8:1-10:18, Christ's present reign at God's right hand is the very way He always intended to fulfill the Old Testament types and shadows of ancient Israel. "Hebrews declares that Christ, by God's ordination, has begun to fulfill the Davidic covenant by ruling over the Church and all powers, authorities, and angels" *(ibid.*, p. 42).

The best that David and his descendants could ever have hoped to achieve from an earthly throne was a literal fulfillment of prophecy (cf. Gen. 15:18; 22:17; 1 Kings 4:20, 21). So David's throne, which was always the Lord's throne (1 Chron. 29:23), is transferred to heaven when Christ ascends it after His resurrection (Acts 2:34-36). As David's greatest "son," He will exceed Solomon's accomplishments (see Luke 11:31). He is the One through whom the prophets are fulfilled (see Matt. 5:17) and God's promises are distributed (see Isa. 55:3). His day (see Matt. 26:64) is our day (see Rom. 8:16-18). From heaven He rules at God's right hand, applying the benefits of His sacrifice as our great High Priest over God's house (cf. Gen. 14:18; Heb. 7:15-17; 10:21). He has also poured out the Holy Spirit (see Acts 2:33) to comfort and build up the church during the New Testament age (see Acts 9:31).

Eventually He will subdue all opposition to His throne, destroy death ("the last enemy"), and subject every element of creation to His Father's government (see 1 Cor. 15:24-28). Like the high priest who capped the typical Day of Atonement by reappearing from behind the veil with his redemptive work accomplished, so our High Priest will climax history by reappearing from heaven "the second time without sin unto salvation" (see Heb. 9:28; cf. Titus 2:13 and Rom. 8:16-19) at the conclusion of the antitypical Day of Atonement. First, the King of kings and Lord of lords will return to raise the faithful dead from their graves and to rescue the faithful living from the beast and the false prophet (see Rev. 19:11-21). Then He will destroy Satan, death, and the grave 1,000 years later in the lake of fire (see Rev. 20:7-15). Natural gives way to supernatural; type meets antitype.

This glorious presentation of Christ culminates a series of divine visits that began before and includes the Incarnation. Christ put in personal appearances among His people at strategic times in redemptive history (for example, the voice that called to Moses from the burning bush, the angel of the Lord who led the Exodus, the Captain of the Lord's Host who visited Joshua) to satisfy His own desire to be with them, to assure them of His love and care, and to reveal Himself progressively. Geerhardus Vos, in his book *Biblical Theology*, points out that the "angel of the Lord," spoke at times as though He were God (Gen. 22:11, 12), then at other times as though God were someone else (verses 15, 16). Only a member of the Trinity could do this without contradicting Himself—by alternately referring to Himself and to other persons in the Godhead. These references to other persons gave witnesses the correct impression that there was more to God than people could grasp from the angel alone—without prematurely disclosing the Trinity. A lesson this advanced might have proved a temptation to polytheism during the early stages of Israel's supernatural education (pp. 72-76).

On some occasions God's appearances took the form of judgments, during which the earth shook or some other phenomenon announced God's awesome presence.

Scholars call these visitations *theophanies* (from the Greek word *theo*, God and *phainein*, to appear). As VanGemeren says: "Each judgment confirms the sovereign rule of our God. He is Lord, and as King over creation, He rules by judgment. Each judgment must be interpreted as a theophany, and each theophany points to the final Day of the Lord. Then all opposition will cease, and the Lord will dwell among His loyal subjects!" *(ibid.,* p. 221).

John uses a series of progressive theophanies in the book of Revelation to feature the earth-heaven connection throughout the New Testament age:

FIGURE 100

voice like a trumpet (1:10)	lightnings, thunderings, and voices (4:5)	voices, thungerings, lightnings, an earthquake (8:5)	lightnings, voices, thunderings, earthquake, great hail (11:19)	voices, thunders lightnings, greatest earthquake, greatest hail (16:18-21)

7 Letters	**7 Seals**	**7 Trumpets**	**7 Crowns**	**7 Plagues**

|——————————— **Historical** ————————————▶|— **Eschatological** —|

Despite the fact that the first four sections cover the same time period, albeit from a different perspective, there is an escalation of phenomena as John proceeds toward the end of the book. That's because the historical section (Rev. 1-14) prepares the readers for and is climaxed by the eschatological (Rev. 15-22), which devotes itself exclusively to the end-time. Intensifying phenomena bring out the progression from the cross to the Second Coming as the world advances toward final judgment and the time arrives when God will completely disclose Himself. The closer to this judgment, the more violent the phenomena. Each theophany points forward to the next as the day of the Lord draws to a close and the King finally wraps things up, because the day is coming when God will actually dwell in the midst of His people and consummate the covenant (Lev. 26:11, 12; Rev. 21:3).

From an eschatological viewpoint, although the King works redemptively throughout the New Testament period, a day will come when He will judge the world, end this age, and His rule will be complete. Not that judgment is entirely reserved for the future. In his own day Peter said that "the time has come for judgment to begin at the house of God" (1 Peter 4:17). That is, all must decide whether to accept or reject Christ during the present age, before the door of probation closes and their fate is sealed forever (Rev. 22:10, 11). In a sense, God's people have been living during the day of the Lord since the Garden of Eden. But as the prophets called the people to repentance, they also spoke of promise and fulfillment, and the beleaguered saints began to look forward beyond their day to the triumph of God's righteousness, when God will destroy His enemies and reward the faithful (Isa. 11).

Although God's people saw fulfillment of prophecy in the fall of cities such as Nineveh, Samaria, and Babylon, things were "being fulfilled differently, and less gloriously than they had expected. . . . The dissonance created between the expectations raised by the prophets and the reality of their situation helped the godly live in the hope of an eschatological dimension of the Day of the Lord. God still had another day, or better other days, in which He holds His own people and the nations accountable for their acts. Thus, the Day of the Lord was a framework for interpreting

284

history, for understanding the present under divine control, and also for projecting a final day of reckoning (the eschatological Day of the Lord). They were given to understand that the Day of the Lord is past, present, and future. The copenetration of history and eschatology helped them live with an edge as they looked in faith to the Lord of creation and the King of the nations" (VanGemeren, p. 222).

FIGURE 101

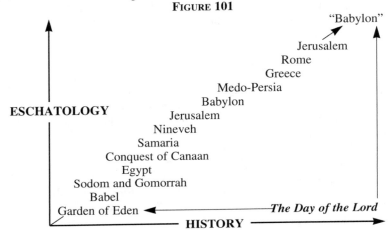

LaRondelle sums things up when he writes: "Christian typology—both in its horizontal and vertical aspects—is characterized by a present *fulfillment* of Old Testament types in Christ's redemptive work, and by hope for the future *consummation* of Christ's kingship in the last Judgment" (p. 44).

Some Specific Examples—Historically, the apostle Paul assumes that both the earthly and the heavenly sanctuaries are real, but there is no comparison. The heavenly "true" is infinitely advanced and absolutely superior to the earthly "copy and shadow" (Heb. 8:5, NIV). "Historical correspondences are interwoven with crucial complexes of earth-heaven correspondences" (Davidson, p. 353) in Hebrews 7-10.

Eschatologically, the "already-not yet" tension conditions Christ's heavenly ministry. He has already inaugurated His kingdom by sacrificing Himself "once for all" and by entering into His high priestly work (Heb. 9:24-26). Although He is currently out of sight, interceding on our behalf in the heavenly sanctuary, Christ will eventually consummate His dealings with sin and "appear a second time . . . to save those who are waiting for him" (verses 27, 28).

Christologically, when Rome crucified Christ, the cross served as the "brazen altar," and the earth as the "court" of the heavenly sanctuary (see Heb. 8:5). The significance of the Levitical priesthood with its ceremonial laws, animal sacrifices, and earthly Temple did not survive the cross. Only an eternal High Priest, who offers Himself instead of others, can qualify to minister in the heavenly courts. So Christ ascended to heaven and assumed His duties over the actual sanctuary/temple there, a priest forever after the order of Melchizedek (that is, both a high priest and a king according to Gen. 14:18). So the New Testament transferred David's throne from its earthly location in Jerusalem to heaven, where Christ ministers at God's right hand (Heb. 1:3, 13; 8:1; 10:12, 13; 12:1, 2; Acts 2:36) and blended redemption with kingship into a single hope. Everyone's salvation depends on Christ's ministry there (Heb. 7:25; 9:12-14, 24-26), from where He will return to finish His redemptive work (9:28) by consummating His kingship.

God challenged the first Adam and his bride to be fruitful and multiply, and to subdue the earth (Gen 1:28). Adam failed. But Christ, the second Adam, and His church will succeed. From His heavenly throne He will gradually bring the earth under His (that is, the Father's) government and ultimately resolve the tension between His heavenly and earthly reign by permanently installing the throne in the new earth (Rev. 22:3).

Ecclesiologically, those individual worshipers who have united under the new covenant to form an eschatological community on earth are the beneficiaries of Christ's heavenly mediation. Although Jesus is currently in heaven, physically separated from them, the Spirit unites the covenant people with Christ through a living connection so that they may receive the benefits of who Christ is and what He does while they remain on earth.

Prophetically, the book of Hebrews argues from the cleansing of the earthly sanctuary to the inescapable necessity of cleansing the heavenly one (9:23). "By *divine design*, the earthly sanctuary, modeled after the heavenly original, with all its cultic functions becomes a prefiguration or *advance-presentation* of the realities connected with Christ's ministry in the heavenly sanctuary (8:5)" *(ibid., pp. 354, 355)*.

Conclusion

God has always been able to communicate remote, supernatural truth through familiar, natural items, because the horizontal and vertical are the two harmonious dimensions of God's one saving work.

Horizontal correspondences provide "the linear dimension" of God's redemptive activity, "which reaches its basic eschatological fulfillment in the historical work of Christ, extends ecclesiologically as the Church appropriates Christ's work, and reaches its consummation at the Parousia [Second Coming]" *(ibid., p. 356)*.

Vertical correspondences provide "an understanding of the link between heaven and earth in the unfolding of God's plan of salvation" *(ibid., p. 357)*. Although the horizontal dimension dominates, it derives its meaning from the vertical: the church appropriates from heaven what Christ has already done in anticipation of what He will yet do, through a spiritual connection with their High Priest while they remain on earth.

So, for example, in the case of the scroll in Revelation 5, the last will and testament of Jesus Christ, which discloses both the heirs and their inheritance.

Horizontally speaking, the seven seals are the events in history through which the church must pass in order to arrive at the reading of the will. Vertically speaking, the seals are also the experiences that will prepare the saints for the inheritance of it.

The New Testament writers did not decide which Old Testament realities served as types. Instead of reading into the Old Testament what they wanted to believe, they recognized which ones continued to apply to the Messianic, end-time congregation— in the light of Jesus Christ. In other words, typology is prospective not retrospective. No wonder C. T. Fritsch says: "It is only in the light of the antitype then, that the full significance of the OT becomes clear. . . . It is the antitype which determines the identity of the OT type, . . . making clear the deeper, spiritual meaning" (C. T. Fritsch, "To 'antitypon,'" in *Studia Biblica et Semitica,* Fetschrift for Th. C. Vriezen; W. C.

van Unnik, ed. [Wageningen: H. Veenman, 1966], p. 101).

The key to understanding both the nature and identity of the type in the Old Testament is the New Testament interpretation of the Old. The discovery of a previously overlooked typological pattern should therefore base itself on sound New Testament authority. So here is a good rule of thumb: "God's saving acts in Israel's history must be applied by a New Testament writer to the future redemption of Christ's people by clear literary allusions to the Old Testament and a clear analogy of theological structure with God to Israel's salvation history" (LaRondelle, p. 48).

Here are some guidelines for interpreting types/prophecy.

---

1. Identify the symbol that you suspect is a type.
2. Apply the guidelines for interpreting symbols.
3. Strip away any ethnic and geographic boundaries.
4. Try to determine its typological significance. For example, Babylon symbolized organized human defiance of God, but it also typifies defiance to the nth degree (rebellion), which seeks to overthrow God and install another in His place.
5. Do not get bogged down comparing or investigating minor details. Focus on broad areas of resemblance, just as the New Testament writers did.
6. Note the points of correspondence and difference/contrast between the suspected type and its alleged antitype.
7. Study your findings in the light of their historical context.
8. Trace their path through Christ and the cross (christologically) to Messianic Israel (ecclesiologically) in its first to second coming context (eschatologically).
9. Consider both its horizontal and vertical dimensions.
10. Innate types (that is, those identified by inspired Bible writers) are the safest foundation for interpretation.
11. Inferred types (those discovered through research) are often less reliable.

How to Use the Typology Work Sheet

1. Follow the guidelines for interpreting symbols found in chapter 3 (pp. 26, 27) to identify the Old Testament symbol, and write down who or what the symbol is between the bold lines of the "Symbol" box in the lower left-hand corner of the page.

2. Follow the "Guidelines for Interpreting Types/Prophecy" on this page (a) to identify the type and write down who or what it is between the bold lines of the "Type" box, and (b) to determine whether you are working with a christological, ecclesiological, or eschatological structure, and mark the appropriate box at the bottom of the page.

3. If you have identified the structure as (a) christological, write the word "inaugurated," or (b) if ecclesiological, write the word "appropriated" along the arrow that points from the Cross to the New Covenant Reality box, or (c) if eschatological, write the word "consummated" along the arrow that points from the Cross to the Antitype box in the upper right-hand corner of the page.

4. Consult an exhaustive concordance and list any typical, corresponding new covenant reality and antitypical texts along with key terms or phrases in their respective boxes.

5. Transfer any observations or insights gained from this typological diagram to the "Analogy of Faith" work sheet.

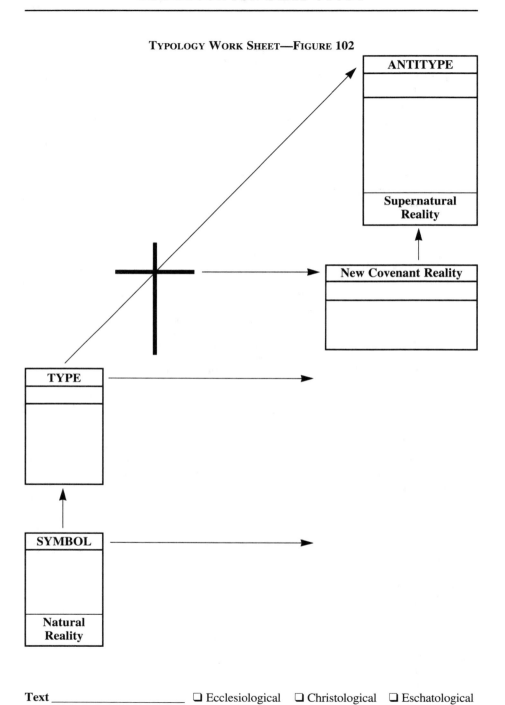

TYPOLOGY WORK SHEET—FIGURE 102

ANTITYPE

Supernatural Reality

New Covenant Reality

TYPE

SYMBOL

Natural Reality

Text _____ ❑ Ecclesiological   ❑ Christological   ❑ Eschatological

How to Use the Prophecy Work Sheet

1. Write your initial text just below the Related OT Prophecies box at the bottom left-hand corner of the page.

2. Refer to the guidelines for identifying and interpreting New Testament midrash in chapter 5 (p. 137) for a quick rundown of the various ways New Testament writers both understood and applied Old Testament texts in the light of Jesus Christ and "Some Guidelines for Interpreting Types/Prophecy" in this chapter (p. 287) to get a broad perspective of things.

3. Use an exhaustive concordance to flesh out all related Old Testament texts, noting their key terms and phrases, and all related New Testament texts that quote or allude to these or similar terms or phrases.

4. List texts from the Old Testament in the Related Old Testament Prophecies box as well as their key terms and phrases in the split box at the bottom right of the page along with any scriptural and/or secular notes concerning their literal fulfillment and any New Testament texts in the appropriate First or Second Advent boxes, referring to "The Prophecy Model" in this chapter and comparing the key terms and phrases that connect them with the original Old Testament text(s).

5. Analyze the structure and flow of thought from the Old Testament to the New. Transfer any observations or insights gained from this prophecy diagram to the "Analogy of Faith" work sheet.

PROPHECY WORK SHEET—FIGURE 103

Key Terms and Phrases

SECOND ADVENT

Application

Consummation

FIRST ADVENT

Application

Partial Fulfillment

Key Terms and Phrases

Related OT Prophecies

Literal Fulfillment   Key Terms and Phrases

CHAPTER 11

BE LOGICAL

A s we saw in chapter 6, sermons are basically extended arguments. Since this is the case, our sermons should reflect logical thinking on the part of the preacher and should also appeal to the congregation's faculties of reason. Sermons that utilize illogical reasoning lack power, and powerless sermons lack effectiveness. And ineffective sermons are a waste of everyone's time—the preacher's and the congregation's.

Introduction

An argument is a group of true or false statements consisting of premises that lead to a conclusion. The premises do not have to come at the beginning, and the conclusion does not necessarily have to come at the end. But an argument should be well constructed, easy to follow, and should appeal to reason rather than to emotion. (Do not infer that emotions have no place in the process of communication.)

The reasoning process that leads to *certainty* is called *deduction*. A deductive argument is valid or invalid depending on whether or not its premises necessarily lead to its conclusion. A deductive argument is *sound* when it is both true *and* valid, arguing *truthfully* as well as *necessarily* to its conclusion.

For instance, we may say:

> "All children are adults.
> All adults are human.
> Therefore, all children are human."

Although this argument is technically valid (that is, the conclusion *necessarily* follows its premises), it is unsound (that is, it will not hold up under all conditions), because one of its premises is untrue (namely, "All children are adults").

The reasoning process that leads to *probability* is called *induction*. An inductive argument may be unjustified even if its premises are true. But it is justified (that is, sound) when its premises are true *and also* lend a high degree of probability to its conclusion.

For example, the mockers in 2 Peter 3:4 doubted Christ's return, because "ever since the fathers fell asleep, all continues just as it was from the beginning of creation" (NASB). These skeptics reasoned that since the laws of nature were still in effect—apparently with undiminished force—there was little evidence to support the cataclysmic Second Coming, whether it would occur sooner or later.

But purely natural premises are not sufficient to argue to a supernatural conclusion, as Peter pointed out in the verses that follow. The God of the cataclysmic return was also the One holding the seemingly undisturbed creation together, delaying His return to give people like them time to repent and be spared.

Belief, Truth, and Justification

In order to argue, you have to know what you are arguing about. So any argument is a claim "to know something, premises, on the basis of which we claim to know something else, conclusions" (Vincent E. Barry, *Practical Logic*, 2nd ed., p. 80). When we claim to know something, "we are not just guessing, musing, or speculating," *(ibid.,* p. 81). We believe it (that is, we consider it to be true). Yet a true proposition accurately describes a state of affairs (an event, condition, or circumstance) regardless of what anyone thinks or believes about it. Truth is independent of our attitude toward it. "A true statement reports an actual state of affairs, whereas a belief statement reports what someone *thinks* is a state of affairs" *(ibid.,* p. 83).

Someone may say, "I think the New Testament writers exaggerated what happened at Calvary," but the cross is still a fact, regardless of what anyone thinks. People may try to argue their case from ignorance, claiming that if you cannot disprove their conclusion, that in itself proves they are correct. But this kind of reasoning is off base, because it shifts the burden of proof from their argument to you, the person hearing the argument. Just because an opponent cannot disprove a conclusion does not prove that the conclusion is true any more than unreasonable (that is, insufficient and inappropriate) evidence can. The only way to justify the claim that you know what you are talking about is to support your conclusions with enough of the right kind of evidence *(ibid.,* p. 86).

Evidence comes through interaction with people and things, and five factors influence whether or not it is enough and the right kind *(ibid.,* pp. 90-92):

1. Physical conditions—firsthand is generally more reliable than secondhand or thirdhand;

2. Sensory ability—some people have sharper senses than others or rely on the accuracy of scientific instruments to enhance those abilities;

3. Background knowledge—education and training are important qualifications and lend credibility to observations;

4. Objectivity—because we all operate on certain assumptions, emotions, and intentions that distort what we propose or evaluate, "the best we can do is to become aware of these biases and minimize their impact on our observations . . . [and] . . . the observations that make up other people's arguments" *(ibid.,* p. 91); and

5. Supporting testimony—corroborating evidence lends credibility to observations.

Fallacies

We also have to be sensible when we present our evidence; otherwise we may argue on the basis of unknowable facts, either in principle or in our particular case. This brings up the matter of fallacies. A *fallacy* is an argument that looks correct but is not.

People frequently serve up "facts" without supporting details. This is known as *the fallacy of unknown fact,* such as, "When I was in college, two out of three students smoked pot." Is the person to whom you present this "evidence" supposed to take this as fact? Maybe it was your impression that two thirds used marijuana, or even if it is true, should you build your argument on something as flimsy as this? It is true that the Holy Spirit can drive home what our senses can neither detect nor confirm for themselves, but should we expect Him to dignify as fact that which we casually pass off as such? Not any more than we may expect Him to bless arguments that view the whole exclusively in terms of group loyalty *(ibid.,* p. 94).

Christians come off as clannish when they size up people, organizations, etc., from limited or narrow points of view, which is *the fallacy of provincialism.* "He's not from our denomination, so I wouldn't trust anything that he says" might influence someone with the same group loyalties, but it is hardly the way to argue truth with someone outside your church. Incidentally, sermons, lessons, or devotionals built on provincial arguments do not fortify congregations to share what they believe with people of other denominations. Not only will they fail to persuade anyone, but also the lack of success may discourage them into doubting what they themselves believe.

Your arguments should be verifiable. Listeners should be able to check the truth or correctness of them for themselves by going to their source. For example, if you use the Bible to build an argument, the persons can examine specific verses in their context. True evidence will withstand public scrutiny or personal investigation. It does not depend on isolation from other points of view to persuade people of its truth. If people whom you attempt to persuade frequently change their minds once they are exposed to old influences, you may need to reexamine your arguments for these two fallacies.

Arguments should also appeal to the inner senses. Your congregation has the capacity to reason—to draw conclusions from the evidence *(ibid.,* p. 102). Reasoning inductively, they may arrive at general conclusions. Reasoning deductively from that general conclusion, they can arrive at particular conclusions. They can experiment with their conclusions and essentially verify or disprove your argument. You can help them in several ways with their "experiments."

You can appeal to authority—something or someone expert outside of yourself— as a secondary source of knowledge. But be careful. Make sure that your "authority" is a real expert. Check its claims against the opinions of other authorities. Experiment for yourself, and verify what the authorities say, if you can. If you are not careful, you may present an expert who really is not one, which is *the fallacy of false authority.*

If you quote an authority and then add, "We went to school together," or attempt to build your credibility by some other means of associating yourself with the authority figure, you will be guilty of *the fallacy of positioning.*

Sometimes the appeal to authority relies on the past to justify the argument in the present. When someone asks "Why?" and your answer goes something like, "That's the way it's always been," you will be guilty of *the fallacy of traditional wisdom.* To the unbelieving mind, the fact that something is a tradition is hardly an endorsement to continue it in the present. Beware of appeals of this kind when you hear phrases like "The pioneers . . . ," "The founding fathers . . . ," "From time immemorial . . . ," "Always . . . ," "For years and years . . . ," "As far back as I can remember . . . ," "When I was a kid, . . ." "We used to . . . ," "Tried and true . . . ," "It says so in . . . ," "Look at the record . . . ," "The lessons of history . . . ," "Used to be . . . ," "We never . . . ," etc. *(ibid.,* p. 110).

Another illegitimate appeal to authority is *the fallacy of popularity* (an argument that tries to justify something strictly because it is popular). For example, a salesperson tries to persuade you to buy something "because all your friends have," or you see a sign over a restaurant that says "Ten Million Sold."

Audiences are also capable of intuition—grasping things without having to reason or sense them, although it is best to subject intuited knowledge to reason and the senses. It must hold up under investigation. Otherwise, flashes of inspiration may turn out to be jumps to conclusions.

Appealing Logically

Your argument should be well-constructed, make sense, and appeal to reason rather than emotion. When we argue psychologically or emotionally rather than logically, we wind up with unsound arguments called "informal fallacies." Informal fallacies are "commonplace errors in reasoning that we fall into because of careless language usage [ambiguity] or inattention to subject matter [irrelevance]" *(ibid.,* p. 47).

Among the fallacies of ambiguity are:

(a) *the fallacy of equivocation*, which confuses the various meanings of a word or phrase. For example, Paul says: "I buffet my body and make it my slave" (1 Cor. 9:27, NASB). He also urges wives (who are the "body" in the marriage relationship) to "be subject to your own husbands" (Eph. 5:22, NASB). Therefore, husbands should beat their wives (that is, their "bodies") in order to keep them in subjection! The fallacy here, of course, derives from inappropriately transferring the meaning of "body" in 1 Corinthians 9:27 to Ephesians 5:22.

(b) *the fallacy of accent*, which depends on emphasis to justify the argument. For example, in reading Exodus 20:8-11 about not working on the Sabbath day the emphasis "Thou shalt *not* do any work" (KJV) emphasizes prohibition, whereas "Thou *shalt* not do any work" stresses God's intention. The point of the text is not that we are forbidden to work on the Sabbath, but that the Creator authorizes us to take the day off from the work that is wearing us out (see Gen. 3:19) in order to demonstrate His ability to rescue people from the killing power of sin (cf. "sanctify" in Eze. 20:12; cf. verses 19, 20).

(c) *the fallacy of composition*, which credits characteristics of the parts to a whole. It assumes that what pertains to the parts is true also of the whole. For example, Elijah mistakenly accused the entire nation of apostasy, when in fact God still had 7,000 other loyal subjects in addition to Elijah (1 Kings 19:14-18).

(d) *the fallacy of division*, which credits to the parts the characteristics of the whole. It assumes that what is true of the whole also pertains to the parts. That is like saying, "Our church is evangelistic. So every member is a soul-winner," when only a few selfless people carry on the work.

The fallacies of irrelevance include:

(a) *the fallacy of ad hominem*, which attacks the person rather than the argument. Instead of establishing the correctness or incorrectness of the argument, ad hominem may belittle a person's character: "He's divorced. I wouldn't trust him if I were you" discounts a person's circumstances: "Mary's not a doctor. What does she know about health?" or turn the argument back on the person: "You have no business telling me to avoid premarital sex. Mom was pregnant when she married you."

(b) *the fallacy of ridicule*, is a variation of ad hominem, which appeals to humor or abuse while attacking something. So instead of discussing the merits, it defuses an opposing view by making a joke that embarrasses opponents or belittles them in the eyes of others: "Smith says he wants to do a man's job? How can he, when he has long hair like a girl?"

(c) *the fallacy of mob appeal*, which arouses the deepest personal emotions to gain support for an argument. One deodorant company capitalized on the emerging feminist consciousness of the eighties to sell its product. It ran a series of successful TV commercials in which a woman refused to share her "strong enough for a man" deodorant with her husband, because it was "made for a woman."

(d) *the fallacy of pity*, which relies on sympathy and guilt to prove a point. So, for example, a youngster who murders his mom and dad might appeal to the jury for clemency on grounds that he is now an orphan (which puts them on a guilt trip) or that his parents drove him to desperation with physical and emotional cruelty (which looks for their sympathy).

(e) *the fallacy of fear*, which threatens harm in order to gain acceptance for its conclusion. The Sanhedrin used this tactic—first with words (Acts 4:15-22) and then with flogging (Acts 5:40)—in an attempt to check the spread of recognition for Jesus through the activities of Peter and John. The rabbi Gamaliel, the apostle Paul's original mentor, pointed out to his co-councilmen the fallacy of such methods (verses 38, 39).

(f) *the fallacy of two-wrongs-make-a-right*, which appeals to other instances of the same wrong in order to justify it. So a teenage boy says to his father, "I'm not the only one around here who does stuff behind your back. Sally makes long-distance calls when you're out of the house" or "Everybody else is doing it." In both cases, since others are also doing wrong—perhaps even the same thing—the teen proposes that his father let him off the hook.

(g) *the fallacy of the straw man*, which transforms the argument into a version that is easier to attack than the original. For example, a bigot claims that admitting people of another race to his club will weaken the membership's chances of gaining community support for its worthwhile projects. He cleverly disguises his racism as a concern for successful programs, because it is a lot easier to keep people of other races out of the club by gaining support for traditional programs than by gaining approval for racism.

(h) *the fallacy of invincible ignorance*, which insists that something is correct, even when there are facts to the contrary. Arguments that use this device to gain support for their conclusions frequently begin with the words, "I don't care what you say . . . ," "All *that* is well and good, but . . . ," "Be that as it may . . . ," "That may be true, but . . . ," etc. The person who uses invincible ignorance has his mind made up, and "doesn't want to be confused with the facts" *(ibid.*, p. 63).

(i) *the fallacy of begging the question*, which argues on the basis of what it sets out to prove. For example, someone insists: "God exists because it says so in the Bible, and the Bible is the inspired Word of God." The conclusion of this argument is that God exists. But the premise, "The Bible is the inspired Word of God" assumes the very thing that it must demonstrate, namely, that God exists. Hence the argument is guilty of "begging the question" *(ibid.*, pp. 63, 64).

(j) *the fallacy of a complex* (loaded, trick, or leading) *question*, which asks a question that assumes its own conclusion. For instance, a presumptuous parent might ask a teen, "Where did you go last night with the friends I told you to stay away from?" and

(k) *the fallacy of irrelevant reason*, which uses premises that have virtually nothing to do with the conclusion. For example, "A member of Congress rises to speak in favor of a particular national health insurance program Congress happens to be debating. The member points out how the people of the United States need sound medical care, how they are troubled by the fear of being unable to pay their medical bills, how they often go without medical treatment for want of money, and so on. While everything the member is saying may be true, it's nonetheless irrelevant to the issue at hand—the merits of *this particular* national health insurance program" *(ibid.*, p. 65).

Making Sense When You Preach

Both inductive and deductive reasoning will help you appeal to the reasoning powers of your congregation. Both have their place and can take varying forms.

Inductive Reasoning—Inductive reasoning includes:

(a) *generalization.* "A generalization is a statement that covers many specifics" *(ibid.,* p. 125). While the most fundamental type of inductive argument concludes with a generalization, it is frequently unjustified (unsound). We generalize when we observe a connection between two specific things and draw a general conclusion about the classes that these things represent (a class is a group of things that share similar properties).

A *universal* generalization claims that something is true for all, every, or any member of a class. For example, "All teens are disrespectful."

A *statistical* generalization alleges that something is true for a percentage of a class. For example, "Most girls nowadays are immoral."

Whether you make a universal or statistical generalization, it is important that you draw on enough specifics, because "inductive generalizations always go beyond their premises" *(ibid.,* p. 128). Based on what we have experienced or researched, we can speculate about the rest of the members of the class. But inductive arguments at best are probable and not certain.

If you want to make the most reliable generalization possible, then see to it that your specifics are *comprehensive* (a broad sampling of the whole); *numerous* (include as many subgroups as possible), and *diverse* (random enough that any member of the group has an equal chance of being sampled). Then allow some *margin for error* in your conclusion. Do not try to be too precise.

We tend to go overboard when we generalize. For example, suppose that you poll the members after a service to determine the local church's stand on an issue. Only half the membership attended, and the members polled are 3 to 1 in favor of the issue. When you include in the poll those who were not at this particular service, however, only 57 percent (instead of the original 75 percent) are in favor. So it would have been better in the first place to say that a *majority* of the membership is in favor of . . .

Four principal fallacies associated with generalization are

• *hasty conclusion* (drawing a conclusion based on insufficient evidence);

• *questionable classification* (classifying something or somebody on the basis of a single prominent feature (for instance, "women's libber");

• *accident* (applying a general rule to a particular case whose special circumstances disqualify the application)—a generalization is designed to apply to the individual cases that fall under it and not to all individual cases (leg raises may strengthen the leg muscles but not those of a paraplegic); and

• *guilt by association* (judging people by the company they keep or the places they hang out)—we assume that likes always attract, that appearances warrant conclusions, and that since something is sometimes the case, it is always the case (for instance, long hair always identifies a "hippie").

(b) *analogy.* An analogy is a special form of comparison that rests on one or more points of similarity. An inductive argument from analogy uses a known similarity between two things as evidence for concluding that the two things are similar in other respects.

"Sometimes we draw analogies in description to help create a picture in a reader's or listener's mind. . . . Other times analogies help in explanation by making the unfamiliar understandable by comparison with the familiar" *(ibid.,* p. 147).

An argument from analogy is really a form of inductive generalization, because it moves from the specific to the general. Jesus' parables are good examples of arguments from analogy.

If you want to strengthen the probability of your analogical arguments, then make sure that you are familiar with more than one of the objects you are using to make the analogy (make sure you have tested enough washes before you recommend a laundry detergent to someone else), that there is a sufficient number of relevant likenesses to warrant the conclusion (the greater the number of similarities, the more likely the conclusion), and that you take the number of differences into account.

Some differences strengthen an analogical argument (for instance, different people sampling the same laundry soap share the same opinion of it). Other differences, or disanalogies, weaken an analogical argument (for example, the laundry detergent you want to recommend has been dependable in warm water, but the party to whom you are recommending it may wash with cold water).

In dealing with analogies, allow a margin for error. (Don't make a parable walk on all fours; it is designed to teach one major spiritual truth, and to push the comparison to every point of likeness you can find is irresponsible exegesis.)

False analogy occurs when we overemphasize insignificant similarities that suit our purpose and ignore significant dissimilarities that do not. For example, you might compare a person who refuses to accept Christ with someone who, though desperate, is unable to see his or her own need, but not with a lunatic who is hurting himself or herself.

(c) *hypothesis.* A hypothesis is a "tentative conclusion that relates and explains a group of different items of information" *(ibid.,* p. 165).

In inductive generalizations or analogies we argue to a probable conclusion on the basis of similar specifics. We try to apply what we have observed to the remaining members of the class that we have not observed. But in the case of hypothetical arguments, we argue to a probable conclusion on the basis of dissimilar specifics in an effort to explain what we have experienced or researched. When detectives investigate a crime, they collect facts and then form a hypothesis to explain what they have observed.

But a hypothesis "shouldn't only account for the observed facts. It should also imply and then explain further facts" *(ibid.,* p. 169). Detectives now draw inferences from their hypothesis about the criminal (alibi, motive, weapon, etc.). If they can verify their inferences, "the hypothesis is supported. If the inferences are not verified, the hypothesis is weakened" *(ibid.,* pp. 169, 170).

A good hypothesis is *relevant* (that is, it explains the problem directly or in connection with other highly probable suppositions). A hypothesis may be relevant for a while, but if what you can deduce from it no longer explains the updated facts, it becomes irrelevant and in need of "reexamination and perhaps modification and amendment" *(ibid.,* p. 175).

The hypothesis should also be *compatible* (that is, it agrees with what is already accepted as true); so, for example, if you develop a hypothesis from a text to explain a problem for the congregation, it needs to agree with what the rest of Scripture has to say about the same problem.

A hypothesis should also be *testable* (that is, it allows for observations that either confirm or disprove it or its inferences). It should hold up under trial. For instance, the idea that the blood of sacrificial animals defiled the sanctuary is confirmed by such verses as Leviticus 16:16.

A hypothesis is *predictive*. A sound hypothesis provides the wherewithal for you to be able to deduce many testable facts from it. The stronger a hypothesis is, the more you will be able to calculate, speculate, and further hypothesize from it.

A hypothesis should be *simple* (that is, it should offer the least complicated explanation of the facts). "A significant factor in deciding in favor of the Copernican theory was that it offered fewer 'epicycles' in its explanation than did the Ptolemaic. Translated, this meant fewer complications. In effect then, Copernicus had done everything Ptolemy had done, but had done it more simply" *(ibid.,* p. 182).

(d) *cause and effect.* A causal statement insists that there is a connection between two things that allows one to have an effect on the other. "A causal argument is an attempt to support a causal statement" *(ibid.,* p. 192). In a causal sequence of more than two things, the last is the *cumulative effect* of all the preceding items; the one nearest to last is the *proximate cause,* and the rest are considered more and more remote.

Causal statements or arguments may rely on any of four different relationships between cause and effect:

• *necessity,* which is a condition that must be present if the effect is to occur. For instance, "The fear of the Lord is the beginning of wisdom" (Prov. 9:10). Here, then, fear of the Lord is a *necessary cause* for wisdom.

• *sufficiency,* which is any condition that, by itself, will bring about the effect, although it is unnecessary for the effect to occur. For example, "Good understanding produces favor" (Prov. 13:15, NASB), and so will mercy and truth (Prov. 3:4).

• *necessity and sufficiency,* which is any condition that must be present for the effect to occur and that will bring about the effect alone and of itself. For instance, "Without faith it is impossible to please him" (Heb. 11:6, KJV). Here faith is the necessary and sufficient cause for pleasing God.

• *contribution,* which is a factor that helps create the necessary or sufficient conditions for an effect. For instance, "You seek Me, not because you saw signs, but because you ate of the loaves, and were filled" (John 6:26, NASB). Miracles do not directly cause people to believe, but they can help create the conditions that promote faith.

There is always the possibility of discounting whatever disagrees with your conclusions or of focusing on one cause in particular when many contributory causes may be involved. Therefore, use a reliable method for establishing a cause-and-effect relationship in your arguments. Barry suggests three (pp. 198-203).

Agreement—If two or more instances of a phenomenon have only one circumstance in common, then that circumstance is probably the cause (or the effect) of the phenomenon. For example, why were so many males in Jerusalem during Passover, Pentecost, and Tabernacles? The Torah required Israelite males to attend these great festivals at Jerusalem (Deut. 16:16), and that could account for the large numbers of men in Jerusalem at those times.

Difference—If an instance where the phenomenon occurs and an instance where it does not have every circumstance in common except one, and if that circumstance occurs only in the former, then that circumstance is probably the cause (or the effect) of the phenomenon. For instance, Pentecost enjoyed the highest attendance in Jerusalem of the three annual festivals. The weather at that time of the year allowed the safest travel for pilgrims and probably accounted for the larger turnout.

Concomitant variation—Whenever a phenomenon repeatedly varies in a particular way while another phenomenon varies in a particular way, then a causal relationship probably exists between them. For example, the more staunchly you resist the devil, the more certainly he will flee from you (James 4:7) or (inversely) the more feeble your resistance, the less certain he will flee from you.

We frequently confuse a correlation with a causal relationship and so misuse the method of concomitant variation. Correlation exists when there is a relationship between *properties*, but cause and effect exists when there is a relationship between two *things*.

Correlations are also symmetrical. They work both ways: from A to B and from B to A. If B is positively correlated with A, then so is A with B. If B is negatively correlated with A, then so is A with B. But in causal relationships, while A may cause B, B may not necessarily cause A. For instance, on the one hand, relentless loyalty to Christ will cause the devil to flee from you, but the devil's fleeing from you may not necessarily cause you to resist him. On the other hand, a correlation exists between submission to God and resistance to the devil (James 4:7). People who submit to God do resist the devil, and people who resist the devil do submit to God.

There are several ways by which we may mistake something for a cause when it is not.

Questionable causation is when we insist that something causes a particular effect even though the evidence warrants no such conclusion. For instance, a South Seas tribe believed that body lice promoted good health, because only healthy tribal members had them. There was a real correlation between having lice and being healthy. However, the lice did not promote health but fed on it; thereby the parasites purposely avoided sickly members of the tribe (*ibid.*, p. 204).

Post hoc ("after this") is when we insist that one event generates another simply because it occurred earlier. For example, a truck driver sins and then loses his job. He thus infers from this that his sin brought on unemployment, as though God punished him for his sin by taking away his job.

Slippery slope is when we object "to a position on the erroneous belief that the position, if taken, will set off a chain of events that ultimately will lead to undesirable action" (*ibid.*, p. 205). For instance, if the church allows such and such, then this will happen, next that, and ultimately all the standards will fall. The fact is that "people who rely on slippery slope appeals do not understand what constitutes a cause" (*ibid.*, p. 205). Change may spell the end of a tradition, but it does not necessarily mean the church will lose its standards. To the contrary, an upgraded application of a divinely proclaimed norm in the present may be necessary for the church to grow, increase its effectiveness, or to overcome a problem.

(e) *statistics*. A statistic is an item of information expressed in numbers. "The President's popularity has dropped 55 percent in the past 10 months" or "Two out of 3 doctors recommend Bayer aspirin."

The government, the media, and a host of advertisers flash percentages, ratios, and odds in front of us every day. They know that people will draw conclusions from them, because "the language of statistics impresses us; it sounds authoritative. And the more precise the statistic, the more convincing. . . . Even the most absurd claims sound plausible when propped up with a statistic" (*ibid.*, p. 218).

What does this have to do with preparing or presenting a sermon, lesson, or devotional? Just this: "In one sense all inductive arguments rely on statistics, since they base their conclusions on a number of observed specifics" (*ibid.*). A number of speakers and teachers appeal to studies, polls, and surveys, which "supposedly use statistics in precise, scientific ways to generate inductive conclusions" *(ibid.)* when they speak or teach. Statistical arguments (arguments that use statistics to support their conclusions) can be misleading and manipulative. You owe it to your God, your audience, and yourself to investigate thoroughly the statistics in your messages before you actually use them.

Studies are the results of investigations into particular subjects that usually draw conclusions from the accumulated data. But before you accept their findings as fact, ask some questions such as these suggested by Barry for a medical study *(ibid.,* pp. 220, 221):

- Who were the subjects involved in the study?
- For how long was the research conducted?
- Who conducted the study—the company itself or some independent agency?
- Who participated in the study—physicians, medical centers, hospitals?
- To which stage of research does the claim refer?
- Test tube, animal, human? How was the study conducted? Were all the variables accounted for? What methods were used to establish causation between product usage and claimed results?
- How extensive was the testing?
- How many subjects were involved? What were their backgrounds? Were they always under control during testing? How were they selected?
- Were follow-up studies conducted? If so, for how long?
- Did the subjects report side effects? At what stages? Did they report cures or relief? How were their reactions different from those using conventional treatment or products?

Polls and surveys are general estimates of public opinion made by questioning a representative sample of people. Accuracy depends on (1) how representative of the group the sample is—not the size of the group or the number of people polled and (2) how close the sampling technique came to allowing each member of the group to have an equal chance of being sampled, not the area of the country or some other method of handpicking the people to question.

Some pollsters, especially in dealing with large groups, ensure randomness through the use of stratified samples, which divide the group into strata according to characteristics, geographical location, etc. and proceed to sample randomly each stratum in proportion to the number of members in each one as compared to the whole group *(ibid.,* p. 223).

Statistical arguments are weak and unreliable when (1) they reason on the basis of a biased sample (one that is not representative of the population under study), (2) the pollster may not be objective, (3) the method or procedure used may introduce bias into the sample, or (4) the people polled may say what they figure the pollster wants to hear, rather than what they actually think, prefer, or do *(ibid.,* pp. 224-227).

Also statistical presentations can be weak if they are based on equivocation (words or visual aids that can be taken in more ways than one). In *verbal equivocation,* the word "average" can be very misleading, since it can be the "mean" (that is, the sum of all the values on a list divided by the number of values listed), the "median" (that is, the value at the middle of the list), or the "mode" (that is, the value that occurs most frequently on the list). In *visual equivocation,* maps, graphs, charts, can be made to say what the presenter wants by changing their scale or distorting their proportions to dramatize or minimize certain features, just as dwelling on a topic or varying the tone or volume of voice emphasizes what a speaker wants to get across.

Statistical rationalization can also be weak because of *biased questions*, which are worded to get a desired response. For instance, "Wouldn't you like to spend your vacation in a beautiful European city this year instead of at home again?" The answer is obviously yes!

A *false dilemma* can also render a statistical report ineffective. A false dilemma deliberately reduces the options, thereby unnecessarily limiting the range of choices, in order to lead people to an inescapable conclusion. Not everything is black and white, this or that, one or the other. But arguments like these take away everything in the middle and leave only the extremes. For example, "Are you for or against increased federal spending?" "You're either with me or against me!" "Either decide tonight, or else face the consequences if Christ comes before tomorrow!"

Concealed evidence (that is, featuring only what favors, while censoring what contradicts the conclusion) can skew a study. Here are some nonstatistical examples. Some medicines tout their benefits while concealing their side effects. An evangelist might present what is easy for people to accept, but conceal doctrines that are not. Here are some statistical examples: Some companies appeal for rate increases by pouting over expenses, without revealing their profits, or by promising improved services with a price tag. Church leaders may paint a rosy picture at the end of the year by focusing on the number of baptisms, when in fact, the membership actually declined through factors such as transfers, apostasies, and apathy.

Deductive Reasoning—The difference between deductive and inductive reasoning is that the conclusion necessarily follows its premises deductively, but only with a high degree of probability inductively.

(a) *categorical propositions*. Inductive and deductive arguments are made up of true or false statements called propositions. Propositions associate groups of things called classes, which have properties or characteristics in common. A categorical proposition insists that one class is included in whole or in part within another. For example, "All mothers are females" alleges that the whole class of "mothers" is included in the class of "females." If we substitute the letter S for the first class, and the letter P for the second, we can restate the proposition, "All S is P." The word "all" quantifies, or makes clear, how many of S are included in P. In this case, every single S. When a proposition takes the form of "All S is P," the quantifier "all" identifies it as a universal statement.

The copulative verb "is" not only "couples" the classes S and P, but it also tells us the quality of the proposition, whether it is affirmative or negative. In this case, affirmative. And since the statement "All S is P" takes the form of a sentence (subject plus verb plus predicate), not only do S and P stand for the two classes involved, but the S also represents the subject, and P, the predicate.

Propositions in the form of "All S is P" are universal affirmatives. If we said, "No S is P," the word "no" is every bit as universal as the quantifier "all"—but in a negative sense. Instead of including every single S, "no" excludes every single S from the class P. So propositions in the form of "No S is P" are universal negatives.

The word "some" refers partially to S, as the words "all" and "no" do completely. So propositions in the form of "Some S is P" are more particular than the universal "All S is P" and so are called particular affirmatives, just as those in the form of "Some S is not P" are more specific than the universal "No S is P" and are particular negatives.

A universal affirmative speaks universally of S, and hence distributes (that is, refers to all the members of the class) S, which is its subject. If we refer back to our original proposition "All mothers are females," we can see that universal affirmatives do not distribute their predicates, P, because we cannot say, "All females are mothers," since not every woman has borne children.

In the universal negative "No girls under 10 are mothers," however, we know immediately that the subject is distributed from the universal quantifier "no." And since we can also say, "No mothers are girls under 10," it is obvious that universal negatives distribute *both* their subjects and predicates.

In the *particular affirmative* "Some men are executives," the quantifier "some" tells us that propositions in this form do not distribute their subjects. What about their predicates? Well, we cannot say, "All executives are men," because plenty of females are in corporate leadership. But we can claim, "Some executives are men." So particular affirmatives do not distribute their predicates either.

In the case of *particular negatives*, the quantifier "some" tells us right away that they do not distribute their subjects. But as the proposition "Some women are not mothers" reveals, we cannot come up with an equivalent to the original proposition by interchanging the subject and predicate ("Some mothers are not women"), because particular negatives do not speak equally of them (that is, they only distribute their predicates, not their subjects).

FIGURE 104

Proposition	Name	Quantity	Quality	Distribution
All S is P	A	universal	affirmative	subject only
No S is P	E	universal	negative	subject and predicate
Some S is P	I	particular	affirmative	neither subject nor predicate
Some S is not P	O	particular	negative	predicate only

(b) *syllogisms.* A syllogism is a deductive argument that contains two premises and one conclusion:

> All Christians are in Christ. (major premise)
> Some church members are Christians. (minor premise)
> Some church members are in Christ. (conclusion)

Categorical syllogisms are composed of three categorical propositions, which contain only *three* terms. In this case: "Christians," "in Christ," and "church members." Each of the terms appears in two of the three propositions. "In Christ," the predicate of the conclusion, is the major term. "Church members," the subject of the conclusion, is the minor term. The premise with the major term is called the major premise, the one with the minor term is the minor premise, and they always appear in the above order: major premise, minor premise, then conclusion.

The form a syllogism takes is determined by the order in which its propositions occur when it is in standard form (that is, its mood) and by the location of its middle term, which appears in the two premises but not in the conclusion (that is, its figure). There are only *four* possible configurations.

In Example 1 (on page 303) the middle term is the subject of the major premise and the predicate of the minor one:

Example 1	M	P	All Christians are in Christ.
	S	M	Some church members are Christians.
	S	P	Some church members are in Christ.

In Example 2 the middle term is the predicate of both the major and minor premises:

Example 2	P	M	All politicians are elected officials.
	S	M	Some church officers are not elected officials.
	S	P	Some church officers are not politicians.

In Example 3 the middle term is the subject of both the major and minor premises:

Example 3	M	P	All married couples are vow-takers .
	M	S	Some married couples are honeymoon veterans.
	S	P	Some honeymoon veterans are vow-takers.

In Example 4 the middle term is the predicate of the major premise and the subject of the minor premise:

Example 4	P	M	Some astronomers are physicists.
	M	S	All physicists are mathematicians.
	S	P	Some mathematicians are astronomers.

Valid syllogisms are a necessity in a logical presentation. According to Barry (pp. 291-299), valid deductive arguments in their standard form

• must contain *only three* class terms that cannot be taken more than one way. Otherwise, the fallacy of equivocation will create an obscure fourth term as in "Unlikely things happen all the time. But what happens all the time is likely. So, unlikely things are likely" *(ibid.,* p. 292). In the major premise "All the time" means "generally," whereas in the minor premise, it means "frequently." So the two phrases, though worded identically, are not equivalents.

• must distribute the middle term in at least one premise or else commit the fallacy of undistributed middle (that is, the middle term is not universalized). Take for example, the argument "All soldiers are killers. Some girls are killers. Some girls are soldiers." The minor premise includes some of the class "girls" within "some killers," because "Some S is P" propositions do not distribute either their subjects or predicates. The major premise, however, does not speak about every killer because "All S is P" propositions do not distribute their predicates. So we cannot tell whether the killers of the minor premise, which include "some girls," are the ones in the major premise. It is impossible then to conclude deductively that "Some girls are soldiers," because we do not know whether they are among the "killers" of the major premise, which include "all soldiers."

• may not distribute the major or minor terms in its conclusion if they are not distributed in their respective premises in order to avoid the fallacies of illicit major or minor terms (that is, referring to every member of a class in the conclusion, when the premises speak only particularly about "some" of them). Let us say that from the premises "All soldiers are killers" and "Some girls are soldiers," we conclude that "All girls are killers." The conclusion obviously overextends the argument, because it overstates the evidence in its premises. They never spoke about "all" girls, only "some."

• may not contain two negative premises in order to avoid the fallacy of exclusive premises. For example, "Some Christians are not spiritual. Some plumbers are not Christians. Some plumbers are not spiritual." Since the subject "plumbers" and the predicate "Christians" both exclude themselves from the middle term "spiritual," the argument fails to establish anything in common between them and cannot draw a conclusion relating one to the other.

• must have a negative conclusion if either of its premises are negative, or else commit the fallacy of drawing an affirmative conclusion from a negative premise. In the argument

> No Christians are pagans.
> Some pagans are former church members.
> Some former church members are not Christians.

the major premise excludes the entire class "Christians" from the whole class "pagans." The minor premise, however, includes part of the class "pagans" within some of the class "former church members." Since Christians and pagans have nothing to do with each other, and some former church members are some of the pagans spoken of in the major premise, then the only thing you can deduce about those former church members is that they have nothing to do with Christians either.

• may not have a particular conclusion, if both its premises are universal to avoid existential fallacy. For example, in

> All sinners are lawbreakers.
> All those who don't believe in Christ are sinners.
> Some of those who don't believe in Christ are lawbreakers.

the universal quantifiers "all" and "no" do not imply that the things they quantify actually exist, but the particular quantifier "some" does. So neither the major nor minor premises imply that sinners or those who don't believe in Christ actually exist. Since the word "some" implies the existence of at least one person who does not believe in Christ, the conclusion claims something beyond the scope of its premises.

Disjunctive syllogisms are another category worth considering. Statements such as

> Either the people are deaf or they refuse to listen.

actually contain two propositions: the people are deaf, and the people refuse to listen. This is a compound proposition, and when compound propositions appear in either-or form, they are called disjunctions. Each proposition is a disjunct, and at least one of them is true—possibly both. If a syllogism contains a disjunction, then we have a disjunctive syllogism.

In a valid disjunctive syllogism, "the categorical proposition denies one of the disjuncts and the conclusion affirms the other" (*ibid.*, p. 302). So, for example:

> Either some people are deaf, or they refuse to listen.
> Some people are not deaf.
> Therefore, some people refuse to listen.

Conditional or hypothetical syllogisms also demand attention. When a compound proposition sets up an if-then condition, it is a conditional or hypothetical proposition. When a syllogism contains a conditional proposition plus a categorical proposition, it is called a mixed-conditional or hypothetical syllogism. The "if" portion is called the *antecedent,* and the "then" portion is called the *consequent.* A syllogism of this type is valid when the categorical proposition affirms the antecedent and the conclusion affirms the consequent. If the categorical proposition affirms the consequent, it does not necessarily lead to the conclusion. For instance,

> If there is singing in the sanctuary, then the service is still going on.
> There is singing in the sanctuary.
> Therefore, the service is still going on.

Sometimes a syllogism has two conditional propositions for premises:

> If a1, then c1: If Jolynn is studying her Bible, then it is morning.
> If c1, then c2: If it is morning, she is spending time with the Lord.
> If a1, then c2: If Jolynn is studying her Bible, she is spending time
>   with the Lord.

(c) *the dilemma.* The dilemma combines conditional and disjunctive propositions into one form. It has a conditional and a disjunctive premise, with either a categorical or disjunctive proposition for a conclusion.

If the conclusion is categorical, it is a *simple dilemma.*

> If a1, then c1; if a2, then c1: If I pray, I'm relaxed; If I stay calm, I'm relaxed.
> Either a1 or a2: Either I pray or I stay calm.
> Therefore, c1: Therefore, I'm relaxed.

If its conclusion is disjunctive, then it is a *complex dilemma.*

> If a1, then c1; if a2, then c2: If I pray, I'm relaxed; If I don't pray,
>   I'm tense.
> Either a1 or a2: Either I pray or I don't pray.
> Therefore, c1 or c2: Therefore, I'm relaxed or I'm tense.

To determine whether a valid dilemma is also sound, you can either *take the dilemma by the horns* by attacking the truth of its conditional premise (perhaps showing that it is a questionable-cause fallacy or a hasty conclusion) or *escape between the horns* "by attacking the disjunction" (contending that it poses a false dilemma, an either-or situation where, in fact, none exists) *(ibid.,* p. 308).

In Conclusion

We believe that human beings were created in the image of their Creator, and this means they are endowed with the power to think as well as to do. Since the ability to think or reason is part of the divine image that appears within humanity, it is important—even imperative—that as preachers we do not denigrate our rational powers but rather appeal to them in our sermons, which are, of course, extended arguments.

CHAPTER 12

JEWISH INSTITUTIONS AND THE SPIRITUAL CONDITION OF ISRAEL IN THE TIME OF JESUS

Effective exegesis of the New Testament requires serious research into the amazing durability of both the Jewish nation and its distinctive way of life. Conservative scholarship credits this extraordinary endurance to the successful union of Israel's cultural and spiritual elements into a single code of life, which we now call Judaism. According to these scholars, the exceptional stability of "certain institutions and practices" that exerted a dynamic influence upon Jews both in Palestine and abroad helped the nation resist paganism and keep the old ways in use. (See Everett F. Harrison, *Introduction to the New Testament*, rev. ed., p. 18.)

The Temple

The Jerusalem Temple remained central to Israel's worship and vital to her existence, at least until A.D. 70 (see Donald E. Gowan, *Bridge Between the Testaments: A Reappraisal of Judaism From the Exile to the Birth of Christianity*, vol. 14, p. 249). Herod undertook its full renovation in 20 B.C.—500 years after the exiles returned from Babylon to restore Solomon's original structure. The reconstruction was completed in various stages during the next 84 years (cf. John 2:20).

Even the first generation of Christians in Palestine revered the impressive 15-story building (see Eric M. Meyers, "Early Judaism and Christianity in the Light of Archaeology," *Biblical Archaeologist*, June 1988, p. 69). As late as the second century of our present era, Jewish-Christian groups "insisted on the validity of the Torah and laws of ritual purity" and "looked forward to the restoration of the Temple" (*ibid.*, p. 73).

Just inside the massive outer walls eight gates allowed worshipers to pass under a ring of walkways supported by pillars. Then a series of courts determined how near specific groups of people could approach the divine presence in the Most Holy Place. Gentiles could penetrate the outermost court of the Gentiles; women, the court of the women; and ritually clean males, the ensuing court of Israel. Custom permitted those who could trace their heritage back to Aaron (cf. 1 Chron. 6:49-53)—more specifically to his sons Eleazar (through Zadok) and Ithamar (through Abiathar, cf. 1 Chron.

24:4-19)—to occupy the court of the priests. They ministered daily in the holy place. Only the high priest could enter the Most Holy Place, and then only once a year.

The post-exilic community anointed their high priests, a rite characteristic of kingship before the exile, but this custom seems to have died out by the Roman era (Gowan, p. 258). These religious leaders even wore the turban and breastplate formerly restricted to Israel's kings.[1]

The significance of the high priestly office did not escape the notice of occupying forces. The Seleucid king Antiochus Epiphanes began the practice of appointing and deposing high priests at will in order to neutralize their power and install men sympathetic to his hellenizing policies. Herod went so far as to eliminate all eligible males from the Hasmonean-Maccabean line. From his time to A.D. 37, procurators controlled the high priesthood by locking the turban and breastplate in the Fortress of Antonia and releasing them only on feast days (ibid.).

Israelites remained ferociously loyal to the Temple until the end. The renowned Jewish historian Josephus, himself a general during the war with Rome (c. A.D. 66-73), described its courageous defense against overwhelming enemy forces (Flavius Josephus, The Wars of the Jews, 5, 6). Only after the Romans set the Temple on fire did the defenders finally lose heart, and the city eventually fell (Harrison, p. 22).

The Synagogue

With their beloved Temple in ruins and its vital sacrifices suspended, the religious leaders regrouped to redefine true worship. The Sadducees, a priestly aristocracy that maintained all along that "the Temple cult was essential, and alone essential" (C.F.D. Moule, The Birth of the New Testament, 3rd ed., revised and rewritten, p. 21) faded from view after A.D. 70.

"The disappearance of the worldly-minded Sadducees, with their outworn sacrificial ritual at the temple, largely divorced from the true religious life of the people, was really on the whole to strengthen essential Judaism" (ibid., pp. 172, 173).

With the Sadducees out of the way, the stage was set for a smoother transition to a religion independent of sacrifice through Pharisaism—a Judaism of study and tradition rather than ritual (see Morton Smith, "The Dead Sea Sect in Relation to Judaism," New Testament Studies 7 [1960, 1961]: 355). The rabbis substituted obedience to the Torah for the old rites and offerings. They appealed to the central place that the law already occupied at the synagogue since the exile. "Surely the exiles had to devise some form of nonsacrificial worship during the years they lived outside of Palestine" (Gowan, p. 281).

Every community where 10 to 12 men gathered could have its own synagogue, a place for the faithful to offer prayers and to hear both the reading and the interpretation of Scripture (ibid., pp. 279, 280). Yet evidence of synagogues during Jesus' day is sparse. One scholar suggests that while the Temple remained standing "a synagogue could well have been nothing more than a large meeting room in a private house, or part of a larger structure set apart for worship. If this was the case, then the argument for house-churches at Capernaum and elsewhere becomes all the more compelling" (Eric M. Meyers and James F. Strange, Archaeology, the Rabbis, and Early Christianity, p. 141).

The proposed synagogue at Masada during the sicarii occupation was a small room with "tiered benches built in and around three sides of the room . . . and under its floor manuscripts were found hidden; later synagogues had a niche in the center of the wall faced by the congregation, which served as the Torah-shrine or *aron*" (Gowan, p. 283).

Generally, however, men sat on stone benches along the walls or on rugs in the center of the room. Some Palestinian synagogues separated the women and children along with the slaves from the rest of the men. Whoever stood up to read then sat down in a large stone chair (that is, "Moses' Seat"), facing the people and expounded on the passage.[2] A study hall for adults, with or without a schoolroom, usually stood off to one side along with a room for receiving visitors.

The ruins of later synagogues are near rivers, lakes, or seashore—probably for the convenience of water for purification rites (*ibid.*), and Acts 16:13 suggests that Paul expected to find one along the banks of the Gangites River at Philippi as early as A.D. 49. Furthermore, a synagogue site remained sacred even after it had been turned to ruins (Albert Rouet, *A Short Dictionary of the New Testament*, p. 101).

The main synagogue service occurred on Sabbath morning, although people could worship daily in the afternoon and attend special services on Monday and Thursday. In the absence of a priest, a layman could offer the blessing and conclude the service (Gowan, p. 287).

The Sanhedrin

Josephus describes the *synedrion* as a political court *(The Life of Flavius Josephus* 12), which apocryphal and New Testament sources describe under the leadership of the ranking high priest (Judith 4:8; Matt. 26:57-68). But rabbinic literature mentions only a council of scholars presided over by a *nasi* (president) and an *ab beth din* (father of the house of judgment)—both Pharisees (Gowan, p. 295; Moule, p. 155, footnote 2). Some scholars reconcile this difference by contrasting the Sanhedrin of priests and elders at Jerusalem with the exclusively rabbinic Sanhedrin after A.D. 70 at Jamnia (Moule, p. 246).

First Maccabees 12:6 refers to a *gerousia* (senate), which operated during the Seleucid decline under Pompey. Gabinius, the Roman administrator of the province of Syria, attempted to weaken Jerusalem's centrality and influence by dividing Judea into five parts, each with its own local council. Caesar reversed the policy, and even in the days of Herod, who dominated the Jewish state, Judea did have a supreme central body "to administer Jewish affairs without interference except in matters that would involve Roman policy or jurisdiction" (Harrison, p. 23).

For example, according to John 18:31, the Sanhedrin lacked authority for putting anyone to death. This observation is consistent with Rome's policy at the time, which withheld the death penalty from captive peoples, because they would certainly use it against those who cooperated with her (Gowan, p. 297). At any rate this essentially political body wielded enormous power. Originally dominated by Sadducees, it came under Pharisaic control after A.D. 70, when it became influenced by the social and religious trends of the period.

The Sects

The Israel of Jesus' day split along four main party lines or "sects," as Josephus called them: the Pharisees, the Sadducees, the Essenes, and the Zealots *(Wars,* 2. 7 1-4; *Antiquities of the Jews,* 13. 5. 9).

The Pharisees were "the driving force in rallying the nation around its religious heritage" (Harrison, p. 24). Essentially laypersons "who banded themselves into brotherhoods committed to the faithful observance of the Law and the traditions of the elders" *(ibid.),* this group evoked the broadest grass-roots appeal of any party in Judaism. Apparently they and the Sadducees came out of the Hasidim movement during the Maccabean revolt.[3]

When the sons of Mattathias had recovered Israel's religious liberty, they assumed both the political and religious leadership, establishing the Hasmonean line of high priests.[4] Naturally the Sadducees, a priestly aristocracy, rejected the Hasmonean takeover, but the Pharisees, "because of their high standards and reputation for faithfulness to the Law, developed naturally as a group providing guidance to a regime founded on the defense of the faith" (Gowan, p. 189).

This honeymoon with the royal family came to an abrupt end when one of them asked the king[5] to renounce the high priesthood and to keep only the kingship for himself *(ibid.).* Both Josephus and the Talmud connect this turn of events with the sudden appearance of the Sadducees and their brief fling with the family in power.

The Pharisees insisted that God gave Moses both an oral as well as a written law at Mount Sinai, despite an apparent contradiction with the inspired record[6] and that Moses handed it down both to Joshua and Israel's elders (see Aboth 1:1). Schools of rabbis and scribes endeavored to make the written law more practical for Israel by drafting rules, customs, and interpretations from the Ten Commandments, which they passed on by word of mouth. The rabbis kept the oral law separate by making it a crime to write it down.

This oral law enjoyed an equal place with the written, so that the whole glorious future prophesied for Israel depended on whether or not she obeyed both the written and the oral laws. When Jesus streamlined the law curriculum for Israel to the written law alone,[7] the Pharisees accused Him of tearing down the law that would bring in the future kingdom.

The gospel writers unanimously rejected this charge by showing that Christ had no intention of lowering Israel's high standards, but rather He wished to heighten them (Moule, pp. 94, 128; cf. Matt. 5:20). Jesus Himself said that He had come to carry the law and the prophecies to a successful conclusion from a different but higher standard than that espoused by the Pharisees (Matt. 5:17-20). Throughout His ministry, "the genuinely religious leaders of Judaism—those Pharisees, and especially those scribes and teachers with whom He came into conflict—did recognize the threat to their system presented by this revolutionary and subversive teacher" *(ibid.,* p. 55).

The rabbis claimed that the men of the Great Synagogue had ordered them to guard the written law by building "a fence [or hedge] around" it (Aboth 1:1). So the rabbis designed a security system that would allow them to catch hedgehoppers in the act—an external religion that focused on actions and behavior. People could prove themselves by *doing* what the system required, and the rabbis could easily get the goods on violators, such as the woman *caught in the act* of adultery (John 8:3, 4).

Jesus preferred to focus on the motives behind human behavior, so instead of resetting the clever traps left by former scholars, He went straight to the source of all law, God's penetrating Word (Heb. 4:12, 13). He simply bypassed the rabbinic traditions and returned to the pure Word of God, which preceded them (Matt. 5:21-48; cf. Matt. 19:8).

The people could tell the difference. According to Matthew, they "were astonished at the power behind His teaching. For his words had the ring of authority, quite unlike those of the scribes" (Matt. 7:28, 29, Phillips).

The Sadducees had their own *halakah,*[8] but unlike the Pharisees, they did not ascribe divine authority to it (Gowan, p. 182). Extremely conservative toward the Bible, these aristocrats accepted only the authority of the written word and preferred literal to figurative interpretation. They considered the Pharisaic interpretations and applications of Scripture unnecessary, because the Bible is self-explanatory and should be taken as is *(ibid.,* p. 181). This restricted canon led to differences with key Pharisaic doctrines, including the resurrection from the dead (see Josephus *Wars* 2. 8. 14; *Antiquities* 18. 1. 3; Mark 12:18; Acts 4:1, 2; 23:8), the existence of angels and spirits (Acts 23:8), and the belief that human affairs are the result of both God's sovereignty and human freedom (Josephus *Wars* 2. 8. 14; *Antiquities* 13. 1. 3).

Whereas the Pharisees relied on obedience and the Sadducees depended on collaboration, the Zealots preferred the use of force to bring in the kingdom. Historians trace these radicals back to Galilee, the seat of extremist insurrection throughout the Roman occupation. In 47-46 B.C., Herod waged a merciless war against outlaws in the Galilean hills, temporarily crushing active Hebrew defiance, but he failed to extinguish the fire of nationalism. Eventually Judas, the son of Ezekias, an outlaw chieftain, later executed, began to preach revolt against Rome in A.D. 6. Josephus blamed him and his teachings for all of Israel's troubles, including the destruction of Jerusalem's Temple in A. D. 70 (Gowan, p. 201).

According to Josephus, this subversive movement surfaced with the Sicarii, vicious dagger-wielding assassins of Romans and Jewish collaborators during the 50s and 60s B.C., and it peaked with the Zealots from A.D. 67-70. Despite a succession of strong personalities, often with unconsecrated motives, Josephus insisted that Judas sired all organized violent Palestinian resistance to occupation forces (Josephus *Wars* 2. 4. 12; *Antiquities* 14. 10. 5).

Zealot groups contended with each other as well as with Rome. Apparently demagogues could sway those loyal to them, even to further their own personal ambitions. For example, according to Josephus, Eleazar, the son of Ananias the high priest, touched off the fatal revolt of A.D. 66, by persuading the priests to stop the daily sacrifice on Caesar's behalf *(Wars* 2. 17. 2).

When Judas' son Menahem led a raid on Herod's storehouse at Masada, Eleazar's followers resisted his monarchial pretensions and killed him. This rivalry continued up to the day Romans invaded Jerusalem in A.D. 70 and found several groups battling each other for supremacy. John of Gischala occupied the upper city and Temple area, while Simon bar Giora controlled the lower city *(ibid.* 2. 19. 2).

The Essenes took a different tack altogether from their contemporaries. They separated themselves from mainstream Israel. Pliny the Elder located them along the shores of the Dead Sea, virtually disconnected from Jewish society *(Natural History* 5.17). Although Philo of Alexandria emphasized their holiness, communal living, and all-male population *(Quod omnis probus liber* 75-91; *Apologia pro Judaeis,* quoted in Eusebius, *Preparatorio Evangelica,* 8.11), Josephus says that some did practice marriage and adopted children *(Wars* 2. 8. 2; *Antiquities* 8. 5. 9). So the Essenes probably operated from several centers, with slightly different practices at each place.

Some scholars connect the people of the Dead Sea Scrolls[9] with the Essenes. If they are correct and if Qumran served as one of those centers, then the Essenes originated with the same Maccabean unrest as did the Pharisees and Sadducees. A cer-

tain "wicked priest," probably a Hasmonean who disregarded the Zadokite requirements for high priesthood, expelled their founder, the so-called "Teacher of
Righteousness," from Jerusalem. Most likely he went into exile at the ascent of the
first Hasmonean high priests Jonathan and Simon around 150-140 B. C. That is when
he apparently began a community in the wilderness for like-minded dissidents
(*Damascus Document* [also known as the *Zadokite Fragment*], 1.5-12).

The scrolls reveal a fervor for study and a catalogue of insights into this separate
society, which carried the Pharisaic passion for holiness to the limit but rejected the
Zealot approach of forcing their *halakah* on those who disagreed with them. Only a
community of parallel thinkers could have agreed to or kept such a strict *halakah*
(Gowan, p. 217), which forbade bowel movements on the Sabbath, cut daily rations
for laughing out of turn, or insisted on repeated baths for purification and acceptance.

Members joined voluntarily through stages of initiation and forfeited their personal belongings upon withdrawal or dismissal from the community. The Qumran
writings also betray a self-righteous conviction that the rest of Israel had forfeited any
hope of entering into the new covenant, because it relied on a corrupt Temple and
priesthood in Jerusalem. So God had called them out of the world and mainstream
Israel to cut the "new covenant" of the "last days" with them. Scroll after scroll interprets the Scriptures as though the Dead Sea people alone were the true remnant of
Israel. One in particular, the *War Scroll*,[10] even insinuates that the kingdom would
come through the combined effort of God *and* the community.

The Diaspora

Jerusalem served as the capital for Jews everywhere, not just for those who lived
in Palestine. Harrison says that Jerusalem was to the Jews what Rome was to the empire (p. 28). Ever since the days of captivity in Babylon, a substantial portion of
Jewish history occurred outside the homeland (Gowan, p. 151), but dispersed[11] Jews
never stopped yearning for Mt. Zion. Pilgrims swarmed the city during the great festivals, and many retired in its vicinity just to finish their lives in the Promised Land
and to be buried there (see John 7:8; Acts 2:5-11). Yet while Palestinian Judaism remained the norm, Diasporan influence continued to mount, especially after A. D. 70.

Many factors contributed to a scattered Israel. First and foremost, the vast majority of captives chose to remain in Babylon (see Ezra 1:3-5) rather than return to
Jerusalem with Zerubbabel. Then there was the large group of Jews that had fled earlier to Egypt with a reluctant Jeremiah, after one of them assassinated the Babylonian
governor, Gedaliah (Jer. 41:16-18). And an increasing number of Jews sought the
commercial opportunities outside of Palestine. "Heavy concentrations of Jews
formed in Alexandria in Egypt, in Cyrenaica, in the major cities of Asia Minor, and
at Rome. Greece and Macedonia had their share also" (Harrison, p. 28).

Eventually extra-Palestinian Jewry revolved around two great centers:
Alexandria and Babylon. Philo, a devout Alexandrian scholar and a contemporary of
Christ, did his best to reconcile the culture shock for Jews in a Greco-Roman world
by attempting to marry Greek philosophy to the Scriptures. He hoped to show that
the Greeks had looked into the same things as reported in the sacred writings, but that
without supernatural revelation, they had fallen short of its inspired insights.

As for Babylon, it gradually supplanted Alexandria as the intellectual and physical extra-Palestinian center for Diaspora Jews, and it emerged as the locus of vigor-
ous rabbinical activity after A. D. 70, which continued there for many centuries, even

until the Islamic invasion (Gowan, p. 153). Scholars there produced their own rendition of the Talmud, the "Babli," which subsequently overtook and finally eclipsed the "Yerushalmi," the much shorter Palestinian version (*ibid.*, p. 383).

[1] Consider Paul's remarks before the Sanhedrin (Acts 23:5).

[2] The procedure was followed at Jesus' hometown synagogue in Nazareth (Luke 4:16-21).

[3] The revolt was led by Mattathias, an aged priest, and his sons Judas, Jonathan, Simon, John, and Eleazar.

[4] Named for their grandfather Hasmoneus, the priest. In 152 B.C. Jonathan accepted the high priesthood as a gift from Alexander Balas, the Seleucid pretender to the throne. But when Israel secured its national independence in 142 B.C., a grateful nation decreed that Simon, who assumed leadership when the enemy captured and killed his brother Jonathan in 143, "should be their . . . high priest forever, until a trustworthy prophet should arise" (1 Maccabees 14:41).

[5] Either John Hyrcanus (134-104 B.C. according to Josephus [*Antiquities* 14. 10. 3]) or Alexander Jannaeus (103-76 B.C., according to Kiddushim 66a).

[6] See Deut. 5:22, where in reference to the Ten Commandments (verses 6-22) Moses said: "These words the Lord spoke unto all your assembly in the mount out of the midst of the fire, of the could, and of the thick darkness, with a great voice, *and he added no more.*"

[7] "The law will not lose a single dot or a comma" (Matt. 5:17, 18, Phillips).

[8] Rules of conduct concerning matters about which the Scriptures are not explicit.

[9] In 1947 the first scrolls were discovered in a cave along the shore of the Dead Sea by a shepherd boy.

[10] It is also known as *The War of the Sons of Light Against the Sons of Darkness.*

[11] "Diaspora" refers to Jews dispersed or scattered around the world.

CHAPTER 13

___

IS THE KING JAMES THE MOST ACCURATE VERSION OF THE NEW TESTAMENT?

Biblical exegesis is more than a careful procedure to lead the unabridged truth out of Scripture. It is also a process aimed at bringing the congregation to the goal intended for the sacred text. Since none of the original documents exist today and those that do exist differ from one another, complete exegesis demands verification of the text before attempts are made to interpret it.

Transmission of the New Testament Text

In the earliest days of the Christian church, apostles wrote letters to the various congregations in their care, sometimes with explicit instructions to share the counsel they had sent[1] "in order to extend its influence and to enable others to profit from it as well" (Bruce Metzger, *A Textual Commentary on the Greek New Testament*, corrected ed., p. xv). Obedient congregations accomplished this by circulating either the original letter or handwritten copies[2] to surrounding churches.

Inevitably "such handwritten copies would contain . . . differences in wording from the original" (Kurt Aland and Barbara Aland, trans. Erroll F. Rhodes, *The Text of the New Testament*, p. 70), most of which arose from accidental causes.[3] "It is certainly no secret that a scribe engaged in copying a manuscript is susceptible to fatigue, especially when copying continuous script. When word divisions are observed . . . the strain is somewhat relieved, but it cannot be entirely avoided" *(ibid.*, p. 280).

Evidence suggests that a tired scribe's eye tended to jump from one thing to another,[4] his mind occasionally wandered,[5] and at times he made errors in judgment,[6] especially with undivided texts or those using abbreviations (see Everett Harrison, *Introduction to the New Testament*, p. 84). Weary writers frequently mistook a letter or a word for another resembling it, omitted portions of the text,[7] or committed errors of repetition.[8] They even confused words or letters that sounded alike.[9]

On the other hand, some manuscripts reveal "deliberate attempts to smooth out grammatical or stylistic harshness, or to eliminate real or imagined obscurities of meaning in the text" (Metzger, p. xvi). Some scribes felt compelled to mend the syntax of documents by willfully altering or introducing words into the text. Aside from changes in spelling (see Harrison, p. 85) and in the form of words,[10] the most obvious type of intentional change is the explanatory supplement (Aland, p. 284), in which the scribe added what he considered to be a more appropriate word or words. In addition to the simple amplification or rounding off of phrases,[11] some copyists actually corrected historical and geographical "errors,"[12] harmonized even whole sections according to parallel passages,[13] and even rewrote inspired material according to their own theological points of view.[14] Others, to avoid omitting the genuine wording, preferred to combine rather than choose between two or more variant readings.[15]

With the tendency of accidental errors and intentional changes to expand and smooth over difficulties in the New Testament text, no wonder most critical exegetes prefer the shortest, most difficult reading that best explains the origin of the other(s) (see Harrison, p. 86; Metzger, Aland, and Greenlee) when they evaluate variants.

The Development of Text Types

As the early church expanded in and around the major metropolitan centers,[16] established congregations provided newer ones with a copy of the Scriptures in use in that territory. The churches prepared duplicates privately, rather than professionally, because *scriptoria*[17] did not appear before A.D. 200 (Aland, p. 55). Although this primitive procedure gradually produced a variety of small textual families[18] ("Mother Manuscripts and Their Children," *ibid.*) as close to the originals as their local standard of copying would allow,[19] actual text types did not begin to take shape until the second half of the third century.[20] That is when the church had the organizational structure, the settled canon of Scripture, and the peaceful setting needed to produce them.

Then came the holocaust initiated by Diocletian,[21] with its systematic destruction of churches and public burning of confiscated or surrendered sacred manuscripts. This created a shortage of texts, which was made critical by the evangelistic explosion during the age of Constantine. "For when Christianity could again engage freely in missionary activity there was a tremendous growth in both the size of existing churches and the number of new churches. There also followed a sudden demand for large numbers of New Testament manuscripts in all provinces of the empire. Privately made copies contributed significantly, but they were inadequate to satisfy the growing need, which could be met only by large copying houses" (Aland, p. 65).

Bishops now opened their own scriptoria to provide replacements for the lost manuscripts and to supply Scripture for the flood of new churches. They established influential manuscript production houses "in all the diocesan centers, or at least in all the provinces of the Church" *(ibid., p. 70)*, which circulated copies of a single or a particular group of manuscripts. These mass-produced copies of the "model texts" flooded and dominated the geographical areas in which their scriptoria circulated them, and eventually a standard, local text emerged.

"As additional copies were made, the number of special readings and renderings would be both conserved and to some extent, increased, so that eventually a type of text grew up which was more or less peculiar to that locality. Today it is possible to identify the type of text preserved in New Testament manuscripts by comparing their characteristic readings with the quotations of those passages in the writings of Church Fathers who lived in or near the chief ecclesiastical centers" (Metzger, p. xvii).

Throughout a period of time these local texts (see B. H. Streeter, *The Four Gospels: A Study of Origins*, pp. 35ff.) spawned stepchildren as they mixed with one another. Although particular church groups continued to preserve local traditions alongside the text promoted by a church center, "on the whole, however, during the earliest centuries the tendencies to develop and preserve a particular type of text prevailed over the tendencies leading to a mixture of texts" (Metzger, p. xvii).

Four main text types emerged from this process. Englishmen Brooke Foss Westcott (1825-1901) and Fenton John Anthony Hort (1828-1892), advancing on the earlier work of Karl Lachmann (1793-1851) and Constantin von Tischendorf (1815-1874), published a critical edition of the New Testament in 1881 that retraced its development from the original autographs as follows:

FIGURE 105
WESTCOTT-HORT MODEL

Original Autographs

ALEXANDRIAN	NEUTRAL	WESTERN
(C, L, 33, Sahidic, Boharic)	B, Aleph	D, Old Latin, Syriac C. (family Theta so far as known)

Syrian Revision (c. **A.D. 310**)

"Syrian" = **(Byzantine)** Text **(A)** E etc.

Textus Receptus

But, by 1924, B. H. Streeter identified Westcott and Hort's *neutral* text with the Alexandrian and rediagrammed its development like this:

FIGURE 106
B. H. STREETER MODEL

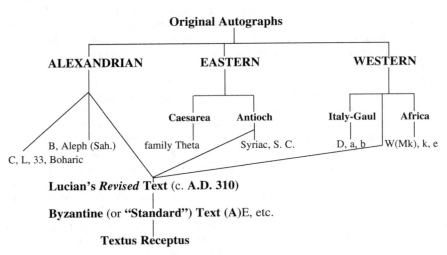

Original Autographs

ALEXANDRIAN	EASTERN	WESTERN
	Caesarea Antioch	Italy-Gaul Africa
B, Aleph (Sah.) C, L, 33, Boharic	family Theta Syriac, S. C.	D, a, b W(Mk), k, e

Lucian's *Revised* Text (c. **A.D. 310**)

Byzantine (or **"Standard"**) Text **(A)**E, etc.

Textus Receptus

The Alexandrian text[22] (Westcott and Hort's "Neutral" text), is generally considered closest to the original. "Until recently the two chief witnesses to the Alexandrian text were codex Vaticanus (B) and codex Sinaiticus (Aleph), parchment manuscripts dating from about the middle of the fourth century. With the acquisition, however, of the Bodmer Papyri, particularly p66 and p75, both copied about the end of the second or the beginning of the third century, evidence is now available that the Alexandrian type of text goes back to an archetype that must be dated early in the second century" (Metzger, pp. xvii, xviii).

The earlier Proto-Alexandrian form (for instance, p66 and p75) features short readings and limited polishing—even less than "the later form of the Alexandrian text itself" (Aland, p. 216).

Most scholars trace the Western text back to the second century, and that is precisely why a significant number question its identity as a text type. For example, Aland says: "In the early period there was no textual tradition in the West which was not shared with the East: there was only the Early text with its characteristics varying from manuscript to manuscript, for in the second century the New Testament text was not yet firmly established. As late as 150, when the first traces of Gospel quotations are found in the writings of Justin Martyr, the manner of quotation is quite free. Earlier examples are even more allusive or paraphrastic. It is not until 180 (in Irenaeus) that signs of an established text appear. While it is possible that this 'Early text' may have had certain characteristics in the West (as a local text), it is impossible to identify any occasion or person with its development in the way that B. F. Westcott and F.J.A. Hort and their modern followers suggest" (*ibid.*, pp. 54, 55).

Bruce Metzger offers a less radical evaluation of the same data. "Though some have held that the Western text was the deliberate creation of an individual or several individuals who revised an earlier text, most scholars do not find this type of text homogeneous enough to be called a textual recension; it is usually considered to be the result of an undisciplined and 'wild' growth of manuscript tradition and translational activity. The Western text can be traced back to a very early date, for it was used by Marcion (and probably Tatian), Irenaeus, Tertullian, and Cyprian. . . . So-called 'Western' texts of the Gospels, Acts, and Pauline epistles circulated widely, not only in North Africa, Italy, and Gaul (which are geographically 'Western'), but also in Egypt and (in somewhat different text forms) in the East" (*ibid.*, pp. 213, 214).

Witnesses to this type of text show up in late third and early fourth century papyri from Egypt (for example, p38, p48), codices from the late fourth to sixth centuries (Codex Bezae, Gospels and Acts [D], codex Claremontanus Pauline Epistles [D], codex Washingtonianus [W]), the Old Latin Fathers (African, Italian, and Hispanic forms), and Syrian Fathers to the middle fifth century (the Sinaitic and Curetonian manuscripts of the Old Syriac, many marginal notes in the Harclean Syriac, and perhaps by the Palestinian Syriac) (see Metzger, p. 214).

"The chief characteristic of Western readings is fondness for paraphrase. Words, clauses, and even whole sentences are freely changed, omitted, or inserted. Sometimes the motive appears to have been harmonization, while at other times it was the enrichment of the narrative by the inclusion of traditional or apocryphal material. Some readings involve quite trivial alterations for which no special reason can be assigned. One of the puzzling features . . . is that at the end of Luke and in a few other places in the New Testament, certain Western witnesses omit words and passages that are present in other forms of text, including the Alexandrian. Although at the close of the last century certain scholars were disposed to regard these shorter readings as original . . . since the acquisition of the Bodmer Papyri many scholars today are inclined to regard them as aberrant readings" (Metzger, pp. xviii, xix).

Although B. H. Streeter identified the Caesarean text from the form of text Origen used at Caesarea, it apparently originated in Egypt.[23] Origen brought the text to Caesarea,[24] where Eusebius and others made use of it (Metzger, p. xix). From there it went to Jerusalem, where Cyril and an Armenian colony located there picked it up. Then Armenian missionaries carried it to Georgia, "where it influenced the Georgian version as well as an uncial Greek manuscript of about the ninth century (Theta, codex Koridethi)" (Metzger, p. xix).

Modern scholars call the Egyptian text that Origen carried to Caesarea the pre-Caesarean text[25] and refer to the text that began to develop there as the Caesarean text proper.[26] This text type is characterized by "its distinctive mixture of Western . . . and Alexandrian readings . . . Evidently its maker . . . in substance . . . followed the Alexandrian text while retaining any Western readings which did not seem too improbable, for the latter was widely current, although the former was the better. One may also observe a certain striving after elegance" *(ibid.)*.

The Byzantine text is the latest of the main New Testament text types. Scholars trace it to Antioch during the peaceful decades preceding the fourth-century persecution initiated by Diocletian. Near the close of this period Lucian of Antioch or some of his associates prepared a recension that deliberately combined elements from earlier types of text.

Metzger summarizes the development of the text throughout this period: "The framers of this text sought to smooth away any harshness of language, to combine two or more divergent readings into one expanded reading (called conflation), and to harmonize divergent parallel passages . . . produced perhaps at Antioch in Syria" (p. xx).

Aland is somewhat more certain: "In Antioch the early form was polished stylistically, edited ecclesiastically, and expanded devotionally. This was the origin of what is called the Koine text, later to become the Byzantine Imperial text. Fourth century tradition called it the text of Lucian" (p. 64).

It just so happened that Antioch enjoyed a prominent school of exegesis stocked with students of Origen's theology and also Arians. During the era of missionary activity ushered in with Constantine, this school supplied the expanding church with a prolific scriptorium and bishops for many dioceses throughout the East. Furthermore, "each of these bishops took with him to his diocese the text of Lucian (i.e., the Koine text), and in this way it rapidly became very widely disseminated even in the fourth century" *(ibid.,* p. 65).

The effort to install Lucian as the primary text among the churches met with such success that Jerome, the late fourth-century father, wrote in the preface to Chronicles in the Roman edition of his Vulgate translation that "in Constantinople and as far as Antioch copies made by the martyr Lucian are regarded as authoritative" *(ibid.,* p. 66).

This text was adopted with some modifications as the received text of the Greek Orthodox Church, witnessed by the fifth century codex Alexandrinus (in the Gospels), the later uncial manuscripts, and the vast majority of minuscule documents (Aland, p. 212; Metzger, p. xx). The Byzantine text, in the especially corrupted Lucian (Koine) form, dominated its rival text types so completely that "except for an occasional manuscript that happened to preserve an earlier form of text, during the period from about the sixth or seventh century down to the invention of printing with movable type (A.D. 1450-1456), the Byzantine form of text was generally regarded as *the* authoritative form of text and was the most widely circulated and accepted" (Metzger, p. xx).

Thus Erasmus and others published a succession of Greek New Testaments—all based on the same text type preserved in the later Byzantine manuscripts.

"Even when it happened that an editor had access to older manuscripts—as when Theodore Beza . . . acquired the fifth or sixth century manuscript that goes under his name today as well as the sixth century codex Claromontanus—he made relatively little use of them, for they deviated too far from the form of text that had become standard in the later copies" *(ibid.*, p. xxii).

Beza published nine editions of the Greek New Testament from 1565-1604, and the King James translators leaned heavily on those from 1588, 1589, and 1598. He popularized and stereotyped the Byzantine form of text, which later came to be known as the Textus Receptus. Bonaventura and Abraham Elzevir, two printers in Leiden, prefaced their Byzantine, second edition of the Greek New Testament (1633): "Therefore you [dear reader] now have the text received [hence, *Textus Receptus]* by all, in which we give nothing changed or corrupted" *(ibid.*, p. xxiii). To do so, they virtually ignored Codex Alexandrinus, the early fifth century manuscript of the *entire* New Testament that *differed dramatically* from the Textus Receptus. Fortunately, this indifference toward anti-Byzantine witnesses did not last.

Later editions did continue to neglect the evidence for a while and perpetuate this injustice to God's Word. As the documents dating closer to the originals surfaced, however, it became evident that the Textus Receptus had deviated from—rather than preserved—the autographs, and attitudes changed: "At first, scholars appended variant readings to the Textus Receptus; then they began to abandon" it (Phillip Wesley Comfort, *The Quest for the Original Text of the New Testament*, p. 26). As early as 1707, for instance, Oxford scholar John Mill published a critical edition of the Textus Receptus. Johann Jakob Wettstein reissued the Elzevir's (Textus Receptus) text with critical footnotes (*c.* 1720). To maintain some level of credibility, he cited manuscripts that both supported or varied from the printed text. A collaborator, Richard Bentley, had intended to supersede the Textus Receptus with a text resembling that of the early third century. He never printed his revolutionary work. That honor went to Johann Albert Bengel, who independently published (*c.* 1730) the first text of the Greek New Testament to vary from the Textus Receptus.

Around 1830 Constantin von Tischendorf discovered an even earlier witness to the original Greek text than Alexandrinus. The German scholar named it *Codex Sinaiticus* for St. Catherine's Monastery near Mount Sinai, where he found the manuscript. Dating from A.D. 360-375, Sinaiticus represented an almost singular attempt by Greek-speaking monks there to preserve the Alexandrian text. Only churches in Greece and Byzantium carried on the work of copying by the fifth century—and they just perpetuated the corrupted Byzantine text. When Karl Lachmann applied classical scholarship to the Greek New Testament one year later (in 1881), he produced a critical text resembling that of the fourth century.

Tischendorf recognized the value of other overlooked documents during his travels. Important texts like Codex Claromontanus, Codex Ephraemi Rescriptus, and Codex Vaticanus (*c.* A.D. 350) became accessible for the first time through his efforts. Vaticanus, for example, had been at the Vatican Library since 1481! He also published many critical editions of the Greek Old and New Testaments. His eighth edition of the New Testament (*c.* 1869-1872) is still a standard today.

During the latter part of the nineteenth century, Samuel P. Tregelles, Henry Alford, Brooke Foss Westcott, Fenton J. A. Hort, and F.H.A. Scrivener developed and published editions of the Greek New Testament from documents predating the "received" text. In 1882 Westcott and Hort explained how they produced *The New Testament in the Original Greek* in 1881. Working from the premise that Codex Vaticanus and Codex Sinaiticus represented the text most closely resembling the original Greek, these English scholars used the two codices as the standard to compile that text from available documents. Streeter later identified this *Neutral* text with the Alexandrian text (see the textual transmission diagrams on pp. 5, 6).

Around 1900, Eberhard Nestle compiled a text of the Greek New Testament that summed up what scholars had learned through the nineteenth century. As additional manuscripts surfaced, however, first his son Erwin (1914-1963) and then Kurt Aland (1956 to the present) updated Nestle's *Novum Testamentum Graece [Greek New Testament]*. Blockbuster discoveries such as the first to third century Oxyrhynchus (1897-1907), Chester Beatty (1931), and Martin Rodmer (1951) papyri, and the fourth century Nag Hammadi Codices (1945-1946) demanded frequent revision of the text. In 1979 Aland and his wife Barbara produced the twenty-sixth Nestle-Aland edition of *Novum Testamentum Graece*. The United Bible Societies Greek New Testament Committee used this Alexandrian text to produce its fourth revised edition in 1993.

The textual revolution also influenced the translation of the Old and New Testaments. In 1885 British scholars—with help from an American delegation—revised the King James Version to produce the *Revised Version* (RV) of the Bible. By 1901 the same American committee had independently revised the work of their English counterparts and issued the *American Standard Version* (ASV). The two versions have at least one thing in common: "Both are extreme efforts at literal translation" (Soulen, p. 26).

In 1952 another American committee, sponsored by the National Council of Churches in Christ, revised the ASV. While their *Revised Standard Version* (RSV) retains much of the King James Version's elegance, it is also more accurate. The RSV's text is much closer to the original than the Textus Receptus. The 1971 *New American Standard Bible* (NASB) is also a revision of the ASV, motivated by a sense of "urgency to update it by incorporating recent discoveries of Hebrew and Greek textual sources and by rendering it into more current English" (Preface to the *New American Standard Bible*). In most instances, the NASB translators followed the then latest, twenty-third, edition of Nestle's *Novum Testamentum Graece*.

In 1966 the American Bible Society published *Good News for Modern Man*, the New Testament portion of *Today's English Version* (TEV) of the Bible. Although it deliberately avoids the technical language of a study Bible, the TEV New Testament is a faithful, highly readable translation of the twenty-sixth Nestle-Aland edition of *Novum Testamentum Graece*.

The New York Bible Society (now the International Bible Society) undertook the financial sponsorship of the *New International Version* (NIV) in 1967. "The first concern of the [NIV's international, transdenominational team of] translators has been the accuracy of the translation and its fidelity to the thought of the Biblical writers. . . . The Greek text used in translating the New Testament was an eclectic one. . . . Where existing manuscripts differ, the translators made their choice of readings according to accepted principles of New Testament textual criticism. Footnotes call attention to places where there was uncertainty about what the original text was. The best current printed texts of the Greek New Testament were used" (Preface to the *New International Version*, 1978).

Breakthrough studies of documents written in languages related to Hebrew and the discovery of additional early Greek manuscripts inspired the Revised Standard Version Bible Committee in 1974 to update its text and to release a *New Revised Standard Version* of the Bible in 1989.

A host of independent Bible translations have come about as a result of the textual revolution, yet they all have one thing in common. In departing from the Textus Receptus and turning to texts that are closer to the originals, text-critical versions of the Bible have dramatically improved on the accuracy of the King James Version of the New Testament.

How to Evaluate Variant Readings

Legitimate interpretation demands a text that faithfully reproduces what the author wrote in his original situation. As Wurthwein reminds us, however: "The history of the text shows clearly that all our witnesses stand far removed from the original text both by time and by the process of transmission. They contain, therefore, not only a great variety of scribal errors . . . but also some actual transformations of the original, both deliberate and accidental. . . . Scholarship cannot rest content with such a situation. By means of textual criticism it attempts to ferret out all the alterations that have occurred and recover the earliest possible form of the text" *(The Text of the Old Testament*, p. 103). This being the case, it only makes sense to compare carefully all the different readings of a passage from ancient sources in order to decide which is the most accurate—that is, most resembles the autograph—before you analyze it.

The best place to start is with the Hebrew Old Testament and Greek New Testament. Most editions list the various readings (with their supporting documentation) usually below the text at the bottom of the page. If you cannot work directly with the biblical languages, you can either: (1) depend on the translators to decide for you which reading to work with or (2) obtain the tools to investigate the text for yourself.

Some Bibles, such as the NASB, the NIV, and the Companion Bible (KJV), offer alternative readings and brief text-critical remarks for both the Old and New Testaments. Others do the same, but like the RSV and NRSV add simple evidence for Old Testament readings and alternatives, usually at the bottom of the page. The *Newberry Bible* (KJV) prints New Testament readings and variants with detailed textual support at the bottom of the page. If you have a computer, there are helpful computer programs available (see the discussion of Bible software on p. 461).

Before you proceed any further, let me express a word of caution. It takes years of training to qualify as a scholar of biblical languages and textual studies. To apply the principles of textual criticism to your passage, you will need guidance—by the Holy Spirit and from experts in the field. As you sort through the various readings and supporting evidence, consider the choices scholars have made—and why they made that choice. Let them teach you about the text that underlies the translation you are using—its sources, tendencies, and accuracy. These insights into the text are fundamental to preparing it for interpretation.

The Sources

The Old Testament—The history of the Old Testament text is as old as the Bible itself. Unfortunately, "woefully little historical evidence is available" from the period before 300 B.C. (Shemaryahu Talmon, "The Old Testament Text," in *Qumran and the History of the Biblical Text,* p. 1). The absence of any original documents forced scholars to draw conclusions about the ancient text and its transmission, secondhand, from copies—all of which date after the first century A.D. Drawing on every available source, they have deduced that before 300 B.C., Old Testament books were (1) originally written and copied in Phoenician (or paleo-Hebrew) script, and in square or Aramaic script toward the end of the period, (2) as individual scrolls rather than codices or collections, (3) at first in purely consonantal form, but gradually with vowels, (4) without spaces or dividing marks between words, (5) according to post-1350 B.C. rules of grammar.

Then, in 1947, the Dead Sea Scrolls, manuscripts dating from the last centuries B.C. and the first century A.D. became available for the first time and revolutionized the field of textual studies. The scrolls come from a crucial period in the history of the transmission of the biblical text and offer firsthand evidence of what happened to it during that time. Instead of relying on speculation as they had in the past, scholars saw for themselves that the Hebrew text from 300 B.C. to 135 A.D., "existed in a variety of textual traditions or text families" (Brotzman, *Old Testament Textual Criticism,* p. 43)—because some of the scrolls resemble the Masoretic text, others the Septuagint tradition, and still others the Samaritan Pentateuch.

Yet, other Hebrew documents retrieved nearby, dating to the Bar-Kochba revolt against Rome (ca. 135 A.D.) show that the variety of text types popular "between the third to first centuries B.C. was replaced by a single and authoritative text type by A.D. 235 at the latest" (Brotzman, *Old Testament Textual Criticism,* p. 44).

Scholars have struggled since, to explain how this happened. One of them, Harvard's Frank Moore Cross, has suggested that each of the Masoretic, Septuagint, and Samaritan traditions developed separately, because they operated in different geographic areas. He hypothesizes that two local texts began to develop independently in Palestine and Babylon during the fifth century B.C. The Jewish community in Palestine, for example, studied and copied the Hebrew Bible throughout the centuries. The Samaritan Pentateuch, for the most part, represents this Palestinian family of texts.

Diaspora Jews took the Scriptures with them to Babylon, where scribes also studied and copied the Scriptures, and after centuries of less-than-perfect transmission produced the Masoretic text.

Other Jews took a text from Palestine with them to Egypt where scholars translated it into Greek (the Septuagint). We are reasonably certain of this because the Septuagint agrees with the Samaritan Pentateuch some 1900 times—when they both disagree with the Masoretic text.

The presence of all three families in the Dead Sea Scrolls proves that (1) both Babylonian and Egyptian text types were recognized in Palestine, and (2) all three began to influence each other there—before the Christian era. According to Cross: "By the first century B.C. or the early first century A.D. . . . [the Babylonian text] . . . became accepted as the official form of the Pentateuch and the Former Prophets within Jewish scribal circles. It was apparently not available in the case of the Latter Prophets, so the Palestinian text type was adopted for these books. This accepted standard text replaced the other families, except as they were reflected in the Septuagint and the Samaritan Pentateuch, and would later be called the Masoretic text"

(Brotzman, *Old Testament Textual Criticism,* p. 46).

You could diagram this *Theory of Local Texts* as follows:

FIGURE 107

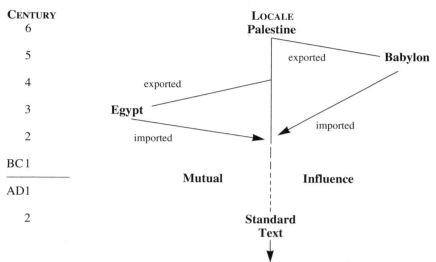

Shemaryahu Talmon, who coedited *Qumran and the History of the Biblical Text* with Cross, feels that his colleague has oversimplified the situation. For him, the three known text types are only survivors of a long process that eliminated many others (pp. 324, 325). Emmanual Tov says that they are only documents that survived the process rather than recension or text types ("A Modern Textual Outlook Based on the Qumran Scrolls," *Hebrew Union College Annual* 53 [1982]:11). In fact, by Tov's reckoning, there are *five* text types at Qumran alone: (1) Qumran indigenous (25%); (2) proto-Masoretic (40%); (3) proto-Samaritan (5%); (4) pre-Septuagint (5%); and (5) independent (25%).

Brotzman rightly points out that Cross, apparently focusing on similarities of the texts, favors a single ancestor—while Talmon and Tov conclude from the differences that more than one prototype is necessary to account for the texts at that time. "Summing up," Talmon says, "we may say that in spite of its appeal the 'local texts' theory cannot really explain satisfactorily the 'plurality of text types' at the end of the pre-Christian era. It could indeed account for the 'limited number of distinct textual families' extant at that time. But," he objects, "one is inclined to attribute this feature of the text transmission to two factors. . . . As a result of undirected, and possibly in part also of controlled processes of elimination, the majority of these variations went out of use. The remaining traditions achieved by and by the status of a textus receptus within the socio-religious communities which perpetuated them. These standardized texts were preserved for us in the major versions of the Hebrew Bible and its translations *(Qumran and the History of the Biblical Text,* pp. 40, 41).

Whether you subscribe to a theory of local texts, or a theory of plural texts, the Qumran evidence certifies one thing for sure: Jewish scribes adopted a standard text by the year 135 A.D. and concentrated, in the years that followed, on the transmission of that text. During the Age of the Talmud, from 135 to 500 A.D., for example, they made mostly external changes to the text—that made it easier to read, understand, and appreciate. In the Masoretic era, they continued to develop the text by creating (1) a graphic system to represent vowels, (2) the accent system, and (3) a system of textual notes.

From 1000 to 1450 A.D., scribes transmitted the Masoretic text with only *minor* changes. But beginning with the first rabbinic Bible around 1516 A.D., scholars began to deal with places where the text may be doubtful. Today there are several critical editions for the study of the Old Testament that utilize ancient versions and other documents to restore the Masoretic text to its purest predecessor.

Sources for Old Testament criticism are sparse. They include

1. manuscripts of the Hebrew Bible

The **Masoretic Text** (MT), the traditional and received text of the Old Testament, punctuated and handed down with vowel points through a centuries-long tradition of careful copying and checking by the Masoretes (Jewish scholars). The earliest copies of the Masoretic text available today, the Cairo Codex (Prophets), ca. 895 A.D., and the Aleppo Codex, ca. 925 A.D. date from the ninth and tenth centuries, approximately 1300 years since the close of Old Testament revelation. It derives from a separate tradition than the Septuagint or the Samaritan Pentateuch called *Proto-MT*—at least for the Pentateuch (the first five books of the Old Testament).

The **Samaritan Pentateuch** [SP], a recension (that is, a purposely created edition) of the Pentateuch—in mostly unpointed Hebrew. It derives from an ancient textual tradition in Palestine called *Proto SP*—that also predates the Masoretic text. Fragments of this tradition appear even among the Dead Sea Scrolls. Preserved as Scripture by the Samaritans, a small but zealous religious sect in Galilee, it represents a late form of the Hebrew text, as it was elaborated and expanded in Palestine. You could trace its history as follows:

FIGURE 108

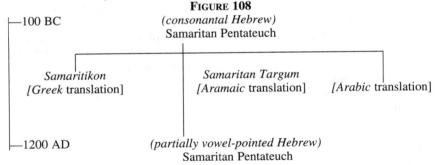

The **Dead Sea Scrolls,** the oldest known copies of the Hebrew Scriptures, witness to every book of the Old Testament except Esther (see the discussion of the scrolls, beginning on p. 379).

2. versions of the Hebrew Bible

The **Targumim** (also spelled targums, the Heberw word for "translation"), Aramaic paraphrases of the Hebrew. As the B.C. Era began to wind down, the majority of Jews in Palestine came to speak and understand Aramaic rather than Hebrew even though readers at synagogue services continued to present the Scriptures in their original language. Religious leaders solved the language difficulty by quickly translating orally and freely into Aramaic, what had just been read in Hebrew. The Jewish community grew to cherish the targums and eventually preserved them in written form. They were also reworked during the fifth century in Babylon to agree with the Masoretic text. Although "Palestinian targums on the Pentateuch contain much additional narrative material . . . they occasionally preserve older, non-Masoretic readings of the canonical text as well" (Ralph W. Klein, *Textual Criticism of the Old Testament,* p. 60). Among those that have survived are: (Pentateuch) Onqelos, Pseudo-Jonathan, and Codex Neofiti I; (Prophets) Jonathan; and (Writings) at least one for each book, with the exception of Ezra-Nehemiah and Daniel, which have none (see the discussion of the targums on p. 376).

The **Peshitta,** a fourth to fifth century reworking of first and second century Christian translations of the Old Testament into an Aramaic dialect, Syriac. Though based primarily on the Masoretic text, it also contains corrections inserted from the Greek Old Testament (the Septuagint, or LXX), especially in Isaiah and the Psalms.

The **Vulgate** is Jerome's Latin translation of the Old Testament—in response to Pope Damasus' commission to revise the Old Latin Bible in 382 A.D. Proceeding in stages, he began by modestly correcting the Psalms according to the LXX and produced the *Roman Psalter.* He continued the process by adjusting his earlier work to both the *Hexaplaric* LXX and Hebrew text, transforming it into the so-called *Gallican Psalter.* Finally, from 390-405 A.D. he completely revised the entire Old Testament, solely on the basis of the Hebrew text. The Council of Trent recognized it as the official Bible of the Roman Catholic Church in 1546.

3. versions of the Greek Old Testament

The **Septuagint** (LXX), the original pre-Christian Greek translation of the Old Testament. It derives its name (which means 70) from the legenc that 72 Jewish scholars from Jerusalem came to Egypt and translated it from the Hebrew scriptures in 72 days (according to the apparently fictitious *Letter of Aristeas).* Actually developed in Alexandria, Egypt, around 200 B.C. by Greek-speaking Jews, it underwent revision in Palestine well into the Christian era. As translators updated it to match developments in the Greek language, the original became known as the Old Greek. Although Septuagint manuscripts lie closer in time to the original Hebrew, they are nevertheless translations of it—into another language. It is frequently referred to as the LXX (the Roman numeral for 70).

Proto-Lucian, a second to first century B.C. revision intended to bring the LXX in line with the Palestinian Hebrew text.

The **Kaige,** also known as Proto-Theodotion, is a turn-of-the-era revision intended to bring the LXX in line with Proto-MT.

Aquila is an extremely literal revision, intended to bring the *Kaige* in line with MT, named for the Jewish scholar who completed it in 130.

Symmachus is a second century revision, intended to bring the *Kaige* (and possibly Aquila) in line with MT. "As a result of his rabbinical exegetical training, we find Symmachus softening or even eliminating many of the anthropomorphisms [human attributes or characteristics ascribed to God for purposes of illustration or explanation] of the Old Testament" (Danker, *Multipurpose Tools for Bible Study,* p. 69).

Theodotion, a second century Jewish revision named for its translator. He based his work on the *Kaige* recension, which is closely related to the Masoretic text, a different tradition than the Palestinian text from which the LXX originally came.

The **Hexapla,** Origen of Alexandria's revision *(c.* A.D. 240-245). Prepared to help with public Bible reading, it lines up six texts in parallel columns: (1) the Hebrew text; (2) a transliteration of the Hebrew words into Greek letters; (3) Aquila; (4) Symmachus; (5) the LXX, edited to bring it in line with MT (even though it was originally based on the Palestinian text); and (6) Theodotion. According to Eusebius, in the Psalms, Origen added three other versions to those previously mentioned, called *Quinta* (fifth), *Sexta* (sixth), and *Septima* (seventh).

Eusebius, a recension of Origen's LXX, named for its author.

Hesychius, a *c.* 300 A.D. recension of Origen's LXX, named for its author.

Lucian, an early revision of Proto-Lucian [and possibly other texts] intended to bring the LXX in line with MT.

To summarize, the Greek versions developed as follows:

GREEK VERSIONS—FIGURE 109

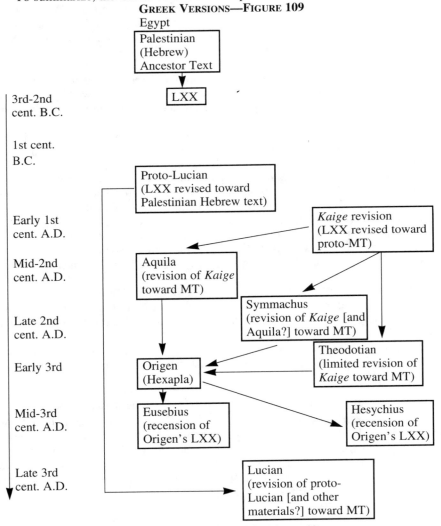

(Adapted from Ellis R. Brotzman, *Old Testament Textual Criticism*, p. 80)

325

4. daughter translations of the Greek Old Testament (translations of the Old Greek translation of the Hebrew or its recensions):

Old Latin (or Itala), are second century and later Christian translations of close copies of the Old Greek in North Africa, Gaul, and Italy (outside of Rome).

Coptic are translations of the Old Greek, for the most part, into the Sahidic (third century), Achmimic, and Boharic (fourth century) dialects of Egypt.

Ethiopic are Semitic translations of the early LXX.

Syriac (Syro-Hexaplar) is a translation of the fifth column of Origen's Hexapla. The translators were Paul of Tella and others from A.D. 615-617.

Gothic, Armenian, Georgian, Slavonic, and **Arabic** are translations more useful for the study of the history of interpretation than for the practice of textual criticism.

(For a comprehensive catalogue of Old Testament documents, see Wurthwein's *The Text of the Old Testament*. For an exhaustive catalogue of the Dead Sea Scrolls, see Scanlin's *The Dead Sea Scrolls and Modern Translations of the Old Testament*.)

The New Testament—The vast sources of New Testament textual criticism include:

1. **Papyri** are the earliest witnesses to the original Greek text, dating back to the first century. Parchment papyri are designated by the letter *p* followed by a number, as in p46, while vellum (calfskin) papyri are labeled by the number 0 followed by Arabic numerals, as in 0171.

2. **Uncials** are third to tenth century codices of the Bible written in capital letters on parchment or vellum—designated by capital letters such as A, B, C, etc., they are frequently known by names associated with their discovery, such as Sinaiticus.

3. **Minuscules** are ninth century and later codices of the Bible written in small cursive or "running" letters. They constitute more than 90 percent of all known biblical manuscripts. Minuscules are labeled with Arabic numerals without a preceding 0 as in 118; some, like the Lake group, appear under headings such as Family 1.

4. **Ancient versions** are early translations of the New Testament into Syriac, Coptic, Ethiopic, Latin, Armenian, Georgian, and Old Slavonic. The form of the Greek text underlying these translations witnesses to its form at the time and place of their origin and development.

5. The **Church Fathers**, either Greek such as Origen or Latin such as Tertullian, quoted, paraphrased, modified, or alluded to the Greek New Testament. Quotations are the most helpful because they most faithfully reproduce the text circulated at that time and place.

6. **Lectionaries** are Greek quotations of Scripture used in public worship and private devotion. They are designated by the small letter *l* followed by the number of the manuscript, as in 159.

A Sound Procedure for Evaluating Variant Old Testament Readings[27]

1. List the variant (that is, variations of the) *readings in your passage*, in addition to the reading adopted by your Bible (your standard text). Your task is to compare the variants with your standard reading and to decide whether or not any of them should replace it. If your Bible does not have critical notes, consult a Hebrew Old Testament that does (if you can work with Hebrew), a Bible program, or another Bible (if you don't). For example:

FIGURE 110

Book: 1 Samuel	Chapter/verse: 5:10			Bible Version: *Biblia Hebraica*			
Readings	**Supporting Evidence**						
	MT	SP	LXX	Version	Translation	Qumran	Other
the ark of the God of Israel				Lucian		4QSam[a]	
the ark of God	x			Kaige			

2. Weigh the evidence and choose a reading.
(a) Consider the *external* evidence.
- **The date and character of the witnesses**
  Ernst Wurthwein weights Old Testament text-critical evidence in the following order: Masoretic text (MT); Samaritan Pentateuch (SP); Septuagint (LXX); Septuagint Editions: Aquila (A), Symmachus (Σ), Theodotion (O); Septuagint Versions: Syriac, Targum, Vulgate, Old Latin, Sahidic, Coptic, Ethiopic, Arabic, and Armenian *(The Text of the Old Testament*, p. 76).
- **The geographical distribution of the witnesses**
  A reading carries more weight if it appears in two or more manuscripts or versions and may actually overrule the Masoretic text.
- **Witnesses should be weighed instead of counted**
  According to Klein, the type of witness is more important than the number: "A variant that occurs in the Dead Sea Scrolls, the Samaritan Pentateuch, or LXX will probably be given more attention than if it appears in a Targum or in one of the daughter translations of the LXX" *(Textual Criticism of the Old Testament*, p. 74).
- **The relationship between the Masoretic text and the Hebrew text of the LXX translator** (adapted from Klein, *Textual Criticism of the Old Testament*, pp. 69-73).

FIGURE 111

The Pentateuch

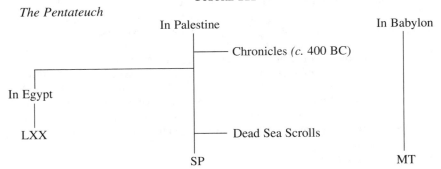

Chronicles, the Dead Sea Scrolls, and SP all share a similar text. The LXX, although developed in Egypt, shares 1,600 readings with the SP against the MT, which came about separately, probably in Babylon (see Frank Moore Cross, "The Evolution of a Theory of Local Texts," 1972 Proceedings of the International Organization for Septuagint and Cognate

Studies [Missoula, Montana: Society of Biblical Literature], pp. 108-126). So if isolated, unrelated texts like LXX and MT agree against SP, the reading is probably preferable to one supported by Chronicles, the Dead Sea Scrolls, SP, and LXX, which represent one local tradition or related traditions.

FIGURE 112

Samuel and Kings

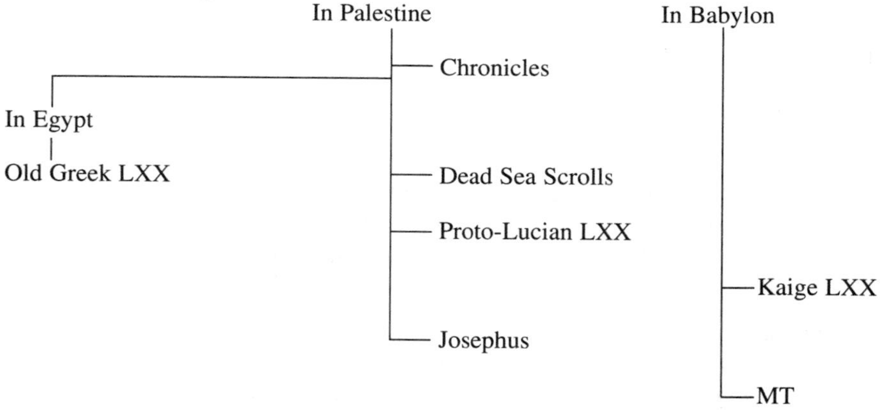

In Palestine   In Babylon

— Chronicles

In Egypt
|
Old Greek LXX   — Dead Sea Scrolls

— Proto-Lucian LXX

—Kaige LXX

—— Josephus

—MT

Although LXX witnesses appeared in Egypt, Palestine, and Babylon, the Palestinian text has more in common with LXX than MT, since the Kaige recension is based on an early (proto) form of MT. Chronicles is based on the local Palestinian text type, to which (4Q Sam) is a witness. The proto-Lucianic recension itself no longer exists, but Josephus used it in the process of writing his histories. Despite its having developed separately, you can still identify authentic proto-Lucian readings from these three traditions when (a) Lucian and 4Q Sam agree, although MT and Kaige have an alternate reading (this means that the reading "the ark of the God of Israel" in the example used earlier is preferable to "the ark of God"); (b) 4Q Sam, MT, and Josephus agree, although Kaige has a different reading; and (c) 4Q Sam and Josephus agree, although Kaige, Lucian, and MT share another reading.

Isaiah, Jeremiah, and Ezekiel

Most of what the prophets said is preserved for us in MT and LXX. In the case of Jeremiah and Ezekiel, however, the two texts are significantly different. The MT is lengthy and expansionist (added to), whereas the LXX is shorter and therefore closer to the original. Although they represent separate traditions, the Dead Sea Scrolls, MT, and LXX of Isaiah are all expansionist texts, making it difficult at times to isolate the best readings and recover the original.

(b) Consider the *internal* evidence.

Errors in transmitting the Hebrew text

• **Accidental, mechanical mistakes in reading, writing, and hearing**

    —*mistaking letters that look alike* [ד (daleth) for ר (resh), יי (yod, nun) for מ (mem), ו (waw) for ר (resh), ב (beth) for כ (koph), ה (heh) for ח (heth), ה (heh) for ת (taw), ו (waw) for י (yod), ע (ayin) for צ (tsadeh), כ (koph) for נ (nun)]

—*mistaking letters that sound alike* ["lo" = לֹ (to him) for לֹא (not); "attah" = עתה (now) for אתה (you), etc.]

—*leaving out what is between two words that end alike* (homoeoteleuton). So, for instance, MT omits the italicized words in the following quotation from the LXX: "And Samuel arose and set out from Gilgal *and went on his way; but the rest of the people went up after Saul to meet the soldiers. Then they came from Gilgal* to Gibeah of Benjamin" (1 Sam. 13:15).

—*leaving out what is between two words that begin alike* (homeoarchion)

—*writing once what appears twice in succession* (haplography). So the MT omits the italicized words in the following citation from the LXX: "Not as a man sees, *does God see*" (1 Sam. 16:7).

—*writing twice what appears once* (dittography). This explains why the MT repeats the words "*and they took it away from the house of Abinadab which is on the hill*" (2 Sam. 6:3) in verse 4 (cf. 4QSam and LXX).

—*incorrectly uniting or dividing words*. Sometimes the space between words was so small that scribes had a difficult time telling where one word ended and another began. As a result, they incorrectly joined or separated words. In the Lachish Ostraca, one scribe actually squeezed words together to fit them in narrow spaces. Consider Amos 6:12, which begins with "Do horses run on rocks?" Some manuscripts continue with "or does one plow *[them] with oxen* (בבקרים)?" instead of "or does one plow *the sea with oxen* (בבקר ים)?"

—*incorrectly pronouncing words*. From the sixth to the ninth centuries, the Masoretes added vowels (pointed the words) to the consonantal text. "The record a traditional pronunciation which at times is mistaken" (Klein, *Textual Criticism of the Old Testament*, p. 79). So the LXX translates the first verb in 1 Samuel 18:11 as though it were *wayyittol* "and he picked up" rather than the Masoretic *wayyatel* "and he hurled."

—*transposing words or letters* (metathesis). Without vowel pointings to guide them, scribes sometimes reversed the order of letters. So the MT has "and he showed a willingness" *(wya'al)* whereas the LXX has "and he exerted himself" *(wyala')* in 1 Samuel 17:39.

—*assimilating the wording of a passage to the wording of the context or a parallel passage*. When the MT has "the hand of the Lord will be against you *and your fathers*," Lucian has "*and your king*." The MT scribe may have allowed the frequent mention of fathers in verses 6 to 8 to unintentionally influence his efforts.

—*including marginal or interlinear comments in the text* (glosses). This offers a possible explanation for the MT version of Isaiah 24:4, where the "heights" mourn *with* the land. The Dead Sea Scroll 1QIs reads "the heights *of* the land mourn." Above the line, however, a scribe wrote the word *'am* (people). Later on another scribe probably inserted the *'am* into the text. Without vowel pointing that Hebrew word can either be understood as people or as the preposition with.

• **Deliberate, conscious alterations**

Some scribes did alter the text at times, but these modifications were "undertaken in good faith, and their purpose was not by any means to bring anything foreign into the text . . . [but] . . . to restore the correct reading, or to avoid what the copyist thought might lead to a misunderstanding" (Wurthwein, *The Text of the Old Testament*, p. 74).

—*changed the spelling or grammar.* Scribes made subjects and verbs agree in person and number, corrected numerals, inserted like "and," "now," "which," "saying," etc. when they thought it appropriate.

—*harmonized difficulties.* So the MT inserts "the third" in the LXX phrase "until evening" in order to harmonize 1 Samuel 20:5 with the time frame found in verses 34, 35.

—*conflated variant readings.* Instead of choosing between variants, some scribes blended them into a single reading in order to avoid omitting the original. So the MT has both the reading of some Hebrew manuscripts, the LXX, and the Syriac, plus an alternate "wherever the spirit wanted to go" in Ezekiel 1:20.

—*supplied subjects and objects* (glosses). Well-meaning scribes inserted implied subjects and objects or substituted them for pronouns in the original text.

—*expanded passages.* Scribes used information from parallel passages to explain the text. So while the MT uses different but complementary reasons for keeping the Sabbath in Exodus 20:11 and Deuteronomy 5:14, 15, 4QDt, a Dead Sea Scroll, adds the reason from Exodus 20:11 to Deuteronomy 5:15.

—*removed difficulties.* At times "certain matters of history, geography, or theology seemed incorrect or even offensive to the copyists and were corrected" (Klein, *Textual Criticism of the Old Testament*, p. 82). Many texts, for example, replace the expression "curse God" with "bless God" in Job 1:5, 11 and 2:5, 9.

—*replaced rare words with common ones.* "It is also understandable that a text which was not only the subject of learned study, but was read and heard repeatedly in the whole Jewish community, should be assimilated to the linguistic needs of the community" (Wurthwein, *The Text of the Old Testament*, p. 74). So the MT replaces the verb *wyphz* (sprang up—LXX, 4QSam]) with the more colloquial *wyqm* (arose) in 1 Samuel 20:34.

In view of the scribal tendency "to simplify and clarify the texts they were copying" (Brotzman, *Old Testament Tectual Criticism*, p. 128), and "to amplify a text by adding words to clarify or smoothe" it out (*ibid.*, p. 128), (1) the shorter, (2) the more difficult reading, (3) that best explains the origin of the others is generally preferable.

Weigh carefully both the internal and external evidence and select the best reading. If your internal investigations prove inconclusive, however, give the preference to the MT.

A Sound Procedure for Evaluating Variant New Testament Readings

1. List the variant (that is, variations of the) *readings in your passage.* Write down each possibility, beginning with the one printed in your Bible text. Group similar readings under one possibility. For instance, the possibility "Jesus delivered his people out of Egypt" includes readings with different word order in the Greek, but they all insist that Jesus did the saving.

FIGURE 113

Book: Jude	Chapter/verse: 5		Bible Version: UBS4, TEV	
Readings	**Supporting Evidence**			
	Alexandrian	Caesarean	Western	Byzantine
the Lord	C*, I, 1175 1409		Syriac-Harklensis	K, 436, 945, 1067, 1292, 1505, 1611, 1844, 2138
Lord	ℵ²			ψ
God	C², 1243 Clement			1846
Jesus	A, B, 33, 81, 322, 1241, 1739, 2344, Coptic-Sahidic, Boharic, Cyril, Origen		Old Latin	1881, 2298
God, the Messiah	p72			
the Lord, Jesus	1735			

2. *Weigh the evidence for each reading and draw an educated conclusion.*
(a) Consider the *external* evidence.[28]
- **The date and character of the witnesses.**
  Generally, the earlier the text type the better, because they are closer in time to the autographs (the originals). Usually Alexandrian texts are the most reliable, although they may contain scholarly corrections of the original. (See the discussion of text types in this chapter.)
- **The geographical distribution of the witnesses**
  Generally witnesses from a variety of places outweigh a single witness, regardless of its character. A reading with the support of good witnesses representing different text types probably "antedates the rise of the local texts instead of having originated in one of the local texts (Greenlee, *Introduction to New Testament Textual Criticism*, p. 116).
- **The genealogical relationship of the texts and families of witnesses**
  Witnesses that share a common ancestor count as only one witness. A proper comparison weighs only that common ancestor against other evidence.
- **Witnesses should be weighed instead of counted**
  It doesn't matter how many witnesses there are if they embody an inferior type of text. The versions, fathers, and lectionaries supplement, corroborate, and are secondary to the Greek manuscript tradition (papyri, uncials, and minuscules).

In the example from Jude given above, the readings *"the* Lord," plus the related reading without the article "Lord" and "Jesus" all have Alexandrian support—the latter with more than the former two combined. The reading *"the* Lord," however, has a wider variety of witnesses, including Western and Byzantine texts.

(b) Consider the *internal* evidence.[29]

• **Transcriptional Probabilities** (from the scribal viewpoint)

(a) In general, the *more difficult reading* is preferable if it makes sense. Scribes were more likely to change something difficult into something easier to understand than the other way around.

(b) In general, the *shorter reading* is preferable. A scribe who deliberately changed the text was more likely to add than to leave something out. "He may add a note of explanation, add a phrase from a parallel account (harmonization), or he may combine two or more readings (conflation)" *(ibid.*, pp. 114-116). He could also intentionally leave out something hard to understand. If the change was accidental, he could either add to the text "by conflation, harmonization, or repetition (dittography); or may omit, by failing to repeat letters which occur twice (haplography), or by accidentally passing from a word or syllable to the same or similar appearing letters farther on (homoeoteleuton)" *(ibid.*, p. 115). Tend to reject familiarized, refined, or smoothed readings.

(c) The reading that *best explains* the origin of the others is preferable. For instance, in Luke 11:2 one scribe has *"our Father, the one in heaven,"* and another simply *"Father."* The second reading is probably the original for two good reasons: (1) the parallel prayer in the earlier and more familiar Matthew 6:9 has the first reading without any variants; (2) a scribe would be more likely to add the words "the one in heaven" either deliberately or accidentally and thus lengthen the shorter reading than to leave them out and shorten the longer one.

(d) In general, *divided rather than conflated* readings are preferable. Conflated readings usually represent a scribe's attempt to avoid choosing between variant readings, deliberately combining them to avoid accidentally omitting the genuine one. Luke 24:53 is a case in point. Some early manuscripts have the disciples *"blessing* God," whereas others have them *"praising* God." Eventually some scribes blended both readings so that the disciples wound up "praising and blessing God."

• **Intrinsic Probabilities** (from the author's point-of-view).

(a) In general the reading characteristic of the author is preferable. Take into account the author's style and vocabulary throughout the book, the immediate context, and parallel passages in other books by the same author. In the Gospels, especially consider the Aramaic background of Jesus' teaching, the literary and theological intent of the Gospel author, and the influence of the Christian community upon the formation and transmission of the passage.

Reconsider Luke 24:53. (1) The *external* evidence favors the reading "blessing" with Alexandrian support over "praising" with Western support, and "praising and blessing" with Western and Byzantine backing.

On the basis of *internal* evidence, (2) either short reading ("praising" or "blessing") is preferable to "praising and blessing." (3) Either "praising" or "praising or blessing" could have generated the reading "blessing." A scribe with the Western tendency to paraphrase could have substituted "praising" for "blessing," and a scribe with the Byzantine bent for conflation could have blended "praising" and "blessing" into a single reading.

(4) "Blessing" is also the most difficult reading. Although "praising"

and "blessing" both occur in reference to God, the word for "blessing" is the more common New Testament choice for blessing human beings not God. A concerned scribe might have deliberately changed "blessing" to "praising" in order to remove the apparent inconsistency.

(5) In addition, Luke-Acts is the text for six of the nine appearances of the Greek word *aineo* (praising) in the New Testament—always in reference to God. Luke-Acts also hosts more than one third of the New Testament occurrences of *eulogeo* (blessing). "Thus both words are common in Luke, with . . . [eulogeo] more frequent but with . . . [aineo] more common in reference to God. Thus *aineo* may be termed somewhat more characteristic of the author, but no strong conclusion is warranted, since Luke uses both words in reference to God" (*ibid.*, p. 122).

All things considered, then, "blessing" is most likely the original text. The external evidence (1) favors it, and it has more internal support (2, 3, 4) than either of the other readings.

In the example from Jude given above, "it is easier to argue [from a textual perspective] that the reading 'Jesus' is the one from which all the others derived than to argue that the reading with 'Lord' [or 'God'] was changed to 'Jesus.' Scribes were not known for fabricating difficult readings" (Comfort, *The Quest for the Original Text of the New Testament,* p. 155). The evidence is, therefore, split between "Lord" and "Jesus." For this reason, translations of critical texts, such as the NIV and NASB, go along with the Nestle 26th edition and the UBS 3rd and 4th editions—reading "the Lord" in the text and "Jesus" in the margin.

Catalogue of Texts and Witnesses

Old Testament—The following names and symbols will help you identify the documents used in Old Testament textual criticism.

BHK	BHS	
A	α′	Aquila
E′	ϵ′	Origen's Quinta
Θ	θ′	Theodotion
	ο ϵβρ	see below: BHK H°
	οι Y′ }	the three later Greek version
	οι λ′ }	Samaritan Pentateuch, A. von Gall's edition
ɯ	ɯ	Samaritan Pentateuch manuscript(s) in A.
	ɯ^Ms(s)	von Gall's critical apparatus
ɯ^T	ɯ^T	Samaritan Targum
	ɯ^W	Samaritan Pentateuch, B. Walton's London Polyglot
Σ	σ′	Symmachus
𝔄	𝔄	Arabic version
𝔄	𝔄	Ethiopic version
	Ambr	Ambrose
Arm	Arm	Armenian version
ℬ	ℬ	Second Rabbinic Bible by Jacob ben Chayyim
	Bo	Bohairic version

BHK	**BHS**	
C	C	Coex Cairensis of the Prophets
	𝕮	Cairo Geniza Hebrew codex fragment
	$𝕮^{2.3 \text{ etc.}}$	Cairo Geniza Hebrew codex fragments
	cit(t)	Citations in Rabbinic and Medieval Jewish literature following V. Aptowitzer
	Cyr	See below: BHK $𝕲^{Cyr}$
E′		See above: E′
Ea 1-27		
Eb 1-30 }	(𝕮)	Fragments with simple Babylonian pointing
Ec 1-24		
	Ed(d)	Editions of the Hebrew text by Kennicott, de Rossi, and Ginsburg; cf. Ms(s)
	Eus	Eusebius Pamphilius of Caesarea
	Eus Onom	Eusebius' *Onomasticon*
Ginsb(urg Mass)	G	C. D. Ginsburg, *The Massorah compiled from Manuscripts*
𝕲	𝕲	Septuagint
	𝕲*	Original Greek text
$𝕲^{\aleph}$	$𝕲^{S}$	Codex Sinaiticus
$𝕲^{n\ c.a,\ c.b,\ c.c}$	$𝕲^{S\ 1.2.3}$	Correctors of Codex Sinaiticus
$𝕲^{A}$	$𝕲^{A}$	Codex Alexandrinus
$𝕲^{B}$	$𝕲^{B}$	Codex Vaticanus
$𝕲^{Beatty}$		Chester Beatty Papyri
$𝕲^{r}$	$(𝕲^{Ms})$	Codex rescriptus Cryptoferratensis
$𝕲^{C}$	$𝕲^{C}$	Codex Ephraemi Syri rescriptus
	$𝕲^{C}$	Greek text of the Catenae
$𝕲^{C(om)pl}$		Septuagint in the Complutensian Polyglot
$𝕲^{Cyr}$	Cyr	Septuagint in Cyril of Alexandria
$𝕲^{D}$	$(𝕲^{Ms})$	Codex Cottonianus of Genesis
$𝕲^{E}$	$(𝕲^{Ms})$	Codex Bodleianus of Genesis
$𝕲^{F}$	$𝕲^{F}$	Codex Ambrosianus
$𝕲^{G}$	$(𝕲^{Ms})$	Codex Colberto-Sarravianus
$𝕲^{\Theta}$	$(𝕲^{Ms})$	Codex Freer
$𝕲^{h}$	$𝕲^{O}$	Hexaplaric recension of the Septuagint
	$𝕲^{Op}$	$𝕲^{O}$ in part
$𝕲^{Mss\ (Holmes-)}_{Parsons}$	$𝕲^{Ms(s)}$	Manuscripts in Holmes-Parson's edition
$𝕲^{62.\ 147\ (Parsons)}$	$(𝕲^{min})$	Minuscules 62 and 147 in Holmes-Parsons
	$𝕲^{22,\ 26,\ etc.}$	Minuscule manuscripts in A. Rahlfs, *Verzeichnis der griechischen Handschriften des AT*
$𝕲^{XI}$	$(𝕲^{maj})$	Uncial no. XI in Holmes-Parsons
$𝕲^{K}$	$(𝕲^{Ms})$	Codex Lipsiensis
$𝕲^{L}$		Largarde's edition
$𝕲^{Luc}$	$𝕲^{L}$	Lucian's recension
	$𝕲^{Lp}$	$𝕲^{L}$ in part
	$𝕲^{I.\ I.\ II}$	Lucianic Subgroups I and II
$𝕲^{M}$	$(𝕲^{M})$	Codex Coislinianus

BHK	BHS	
𝕲ᴺ	(𝕲ᴹ)	Codex Basiliano-Vaticanus
𝕲ᴾᵃᵖ ᴸᵒⁿᵈ	𝕲ᵁ	British Museum Papyrus 37
𝕲Q	𝕲Q	Codex Marchalianus
	𝕲ᴿ	Codex Veronensis
𝕲ⱽ	𝕲ⱽ	Codex Venetus
𝕲ⱽⁿ		Aldine edition
𝕲ᵂ	(𝕲ᴹˢ)	Codex Atheniensis
	𝕲ᵂ	Septuagint fragment edited by H. Hunger
	𝕲⁻ˢ ᵉᵗᶜ·	Greek tradition except for 𝕲ˢ etc.
	Ga	Psalterium Gallicanum
	Gn R	Genesis rabba, see cit(t)
ჩᵒ	o εβρ΄	Origen's Hebrew text
Hie(r)	Hier	Jerome
Hill	Hill(el)	Codex Hillel
	jJeb	Jerušalmi Jebamot, see cit(t)
	Jos Ant	Flavius Josephus, *Antiquities of the Jews*
Jerich	Jericho	Codex Jericho
	Just	Justin Martyr
K	K	Kethib
Kᴼᶜᶜ	Kᴼᶜᶜ	Kethib of the Western Masoretes
Kᴼʳ	Kᴼʳ	Kethib of the Eastern Masoretes
ϰ	ϰ	Coptic version
Ka 1-22 } Kb 1-15 } Kc 1-14 }	(ꟍ)	Fragments with complex Babylonian pointing
L	L	Codex Leningradensis
𝔏	𝔏	Old Latin versions
	𝔏⁹¹	Codex Legionensis
	𝔏⁹³	Copy of Codex Legionensis
	𝔏⁹⁴	Incunabulum 54 marginalia
	𝔏¹¹⁵	Naples Codex Lat. 1 (formerly Vindob. 17)
	𝔏¹¹⁶	Fragmenta Quedlinburgensia and Magdeburgensia
	𝔏¹¹⁷	Fragmenta Vindobonensia
𝔏(Berger)		Old Latin version edited by Berger
	𝔏ᶜʸ	Cyprian's Testimonia
𝔏ᴰ		Old Latin version edited by Dold
	𝔏ᴳ	Codex Parisinus Latinus
	𝔏ᵍˡ	Old Latin Glossarium
𝔏ʰ		Old Latin version in the Würzburg palimpsests
𝔏ᴸ		Codex Lugdunensis
𝔏ᴸᵍ	𝔏ᴸᵍ	Codex Legionensis margin
	𝔏ᴿ	Codex Veronensis
	𝔏ˢ	Fragments from St. Gall
	𝔏ᵀᴱ	Tertullian, *Adversus Marcionem*
𝔏ⱽⁱⁿᵈ		Palimpsestus Vindobonensis
𝔪	𝔪	Masora, Masoretic text
Mas		Masora of Codex Leningradensis

BHK	**BHS**	
Mm, Mas, M	Mm	Masora magna
Mp	Mp	Masdora parva
MSS	Ms(s)	Hebrew manuscripts in the editions of Kennicott, de Rossi, and Ginsburg
	Mur	Manuscripts found in Wadi Murabba'at
	Naft	Ben Naftali
Occ	Occ	Western Masoretes
Ochla	Okhl	*Okhla weOkhla,* Frensdorff's edition
Or	Or	Eastern Masoretes
Orig	Orig	Origen
	Pes R	Pesiqta Rabba, see cit(t)
Q	Q	Qere
Q^{Occ}	Q^{Occ}	Qere of the Western Masoretes
Q^{Or}	Q^{Or}	Qere of the Eastern Masoretes
	ℚ	Qumran manuscripts
	ℚ^a	1QIsa^a
	ℚ^b	1QIsa^b
	1QGenAp	1QGenesis Apocryphon
	1QM	1QMilhama
	4QPs^b	Ps. 91-118, edited in *CBQ* 26 (1964), pp. 313-322
S	S^W	Syriac Peshitta in the London Polyglot
	S	Syriac Peshitta, consensus of S^A and S^W
S^A	S^A	Codex Ambrosianus
S^{Aphr}		Syriac Bible quotations in Aphraates
	S^B	Codex Londoni British Museum Add. 14,431
	S^C	Codex Leningradensis Public Library No. 2
	S^D	Codex Londoni British Museum Add. 14,442
S^h	Syh	Syrohexaplaric text
S^L	S^L	Syriac Peshitta edited by Lee
	S^M	Syriac Peshitta, Mosul edition
	S^{Mss}	Syriac Peshitta manuscripts
S^U	S^U	Syriac Peshitta, Urmia edition
	S$^{Jac edess}$	Syriac version of Jacob of Edessa
	S$^{Bar Hebr}$	Readings in the Scholii of Bar Hebraeus
Sah	Sa	Sahidic version
	Samar	Samaritan pronunciation according to P. Kahle
Seb	Seb	Sebir
Sev	Sev	Codex Severi
Sor	Sor	Soraei (= Masoretes of Sura)
ℭ	ℭ	Targum
	ℭ$^{Ms(s), Ed(d)}$	Targum manuscripts or editions cited in Sperber's critical apparatus
ℭ^B		Targum in the Second Rabbinic Bible
	ℭ^{Buxt}	Targum, Buxtorf edition
	ℭ$^{ed princ}$	Targum, editio princeps, Leiriae 1494
ℭ^J	ℭ^J	Targum Pseudo-Jonathan
ℭ^{JII}	ℭ^{JII}	Targum Jerušalmi II

BHK	BHS	
ᴄᴸ	ᴄᶠ	Codex Reuchlinianus, edited by Lagarde (BHK) or from Sperber's critical apparatus (BHS)
ᴄᴹ		Merx, *Chrestomathia targumica*
ᴄᴼ	(ᴄ)	Targum Onkelos
ᴄᴾ	ᴄᴾ	Palestinian Targum
ᴄᴾʳ		Targum, Praetorius edition
ᴄᵂ		Targum, London Polyglot
	Tert	Tertullian
Tiq Soph	Tiq Soph	Tiqqune Sopherim
	Tyc	Tyconius
𝔳	𝔳	Latin Vulgate version
𝔳ᴬ		Codex Amiatinus
Varᴮ		Variants in Baer's edition
Varᴱ¹·²·³		Variants in the three Erfurt codices
V(ar)ᶠ		Variants in the first Firkowitsch collection
V(ar)ᴳ		Variants in Ginsburg's edition
V(ar)ᴶ		Variants in Yemenite manuscripts
V(ar)ᴷᵃ		Variants in Babylonian Mss collected by Kahle
V(ar)ᴷᵉⁿ	Vᴷᵉⁿ ⁹⁶ ᵉᵗᶜ·	Variants cited in Kennicott's edition
V(ar)ᴹ		Variants in Michaelis' edition
V(ar)ᴼ		Variants in the Scholastic Odo
V(ar)ᴾ	Vᴾ	Variants in the Petersburg Prophets Codex
V(ar)ᵖᵃˡ		Variants in fragments with Palestinian pointing
Varˢ	Vˢ	Variants in Strack, *Grammatik*
V(ar)ᵂ		Variants in Wickes
	Vrs	All or most of the versions
c ᵃˢᵗ	c ᵃˢᵗ	with asterisk
c ᵒᵇ	c ᵒᵇ	with obelos
conj		conjecture
dittogr	dttg	dittography
gl(oss)	gl	gloss
haplogr	hpgr	haplography
Hex, hex		Hexapla, Hexaplaric
homoeoarct	homark	homoioarcton
homoeotel	homtel	homoioteleuton

Here are some helpful notes concerning some Septuagint (LXX) manuscripts:

Papyri—These are the oldest witnesses to the text, dating to the seventh century and earlier:

> **Papyrus 967-968**: third century witness to the Old Greek text of Daniel
>
> **Rylands Papyrus Greek 458**: second century B.C. (hence, pre-Christian) copy of the LXX, containing Deuteronomy 23:24-24:3; 25:1-3; 26:12, 17-19; 28:31-33.
>
> **Papyrus Fouad 266**: first or second century B.C. manuscript, containing parts of Deuteronomy 18, 20, 24-27, and 31.
>
> **Dead Sea Scroll** fragments of Exodus 28, Leviticus 2-5, 26, and Numbers

3, 4, dating to the turn of the era.

Uncials—Fourth to tenth century manuscripts written in all capital (uncial) letters.

Codex Vaticanus (B): fourth century manuscript, inferior in Deuteronomy and Chronicles, and more like Origen's Hexaplaric recension than the Old Greek in Isaiah.

Codex Sinaiticus (or S): fourth century manuscript, much like Vaticanus but lacking most of the Pentateuch.

Codex Alexandrinus (A): fifth century manuscript, containing most of the book of Genesis, but heavily influenced by the Hexapla in some books.

Codex Bodleianus (I): ninth century manuscript of the Psalms with marginal inserts from Aquila, Symmachus, and Theodotion, and from the Hexapla's Quinta (fifth) and Septima (seventh) columns. (See the discussion above under the heading "Sources.")

Codex Marchalianus (Q): sixth century manuscript of the minor prophets, replete with marginal notes from Aquila, Symmachus, and Theodotion, and diacritical symbols from the Hexapla.

Codex Washingtonianus (W): latter third century manuscript of the minor prophets that appears related to the Kaige.

Minuscules

Although these are the latest manuscripts (written in all lower case letters), dating from the ninth century and later, they are copies (or copies of copies) of very old manuscripts. So "while the manuscripts b, o c2, and e3 come from the tenth-fourteenth centuries, they are our only witnesses to the Lucianic recension for Samuel and Kings which was made in the fourth century!" (Klein, *Textual Criticism of the Old Testament*, pp. 56, 57). Archaeologists and scholars have recovered more than 1,500 minuscule documents to date.

New Testament—Unless you know whether the texts and witnesses that support the various readings in your passage are either Alexandrian, Caesarean, Western, or Byzantine, you cannot properly evaluate the accuracy of your text. Here is a table of principal texts and witnesses arranged under five biblical classifications: (1) Gospels, (2) Acts, (3) General (Catholic) Epistles, (4) Paul and Hebrews, and (5) Revelation. Entries in each of the four categories are, in order, the chief (a) papyrus, (b) uncial, and (c) minuscule texts (if any); then the witness of any (d) versions, or (e) Fathers.

(1) Gospels

Alexandrian

p1, p3, p4, p5, p7, p19, p22, p28, p35, p37, p39, p52, p53, p62, p64/67, p66, p69, p70, p71, p75, p77, p80, p82, p86

$\aleph$, B, C, L, Q, T, W Luke 1-8:12; John, Z, Δ, Ξ, Ψ, 054, 059, 060, 071, 0162 20, 33, 164, 215, 376, 579, 718, 850, 892, 1241, 1342 (Mark)

Coptic-Boharic, Coptic-Sahidic

Athanasius of Alexandria, Cyril of Alexandria, Origen

Caesarean

p45

θ, W (Mark 5ff), N, O, Σ, Φ

fam 1, fam 13, 28, 565, 700, 157, 1071, 1604

Gregorian, Armenian, Syriac-Palestinian

Eusebius, Cyril of Jerusalem, Origen

Western
p25
D, W (Mark 1-5) 0171
Old Latin (especially Italian e, k), Syriac-Sinaitic, Syriac-Curetonian
Tertullian, Ireneaus, Clement of Alexandria, Cyprian, Augustine

(2) Acts

Alexandrian
p8, p50
ℵ, A, B, C, Ψ, 048, 076, 096, 0189
6, 33, 81, 104, 326, 1175
Coptic-Boharic, Coptic-Sahidic
Athanasius of Alexandria, Cyril of Alexandria, Clement of Alexandria, Origen

Caesarean
p45
I
1
Cyril of Jerusalem

Western
p29, p38, p41, p48
D, E. 066
257, 440, 614, 913, 1108, 1245, 1518, 1611, 1739, 2138, 2298
Old Latin, Syriac-Harklensis (variant reading in the margin)

Byzantine
H, L, S, P
Most minuscules
Gothic later versions
Later Fathers

(3) General (Catholic) Epistles

Alexandrian
p9, p20, p23, p72, p74, p78
ℵ, A, B. C, P, Ψ, 048, 056, 0142, 0156, 0173
33, 81, 104, 323, 326, 424, 1175, 1739, 2298
Coptic-Boharic, Coptic-Sahidic
Athanasius of Alexandria, Cyril of Alexandria, Clement of Alexandria, Origen

Western
p38
D, E
Old Latin, Syriac-Harklensis (variant readings in the margin)
Ireneaus, Tertullian, Cyprian, Augustine, Epiphanius

Byzantine
p54
H, K, L, S, 0206
42, 398
Most other minuscules
Gothic, later versions
Later Fathers

(4) Paul and Hebrews

Alexandrian
p10, p12, p13, p15, p16, p17, p26, p27, p30, p32, p40, p46, p49, p51, p65, p87
ℵ, A, B, C, H, I, M, P, Ψ, 048, 081, 088, 0172, 0220
6, 33, 81, 104, 326, 424, 1175, 1739, 1908
Coptic-Boharic, Coptic-Sahidic
Western
D, E, F, G, 048 (Titus, Timothy, Philemon)
88, 181, 915, 917, 1836, 1898, 1912
Old Latin
Byzantine
K, L, 0176
Most other minuscules
Gothic, later versions
Later Fathers

(5) Revelation

Alexandrian
p18, p24, p47, p85
ℵ, A, C, P, 027, 0169
61, 69, 94, 241, 254, 1006, 1175, 1611, 1841, 1852, 2040, 2053, 2344, 2351
Western
F
Old Latin
Byzantine
046, 0163, 0169
82, 93, 429, 469, 808, 920, 2048
Most other minuscules
Gothic, later versions
Later Fathers

In recent years scholars have expressed uncertainty about whether or not there actually was a defined *Caesarean* text type. The Alands have proposed an alternative five-category system that the United Bible Societies' Greek New Testament Committee adopted to compile its editions of the Greek New Testament. The categories, in declining order of weight, are:

Alexandrian

Category I:	Manuscripts of a special quality that should always be considered in establishing the original text.
Category II:	Manuscripts of a special quality, distinguished from Category I by the presence of alien (especially Byzantine) influences. They are, nevertheless, very important for establishing the original text.

Independent

Category III:	Manuscripts of a distinctive character, though of varied origin, with considerable Byzantine influence. They are usually important for establishing the original text.

Western
  Category IV: Manuscripts of the D text that can help one trace other traditions.

Byzantine
  Category V: Manuscripts with a purely or predominantly Byzantine text or with a text too brief or colorless to be of any real importance for establishing the original text.

When you work with your passage, (1) list the variant readings and (2) enter each item of supporting evidence under its category according to the table. For example:

FIGURE 114

Book: Jude	Chapter/verse: 5			Bible Version: UBS4, TEV	
Readings	**Supporting Evidence**				
	I	II	III	IV	V
the Lord		C, L, 1175, 1292, 1409	436, 945, 1067, 1505, 1611, 1844, 2138		K
Lord					
God	1243	C²	1846		
Jesus	A, B, 33, 1241, 1739	81, 322	1881, 2298		
God, the Messiah	p72				
the Lord, Jesus		1735			

Compare this with the previous chart for Jude 5 on page 521. Notice: Although the nomenclature is different from the traditional four text system, the evidence is essentially weighed the same and leads to similar conclusions.

The following table charts most known Greek manuscripts according to their apparent dates (by Aland's conservative reckoning) on the left, and assigned categories across the top. (For an exhaustive catalogue of Greek manuscripts and witnesses, see Aland, *The Text of the New Testament*.)

	Category I	Category II	Category III	Category IV	Category V
2nd	ρ^{52}				
2nd/	ρ^{32}, ρ^{46},				
3rd	$\rho^{64\text{-}67}$, ρ^{66}, ρ^{77}, 0189				
3rd	ρ^{1}, ρ^{4}, ρ^{5}, (ρ^{9})			ρ^{29}, ρ^{48}	(ρ^{9}), (ρ^{12}), (ρ^{80})
	(ρ^{12}), ρ^{14}, ρ^{20}			$(\rho^{69}?)$	(0212)
	ρ^{22}, ρ^{23}, ρ^{27}, ρ^{28},				
	ρ^{30}, ρ^{39}, ρ^{40}, ρ^{45},				
	ρ^{47}, ρ^{49}, ρ^{53}, ρ^{65},				
	(ρ^{69}), ρ^{70}, ρ^{75},				
	(ρ^{80}), ρ^{87}, 0220				
3rd/	ρ^{13}, ρ^{16}, ρ^{18},			ρ^{38}, 0171	
4th	ρ^{37}, ρ^{72}, ρ^{78}, 0162				
4th	ρ^{10}, ρ^{24}, ρ^{35},	ρ^{6}, ρ^{8}, ρ^{17}	ρ^{88}, 058?, 0169		(ρ^{7}), (ρ^{25}), (0230)
	ℵ(01), B(03)	ρ^{62}, ρ^{71},	0188, 0206, 0207,		

	Category I	Category II	Category III	Category IV	Category V
		ρ^{81}, ρ^{86}, 0185	0221, 0228, 0231, 0242		
4th/ 5th	057	ρ^{19}, ρ^{51}, ρ^{57}, ρ^{82}, ρ^{85}, 0181, 0270	ρ^{21}, ρ^{50}, 059, 0160, 0176, 0214, 0219		
5th	A (02 exc. Evv.), 0254	ρ^{14}, C (04), I (016), T (029), 048, 077, 0172, 0173, 0175, 0201, 0240, 0244, 0274	A (02 Evv), W (032), 062, 068, 069, 0163, 0166, 0182, 0216, 0217, 0218, 0226, 0227, 0236, 0252, 0261	D^{ea} (05), (0165?)	Q (026), 061, (0174), (0264), (0267)
5th/ 6th		ρ^{56}, 071, 076, 088 0232, 0247	ρ^{54}, ρ^{63}, 072 0170, 0186, 0213		
6th		076, 088, 0232, 0247	0170, 0186, 0213		
6th		ρ^{33+58}, D^p (06) E^a (08), 073, 081, 085, 087, 089, 091, 093, (1 Pet), 094, 0184, 0223, 0225, 0245	ρ^{2}, ρ^{36}, ρ^{76}, ρ^{83} ρ^{84}, H^p (015), Z (035), Ξ (040), 060, 066, 067, 070, 078, 079, 082, 086, 0143, 0147, 0159, 0187, 0198, 0208, 0222, 0237, 0241, 0246, 0251, 0260, 0266		N (022), O (023) p^c (024), R (027), Σ (042), Φ (043), 064, 065, (080), 093 (Acts), 0253, (0263), 0265?
6th/ 7th	ρ^{26}	ρ^{43}, ρ^{44}, ρ^{55}, 083	ρ^{3}, 0164, 0199		
7th	p^{74}, 098	P^{11}, ρ^{31}, ρ^{34}, ρ^{68}, ρ^{79}, 0102, 0108, 0111, 0204	p^{59}, 096, 097, 099, 0106, 0107, 0109, 0145, 0167, 0183, 0200, 0209, 0210, 0239, 0259, 0262		(ρ^{73}), 0104, 0104, 0211, (0268)
7th/ 8th		ρ^{42}, ρ^{61} L^c (019),	p^{60} p^{41}, 095, 0126,		
8th	0118	0101, 0114, 0156, 0205, 0234	0127, 0146, 0148, 0161, 0229, 0233, 0238, 0250, 0256		E^e (07), 047, 054?, 0116, 0134
8th/ 9th		Ψ (044, Cath)	Ψ (044, exc. Cath)		
9th	33 (Acts-Paul)	Θ (038), 0155, 33	F^p (010), G^p (012) p^{apr} (025 exc.		F^e (09), G^e (011), H^e (013), H^a (014),

	Category I	Category II	Category III	Category IV	Category V
		(Evv), 892	Acts, Rev), (037), 050, 0122, 0128, 0130, 0131, 0132, 0150, 0269, 0271, 565		K^c (017), $K^φ$ (018), $L^φ$ (020), M (021), $p^{πr}$ (023 Acts, Rev), U (030), V (031), Y (034), Λ (039), Π (041) Ω (045), 049, 053?, 063, 0120, 0133, 0135, 0136?, 0151, 0197, 0248, 0255, 0257, 0272, 0273?, 461
9th/ 10th		1841 (Rev)	0115, 1424 (Mk)		1424 (exc. Mk), 1841 (exc. Rev)
10th	1739 (exc. Acts)	0177, 0243?, 1739 (Acts), 2329, 2464	051, 075, 0105, 0121a, 0121b, 0140, 0141, 0249, 307, 1582, 1836, 1845?, 1874 (Paul), 1875, 1891 (Acts), 1912, 2110, 2193, 2351		S (028), X (033), r (036), 046, 052, 0256, 0142, 1874 (exc. Paul), 1891 (exc. Acts)
11th	1243 (Cath), 2344 (Rev)	81, 323 (Cath), 1006 (Rev), 1175, 1854 (Rev), 2344 (Cath)	28, 104 (exc. Rev), 181 (exc. Rev), 323 (exc. Cath), 398 (Cath), 424, 431 (Acts, Cath), 436, 451 (Paul), 459 (Paul, 623, 700, 788, 945 (Acts, Cath), 1243 (exc. Cath), 1448 (Cath), 1505 (exc. Evv), 1838, 1846 (exc. 2138 (exc. Rev), 2147 (Cath), 2298, 2344 (exc. Cath, Rev), 2596		103, 104 (Rev), 398 (exc. Cath), 431 (Evv, Paul), 451 (exc. Paul), 459 (exc. Paul), 945 (Evv, Paul), 1006 (Evv), 1448 (exc. Cath), 1505 (Evv), 1846 (Acts), 1854, (exc. Rev), 2138 (Rev), 2147 (exc. Cath)
11th/ 12th		1735 (Cath)	256 (Paul), 1735 (exc. Cath), 1910		256 (exc. Paul)
12th	1241 (Cath)	36a (Acts), 1611 (Rev), 2050, 2127 (Paul)	1 (Evv), 36a (Cath), 88, 94? (Rev), 157, 180 (Acts), 326, 330 (Paul, 346, 378 (Cath), 543, 610 (Acts), 826, 828, 917 (Paul), 983, 1071, 1241, (exc. Acts, Cath), 1319 (Paul), 1359		1 (Acts-Paul), 180 (exc. Acts), 189 (Acts-Paul), 330 (exc. Paul), 378 (exc. Cath), 610 (Cath), 911, 917 (exc. Paul), 1010, 1241 (Acts), 1319 (exc. Paul), 1359 (exc. Cath),

	Category I	Category II	Category III	Category IV	Category V
			(Cath), 1542b (Mk), 1611 (exc. Rev), 1718, 1942, 2030, 2412 (Cath), 2541 (Cath), 2744		1542b? (Lk), 2127 (exc. Paul), 2412? (exc. Cath), 2541? (exc. Cath)
12th/13th			1573 (Paul)		1573 (exc. Paul)
13th	2053, 2062	1292 (Cath), 1852 (Cath)	6 (Cath, Paul), 13, 94 (exc. Paul, Rev), 180 (Acts), 206 (Cath), 218 (Cath, Paul), 263 (Paul), 365 (Paul), 441, 442, 579, 614, 720 (Cath), 915, 1292 (exc. Cath), 1398 (Paul), 1563?, 1642 (Acts), 1852 (exc. Cath, Rev), 2374 (Cath), 2400 (Paul), 2492 (Cath, Paul) 2516 (Paul), 2542, 2718		6 (Evvy, Acts), 94? (Paul), 180 (exc. Acts), 206 (Acts, Paul), 218 (Evv, Acts), 263 (exc. Paul), 365 (exc. Paul), 597, 720 (exc. Cath), 1251?, 1398 (exc. Paul), 1642 (exc. Acts), 1852 (Rev), 2374 (exc. Cath), 2400 (exc. Paul), 2492? (exc. Cath, Paul), 2516 (exc. Paul)
13th/14th		1342 (Mk)	1342 (Mk)		
14th	2427	1409 (Acts, Cath), 1506 (Paul), 1881	5 (Acts-Paul), 209 (Evv, Rev), 254 (Cath), 429 (exc. Paul, Rev), 453, 621, 629, 630, 1067, 1506 (Evv), 1523, 1524 (Cath), 1678, 1842, 1877 (Paul), 2005, 2197, 2200 (exc. Rev), 2377		5 (Evv), 189 (Evv), 209 (exc. Evv, Rev), 254 (exc. Cath), 429 (Paul), 1409 (Evv, Paul), 1524 (exc. Cath), 1877 (exc. Paul), 2200 (Rev)
14th/15th			2495		
15th		322 (Cath)	69 (exc. Acts), 205 (Evv, Rev), 209 (Rev), 322 (exc. Cath), 467 (Paul), 642 (Cath), 1751, 1844, 1959, 2523 (Paul), 2652 (Cath)		69 (Acts), 181 (Rev), 205 (Acts, Paul), 429 (Rev), 467? (exc. Paul), 642 (Acts, Paul), 886(?), 2523 (exc. Paul), 2652 (Paul)
16th			61 (Cath, Paul, Rev), 522 (Acts), 918 (Cath), 1704 (Acts), 1884		61 (Evv, Acts), 522 (exc. Acts, Cath), 918 (Paul), 1704 (exc. Acts)
16th/17th and later			849, 2544 (Paul)		2544 (Cath)

[1] For example, Col. 4:16; cf. 1 Thess. 5:27.

[2] "The circulation of all the New Testament writings began where they were first written—the genuine letters were the only exceptions (their circulation began from their earliest destinations). As copies multiplied, their circulation became steadily wider, like the ripples from a pebble cast into a pond. . . . Meanwhile every copy made from another copy repeated the same pattern of expansion, like another pebble cast into a pond making a new series of ripples. These rippling circles would intersect. Two manuscripts in a single place (each with its own range of textual peculiarities, depending on its distance from the original text) would influence each other, producing a textual mixture and starting a new pattern of ripples—a process which would be repeated continually" (Aland and Aland, p. 70).

[3] So Aland, Metzger, Greenlee, and Harrison, but E. C. Colwell attributes most to "theological and dogmatic reason" (*What Is the Best New Testament?* p. 53, note 22, quoted in Harrison, p. 85).

[4] The same holds true for scribes who were distracted, interrupted, or careless.

[5] Such wandering of the mind resulted in substitution of synonyms, variation in the sequence of words, transposition of letters, and assimilation of the wording from another similar passage (Metzger, p. 193). The inadvertent attraction of cases by neighboring words (for instance, nominative *epignosis* to the genitive *epignoseos* in Rom. 3:20) (Aland, p. 280).

[6] This accounts for the insertion of marginal notes into the actual text. (See Metzger, p. xv, and Harrison, pp. 84, 85.)

[7] Because of similar letters at either the beginning (homeoarcton) or the ending (homoeoteleuton) of a word.

[8] Either superfluous repetition (dittography) or failure to repeat (haplography) a word. Both are unintentional errors.

[9] This is called itacism and is a frequent error when one scribe took dictation from another.

[10] For instance, in Rev. 1:15 the genitive *pepuromenes* has been changed to either a dative or nominative. In Rev. 1:6 the indicative has been replaced with a participle (*poiesanti*) to agree with the string of participles in verse 5 (see Metzger, p. 197).

[11] So, for instance, "Jesus" could become "Jesus Christ" or "Lord Jesus" or "Lord Jesus Christ" or even "our Lord Jesus Christ" (Aland, p. 285). Matthew 9:13 appears to have been expanded from simply "For I came not to call the righteous, but sinners" to "For I came not to call the righteous, but sinners to repentance," because of the influence of Luke 5:32 (Metzger, p. 198).

[12] The church father Origen (c. A.D. 185-254) admitted to changing "Bethany" in John 1:28 to "Bethabara" (Harrison, p. 85; Metzger, p. 199). Concerned scribes changed "the prophet Isaiah" in Mark 1:2 to "the prophets" and replaced "after three days" in Mark 10:34 with "on the third day."

[13] Some scribes used Matt. 6:9-13 to fill out the Lord's prayer in Luke 11:2-4 (J. Harold Greenlee, *Introduction to New Testament Criticism*, p. 67).

[14] Some scribes decided to change the references to Joseph and Mary in Luke 2 in order to safeguard the doctrine of Christ's virgin birth. In verses 41 and 43 they replaced the words "his parents" with "Joseph and Mary," and in verses 33 and 48 they either substituted the name "Joseph" for "father" or left out "father" altogether (Metzger, pp. 202, 203).

[15] An example of this technique, which is called conflation, is found in some later versions of Luke 24:53. Some early manuscripts say that the disciples "were continually in the temple *blessing* God," whereas others insist that they "were continually in the temple *praising* God." Eventually some scribes "put the two together and so they invented the reading, 'were continually in the temple, *praising and blessing* God'" (Metzger, p. 200).

[16] Such as Alexandria, Antioch, Constantinople, Carthage, or Rome.

[17] These were professional copying houses that later mass-produced copies and overpowered the textual influence(s) of individual copyists. They employed professional scribes to produce a large number of manuscripts at a time, usually from a single model text.

[18] This method generated one copy at a time, limiting both the number and influence of the manuscripts it produced.

[19] The "early text," the text prior to the third and fourth centuries A.D., by and large reflected the peculiarities of individual copyists (Aland, p. 64).

[20] c. A.D. 260-303—the period following the persecutions of Decius and Valerian.

[21] It lasted 10 years in the West and longer in the East.

[22] The text developed through the influence of the powerful (thanks to the effective centralization of its patriarchs) scriptorium at Alexandria, Egypt (Aland, p. 56). Metzger says that "it is widely agreed that the Alexandrian text was prepared by skillful editors, trained in the scholarly traditions of Alexandria" (p. 215).

[23] An eastern text dated from the early third century and attested by the Chester Beatty Papyrus p45. (Metzger, pp. xix, xx).

[24] Caesarea was the cultural and ecclesiastical center of the region (Aland, p. 66).

[25] "Preserved in p45, W (in Mark 5:31-16:20), fam. 1, fam. 13, 28, and many Greek lectionaries" (Metzger, p. 215).

[26] The form proper is found in Theta, 565, and 700, many of the citations of Origen and Eusebius, and the Old Armenian and Old Georgian versions *(ibid.,* p. 215).

[27] "Only the reading which best satisfies the requirements of both external and internal criteria can be original" (Aland, p. 275).

[28] "Criticism of the text must always begin from the evidence of manuscript tradition and only afterward turn to a consideration of internal criteria" *(ibid.).*

[29] "Internal criteria can never be the sole basis for a critical decision, especially when they stand in opposition to the external evidence" *(ibid.).*

CHAPTER 14

HOW DID WE GET THE NEW TESTAMENT?

Before He ascended to God's right hand, Jesus entrusted His apostles with the task of guarding the early church from error. Through them He planned to provide the first congregations with a "living voice of authority as to what was and what was not the gospel" (Harry R. Boer, *A Short History of the Early Church*, p. 71) despite His physical absence. So He appointed apostles to "deliver"[1] what they had "received" from Him (see 1 Cor. 11:2, 23; 15:1, 3; Gal. 1:12) to the churches and to charge the saints to keep this "tradition"[2] handed down from Christ, which they had "received" from the apostles (see Gal. 1:9; Phil. 4:9; 1 Thess. 2:13; 4:1; 2 Thess. 3:6).

Introduction

John says that Christ expected these apostolic eyewitnesses (see John 15:27; 2 Peter 1:16; 1 John 1:1-4) to testify about Him in collaboration with the Spirit of Truth (see John 14:17; 15:26, 27; cf. 2 Peter 1:20, 21), whom the Father had commissioned to remind the world of Him and everything He said during His earthly ministry (see John 14:26; 15:26). In this way they handed down the curriculum for discipling the nations[3] and laid the foundation upon which Christ intended to build His church both during and after the apostolic period (see Eph. 2:20; John 17:20, 21; cf. 2 Peter 1:19). The apostle Peter said this very thing when he explained to his readers: "I think it is right to refresh your memory as long as I live in the tent of this body. . . . And . . . after my departure . . ." (2 Peter 1:12-15, NIV; "departure" is a symbol or maybe a euphemism for death).

Death may have silenced the living voice of Peter and the other apostles, but their teaching "lived on in spoken and in written tradition" *(ibid.)* as an aid to the church in its search for a clear standard of authority in their absence. "In the case of the authority of bishops, the standard was their relationship to the apostles by lawful ordination. In the case of the authority of sacred writings, the standard was apostolic authorship or authorship by a writer closely related to one of the apostles" *(ibid., p. 73)*.

Although the church naturally believed that the men who had been with Jesus "from the beginning" of His public ministry (John 15:27 cf. Acts 1:21 22) could produce the most authentic presentations of Christ, it still took her nearly four centuries to sanction the collection of 27 books, which we have to this day. The church did not create the official canon (the collection of sacred writings by which truth is measured); she confirmed it. The final collection did not come as the result of any official announcement either by a single church leader or any ecclesiastical synod.

Instead, any "official declarations merely confirmed that the church had long accepted these books as God's Word" *(ibid.)*.

Because the church recognized that Christ continued the work of salvation already begun in the Old Testament, she also considered herself the end-time Messianic Israel—God's true covenant people. Tracing her heritage to the Old Testament, she saw herself as the rightful owner and interpreter of God's Word (see Acts 4:23-30) and appropriated the Bible used by Jews all around the Greek-speaking world (the Septuagint, or LXX, translation of the Old Testament) for herself.

In so doing, the church also assumed the Jewish doctrine of divine inspiration *(The Seventh-day Adventist Bible Commentary* [SDABC], vol. 5, p. 124). Convinced that the Spirit behind Old Testament prophecy also generated the gospel (see 1 Peter 1:10-12), she searched for a standard from a spiritual perspective and gradually recognized which works the Spirit inspired and which it did not *(ibid.,* p. 132). In a sense, then, "both the writing of the books of the New Testament and their acceptance by the church took place under the guidance of the Holy Spirit' (Boer, p. 73).

Factors Affecting the New Testament Canon

The early church considered the teachings of Jesus, handed down from Him through His apostles, on the same inspired level as the sayings of the Old Testament. Peter indicated this in his second epistle concerning apostles in general (2 Peter 3:2) and Paul in particular (2 Peter 3:15, 16).

Luke knew of several secondhand attempts to draw up a faithful account of the way Christ and His work had fulfilled Old Testament prophecy according to apostolic tradition (Luke 1:1-4). Satisfied that this method produced authoritative results, Luke undertook what amounts to forming a primitive Gospel canon, carefully sifting through and organizing all the available material about Jesus into a single document for the purpose of strengthening converts in the faith (verse 4; cf. Matt. 28:20).

Unfortunately the orthodox were not the only ones seeking a clear-cut church standard from apostolic tradition. The heretic Marcion separated himself from the mainline church at Rome in A.D. 144 and soon drafted his own New Testament canon (J.N.D. Kelly, *Early Christian Doctrines*, p. 57). Unable to reconcile the God of the Old Testament with the God of Jesus Christ, Marcion rejected most of today's canon, approving only Luke's gospel and 10 of Paul's epistles, less any passages "infected with a Jewish [Old Testament] outlook" *(ibid.)*.

Marcion's action, along with quotations by various church fathers,[4] seems to suggest that the early Christian community already recognized the authority of certain books. Although no official collection of Christian writings existed at the time, Marcion's abridged list did force the church "to take a stand with regard to what books could justly claim the status of Scripture " (*SDABC*, vol. 5, p. 126), so that by A. D. 150 an apologete like Justin Martyr wrote with high regard for all four canonical Gospels (First *Apology* 66; 67; *Dialogue With Trypho* 103; 106), and his disciple Tatian combined them into a harmony called the *Diatessaron*.[5]

In A.D. 156 Montanus, a former pagan priest from Phrygia, began a movement that emphasized ecstatic experiences in the Spirit—a throwback to the wild, prophetic religion from which he had come. He taught that as the Old Testament was the age of the Father and the New Testament was that of the Son, so the era inaugurated at Christ's ascension is the age of the Paraclete, who spoke through the prophet Montanus and the two women who had abandoned their husbands to help him (Boer, p. 63).

About the same time, Valentinus of Alexandria, the most articulate spokesperson for another heresy—Gnosticism—did his best to blend Christianity with Greek and Oriental ideas. Gnostics claimed access to secret, esoteric knowledge of God that was unavailable through normal channels.

Development of the New Testament Canon

With Montanus and Marcion threatening to dilute the apostolic tradition with a flood of additional "revelation," the church responded. As a result, a definite collection of sacred books based on apostolic tradition appeared around the end of the second century.

An Italian scholar named Ludovico Muratori discovered the earliest known catalogue of New Testament books. In 1740 he found the fragment of an ancient Western manuscript in the library of a monastery at Milan. Written about A.D. 170, it lists certain books fit for reading at public worship and also others that are not. Its author recognized the whole New Testament except for Hebrews, James, the two Petrine epistles, and 3 John. He also included the Apocalypse of Peter, endorsed the Shepherd of Hermas for reading only, and branded the Marcionite and Gnostic books as unfit (Kelly, p. 59).

Prominent church fathers contributed their witness to the emerging canon. Irenaeus of Lyons, for example, recognized the four Gospels, but he ignored[6] the books of Hebrews, James, 2 Peter, 3 John, and Jude, while granting Hermas' Shepherd canonical status (*Against Heresies* 3. 11. 8). Tertullian of Carthage defended the four Gospels against Marcion and recognized 13 of Paul's epistles plus the book of Acts. Although he quoted from Hebrews, he denied it a place in the canon, thinking that Barnabas, not Paul, had written it.

Since the Eastern church did not distinguish between apostolic and nonapostolic writings, one of its eminent representatives, "Clement of Alexandria . . . showed a more liberal attitude toward the sacred writings than was common in the west" (*SDABC*, vol. 5, p. 127). So in addition to the four canonical Gospels, he also quoted (as somewhat lesser authorities) the apocryphal[7] gospels of the Hebrews and the Egyptians, 14 of Paul's books,[8] 1 Peter, 1 and 2 John, Jude, Acts, and Revelation— plus the apocryphal Epistle of Barnabas and the Apocalypse[9] of Peter, with assorted other noncanonical writings already rejected in the Western church, as attested by Tertullian and the Muratorian Fragment (see *SDABC*, vol. 5, pp. 127, 131).

By the end of the second century some in the West still doubted James, 2 Peter, 3 John, and Hebrews, while the East felt free to use certain apocryphal writings. The principle of apostolicity helped the church (1) recognize true canonical books, (2) ultimately reject books that lacked this indispensable stamp (for instance, the Didache, the Shepherd of Hermas, and the Apocalypse of Peter), and (3) eventually accept the books of Hebrews, James, 2 Peter, 2 and 3 John, Jude, and Revelation.

In addition, however, the church also used the content of a book to distinguish between canonical and extracanonical writings. This touch-and-go process called for painstaking "evaluation of a book in terms of its inner consistency, its agreement with the rest of Scripture, and its conformity with Christian experience" (*ibid.*, p. 132). This supplementary principle complemented apostolicity so that the church could rightfully reject even those books that claimed apostolic authorship while containing heretical elements—especially the Gnostic gospels, epistles, and apocalypses.

At the turn of the third century the West had arrived at a fairly fixed New Testament canon. Because it was a disciplined church with relatively few scholars, the canon developed more swiftly there than in the East. Only 2 Peter, James, 3 John, and Hebrews awaited full recognition and a handful of apocrypha, final rejection.

In the East, however, theologians debated the canonicity of Revelation. When Origen[10] took the perennial orthodox position and endorsed the book, some of his students attacked it. One in particular, Dionysius, bishop of Alexandria, led a movement there to disprove Revelation's apostolic authorship, "because its vivid picture of the reality of the judgment and the heavenly kingdom did not agree with their allegorical and spiritualized theology" *(ibid.,* p. 129).

In A.D. 325 the noted church historian, Eusebius, divided the books under consideration for canonicity into three classes. First he wrote of the "recognized" books (the four Gospels; Acts; 14 Pauline Epistles, including Hebrews; 1 John; 1 Peter; and Revelation). Then there were the "disputed" books, which he subdivided into two groups: those known to most[11] Christians (James, Jude, 2 Peter, 2 and 3 John), and those that were not genuine[12] (the Acts of Paul, the Shepherd of Hermas, the Apocalypse of Peter, the Epistle of Barnabas, and the Didache). The final class of "absurd and impious" writings included such Gnostic works as the Gospels of Peter, Thomas, and Matthias *(Ecclesiastical History* 3. 25). If we combine Eusebius' recognized books with the disputed books "known to most," we have the 27-book collection that we today call the New Testament.

In A.D. 367 Anthanasius of Alexandria issued his 39th Festal (Easter) Letter, in which he endorsed the same 27 books, while suggesting that the apocryphal books of the Didache and Shepherd of Hermas might prove useful in preparing candidates for baptism (see *SDABC,* vol. 5, pp. 129, 130). Under the influence of Eastern theology, the Latin fathers in the West gradually acknowledged the Pauline authorship of Hebrews. Eventually, its leaders (for example, Jerome, Hilary of Poitiers, Lucifer of Cagliari, Vigilius of Thapsus, Ambrose, and Augustine) accepted Hebrews as canonical—a "trend . . . legalized at the synod of Rome in A.D. 382" *(ibid.,* p. 131). Two subsequent synods, held in Hippo Regius (A.D. 393) and Carthage (A.D. 397) under Augustine's leadership, made the canon of 27 books—including Hebrews—official. By and large, the church in both the East and West followed the African example, "although the process was not everywhere complete until at least a century and a half later" (Kelly, p. 60).

---

[1] The Greek verb is *paradidonai,* which means to hand down or to pass along.

[2] "Tradition" translates the noun *paradosis.*

[3] According to Matt. 28:19, 20, Christ commissioned His followers to make disciples by baptizing converts and training them *"to obey everything I have commanded you."* The apostolic tradition provided the material for this training program.

[4] Including Clement of Rome, Ignatius of Antioch, and Polycarp of Smyrna.

[5] The word literally means "through four," the standard Gospel format circulated in the Syriac-speaking churches during the next two centuries. Influenced perhaps by his vegetarian principles (he belonged to the Encratites, a Syrian sect that avoided flesh foods), Tatian changed John the Baptist's diet from "locusts" to "milk and honey" (Mark 1:6).

[6] It is uncertain whether this was intentional or otherwise.

[7] These are certain writings that derive their name from the Greek word which carries the idea of something hidden or secret. Heretical authors tried to pass off these esoteric writings as genuine to the church, as though they had the endorsement of Christ or the apostles. They answered the public demand for additional information concerning either Christ's life or apostolic activities in the form of sayings slanted to the author's heretical views, yet purportedly these sayings come from the lips of either Jesus or some other influential New Testament figure (see Harrison, pp. 121-129).

[8] The Eastern church accepted Hebrews as authentically Pauline without hesitation.

[9] Apocalypses are writings born of suffering and persecution but having a happy eschatological ending. In this case, the third-century Apocalypse of Peter uses Jesus' crucifixion and humiliation "as a model for understanding early Christian history in which a faithful Gnostic remnant is oppressed by those who name themselves bishop and also deacons" (James Brashler, "Apocalypse of Peter," *The Nag Hammadi Library*, ed. James N. Robinson, p. 339).

[10] Origen was the Father who became the first great theologian of the church. Born and educated in Alexandria, ordained in Palestine, and a guest in several cities from A.D. 230 on, he died during the Decian persecution in A.D. 254. His students served as bishops for dioceses throughout the East (see Kurt Aland and Barbara Aland, *The Text of the New Testament*, pp. 65ff).

[11] That is, those held in a favorable light.

[12] That is, those held in an unfavorable light.

CHAPTER 15

WHERE DID MATTHEW, MARK, AND LUKE GET THEIR GOSPELS?

I t does not take long. Some people can tell after only one reading: all Gospels are not alike. First, they usually notice that John's Gospel stands out from the rest. Its distinctive structure and content set it apart in a class of its own. Second, they cannot help seeing how the other three Gospels resemble one another.

Introduction

Scholars call Matthew, Mark, and Luke the Synoptic[1] Gospels because of their remarkably similar structure and scope. There are, however, also striking differences between them, and scholars since the early days of the church have tried to explain how canonical accounts of Christ's life can be so much alike, yet so different. "The Synoptic problem, then, has to do with the mutual relations of these accounts. It takes no notice of the Fourth Gospel" (Everett F. Harrison, *Introduction to the New Testament*, rev. ed., p. 142).

The Synoptic Problem

Attempts at solving this Synoptic problem shifted during the eighteenth century from a concern with explaining the differences to accounting for the similarities (*ibid.*). These agreements are not identical, but they are close enough to consider them points of contact between the Synoptic trio. B. F. Westcott's overview (*An Introduction to the Study of the Gospels*, 5th ed., p. 191) reduces the situation to percentages.

FIGURE 115

Gospel	Peculiarities	Similarities
Mark	7	93
Matthew	42	58
Luke	59	41
John	92	8

Notice that Mark has the least unique material, while John has virtually nothing in common with the other three Gospels. If we discount the so-called long ending for Mark (16:9-20), "scarcely 30 verses remain that are truly unique . . . 1:1; 2:27; 3:20, 21; 4:26-29; 7:2-4; 3:2-37; 8:22-26; 9:29, 48, 49; 14:51, 52" (Harrison, p. 143).

These statistics could support either the idea that Matthew and Luke drew substantial amounts of material from Mark, or that Mark relied on Matthew and Luke for the bulk of his subject matter. The church fathers considered Matthew the source document from which Luke and Mark derived their material. Griesbach said that Mark depended on both Matthew and Luke. Scholars during the past century and a half, however, lean toward Mark as the source document.

But if that is true, then why did Matthew and Luke overlook some important details in Mark's gospel?[2] And why do Mark's narratives "tend to be somewhat longer than the parallels in the other Synoptics" (Harrison, p. 143)? Is this not strong evidence that he enlarged on their briefer accounts, rather than the other way around? Where did Matthew get nearly one third of his unique material? Why did he share about 200 of his verses exclusively with Luke? Why are Luke's versions of the nativity, parables, and the passion so much lengthier than those of Matthew or Mark?

Most scholars, working from the presupposition that the New Testament makes sense only against its first-century situation, launched a campaign to reconstruct the New Testament historical background, hoping that this would lead to some answers. But it was inevitable that their critical search would lead to a full-scale inquiry into the origins of apostolic material (Donald Guthrie et al., *Biblical Criticism: Historical, Literary, and Textual*, p. 98).

Approaches to the Problem

Two schools of Gospel research have dominated the past 150 years. "The earlier stages of this investigation involved the literary analysis of the written Gospels. At the close of World War I attention shifted to the preliterary stages of the Gospels, and what is called form criticism was applied to the units of tradition about Jesus that had circulated by word of mouth before they were incorporated in written Gospels" (Bruce Metzger, *The New Testament: Its Background, Growth and Content*, pp. 79, 80).

Any expedition into Gospel origins is bound to employ the explorer's views on inspiration. A great many Christians, for example, accept the prophetic model[3] as the only valid one for inspiration. These individuals have a hard time dealing with the Lucan model (see George E. Rice, *Luke a Plagiarist?*), in which a genuinely inspired person assembles and arranges a canonical Gospel from available sources, albeit under divine guidance.

"Such an understanding of prophecy, and of the prophet as the model for understanding the inspiration of Scripture, continued its influence in the church through the Middle Ages and into the period of the Reformation. . . . This view of inspiration continues to dominate the thinking of the conservative Christian scholars of our time, and is probably also the model assumed by most people who are untrained in theology" (Paul Achtemeier, *The Inspiration of Scripture: Problems and Proposals*, p. 30).

Literary Criticism—Several source theories have gained support in recent years. The idea that the Synoptists made use of each other's documents—immediate dependence (Harrison, p. 145)—accounts for material common but not unique to their Gospels. Another theory, which proposes that all three Synoptists drew their material from the same mythical, primitive document, also fails to account for differences—the so-called *Urevangelium* or "ancestor Gospel" theory *(ibid.)*. Schleiermacher suggested that Jesus' sayings and deeds were preserved in fragments. What the Synoptists drew from the same fragments is common to all; what they derived from different fragments is not. While this suggestion seems to explain the existence of contextual similarities and differences, this "fragmentary theory" reduces structural agreement to a coincidence *(ibid.,* p. 146).

The most popular of all source theories has to be the revolutionary two-document hypothesis, which looks toward Mark as the document from which the Synoptists derived material in common with Mark, and an undetermined source labeled "Q,"[4] responsible for material that is not. Proponents of this scheme point to various structural, stylistic, and linguistic features for support. (See Metzger, *The New Testament: Its Background, Growth, and Contents,* pp. 81-83 for a more thorough discussion.)

For example, the other two Synoptists seem to depend structurally on Mark. Whenever one offers a sequence different from Mark, the other agrees with Mark, and the other two never agree in sequence against Mark. Since they offer a more polished style and language, it is easier to believe that Matthew and Luke improved on Mark than the reverse, when both of them deleted troublesome passages in their parallel accounts,[5] softened Mark's blunt remarks concerning church leaders,[6] revised any questionable statements about Jesus,[7] intensified those that magnify Christ,[8] and display a more advanced theology than Mark's.

"For example, in the parable of the wicked tenants, according to Mark 12:8, when the owner of the vineyard sent his son to the vineyard to get some of the fruit, the tenants 'took him and killed him, and cast him out of the vineyard.' Matthew and Luke, however, finding in the parable a parallel to what happened to Jesus when He was crucified *outside* the city walls, alter the sequence of clauses so to read, 'they cast him out of the vineyard and killed him' (Matt. 21:39; Luke 20:15)" (Metzger, pp. 82, 83).

The rest of Matthew and Mark is supposed to be the result of a theoretical document called Q. Although some literary critics believe that Q circulated in oral form, the majority of them "hold that it was reduced to writing, perhaps in Aramaic and then in Greek, before it was utilized by Matthew and Luke" *(ibid.,* p. 83).[9]

Literary critics have reviewed, revised, and refined this basic two-document theory. Vincent Taylor, and especially B. H. Streeter, advanced the idea that Luke wrote his gospel in stages. The original draft[10] came as a result of Luke combining his unique material[11] with "Q." Later on, after coming upon Mark's document, he updated his own version and put out a larger edition that included significant portions from it.

Most New Testament scholars reject the concept of a "Proto-Luke" but accept the "four-document hypothesis."[12] It provides a broader base for the Synoptic tradition and elevates the status and reliability of non-Markan material (Harrison, p. 150).

Form Criticism—Shortly after World War I, dissatisfied source critics in Germany shifted their attention from an examination of *written* Gospel sources to an investigation of the *oral* traditions that preceded and precipitated them. In point of fact, Luke does allude to oral as well as written sources in his introduction.[13] Apparently the early church reminded its members of Christ's activities mainly by preaching rabbinic style. This method assured a high degree of fidelity as its practitioners first memorized then quoted the original material word for word.[14]

In addition, early Christians kept their accounts brief and to the point for accurate transmission. Form critics reduced these oral units[15] into literary forms that they labeled pronouncement stories,[16] miracle stories,[17] parables,[18] Jesus stories,[19] "I" sayings,[20] and "legends."[21]

Instead of concentrating their attention on literary concerns, form critics seek to reconstruct the conditions in the infant church in which the Gospels took shape (the *sitz-im-leben,* or life situation), because the Christian community frequently applied what it could remember of Christ to its current situation.

"There is no reason to doubt that a significant proportion of the words and events included in the Gospels are there not only because they figured in the life of Jesus, but also because they served some vital need in the life of the early church" (Metzger, p. 86).

In consideration of these factors, scholarship shifted its attention "to the practical interests and needs of the early church in which the gospel traditions circulated. It was now more fully appreciated that the history of Jesus was never viewed as a mere incident in the past; it was seen rather as a vital power always operative, challenging and controlling the lives of His followers in the present. This continued use of His words and deeds was bound to shape their telling and to bring out what was deep and rich in every event" (ibid., p. 85).

In a way reminiscent of rabbinic midrash, this oral tradition kept Christ's words and deeds from the past current and meaningful for His people.[22] But because the church leaders adapted these sayings for guidance in doctrinal, liturgical, and practical matters "they were liable in this way to a certain, or rather an uncertain, amount of modification" in order to bring out more clearly their meaning when applied to new situations (ibid., p. 86).

When the Synoptists compiled their Gospels, they chose material from the available traditions to meet the need of the target population they had in mind and "preserved, therefore, . . . not a photographic reproduction of the words and deeds of Jesus, but an interpretive portrait delineated in accord with the special needs of the early church" (ibid.).

On these grounds, hardcore form critics question the historicity of the Jesus portrayed in the Gospels. They suspect that the Christian community's attempts to reinterpret Christ's words and deeds led to distortion of their original meaning. And so these form critics reject most Gospel material as myth.

But three factors argue against this conclusion. First, the apostles and other eyewitnesses[23] mentioned in Luke 1:2 checked the spread of fantasy (see 2 Peter 1:16) rather than caused it. Second, the efficiency of rabbinical teaching methods would militate against distortion.[24] And finally, the Gospels developed in a community with a teachable spirit under divine guidance, in a church that walked "in the fear of the Lord and in the comfort of the Holy Ghost" (Acts 9:31).

As Metzger puts it: "The fact, for instance, that certain of Jesus' parables were recast in the retelling so as to deal more directly with new problems in the developing church, so far from supporting the opinion of some form critics that the early Christian communities invented a large part of the contents of the Gospels, points rather to the tenacity with which the church retained the words of Jesus and merely readapted them to meet new situations" (ibid., p. 87).

The fact that the church retained those sayings by which Jesus implied He would return shortly to establish His kingdom (see, for instance, Mark 9:1 and Matt. 10:23), despite increasing embarrassment over its delay in a mocking world, argue for the accuracy and integrity of the Gospel tradition.

Redaction Criticism—Since the close of World War II, the pendulum of research has swung away from preoccupation with the Synoptists as editors. Now biblical scholars concentrate on them as writers. In reaction against certain form critical extremists, scholars today focus on the Synoptic Gospels as *unified compositions*, each with its own emphasis and point of view, rather than a collection "made up of isolated units of tradition (stories, sayings, etc.), which have been put together in their present form either by the Evangelist or by the transmitters of the tradition, who precede the Gospels" (Christopher Rowland, *Christian Origins From Messianic Movement to Christian Religion*, p. 325).

Instead of zeroing in on the tradition common to all three Synoptics, redaction critics prefer to deal with what is unique to each one. And that is good. Unfortunately, because of its form critical roots, redaction criticism tends to operate from a skeptical point of view toward the historicity of Gospel materials. As a result, redaction critics treat the Gospel writers as theologians rather than historians. But as Donald Guthrie observes: "It is not a question, for example, of Luke's being a theologian or a historian but of his being a theologian as well as a historian" (p. 108).

Luke said that he had drawn up "an orderly account" (Luke 1:3), and most Christians have difficulty reconciling this with a Gospel supposedly developed from a thematic approach that ignores chronology. "When people come to realize that many of the events in Jesus' ministry have been moved out of their historical sequence, some begin to fear that perhaps the Gospels are not historically accurate. This is a needless fear. First of all, each event recorded by the Gospel writers did take place historically. Second, using historical events in connection with other historical happenings to establish a truth about Jesus or to illustrate a spiritual teaching He was presenting, does not make these events unhistorical, even if they are presented out of chronological sequence" (Rice, p. 25).

We must remember that the Synoptists as authors and theologians arranged historical material to address the special needs of their readers.[25] Whereas form critics set aside the work of the Gospel writers[26] in order to get at the units of tradition they chose, redaction critics recognize the need "to see what each evangelist has done with his sources by omission, addition, or alteration to suggest his theological as distinct from his literary concern" (Harrison, p. 162). They want to determine each Gospel component's literary contribution to the Synoptist's overall purpose, as well as to recapture its preliterary role in the early church.

Although redaction critics generally deny the historicity of Synoptic materials and proceed from a purely theological point of view, it is equally unwarranted "to regard the Gospels as a journalist's verbatim report of what happened yesterday. What the evangelists have preserved for us is not a photographic reproduction of all the words and deeds of Jesus, but something more like four interpretive portraits. Each of these portraits presents distinctive highlights of Jesus' person and work, and, taken together, the four provide a varied and balanced account of what Jesus said and did" (Metzger, p. 99).

The literary, form, and redaction critical disciplines can teach us a great deal about the Synoptics. Apparently the writers gathered historical data from reliable written and preliterary sources through reading, oral interviews, and community worship, where authorized spokespersons and teachers recalled and applied the words and deeds of Jesus to crises and everyday life.

Because Jesus taught in the Aramaic and Greek languages, the Christian community began the Gospel tradition by circulating bilingual accounts of His sayings and activities, by word of mouth. The presence of eyewitnesses, plus the highly successful rabbinic style of teaching prevented fabrication and assured accurate transmission in the tradition. Eventually the community translated everything into Greek—"sometimes literally, mostly, however, literary and interpretive, but generally bearing the stamp upon it, in one feature or another, of its Aramaic origin"

(Matthew Black, *An Aramaic Approach to the Gospels and Acts*, 2nd. ed., p. 206), though it is uncertain whether this happened orally or in writing.

Matthew and Luke probably used Mark's Gospel, and at least Luke depended on testimony from eyewitnesses plus ministers of the word. After the research stage they shaped their material to meet the needs of a certain target population. And this shaping reflected both their interests as authors and understanding as theologians. And all the while "the Spirit guided throughout the whole process. . . . God was working in and through these men to accomplish a special task which was vital to the success of His cause throughout the generations of time" (Rice, pp. 27, 28).

Rhetorical Criticism—In 1968 Old Testament scholar James Muilenberg coined the term *rhetorical criticism* to label a method of analyzing Scripture that he considered a supplement to form criticism. Form critics traditionally searched and reduced sources to an impersonal collection of typical ltierary forms, respresentative of their genre. Muilenberg contended that rhetorical critics search for what is unique and personal to the specific work and its author so as "to trace the movment [flow] of the writer's thought" (Richard N. Soulen, *Handbook of Biblical Criticism*, 2nd ed rev., p. 169).

Some scholars disagree with Muilenberg. Instead of a supplement or a separate discipline, they see rhetorical criticism as "the renewal of a proper but neglected aspect of the form critical method" *(ibid.)*. For example, form critics have generally ignored the thought and setting of the Gospel writers themselves. With their emphasis on the unique and personal, however, rhetorical critics have form critics reexamining "the relation of genre to setting, or oral to written traditions, of form to content, of the conventional or typical to the unique within the text" *(ibid., p. 72)*. Some form critics have already admitted that their assumptions are too general and that they need to take other distinctive factors into account besides the forms that words take if they are to properly analyze a text.

Rhetorical critics proceed from one literary unit to the next in order to map out structures and analyze contents for patterns. First, they determine each unit's opening and closing (inclusio) so as to capture each overall structure. Then they search for patterns of literary devices that occur with them—either conventional (parallelism, chiasmus, anaphora, epiphor, paranomasia, diatribe, irony, etc.) or unconventional (see James Muilenberg, "Form Criticism and Beyond," *Journal of Biblical Literature*, March 1969, pp. 1-18).

Matthew does, for example, distinctively weave his gospel around five great discourses, concluding each section with the words, "Now when Jesus had finished" (7:9b; 11:1; 13:53; 19:1; 26:1). These five pericopes (self-contained units or sections of Scripture) recall the five books of the Torah. As a result, Christ comes across as a new Moses who will lead God's people into the promises.

Mark, in point of fact, does move quickly from one episode in Jesus' life to the next, often (some 40 times) using the adverb "immediately." This rapid transition from one action scene to another emphasizes more what Christ did than what He said.

And Luke indeed emphasizes prayer, especially Jesus' praying before important occasions; for instance, His baptism (3:21; cf. 5:16; 6:12; 9:18, 28, 29; 11:1; 22:32, 41; 23:34, 46). In this way he presents Jesus in close contact with and in complete dependence upon His heavenly Father at crucial moments in His life and ministry.

Narrative Criticism—Although the historical-critical method has dominated biblical studies since the eighteenth century, it is not the last word in scriptural investigation. "Actually a conglomeration of approaches . . . [that seek] . . . to reconstruct the life and thought of biblical times through an objective, scientific analysis of biblical material . . . fail to take seriously the narrative character of the Gospels" (Mark Allan Powell, *What Is Narrative Crisitcism?* p. 2).

Source critics want to describe the persons or documents from which the gospels originated; *form* critics attempt to define the *Sitz-im-leben* or real life setting of the component traditions that make up the gospels; and *redaction* critics derive key information about the evangelists as editors and theologians from the way they chose and arranged the material in their Gospels. But each of these approaches is limited by an intense focus on the historical circumstances behind the Gospels and virtually ignores their literary character. Narrative critics, on the other hand, see the Gospels as "stories about Jesus, not compilations of miscellaneous data concerning Him. They are intended to be read from beginning to end, not dissected and examined to determine the relative value of individual passages" *(ibid., p. 2).*

Narrative critics are not out to uncover the process that produced the existing text but to study its finished form. Instead of dissecting the text, they are concerned with what holds it together. While the historical critic looks through the Gospels to catch a glimpse of the New Testament world, the narrative critic looks at the whole text to learn what can be gleaned from it. For them text is an end in itself, with a message for the reader from the author—not the final edition of "something that has evolved through sequential stages" *(ibid., p. 9),* which makes it possible to recapture its origins.

To the narrative critic, the Gospels are more than historical souces of material about Jesus and the early church—but narratives, literary compositions that "invite the reader to participate in the passage . . . and attempt to evoke a particular response" *(ibid., p. 2).* Instead of extracting "information about the ancient world, such as how people dressed, ate, married, and went to war . . . [they want to know] . . . What is the plot? How are characters developed? What effect does the story have on its readers and why does it have that effect?" *(ibid., p. 3).* They treat the text as "the middle component in an act of communication . . . [not] . . . the end product of a process of development" *(ibid., p. 9.)*

For the most part, narrative critics do not treat the Gospels like secular literature. They recognize the difference between them and ordinary books, and they have made important contributions to the field of biblical studies.

As a text-centered approach to Bible study narrative criticism encourages the interpreter to let the Bible explain itself and to make the most of socio-historical research. In effect, it has ruptured the historical-critical membrane that separates scholarship from the plain sense of Scripture. Because it deals with a text as is, narrative criticism also encourages Bible students to go ahead and examine the text, even though its historical origins remain uncertain. From a narrative-critical perspective, for example, you don't have to settle on a solution to the "Synoptic problem" before you can interpret Matthew's, Mark's and Luke's gospels.

Narrative-criticism also subjects texts to analysis that can either corroborate or call for reevaluation of the traditional findings of historical-criticism. Some narrative critics, for example, have advanced the idea that Mark presents the disciples in a negative light to arouse sympathy from his readers rather than a negative reaction toward them. As a result, scholars are beginning to reinvestigate perennial views of Mark's purpose for doing so.

On the whole, the effect of narrative criticism on the faith community has been positive and constructive. Students of the Bible can strengthen their expositions of

Scripture by asking questions about events, characters, and settings in the text from a narrative-critical perspective.

The following guidelines are adapted from Mark Allan Powell's *What Is Narrative Criticism,* pp. 103-105:

Events

1. What happens in this passage?
2. Does it mark a turning point, or does it logically carry on what has happened already?
3. Is it out of sequence? Is it sketchy or detailed? Is it unique, occasional, or repeated?
4. Is it the result of something that happened already, or the cause, direct or indirect, or something that happens afterward?
5. Is there evidence of conflict? How does it compare with conflict elsewhere in the narrative? Is it eventually resolved? Does this event help to develop and ultimately resolve the conflict?
6. What role does this event play in the overall story? What does it contribute to the plot as a whole?

Characters

1. Who appear in this episode? Do they appear elsewhere in the narrative? Do they respect a character group that fulfills a single role in the story?
2. Does the narrator tell us about the characters? Do they represent themselves, or are they presented through other characters? Is this consistent with the way we learn about these same characters elsewhere in the narrative?
3. Are the characters oriented toward truth or untruth? Is this consistent with their characterization elsewhere in the narrative?
4. What traits do these characters have? Are they derived, or the cause of other traits? Are they consistent with traits the characters exhibit elsewhere in the narrative? Do the characters have potentially conflicting traits, consistent and predictable traits, or a single trait with a superficial role in the story?
5. Is the reader likely to empathize either idealistically or realistically with any of these characters? What is the attitude of the narrator or leading character toward the characters? Will the reader regard the characters with sympathy or antipathy?

Setting

1. What are the time, location, and social settings of this episode? Are they unique or repeated elsewhere in the narrative? What do they contribute to the overall mood of the narrative?
2. How does the physical environment affect the actions of the characters in this episode? Through what sensory data do the characters describe their physical surroundings and is this typical for the narrative? Do any other of the physical features have symbolic connotations either here or elsewhere in the narrative? Is there evidence of paradox between connotations of protection or security, on the one hand, versus confinement on the other—or do they connote danger in one setting and freedom in another? Is there evidence of opposition by contrast (such as country and city, solitude and society, or land and sea)?
3. Does the episode mention the point in time, or the amount of time during which it occurs? Does it tell us the actual time or at what time it occurs (e.g., nighttime)? Does the kind of time suggest some special significance (e.g., nighttime

could suggest a desire for secrecy or a need to be enlightened)? Should what happens here be interpreted in terms of (a) mortal time measured by calendars, watches, clocks, and sundials; (b) monumental time, the broad sweep of time that both includes and transcends history; or (c) salvation history?

4. What is the cultural context for what happens in this episode? What do the characters or author assume the readers know about political institutions, class structures, economic systems, social customs, etc.? How does this information affect the interpretation of this particular episode within the context of the narrative as a whole?

Overall Interpretation

1. What rhetorical devices are used to report this episode? Is there any intentional symbolism or irony? What narrative patters are used in structuring this passage and its immediate context?

2. What does this episode, as understood within the context of the entire narrative, tell us about its author? What values, ideas, priorities, or preferences seem to govern the way in which this story is told?

3. What effect does the narrative seem to assume that this episode will have upon its readers? What elements of the narrative work to produce this effect?

---

[1] New Testament scholar J. J. Griesbach (1745-1813) coined the term from the compound Greek word *syn-opsis,* which means a seeing together.

[2] Compare Mark 9:14-29 with Matt. 17:14-20 and Luke 9:37-42.

[3] The prophetic model is based on the idea that genuinely inspired people get their words from God and no one else.

[4] The letter comes from the word "Quelle," which is German for source.

[5] For instance, both other Synoptists see a conflict with 1 Sam. 21:1-7 and so omit Mark's reference to Abiathar (Mark 2:26) from their parallels (Matt. 12:3, 4; Luke 6:3, 4).

[6] The church members grew to respect the apostles as "pillars of the church" (Gal. 2:9; cf. Eph. 2:20). Matthew omits accusations (see Mark 6:52), shameful (see Mark 9:33-35) and nonplussed behavior (see Mark 9:32), while Luke tones down Peter's cursing (see Mark 14:71) to irate denial (Luke 22:60) and drops the words "Get thee behind me, Satan!" (KJV) in his parallel to Mark 8:33.

[7] Only Mark reports that Jesus' friends thought He was beside Himself (Mark 3:21), emphasizes His human emotions (Mark 3:5; 6:6; 10:21) or humanity (Mark 1:45; 5:9, 30; 6:38, 48; 8:12; 9:16, 21, 33; 14:14; cf. their parallels).

[8] Mark refers to Jesus as Lord only once (11:3), whereas Luke does so 16 times and Matthew 19 times. Compare also "all who were sick" "and he healed many" (Mark 1:32, 34, RSV) with "They brought to him many . . . and he cast out the spirits with a word, and healed all who were sick" (Matt. 8:16, RSV). Matthew emphasizes the instantaneous nature of Christ's power with instant healing (Matt. 15:28; 17:18) and immediate withering for the fig tree (Matt. 21:19, 20), which Mark seems to suggest took a day (Mark 11:20, 21).

[9] Compare the work of Roman Catholic scholar Leo Vaganay and Pierson Parker (see Harrison, pp. 151, 152).

[10] Streeter called it "Proto-Luke" and said that it originally began with Luke 3:1.

[11] This was a Caesarean source that he labeled "L." Matthew's unique subject matter, he said, came from a Jerusalem source "M." "Q" is supposed to have originated in Antioch.

[12] See Archibald Hunter, *The Work and Words of Jesus,* rev. ed., for a thorough treatment of the Synoptic Gospels from this approach.

[13] In Luke 1:1-4 he includes himself among those who draw up Gospel accounts based on the testimony of eyewitnesses. Willard Swartley proposes that Luke's "ministers of the word" (*hyperetai*) were people "specially chosen to memorize the sermons, parables, and deeds of Jesus" (quoted by Rice, p. 22).

[14] Practitioners meticulously avoided making any alterations to the original material.

[15] That is, missionary preaching, sermons, liturgy, and catechetical instruction.

[16] Vincent Taylor used this term for Gospel units that feature controversy between Jesus and His antagonists (for instance, Matt. 17:24-27). After describing the situation, the story presents an objection

against Jesus and/or His followers, which is balanced against a rebuttal from Jesus, which is followed by a pronouncement or famous saying that drives home Christ's point. This saying later served as a principle of action for the primitive church in its conflict with the Jewish authorities (for example, verse 27).

[17] These are accounts of Christ as a wonder-worker that were kept brief so as to assure accurate transmission. They begin with the illness and condition of the sufferer, feature Jesus' wonder-working response, and climax with the saving effect of His power.

[18] Since God made both heaven and earth, Jesus illustrated or explained heavenly realities by "placing them alongside" (the root meaning of the Greek word for parable) familiar corresponding earthly ones.

[19] That is, passages that portray Jesus in a supernatural manner.

[20] That is, words of wisdom, prophecies, and legislation concerning such things as prayer, fasting, divorce, and forgiveness.

[21] That is, stories about the death, burial, and resurrection of Jesus, which some form critics, such as Schweitzer and Bultmann, consider to be virtually ahistorical.

[22] See the discussion on page 211 of this book regarding midrash and the New Testament.

[23] See footnote 13 and Swartley, pp. 28-31. Rice says that the word translated "delivered" (*paradosan*) "is derived from two words, *paradidomi* and *paralambano*, that had become technical terms in the New Testament for the transmission of oral teaching" (p. 23).

[24] According to Matt. 23:1-3 the scribes and Pharisees held a legitimate teaching office in Israel (handed down from Moses) to teach the commands, decrees, and laws of the Lord (see Deut. 6:1). This they did with such fidelity that Jesus said: "So you must obey them and do everything they tell you" (Matt. 23:3, NIV). Unfortunately, they lived by a code, that is, the oral tradition, which frequently contradicted and neutralized the spirit of God's law (see Matt. 15:1-9). So Jesus warned the people: "But do not do [that is, live by] what they do [that is, live by], for they do not practice what they preach" (23:3, NIV).

[25] Luke says that "it seemed good also to me to write an orderly account for you, most excellent Theophilus" (Luke 1:3, NIV). Clearly, "orderly" has something to do with the special needs of Theophilus, who had been exposed to oral and perhaps written traditions. (For the form critical perspective, see Vernon Neufeld, *The Earliest Christian Confessions*; Bruce Metzger, ed., *New Testament Tools and Studies*, vol. 5, pp. 7-10; and E. Earle Ellis, *Prophecy and Hermeneutic in Early Christianity*. For a more conservative approach see the way that Walter Kaiser, Jr., deals with "The 'Testimony Book' Hypothesis" in *The Uses of the Old Testament in the New*, pp. 10-13.)

[26] The Gospel writers supposedly merely wrote what was necessary to segue from one isolated unit to another and so give the appearance of one continuous account.

CHAPTER 16

BIBLICAL DATA FOR THE FOUR GOSPELS

The New Testament writers lived in the first century. As children of their times, they used the language and lived by the customs of the day. Since we are 19 centuries removed from their in-life-situation,[1] any examination of the New Testament requires a thorough investigation into the authorship, date, and purpose of writing, characteristics, and background that constitute its proper historical setting. Such research often demands that we evaluate conflicting internal and external evidence for the most compelling argument.

Introduction

Those who tend to doubt the authenticity and/or historicity of the New Testament documents generally favor external sources, but for those who regard the New Testament accounts as trustworthy, the self claims of the text carry the greatest weight. Although presuppositions may vary, it is important for liberals and conservatives alike to recognize that only when we explore these ancient writings in their biblical milieu is it possible to understand the text.

The Gospel According to Matthew

Authorship—The early church fathers unanimously supported the understanding that the apostle Matthew authored the Gospel bearing his name, although this Gospel itself claims nothing to that effect. Objections to this tradition proceed along two lines.

Some critical scholars contend that the author failed to write with the personal touch of an eyewitness, but Matthew apparently made a practice of removing local color—even when he borrowed from Mark. Perhaps he simply trimmed the fat, so to speak, to make room for deserving extra-Markan material.

Others wonder why an eyewitness like Matthew would depend so heavily on Mark. Some suggest that he agreed with what Mark said and how he expressed himself and so incorporated large segments of Mark's Gospel. Another ancient tradition insists that Mark derived the substance of his Gospel from Peter (see Irenaeus *Against Heresies* 3. 1. 2) so that Matthew actually depended on the apostolic leader when he relied on Mark's account.

Date and Place of Writing—Papias, the bishop of Hieropolis (*c.* A.D. 130-140) (Eusebius *Ecclesiastical History* 3. 39. 16), the church historian Eusebius Pamphyli (*ibid.* 5. 10. 3), and the Church Fathers Irenaeus (*Against Heresies* 3. 1. 1), Origen (*Ecclesiastical History* 6. 25. 4), and Jerome (De *Virus Illustribus* 3) all testify to a Semitic (that is, either Hebrew or Aramaic) original for Matthew, although they per-

362

sonally never worked with anything but Greek documents.

However, Jerome eventually admitted that he had confused Matthew's Gospel with the noncanonical Gospel of the Hebrews. Firsthand examination of the Greek of the Gospel of Matthew casts doubt on a Semitic original for various reasons: (1) the Greek of the Gospel of Mark accounts for most of Matthew; (2) the Septuagint is the chief source for quotations from the Old Testament that appear (a) in all three Synoptics and (b) in Matthew only,[2] and (3) the translation Greek in Matthew, which (a) uses the rare construction *men . . . de* (on the one hand . . . on the other) nearly 20 times in material from Q and (b) has an exceptionally high frequency of the genitive absolute.[3]

Nevertheless, both external and internal evidence argue for a Palestinian origin. The Gospel's Jewish flavor is unmistakable, and Matthew 5:43, unparalleled in the Old Testament, is similar to a statement found in the Dead Sea Scroll known as the *Manual of Discipline* (1Qs i. 4. 10). Although the church fathers favored Judea as the point of origin for Matthew's Gospel (see Harrison, p. 174), modern scholars trace Matthew back to the Syrian city of Antioch, because of its sizable Jewish community since the Seleucid heyday and its early knowledge of Matthew.[4]

Some scholars argue that such strong Jewish character demands an early date— around A.D. 50, when the church geared its evangelism to Jews and Jewish converts dominated its ranks (see Acts 11:19). But those who believe that Matthew depended on Mark have to date his Gospel later than that in order to give Mark time to circulate and gain recognition. Accordingly they see the Gospel according to Matthew written sometime between A.D. 70 and 80. They appeal to certain internal evidence to support their claims: (1) use of the supposedly late trinitarian baptismal formula in 28:19;[5] (2) the apparent influence of Jerusalem's fall in A.D. 70[6] on the Olivet Discourse; and (3) the sense that the church is already established and well-organized.

But the most convincing argument is the way that Matthew arranged his material, apparently to deal with an advanced state of tension between the Christian and Jewish communities of his day. Although Israel's religious leaders stoned Stephen to death in A.D. 34 and murdered James, the Lord's brother, at Jerusalem in A.D. 62, not until Christian residents abandoned Jerusalem just before its fall[7] did the Jews condemn Christians as a whole.

In the wake of this national tragedy, Rabbi Johanan ben Zakkai convened a council of Pharisaic scholars at Jamnia[8] to consolidate what remained of the shattered Jewish state and to lay the foundation for future rabbinic Judaism. The spread of subversive Christian teachings probably explains why a consensus arose among Jews for a distinctively Jewish canon over against the LXX, which Christian evangelists had used with so much success.

And so under the leadership of Rabban Gamaliel II, the rabbis instituted the *Birkat Ha-minim*, the twelfth benediction of 18 pronounced at the weekly synagogue service. This new addition to the benedictions required everyone present to recite together: "And let Christians and *minim* perish in a moment, let them be blotted out of the book of the living and let them not be written with the righteous" (W. D. Davies, *The Setting of the Sermon on the Mount*, p. 275).[9]

Destination and Purpose—Harrison suggests that Matthew may have contributed to this outbreak of hostility by insisting that the very Jesus who was hated by the Jewish leaders was indeed God's Messiah.[10] Writing probably to a predominantly Jewish audience, Matthew works hard to show that Jesus either directly or indirectly fulfilled the Old Testament prophecies. And so he traced Jesus back to Abraham

(Matt. 1:1-17), emphasizing Him as the Son of David (see Matt. 1:1, as an example); did not explain Jewish customs; and used Jewish terminology.[11]

But Matthew does not limit his message to Jews alone. He records the coming of *Gentile* magi to worship Jesus, God's anointed King of kings (2:1-12; cf. 1 Kings 4:21), Jesus' explanation that the sower's field "is the world" (Matt. 13:38), and the Great Commission to go to "all the world" (Mark 16:15). So Matthew intended his Jewish Gospel for people everywhere, and he shows his concern that *every* reader become *personally* acquainted with the Old Testament in order to understand the full significance of Jesus.

Indeed, Matthew wants to prevent any attempt to detach the Gospel from the Old Testament, because that would sever its biblical-historical-theological moorings, setting it hermeneutically adrift. His aim from the start is to prove that Jesus is the promised Messiah, and he does this by showing that the Old Testament is fulfilled Christologically, ecclesiologically, and eschatologically in the Person and work of Messiah Jesus. The heart of his argument is the way that Jesus recapitulates the history of national Israel in the significant events of His own life:

National Israel	**Jesus**
God's "son" (Hosea 11:1)	God's Son (Matt. 2:15)
Baptized at Red Sea (1 Cor. 10:1, 2)	Baptized in the Jordan (Matt. 3:13-17)
Rebaptized in Jordan (Joshua 4:14-17)	
Receives law at Mount Sinai, fails test, and wanders 40 years in wilderness	Passes 40-day wilderness test and goes to mount to give the law (Matt. 4:1-11; 5-7)
Stiff-necked and impotent	Obedient and powerful (Matt. 8-20)
Suffers, dies, raised from the dead, is born again, but it and following generations fail to bless all the families of earth, and go on to glory	Suffers, dies, raised from the dead in order to raise up through new birth a people in which all families shall be blessed and share His glory (Matt. 21-28)

Structure—Jesus does not replace the nation. Rather, Israel *continues* through Him as the final, eschatological branch in the elect family tree. A homegrown prophet, Jesus urged the nation to join Him and return to God's ways. When the nation resisted, He forged ahead on the road assigned to Israel—even when He had to go it alone.[12]

The result is that Christ, the Elect One, obtained exclusive rights to God's promises, and people need to unite with Him by baptism to enjoy those promises, as the nation once identified itself with Moses by baptism at the Red Sea. So it is that Matthew structures his Gospel around this Moses typology (see W. D. Davies, pp. 1-94), with five discourses by Jesus, recalling that Moses also had five books.

FIGURE 116

Birth	FIVE DISCOURSES					Last Supper Death Resurrection Commission
	1	2	3	4	5	
1:1-2:23	Sermon on the Mount	Commission Instruction of the 12	Kingdom Parables	Humility and Forgiveness	Woes and Olivet	26:2-28:20
Narrative	3:1-4:25	8:1-9:35	11:1-12:50	13:54-17:21	19:2-22:46	
Discourse	5:1-7:27	9:36-10:42	13:1-52	17:22-18:35	23:1-25:46	
Transition	7:28, 29	11:1	13:53	19:1	26:1	

The Gospel According to Mark

Authorship, Date, and Place—The early church attributed this book to Mark. Papias said that Mark had served as Peter's interpreter or translator to reduce the Aramaic discourses to Greek (Harrison, p. 182) in an accurate but not necessarily chronological way as he recorded Peter's memories of what Jesus said and did (see Eusebius *History* 3. 39. 15). Peter refers to Mark with affection, calling him "my son," perhaps hoping Mark would carry on the work after his death, much as Paul apparently yearned that Timothy would for him (1 Peter 5:13; cf. 1 Cor. 4:17).

Irenaeus concurs and claims that Mark wrote his account at Rome some time after Paul and Peter died there *(Against Heresies* 3. 1. 2). The traditional setting for their martyrdom is the persecution that followed Nero's torching of Rome in A. D. 64, when he tried to blame the Christians for it. Presumably this places the writing of Mark's Gospel somewhere between A.D. 65 and 70, although some still argue that Mark may have written substantial portions of it before Peter died.[13]

The Muratorian Canon apparently opens with its scribe saying that Mark did not attend all the events recorded in his Gospel, which also seems to support the contention that he recorded material from Peter (quoted in Henry Bettenson, *Documents of the Christian Church*, 2nd ed., pp. 38, 39). Clement of Alexandria places the writing of Mark's Gospel during Peter's lifetime, probably for apostolic weight and endorsement *(History* 2. 15. 2; 6. 14. 6, 7).

Most scholars identify Mark the Gospel writer with John Mark, Barnabas' cousin and Paul's coworker (Acts 12:25; 13:5), who had a falling out with the fiery apostle (Acts 15:36-39) but eventually won his way back into Paul's confidence (Col. 4:10; cf. 2 Tim. 4:11).

Destination and Purpose—Since tradition associates his Gospel with Rome, most scholars consider that it was intended for the Christians at Rome or at least for Gentile readers. Mark explains Jewish customs (7:2-4; 15:42), translates Aramaic words (3:17; 5:41; 7:11, 34; 15:22), and seems to play to the special interests of Roman believers with his emphasis on persecution and martyrdom (8:34-38; 13:9-13). A Roman destination helps explain Mark's overnight acceptance and rapid distribution.

Certain features imply that Mark may have intended to encourage the Roman church, which was the object of Nero's fierce persecution. So we find a number of references to suffering and discipleship (1:12, 13; 3:22-30; 8:34-38; 10:29, 30, 33, 34, 45; 13:8, 11-13) and see Jesus content to carry out His mission, even though it would lead to a horrible death (10:45).[14] We also discover that persecution is not a time to harden the heart. People who do so fail to appreciate Christ and His ministry (3:5), and ultimately they wind up candidates for judgment and so remain outside the circle of His protection (14:61-64).

Characteristics and Structure—1. Mark emphasizes the *kerygma* or gospel message to the unsaved that was at the core of Jesus' preaching (1:14, 15). It is worth dying for (8:35; 10:29) and proclaiming to the whole world (13:10; 14:9).

2. Mark features Messianic secrecy, with Jesus warning both disciples and the beneficiaries of His miracles to keep silent about who He was and what He had done for them (1:44; 8:30). Harrison offers three reasons for this. First, Jesus wanted to avoid crowds so that He could give time to His disciples (9:30, 31). Second, Jesus wanted to postpone apostolic conclusions concerning His mission before He successfully completed His earthly task. Third, Jesus wished to prevent public misunderstanding concerning His mission in order not to excite false revolutionary hopes (*Introduction to the New Testament*, pp. 187, 188).

3. Mark stresses that huge crowds gathered around Jesus (1:33).

4. Mark wrote in unpolished Greek, with the kind of broken sentences (2:10; 11:32)[15] and blend of the historical present with past tenses, parenthetical remarks,[16] and colloquialisms necessary to reproduce Peter's style of speech (Harrison, p. 188).

5. Mark is an action Gospel. It is brief, to the point, and sprinkled 40 times with the adverb *euthys* (immediately).

6. Mark presents an emotional Jesus, who was compassionate (1:41), offended for God (10:14), and distressed and sorrowful (14:33, 34). Mark says that twice the Saviour even sighed (7:34; 8:12).

7. Mark uses words to emphasize Jesus as a teacher, although he records fewer actual teachings than the other Gospels.[17] Perhaps this way he shows that even when He preached, Christ was educating or reeducating Israel and the world concerning God and the plan of salvation.

8. Mark has a high Christology, identifying Christ immediately as God's Son (1:1), yet he does not ignore Christ's humanity (3:5).

9. Mark dwells on Christ's passion, devoting more than two fifths of his Gospel to it (see 10:32-35).

Literary critics argue that Mark's Gospel account should end with 16:8 rather than 16:20. Indeed, the most reliable witnesses omit verses 9 through 20.[18] Ernst Lohmeyer explains the abrupt ending by interpreting the announcement in verse 7 that Christ would rejoin His disciples in Galilee as more than a pledge to appear after the Resurrection. He says that it is a promise (with eschatological overtones) to come again (see Harrison, p. 189). Most scholars accept the shorter ending but remain unconvinced of Lohmeyer's explanation. An outline goes something like this:

FIGURE 117

Preparation	Christ's Public Ministry					Completion
	Galiliee			Judea	Perea	
Early	Later	Delay	Final			
1:14-3:12	*3:13-6:29*	*6:30-9:32*	*9:33-50*	*10:1-31*	*10:32-52*	
						Triumphal Entry
						Temple Cleansing
Baptism						Controversies
Temptation						Olivet Discourse
						Anointing
						Arrest and Trial
						Crucifixion
						Resurrection
1:1-13						11:1-16:8

The Gospel According to Luke

Authorship—This Gospel was written anonymously, but certain factors point to Luke the physician as its author.

1. Internal evidence contends for the same author as the book of Acts. Both books begin with a prologue addressed to a certain Theophilus, and Acts apparently picks up where the Gospel (Luke's "former treatise")[19] leaves off.

In Colossians 4:14 Paul mentions that Luke, one of his traveling companions, was a physician. The writer of Acts was evidently someone who accompanied Paul on his travels[20] and was acquainted with details of the apostle's imprisonment in Rome. Luke remained faithful to the end and quite possibly was the last believer to see Paul alive (see 2 Tim. 4:11). Studies by W. K. Hobart and A. Harnack argue forcefully that a medical man probably composed Luke-Acts, although H. J. Cadbury has shown convincingly that someone without a medical background could have written either book ("The Style and Literary Method of Luke," *HTS*, VI, p. 41).

2. Tradition also casts its vote for Luke. The early church fathers knew of the good doctor's travels with Paul and considered him to be the "scribe" who put Paul's "gospel" (Rom. 2:16) in writing (see Irenaeus *Against Heresies* 3. 1. 1 and the Muratorian Canon).

It is difficult, however, to reconcile this with Luke's own claim that he had compiled material from many witnesses (Luke 1:1-4). Equally unjustified are Origen's and Jerome's attempts to connect Luke with the brother "whose praise is in the gospel throughout all the churches" (2 Cor. 8:18, KJV). But unwarranted assumptions cannot discount the weight of so much testimony that points to Luke as the writer of this Gospel.

Even when the Anti-Marcionite and the Monarchian prologues to the third Gospel disagree over his age at death and on his final resting place,[21] they still add their voices in support of Luke's authorship.

Date and Place of Writing—Luke and Acts are a single work written in two volumes, with the latter a sequel to the former. Acts fails to mention two significant first-century events: the burning of Rome in A.D. 64 and the fall of Jerusalem in A.D. 70. Why would Luke avoid referring to the fire, when Nero shielded himself from suspicion by first blaming and then persecuting the Christian community for it? And how could he overlook the Jewish War with Rome, which ended with a dismantled Temple—just as Christ had announced years earlier?

Consequently, since Acts ends abruptly with events dating to A.D. 62, most conservative scholars opt for a date around A.D. 63 for the Gospel. But if Luke depended on Mark, how could this be? Well, first of all, Luke knew Mark personally. They traveled together with Paul (see Col. 4:10, 14), and the two probably discussed much of their common material during Paul's imprisonment at Rome in the early 60s. Although some scholars look to the two years Luke spent in Caesarea as the time of writing, he most likely completed the necessary research and penned his Gospel in Rome.

Style and Characteristics—1. Luke wrote an elegant brand of Greek and was versatile enough to include both classic (see the prologue in Luke 1:1-4) and Semitic (see 1:5-2:52, which closely resembles LXX Greek) elements. His vocabulary was sufficiently rich that it gave local color to each episode.

2. As a precedent to its role in Acts, Luke's Gospel features the Spirit's central function in Christ's life and ministry (see 1:15, 35; 3:22; 4:1, 2, 14, 18; 10:21).

3. Luke depicts both Jesus and His earthly parents as meticulously obedient to the law in order to show that Jesus built His unusual wisdom and understanding of God's will on the lawful foundation that they laid. As model disciples, Mary and Joseph lived "according to the custom of the law" (2:27, NKJV), fervently attended the annual feasts (2:41), and strictly adhered to lawful Jewish practices.[22] Jesus Himself (despite their parental negligence,[23] His unique connection with a heavenly Father, and His superior intelligence) continued to honor Joseph and Mary with obedience according to the fifth commandment (Ex. 20:12; Deut. 5:16).

4. Luke refers to angels more than 20 times in order to reveal the last-day flavor of the Gospel message (for instance, Luke 1:11, 26; 2:9, 13).

5. By liberally using the Greek verb *dei* (it is necessary), Luke emphasizes Christ's personal awareness that His heavenly Father assigned Him to His redemptive mission.

6. Luke is the only evangelist to bind sacred narrative to sacred history (see Harrison, p. 205; 2:1, 2; 3:1).

7. Luke shows special interest in the poor, concern for the sinner, and the role of women.

8. Luke highlights prayer, especially on those occasions when Jesus prepared Himself for important events (see Luke 3:21; 5:16; 6:12; 9:18, 28, 29; 11:1; 22:32, 41; 23:34, 46). He also features various concepts, including joy, forgiveness, weeping, love, friendship, peace, glory, the kingdom of God, and the kingship of Jesus.

9. Luke presents Jesus as a frequent minister to people in their homes, thus emphasizing the significance of the family unit to the Saviour.

10. Luke goes beyond Matthew's intention to show the way that Christ fulfilled the Old Testament, by presenting Christ and His ministry as the crucial continuation of the historical process by which God intends to carry out His saving purpose, which theologians refer to as Heilsgeschichte (salvation history).

Purpose—Luke implies that he decided, because of his extensive personal investigation into authentic materials "handed down" from eyewitnesses and related by experts concerning the public life of Christ, "to write an orderly account for you, most excellent Theophilus, so that you may know the certainty of the things you have been taught" (Luke 1:3, 4).

Charles H. Talbert suggests that "certainty was essential if the Lukan biography of Jesus was to serve its practical purpose. Ancient biography, even of a literary type, often aimed at instruction in values . . . which, it was believed, could be most graphically communicated when shown incarnated in living personalities. Hence biographies often became hagiographies. As D. R. Stuart has put it, Aristixenus' life of Pythagoras and the Pythagoreans consisted of 'preachments in which he sought to glorify the master and the ideals for which the master stood, and to correct the vulgar errors according to which popular belief had deformed the Pythagorean way of life.' . . . The emulation of the hero's way of life was the goal of such biography, but this was not understood as simply a blind and unthinking repetition of acts performed by the great person. Rather one was expected to learn from the hero how to order one's life. Without necessarily performing the same actions, the reader . . . was expected to emulate the values of the hero in his or her own context. . . . If the third gospel is biography, then the work and words of Jesus are narrated with the intent that they be emulated—not in a mechanical way but with imagination and conviction, and not through one's own strength but through the power of the Holy Spirit. That the evangelist repeatedly portrays Jesus as a model for disciples conforms to the preceding assessment of the gospel as a type of ancient biography" (*Reading Luke: A Literary and Theological Commentary on the Third Gospel*, pp. 4, 5).

   Structure—

FIGURE 117

Prologue 1:1-4	Expectations 1:5-4:15	Exploits 4:16-23:56a	Exultation 23:56b-24:53
	Anointed *4:16-9:50*	Advisor *9:51-19:44*	Martyr *19:45-23:56a*

The Gospel According to John

Authorship—Although the Gospel identifies its author as "the disciple whom Jesus loved" (21:20-24), any attempt to connect this identification with a specific personality must weigh the strength of both external and internal evidence.

External evidence makes a strong case for the apostle John. The early church fathers did not concern themselves with matters of authorship, so testimony in favor of Johannine authorship begins with two documents from the late second century: the Muratorian Fragment and the Anti-Marcionite prologue to the Gospel. Irenaeus, Tertullian, and Clement of Alexandria—church fathers contemporary with this period—all agree that John was the author. Church leaders Polycarp of Smyrna and Pothinus of Lyons sat at John's feet, and Irenaeus knew both of them personally.

Irenaeus himself recalls how he used to sit in Polycarp's house and listen to him describe the old days with John and others who had spent time with Jesus ("Epistle to Florinus" in Eusebius Pamphyli, *Ecclesiastical History*, V. xx. 6). He passed on testimony from John's protégé, Polycarp, when he said that the apostle John wrote his Gospel after the Synoptic evangelists and while living at Ephesus (*Against Heresies*, III. 1. 1).

Internal evidence does not identify the author by name, but it does tell us a great deal about him. Certain details betray his Jewish Palestinian background, such as his familiarity with Hebrew customs and the law (7:22), insights into Jewish-Samaritan hostilities (4:9), awareness of popular Messianic expectations (1:20, 21; 7:40-42), acquaintance with the local geography,[24] and descriptions of things only an eyewitness would relate.[25]

The text seems to narrow down the identity of "the disciple whom Jesus loved" to one of the Twelve (see 13:23-25; 19:25-27; 20:2-10; 21:7, 20-24). When you consider that the Synoptics single out James, Peter, and John as the inner circle of the Twelve (see Mark 5:37/Luke 8:51; Mark 9:2/Matt. 17:1/Luke 9:28; Mark 14:33/Matt. 26:37), that Herod had James put to death around A.D. 44 (see Acts 12:2), and that Peter died a martyr's death at Rome during the reign of Nero (about A.D. 64; see 1 Peter 5:1, 13; John 21:18, 19; 1 Clement 5:1-6:1), it is not hard to subtract two from three and wind up with John.

Critics point out that John's account sharply differs from the Synoptic Gospels. There are no parables proper in John, but that is because he formats his material according to the trend at the turn of the first century away from rabbinic techniques toward one-on-one debates.[26] The Synoptic Gospels report events in which John figured prominently, events that the fourth Gospel fails to mention—probably because the earlier evangelists merely cover them as journalists, while John interprets these events and allows them to color his thinking.[27]

Critics also accuse the fourth Gospel of being too idealistic. They cannot reconcile the gradual disclosure of Jesus' Messiahship in the Synoptics with John's insistence that some knew His identity from the beginning (see John 1:41). But there is nothing unusual about a disciple of John the Baptist repeating his teacher's convictions. As for material not found in the other three Gospels, John usually provides details with which others could seriously sabotage his credibility had he fabricated anything.[28]

Date and Place of Writing—Tradition holds that John wrote this account at Ephesus between A.D. 85 and 95. But since John apparently did not depend on the Synoptics, he could have written his Gospel first. Some critical scholars date his work anywhere from the 50s to the 70s. They point out that Paul's theology in Romans is every bit as developed as that in John and that John apparently refers to an existing feature at Jerusalem, which was destroyed in A.D. 70, when he says "there is" rather than "there was" a pool near the Sheep Gate (5:2). But John likes to use the historical present when he describes the past to give his readers a sense of being there at the time.

So no critical argument has enough weight to displace the testimony of Clement of Alexandria, who said that John wrote his Gospel to supplement the earlier ones; and the witness of Irenaeus, who said that the other three gospels came first, and "then John . . . produced his gospel while he was living at Ephesus in Asia" (Eusebius *Ecclesiastical History* 5. 8). Polycarp verifies Ephesus as John's place of residence, and Polycrates mentions Ephesus as his place of burial (Harrison, p. 217). Attempts at locating John elsewhere work from indirect rather than direct sources or depend on unsubstantiated tradition.[29]

Purpose and Destination—The writer himself plainly states his purpose when he says: "These [things] are written that you may believe that Jesus is the Christ, the Son of God, and that by believing you may have life in his name" (John 20:31, NIV). John says that he prepared this Gospel to persuade his audience that Jesus is God's Anointed, the Messiah, and thereby bring them into the fold of those who have eternal life.

This audience is obviously Greek-speaking, but not entirely Greek. The fourth Gospel has a universal scope (see 3:16; 10:16; 12:32), aimed at readers outside Palestine (see 7:35; 10:16; 11:52), but use of the term *Messiah* gives it a Hebraic flavoring (see 1:41; 4:25).

Some scholars suggest that John wrote to Jews of the Dispersion to prevent them from making the same mistake as their Palestinian brethren concerning Jesus, but the audience is broader than that. Since John presents Jesus and His ministry as the continuation of the historical process by which God intends to rescue a people—regardless of their national origin—from sin and death, it appears that John is saying that true believers must come to grips with the Old Testament before they can appreciate Christ and enter into eternal life. This fits well with the purpose stated in John 20:31: "whether to constrain the unsaved to believe or to deepen faith among believers" (see Harrison, p. 226).

Characteristics—1. John presents Jesus as God's *logos* (His eternal spoken Word-in-action) incarnate (John 1:1-18). As that Word brought forth God's will from nothing, so He brings forth a people according to God's will from fallen humanity (17:6). As that Word never returns to God void, so Christ will accomplish His divine task (17:4). As what this Word produces is "very good" (Gen. 1:31), that is, it brings about exactly what God has in mind, so the Word Itself must epitomize the One Who sent/spoke it. Hence Christ is the perfect representation of His Father (John 12:49, 50 cf. 14:9; 17:8, 9), sent to reveal the Father and to give life to a chaotic world.

2. The ultimate aim of John's Gospel is that everyone who reads it should have eternal life. The Father has this life (John 5:26), which shines through the Son to this dark world (1:4) so that those who believe in Him may, through the Spirit (3:8), also possess it (3:36). To know *both* the father and the Son whom He has sent *is* eternal life (17:3), and Christ nourishes this new life that glorifies God when it bears fruit (15:9-17)[30]—and the more fruit the better (15:8) for those who remain joined to Him (15:17; cf. 6:25-59).

3. The lack of references to the church or its government (cf. Matthew 18; see Harry R. Boer, *The Four Gospels and Acts: A Short Introduction*, p. 75) has led some to conclude that the fourth Gospel concerns itself solely with the individual believer and his or her personal relationship with Christ. But John's preference to interpret rather than to report the significant events during Christ's earthly ministry explains the fourth Gospel's approach to the church and its sacraments.

John presents a unified people of God, assembled from those who embrace the apostolic tradition throughout all the generations of the church age (John 17:20) and intimately connected with one another, Christ, and the Father (verses 20-26). John promotes the idea of a close Christian community with such illustrations as the vine and its branches (15:1-17) and the shepherd and his flock (10:1-21) and points to its organization by relating Jesus' authorization of Peter to feed His sheep and His lambs (21:15-17).

John may not mention baptism by name, but passages like 3:5 and 13:10, 11 certainly bring the ordinance to mind. John seems to say that the deeper meaning of baptism is renewal of the whole person, which is maintained through daily confession and forgiveness as represented by foot washing. The author of the fourth Gospel appears silent also concerning the Lord's Supper, but notice his emphasis in the Bread of Life discourse (John 6:25-59) and the way he illustrates our need for continuous union and fellowship with Christ as a vine on which grapes for wine grow (15:1-17). John is so sacramental minded that he combines the life we celebrate with Communion wine and the renewal we celebrate through baptismal water into a single symbol of new life gained through His sacrificial death, flowing from the pierced side of our crucified Saviour (19:34).

4. John presents an advanced, but not radical, eschatology. In the Old Testament the end lies in the remote future. In the Synoptic Gospels it is "at hand." But for John it has invaded the present and influences the here and now. Although the resurrection to life (John 6:39, 40, 44; 11:23, 24), reunion with Christ (14:1-3), and judgment (5:28, 29) are still future, in some measure these things are already realized during the present evil age. Obedience unto death is a triumph, not a tragedy (21:19). Those who answer Christ's call enjoy the life of the future today (5:24; cf. 12:25). Christ raises His followers from the dead through regeneration (11:23-26), and the wicked one already stands condemned (16:11).

Structure—

FIGURE 119

Prologue Preliminaries	Public Ministry	Private Instruction	Personal Suffering	Finale Epilogue
1:1-51	2:1-12:50	13:1-17:26	18:1-19:42	20:1-21:25

---

[1] That is, their *sitz-im-leben*, which includes circumstantial as well as cultural and historical factors.

[2] Apart from those with the introductory fulfillment formula.

[3] About 1 out of every 20 verses has the genitive absolute. Compare this frequency with that found in the LXX version of the Pentateuch, which averages about 1 instance in every 140 verses.

[4] The early second-century church father Ignatius seems to have quoted Matt. 10:16 in his *Epistle to Polycarp* (2:2) and alluded to the exclusive material in Matt. 3:15 when he wrote *To the Smyrnaeans* (1:1).

[5] The book of Acts, reporting on early church expansion, has baptism in the name of Christ only, but chapter 9 of the late first-century or early second-century work known as *The Didache* (*The Teaching of the Twelve Apostles*) reports that those already baptized have been baptized in the name of the Lord, although earlier (in chapter 7) it called for baptism in the name of the Father, Son, and Holy Spirit.

[6] Those who challenge the text and its historicity often have difficulty with the predictive nature of prophecy. They feel that statements such as "Not one stone will be left here upon another" (Matt. 24:2) must come after the fact. Nevertheless, "it is possible to hold that the Gospel preserves our Lord's prophetic utterances even though the date of writing was after the event in question" Harrison's *Introduction to the New Testament*, p. 175).

[7] Christians fled from Jerusalem to Pella in obedience to the Lord's instruction in Matt. 24:15-25 (cf. Mark 13:14-23; Luke 21:20-24).

[8] Scholars have long referred to the Council of Jamnia, but because of the lack of solid evidence for such a meeting, scholarly consensus now regards the term as a kind of shorthand for a series of meetings, some of which were probably more or less informal, that occurred throughout a period of several decades. Some scholars wonder if the term Council of Jamnia has outlived its usefulness and should disappear from our vocabulary.

[9] Although W. D. Davies is considered a reliable authority, the exact wording of this "blessing [the term *blessing* is sometimes used with just the opposite of its literal meaning, hence curse; this usage is common, for example, in the book of Job, where the Hebrew word for blessing is translated into English as curse] of the wicked/heretics" is problematic. In fact, the wording appears to have been fluid, changing throughout the years. (This expanded reading supposedly comes from the pen of Rabbi Samuel the Small.)

"May no hope be left to the slanderers; but may wickedness perish as in a moment; may all Thine enemies be soon cut off, and do Thou speedily uproot the haughty and shatter and humble them speedily in our days. Blessed be Thou, O Lord, who strikest down enemies and humblest the haughty" (*Jewish Encyclopedia*, Vol. XI, p. 271).

"And for slanderers let there be no hope, and let all wickedness perish as in a moment; let all thine enemies be speedily cut off, and the dominion of arrogance do thou uproot and crush, cast down, and humble speedily in our days. Blessed art thou, O Lord, who breakest the enemies and humblest the arrogant" (Jakob Jocz, *The Jewish People and Jesus Christ*, p. 53).

An older version has been found in the Cairo *Genizah*: "For the renegades let there be no hope, and may the arrogant kingdom soon be rooted out in our days, and the Nazarenes and the *minim* perish as in a moment and be blotted out from the book of life and with the righteous may they not be inscribed. Blessed art Thou, O Lord, who humblest the arrogant" (*ibid.*). There is no consensus on the dating of this rendition of the twelfth blessing.

[10] This fact was clear to those who had a close connection to God (Matt. 16:16, 27).

[11] For example, Matthew uses the word "heaven" as a substitute for "God," as did Jews of his day. He also uses terms such as "kingdom of heaven" and "Father in heaven" in accord with Jewish custom—all done because of reverence for God's name.

[12] He went to His death in the nation's place as the Suffering Servant (Isa. 40-53) in order to complete the task given to Abraham (Gen. 12:1-3 cf. Isa. 49:6) Christologically, ecclesiologically, and eschatologically (Matt. 28:18-20).

[13] For example, Adolph Harnack suggests between A.D. 50 and 60. C. C. Torrey, banking on an Aramaic original, suggested around A.D. 50. T. W. Manson put the date somewhere between A.D. 58 and 65.

[14] Compare this with the language in Isa. 53 about the suffering servant.

[15] That is, asyndeton and anacoluthon.

[16] That is, to throw in some guidelines for interpretation.

[17] Mark applies the words "teach," "teacher," "teaching," and "rabbi" to Jesus 12 times.

[18] Codices Sinaiticus (aleph) and Vaticanus (B) stop with verse 8.

[19] That is, which covers "all that Jesus began to do and to teach, until the day when He was taken up" (Acts 1:1, 2, NASB).

[20] This is deduced from the "we" and "us" passages in Acts 16:10-17; 20:5-21:18; 27:1-28:16.

[21] The Anti-Marcionite prologue claims that he died in Boeotia at the age of 84. The Monarchian prologue says that he died in Bithynia at the age of 74.

[22] Mary and Joseph brought Baby Jesus for circumcision on the eighth day (Luke 2:21; cf. Lev. 12:3) and offered birds for Mary's purification after childbirth (Luke 2:24; cf. Lev. 12:6, 8).

[23] With one year to go before His initiation into the adult community in Israel, Mary and Joseph brought Jesus to Jerusalem to prepare Him for His first Passover, which would take place when He became 13 years old the following year. However, although the practice of bar mitzvah is very old, we cannot be certain that it was practiced during Jesus' lifetime.

[24] For example, he gives the distance between Jerusalem and Bethany as 15 stadia, or two miles (11:18), and he also mentions the tiny town of Cana by name (2:1; 21:2).

[25] For instance, he refers to the fragrance spreading throughout Simon's house in Bethany after the perfume jar had been broken open (John 12:3).

[26] Compare Justin Martyr's debate with Trypho at Ephesus around A.D. 134-137.

[27] Compare, for instance, the transfiguration with John's statement in John 1:14; the Lord's Supper with John's discourse on the Bread of Life (6:25-59); and the way John substitutes Jesus' pleading priestly prayer for the agonizing one at Gethsemane (17:1-26).

[28] Consider, for example, the story of raising Lazarus from the dead, which includes names (Mary and Martha), a place (Bethany), and a time (just before the Passion Week).

[29] Some have suggested Alexandria, because of alleged influence by Philo on the *logos* doctrine and because Egyptian Gnostics used the Gospel in their writings. Others favor Antioch, because Ignatius seems to depend on this Gospel in his writings and because of an appended note in Syriac found in the Armenian version of Ephraem's commentary on Tatian's Diatessaron, claiming that John wrote his Gospel there (see Harrison, pp. 217, 218).

[30] That is, the fruit of love for one another as Christ loves us.

PART 3

APPENDICES

APPENDIX A

EXEGESIS AIDS AND THE BOOK OF JUDE

H ere are samples of the exegesis aids that you can use to help you interpret Scripture more effectively.

The sections in this appendix will follow the six types of analysis discussed in Section 1 of this book.

Sample Primary Analysis

I. CONTEXTUAL ANALYSIS—Book

A. The Canonical Context

The controlling context is the one everlasting covenant, God's promise-plan to all who believe in Messiah Jesus.

B. The Book Context

1. Complete a *biblical data chart* and attach it to this study.

FIGURE 120

Biblical Data for the Book of Jude			Date May 22, 1992	
DATA	**SDA Bible Dictionary**	**NIV Study Bible**	**ICC Commentary: Jude**	**My CONCLUSIONS**
AUTHOR	Jude, the servant of Jesus and brother of James (cf. Matt 13:55; Mark 6:3)	Judas, the Lord's brother (cf. Matt. 13:35; Mark 6:3; John 7:3-10; Acts 1:14; 1 Cor. 9:5; Gal. 1:19	Judas, the Lord's brother (cf. Matt. 13:55; Mark 6:3; 1 Cor. 9:5); Hegesippus, Eusebius, Clement of Al.	Jude, the Lord's brother
WHEN?	The latter half of the first century	If later than 2 Peter, c. A.D. 80; earlier, c. A.D. 65; some of his readers may have heard the apostles (verses 17, 18)—so earlier date seems preferable	Contemporary with 2 Peter; He wrote first and sounded the alarm for Jude, who wrote of his particular interest in the late 60s	Sometime between A.D. 50-80; Probably around A.D. 50-65
FROM WHERE?	?	?	?	Jerusalem? (cf. Acts 15:22, 23)
TO WHOM?	Believers everywhere	Believers everywhere	Believers influenced by Corinth	Believers, especially those in Asia Minor
WHY?	A warning against similar heresies as found in John's Gospel and epistles (cf. verse 3 with Peter's Epistles)	To combat the same error found in 2 Peter and in Paul's epistles (Acts 20:29, 30; Rom. 6:1; 1 Cor. 5:1-11; 2 Cor. 12:21)	To battle the same heresies as found in Paul's and Peter's epistles (false teachers caught up in an early form of Gnosticism)	To destroy the peaceful coexistence of orthodox and heretical factions within the church
MAIN THEME	The Lord delivers and destroys—so remain faithful	The truth about God's saving grace	?	Don't take your salvation for granted.
KEY VERSES	Verses 20-23	?	?	Verse 5

2. Sketch out a flow chart to trace the progressive steps that the author took to unfold his purpose and to reach his goal.

FIGURE 121

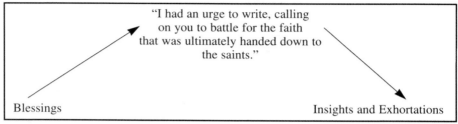

"I had an urge to write, calling on you to battle for the faith that was ultimately handed down to the saints."

Blessings   Insights and Exhortations

C. The Section Context
    1. Where are the *natural breaks* in the text that divide the book into sections?
- Does the author *announce* his theme for the section?
- Is there any *repetition?*
- Do the words "then," "therefore," "wherefore," "but," "nevertheless," or "meanwhile" appear in the text? They could indicate a transition in the author's thought.
- Do *rhetorical questions* signal a switch to a new theme or section?
- Did the author leave out any *conjunctions?* insert *explanations?* or jump to the *next thought* without finishing the sentence?
- Are there any changes in *time? location? setting? grammar?*

    2. Prepare a section map according to your findings.

FIGURE 122

GREETINGS	CONCERNS	INSIGHTS	EXHORTATIONS	BENEDICTION
Called	Battle	Remind	Keep	Stand
Verses 1, 2	Verses 3, 4	Verses 5-15	Verses 16-23	Verses 24, 25

D. The Immediate Context
How does the passage *connect* with what comes *before? after?*
    1. Is it tied to *facts, events, people,* or *places* in the previous or following text?

facts, events, and **people**

    2. Does it depend on what the writer said *previously,* or is it part of a *developing argument?*

both

    3. Does it develop the significance of some historical *figure, fact,* or *circumstance?*

Yes. Jude's readers could meet the same fate as the people in the wilderness, the fallen angels, and the cities around Sodom and Gomorrah, if these men, like the instigators before them, remain incognito, to spread freely their evil among them.

II. STRUCTURAL ANALYSIS
  A. What *type* of literature are you dealing with?
    1. Is it *prose, poetry, narrative, wisdom,* or *apocalyptic?*

> *Prose*—A sermon in the form of a letter; not a real letter, but a small polemical tract without any specific addressees.

  2. Write out your *observations* on the back of this sheet. Then summarize them here.

> Jude rushes right into his purpose for writing (verse 3), and after he exposes the false teachers, by alternating examples from the past with dangers in the present, he repeatedly reminds his readers of the danger these men present to the faithful. These reminders clearly define the way that Jude organized his thoughts as he leads us from one major thought unit into the next

  B. Prepare a textual evaluation of the biblical text.
  C. Scan the text, one sentence at a time; mentally identify each *part of speech.*

FIGURE 123

Book: Jude	Chapter/verse: 5		Bible Version: UBS4, TEV	
Readings	**Supporting Evidence**			
	Alexandrian	Caesarean	Western	Byzantine
the Lord	C*, I, 1175 1409		Syriac-Harklensis	K, 436, 945, 1067, 1292, 1505, 1611, 1844, 2138
Lord	ℵ			ψ
God	C², 1243 Clement			1846
Jesus	A, B, 33, 81, 322, 1241, 1739, 2344, Coptic-Sahidic, Boharic, Cyril, Origen		Old Latin	1881, 2298
God, the Messiah	p72			
the Lord, Jesus	1735			

FIGURE 124

Book: Jude	Chapter/verse: 5		Bible Version: UBS4, TEV		
Readings	Supporting Evidence				
	I	II	III	IV	V
the Lord		C, L, 1175, 1292, 1409	436, 945, 1067, 1505, 1611, 1844, 2138		K
Lord					
God	1243	C²	1846		
Jesus	A, B, 33, 1241, 1739	81, 322	1881, 2298		
God, the Messiah	p72				
the Lord, Jesus		1735			

D. Prepare a structural draft of your text.
  1. Identify clauses and phrases.
  2. Figure out the relationship between clauses.
  3. Count the number of clauses and phrases directly related to each other.

STRUCTURAL DRAFT—FIGURE 125

	CLAUSES			PHRASES		SENTENCES
VS	Intro	Type	Relation	Intro	Type	Type
1				Jude	Subj.	
				a bondslave	Appo.	Complete Subj.
				and brother	Appo.	
				to the called	Prep.	Incompl. Pred.
	those who	Adj.	Dep./Coor.	by	Prep.	
	who	Adj.	Dep./Coor.	in	Prep.	
2	Grace	Noun				Simple
	peace	Noun				
	and mercy	Main	Ind.			
3	While	Adv.	Dep.			Complex
				about	Prep.	
	I	Main	Ind.	calling	Part.	
				to battle	Infin.	
	that was	Adj.	Sub.			
4	because	Adv.	Sub.			
	who	Adj.	Sub.			
	ungodly	Appo.				
	who turn	Adj.	Sub.			
	and deny	Adj.	Sub./Coor.			
5	So I	Main	Ind.			Complex
	though	Adv.	Sub.			
	that	Noun	Sub.	after	Adv.	
				from	Prep.	
	who	Adj.	Sub.			

	CLAUSES			PHRASES		SENTENCES
VS	Intro	Type	Relation	Intro	Type	Type
6	and He	Noun	Coor.			
	those who	Adj.	Sub.			
	who did not	Adj.	Sub.			
	but	Adj.	Sub./Coor.	in	Prep.	
				under	Prep.	
				for	Prep.	
7	Just as	Adv.	Sub.			
	which indul.	Adj.	Sub.	the same	Adv.	
	and went	Adj.	Sub./Coor.	as	Prep.	
				by	Prep.	
8	nevertheless	Adv.	Sub.	in	Prep.	
9	Even Mich.	Main	Ind.			Compound
	when he	Adv.	Sub.	with	Prep.	
	and argued	Adv.	Sub./Coor.	about	Prep.	
				against	Prep.	
	but said	Main	Coor.			

E. Prepare a *paragraph map*.
   1. Break down each section into *groups of verses* that deal with *a single topic* or *a series of events* relating to only one actor or participant in the same time setting and location. Look for these indicators:
      a. In *prose, narrative, wisdom,* or *apocalyptic* literature:
         i. *repeated* terms or concepts
         ii. *rhetorical* questions and *vocative* forms of address
         iii. *sudden* changes in the text (e.g., in *key* actors)
         iv. *development* of the last topic from a previous paragraph
      b. In *poetry:*
         i. *recurring* refrains
         ii. the word *selah*
         iii. *alphabetic* acrostics
         iv. *changes* in rhythm or length of the last line in a poetic unit
         v. *repeated* catchwords, such as "O Lord"
         vi. *parallelism* (e.g., chiasmus)
         vii. a single word *standing outside* the balance/parallel (anacrusis)
         viii. parallels *separated* by more than one line (distant parallelism)
   2. *Map* the paragraph divisions with a chart, using verses for coordinates:
      a. Record the way several Bibles divide the text.
      b. Show your own conclusions.

FIGURE 126

NASB	KJV	RSV	NIV	NKJV	My Own
1	1	1	1	1	1
3	3	3	3	3	3
5		5		5	5
				11	
				16	16
17	17	17	17		
				20	
24	24	24	24	24	24

F. Prepare a *structural analysis.*
1. Preserve the writer's flow of thought.
2. Carefully position each term to show coordination, subordination, and connection.
3. Set off the structural signals in the text.
4. Preserve the writer's syntax.

FIGURE 127
STRUCTURE OF THE BOOK OF JUDE

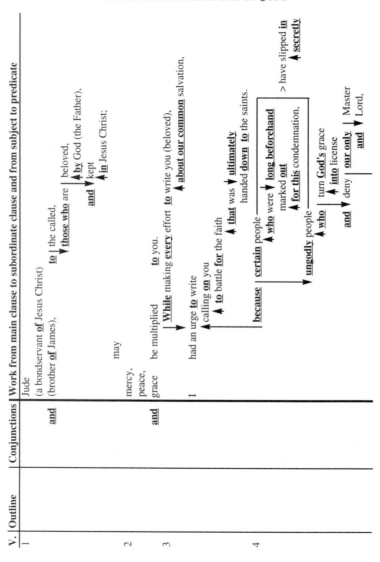

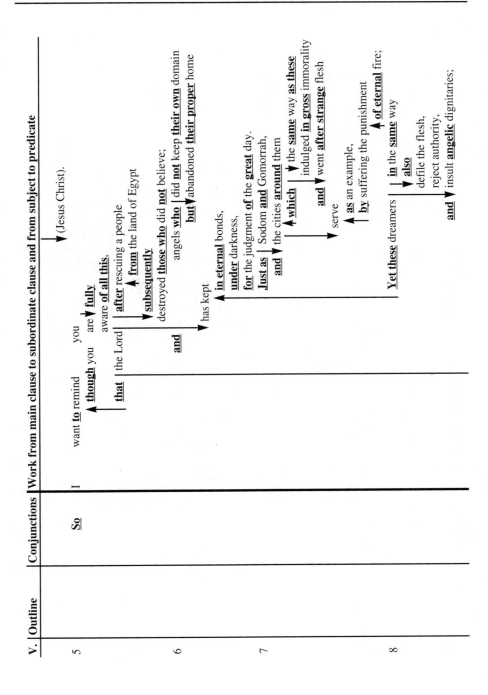

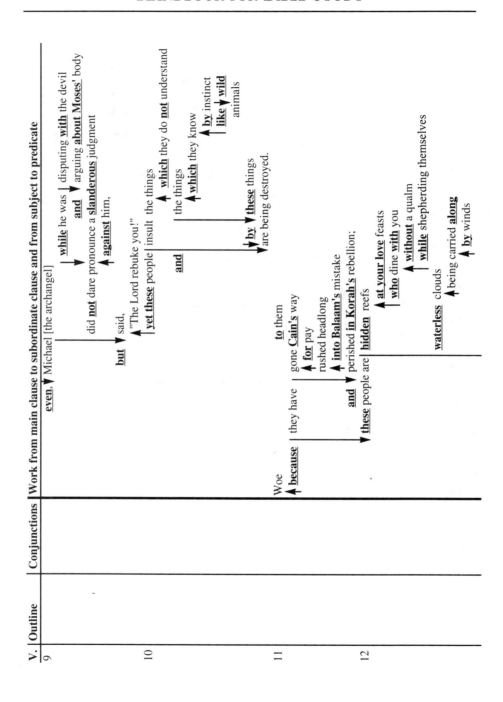

V.	Outline	Conjunctions	Work from main clause to subordinate clause and from subject to predicate
13			autumn trees
			fruitless
			doubly dead
			uprooted
			wild waves **of** the sea
			bringing **their own** shame
			to the surface
			like foam
			wandering stars **for whom** the **black** darkness is reserved
			forever.
14		**Even**	Enoch [the **seventh from** Adam] prophesied saying, "Look, the Lord is coming **with many** thousands **of His holy** ones
			about these people
15			**to** execute judgment
			upon all
			and convict the ungodly
			of all **their ungodly** deeds
			which they have done **in** an **ungodly** way
			and the **harsh** things
			which ungodly sinners have spoken
			against Him."
16			**These** people are grumblers
			[chronic complainers] **who** walk **according to their own** lusts
			and speak **patronizingly**
			by flattering people
			for the sake **of** advantage;

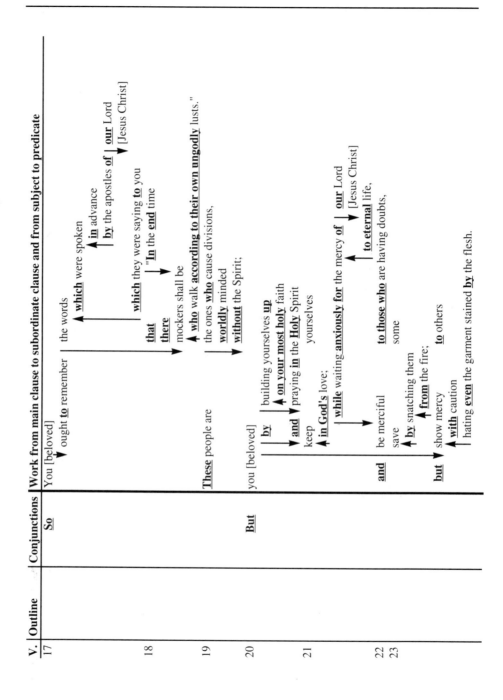

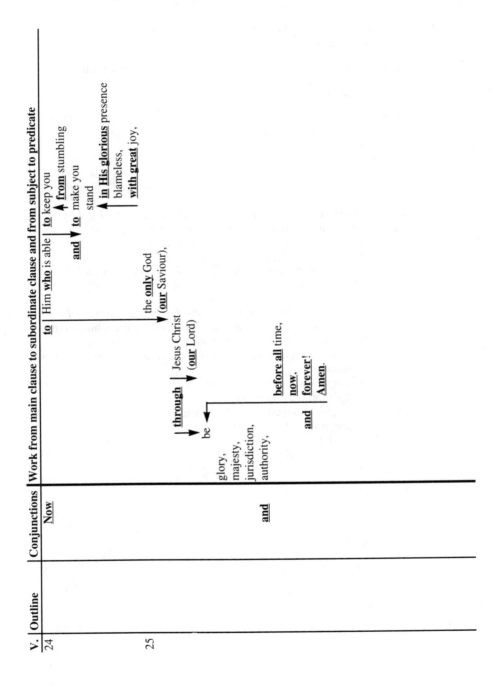

v.	Outline	Conjunctions	Work from main clause to subordinate clause and from subject to predicate
24		Now	to Him who is able to keep you to make you stand from stumbling in His glorious presence blameless, with great joy, to the only God (our Saviour), through Jesus Christ (our Lord)
25		and	be glory, majesty, jurisdiction, authority, before all time, now, and forever! Amen.

G. Convert your structural analysis into a *structural diagram.*
  1. *Code* your analysis:

Part of Speech	Highlight in	or	Mark with
relative pronoun	orange		○
preposition	green		◇
adjective	yellow		□
conjunction	pink		▷
adverb	blue		△

  2. Make appropriate *grammatical/syntactical* notes alongside key words, phrases, and clauses—from your grammar review, etc.
  3. Isolate the stated or implied *theme proposition* or *topic sentence:*
      a. for *each* paragraph
      b. whether at the paragraph's *beginning, middle,* or *end*
          i. by singling out the *main* clause *syntactically* rather than *logically.*
          ii. by tracking the *flow* of thought along the trail of phrases, clauses, and sentences that the author left behind in the text.
  4. *Outline the structure* [for teaching or study] in the main margin:
      a. Roman numerals, lined up with theme propositions or topic sentences
      b. Letters, working from capitals to lowercase, lined up with main and subordinate subpoints.
  5. *Reflect any insights* gained so far by labeling
      a. theme propositions or topic sentences
      b. subpoints

FIGURE 129

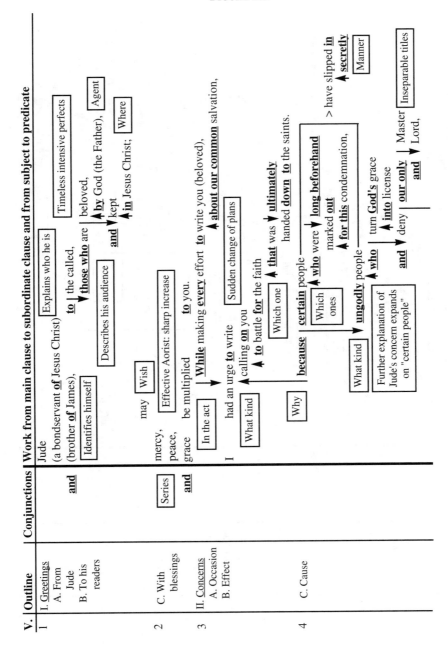

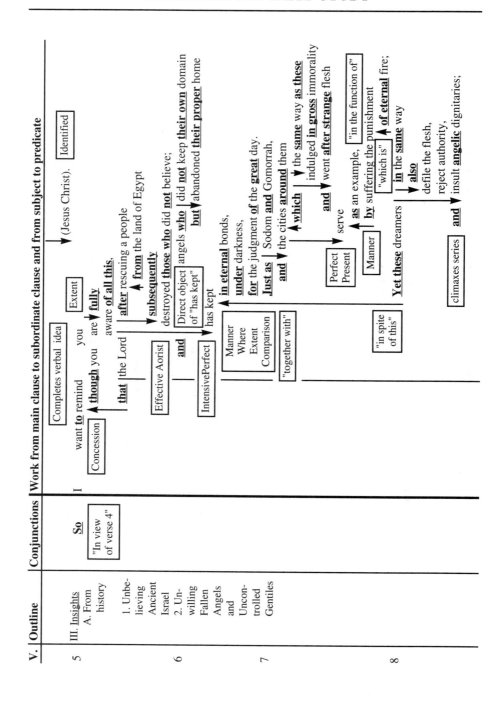

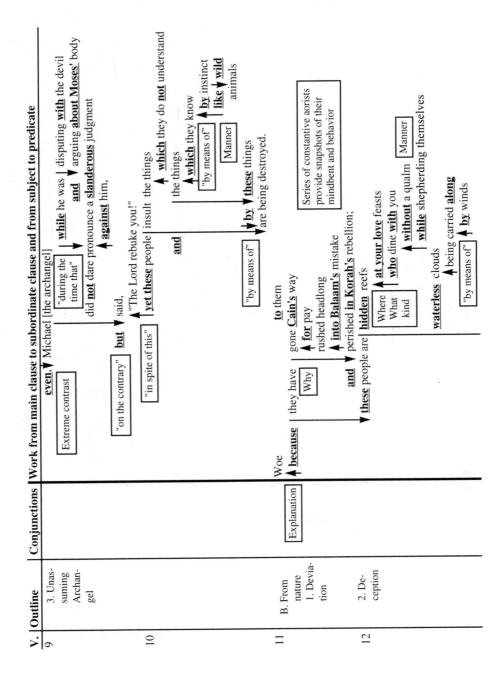

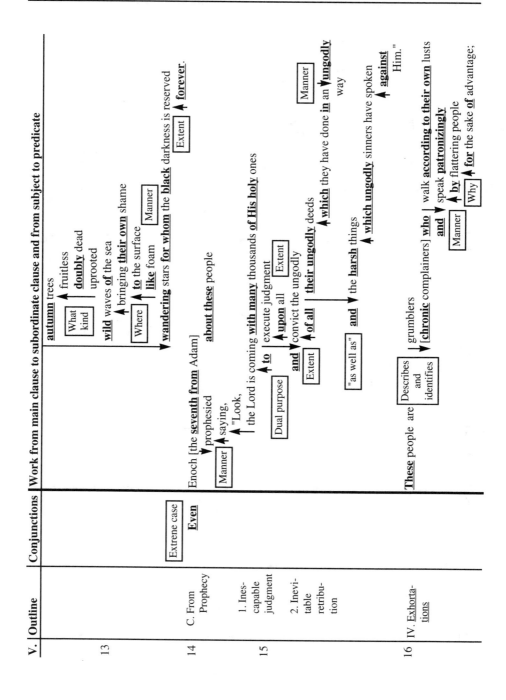

V.	Outline	Conjunctions	Work from main clause to subordinate clause and from subject to predicate

13 — C. From Prophecy

14 — 1. Inescapable judgment — Even [Extreme case]

15 — 2. Inevitable retribution

16 — IV. Exhortations

Diagram content (Jude 13–16):

autumn trees — fruitless, doubly dead, uprooted [What kind]

wild waves of the sea — bringing their own shame [Manner] — to the surface [Where] — like foam [Manner]

wandering stars for whom the black darkness is reserved forever [Extent]

Enoch [the seventh from Adam] prophesied [Manner] saying, "Look, the Lord is coming with many thousands of His holy ones about these people

to execute judgment upon all [Extent] [Dual purpose]

and convict the ungodly of all [Extent] their ungodly deeds

"as well as" and the harsh things

which ungodly sinners have spoken against Him." [Manner]

which they have done in an ungodly way [Manner]

These people are grumblers [Describes and identifies] [chronic complainers] who walk according to their own lusts

and speak patronizingly by flattering people [Manner] for the sake of advantage; [Why]

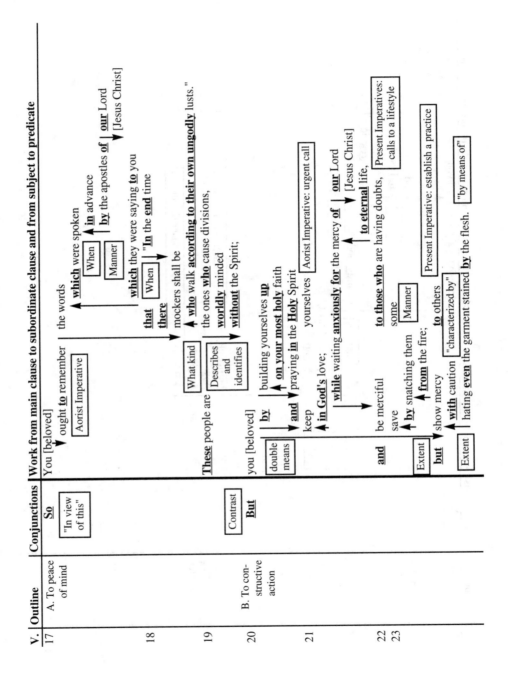

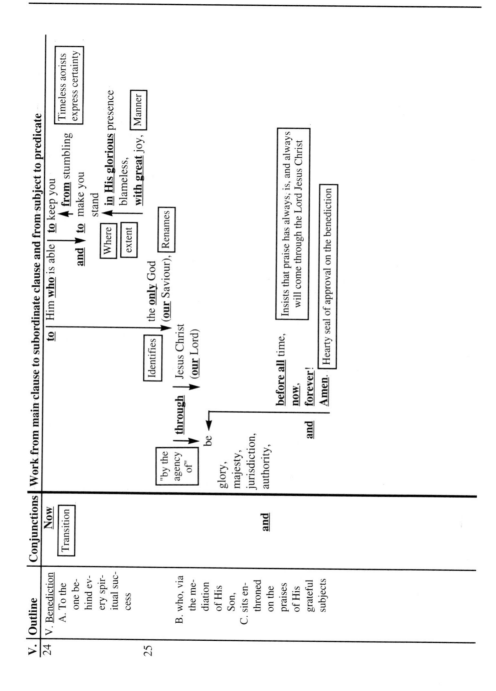

V.	Outline	Conjunctions	Work from main clause to subordinate clause and from subject to predicate
24	V. Benediction A. To the one behind every spiritual success	Now [Transition]	to	Him who is able	to keep you → from stumbling	Timeless aorists express certainty	and to make you stand	[Where] [extent]	in His glorious presence blameless, with great joy, [Manner] the only God (our Saviour), [Renames]
25	B. who, via the mediation of His Son, C. sits enthroned on the praises of His grateful subjects	and	[Identifies]	Jesus Christ (our Lord) [through] "by the agency of" be glory, majesty, jurisdiction, authority, before all time, now, and forever! Amen.	Insists that praise has always, is, and always will come through the Lord Jesus Christ Hearty seal of approval on the benediction

III. VERBAL ANALYSIS

A. Get acquainted with unfamiliar words.

FIGURE 130

UNFAMILIAR WORD	V.	PART OF SPEACH	STRONG'S NUMBER	ROOT MEANING FROM BIBLE DICTIONARY, *THEOL. WORDBOOK OF OT*, VINE'S *EXPOSITORY DICT. OF NT*
Kept	1	verb	5083	to guard by keeping an eye on; to preserve
Mercy	2	noun	1656	spared what one truly deserves
Be merciful	22	verb	1653	passive—to feel sympathy/compassion for
Show mercy	23			active—to show kindness by giving or helping
Grace	2	noun	5845	a gift of what one does not deserve
Peace	2	noun	1515	the bliss generated by the covenant life
Common	3	adjective	2839	shared by all or at least several
Salvation	3	noun	4991	rescue or safety
Necessary	3	adjective	318	compulsive, inescapable, unavoidable
Appealing	3	participle	3870	to urge—to pursue a course of action
Contend	3	infinitive	1864	to struggle on behalf of
Delivered	3	verb	3860	to hand down or over, to entrust
Grumblers	16	noun	1113	people who complain under their breath
Complainers	16	noun	3202	malcontents who can't accept their situation
Lusts	16	noun	1939	strong desires inconsistent with God's will
Walk	16	verb	4198	to go one's way; to follow one's routine
Patronizingly	16	adverb	5246	pompous; high and mighty; exaggerated
Flattering	16	participle	2850	selfishly telling others what they want to hear
Mockers	18	noun	1703	people who toy with or ridicule others
Save	22	verb	4982	to rescue from danger, suffering, sickness
Fear	23	noun	5401	"caution" brought on by intimidation

STUDY WORD *Sensual/psychikos*   **Passage Jude 19**   Date 5/20/94

DESCRIPTIVE STUDIES/Describe the word in its own context
   What is it? **Predicate adjective**

   What does it do in the sentence?
      It describes the character and condition of those who cause division in the church.

   Is it literal or figurative? **Literal**

DISTRIBUTIVE STUDIES/Where can you learn the most about the word?
   How many times does the root word appear in the Bible? **Six times (1 Cor. 2:14; 15:44 [two times], 46; James 3:15; Jude 19.**

   What historical period has the highest concentration of occurrences?
      James (A.D. 45-60); Jude (A.D. 50-65); 1 Corinthians (A.D. 55-57)

   Is your book from this period? **Yes**

   Is your Bible writer the most frequent user of it? If not, who is, and how does he use it? Did he influence your Bible writer? How?

No. Paul uses it more than anyone else, but it is possible that he influenced Jude (cf. "devoid of the Spirit" with 1 Cor. 2:14).

Establish the range of meanings. How did
earlier Bible writers use it?

later Bible writers use it? **It does not appear in later writings.**

contemporary Bible writers use it?
James 3:15 (KJV—"sensual;" NASV—"natural"; NIV—"unspiritual")—associated with jealousy, selfish ambition, disorder, every evil thing (verse 16); it was the label for unreasonable, harsh, judgmental, hostile, hypocritical, and unstable people (verse 17). First Cor. 2:14 describes someone who lives on a purely natural, Spiritless plane; 1 Cor. 15:44 contrasts the body in this life with the resurrection body; 1 Cor. 15:46 describes what comes first on a lower plane before the spiritual.

Can you make out any earlier, contemporary, or later trends?
Yes. Earlier writers in general associate it with people who have no connection with the Holy Spirit.

Does your Bible writer fit or deviate from these trends? agree with any earlier, contemporary, or later authors? How does this affect your understanding of the word?
Yes. There is considerable agreement, which fortifies the certainty of any definition.

COGNATE/COMPARATIVE STUDIES/Compare with nonbiblical sources.

What are the root meanings of any equivalent words from the Mesopotamian, Greco-Roman, or Jewish world?
Psychē (= soul, life) has been traced back to the Indo-European root bhes, from which German gets the word blasen (to blow). So originally, psychē referred to the breath that brings humans to life. The Greeks believed that the psychē temporarily combined with the body (see Plato Cratylus 400c; Laws 873a, b; and Homer Iliad 23. 34ff.; Odyssey 11. 387) and that the body lost its life when it left (Homer Odyssey 14. 426), whereas the Hebrews considered the soul (nephesh) the result when God's "breath of life" (ruach) enters the human body (Gen. 2:7). According to Psalm 146:3, 4, when this breath leaves the body at death, the soul ceases to exist, but the Greeks believed that the soul is immortal (Plato Republic 10. 608d) and that it did not reach its peak until it was separated from the body (Plato Phaedo 66e-67a), although it had to pass through several incarnations "to turn away from worldly values such as riches and power and to devote itself to truth and goodness in imitation of the gods" (George E. Thomas, Religious Philosophies of

the West, p. 25). So to an ancient Greek when something was *psychikos*, it was alive, animated by the *psyche*, but it was still physical and of this world.

Determine the range of meanings from inscriptions or documents:
earlier than your text:
- **The opening prayer of the Liturgy of Mithras referred to "my human *natural* powers."**
- **The adjective occurs in a document describing *natural* gifts to the god Mercury on behalf of a deceased wife.**

later than your text: **Not applicable**

contemporary with your text: **Not applicable**

Can you make out any earlier, contemporary, or later trends?
Yes. Whatever is associated with the *psychē* is earthly, connected with life in this world, and separated from the higher realm to which the Greeks believed the soul would escape.

Does your Bible writer fit or deviate from these trends? agree with any earlier, contemporary, or later authors? How does this affect your understanding of the word?
Jude was a Hebrew, trained in the scriptures of the Old Testament. In all likelihood he did not share the Greek view of the soul, but he would agree that "the soul" (to him, the whole person: body plus breath of life) is separated from God in its natural state and that people who are *psychikos* live on a lower plane (verse 10) and are strongly motivated by money and power (verse 11).

CONTEXTUAL STUDIES/Consider the context of your word.

Does the author define what he means?
Yes. The appositive phrase "devoid of the Spirit" explains that these people were *unspiritual*—they had nothing to do with God's Spirit.

Does the author attach any explanations? **See above.**

Does the structure of the author's argument (logically, syntactically, or semantically) affect the term?
Yes. This isn't the first time that Jude describes "these men." Verses 10-18 shed considerable light on his opinion of the sensual person.

ATTEMPTED DEFINITION/In pencil
Sensual people lead selfish, Spiritless lives on a much lower plane that

the abundant life that Christ gives. Without the Spirit, they depend entirely on natural instincts and still suffer from every human vice and weakness that stands between humans and salvation. Consequently, they naturally oppose the Spirit and work against Him, dividing rather than uniting flock, selfishly exploiting church members and their circumstances for personal gain. Instead of building up the saints, they mercilessly tear them down by pouncing on the weak, ignoring the helpless, and hating the sinner instead of the sin.

VERIFICATION/Compare your findings with reference materials.

Source	Differences
7 SDABC 709	
3 JFB 653, 654	
5 EGT 273	
Kelly: *Epistle of Jude*, pp. 284, 285	
Bigg: *St. Jude*, p. 339	

DEFINITION/Adjusted or affirmed, in pencil

Sensual people lead selfish, Spiritless lives on a much lower plane that the abundant life that Christ gives. Without the Spirit, they depend entirely on natural instincts and still suffer from every human vice and weakness that stands between humans and salvation. Consequently, they naturally oppose the Spirit and work against Him, dividing rather than uniting flock, selfishly exploiting church members and their circumstances for personal gain. Instead of building up the saints, they mercilessly tear them down by pouncing on the weak, ignoring the helpless, and hating the sinner instead of the sin.

B. Identify and explain any symbols or figures of speech

FIGURE 131

VERSE	SYMBOL OR FIGURE OF SPEECH	EXPLANATION
4	"turn God's grace into license"	use liberty as an excuse for license
6	"own domain"	original position assigned to the fallen angels, which they deserted to side with Lucifer against God and subsequently forfeited upon eviction from heaven
	"kept in eternal bonds under darkness for the judgment of the great day"	the fallen angels cannot escape the terrible destiny that awaits them in the lake of fire, which God originally prepared exclusively for them and their leader—based on deep, dark, subterranean Tartaros, the lengendary prison house of Greek mythology.
7	"went after strange flesh"	desired sexual relations with members of their own, rather than the God-appointed opposite sex
8	"dreamers"	in the sense that they pose as prophets

Verse	Symbol or Figure of Speech	Explanation
	"insult angelic dignitaries"	talk disrespectfully to superior celestial beings who have authority over them
10	"wild animals"	creatures that live entirely by natural instinct and surrender themselves to the guidance of their own self-destructive appetites
11	"Cain's way"	who insisted on his way, even though God plainly showed him another, and was willing to kill for it
	"Balaam's mistake"	who tried to exploit for personal advantage the gifts God had given him
	"perished in Korah's rebellion"	deserve the same fate as Korah and his supporters for imitating his rebellious attitude and carrying out similar subversive activities among God's people
12	"hidden reefs"	like hidden rocks beneath the ocean surface, they cause the unsuspecting weak to shipwreck on their rebellious self-righteousness
	"without qualm—themselves"	the ridiculous picture of sheep defying the authority of their shepherds to watch over them, taking care of themselves, believing no harm will come to them
	"waterless clouds carried along by winds"	teachers should shower their pupils with the truth by word and example, but these men are like clouds that only hide the sun and blow by without yielding any rain
	"autumn trees, fruitless, doubly dead, uprooted"	just as waterless clouds disappoint the gardener, so do the trees of fall, when things stop growing and their branches are bare; these trees are not only dead for the season (fruitless); they are also dead forever (uprooted)—and so, doubly dead. In a spiritual sense, we could infer that these men were once fruitless, dead in trespasses and sins, and are now uprooted from Christ, the vine, through apostasy—dead all over again.
13	"wild waves of the sea, bringing their own shame to the surface—like foam"	like the raging waves of a stormy sea that dredge up garbage from the ocean bottom—first to the surface, then along the shore, so unbridled passions bring out the worst in these men—first personally, then socially on the lives of those around them
	"wandering stars"	Unlike fixed stars, which are reliable for navigation, wandering stars neither stay put nor follow a predictable path in the heavens. Although this could refer to comets or planets, which come and go, Jude probably has meteors in mind. Just as they flash briefly and brilliantly across the night sky, then disappear forever into the darkness, so these men, after a meteoric climb and a blaze of publicity, will vanish from view—never to return again.

VERSE	SYMBOL OR FIGURE OF SPEECH	EXPLANATION
14	"Enoch . . . prophesied"	not the actual patriarch, but the popular apocalyptic book circulated in Jude's day, bearing his name; Jude frequently alludes to and even quotes from this uninspired work—not to give it canonical credibility, but to use its well-known phrases as a vehicle for reaching people with the truth
16	"grumblers"	who speak in a derogatory way, under the breath
	"chronic complainers"	malcontents, who can't accept their own circumstances, so they find fault with everything
	"walk according to their own lusts"	allow human desire to determine how they should live
	"speak patronizingly"	to speak in an obnoxious, offensively condescending manner, telling people what they want to hear, for the sake of getting something out of them
18	"mockers"	scoffers who ridicule God's law as a standard, laugh at those who try to keep it, and belittle any notion of a decisive judgment to come
20	"building yourselves up regularly on your most holy faith"	the daily activity of drawing on the divine nature for growth through the vine-relationship with Christ
	"praying relentlessly in the Holy Spirit"	Since we don't even know how to pray (Rom. 8:26) we should communicate our needs and devotion to God as His Spirit leads and helps us (verse 27).
21	"keep yourselves in God's love"	instead of taking God's love for granted, we should cooperate with and obey God on a regular basis
	"while waiting and anxiously for the mercy of our Lord Jesus"	the divine attribute of compassion, on which our destiny depends, that will propel Christ earthward at the climax of our need—at the Second Coming
22	"those who are having doubts"	those who haven't reached a settled opinion or are questioning things they once believed are weak in the faith and consequently in danger of being misled and falling away
23	"snatching them from the fire"	braving the flames like a fireman to pluck souls from the brink of certain consumption in the fire of God's wrath—because no one can go so far that we should give up on him or stand by and let him be destroyed
	"show mercy with caution, hating even the garment	Jude probably has blotches of runny discharge from festering, leprous sores in mind here. Commonly considered typical of sin, leprosy was also considered

VERSE	SYMBOL OR FIGURE OF SPEECH	EXPLANATION
	stained by the flesh"	highly contagious. Just as people needed to exercise caution when aiding lepers, so believers should also be careful when coming to the aid of sinners. If they count themselves better than sinners or beyond the sinner's sin, believers may find their own lives soiled with the very same stains. Like Christ, we should learn to hate the sin that stains lives and to love the sinner.

IV. CULTURAL ANALYSIS

A. History

  1. Key characters or groups:

     a. *Jude*—Greek for Judah ("Let God Be Praised"), the brother of Jesus (Mark 6:3; Matt. 13:55). Apparently married, he took his wife with him on trips (1 Cor. 9:5; cf. Acts 1:14). At one time he opposed Jesus (John 7:5), but here he introduces himself in verse 1 as Christ's willing bondservant.

     b. *God the Father*—Author of our salvation

     c. *Jesus Christ*—Captain of our salvation

     d. *Children of Israel*—They heard the gospel but failed to mix it with faith (Heb. 4:2). They hardened their hearts and rebelled against God at Kadesh Barnea (Heb. 3:8), disqualified themselves from entering the Promised Land (verses 9-11), and wandered in the wilderness until they died (verse 17).

     e. *Fallen angels*—They gave up heaven to side with Lucifer against God; the lake of fire was made for them and their leader (Matt. 25:41).

     f. *The devil*—He is the diabolical founder and ongoing leader of resistance to God's government.

     g. *Moses*—He was the shepherd of Israel, who led the people out of Egypt, across the wilderness, up to the border of the Promised Land by Mt. Nebo, where he died and presumably was buried.

     h. *Michael*—He was the prince of God's people, also called Jesus Christ.

     i. *Cain*—He was Adam and Eve's son. He had to have his own way, even though God showed him another and better way, and he slew his own brother Abel for it.

     j. *Balaam*—He was a prophet who tried to use God's gift for personal advancement, and eventually he led many Israelites into apostasy (Num. 22-24).

     k. *Korah*—He was one of the Israelites set free from Egypt. He led an unsuccessful revolt against Moses and Aaron in the wilderness. At issue was Aaron's exclusive right to offer incense before the Lord (Num. 16).

     l. *Enoch*—He was the seventh patriarch from Creation. God translated him. That is why the author(s) of Enoch attached his name to their work—he was a historical heavyweight.

B. Anthropology—**Nothing applicable**

C. Geography

1. *Sodom and Gomorrah*—These cities were blessed with fertile land, wealth, Lot's influence, and Abraham's favor. God eventually had to destroy them because of their gross immorality and perverse sexual activities.

2. *Cities around Sodom and Gomorrah*—Admah and Zeboim were influenced by Sodom and Gomorrah and destroyed along with them. A third city, Zoar, was spared (Isa. 15:5; Jer. 48:34).

3. *Sinai Peninsula*—When the Israelites left Goshen, the most fertile area of Egypt, God deliberately led them toward the Promised Land by a long, roundabout journey across this desert wasteland. Their trip was rich with spiritual lessons.

4. *Astronomy*—The ancients interpreted the regularity of the heavens as evidence of God's authority over His creation and of the creation's obedience to Him. Anything that refused to stay in its place or follow its God-given course symbolized defiance and rebellion.

D. Material goods

Love feasts—Meals were always important to God's people because of their rich fellowship. Acts 2:46 mentions community meals in the homes of church members at Jerusalem after Pentecost. This text probably refers to the early church's celebration of the Lord's Supper, which was originally a full hunger-satisfying meal according to the way that Luke 22:20 and 1 Corinthians 11:25 describe the final meal in the upper room before Jesus' death.

E. Socioreligious situation—**Not applicable**

F. Economics—**Not applicable**

G. Politics

1. The Children of Israel met fierce resistance along the way to the Promised Land, especially from the Amalekites. The Egyptians pursued them as they left Egypt; mortal combat awaited them as they headed toward a showdown with the inhabitants of the land.

2. Sodom and Gomorrah led a loose confederacy of five cities on the plan, including Admah, Zeboim, and Zoar, which paid tribute money for 12 years to a group of foreign conquerors led by King Chedorlaomer. When they rebelled in the thirteenth year, the king retaliated and routed the rebels. Yet Abraham defeated the army, freed his nephew Lot, and restored the captives and their possessions to the five cities (see Gen. 14:1-15).

3. God gave the territory belonging to the five cities, as well as the rest of Palestine, to Abraham and his descendants.

V. THEOLOGICAL ANALYSIS

A. The analogy of antecedent Scripture

FIGURE 132

VERSE	ANTECEDENT TEXTS [BRACKET NONBIBLICAL REFERENCES]
1	1 Cor. 1:2; 1 Peter 1:1
2	1 Peter 1:2; 2 Peter 1:2
3	2 Peter 3:1, 8, 14, 17; 1 Peter 2:11; 4:12
5	Num. 14:35b
6	[1 Enoch 10:4-6]; 2 Peter 2:4, 9
7	Gen. 19:4-25; 2 Peter 2:6-10
8	Gen. 19:5; [Testament of Asher 7:1]
9	[Assumption (Testament) of Moses 11:5-8]*; Deut. 34:6; Zech. 3:2
11	Num. 16; 22; 25:1-3; 31:8, 16; Neh. 13:2; Deut. 23:4; 1 Peter 5:2; 2 Peter 2:10
12	Eze. 34:8; Prov. 25:14; Eph. 4:14; 2 Peter 1:8, 9; 2:13, 20-22
13	Isa. 14:12; 57:20; 2 Peter 2:17; [Assumption (Testament) of Moses 10:5, 6
14	Gen. 5: Ps. 118:17; Deut. 33:2; [Enoch 1:9; 60:8; 93:3; Book of Jubilees 7:39]
15	[Enoch 27:2]
16	Ex. 15:24; 16:8; 17:3; Lev. 19:15; Num. 11:1, 14-23, 25-29; 14:29; Ps. 143:8, 11; 1 Peter 4:9; 2 Peter 2:18; [Assumption (Testament) of Moses 7:7, 9; 5:5]
17	Acts 20:29; 1 Tim. 4:1; 2 Tim. 3:1-5; 2 Peter 3:2, 3
18	1 Peter 1:20; 2 Peter 2:12; 3:3; [Assumption (Testament) of Moses 7:1]
19	1 Cor. 2:14; 15:44; 2 Peter 2:1; [Assumption (Testament) of Moses 7]
20	Rom. 8:26; 1 Cor. 3:9-17; 12:3; 2 Peter 1:4
21	1 Tim. 5:22; James 1:27; 1 Peter 1:3; [Enoch 27:3, 4]
23	1 Cor. 3:9-17; cf. 1 Peter 5:9
24	Rom. 16:25; Eph. 3:20; 2 Peter 1:10; cf. Acts 6:6; Eph. 6:13; Col. 1:22
25	Rom. 16:27; 1 Peter 4:11

*In 1861 A. M. Ceriani discovered the only existing copy of this document—a Latin palimpsest (a manuscript written on recycled parchment) dating to the sixth century—at the Ambrosian Library in Milan. He identified it as the Assumption of Moses "on the basis of a passage from the Acts of the Council of Nicea that appeared to cite 1:14, and perhaps parts of 1:6 and 1:9" as "having been written in the book of the Assumption of Moses" (J. Priest, "Testament of Moses" in *The Old Testament Pseudepigrapha*, vol. 1, ed. by J. H. Charlesworth, p. 925). Since Ceriani's manuscript deals entirely with Moses' farewell, most scholars prefer to call it the *Testament* rather than the *Assumption* of Moses—and so it appears as "Assumption (Testament) of Moses" above. The Acts of the Council of Nicea also claims, as do many other early texts, that the dispute over Moses' body between the archangel Michael and the devil is a part of the Assumption of Moses. That part, however, is missing from the Testament of Moses, which implies that it is either lost or part of another but as yet undiscovered work that itself is called the Assumption of Moses.

Observations:

- **Jude wrote his epistle in Midrashic style. He introduces quotations with *de* [but] (verse 9), *hoti* [that] (verses 5, 18) [because] (verse 11), and *legein* [saying] (verse 14); cf. 2 Cor. 10:17; Gal. 3:11; Mark 12:26.**
- **Verses 5-7—Implicit midrashim express thematic summaries of Old Testament passages (cf. Rom. 3:10-18; 1 Cor. 2:9; 2 Cor. 6:16-18;**

Gal. 4:22; 2 Peter 3:5, 8).
- Verse 11—Shift in tense and generalized wording suggest an application of an earlier (prophet's) condemnation of disobedient persons.
- Verses 9, 14, 15, 18—Apocryphal elaborations of the Old Testament and an apostolic prophecy are here regarded as a faithful interpretation of inspired teachings (cf. verse 18 with Acts 20:29; 1 Tim. 4:1, 2; 2 Tim. 3:1; 2 Peter 3:3).

B. The analogy of faith—sensus plenior or typology (attach any typology or prophecy work sheets)

FIGURE 133

VERSE	PROSPECTIVE TEXTS [BRACKET ANY NONBIBLICAL REFERENCES]
5	Ex. 12:51; Num. 26:64, 65; 1 Cor. 10:1-10; Heb. 3:16-19; 2 Peter 1:12-15; 2:4, 9; 3:1-5; 1 John 2:20
6	Matt. 25:41, 46; 2 Peter 2:4, 9
7	Gen. 19:24, 25; Deut. 29:23; Hos. 11:8; Mal. 4:1-3; 2 Thess.1:8-10; 2 Peter 2:2, 6; 3:7
11	Gen. 4:3-8; Num. 31:16; 16:1-3, 31-35; Heb. 11:4; 2 Peter 2:15; 1 John 3:12
18	Acts 20:29; 1 Tim. 4:1; 2 Tim. 3:1-5; 4:3; 2 Peter 3:3

Observations:

According to the apostle Paul in 1 Corinthians 10:6, the events and experiences of ancient Israel in the wilderness "took place as *types* (KJV, "examples") of us"—Messianic Israel, the Christian church. So the church and its experiences are more than similar or parallel to what happened long ago; they are an extension of what began with ancient Israel, continues through Jesus Christ, and will eventually climax at His second coming.

What happened to those who murmured, forfeited their salvation, and died short of God's promises in the wilderness *prefigures* what will certainly happen to those Christians in Paul's day and ours who persist in sin (Jude 5; cf. verses 4, 16; Davidson, p. 291). Even the rebellious angels who gave up their place in heaven to side with the enemy cannot escape the judgment (verse 6; cf. verse 8), which Jesus Himself said is the destiny for those who mistreat His brethren (verse 12; cf. Matt. 25:41). Sodom and Gomorrah and the nearby cities that imitated them, indulging in gross immorality, symbolize how final the judgment of eternal fire is (verse 7; cf. verse 8). Yet, despite all this evidence the people who prompted Jude's letter, like the misguided souls (verses 5-7), are (pipe) dreamers who live in the unreal world of their imaginations (verse 8). Caught up in Cain's envy, Balaam's error, and Korah's rebellion (verse 11), they are exposed for the Spiritless mockers that they are (verses 18, 19). The epitome of what these three infamous antiheroes merely foreshadowed, the scoffers take unlawful liberties not only at the expense of those in authority (verses 8-10), but also of the rank-and-file membership (verses 18, 19).

Sample Supplemental Analysis—Focusing on Jude 16-23, Based on the Primary Analysis of the Whole Book

I. CONTEXTUAL ANALYSIS/Passage—**Jude 16-23**

    A. What section of its book is your passage in? **Exhortations**

    B. How does your passage fit *immediately* into its section?
    Jude shifts gears at verse 16, from opening eyes to unseen dangers (verses 5-15) to outlining a course of action for those who have heard the alarm.

II. STRUCTURAL ANALYSIS

    A. Is your passage a single literary type? **Yes**

    B. What is it or are they? **Prose**

    C. How does this relate your text to the rest of its book?
    It relies on what came before it and brings the letter to a climax.

    D. Label the paragraphs in your text:

FIGURE 134

Topic/Theme	Verse(s)
Exhortation to peace of mind	16-18
Exhortation to constructive action	19-23

    E. Outline your passage with topic sentences or theme propositions as main headings and their supporting arguments as subpoints.

I. Exhortation to Peace of Mind

    A. These men are

        1. grumblers

        2. chronic complainers

            a. who walk according to their own lusts

            b. who speak patronizingly, by flattering people for the sake of advantage

    B. But you, beloved, ought to remember the words

        1. which were spoken

            a. in advance

            b. by the apostles of the Lord Jesus Christ

        2. which they were saying to you that

            a. there shall be mockers

                i. in the end time

                ii. who walk according to their own ungodly lusts

II. Exhortation to Constructive Action

    A. These men are

        1. the ones who cause divisions

        2. wordly minded

        3. without the Spirit

    B. But you, beloved,

        1. keep yourselves in God's love

            a. by building up yourselves on your most holy faith

            b. by praying relentlessly in the Holy Spirit

    2. be merciful
       a. to those who are having doubts
       b. while waiting anxiously for the mercy of our Lord Jesus Christ to eternal life
    3. save others by snatching them from the fire
    4. show mercy
       a. to others
       b. with caution, hating even the garment stained by the flesh

III. VERBAL ANALYSIS

A. What does the language contribute to your understanding of the passage?
  1. **Meanings**
    a. **be merciful/show mercy (same word)—two sides of the same coin; the tenderness and kindness of mercy**
  2. **Grammar**
    a. *walking, flattering, dividing*—**present participles indicate a pattern of behavior**
    b. *spoken in advance*—**perfect participle coupled with the imperfect verb**
    c. *keep, be merciful, save, show mercy*—**Aorist imperative followed by present imperatives call on the readers to make a definite, on-the-spot decision from which they may generate lifestyle choices.**
    d. *building, praying*—Present participles suggest a routine or lifestyle for the faithful saint until Christ returns.
    e. *waiting anxiously*—Present participle coupled with the present imperatives *be merciful, save, show mercy,* suggests that the saints should be reaching out, not sitting back, while they eagerly await Christ's return.
  3. **Symbolism/figures of speech**
    a. *mocker*—**brings out the idea of contempt for authority**
    b. *building/praying*—**describe a life dependency upon the Comforter**
    c. *keep*—**brings out the idea of not taking God's love for granted**
    d. *snatching/showing mercy with caution*—**describe bravery, not carelessness**

IV. CULTURAL ANALYSIS

A. History—**Not applicable**
B. Anthropology—**Not applicable**
C. Geography—**Not applicable**
D. Environmental Studies
  1. Socio-religious situation
    a. *apostles*—**Christ's authorized heralds**
    b. *Holy Spirit*—**Agent of restoration, who brings all under Christ's lordship**
    c. *Lord Jesus Christ*—**Captain of our salvation**

V. THEOLOGICAL ANALYSIS

A. How does your passage relate to

1. what God said earlier in the Old Testament?
   a. **Just as there were chronic complainers in Israel under Moses, there are also malcontents in the church under Jesus Christ.**
   b. **Just as the prophets had authority to speak for God, and their word stood firm, so the apostles were authorized to speak for the Lord, and their word is still valid.**
2. what God said earlier in the New Testament?
   a. **Peter and Jude issued strikingly similar warnings in their epistles (cf. Jude 6 with 2 Peter 2:4; Jude 7; with 2 Peter 2:6) and call upon the saints to make similar decisions (cf. Jude 17 with 2 Peter 3:2).**
   b. **Apparently Jude learned from Peter that the apostolic prediction of infiltration by evildoers had come true and so discarded his original letter in order to write about many of the same concerns expressed by that other apostle in his second epistle (cf. Jude 4 with 2 Peter 2:1).**
3. what the author said earlier in his book?
   a. **Jude continues to alternate from the past to the present as he urges his readers to defend the authentic faith handed down to them by the Lord Jesus Christ through His authorized spokesmen, the apostles.**
   b. **Having alerted his readers to the threat these men represent to the church, Jude challenges them to take a personal stand that will both work in their favor and thwart these men and their evil influence on the church.**

B. How does your passage relate to
1. what the author says later in his book?
   a. **These verses set the stage for a crescendo of praise to the God who is able to keep the saints from stumbling despite the evil influence of these men until Christ presents the saints faultless before the throne. He is the one who supplies and sustains the love and mercy that characterize His true people throughout this present evil age (verses 22, 23).**
   b. **Despite the efforts of these evildoers, Jesus is still the eternal One through whom the Father has received, is receiving, and will continue to receive the glorious tribute to which He is entitled (verse 25).**
2. what God says in the latter part of the Old Testament?
   a. **The later prophets shifted away from reform and a return to the glories of the past to regeneration and transformation toward greater glories in the future.**
   b. **The consummation of the mystery of godliness, respresented by a faultless church perfected and presented by Christ (verse 24), coincides with the climax of the mystery of iniquity, promoted and personified in the last days by these men (verses 11-15).**
   c. **God told the priest Zerubbabel not to rebuild His dwelling place by human might or power but by His Spirit (Zech. 4:6),**

and only those who live out the priesthood of the belivers by God's Spirit (as described in verses 20-23) are actually rebuilding His Temple, the church. He can overcome any obstacle so that nothing can stand in His way—not even evildoers with much influence.

3. what God says later in the New Testament?

    a. **Just as the glorious scenes of triumph in the book of Revelation follow a season of internal conflict in the church (described in the seven letters to the seven churches that span the present evil age), so Jude paints a glorious finish for the church after it endures the division and strife engineered by these deceivers.**

    b. **Christ is the only One worthy to open the scroll, the only One able to bring the saints through the events that stand between them and their inheritance and that they must experience in order to qualify for it (cf. Rev. 5:9-13; Jude 24, 25).**

VI. HOMILETICAL ANALYSIS/The Perry Method—Jude 16-23

A. What is the *author's subject* of the text?

Ungodly men have secretly infiltrated the flock, and they pose a serious threat to unsuspecting members.

B. What does the *author emphasize* in the text?

How the members can counteract the subversive efforts of these men.

C. What *type of audience* will I face?

Believing

D. What *type, style,* and *category* of sermon should I use?

Life-situation. Expository. Steps.

E. What is the *title* of my message?

"Mere Christianity"

F. What is my *strong opening statement*?

Anyone who has ever handled an emergency knows that you cannot put off a serious situation. Unexpected problems demand immediate attention.

G. How can I *illustrate* this?

An ordinary man rescues a drowning flight attendant from the icy Potomac River because it was the only thing he could do.

H. What can I *explain* to move into a *biblical setting*?

That's the way emergencies are. They put us on the spot and force us to do things we hadn't planned on. According to verse 3, Jude was already working on a letter when he got wind of false teacher/prophets who threatened the peace and safety of his readers. The news forced him to change his plans, toss the first letter aside,

and write the letter we have in our Bibles today. Ungodly men had wormed their way into the flock, spreading heresy and setting a bad example among the sheep (verse 4). The flock did not recognize the danger, so Jude exposed these men for what they were by comparing them with infamous people and things in Israel's past.

I. State the *theme* of the message.
The same still holds true today. Unless someone warns the flock that wolves in sheep's clothing are loose in the fold, many sheep may be led astray, and entire flocks might be wiped out.

J. What is my *transitional sentence*?
These men were destroying the doctrines—the precious truths Jesus died for—and they were tearing the church apart. There was no time to waste, so Jude called on God's people to battle for the faith. Today we face a similar danger. The doctrines are under attack, and churches are being torn apart because of it. Different theologies pull congregations this way and that. Old friends find themselves on opposite sides of divisive issues, and there's a tension in the air where there used to be peace. Every day some member asks me, "Pastor, what can I do about this? How do we deal with it?" Jude's readers faced the same problems we're having today. Doesn't it make good sense to find out how an inspired writer advised them to handle their situation? If we take the time to examine his instructions, step by step, each one of us should leave here today able to put together a winning strategy that will help us deal with this problem and reunite our members.

K. What are the *main points, subpoints,* and *applications* of the message?
1. Keep yourselves in God's love (verses 20, 21a)

Jude advises everyone who battles for the faith to keep himself or herself in the mainstream of God's love, and his reasons will become obvious before He is through speaking to us today. For now focus on *how* he says we do that.

a. By building yourselves up regularly on your most holy faith

b. By praying relentlessly in the Holy Spirit

2. Be merciful to those who are having doubts (verses 21b, 22)

God is sensitive to our needs. He really cares . . . feels our pain . . . hurts when we hurt. According to Jude, Jesus will never be more merciful than when He returns at the Second Coming—at the climax of the war—when He comes to take us home in our greatest hour of need. While we wait for this final mercy, we should be merciful to each other, especially to those who are having doubts. The attack on doctrine has shaken the faith of some and left them unsure about things.

In the mainstream of God's love, remember . . .

a. People who are struggling, whether new converts or disenchanted veterans, need love and patient care—not doctrine and criticism—as they work through things. They need mercy from merciful brothers and sisters who . . .

b. Allow their needs, rather than your own insecurities and fears, to motivate you.

3. Save others by snatching them out of the fire (verse 23a)

Our God specializes in rescuing people from hopeless situations . . . from the iron furnace of Egypt (Deut. 4:20) and from the fiery furnace (Daniel 3).

You must not allow your differences to make you decide whom you care about . . . and for whom you are willing to take risks. Not just feelings, but your actions . . . putting your own life on the line, braving the flames like a firefighter to pluck souls from what appears to be certain death. In the mainstream of God's love . . .

a. Remain concerned about other people's salvation—not just your own . . . or of those who agree with you.

b. Don't give up on anyone—no matter how far gone he or she may seem to you. And don't stand by and let your brother or sister be destroyed.

L. What is my *summarizing or climactic illustration*?

St. Augustine's friend, Alypius, who went back to the arena and wound up returning to his old lifestyle

M. How will I make an *appeal or call for a decision*?

There is a danger when people have different opinions to be too sure of themselves. According to verse 23, we should work for the salvation of others—with caution. Just as leprosy is contagious and spots clothing, so does sin. Taking sides may change the way you look at other people, especially those who disagree with you. You may start looking down on them or put yourself on a pedestal, and that is a dangerous place to be.

Avoid thinking that you are above the sinner or beyond his or her sin when you help him or her lest you find the fabric of your life soiled with the same stains . . . just like Alypius. The wisest thing to do is this: separate the sinner from his or her sin by recognizing that grace is the only thing that separates you from him or her.

APPENDIX B

REPRODUCIBLE BLANK EXEGESIS AIDS

Here are three sets of exegesis sheets that you may reproduce as often as you need them.

The *primary* sheets serve a double purpose. They allow you to focus on a *particular passage* while at the same time studying an *entire book* as a unit.

The *supplementary* sheets build on the primary work sheets, allowing you to take advantage of the more extensive earlier study as you focus on *other* texts from the *same* biblical book.

The *homiletical* analysis work sheets bring either your primary or supplemental study to a climax by allowing you to present what you have learned in a way that brings out from the target text the biblical author's meaning to your contemporary audience.

Primary Work Sheets

I. CONTEXTUAL ANALYSIS	Book:	Date:

A. The *Canonical* or Controlling Context—**the one everlasting covenant, God's promise/plan to all who believe in Messiah Jesus.**

B. The *Book* Context
   1. Complete a **biblical data chart**. (Attach it to this study.)
   2. Sketch out a **flowchart** to trace the progressive steps that the author took to unfold his purpose and to reach his goal.

FLOWCHART

Biblical Data for the Book of _____ Date _____				
DATA	DICTIONARY	INTRODUCTION	COMMENTARY	CONCLUSIONS
Author				
Date Written				
From where?				
To whom?				
Why?				
Main theme				
Key verses				

C. The *Section* Context

    1. Where are the **natural breaks** in the text that divide the book into sections?

- Does the author **announce his theme** for the section?
- Is there any **repetition**?
- Do the words *then, therefore, wherefore, but, nevertheless,* or *meanwhile* appear in the text? They could indicate a **transition** in the author's thought.
- Do **rhetorical questions** signal a switch to a new theme or section?
- Did the author leave out any **conjunctions**? insert **explanations**? or **jump to the next thought** without finishing the sentence?
- Are there any changes in **time? location? setting? grammar?**

    2. Prepare a **section map** according to your findings.

Section Map

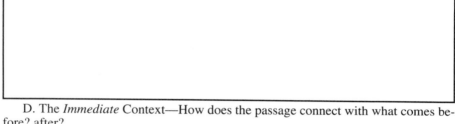

D. The *Immediate* Context—How does the passage connect with what comes before? after?

    1. Is it tied to **facts, events, people,** or **places** in the previous or following text?

    2. Does it depend on what the writer **said previously**, or is it part of a developing argument?

    3. Does it develop the significance of some historical **figure, fact,** or **circumstance**?

II. STRUCTURAL ANALYSIS

A. What *type of literature* (genre) is this?

    1. Is it **prose, poetry, narrative, wisdom,** or **apocalyptic** literature?

    2. Write your observations on the back of this sheet. Summarize them here:

B. Prepare a textual evaluation of the biblical text.

EVALUATING THE OLD TESTAMENT BIBLICAL TEXT

Book:	Chapter/verse:				Bible Version:		
Readings	**Supporting Evidence**						
	MT	SP	LXX	Version	Translation	Qumran	Other

EVALUATING THE NEW TESTAMENT BIBLICAL TEXT

Book:	Chapter/verse:		Bible Version:	
Readings	**Supporting Evidence**			
	Alexandrian	Caesarean	Western	Byzantine

EVALUATING THE NEW TESTAMENT BIBLICAL TEXT

Book:	Chapter/verse:			Bible Version:	
Readings	Supporting Evidence				
	I	II	III	IV	V

C. Scan the text one sentence at a time. Mentally identify each *part of speech*.

D. Prepare a **structural draft** of the text.

    1. Identify clauses and phrases.

    2. Figure out the relationship between clauses.

    3. Count the number of clauses and phrases directly related to one another.

STRUCTURAL DRAFT

	CLAUSES			PHRASES		SENTENCES
Vs.	Intro.	Type	Relation	Intro.	Type	Type

E. Prepare a **paragraph map**.
  1. Break down each section into *groups of verses* that deal with a single topic or a series of events relating only to one actor or participant in the same time setting and location. Look for these indicators:
    a. In **prose, narrative, wisdom,** or **apocalyptic** literature:
      i. *repeated* terms or concepts
      ii. *rhetorical* questions and *vocative* forms of address
      iii. *sudden changes* in the text (for example, in key actors)
      iv. *development* of the last topic from a previous paragraph
    b. In **poetry**:
      i. *recurring* refrains
      ii. the word *selah*
      iii. *alphabetic* acrostics
      iv. *changes* in rhythm or length of the last line in a poetic unit
      v. *repeated catchwords* such as "O Lord"
      vi. *parallelism* (for instance, chiasmus)
      vii. a single word *standing outside* the balance/parallel (anacrusis)
      viii. *parallels separated* by more than one line (distant parallelism)
  2. Map the paragraph divisions with a chart, using verses for coordinates.
    a. Record the way several Bibles divide the text.
    b. Show your own conclusions.

PARAGRAPH MAP

					My Own

F. Prepare a **structural analysis**.
  1. Preserve the writer's flow of thought.
  2. Carefully position each term to show coordination, subordination, and connection.
  3. Set off the structural signals in the text.
  4. Preserve the writer's syntax.
G. Convert your structural analysis into a **structural diagram**.
  1. Code your analysis:

Part of Speech	Highlight in	or	Mark with
relative pronoun	orange		○
preposition	green		◇
adjective	yellow		□
conjunction	pink		▷
adverb	blue		△

2. Make appropriate grammatical/syntactical notes alongside key words, phrases, and clauses. (See chapter 7—A Grammar for English Bible Study.)
3. Isolate the stated or implied **theme proposition** or **topic sentence**
    a. for each paragraph.
    b. whether at the paragraph's beginning, middle, or end
        i. by singling out the main clause syntactically rather than logically.
        ii. by tracking the flow of thought along the trail of phrases, clauses, and sentences that the author left behind in the text.
4. Outline the structure for teaching in the main margin.
    a. Roman numerals should be lined up with theme propositions or topic sentences.
    b. Letters, working from capitals to lowercase, should be lined up with main and subordinate subpoints.
5. Reflect any insights gained so far by labeling
    a. theme propositions or topic sentences
    b. subpoints

STRUCTURAL ANALYSIS WORK SHEET
(for Greek or English)

Book	Chapter	Verses	Bible version	Date
Vs.	Outline	Conjunctions	MAIN SUBJECTS	MAIN VERBS/ADVERBS	MAIN OBJECTS

STRUCTURAL ANALYSIS WORK SHEET
(for Hebrew)

Book	Chapter	Verses	Bible version	Date		
				Outline	Vs.	
PREDICATE ← SUBJECT, SUBORDINATE clause → ← MAIN clause →						

III. VERBAL ANALYSIS

A. Get acquainted with unfamiliar words. Make a **chart of unfamiliar words** and do a **word study**.

CHART OF UNFAMILIAR WORDS

UNFAMILIAR WORD/VERSE	VS.	PART OF SPEACH	STRONG'S NUMBER	ROOT MEANING FROM BIBLE DICTIONARY, *THEOL. WORDBOOK OF OT*, VINE'S *EXPOSITORY DICT. OF NT*

Word Study

Study Word _____   Passage _____   Date _____

DESCRIPTIVE STUDIES	Describe the word in its own context

What is it?
What does it do in the sentence?
Is it literal or figurative?

DISTRIBUTION STUDIES	Where can you learn the most about the word?

How many times does the root word appear in the Bible?
What historical period has the highest concentration of occurrences?
Is the book you are studying from this period?
Is your Bible writer the most frequent user of this word? If not, who is, and how does
      he use it? Did he influence your Bible writer? How?

Establish the range of meanings. How did
* earlier Bible writers use it?

* later Bible writers use it?

* contemporary Bible writers use it?

Can you make out any earlier, contemporary, or later trends?
Does your Bible writer fit or deviate from these trends? agree with any earlier, contem-
      porary, or later authors? How does this affect your understanding of the word?

COGNATE/COMPARATIVE STUDIES	Compare with nonbiblical sources

What are the root meanings of any equivalent words from the Mesopotamian, Greco-
      Roman, or Jewish world?

Determine the range of meanings from inscriptions or documents
* earlier than your text:

* later than your text:

* contemporary with your text:

Can you make out any earlier, contemporary, or later trends?

Does your Bible writer fit or deviate from these trends? agree with any earlier, contemporary, or later authors? How does this affect your understanding of the word?

CONTEXTUAL STUDIES	Consider the context of the word

Does the author define what he means?

Does the author attach any explanations?

Does the structure of the author's argument (logically, syntactically, or semantically) affect the term?

Does the author use this same word in another context? How?

Does he use any other words in this or another book to communicate the same idea? How does this affect your understanding of the word?

ATTEMPTED DEFINITION	In pencil

VERIFICATION	Compare your findings with reference materials

Source	Differences

B. Identify, classify, and explain any symbols or figures of speech.

Verse	Symbol/Figure of speech	Type	Explanation

IV. CULTURAL ANALYSIS

A. *History:* Biblical data chart items in greater depth, events that lead up to, occur simultaneous with, and come after the text. Ask yourself:

1. What is going on in this passage? What events lead up to this situation? Investigate more closely and thoroughly questions, such as Who writes or speaks in the passage? Who is the original audience for the passage/historical situation? Where does the audience live? What are its present circumstances? What is the author's reason for writing/speaker's reason for talking? How do the passage and its circumstances fit into the author's flow of thought?

2. Is the situation in the passage strictly the result of internal developments in Israel, or did other parts of the ancient world have something to do with its realization? Do other passages dealing with the same or similar situations shed any light on its circumstances?

3. What comes next? Does the passage conclude an episode, or is it part of any new developments? How does the passage fit into the flow of secular Old Testament/New Testament history? Into the sweep of redemptive history?

B. *Anthropology:* Social and civil institutions; psychology of the writer, speaker, or key characters; occupations, titles, relationships, and property. Ask yourself:

1. Is the milieu of my passage Israelite or Gentile?

2. What social, civil, or religious institutions does the passage involve? At what state in Israel's history do they occur? What is their meaning or significance in this context? Do the people, places, or things in the passage relate only to ancient Israel, or are they Old Testament projections/New Testament editions of realities to come in the Messianic Age?

3. Do any other passages or outside sources help explain the cultural situation of the author or audience? Does the author refer to something common and universal or local and provincial?

C. *Geography:* The climate; relation to the sea, rivers, desert, mountains, roads; the kind of terrain; population density/distribution. Ask yourself:

1. Does the passage have a geographical setting? In which nation, region, tribal territory, and village do the events and concepts of the passage apply? Is it a northern or southern passage? Does it have a national or regional perspective?

2. Do climate, topography, or local features figure prominently in the passage? If so, what is their significance? What can they tell us about the importance and meaning of people, places, and things in the text? Can other passages or outside sources (for instance, maps, etc.) help explain these issues and open up our understanding of the passage?

D. *Material Goods:* Everyday living items; homes; furnishings; food; clothing; transportation. Ask yourself:

1. Does the text mention everyday items? What are they? What do they tell me about the origins, the practices, or the social-commercial contacts of the people in this passage?

2. What can I tell about the people in the passage from what they wear? where they live? what they eat? what animals they own?

E. *Socioreligious Situation:* Customs at birth, marriage, and death; the place of worship: the tabernacle, Temple, synagogue, Christian congregation; priests; ministers; roles of the city gate to the legal side of life, and of the city itself to Law and order, and labor. Ask yourself:

1. Can I recognize any customs in this passage from what is said? or implied? from items? from times? from frequency? or seasons? from the location? from places of origin; from names? What do these customs tell me about the people involved?

2. Does the text offer any clues about the society in which these people lived? Are they agrarian? nomadic? urban? suburban? What can I deduce or infer from these clues concerning their views of law and order? of justice? of government? of opportunities to succeed? to stay safe?

3. Where, how, and when do they worship? daily? weekly? seasonally? Are there any traces of religious syncretism? extremism?

F. *Economics:* Trade and commerce; agriculture; craftsmen and their products; travel by sea and land; the lingering effects of catastrophes, weather, and war. Ask yourself:

1. How do the people in the passage earn a living? What effect would this have on their view of society? of life? of God? of religion?

2. What can I tell about them from their occupations? What does their work say about what others thought of them? what they thought of themselves? their roots? contacts? any influence they may have had? any influences on them?

3. Are the people in the passage living in a war-torn, weather-driven, disaster-prone economy? What does this tell you about their views of society? of life? of God? Would they tend to interpret natural, social, or historical events differently from people living elsewhere? under different conditions? Would they tend to be less, more, or equally superstititious? extremist? indifferent?

G. *Politics:* Ruler/newsmaker vital statistics, past history, the international situation. Ask yourself:

1. Are any rulers or key political figures/groups in, or influencing, the text? Who are they? Where do they come from? What do they do?

2. Does anything about them deserve further investigation? How did they get to occupy their current positions? Does their childhood, a crisis, or some other significant person or event explain anything I need to know?

3. Are forces in motion that have a bearing on them or their situation? on the

people with whom they are intimately connected? How do they fit into the past, current, future political picture?

V. THEOLOGICAL ANALYSIS

A. The analogy of antecedent scripture.

Verse	Antecedent Texts [Bracket nonbiblical references]

Observations

B. The analogy of faith—sensus plenior or typology

Verse	Prospective Texts [Bracket nonbiblical references]

Observations

Supplementary Exegesis Work Sheets—Passage Study

I. CONTEXTUAL ANALYSIS	Passage	Date

A. What *section* of its book is your passage in?

B. How does your passage fit *immediately* into its section?

II. STRUCTURAL ANALYSIS	

A. Is your passage a single *literary type*?

B. What is it, or what are they?

C. How does this relate your text to the rest of the book?

D. Label the *paragraphs* in your text.

Topic/Theme	Verse(s)

E. Outline your passage with topic sentences or theme propositions as the main points and their supporting arguments as subpoints.

432

III. VERBAL ANALYSIS	

A. What does the language contribute to your understanding of the passage?
    1. Meanings

    2. Grammar

    3. Symbolism/Figures of Speech

IV. CULTURAL ANALYSIS	

A. History

B. Anthropology

C. Geography

D. Environment

V. THEOLOGICAL ANALYSIS	

A. How does your passage relate to
    1. what God said earlier in the Old Testament?

    2. what God said earlier in the New Testament?

    3. what the author said earlier in his book?

B. How does your passage relate to
    1. what the author says later in his book?

    2. what God says later in the Old Testament?

    3. what God says later in the New Testament?

Homiletical Analysis Work Sheets
(for primary or supplemental study)

VI. HOMILETICAL ANALYSIS	The Perry Method

A. What is the *author's topic* of the text?

B. What is the *author's thrust* in the text?

C. What *type of audience/congregation* will I face?

D. What *type, style,* and *category* of sermon should I use?

E. What is the *title* of my message?

F. What is my *strong opening statement*?

G. How can I *illustrate* this?

H. What can I *explain* to move into the *biblical setting*?

I. What is the *theme* of my message?

J. What is my *transitional sentence*?

K. What are the main *points, subpoints,* and *applications* of my message?

L. What is my *summarizing* or *climactic illustration?*

M. How will I *make an appeal* and *call for a decision?*

VI. HOMILETICAL ANALYSIS	The Crum Method

A. What is the *author's topic* of the text?

B. What is the *author's thrust* in the text?

C. What *type of audience* will I face?

D. What *type, style,* and *category of sermon* should I use?

E. What is the *title* of my message?

F. With what *symptomatic behavior* do I want my listeners to identify?

G. What is the *root cause* of this behavior?

H. What are the *resulting consequences* and *general outcome* for those who behave this way?

I. What *gospel material* can I introduce at this point to prevent this helpless situation from appearing hopeless?

J. What *new results* will motivate the listener to choose the gospel and the beautiful ending that comes with it, over this behavior and its ugly outcome?

VI. HOMILETICAL ANALYSIS	The Lowery Method

A. What is the *author's topic* of the text?

B. What is the *author's thrust* in the text?

C. What *type of audience* will I face?

D. What *type, style,* and *category of sermon* should I use?

E. What is the *title* of my message?

F. *Disturb* the listeners' *status quo.*

G. *Analyze* the *discrepancy.*

H. *Disclose* the *clue* to resolution.

I. *Challenge* the listener to a *gospel experience.*

J. *Anticipate consequences, appeal,* and *call for a decision.*

VI. HOMILETICAL ANALYSIS	Monroe's Motivational Sequence

A. What is the *author's topic* of the text?

B. What is the *author's thrust* in the text?

C. What *type of audience* will I face?

D. What *type, style,* and *category of sermon* should I use?

E. What is the *title* of my message?

F. *Get* their *attention.*

G. *Show* the *need.*

H. *Satisfy* the *need.*

I. *Help* them to *visualize* it.

J. *Call* them *to action.*

SELECTED
BIBLIOGRAPHY

Achtemeier, Paul J. *Harper's Bible Dictionary*. San Francisco: Harper and Row, Publishers, 1985.

——— , and Elizabeth Achtemeier. *The Old Testament Roots of Our Faith*. Rev. Ed. Peabody: Hendrickson Publishers, 1996.

———.*The Inspiration of Scripture: Problems and Proposals*. Philadelphia: Westminster Press, 1980.

Aharoni, Yohanan. *The Land of the Bible: A Historical Geography*. Rev. ed. trans. by A. F. Rainey. Philadelphia: Westminster Press, 1979.

——— , and M. Avi-Yonah. *The Macmillan Bible Atlas*. New York: Macmillan Press, 1968.

Aland, Kurt, and Barbara Aland. *The Text of the New Testament*. Trans. by Erroll F. Rhodes from the German ed. Stuttgart: Deutsche Bibelgesellschaft, 1981; reprint, Grand Rapids: Wm. B. Eerdmans Publishing Co./Leiden: E. J. Brill, 1987.

——— , Matthew Black, Carlo M. Martini, Bruce M. Metzger, and Allen Wikgren. *The Greek New Testament*. 3rd ed., United Bible Societies. Stuttgart: Wurttemberg Bible Society, 1975.

Albright, William F. *The Archaeology of Palestine*. Gloucester: Peter Smith Publisher, Inc., 1971.

———.*The Biblical Period From Abraham to Ezra: A Historical Survey*. New York: Harper and Row, Publishers, 1963.

———.*Yahweh and the Gods of Canaan: A Historical Analysis of Two Contrasting Faiths*. Garden City, N.Y.: Doubleday and Co., 1968.

Alexander, George M. *The Handbook of Biblical Personalities*. New York: The Seabury Press, 1962.

Andreasen, M. L. *The Sanctuary Service*. Washington, D.C.: Review and Herald Publishing Association, 1937.

Arthur, Kay. *How to Study Your Bible: Precept Upon Precept*. Eugene: Harvest House Publishers, 1994.

———. *The International Inductive Study Bible*. Eugene: Harvest House Publishers, 1993.

Avi-Yonah, M. *The Holy Land From the Persian to the Arab Conquests (536 B.C. to A.D. 640): A Historical Geography*. Grand Rapids: Baker Book House, 1966.

Baerg, Harry J. *Bible Plants and Animals*. Hagerstown, Md.: Review and Herald Publishing Association, 1989. 3 vols.

Balz, Horst, and Gerhard Schneider, eds. *Exegetical Dictionary of the New Testament*. Grand Rapids: William B. Eerdmans Publishing Co., 1990. 3 vols.

Banks, Robert. *Paul's Idea of Community*. Peabody: Hendrickson Publishers, 1994.

Barber, Cyril J. *Introduction to Theological Research*. Chicago: Moody Press, 1982.

Barker, K. *The NIV Study Bible*. Grand Rapids: Zondervan Publishing House, 1985.

Barr, James. *Comparative Philology and the Text of the Old Testament*. [Winona Lake, Indiana]: Eisenbrauns, [1987].

————. *Semantics of Biblical Language*. Oxford: The University Press, 1961.

Barrett, C. K., ed. *The New Testament Background: Selected Documents*. London: S.P.C.K., 1956; reprint, New York: Harper and Row, Publishers, 1961.

Barry, Vincent E. *Practical Logic*. 2nd ed. San Francisco: Holt, Rhinehart, and Winston, 1980.

Bauer, W. *A Greek-English Lexicon of the New Testament and Other Early Christian Literature*. Trans. by W. F. Arndt, and F. W. Gingrich from the 4th German ed. Chicago: University of Chicago Press, 1957.

Baybrook, Gar. *Will You Be the Speaker?* Mountain View: Pacific Press, 1961.

Bennett, Boyce M., Jr., and David H. Scott. *Harper's Encyclopedia of Bible Life*. Rev. by Madeline S. and J. Lane Miller. New York: Harper and Row, Publishers, 1978.

Berg, Orley. *Treasures in the Sand*. Boise, Idaho: Pacific Press Publishing Association, 1993.

Berkhof, L. *Principles of Biblical Interpretation*. Grand Rapids: Baker Book House, 1980.

Bettenson, Henry, ed. and trans. *Documents of the Christian Church*. 2nd ed. New York: Oxford University Press, 1963.

————. *The Later Christian Fathers*. London: Oxford University Press, 1970.

Bigg, C. *Epistles of St. Peter and St. Jude*. The International Critical Commentary. Ed. S. R. Driver, A. Plummer, and C. A. Briggs. Edinburgh: T and T Clark, 1978.

Bigger, Stephen, ed. *Creating the Old Testament: The Emergence of the Hebrew Bible*. [Cambridge, Mass.]: Blackwell, 1989.

Black, Matthew. *An Aramaic Approach to the Gospels and Acts*. 2nd ed. Oxford: Clarendon Press, 1954.

Blackwood, Andrew W. *Preaching From the Bible*. Nashville: Abingdon-Cokesbury Press, 1941.

Blaiklock, Edward M., and R. K. Harrison, eds. *The New International Dictionary of Biblical Archaeology*. Regency Reference Library. Grand Rapids: Zondervan Publishing House, 1983.

Blass, F., and A. Debrunner. *A Greek Grammar of the New Testament and Other Early Christian Literature*. Trans. and rev. of the 9th-10th German ed. incorporating supplementary notes of A. Debrunner by R. W. Funk. Chicago: University of Chicago Press, 1961.

Boer, Harry R. *The Four Gospels and Acts: A Short Introduction*. Grand Rapids: William B. Eerdmans Publishing Co., 1982.

————. *A Short History of the Early Church*. Grand Rapids: William B. Eerdmans Publishing Co., 1979.

Bork, Paul F. *The World of Moses*. Nashville: Southern Publishing Association, 1978.

Boyd, Robert T. *Paul the Apostle*. Iowa Falls: World Publishing, 1995.

Braga, James. *How to Prepare Bible Messages*. Rev. ed. Portland: Multnomah Press, 1981.

Bright, John. *The Authority of the Old Testament*. Nashville: Abingdon, 1967; reprint, Grand Rapids: Baker Book House, 1975.

————. *A History of Israel*. 2nd ed. Philadelphia: Westminster Press, 1972.

Broadus, John A. *On the Preparation and Delivery of Sermons*. Rev. by Jesse B. Weatherspoon. New York: Harper and Brothers, 1944.

Brooks, James A., and Carlton L. Winebery. *Syntax of New Testament Greek*. Washington: University Press of America, 1979.

Brotzman, Ellis R. *Old Testament Criticism*. Grand Rapids: Baker Book House, 1994.

Brown, Colin, ed. *The New International Dictionary of New Testament Theology*. Trans. with additions and revisions from the German. Wuppertal: Theologischer Verlag Rolf Brockhaus, 1967; reprint, Grand Rapids: Zondervan Press/Exeter, Devon: The Paternoster Press, Ltd., 1975. 3 vols.

Brown, F., S. R. Driver, and C. A. Briggs. *A Hebrew and English Lexicon of the Old Testament With an Appendix Containing the Biblical Aramaic*. Oxford: Clarendon Press, 1907.

Bruce, F. F. *Jesus and Christian Origins Outside the New Testament*. London: Hodder and Stoughton, Ltd., 1974; reprint, Grand Rapids: William B. Eerdmans Publishing Co., 1982.

————. *New Testament Development of Old Testament Themes*. Exeter: The Paternoster Press, 1968; reprint, Grand Rapids: William B. Eerdmans Publishing Co., 1969.

————. *New Testament History*. Nelson's Library of Theology; London: Thomas Nelson, 1969; reprint, Garden City, N.Y.: Doubleday, 1971.

Bucke, Emory Stevens. *Interpreter's Dictionary of the Bible*. Nashville: Abingdon Press, 1976. 5 vols.

Bullinger, E. W. *The Companion Bible*. London: Marshall, Morgan and Scott, Ltd. Grand Rapids: Zondervan Publishing House, 1974.

Burgess, David F., ed. *Encyclopedia of Sermon Illustrations*. St. Louis, Missouri: Concordia Publishing Co., 1988.

Burgess, E. *Christ, the Crown of the Torah*. Grand Rapids: Zondervan Publishing House, 1986.

Burton, Ernest DeWitt. *Syntax of the Moods and Tenses in New Testament Greek*. Chicago: The University of Chicago Press, 1900; reprint, Grand Rapids:

Kregel Publications, 1976.

Caird, G. B. *The Language and Imagery of the Bible*. Philadelphia: Westminster Press, 1980.

The Cambridge Annotated Study Bible (NRSV). Notes and references by Howard Clark Kee. New York: Cambridge University Press. 1993.

Campbell, Anthony, and Mark A. O'Brien. *Sources of the Pentateuch: Texts, Introductions, Annotations*. Minneapolis: Fortress Press, 1993.

Carroll, John T. and Joel B. Green, ed. *The Death of Jesus in Early Christianity.* Peabody: Hendrickson Publishers, 1995.

Cartlidge, D. R., and D. L. Dungan, ed. *Documents for the Study of the Gospels*. London: Collins Liturgical Publications/Philadelphia: Fortress Press, 1980.

Chamberlain, William Douglas. *An Exegetical Grammar of the Greek New Testament*. The Macmillan Co., 1941; reprint, Grand Rapids: Baker Book House, 1979.

Charlesworth, J. H., ed. *John and Qumran*. London: Geoffrey Chapman, 1972.

———, ed. and trans. *The Odes of Solomon*. Oxford: Clarendon Press, 1973.

———, and Walter P. Weaver, eds. *The Old and the New Testaments: Their Relationship and the "Intertestamental" Literature*. Valley Forge, Pennsylvania: Trinity Press International, 1993.

———, ed. *The Old Testament Pseudepigrapha*. Garden City, N.Y.: Doubleday, 1983-1985. 2 vols.

Chilton, Bruce D. *A Galilean Rabbi and His Bible: Jesus' Use of the Interpreted Scripture of His Time*. Good News Studies 8. Wilmington, Del.: Michael Glazier, Inc., 1984.

Clowney, Edmund P. *Preaching and Biblical Theology*. Grand Rapids: William B. Eerdmans Publishing Co., 1961.

Cochrane, C. N. *Christianity and Classical Culture: A Study of Thought and Action From Augustus to Augustine*. New York: Oxford University Press, 1957.

Cohen, A. *Everyman's Talmud*. New York: Schocken Books, 1975.

Comfort, Philip Wosley. *Early Manuscripts and Modern Translations of the New Testament*. Wheaton: Tyndale House Publishers, 1990.

———. *The Quest for the Original Text of the New Testament*. Grand Rapids: Baker Book House, 1992.

Conzelman, H. and A. Lindemann. *Interpreting the New Testament*. Peabody: Hendrickson Publishers, 1988.

Cook, J. M. *The Persian Empire*. New York: Shocken Books, 1983.

Cooper, Douglas. *Stranger to the World; A Contemporary Look at the Life and Times of Christ: The Early Years*. Boise, Idaho: Pacific Press, 1990.

Craigie, Peter C. *Ugarit and the Old Testament*. Grand Rapids: William B. Eerdmans Publishing Co., 1983.

Crim, Keith, ed. *The Interpreter's Dictionary of the Bible*, Supplementary Volume. Nashville: Abingdon Press, 1976.

Cross, Jr., and Frank Moore. *The Ancient Library of Qumran and Modern Biblical*

Studies. Rev. ed. Grand Rapids: Baker Book House, 1980.

———, and Shemaryahu Talmon, eds. *Qumran and the History of the Biblical Text.* Cambridge: Harvard University Press, 1975.

Crossan, John Dominic. *Jesus: A Revolutionary Biography*. San Francisco: Harper, 1994.

Crum, Milton, Jr. *Manual on Preaching*. Valley Forge, Pa.: Judson Press, 1977.

Cullman, Oscar. *The Christology of the New Testament*. Rev. ed. rans. by Shirley C. Guthrie and Charles A. M. Hall from the German. Tubingen: J.C.B. Mohr (Paul Siebeck), 1957; reprint, London: SCM Press, Ltd./Philadelphia: Westminster Press, 1959.

Culley, Robert C. *Studies in the Structure of Hebrew Narrative*. Philadelphia: Fortress Press, 1976.

The Daily Walk Bible. Wheaton, Ill.: Tyndale House Publishers, 1988.

Damsteegt, P. G. *Foundations of the Seventh-day Adventist Message and Mission*. Grand Rapids: William B. Eerdmans Publishing Co., 1977.

Dana, H. E., and J. R. Mantey. *A Manual Grammar of the Greek New Testament*. New York: Macmillan, 1927.

Danby, Herbert. *The Mishnah: Translated From the Hebrew With Introduction and Brief Explanatory Notes*. Oxford: Oxford University Press, 1933.

Danker, Frederick W. *Multipurpose Tools for Bible Study*. St. Louis: Concordia Publishing Co., 1970.

Daube, David. *The New Testament and Rabbinic Judaism*. Peabody: Henderickson, 1992.

Davidson, Richard M. *Typology in Scripture*. Vol. 2, Andrews University Doctoral Dissertation Series. Berrien Springs, Mich.: Andrews University Press, 1981.

Davies, W. D. *Paul and Rabbinic Judaism: Some Rabbinic Elements in Pauline Theology*. London: S.P.C.K., 1948.

———. *The Setting of the Sermon on the Mount*. Cambridge: Cambridge University Press, 1984; reprint, 1966.

Dearman, J. Andrew. *Religion and Culture in Ancient Israel*. Peabody: Hendrickson Publishers, 1992.

DeHaan, Dennis J., ed. *Windows on the Word: Usable Illustrations for Any Occasion*. Grand Rapids: Baker Book House, 1984.

Deissman, G. A. *Bible Studies*. Trans. by Alexander Grieve; Edinburgh: T and T Clark, 1923; reprint, Winona Lake, Ind.: Alpha Publications, 1979.

———. *Light From the Ancient East: The New Testament Illustrated by Recently Discovered Texts of the Graeco-Roman World*. 4th ed. New York: Harper and Brothers, 1922; reprint, Grand Rapids: Baker Book House, 1965.

Detzler, Wayne A. *New Testament Words in Today's Language*. Wheaton, Ill.: SP Publications, 1986.

deVaux, Roland. *Ancient Israel*. New York: McGraw-Hill, 1965. 2 vols.

Dobson, John H. *Learn New Testament Greek*. Grand Rapids: Baker Book House, 1992.

Dodd, C. H. *Interpretation of the Fourth Gospel*. Cambridge: University Press, 1953.

Douglas, J. D. *New Bible Dictionary*. Wheaton, Ill.: Tyndale House Publishers, Inc., 1982.

Dyrness, W. *Themes in Old Testament Theology*. Downers Grove, Ill.: InterVarsity Press, 1979.

Earle, Ralph. *Word Meanings in the New Testament*. Kansas City, Mo.: Beacon Hill Press, 1974-1984; reprint, Grand Rapids: Baker Book House, 1986. 6 vols.

Edersheim, A. *The Life and Times of Jesus the Messiah*. 3rd. ed. New York: Longmans, Green, 1886; reprint, Grand Rapids: William B. Eerdmans Publishing Co., 1947, 1972. 2 vols.

————. *Sketches of Jewish Social Life: In the Days of Christ*. Grand Rapids: William B. Eerdmans Publishing Co., 1982.

————. *The Temple: Its Ministry and Services: As They Were at the Time of Jesus Christ*. Grand Rapids: William B. Eerdmans Publishing Co., 1983.

Ehrlich, Eugene, Stuart B. Flexner, Gorton Carruth, and Joyce M. Hawkins, eds. *Oxford American Dictionary*. New York: Avon Books, 1986.

Eisenman, Robert, and Michael Wise. *The Dead Sea Scrolls Uncovered*. New York: Penguin, 1993.

Ellis, E. Earle. *The Old Testament in Early Christianity*. Grand Rapids: Baker Book House, 1992.

————. *Paul's Use of the Old Testament*. By the author, 1957; reprint, Grand Rapids: Baker Book House, 1981.

————. *Prophecy and Hermeneutic in Early Christianity*. Vol. 18, Wissenschaftliche Untersuchungen zum Neuen Testament. Tubingen: J.C.B. Mohr (Paul Siebeck)/Grand Rapids: William B. Eerdmans Publishing Co., 1978.

Eusebius. *Ecclesiastical History*. Trans. with an introduction by C. F. Cruse. Grand Rapids: Baker Book House, 1955-1981.

Evans, Craig A. *Noncanonical Writings and New Testament Interpretation*, Peabody, Mass.: Hendrickson Publishers, 1992.

Fee, Gordon D. *New Testament Exegesis*. Philadelphia: Westminster Press, 1983.

Finegan, J. *The Archaeology of the New Testament: The Life of Jesus and the Early Church*. Princeton, N.J.: Princeton University Press, 1969.

Finegan, Jack. *The Handbook of Biblical Chronology*. Peabody: Hendrickson Publishers, 1996.

Fishbane, Micahel. *Biblical Interpretation in Ancient Israel*. London: Oxford, 1989.

Fohrer, George, ed. *Hebrew and Aramaic Dictionary of the Old Testament*. Hawthorne, N.Y.: Walter DeGruyter Publishers, 1973.

France, R. T. *Jesus and the Old Testament: His Application of Old Testament Passages to Himself and His Mission*. Wheaton: Tyndale House Publishers, 1971; reprint, Grand Rapids: Baker Book House, 1982.

Freedman, David Noel, ed. *The Anchor Bible Dictionary*. New York: Doubleday, 1992. 6 vols.

Friberg, Barbara, and Timothy Friberg, eds. *Baker's Greek New Testament Library*. Grand Rapids: Baker Book House, 1981-1984. 4 vols.

Freund, W.H.C. *Martyrdom and Persecution in the Early Church*. Grand Rapids: Baker Book House, 1981.

Froom, Leroy E. *Movement of Destiny*. Washington, D.C.: Review and Herald Publishing Association, 1971.

Fuller, Daniel P. *Gospel and Law: Contrast or Continuum? The Hermeneutics of Dispensationalism and Covenant Theology*. Grand Rapids: William B. Eerdmans Publishing Co., 1980.

Gall, James. *Layman's English-Greek Concordance*. Grand Rapids: Baker Book House, 1975.

Gardiner, Sir Alan. *Egypt of the Pharaohs: An Introduction*. Oxford: Clarendon Press, 1961.

Gevirtz, Stanley. *Patterns in the Early Poetry of Israel*. Chicago: University of Chicago Press, 1964.

Gianotti, Charles R. *The New Testament and the Mishnah: A Cross-Reference Index*. Grand Rapids: Baker Book House, 1933.

Gilbert, F. C. *The Jewish Problem*. Takoma Park, Md.: Review and Herald Publishing Association, 1940.

————. *Messiah in His Sanctuary*. Payson, Ariz.: Leaves of Autumn Books, 1985.

————. *Practical Lessons From the Experience of Israel for the Church of Today*. South Lancaster, Mass.: South Lancaster Printing Co., 1902.

Gilbertson, Merrill T. *The Way It Was*. Minneapolis: Augsburg Publishing House, 1959.

Glatzer, N. N. *Philo Judaeus: The Essential Philo*. New York: Schocken Books, 1971.

Gowan, Donald E. *Bridge Between the Testaments: A Reappraisal of Judaism From the Exile to the Birth of Christianity*. 2nd. ed., revised. Pittsburgh: Pickwick Press, 1982.

————. *Eschatology in the Old Testament*. Philadelphia: Fortress, 1986.

Grant, Michael. *From Alexander to Cleopatra: The Hellenistic World*. New York: Charles Scribner's Sons, 1982.

Grant, Robert M. *A Short History of the Interpretation of the Bible*. New York: Macmillan Co., 1963.

Gray, John. *Archaeology and the Old Testament World*. New York: Harper and Row, 1962.

Green, Michael P., ed. *Illustrations for Biblical Preaching*. Grand Rapids: Baker Book House, 1989.

Greenlee, J. Harold. *A Concise Exegetical Grammar of New Testament Greek*. 5th ed. rev. Grand Rapids: William B. Eerdmans Publishing Co., 1986.

————. *Introduction to New Testament Textual Criticism*. Grand Rapids: William B. Eerdmans Publishing Co., 1980.

Guthrie, D., ed. *Biblical Criticism: Historical, Literary, and Textual*. Grand Rapids:

Zondervan Publishing House, 1979.

——. *New Testament Introduction*. 3rd ed. Downers Grove, Ill.: InterVarsity Press, 1970.

Habershon, A. *Hidden Pictures in the Old Testament*. Grand Rapids: Kregel Publications, 1982.

Hallo, William W., and William Kelly Simpson. *The Ancient Near East: A History*. New York: Harcourt, Brace, Jovanovich, Inc., 1971.

Hamell, P. J. *Handbook of Patrology*. Staten Island, N.Y.: Alba House, 1968.

Hanna, Robert. *A Grammatical Aid to the Greek New Testament*. Grand Rapids: Baker Book House, 1983.

Hanson, Paul D. *The Dawn of Apocalyptic*. Rev. ed. Philadelphia: Fortress Press, 1979.

Hardy, W. G. "The Greek and Roman World." Canadian Broadcasting Corp., "University of the Air," 1960. Rev. ed. Cambridge: Schenkman Publishing Co., 1962.

Harper Study Bible. New York: Harper and Row, Publishers, 1964.

Harper, William Rainey. *Elements of Hebrew by an Inductive Method*. Rev. by J. M. Powis Smith. Reprinted Berrien Springs, Mich.: Andrews University Press, 1978.

Harris, R. Laird, Gleason L. Archer, Jr., and Bruce K. Waltke, eds. *Theological Wordbook of the Old Testament*. Chicago: Moody Press, 1981. 2 vols.

Harrison, E. F. *Introduction to the New Testament*. Revised ed. Grand Rapids: Baker Book House, 1971; reprint, 1982.

Harrison, R. K. *Biblical Hebrew*. Kent: Hodder and Stoughton, 1986.

——. *Introduction to the Old Testament*. Grand Rapids: William B. Eerdmans Publishing Co., 1969; reprint, 1977.

——, ed. *Major Cities of the Biblical World*. Nashville: Thomas Nelson, Publishers, 1985.

Hasel, Gerhard. *Understanding the Living Word of God*. Vol 1, Adventist Library of Christian Thought. Mountain View, Calif.: Pacific Press, 1980.

Haskell, Stephen N. *The Cross and Its Shadow*. South Lancaster, Mass.: The Bible Training School, 1914.

Hatch, E., and H. Redpath. *A Concordance to the Septuagint and the Other Greek Versions of the Old Testament (Including the Apocryphal Books)*. Oxford: Clarendon Press, 1897; reprint, Grand Rapids: Baker Book House, 1983. 3 vols.

Hatch, Edwin. *The Influence of Greek Ideas and Usages Upon the Christian Church*. Peabody: Hendrickson Publishers, 1995.

Haynes, Carlisle B. *The Divine Art of Preaching*. Washington, D.C.: Review and Herald Publishing Association, 1939.

Hendriksen, William. *More Than Conquerors*. Grand Rapids: Baker Book House, 1982.

Hennecke, Edgar. *New Testament Apocrypha*. Ed. by Wilhelm Schneemelcher; trans. by R. McL. Wilson. Tubingen: J.C.B. Mohr, 1959; Philadelphia: Westminster Press, 1963. 2 vols.

Herodotus. *The Histories*. Trans. by Aubrey de Selincourt. Rev. with an introduction and notes by A. R. Burn. Harmondsworth: Penguin Books, 1954.

Hill, Gary. *The Discovery Bible: New American Standard New Testament*. Chicago: Moody Press, 1987.

Holbrook, Frank B. *The Atoning Priesthood of Jesus Christ*. Hagerstown: Review and Herald Publishing Association, 1996.

————, ed. *Issues in the Book of Hebrews*. Vol. 4, Daniel and Revelation Committee Series. Hagerstown, Md.: Review and Herald Publishing Association, 1989.

————. *Seventy Weeks, Leviticus, Nature of Prophecy*. Vol. 3, Daniel and Revelation Committee Series. Hagerstown, Md.: Review and Herald Publishing Association, 1986.

————. *Symposium on Daniel*. Vol. 2, Daniel and Revelation Committee Series. Hagerstown, Md.: Review and Herald Publishing Association, 1986.

————. *Symposium on Revelation*. Daniel and Revelation Committee Series. Hagerstown, Md.: Review and Herald Publishing Association, 1992. 2 vols.

Holladay, W. L. *A Concise Hebrew and Aramaic Lexicon of the Old Testament Based on the First, Second, and Third Editions of the Kohler-Baumgartner Lexicon in Veteris Testamenti Libros*. Leiden: E. J. Brill/Grand Rapids: William B. Eerdmans Publishing Co., 1971.

Holmes, C. Raymond. *It's a Two-Way Street*. Washington, D.C.: Review and Herald Publishing Association, 1978.

Horn, Siegfried. *The Seventh-day Adventist Bible Dictionary*. Vol. 8, *Seventh-day Adventist Bible Commentary*, ed. Francis D. Nichol. Washington, D.C.: Review and Herald Publishing Association, 1956; rev. ed. 1981.

Hudson, D. F. *New Testament Greek*. London: English Universities Press, 1973.

Hunter, Archibald. *The Words and Work of Jesus*. Rev. ed. Philadelphia: Westminster Press, 1977.

Hyde, Gordon, M., ed. *A Symposium on Biblical Hermeneutics*. Washington, D.C.: Review and Herald Publishing Co., 1974.

Jamieson, Robert, A. R. Fausset, and David Brown. *A Commentary, Critical, Experimental, and Practical, on the Old and New Testaments*. Reprint, Grand Rapids: William B. Eerdmans Publishing Co., 1982.

Jellicoe, Sidney. *Septuagint and Modern Study*. Winona Lake, Ind.: Eisenbrauns, 1989.

Jensen, Irving L. *Jensen's Survey of the Old Testament and New Testament*. Chicago: Moody Press, 1981.

Jeremias, J. *Jerusalem in the Time of Jesus: An Investigation Into Economic and Social Conditions During the New Testament Period*. Trans. by F. H. and C. H. Cave. Philadelphia: Fortress Press, 1969.

Johns, Alger F. *A Short Grammar of Biblical Aramaic*. Vol. 1, Andrews University Monographs. Berrien Springs, Mich.: Andrews University Press, 1963.

Johns, Warren H., Tim Poirier, and Ron Graybill, eds. *A Bibliography of Ellen G. White's Private and Office Libraries*. Washington, D.C.: The Ellen G. White

Estate, 1982.

Jones, Edgar. *Discoveries and Documents*. London: Epworth Press, 1974.

Jones, G. Curtis. *1,000 Illustrations for Preaching and Teaching*. Nashville: Broadman Press, 1986.

Josephus, Flavius. *Complete Works*. Trans. by William Whiston. Edinburgh: William P. Nimmo, 1867; reprint, Grand Rapids: Kregel Publications, 1960.

Juel, Donald. *Messianic Exegesis: Christological Interpretation of the Old Testament in Early Christianity*. Minneapolis: Fortress Press, 1992.

Kaiser, Walter C., Jr. *Toward an Exegetical Theology*. Grand Rapids: Baker Book House, 1981.

———. *The Uses of the Old Testament in the New*. Chicago: Moody Press, 1985.

———, and Moises Silva. *An Introduction to Biblical Hermeneutics*. Grand Rapids: Zondervan Publishing House, 1994.

Kautzsch, E. *Gesenius' Hebrew Grammar*. 2nd Eng. ed., A. E. Cowley. Oxford: Clarendon Press, 1910.

Keach, Benjamin. *Preaching From the Types and Metaphors of the Bible*. Grand Rapids: Kregel Publications, 1994.

Keil, C. F., and F. Delitzsch. *Commentary on the Old Testament in Ten Volumes*. Reprint, Grand Rapids: William B. Eerdmans Publishing Co., 1975.

Kelly, J.N.D. *Early Christian Doctrines*. rev. ed. New York: Harper and Row, Publishers, 1978.

———. *A Commentary on the Epistles of Peter and Jude*. Grand Rapids: Baker Book House, 1982.

Kenyon, Kathleen M. *The Bible and Recent Archaeology*. Atlanta: John Knox Press, 1978.

Kitchen, K. A. *Ancient Orient and Old Testament*. Downers Grove, Ill.: InterVarsity Press, 1966.

———. *The Bible in Its World: The Bible and Archaeology Today*. Downers Grove, Ill.: InterVarsity Press, 1977.

Kittel, Bonnie Pedrotti, Vicki Hoffer, and Rebecca Abts Wright. *Biblical Hebrew: A Text and Workbook*. New Haven: Yale University Press, 1989.

Kittel, G., and G. Friedrich, eds. *Theological Dictionary of the New Testament*. Trans. by G. W. Bromiley; Grand Rapids: William B. Eerdmans Publishing Co., 1964. 10 vols.

Klein, Ralph W. *Textual Criticism of the Old Testament*. Philadelphia: Fortress Press, 1974.

Knight, Douglas, and Gene Tucker, eds. *The Hebrew Bible and Its Modern Interpreters*. Atlanta, Georgia: Scholars Press, 1985.

Knight, George A. F. *Servant Theology*. The International Theological Commentary. Nashville: Abingdon Press, 1965; reprint, rev. ed. Edinburgh: Handsel Press/Grand Rapids: William B. Eerdmans Publishing Co., 1984.

Knight, George R., Gen. ed. *The Abundant Life Bible Amplifier*. Boise: Pacific Press Publishing Association, 1996.

Knight, Walter R. *3,000 Illustrations for Christian Service*. Grand Rapids: William B. Eerdmans Publishing Co., 1954.

————. *Knight's Master Book of New Illustrations*. Grand Rapids: William B. Eerdmans Publishing Co., 1956.

————. *Knight's Treasury of Illustrations*. Grand Rapids: William B. Eerdmans Publishing Co., 1963.

Kubo, Sakae, and Walter Specht. *So Many Versions? Twentieth-Century English Versions of the Bible*. Grand Rapids: Zondervan Publishing House, 1975.

Ladd, George E. *A Theology of the New Testament*. Grand Rapids: William B. Eerdmans Pubishing Co., 1974.

Lambdin, Thomas O. *Introduction to Biblical Hebrew*. New York: Charles Scribner's Sons, 1971.

Lampe, G.W.H. *A Patristic Greek Lexicon*. Oxford: Clarendon Press, 1961.

LaRondelle, Hans K. *Chariots of Salvation: The Biblical Drama of Armageddon*. Hagerstown, Md.: Review and Herald Publishing Association, 1987.

————. *Deliverance in the Psalms: Messages of Hope for Today*. Berrien Springs, Mich.: First Impressions, 1983.

————. *The Israel of God in Prophecy: Principles of Prophetic Interpretation*. Vol. 13, Andrews University Monographs, Studies in Religion. Berrien Springs, Mich.: Andrews University Press, 1983.

Larson, Craig Brian, ed. *Illustrations for Preaching and Teaching*. Grand Rapids: Baker Book House, 1994.

LaSor, William Sanford. *The Dead Sea Scrolls and the New Testament*. Grand Rapids: William B. Eerdmans Publishing Co., 1972; reprint, 1983.

————. *Israel: A Biblical View*. Grand Rapids: William B. Eerdmans Publishing Co., 1976.

Latourette, K. S. *A History of Christianity*. New York: Harper and Row, Publishers, 1975. 2 vols.

Lenski, R.C.H. *The Sermon: Its Homiletical Construction*. Grand Rapids: Baker Book House, 1969.

Leon, Harry J. *The Jews of Ancient Rome*. Upd. ed. Peabody: Hendrickson Publishers, 1995.

Leon-Dufour, Xavier. *Dictionary of the New Testament*. Trans. from the 2nd (revised) French ed. by Terrence Prendergast. San Francisco: Harper and Row, Publishers/Toronto: Fitzhenry and Whiteside, Ltd., 1980.

Levenson, Jon D. *The Hebrew Bible, the Old Testament, and Historical Criticism: Jews and Christians in Biblical Studies*. Philadelphia: The Westminster Press, 1993.

Liddell, H. G., and R. Scott. *A Greek-English Lexicon*. 9th ed., H. Stuart Jones, and R. Mckenzie. Oxford: Clarendon Press, 1940.

Lightfoot, J. B. *The Apostolic Fathers*. Ed. and completed by J. R. Harmer. London: Macmillan and Co., 1891; reprint, Grand Rapids: Baker Book House, 1956-1980.

————. *Commentary on the New Testament From the Talmud and Hebraicia*. Peabody, Mass.: Hendrickson Publishers, 1989. 4 vols.

Lightfoot, John. *Commentary on the New Testament From the Talmud and Hebraica.* Peabody: Hendrickson Publishers, 1983. 4 vols.

———, ed. and trans. *The Apostolic Fathers* Parts I, II. Peabody, Mass: Hendrickson Publishers, 1989. 5 vols.

Lisowsky, G., and L. Rost. *Konkordanz zum Hebraischen Alten Testament nach dem von Paul Kahle in der Biblia Hebraica editit R. Kittel besorgten Masoretischen Text.* 2nd ed. Stuttgart: Wurttembergische Bibelanstalt, 1958.

Longnecker, Richard N. *The Christology of Early Jewish Christianity.* London: SCM Press, Ltd., 1970; reprint, Grand Rapids: Baker Book House, 1981.

Lowry, Eugene M. *The Homiletical Plot.* Atlanta: John Knox Press, 1980.

Lund, Nils. W. *Chiasmus in the New Testament.* Peabody, Mass.: Hendrickson Publishers, 1994.

Malina, Bruce J. *The New Testament World: Insights From Cultural Anthropology.* Atlanta: John Knox, 1981.

———. *On the Genre and Message of Revelation.* Peabody: Hendrickson Publishers, 1995.

———. *Windows on the World of Jesus.* Louisville: Westminster/John Knox, 1993.

Mansell, Donald E., ed. *Revival and Reformation.* Washington, D.C.: Review and Herald Publishing Association, 1974.

Mansoor, M. *The Dead Sea Scrolls: A Textbook and Study Guide.* 2nd ed. Grand Rapids: Baker Book House, 1983.

Mare, W. Harold. *The Archaeology of the Jerusalem Area.* Grand Rapids: Baker Book House, 1987.

Matthews, Victor H. and Don C. Benjamin. *Social World of Ancient Israel. 1250-587 BCE.* Peabody: Hendrickson Publishers, 1993.

Matthiae, Paolo. *Ebla: An Empire Rediscovered.* Garden City, N.Y.: Doubleday and Company, Inc., 1980.

Maxwell, C. Mervyn. *Tell It to the World: The Story of Seventh-day Adventists.* Rev. ed. Mountain View, Calif.: Pacific Press, 1982.

McDonald, Lee Martin. *The Formation of the Christian Biblical Canon.* Rev. Ed. Peabody: Hendrickson Publishers, 1995.

McNamara, M.S.C., Martin. *Palestinian Judaism and the New Testament.* Good News Studies 4. Wilmington, Del.: Michael Glazier, Inc., 1983.

———. *Targum and Testament; Aramaic Paraphrases of the Hebrew Bible: A Light on the New Testament.* Shannon: Irish University Press/Grand Rapids: William B. Eerdmans Publishing Co., 1972.

McQuilkin, Robertson. *Understanding and Applying the Bible.* Chicago: Moody Press, 1992.

Mead, Frank S., ed. *The Encyclopedia of Religious Quotations.* Old Tappan, N.J.: Fleming H. Revell Co., 1985.

Meeks, Wayne A. *The First Urban Christians: The Social World of the Apostle Paul.* New Haven, Conn.: Yale University Press, 1983.

Meyers, Eric M., and James F. Strange. *Archaeology, the Rabbis, and Early Christianity*. Nashville: Abingdon Press, 1981.

––––. "Early Judaism and Christianity in the Light of Archaeology." *Biblical Archaeologist* 51 (June 1988).

Metzger, Bruce M. *An Introduction to the Apocrypha*. New York: Oxford University Press, 1957.

––––. *The New Testament: Its Background, Growth, and Content*. Nashville: Parthenon Press, 1982.

––––. *The Text of the New Testament: Its Transmission, Corruption, and Restoration*. 2nd ed. Oxford: Oxford University Press, 1968.

––––. *A Textual Commentary on the Greek New Testament*. Corrected ed., United Bible Societies. Stuttgart: Biblia-Druck GmbH, 1975.

Mickelsen, A. Berkeley. *Interpreting the Bible*. Grand Rapids: William B. Eerdmans Publishing Co., 1982.

Monroe, Alan H. *Principles and Types of Speech*. Rev. ed. Chicago: Scott Foresman, 1939.

Montefiore, C. G., and H. Loewe, eds. *A Rabbinic Anthology*. New York: Schocken Books, 1974.

Morris, Leon. *Apocalyptic*. Grand Rapids: William B. Eerdmans Publishing Co., 1972; reprint, 1983.

Moule, C.F.D. *The Birth of the New Testament*. 3rd ed., revised and rewritten. New York: Harper and Row, Publishers/Toronto: Fitzhenry and Whiteside, Ltd., 1982.

––––. *An Idiom Book of New Testament Greek*. 2nd ed. Cambridge: University Press, 1959.

Moulton, James Hope, and George Milligan. *The Vocabulary of the Greek Testament: Illustrated From the Papyri and Other Non-Literary Sources*. Grand Rapids: William B. Eerdmans Publishing Co., 1930; reprint, 1982.

––––, W. F. Howard, and Nigel Turner. *Grammar of New Testament Greek*. Herndon, Virg.: T & T Clark, 1906, 1963, 1976. 4 vols.

Moulton, R. G. *The Literary Study of the Bible*. Boston: D. C. Heath, Publishers, 1895; reprint, rev. and partly rewritten, 1899.

Moulton, W. F., and A. S. Geden, eds. *A Concordance to the Greek Testament According to the Texts of Westcott and Hort, Tischendorf and the English Revisers*. Edinburgh: T and T Clark, 1897; 4th ed., revised and ed. by H. K. Moulton, 1963.

Mouton, Boyce. *Words Are Windows: Word Studies and Illustrations From the Bible*. Joplin: College Press Publishing Company, 1995.

Mowinckel, S. *He That Cometh*. Trans. by G. W. Anderson from the Norwegian. Copenhagen: G.E.C. Gad, 1951; reprint, Nashville: Abingdon Press, 1954.

––––. *The Psalms in Israel's Worship*. Trans. by D. R. Ap-Thomas from the Norwegian. Oslo: H. Aschehoug and Co., 1951; reprint, Nashville: Abingdon Press, 1979. 2 vols.

Musurillo, Herbert. A. *The Fathers of the Primitive Church*. New York: The New American Library, 1966.

Musaph-Andriesse, R. C. *From Torah to Kabbalah*. New York: Oxford University Press, 1982.

Naden, Roy C. *The Lamb Among the Beasts*. Hagerstown: Review and Herald Publishing Association, 1996.

Neufeld, Vernon. *The Earliest Christian Confessions*. Vol. 5, New Testament Tools and Studies, ed. by Bruce M. Metzger. Grand Rapids: William B. Eerdmans Publishing Co., 1963.

New Open Bible, The. Nashville: Thomas Nelson Publishers, 1990.

New Oxford Annotated Bible With Apocrypha, The. (NRSV) New York: Oxford University Press, 1994.

Newberry, Thomas. *The Newberry Reference Bible*. London: Hodder and Stoughton, 1893; reprint, Grand Rapids: Kregel Publications, 1973.

Nichol, Frances D. *Ellen G. White and Her Critics*. Washington, D.C.: Review and Herald Publishing Association, 1951.

———, ed. *The Seventh-day Adventist Bible Commentary: The Holy Bible With Exegetical and Expository Comment in Seven Volumes*. Washington, D.C.: Review and Herald Publishing Association, 1953; reprint, ev. ed., 1976. 8 vols.

Nicole, Roger, ed. *The Topical Chain Study Bible*. Nashville: Thomas Nelson Publishers, 1983.

Nicoll, W. Robertson, ed. *The Expositor's Greek Testament*. reprint, Grand Rapids: William B. Eerdmans Publishing Co., 1983. 5 vols.

Nickelsberg, George W. E. *Jewish Literature Between the Bible and the Mishnah*. Philadelphia: Fortress Press, 1981.

———, and Michael E. Stone. *Faith and Piety in Early Judaism: Texts and Documents*. Philadelphia: Fortress Press, 1983.

Nock, Arthur Darby. *Early Gentile Christianity and Its Hellenistic Background*. New York: Harper and Row, 1964.

Novak, A. *Hebrew Honey: A Simple and Deep Word Study of the Old Testament*. Houston, Tex.: J. Countryman Publishers, 1987.

Osburn, Carroll D., ed. *Essays on Women in Earliest Christianity*. Vols. 1, 2. Joplin: College Press Publishing Company, 1995.

Oxtoby, Gurdon C. *Prediction and Fulfillment in the Bible*. Philadelphia: Westminster Press, 1966.

Packer, J. I., Merrill C. Tenney, and William White, Jr., eds. *Daily Life in Bible Times*. Nashville: Thomas Nelson, Publishers, 1982.

———. *The World of the Old Testament*. Nashville: Thomas Nelson, Publishers, 1982.

Palmer, W. Robert. *How to Understand the Bible*. Rev. Ed. Joplin: College Press Publishing Company, 1995.

Patte, Daniel. *Structural Exegesis: From Theory to Practice*. Philadelphia: Fortress Press, 1978.

———. *What Is Structural Exegesis?* Guides to Biblical Scholarship Series. Philadelphia: Fortress Press, 1976.

Perry, Lloyd M. *Biblical Preaching for Today's World.* Chicago: Moody Press, 1973.

Perschbacher, Wesley J. *New Testament Greek Syntax.* Chicago: Moody Press, 1995.

Pettinato, Giovanni. *The Archives of Ebla: An Empire Inscribed in Clay.* Garden City, N.Y.: Doubleday and Company, Inc., 1981.

Pierson. Robert H. *501 Adventist Illustrations and Stories.* Nashville: Southern Publishing Association, 1965.

———. *What Shall I Speak About?* Nashville: Southern Publishing Association, 1966.

Porter, Stanley E. *Idioms of the Greek New Testament.* Sheffield: Sheffield Press, 1992.

Powell, Ivor. *Bible Cameos.* Grand Rapids: Kregel Publications, 1991.

———. *Bible Highways: 130 Illustrations.* Grand Rapids: Kregel Publications,1985.

Powell, Mark Allan. *What Is Narrative Criticism?* Minneapolis: Fortress Press, 1990.

Precept Ministries. *International Inductive Study Bible.* Portland, Ore.: Multnomah Press, 1992.

Pritchard, J. B., ed. *The Ancient Near East.* Princeton: Princeton University Press, 1973-1975. 2 vols.

Rahlfs, A., ed. *Septuaginta, id est, Vetus Testamentum Graece iuxta LXX interpretes.* 2 vols. 8th ed. Stuttgart: Wurttembergische Bibelanstalt, 1965.

Ramm, Bernard. *Protestant Biblical Interpretation.* Rev. ed. Boston: W. A. Wilde Co., 1956.

Rice, George. *Luke a Plagiarist?* Mountain View, Calif.: Pacific Press Publishing Association, 1973.

Richards. H. M. S. *Radio Sermons.* Washington, D.C.: Review and Herald Publishing Association, 1952.

Richardson, Alan. *An Introduction to the Theology of the New Testament.* New York: Harper and Brothers, 1958.

———, ed. *A Theological Wordbook of the Bible.* New York: Macmillan Co., 1950.

———, and W. Schweitzer, eds. *Biblical Authority for Today.* Philadelphia: Westminster Press, 1951.

Richardson, William. *Paul Among Friends and Enemies.* Boise, Idaho: Pacific Press, 1992.

Ridderbos, Herman. *Paul: An Outline of His Theology.* Trans. by John Richard DeWitt. Grand Rapids: William B. Eerdmans Publishing Co., 1975.

Ringgren, H. *Israelite Religion.* Trans. by David E. Green from the German. Stuttgart: W. Kohlhammer Verlag, 1963; reprint, Philadelphia: Fortress Press, 1966.

———. *Religions of the Ancient Near East.* Trans. by John Sturdy from the Swedish. Stockholm: Svenska Bokforlaget/Bonniers, 1967; reprint, with additions and alterations by the author. Philadelphia: Westminster Press, 1974.

———, and G. Johannes Botterweck. *Theological Dictionary of the Old Testament.* 5 vols. Grand Rapids: William B. Eerdmans Publishing Co., 1974-1986.

Roberts, F. *To All Generations: A Study of Church History*. Grand Rapids: Bible Way, 1981.

Robertson, O. Palmer. *The Christ of the Covenants*. Grand Rapids: Baker Book House, 1980.

Robinson, Haddon W. *Biblical Preaching*. Grand Rapids: Baker Book House, 1980.

Robinson, J. M., ed. *The Nag Hammadi Library in English*. Trans. by members of the Coptic Gnostic Library Project of the Institute for Antiquity and Christianity. Leiden: E. J. Brill, 1977; reprint, New York: Harper and Row, Publishers/Toronto: Fitzhenry and Whiteside, Ltd., 1981.

Roetzel, Calvin J. *The World That Shaped the New Testament*. Atlanta: John Knox Press, 1985.

Rosenthal, Franz, ed. *An Aramaic Handbook*. Wiesbaden: Otto Harassowitz, 1967. 4 vols.

Rost, Leonhard. *Judaism Outside the Hebrew Canon*. Nashville: Abingdon, 1976.

Rouet, Albert. *A Short Dictionary of the New Testament*. Trans. by The Missionary Society of St. Paul the Apostle in the State of New York. Ramsey, N.J.: Paulist Press, 1982.

Roux, Georges. *Ancient Iraq*. London: George Allen and Unwin, Ltd., 1964. 2nd and rev. ed., Harmondsworth: Pelican Books, 1982.

Rowland, Christopher. *Christian Origins: From Messianic Movement to Christian Religion*. Minneapolis: Augsburg Publishing House/London: S.P.C.K., 1985.

————. *The Open Heaven: A Study of Apocalyptic in Judaism and Early Christianity*. London: S.P.C.K., 1982.

Russell, D. S. *Apocalyptic: Ancient and Modern*. Philadelphia: Fortress Press, 1968.

————. *Between the Testaments*. London: SCM Press Ltd./Philadelphia: Fortress Press, 1960; rev. ed., 1965.

————. *The Method and Message of Jewish Apocalyptic*. London: SCM Press/Philadelphia: Westminster Press, 1964.

————. *Prophecy and the Apocalyptic Dream*. Peabody: Hendrickson Publishers, 1994.

Sanders, E. P. *Paul and Palestinian Judaism*. London: SCM Press, Ltd./Philadelphia: Fortress Press, 1977.

Scanlin, Harold. *The Dead Sea Scrolls and Modern Translations of the Old Testament*. Wheaton, Ill.: Tyndale House Publishers, Inc., 1993.

Schaff, Philip, and Roswell D. Hitchcock, eds. *The Topical Reference Bible*. Gordonsville: Dugan Publishers, Inc., n.d.

Schmittals, W. *The Apocalyptic Movement*. Nashville: Abingdon, 1975.

Schneemelcher, Wilhelm, ed. *New Testament Apocrypha*. rev. Trans. by R. McL. Wilson. Louisville: Westminster/John Knox Press, 1992. 2 vols.

Schoville, Keith N. *Biblical Archaeology in Focus*. Grand Rapids: Baker Book House, 1978.

Schwantes, Siegfried J. *The Biblical Meaning of History*. Mountain View, Calif.: Pacific Press, 1970.

Shanks, Hershel, ed. *Recent Archaeology in the Land of Israel*. Washington, D.C.: Biblical Archaeology Society, 1985.

———, ed. *Understanding the Dead Sea Scrolls*. New York: Vintage Books, 1993.

Shea, William H. *Prophetic Interpretation*. Vol. 1, Daniel and Revelation Committee Series. Washington, D.C.: Review and Herald Publishing Association, 1982.

Silva, Moises. *Biblical Words and Their Meaning*. Grand Rapids: Zondervan Press, 1983.

Smith, Morton. "The Dead Sea Sect in Relation to Judaism." *New Testament Studies* 7. 1960-1961.

Smith, Ralph. L. *Micah-Malachi*. Vol. 32, Word Biblical Commentary. Waco, Tex.: Word Books, 1984.

Soulen, Richard N. *Handbook of Biblical Criticism*. 2nd ed. Atlanta: John Knox Press, 1981.

Spicq, Ceslas, O.P. trans. by James Ernest. *Theological Lexicon of the New Testament*. Peabody, Mass.: Hendrickson Publishers, 1994. 3 vols.

Stern, David H. *The Jewish New Testament*. Clarksville, Md.: Jewish New Testament Publications, 1989.

———. *The Jewish New Testament Commentary*. Clarksville, Md.: Jewish New Testament Publications, 1992.

Stowe, Calvin. *Origin and History of the Books of the Bible*. Hartford: Hartford Publishing Co., 1867.

Strack, Hermann and Gunter Stemberger. *Introduction to the Talmud and Midrash*. Minneapolis: Fortress, 1992.

Strand, Kenneth A. *Interpreting the Book of Revelation*. 2nd ed. Worthington, Ohio: Ann Arbor Publishers, 1982.

Streeter, B. H. *The Four Gospels: A Study of Origins*. London: Macmillan and Co., Ltd., 1956.

Strong, J. *The Exhaustive Concordance of the Bible*. McLean, Va.: MacDonald Publishing Co., n.d.

Stuart, Douglas. *Old Testament Exegesis*. Philadelphia: Westminster Press, 1980.

Summers, Ray. *Essentials of New Testament Greek*. Nashville: Broadman Press, 1950. Sundberg, A. C., Jr. "On Testimonies." *Novum Testamentum* 3 (1959).

Sundberg, A. C., Jr. "On Testimonies." *Novum Testamentum* 3 (1959).

Swartley, Willard M. *Israel's Scripture Traditions and the Synoptic Gospels*. Peabody: Hendrickson Publishers, 1993.

Swete, H. B. *An Introduction to the Old Testament in Greek*. rev. ed. R. R. Ottley; reprinted New York: KTAV, 1968.

Talbert, Charles H. *Reading Luke: A Literary and Theological Commentary on the Third Gospel*. New York: Crossroad Publshing Co., 1982.

Tate, W. Randolph. *Biblical Interpretation*. Peabody: Hendrickson Publishers, 1996.

Terry, Milton S. *Biblical Hermeneutics: A Treatise on the Interpretation of the Old and New Testaments*. Grand Rapids: Zondervan Publishing House, 1974.

Thiele, Edwin R. *The Mysterious Numbers of the Hebrew Kings.* Academie Books. Grand Rapids: Zondervan Publishing House, 1983.

Thomas, D. W., ed. *Documents From Old Testament Times.* Trans. with introductions and notes by members of the Old Society for Old Testament Study. London: Thomas Nelson and Sons, Ltd., 1958; New York: Harper and Row Publishers, 1961.

The Thompson Chain Reference Bible. Indianapolis: B. B. Kirkbride Bible Co., 1964; reprint, Grand Rapids: The Zondervan Corporation, 1983.

Thompson, Leonard L. *Introducing Biblical Literature: A More Fantastic Country.* Englewood Cliffs, N.J.: Prentice-Hall, Inc., 1978.

Tixeront, J. *A Handbook of Patrology.* Trans. from the 4th French ed. by S. A. Raemers. St. Louis: B. Herder Book Co., 1951.

Tov, Emmanual. *Textual Criticism of the Hebrew Bible.* Minneapolis: Fortress, 1993.

————, *The Text-Critical Use of the Septuagint in Biblical Research.* Winona Lake, Ind.: Eisenbrauns, 1981.

Tucker, Ruth A. *Sacred Stories.* Grand Rapids: Zondervan Publishing House, 1984.

Turner, Nigel. *Grammatical Insights Into the New Testament.* Edinburgh: T & T Clark, 1965.

Turner, R. Edward. *Proclaiming the Word: The Concept of Preaching in the Thought of Ellen G. White.* Vol. 12, Andrews University Monographs, Studies in Religion. Berrien Springs, Mich.: Andrews University Press, 1980.

Typical Evangelistic Sermons. By Eighteen Seventh-day Adventist evangelists. Takoma Park, Md.: Review and Herald Publishing Association, 1940-1942. 2 vols.

Unger, Merrill F. *Archaeology and the New Testament.* Academie Books. Grand Rapids: Zondervan Press, 1962.

————. *Archaeology and the Old Testament.* Grand Rapids: Zondervan Publishing House, 1954.

————. *Principles of Expository Preaching.* Grand Rapids: Zondervan Publishing House, 1955.

Unger, Merrill F., and William White, Jr., eds. *Nelson's Expository Dictionary of the Old Testament.* Nashville: Thomas Nelson Publishers, 1980.

VanderKam, James C. *The Dead Sea Scrolls Today.* Grand Rapids: William B. Eerdmans Publishers, 1994.

VanGemeren, Willem. *Interpreting the Prophetic Word.* Academie Books. Grand Rapids: Zondervan Press, 1990.

Van Groningen, Gerard. *Messianic Revelation in the Old Testament.* Grand Rapids: Baker Book House, 1990.

Vine, W. E. *An Expository Dictionary of New Testament Words.* Nashville: Thomas Nelson Publishers, 1985.

Vitrano, Stephen P. *So You're Not a Preacher.* Washington, D.C.: Review and Herald Publishing Association, 1977.

————. *How to Preach: A Practical Guide to Better Sermons.* Hagerstown, Md.: Review and Herald Publishing Association, 1991.

Vermes, G. *The Dead Sea Scrolls in English.* 2nd ed. Harmondsworth: Penguin Books, 1983.

Vos, Geerhardus. *Biblical Theology: Old and New Testaments.* Grand Rapids: William B. Eerdmans Publishing Co., 1948; reprint, 1975.

————. *The Pauline Eschatology.* Princeton: Princeton University Press, 1930; reprint, Grand Rapids: Baker Book House, 1979.

————. *The Self-Disclosure of Jesus.* Princeton: Princeton University Press, 1926; ed. and rewritten by Johannes G. Vos. Grand Rapids: William B. Eerdmans Publishing Co., 1953.

Waldman, Nahum M. *The Recent Study of Hebrew.* Grand Rapids: William B. Eerdmans Publishing Company, 1989.

Walker, Williston. *A History of the Christian Church.* 3rd ed. New York: Charles Scribner's Sons, 1970.

Wallenkampf, Arnold V., and W. Richard Lesher, eds. *The Sanctuary and the Atonement: Biblical, Historical, and Theological Studies.* Washington, D.C.: Review and Herald Publishing Association, 1981.

Walton, John H. *Ancient Israelite Culture in Its Cultural Context: A Survey of Parallels Between Biblical and Ancient Near Eastern Texts.* Regency Reference Library. Grand Rapids: Zondervan Publishing House, 1989.

Weingreen, J. *A Practical Grammar for Classical Hebrew.* New York: Oxford University Press, 1959.

————. *Introduction to the Critical Study of the Text of the Hebrew Bible.* New York: Clarendon Press, 1982.

Wenham, J. W. *Elements of New Testament Greek.* Cambridge: Cambridge University Press, 1979.

Were, Louis F. *The Battle for the Kingship of the World.* Victoria, Australia: By the author, Box 363F, G.P.O., Melbourne, n.d.; reprint, Berrien Springs, Mich.: First Impressions, 1983.

————. *The Certainty of the Third Angel's Message.* Victoria, Australia: By the author, Box 363F, G.P.O., Melbourne, 1945; reprint, Berrien Springs, Mich.: First Impressions, 1979.

————. *The Kings That Come From the Sunrising.* Victoria, Australia: By the author, Box 363F, G.P.O., Melbourne, n.d.; reprint, Berrien Springs, Mich.: First Impressions, 1983.

————. *Middle East Ferments and the Antichrist.* Victoria, Australia: By the author, Box 363F, G.P.O., Melbourne, 1958.

————. *The Moral Purpose of Prophecy.* Victoria, Australia: By the Author, Box 363F, G.P.O., Melbourne, 1949; reprint, Berrien Springs, Mich.: First Impressions, 1980.

————. *The Woman and the Beast in the Book of Revelation.* Victoria, Australia: By the Author, Box 363F, G.P.O., Melbourne, 1952; reprint, Berrien Springs,

Mich.: First impressions, 1983.

Westcott, B. F. *An Introduction to the Study of the Gospels*. 5th ed. London: Macmillan and Co., 1875.

White, Arthur L. *The Ellen G. White Writings*. Washington, D.C.: Review and Herald Publishing Association, 1973.

————. *Toward a Factual Concept of Inspiration II: The Role of Visions and the Use of Historical Sources in the Great Controversy*. Washington, D.C.: The Ellen G. White Estate, 1978.

White, Ellen G. *The Acts of the Apostles*. Mountain View, Calif.: Pacific Press Publishing Association, 1911.

————. *Christ in His Sanctuary*. Mountain View, Calif.: Pacific Press Publishing Association, 1969.

————. *Christ's Object Lessons*. Washington, D.C.: Review and Herald Publishing Association, 1941.

————. *Counsels to Parents, Teachers, and Students Regarding Christian Education*. Mountain View, Calif.: Pacific Press Publishing Association, 1913.

————. *The Desire of Ages*. Mountain View, Calif.: Pacific Publishing Association, 1940.

————. *Early Writings*. Washington, D.C.: Review and Herald Publishing Association, 1945.

————. *Evangelism*. Washington, D.C.: Review and Herald Publishing Association, 1946.

————. *Gospel Workers*. Rev. ed. Washington, D.C.: Review and Herald Publishing Association, 1948.

————. *The Great Controversy Between Christ and Satan*. Mountain View, Calif.: Pacific Press Publishing Association, 1911.

————. Letter 12, 1890.

————. Letter 61, 1896.

————. Manuscript 59, 1900.

————. *Patriarchs and Prophets*. Mountain View, Calif.: Pacific Press Publishing Association, 1913.

————. *Prophets and Kings*. Mountain View, Calif.: Pacific Press Publishing Association, 1943.

————. *Review and Herald* (June 18, 1889; Mar. 24, 1890; Dec. 15, 1891; Dec. 20, 1892; Aug. 7, 1894; Jan. 20, 1903).

————. *Selected Messages From the Writings of Ellen G. White*. Washington, D.C.: Review and Herald Publishing Association, 1958. 3 vols.

————. *Testimonies for the Church*. Mountain View, Calif.: Pacific Press Publishing Association, 1948. 9 vols.

————. *Thoughts From the Mount of Blessing*. Mountain View, Calif.: Pacific Press Publishing Association, 1943.

Wigram, G. V. *The Englishman's Greek Concordance of the New Testament*.

London: 1839; 9th ed., 1903; reprint, London: Samuel Bagster and Sons/Grand Rapids: Zondervan Press, n.d.

———. *The Englishman's Hebrew and Chaldee Concordance of the Old Testament.* London: 1843; reprint, London: Samuel Bagster and Sons/Grand Rapids: Zondervan Press, n.d. 2 vols.

Wilken, Robert L. *The Christians as the Romans Saw Them.* New Haven, Conn.: Yale University Press, 1984.

Williams, Ronald J. *Hebrew Syntax: An Outline.* 2nd ed. Toronto: University of Toronto Press, 1976; reprint, 1982.

Wilson, Marvin R. *Our Father Abraham.* Grand Rapids: Wm. B. Eerdmans Publishing Company, 1989.

Wilson, William. *Wilson's Old Testament Word Studies.* McLean, Va.: MacDonald Publishing Co., n.d.

Wurthwein, Ernst. *The Text of the Old Testament.* 2nd ed. Grand Rapids: William B. Eerdmans Publishing Co., 1994.

———. *The Text of the Old Testament.* Trans. by Erroll F. Rhodes from the 4th German ed. Stuttgart: Wurttembergische Bibelanstalt, 1973; reprint, Grand Rapids: William B. Eerdmans Publishing Co., 1979.

Xenophon. *Anabasis*: Books 1-4. Ed. with an introduction, notes, and vocabulary by Maurice W. Mather, and Joseph William Hewitt. Norman, Okla.: University of Oklahoma Press, 1962.

Yamauchi, E. *The Archaeology of New Testament Cities in Western Asia Minor.* Baker Studies in Biblical Archaeology. Grand Rapids: Baker Book House, 1980.

———. *Greece and Babylon: Early Contacts Between the Aegean and the Near East.* Baker Studies in Biblical Archaeology. Grand Rapids: Baker Book House, 1967.

Yandian, Bob. *Proverbs: Principles of Wisdom.* Tulsa: Harrison House, 1985.

Young, Brad H. *Jesus the Jewish Theologian.* Peabody: Hendrickson Publishers, 1995.

Young, E. J. *An Introduction to the Old Testament.* Grand Rapids: William B. Eerdmans Publishing Co., 1949; Rev. and reprint, 1964.

Young, R. *Analytical Concordance to the Bible.* McLean, Va.: MacDonald Publishing Co., n.d.

Young, Richard A. *Intermediate New Testament Greek: A Linguistic and Exegetical Approach.* Nashville: Broadman and Homan Publishers, 1994.

Zerwick, S.J., Maximilian. *Biblical Greek: Illustrated by Examples.* Eng. ed. adapted from the 4th Latin ed. by Joseph Smith, S.J. Rome: Scripta Pontificii Instituti Biblici 114, 1963.

Zodhiates, Spiro, ed. *The Complete Word Study New Testament and Dictionary.* Iowa Falls: World Bible Publishers, 1992.

———. ed. *The Complete Word Study Old Testament.* Iowa Falls: World Bible Publishers, 1994.

———. *The Epistles of John.* Chattanooga: AMG Publishers, 1996.

———. *The Hebrew-Greek Key Study Bible.* Chattanooga: AMG Publishers, 1984.

DIRECTORY OF BIBLE STUDY SOFTWARE

acCordance
The Gramcord Institute
2218 NE Brookview Drive
Vancouver, WA 98686

Anchor Bible Dictionary
Bantam/Doubleday/Dell
Garden City, NY

Bar-Ilan's Judaic Library
Bible Scholar
Torah Scholar
Torah on CD-ROM
Torah Educational Software
750 Chestnut Ridge Road
Spring Valley, NY 10977

The Bible Companion
White Harvest Software, Inc.
P.O. Box 40868
Raleigh, NC 27629-0968

The Bible Library
Ellis Enterprises
4205 McAuley Boulevard #385
Oklahoma City, OK 73120

BibleScript
Galaxie Software
6302 Galaxie Road
Garland, TX 75044

Bible Windows
Silver Mountain Software
1029 Tanglewood
Cedar Hill, TX 75104

BibleWorks for Windows
Hermeneutika
P.O. Box 98563
Seattle, WA 98198

The Holy Scriptures for Windows
Christian Technologies
P.O. Box 2201
Independence, MO 64055

The Judaic Classics Limited Edition
The Soncino Talmud
Davka Corporation
7074 Western Avenue
Chicago, IL 60645

Logos Bible Software
2117 200th Avenue West
Oak Harbor, WA 98277

The Master Christian Library
Ages Software
P.O. Box 1926
Albany, OR 97321

The New Oxford Annotated Bible With
Apocrypha, Electronic Edition. (NRSV)
200 Madison Avenue
New York, NY 10016

Online Bible U.S.A.
P.O. Box 21
Bronson, MI 49028
[PC users]

Online Bible for Macintosh
Attention: Ken Hamel
P.O. Box 545
Beershèba Springs, TN 37305

PC Study Bible for Windows
BibleSoft
22014 7th Avenue South
Seattle, WA 98198

Quickverse for Windows
Parsons Technology
1 Parsons Drive
P.O. Box 100
Hiawatha, LA 52233

Seedmaster for Windows
White Harvest Software, Inc.
P.O. Box 97153
Raleigh, NC 27624

Thompson Chain HyperBible
Kirkbride Technology
335 West 9th Street
Indianapolis, IN 46202

Torah La-Am Library
Torah Productions, Inc.
3070 North 51st Street
Suite 510A
Milwaukee, WI 53210

Verse Search
Bible Research Systems
2013 Wells Branch Parkway, #304
Austin, TX 78278

WordSearch for Windows
NavPress Software
P.O. Box 35006
Colorado Springs, CO 80935

MISCELLANEOUS

Bible Map Inserts, Flip Charts, Transparencies
All Church Technical Service
Fayetteville, AR 72701